MALT WHISKY YEARBOOK 2019

First published in Great Britain in 2018 by
MagDig Media Limited

© MagDig Media Limited 2018

ISBN 978-0-9576553-5-5

MagDig Media Limited
1 Brassey Road
Old Potts Way, Shrewsbury
Shropshire SY3 7FA
ENGLAND

E-mail: info@maltwhiskyyearbook.com
www.maltwhiskyyearbook.com

Contents

Introduction

I´ve spent some time lately thinking about whisky and what it means to me and what it means to other people. I recall some of the comments I received from friends when I wrote the first edition of the Malt Whisky Yearbook fourteen years ago. Some of them thought it was a brilliant idea because "malt whisky is really trendy right now." Even though I appreciated the backup from people close to me, I couldn´t agree. I just couldn´t see whisky as a trend and at the same time I hated using the word lifestyle just because you chose to drink whisky. There was something else to it. When you spend time with whisky friends it´s not just about the drink. There are so many other aspects of whisky involved that means something; the land, the history, the people, the traditions... and all of a sudden I had written another book on that topic. But I digress.

Struggling to find one simple line to encapsulate my interest in whisky, Bob Dylan came to rescue. In the "Ballad of Frankie Lee and Judas Priest" he sings "It's not a house," says Judas Priest. "It's not a house, it's a home." That´s what whisky is to me – a home. A house is where you dwell for a period of time but a home is where you spend time with people and things that you love.

As usual, my excellent team of whisky writers have excelled themselves this year and have contributed with some fascinating articles;

Sherry matured whisky is adored around the world but there´s more to it than meets the eye. Gavin D Smith scrutinizes the many aspects of sherry casks.

In turbulent times, man has always looked for comfort in days gone by. Neil Ridley explains why whisky nostalgia is sweeping the whisky business at the moment.

Just when we thought we had come to grips with the term 'terroir' there´s another aspect of what influences the flavour. Joel Harrison thinks we should look into the air to get the whole picture.

With close to two million distillery visits last year, whisky tourism has become increasingly popular. Becky Paskin has met with some of the Scotch producers to get their views.

If you invest in rare whiskies, there´s a fair chance of making a good return. But some say the very soul of whisky is being lost if you don´t drink it. Jonny McCormick has listened to both sides.

Are we enjoying a golden age for Scotch whisky and if so, how long will it last? Charles MacLean thinks there´s a great confidence in the future from the producers.

We´re all used to judging a whisky by it´s flavour but there´s so much more to it than that. Ian Wisniewski invites us all to feel the whisky.

How can whiskies from the 'new world' compete with the classics? Ian Buxton discusses everything from shelf space and cash flow to authenticity and branding.

Japanese whisky is hot but difficult to get, yet there´s another problem at hand. Stefan Van Eycken thinks that the lack of rules and regulations could damage the category´s credibility.

In Malt Whisky Yearbook 2019 you will also find the unique, detailed and much appreciated section on Scottish malt whisky distilleries. It has been thoroughly revised and updated, not just in text, but also including numerous, new pictures, new distilleries and tasting notes for all the core brands. The chapter on Japanese whisky is completely revised and the presentation of distilleries from the rest of the world has been expanded. You will also find a list of more than 150 of the best whisky shops in the world with their full details and suggestions where to find more information on the internet. The Whisky Year That Was provides a summary of all the signficant events during the year. Finally, the very latest statistics gives you all the answers to your questions on production and consumption.

Thank you for buying Malt Whisky Yearbook 2019. I hope that you will have many enjoyable moments reading it and I can assure you that I will be back with a new edition next year.

Malt Whisky Yearbook 2020 will be published in October 2019.
If you need any of the previous thirteen volumes of Malt Whisky Yearbook,
some of them are available for purchase (in limited numbers) from the website
www.maltwhiskyyearbook.com

Acknowledgements

First of all I wish to thank the writers who have shared their great specialist knowledge on the subject in a brilliant and entertaining way – Ian Buxton, Stefan Van Eycken, Joel Harrison, Charles MacLean, Jonny McCormick, Becky Paskin, Neil Ridley, Gavin D. Smith and Ian Wisniewski.

A special thanks goes to Gavin who put in a lot of effort nosing, tasting and writing notes for more than 100 different whiskies. Thanks also to Stefan for the Japanese notes. I am also deeply grateful to Philippe Jugé for his input on French distilleries.

The following persons have also made important photographic or editorial contributions and I am grateful to all of them:

Kevin Abrook, Beatriz Alarcon-Zlatkis, Iain Allan, Alasdair Anderson, Russel Anderson, Duncan Baldwin, Dana Baran, Adam Barber, Laura Beadell, Kirsteen Beeston, Jodi Best, Graham Bowie, Keith Brian, Ross Bremner, Andrew Brown, Graham Brown, Jennifer Brown, Alex Bruce, Gordon Bruce, Mark Brunton, Simon Buley, Sebastian Bunford-Jones, Danni Burnett, Stephen Burnett, Peter Campbell, Stuart Cassells, Ian Chang, Oliver Chilton, Claire Clark, David Clark, Suzanne Clark, Francis Conlon, Lucy Coomber, Graham Coull, Jason Craig, Laura Craik, Andrew Crook, Nathan Currie, Alasdair Day, Paul Dempsey, Scott Dickson, Gordon Dundas, Lukasz Dynowiak, Lucie Ellis, Graham Eunson, Diane Farrell, Andy Fiske, Robert Fleming, John Fordyce, Dave Francis, Callum Fraser, Hamish Fraser, Josh Fraser, Karen Fullerton, Graeme Gardiner, Calum Gee, Ewan George, Sharon Gibson, Archie Gillies, Tomer Goren, Kenny Grant, Pierrick Guillaume, Daryl Haldane, Wendy Harries Jones, Emily Harris, Annelise Hastings, Mickey Heads, Lucinda Hodge, Paul Hooper, Liam Hughes, Robbie Hughes, Caryn Inglis, Kevin Innes, Helen Jagger, Sandy Jamieson, Jemma Jamieson, Håkan Jarskog, Tara Karimian, Pramod Kashyap, David Keir, Sarah Kingsbury, Andrew Laing, Gillian Lamont, Graeme Lilwall, Allan Logan, Alistair Longwell, Sarah McAlaney, Iain McAlister, Des McCagherty, Alan McConnochie, Alistair McDonald, Andy Macdonald, John MacDonald, Christy McFarlane, Sandy Macintyre, Doug McIvor, Bethan Mackenzie, Drew McKenzie Smith, Jaclyn McKie, Julia Mackillop, Paul Mclean, Ian MacMillan, Angus MacRaild, James MacTaggart, Ian McWilliam, Graham Manson, Jennifer Masson, Freya Matley, Santiago Mignone, Amy Millen, Ann Miller, Andrew Millsopp, Henric Molin, Rune Molvik, Katy Moore, Carol More, Gareth Morgan, Jake Mountain, Robert Muir, Neil Murphy, Andrew Nairn, Ingemar Nordblom, Nathan Nye, Sietse Offringa, Gemma Paterson, Marc Pendlebury, Sean Phillips, Lars Ragnå, Struan Grant Ralph, Ian Renwick, Fiona Reyner,Chris Riesbeck, Stuart Robertson, Brian Robinson, Colin Ross, Zoe Rutherford, Colette Savage, Emily Senn, Lila Serenelli, Steven Shand, Kristy Sherry, Daniel Smith, Alison Spowart, Greig Stables, Marie Stanton, Tristan Stephenson, Reto Stoeckli, Dan Szor, Christian Svantesson, Duncan Tait, Cheryl Targos, Eddie Thom, Annabel Thomas, Phil Thompson, Andrew Thomson, Jackie Thomson, Laura Thomson, Ruth Thomson, John Torrance, Louise Towers, Kaitlyn Tsai, Jennifer Turkington, David Turner, Perry Unger, Mark Van Der Vijver, Stewart Walker, Jennifer Watson, Ranald Watson, Mark Watt, Iain Weir, Nick White, Ronald Whiteford, Anthony Wills, Alan Winchester, Jamie Winfield, Kristoffer Wittström, Magnus Wittström, Nicole Wood, Stephen Woodcock, Allison Young, Fiona Young, Derek Younie.

Finally, to my wife Pernilla and our daughter Alice, thank you for your patience and your love and to Vilda, our labrador and my faithful companion in the office during long working hours.

Ingvar Ronde
Editor
Malt Whisky Yearbook

MATUSALEM
DAL 6 7 0 2
DALMORE
200

The many faces of Sherry Casks

by Gavin D Smith

"Sherry cask matured"
is a definitioin which is often tossed around
without much reflection of what it actually means. And as we shall see,
it can mean many things.

What we tend to refer to as 'sherried,' 'sherry cask matured' or 'sherry cask seasoned' Scotch whiskies have a cache about them, a sense of luxury and indulgence that allows them to command premium prices. But how much do we really know about the way they have been matured? Surely, they have all been aged in casks that had sherry in them at some point? A 'sherry cask' is a 'sherry cask', isn't it? As we shall see, the reality is far more complex and nuanced than that.

Many consumers assume that a sherry cask which has been used to mature whisky previously had a similar function with sherry, helping to age the product in Spanish bodegas. However, comparatively few 'bodega casks' as they are known find their way into the Scotch whisky industry, and the vast majority instead have been 'seasoned' with sherry specifically for future use with whisky. They are not a by-product of sherry-making.

Similarly, when we talk about a 'sherry cask,' the style of sherry with which it has been seasoned or which it previously held in a bodega makes a significant difference to its influence on whisky subsequently matured in it. Additionally, has the 'sherry cask' been made from European or American oak? Again, each will impart their own characteristics to whisky. Finally, do we mean that the whisky has been matured 'full-term' in sherry casks, has it undergone a period of secondary maturation or simply short-term 'finishing' in a sherry cask after initial Bourbon barrel ageing?

Whyte & Mackay's Master Blender and Dalmore single malt whisky-maker Richard Paterson declares that "Many consumers don't understand the use of sherry casks – they just think if a whisky has been matured in sherry casks, they're getting something 'better.' When I'm conducting tastings around the world, I often have to explain what sherry is, especially in the Far East."

Historically, the use of sherry casks in the Scotch whisky industry was inextricably linked with Britain's great love affair with the Spanish fortified wine. Sherry was imported in casks and either sold directly from merchants or bars or was bottled in the UK. The empty casks had little value and were certainly not worth shipping back to Spain.

The casks in question were known as 'transport casks,' and were coopered from locally-sourced Spanish oak rather than the more expensive imported American oak which the bodegas reserved for the construction of the long-lasting 'bodega casks' in which sherry was matured.

The availability of these transport casks suited the Scotch industry very well as it expanded exponentially during the second half of the 19th century, and the profile of Scotch single malts was shaped to a significant degree by the use of former sherry casks, even when they were refilled with whisky several times. However, as Britain fell out of love with sherry, so fewer casks were available for Scotch distillers, and the Spanish Civil War (1936-39) made supplies almost impossible to find. This coincided with a ruling of March 1938 that US Bourbon could only be matured in new casks, and not in ones that had already been used. So it was that as sherry casks became rare in the UK, there was an abundance of Bourbon casks available to Scotch distillers to fill the void, and Bourbon casks became the prevailing maturation influence on Scotch single malts.

However, some traditionalists still managed to source sherry casks, and malts such as Macallan, Dalmore, Glenfarclas, GlenDronach and Highland Park continued to be associated with the use of sherry wood for maturation purposes. The shortage of sherry casks was exacerbated when, in 1986, Spain decreed that all sherry must be bottled in its country of origin.

This led to a significant increase in the existing practice of using paxarette to rejuvenate well-worn casks and extend their working lives. Paxarette, also known as pajarete, is a dense Spanish sweet wine, usually made from Pedro Ximinez grapes, to which arrope – boiled down must – is added. As pajarete, it was well-known in Britain as a dessert wine as far back as the 18th century.

When it came to Scotch whisky, paxarette was blown into casks in a vacuum chamber so that it penetrated the outer layers of the oak. Writing in The Science and Technology of Whiskies (1989), JM Philip notes that "A typical current cooperage procedure in the Scotch whisky industry is to add 500ml of Paxarette per hogshead, or 1 litre per butt, pressurise at 48 kPa (7psig) for 10 min and then disgorge any unabsorbed Paxarette."

In theory, paxarette merely helped return exhausted casks to a state where they would again impart sherry characteristics to the whisky being matured in them, but in practice it seems that it was not necessarily restricted to casks which had experienced several fills, and actually gave a veneer of greater sophistication to the whisky, as well as influencing its aroma, and, perhaps most importantly, its colour. To be convincing to the consumer, a 'sherry cask matured' whisky had to look the part.

Finally, in 1989, the Scotch Whisky Association banned paxarette as an 'illegal additive' to Scotch whisky, though the use of caramel colouring - known as E150a – continues to be permitted.

There is a school of thought that considers the presence of paxarette to be the main reason why some sherry-cask whiskies distilled and matured during the 1970s and '80s have such a different character profile to those bottled today.

Writing at www.maltmaniacs.net, Michel Van Meersbergen declares that "antique sherried whisky" was "More intense, more creamy, sometimes that great dirty edge to it." After exploring various possible reasons why this might be so, Van Meersbergen concludes that "I've got a dead feel the sherry signature we like so much in the old style whisky is for a huge part generated by Paxarette."

Paxarette is banned

By the time paxarette was banned, a number of Scotch whisky distillers were putting in place programmes with Spanish cooperages and bodegas to ensure a reliable supply of sherry casks. These programmes involve 'seasoning' new, toasted casks with relatively young sherry, which is used several times before being distilled into sherry vinegar.

Sherry casks being charred

Seasoning has the effect of removing undesirable elements from the wood, but when 'transport casks' were used for subsequent whisky maturation, the sherry with which they were filled was mature and ready for drinking, which may explain a key difference between 'old' sherried whiskies and current ones.

When it comes to wood, no company in the Scotch whisky industry has taken the subject more seriously than Edrington.

There is a very good reason for this – namely that in Highland Park and The Macallan, Edrington has two of the best-known and best-selling whiskies associated with sherry wood maturation, with The Macallan in particular having established its reputation as one of the world's great single malts partly due to its use of sherry casks. Today, Edrington is responsible for around 95% of all sherry being imported into Scotland.

Stuart MacPherson is Edrington's Spanish Operations Manager & Master of Wood, and he explains that "Edrington has the largest number of sherry casks manufactured on an annual basis to our specifications. At the moment the market price for sherry casks are around £,1000 for a 500-litre butt.

"In Spain we use a number of cooperages in Jerez [the sherry 'capital' of the country] and our main seasoning bodegas are González Byass and William & Humbert, although we do use some smaller family-owned bodegas. All our casks are made to our specifications which include toasting levels, timings and specification of timber.

"The casks are seasoned with an Oloroso which by definition must be a minimum of two years old. We specify dry Oloroso to season our casks, and this is probably due to a number of factors. Basically, due to wine production, Oloroso volumes are more readily available because of the amount of wines that Oloroso is the base for. Another factor is the slightly higher ABV and the fact that the wine is oxidised, unlike Fino, where the ABV is lower. By using an older wine (Oloroso) you will extract less from the wood, leaving some of the compounds beneficial to the maturation of whisky."

Edrington's casks spend 18 months being seasoned with sherry before they are emptied and transported to Scotland, and some 70% are made from European oak and 30% from American oak. The latter is

A cooperage in Spain

harvested in Ohio and after being dried it is exported in staves to Jerez to be coopered into casks.

MacPherson says that "The main differences between the two types are related to colour and flavour characteristics and this can be attributed to specific chemical compounds within the different species of trees. European oak has a tighter grain and more porous structure, as well as a high level of tannins that give you dried fruit, spice like cinnamon and nutmeg, and even chocolate flavours. American oak gives the whisky a lighter colour and characteristics of vanilla, honey, nuts and ginger."

If The Macallan has a lengthy association with sherry casks, then so too has Dalmore. Distillery owner Andrew Mackenzie prided himself on maturing whisky for much longer than many of his rivals, and records show that as early as 1882, Mackenzie was maturing his whisky for at least 12 years. Much longer maturation was also practiced, with whisky distilled in 1878 being transferred from new casks – termed 'Distillery Wood' – to 'Sherry Wood' in 1890, only to be allowed to age for a further 18 years before bottling as a 30 year old. An earlier example, distilled in 1868, was re-filled from distillery wood to sherry wood in 1880, finally being bottled as a 23 year old in 1891.

Andrew Mackenzie forged a strong and lasting relationship with the sherry house of Gonzales Byass to obtain quality casks, and the relationship between the two persists to this day. The man charged with fostering it from the Scottish end is Richard Paterson, who is passionate about the single malt's maturation programme.

Paterson says that "Since Emperador Inc took over Whyte & Mackay in 2014, we're part of group that is very big in sherry. They own the Harvey's and Garvey's brands. However, most of our casks come from Gonzales-Byass and we have exclusive use of their Apostoles and Matusalem casks, which previously held 30 year old sherry. We also get aged Pedro Ximinex [also known as PX] casks from them.

"The Apostoles and Matusalem casks all come from the bodega, they're genuine bodega casks which have been used to mature sherry, and we also season some casks. We have casks coopered and filled with Amoroso-style sherry – which is 75% fino

Master Blender Richard Paterson draws a sample from one of Whyte & Mackay´s many sherry casks

and 25% PX – and stored in bodegas for over a year. The Amoroso-style sherry will be between eight and 15 years old. At the cooperages we specify a toasting level of 3mm, 4mm or even 5mm, and the casks are a mix of American white oak and European oak.”

Paterson is keen to stress that ”It's not about just any sherry cask. Using sherry casks isn't a quick fix, you have to find the right sherry style to suit your whisky. The body and weight of the Matusalem casks is 100% compatible with the DNA of Dalmore – rich, medium to heavy, with chocolate orange notes. In particular, sherry styles such as Matusalem suits the older Dalmores very well. You have to have muscle and structure in the spirit for it to cope well with sherry, particularly over prolonged periods of time. Oloroso sherry would overwhelm a light, floral spirit. If sherry suits your style of spirit then use it – if not, leave it alone.

”In addition to what we do in Spain, we also have Amoroso-style sherry shipped in bulk to Scotland, where it is used to season casks at our Invergordon grain distillery and bonding complex, close to Dalmore. The majority of this sherry comes from Harvey's.”

Paterson observes that ”Sherry should never be used to change the character of the whisky. It's only there to give it an extra dimension. A seasoning for six months with very young sherry may suit some distillers, but it's not our style for Dalmore. However, when demand is great, people will cut corners. They'll fill younger whisky into sherry casks for a quick finish.

”When done with integrity, using sherry casks well is a very expensive and lengthy process. It can be time consuming, too, as there is no guarantee that every sherry butt will give you exactly what you want – they need to be checked and nosed regularly. They can be much less predictable than Bourbon casks.”

Like Edrington and Dalmore, Glenfarclas has a long-standing relationship with a Spanish bodega, namely Miquel Martin in Jerez. ”We've been using them since the early 1980s,” says the distillery's Production Manager Callum Fraser. ”Each year we buy approximately 1,120 butts and 800 hogsheads, all of which have been seasoned with Oloroso sherry for around five years.”

John and George Grant of Glenfarclas - a distillery defined by the use of sherry casks

By way of an experiment, back in the mid-1970s Glenfarclas filled a dozen types of wood with spirit on the same day and laid the casks together in the same warehouse. The casks included Fino, Amontillado, Oloroso and South African sherries. As company chairman John Grant later remarked, "From this exercise we decided Oloroso sherry gave us the flavours we liked best."

Callum Fraser adds that "I like to use second-fill casks, as I feel that first-fill sherry casks can be quite overpowering, and personally I like to taste the spirit quality coming through. We do, however, use some first-fill casks, as well as second, third and fourth-fills. We can do this because we do all our vattings on site, so this means that we have a complete history of all the wood we are filling."

While Glenfarclas majors in ex-Oloroso sherry casks, GlenDronach distillery at Forgue in Aberdeenshire tends to work with both Oloroso and Pedro Ximinez. Master Blender Rachel Barrie explains that "The GlenDronach prides itself on exclusive maturation in Spanish oak sherry cask from Andalucía, specifically focusing on PX and Oloroso. These are the largest casks available for whisky maturation and their extremely porous wood allows for the highest possible levels of interaction between wood and whisky. The higher levels of tannins in Spanish oak also promote the consistently rich and full-bodied nature of The GlenDronach."

As with Richard Paterson and Dalmore, Barrie points out that GlenDronach works well with sherry wood because "It's a true Highland style: a heavy and robust spirit, which is why it is perfect for a long maturation period in sherry casks."

She adds that "We have been able to increase supply of the highest quality Spanish oak sherry casks (a huge investment for the business), which continues to contribute immensely to the richest and finest aged single malts, particularly for The Glen-Dronach but also our other distilleries BenRiach and Glenglassaugh."

"The GlenDronach focuses on the marriage of fruity and nutty Oloroso sherry casks and intensely rich Pedro Ximénez casks. Alongside the flavour, Oloroso casks give The GlenDronach its signature depth in colour. Pedro Ximénez casks on the other hand provide the signature richness and depth in flavour of The GlenDronach."

GlenDronach 18 year old is matured solely in Oloroso casks, and according to Rachel Barrie "It is the most muscular and full-bodied sherried malt of the core range, with the Oloroso giving it the oily flavours such as raisins and stewed fruits. The 21 year old is a marriage of PX and Oloroso, and this marriage brings more elegance and flavours such as roasted coffee beans and brown sugar."

Barrie's role involves 'finishing' a number of whiskies in sherry casks – for example, Peated GlenDronach, BenRiach 17 year old PX Sherry and Glenglassaugh Revival – so she is ideally positioned to pronounce on how to do sherry cask finishing well. "The 'secret' is making sure you have a great

A SHERRY 101

Sherry is produced in the Jerez region of southern Spain, the country's oldest wine-growing area. All sherry must, by law, be made from grapes grown there, and the sherry itself has to be aged in the region.

Sherry's denominacion de origin embraces three specific areas, namely Jerez de la Frontera, San-lúcar de Barrameda and El Puerto de Santa María. Jerez enjoys a special micro-climate because of its geographical location. The lime albariza soils which were once covered by the ocean give sherry even more uniqueness and style.

Harvest of the three grape varieties used for sherry tends to take place at the end of August or early September. The grapes in question are Palomino, Pedro Ximénez and muscatel, and it is use of these three very different grapes that give the broad spectrum of tastes enjoyed by sherry.

The grapes are immediately pressed after harvest to limit spoilage, except with Pedro Ximenez, as that is laid out on esparto grass to dry and intensify the sugar. The mosto de yema (must) is then transferred into temperature-controlled stainless-steel vats for vinification.

The secret that defines sherry is flor, a layer of living organisms (yeast) that sits on top of the wine, protecting it from any contact with the air. After the process of fermentation has finished, the wine is assessed and the subsequent style is decided upon. Lighter, clear wine will be aged biologically to become Fino or Manzanilla. Some will go through an oxidative ageing by which the wine has direct contact with the air, making it into an Oloroso.

The wine/sherry is aged in American butts, then matured according to the solera and criaderas system. The butts are stacked with the oldest at the bottom. Once the sherry is taken out of the butt it is immediately filled from the butt on the next level above. This system gives the young sherry body and the older sherry youth.

---

quality spirit to start off with," she declares, "and then identifying the cask type/finish that will best complement your spirit characteristics and ensure that your wood quality matches that of your spirit."

On the subject of 'finishing,' Diageo has long been considered highly competent at the process, as exemplified by its Distillers Edition range, introduced in the late 1990s, initially with its six Classic Malts, but with subsequent editions such as Caol Ila and, for a time, Royal Lochnagar.

Each malt – presented as a vintage – is paired with the most compatible style of sherry available, so Lagavulin is finished in Pedro Ziminex casks, Glenkinchie in Amontillado casks, and Oban in Montilla Fino casks.

Apart from the Distillers Editions, Diageo has released few single malts with significant sherry cask influence, apart from a number in the annual Special Releases programme. With the latest addition to the Talisker portfolio, however, the company has committed itself to sherry in the most authentic way possible.

Talisker 40 year old is the first release is what is called The Bodega Series, and a Diageo spokesperson says that the series will be "celebrating age-old sherry relationships dating as far back as the 1900s. Adding to the Talisker portfolio, this new and exclusive series of single malt releases will offer collectors a taste of historic wineries of the renowned 'Sherry Triangle,' where Talisker once sourced its casks."

Working with the Sherry Masters at Bodega Delgado Zuleta in the Marco de Jerez region, Diageo's blenders selected refill casks of 40 year old Talisker and transferred their contents into five ex-sherry casks that previously held the Bodega's 40 year old Amontillado sherry for an unspecified period prior to bottling.

Talisker's global brand ambassador Donald Colville says that "Throughout the ledgers and archives we have, we go back to the early 1900s and see the different types of sherry casks used at Talisker to mature the whisky, and Delgado was being used as a key supplier of casks to the distillery."

As we pointed out at the start of this article, there is really no such thing as just a 'sherry cask'!

Gavin D Smith is one of Scotland's leading whisky writers and Contributing Editor Scotland for Whisky Magazine. He regularly undertakes writing commissions for leading drinks companies and produces articles for a wide range of publications, including Whisky Magazine, Whisky Magazine & Fine Spirits – France, Whisky Etc, Whisky Advocate, Whiskeria, Whisky Quarterly and The Cask.
He is the author and co-author of some 30 books, and recent publications include The Dalmore Presents History in the Making – Richard Paterson 50 Year Anniversary and a new and fully updated edition of Michael Jackson's Whisky the Definitive World Guide, co-written with Dominic Roskrow.

DEWAR'S
The Jubilee Spirit
AWARDED
50 MEDALS
PERTH
50 Gold
and
Prize Medals
50 Gold
and
Prize Medals
BY APPOINTMENT
"White Label"
FINEST SCOTCH WHISKY
OF GREAT AGE
John Dewar & Sons
DISTILLERS.
London Offices,
Dewar House Haymarket. S.W.1.
PERTH
Nothing more refreshing

Whisky Nostalgia

by Neil Ridley

With so many people today succumbing
to a touch of nostalgia one may wonder what triggered it.
Do we want to escape our everyday life to seek refuge in a time
where we felt safe and content? And how does this
trend influence the whisky makers?

Feeling a strange, warming, fuzzy fondness in your bones about a favourite whisky brand? Can't stop thinking that the past was in some way better than the present? Chances are, you're suffering from an acute case of Nostalgia'itis: a syndrome, which is seemingly sweeping the whisky business at the moment. Read on about the symptoms and what to do if you're beginning to have feverishly protective feelings towards Port Ellen all of a sudden.

If you've been an avid MWYB reader since 2012, you may be aware from a number of my previous articles that I'm a man of 'a certain age' when it comes to how a whisky brand's marketing department would categorise me. By this, i'm not a Millennial (the supposed golden goose for the future of global whisky sales) but stuck somewhere in the middle of Generation X: a weird, sprawling mass of people born between 1965 and 1984 with money to spend. I say sprawling because the distinct differences in culture and consumption between the 60s, 70s and

Elliot Wilson, strategy director at The Cabinet

80s are perhaps more pronounced than any time period before or after.

The one thing that brings this rag-tag group together is a mental state which leads us to look back rather fondly on the past; a misty-eyed charm that seems to surround elements of our memories like a comforting fog: be it a 1980s games console, a pair of vintage 70s trainers or the resurgence of vinyl records.

Delving into the past is a powerfully emotive driver of sales for both business and the creative arts. For every groundbreaking new film, we have a reboot or curation of something vintage: for instance, last year's Blade Runner 2049; the 'new' Star Wars trilogy, and on the small screen, Netflix's hugely successful Stranger Things, which for people like me, resembles a scarily accurate scrapbook of a brilliant childhood: Dungeons and Dragons; Nintendo; BMX bikes; cassette players; the Millennium Falcon and 80s synth pop.

It´s arguable that nostalgia is something which has helped to propel whisky sales to its headiest numbers in recent memory. The latest figures reveal that exports of single malt Scotch are as buoyant as ever. According to official HMRC data, sales grew by 14.2% in 2017 to £1.17 billion. Authenticity is clearly a big part of Scotch's continued success, as is playing heavily on its past. Both of these cues have manifested themselves in nearly every aspect of whisky NPD: from recreating old liquid, the labels on the bottle and the product launches themselves.

So what is it that we find so compelling about the past?

Why heritage is important

"Humans have a fear of loss that is greater than the potential joy of gain," thinks Ken Grier, the former Creative Director of Edrington's The Macallan, and the man behind the incredible new distillery: a grand architectural statement which very much looks forward in its design and aesthetic, rather than a white walled, pagoda-roofed past. "Because whisky is very often seen as a heritage category it is easy to put on rose tinted spectacles."

It's a point that clearly resonates with Elliot Wilson, Strategy Director at The Cabinet, an agency which specialises in the design and development of new and revitalised spirits brands, including several leading whisky brands.

"I think that before we look at what role 'nostalgia' plays in the design of brands, old and new, we must

The Johnnie Walker ads may have changed over time but the Striding Man is still very much a part of the message

first look at why people are harking back to times gone by and why demonstrating heritage in drinks brands has been so important over the last decade," points out Wilson. "It will come as no surprise that the impulse to be attracted and drawn to things that allow us to escape the drudgery of everyday modern life is appealing and why drinks brands, which specialise in escapism, have utilised this narrative."

This escapism concept – let's call it, for the sake of argument, The Strangers Things Principle seems to be really resonating in extraordinary ways with the Generation X demographic. There seems to be a confluence of things, which, when combined, (almost a little like the Flux Capacitor in a time-travelling DeLorean) provide a powerfully emotive historical driver of nostalgic purchases, including whisky.

I was keen to explore the psychology of this further, so I enlisted the help of Brett Templeton, Managing Director of Pluralthinking, an insight, thinking and cultural intelligence agency working exclusively for the drinks industries. Templeton is, to all intents and purposes, a guru in gathering the collective thinking of generations, their spending habits and emotional/psychological touch points, so I suspect he might be able to spot the distinct symptoms of Nostalgia'itis at 1000 paces.

"Nostalgia is indeed a huge theme that we are seeing across our work in cultural intelligence. Different people use nostalgia in their lives in different ways, but ultimately it's about identity. Reminding ourselves who we are – and where we have come from – is a big part of it; childhood memories," he explains. "For me, it's the recollection of my dad always insisting on his Campari and Soda aperitif – a habit he had picked up on family holidays in Italy in the 70s. Nostalgia can anchor us in who we are. People remember the simple joys of making the best of what they had and are asserting their identity as part of an (almost forgotten) tribe."

"One key thing that I have observed is that we also co-opt the nostalgia of others," he continues, "immersing ourselves in an idealised version of a past that we were never actually part of. Americana [muscle cars, diners, plaid shirts, baseball caps, and more pertinently, American whiskey] is a classic example of that."

So how do you feel it particularly manifests itself in the whisky world?

"When it goes that way, it's pure escapism, or a celebration of a set of values that we feel is somehow 'lost' from our own time," he explains. "In drinks, nostalgia takes a number of forms that you could essentially divide into the 'maker's world' and the 'drinker's world'. In the 'maker's world' the nostalgia is usually around a founder myth, a sense of struggle, authenticity, hard graft, comradeship, artisan skill – all things that we feel that we have lost as a society."

"In the 'drinker's world'," he continues, "nostalgia is often about a period of excitement, glamour or perceived sophistication, typically placed around times of great change in society – the Belle Epoque, 20s Berlin, Prohibition, the dolce vita of 50's and 60s Europe, when a dull world was opening up, democratising, when rules were being broken and societies redrawn. Again, it's about evoking and channelling a sense of loss or an escapist desire to step into an age perceived as less mundane than our own."

Wowzers… In a few short minutes on the comfy couch, presided over by Mr Templeton, I can see just how these powerfully nostalgic principles have begun to subliminally define many of the whiskies

I am enjoying. In fact, time for a some deeper analysis. Let's start off with the first thing we see, shall we: the label and bottle design.

The nostalgic look

It probably won't have escaped your attention that lately, let's say particularly within the last 5-6 years, that the look of a whisky bottle has generally moved historically backwards in terms of the aesthetics on display. You know where I am going here: The faux Victoriana font at a jaunty angle. The twirly edging sketches around the label. The 'Established in xxxx' making a strong presence at the bottom like a cornerstone and the muted, washed out tones of bygone generations in the colour schemes.

Yes these things do look pretty. That much I won't disagree with. But when you begin to analyse them in detail, they're all a little like a pre-determined nostalgic route map, purposefully designed to take the drinker on a journey back into the past, whether there is any genuine authenticity or not at the final destination.

An escape to days gone by

The Victorian-style labels appeal to our nostalgic minds

Richard Paterson introducing The Shackleton blended malt

I'm beginning to wonder if we are reaching a point where bottle design has become too swamped with these 'authenticity cues' and are they perhaps now beginning to act in a counter-productive way.

The Cabinet's Elliot Wilson has a theory here. "As with anything attractive or appealing or most importantly, successful, there will always be followers and copycats trying to jump on the band wagon. This is not to say that there are not many very good, credible and appealing brands that have been created in the vision of the category leaders, but it does mean that for every good copy there are a ton of very bad interpretations of this style and approach. This mostly comes from brands and businesses that have not understood what is at the heart of these brand's successes and are unable or unwilling to do what is required to execute this type of brand well."

So how can whisky companies appeal to a new age of drinker? certainly one which isn't as affected or influenced by the Victoriana imagery, angled fonts and other cues which are popular now?

"This is the billion-dollar question," continues Wilson. "It's certainly not the packaging which is stopping young drinkers turning onto Scotch whisky. You only have to look at the gin, rum and tequila markets to see that all the things that are important in finely crafted whisky brands are equally important in the packaging of these alternative and much more appealing categories. The answer is not to reappraise the branding of the great whisky brands per se - maybe in some instances - but to look at how the liquid is brought to these younger audiences and to understand and tap into new and interesting ways of talking to them, in places that they frequent."

Nikki Burgess, UK and Ireland Marketing Director for Proximo Spirits (which includes Bushmills Irish whiskey and rising star of the rum world, Kraken in its diverse portfolio) has a similar hypothesis.

"Victoriana has been fashionable as a look but it is perhaps waning," she asserts. "Nostalgia will perhaps continue but with a different look. It's inevitable that when brands like [William Grant & Sons'] Hendricks gin are so successful, with its Victoriana image, [arguably a huge influence now on new craft whisky brands, such as Douglas Laing's blended malt Scotch range, and the reintroduction of older brands, such as John Dewar & Sons' Last Great Malts collection – particularly the Craigellachie series] others will wish to copy. A modern interpretation of authenticity cues, which sometimes has an 'old fashioned' or nostalgic look, has become a language which is useful and denotes a certain product positioning (e.g. "craft"). Sometimes this isn't really true to the product, but that's disingenuous marketing rather than the idea that the cues themselves are, or should be, counter productive."

Ok, but what about when it comes to a nostalgic take on the liquid inside our beautifully 'vintagised' bottles?

Certain brands, such as Whyte & Mackay's Shackleton blended malt have gone to the extremes (quite literally, if you consider the Antarctic a challenging environment) to grab drinkers attention with a reflection of the past. Originally released back in 2011 as a modern day recreation of MacKinlay's Rare Old Highland Malt, (the whisky discovered by archaeologists who were exploring the site of Shackleton's base camp – and recently relaunched in 2017 under the 'Shackleton' banner,) the liquid and pack very much attempts to draw the drinker into the world of its namesake explorer.

"It has been a great honour to create this whisky as a testament to Sir Ernest Shackleton," explains Richard Paterson, Whyte & Mackay's Master Blender. "His character and his story remain a true inspiration and I wanted to capture the essence of Sir Ernest within this whisky."

For all the skill and experience that Paterson undoubtedly brings, it would be near impossible – and perhaps unwise to create an 'exact' facsimile of a liquid which was bottled well over 100 years before, given that many of the original malt whiskies – and distilleries – used in the blend are unlikely to exist any more and that the modern drinker's palate is significantly different to those of the past. However, there is clearly a fervent consumer interest at what the past 'might' taste like. Another example here is the growing success of nostalgia-based whisky shows such as the Whisky Exchange's Old & Rare, which brings out curious fans from all over the UK, in search of dusty old vintage bottlings from the yesteryear.

What's intriguing is that for as many enjoyable

The upcoming resurrection of Port Ellen (and Brora) - a good example where nostalgia has played its part

'time capsule' whiskies I have had the privilege of trying (particularly vintage blends bottled in the 40s and 50s onwards, for example) there are equally as many which were truly awful. By that I mean they were poor, harsh, youthful and spirity, or simply gone bad: containing faults which have most likely developed over time in the bottle. But without jumping in the DeLorean and bringing back a few fresh bottles from the yesteryear, we have no real way of knowing where these flaws and the actual recipes converge. So to quote my father for a second – a man who is equally part-historian and part-technocrat: 'yes, that new housing estate may well have once all been green fields, but there was once an awful lot of cow shit down there too.'

Comfort and a safe place

"Nostalgia for me definitely provides a strong foundation in drinking", thinks Martyn 'Simo' Simpson, the new owner of legendary Soho whisky retailer, Milroy's, and a man who is perhaps perfectly placed to reflect on the importance of the past, but also the future, given the heritage of the Milroy's brand, (which dates back to the early 1960s) and the need to innovate and cater for a more modern drinker. "Subconsciously we can't help but think that when we see history on any bottle we think it's good, because it has been around for long time. Whether it is actually a good drink or not is another matter, but it provides a comforting foundation for when we are torn between what to drink."

So why do you think certain ages of drinkers are seemingly obsessed with reissues of old products or recreations? "We all have our go-to safe place in life. I think that's probably where this comes from," he

suggests. "Sometimes people need that safe place, something that provides stability; they know what it is. There are no surprises and they feel a sense of comfort from it."

Comfort. A Safe Place. Foundation. Escapism.

Words that are definitely interchangeable with nostalgia. Are modern times – and by consequence, modern whiskies really that bad? Of course not, but there is definitely a reason people retreat into the safety of the past.

"The world feels like a very challenging and complex place right now," thinks Brett Templeton, "so what better way to escape it than to remind oneself of the delight felt opening a box of Nike Air Max or the original i-phone (which you can now have the latest tech inserted into, should you be able to find one). We can use nostalgia to retreat, briefly, into a simpler world, one where we ourselves were younger, which is no bad thing. At worst, some nostalgia is just an excuse for age-inappropriate behaviour. I await the return of the roller disco," he smiles.

We've discussed nostalgic design and recreating liquids from the past, but what about the nostalgia of rebuilding actual 'lost' distilleries themselves?

Last October's announcement by Diageo to bring two cult distilleries back to life is an intriguing example where nostalgia surely plays a significant role. At the time of their closure in 1983, both Port Ellen and Brora were by all accounts, fairly unremarkable distilleries in a broad DCL portfolio, facing some tough times economically. However, the proverbial ugly ducklings matured into deliciously tasty beasts and Diageo's £35 million investment plans to re-energise both facilities from next year has been widely applauded by fans – and the wider industry – as a positive step forward.

As excited as I am about the news, the cynic in me wonders just what an entirely new generation of drinker will think, when the first new whiskies potentially become available, as we approach the year 2030, or thereabouts, assuming the whisky won't just be bottled as a 3 year old or NAS release? Will they view them with the same misty-eyed reverence that today's drinkers do, given that they're unlikely to share very much in common?

The same applies to Rosebank distillery, the Lowlander (and personal favourite of mine) which was sidelined in 1993, the former site, name and remaining stocks now under the ownership of Ian MacLeod Distillers. It's a question I pose to Gordon Dundas, International Brand Ambassador for the company.

"Whether it is thought of as an old distillery or new does not make any difference to us," he explains. "Of course the name will, in some consumers, conjure up memories of the old Rosebank but equally it is a new incarnation and has to stand up as a brand in the modern whisky market, which will have evolved even more in 10 years. We do have all the remaining stocks of Rosebank and are currently working on the Rosebank positioning to ensure the newly created whisky is at the centre of the brand."

So how hard will it be to get the same whisky as before from the newly kitted out facility? Is it better to go for something similar but more forward thinking, rather than get mired up trying to recreate a nostalgic liquid that no longer exists?

"It will of course be difficult even with the same principles of Oregon pine washbacks, triple distillation with the same shape stills and worm tub condensers," continues Dundas. "Production methods have changed and we know more about wood and maturation as an industry, but the Lowland region and location is why Rosebank was different, so we want to stay true to those principles and create a whisky that celebrates what was a stunning single malt."

Looking back fondly on the past seems to be a recurring trait in today's society. Does the current climate of unease and uncertainty make us remember the past more rosily than it actually was, as a defence mechanism? I'm beginning to think so.

After attending a talk by Will Rowe, CEO of the media agency Protein at the Global Drinks Forum in Berlin late last year it became clear to me that my generation seems to have conveniently forgotten the bits that we didn't like so much, in favour of the heart-warming nostalgic bits. Rowe asserted that major drinks companies must be more adaptable and be very careful if they are engaging in nostalgia-driven marketing, especially when it comes to the emerging Generation Z drinkers of the future, who simply don't share our current fondness of the past, or particularly resonate to any of the same emotional references points that the current generation does.

So there you have it. Maybe that old Nintendo console was a bit rubbish after all. Time to relax, tune into New Music Monday on my Spotify account and drink a modern no age statement whisky.

Something tells me it's all going to be fine in the future. Stranger things have indeed happened….

m left; Tom Bruce-Gardyne, Gordon Dundas and Leonard Russell sampling Rosebank single malt outside the closed distillery.

Neil writes about whisky and other fine spirits for a number of publications globally, including The Daily and Sunday Telegraph. He is the former chairman of the World Whiskies Awards and regularly presents a drinks feature on the popular TV show, Channel 4 Sunday Brunch. His first book, (written with Gavin D. Smith) 'Let Me Tell You About Whisky' was published in 2013 and since then, he has co-authored 'Distilled', with Joel Harrison, which is now printed in thirteen languages, winning the Fortnum & Mason Drink Book Of The Year in 2015. His latest book, 'Straight Up...' celebrates the finest drinking experiences on every continent.

David Vitale, founder and owner of The New World Whisky Distillery - producers of Starward single malt

Something's in the Air

by Joel Harrison

Single malt is made the world over, often using Scottish barley, Scottish fermentation equipment and Scottish stills. But what is it that makes the single malt from Tain so different to single malt from Texas or Taiwan? Despite the clear difference in local terroir, perhaps it has more to do with the local maturation environment, or the 'airroir'.

There is a fashion at the moment to dig deep into one's own ancestry; to look at who you really are. Not with hours spent digging through family archives, dusting off letters from far-flung forefathers to their friends and family, but a more scientific way of swabbing some DNA into a tube to be sent away for proper chemical analysis, where the far reaches of your origins are exploded, and your true lineage is revealed. This is not a nature versus nurture debate: this is science; fact; truth.

In the lead up to the 2018 Football World Cup, one leading brand of DNA ancestry tests released a promotional video where it engaged with eight football legends from the past to see how well they represented their country. Legends such as Germany captain Lothar Matthäus, England wizard John Barnes and the French forward Robert Pirès. Surely you don't get much more German than a man with a surname that includes an umlaut; as British as a John; as French as a player born in Reims, the capital of Champagne.

Ian Palmer in front of Inchdairnie Distillery

Yet the results showed the opposite. England's Barnes had a healthy portion of celtic DNA, while Pirès had his French bubbles burst, when the test showed him to be mostly Italian. And it turns out that Matthäus' bratwurst might actually be a banger, as his results showed that he is as English as he is German. One wonders if the Russian linesman from the 1966 World Cup Final was doing the testing that day…

The most striking thing from this whole exercise was that each and every player felt they belonged to the country which they had represented in their professional sporting career. It was the country that taught them the game, that nurtured their natural talent, which platformed them on a world stage; the country in which they matured as a player and as a person.

What would happen if we could give a DNA test to different single malt whiskies? How would they fair?

Of course, wherever you are in the word, single malt whisky will be made of just three key ingredients: malted barley, water and yeast. Run the process through Scottish equipment, using Scottish barley and mature in oak casks, and you have Scotch, right?

Nope. Only, of course if the production processes and maturation take place in Scotland.

A Scotch producer can use all-Scottish barley and all-Scottish equipment, or no Scottish equipment and barley from anywhere in the world, yet it is the environment where the spirit matures that really makes it Scotch.

For it is here, in maturation, that the nationality of the spirit is thrust upon it. The determinism for the country it is to represent is set, no matter what the DNA test may say.

Challenge the dogma

Officially opened in May 2016 in the Kingdom of Fife, InchDairnie is an unusually large distillery for such a new build, but the team behind the engineering and construction was able to draw on over four decades of Scotch whisky production experience from Ian Palmer, the Managing Director of owners John Fergus & Co.

The distillery is a tapestry of what Palmer believes to be the best tools for the job of making single malt spirit: a mash filter from Belgium, and copper stills from Italy which produce a spirit that goes on to mature in casks from America and Spain, to deliver a product that, after three years in oak, can be labelled as 'Scotch'.

Talking about his eclectic section of distillation equipment, Palmer confidently explains that, "as a brand new business we wanted to do something to help us stand out from the crowd, within the single malt Scotch world. It made no sense to do what everyone else was doing, so we chose equipment that helps us to pull different flavour levers and to have as many of those as possible".

Jared Himstedt, Balcones Master Distiller

"We wanted to challenge the dogma", he continues. "For us it was all about producing 'flavour'. This means sourcing equipment, such as our mash filter from Belgium and stills from Italy, and other pieces from a number of different suppliers across Europe."

But what about the base product? "When it comes to our barley, at the moment we source it from Scotland, but we are certainly looking at strains and cereals from the rest of the UK, the EU and the rest of the world, as we are after flavour", Palmer says, with a notable passion in his voice.

At InchDairnie there is a clear drive to produce the best possible malt spirit, made in Scotland but with pure European DNA. However, when it comes to the maturation, there is no flinching from Palmer about the effort they have gone to, and the details they have looked at, to ensure the best possible Scotch whisky develops in its casks.

"It was important to us to build warehousing and mature on-site", Palmer explains. "We deliberately chose Fife, an east coast location, slightly south of the country and, like Speyside and Islay, it has its own little climate. It is slightly dryer than the rest of the country. But you still have to remember this is Scotland, where it pours down all the time, so that's very much a relative statement."

It is not just the minutiae of production details which are important to Palmer, but clearly also the maturation environment in which his precious, dili-gently made Scotch malt spirit will mature.

From Fife, take a flight west over the Atlantic to the American Deep South and the state of Texas. A couple of hours drive from Dallas is the University town of Waco, home to the Balcones distillery. Here, the team is making American bourbon, distilling and ageing rum and corn whisky, but their biggest selling product is single malt whisky. Texan single malt whisky. Made using Scottish barley, on Scottish equipment, including shiny new Scottish copper pot stills. Yet this spirit is less Scottish than that made at InchDairnie, on equipment sourced from Europe and barley that may come from anywhere.

"We have always used pot stills and for us Scottish ones are the gold standard," says Balcones Master Distiller Jared Himstedt. "At our core we are malt guys and pot stills make our favourite whiskies. It is the tradition we are interested in pursuing, even when making corn, rye or bourbons."

"We source most of our barley from Scotland. We use Simpson's Golden Promise which has a long history in Scotch distilling but has fallen out of favour the last few decades, being replaced by varieties that have higher yield and we make our grain choices on flavour rather than just yield, so to continue using a very traditional and historic barley made a lot of sense, especially since it is a slowly vanishing style of malt that we love and want to preserve." Here Himstedt echoes the passion for yumminess-over-yield, which Ian Palmer at InchDairnie shares.

Highland Park warehouse

With these ideals at their forefront, and a fully Scottish production process from barley to barrel, what is that makes Balcones single malt a 'Texas single malt'?

"A huge part of what makes our whisky "Texas" is the climate," Himstedt explains. "Texas maturation is quite unique and a bit extreme. We regularly have temperature swings of 20-30 degrees in a day. 8-9 months a year we are having swings like this, which means the spirit is getting pushed/sucked deep into the wood and then squeezed back out way more often than in the traditional whisky regions of the world."

"Our humidity in the summers reaches close to 100% but is much drier in the "cold" months and we have adjusted and continue to tweak every other part of our process to work with our central Texas climate and maximize its impact while maintaining a balanced process and end result." And it is this end result which makes the drink, and defines this single malt as Texan.

As with so many other whisky-making nations that have a hot and humid maturation environment, the angels' share at Balcones hits around 10-12% the first year, moving closer to 5-6% the second year. After 4-5 years, Himstedt says his "barrels can be almost half empty and gain around 3% abv each year, until 3-5 years where we can climb from 62.5% barrel entry proof to over 68% abv".

This is Scotch single malt spirit by production value, yet the finished product is very different. And here is where the talk of the importance of 'place' comes in. However, is not about the whisky's 'terroir', but the whisky's 'airroir': the complex maturation environment of seasonal swings in the heat and humidity of the local air.

The devil is in the details

Let's head back to Scotland and look for a moment at this micro-airroir in action. Craig Owen is the man who heads up the scientific side of maturation for two of Scotland's most well known single malts, Highland Park and The Macallan. His official title is 'Laboratory and Scientific Research Manager'; a title which reflects his 13 years of experience into maturation research at The Scotch Whisky Research Institute, before a further five years at Edrington.

Owen's first point to me is not to forget the cask, stating that, "generally the main contribution towards Scotch whisky is the cask, but the location is also very important for the flavour delivery".

The devil is in the detail according to Owen. "There will certainly be differences in maturation due to environmental conditions. The locations are important, as is the design of the warehouse and how it deals with the local environment. In Orkney, the warehouses are of a smaller dunnage style with slate roofs and earth floors; this is all to keep the conditions as stable as possible. The floors help release moisture into the air".

By contrast, Owen explains that in Speyside Edrington employ, "large racked warehouses made from metal, with concrete floors help to manage the ambient environment around our casks. How the warehouse design deals with the local environment is key. The central belt is warmer and you get a slightly quicker maturation than in Speyside, and again, in Orkney".

"Our maturation is very slow in Scotland", Owen notes. "Maturation is all about the absorption of immature notes followed by the extraction of flavours from the wood, and then an element of rounding and smoothing through oxidation. This is what sets Scotch apart: the slowness of maturation due to our colder temperatures".

Despite describing it as one of the "subtleties of Scotch whisky maturation", Owen is clear that it is this unique airroir which defines single malt from Scotland. By way of example, he notes "the majority of our Highland Park is matured on Orkney for a reason, as the warehouses and the location, at a subtle level, are important".

Of course, both Highland Park and The Macallan have been producing spirit for centuries, and the environment in which that spirit matures is part of the final overall character of each malt. However, what if you already understand your maturation environment, but are yet to make a malt spirit to mature in it? This was the position David Vitale found himself in, when starting The New World Whisky Distillery, which makes Starward single malt in Melbourne, Australia.

You don't need to be a global traveller to have experienced the extreme weather conditions in this part of the world; the band Crowded House sent a musical postcard of their experiences of the local environment through their song 'Four Seasons In One Day', so when Vitale started to make single malt in Melbourne, he knew he was going to face a challenge with maturation.

"We knew we wanted to use Australian brewing barley to start with, and we knew we wanted to fill into ex-Australian wine barrels which are made from French or American oak, so at the very start, before we did anything, we had to develop a spirit that would work with the 'Elemental Maturation' environment that we have here in this part of Australia," he notes.

"I think we have the hardest working casks in the world of whisky," he claims. "Our alcohol content rises consistently across the years we are maturing, so we fill at 55% and after three and a half years, our whisky is up to 62% abv. This unique environment is critical to what makes our whisky, our whisky. If we weren't careful in our spirit development, we would have ended up simply with eau de oak."

It was this retro-engineering of the spirit that allowed Starward to retain flavour in the face of such aggressive maturation. "The new make spirit we developed was high in flavour and designed specifically for shorter maturation than, say, Scottish spirit. If you were to mature this in Scotland, it would come out as a lighter product than with our maturation here in Melbourne," Vitale explains.

In Taiwan, the award-winning single malt Kavalan, from the King Car distillery built their process around traditional Scottish production methods, as well as equipment, but tweaked the spirit production to accommodate the local airroir. Master Distiller Ian Chang explains that they "use Scottish copper pot stills but with English malts to produce our single malt whisky. The method that we adopt is indeed the traditional Scottish method but with a few changes in order to suit the subtropical Taiwan climate".

"With our subtropical climate of the summer heat, it is very helpful for our rapid extraction process. With our winter's cold Siberian air, it is very good for oxidation and maturation of the spirit. With the two processes taking place intermittently year-to-year, our spirit naturally "matures" in a short period of time. Our annual average temperature is 25°C, with an average humidity of around 90%. So, warm and humid throughout the year", notes Chang.

It is a "combination with the climate" which Chang says makes their whisky "very special and very Taiwanese. By that we mean clean, complex and rich in character". And as Chang quipped at the World Whisky Forum in 2018, "because of earthquakes, the whisky maturing in our warehouses is like something from James Bond: shaken, not stirred".

The Scottish style of maturation however has always been a Holy Grain for single malt distillers. This can be seen as far back as 1918, when Masata-

Kavalan´s Master Distiller, Ian Chang

The old warehouse at Karuizawa Distillery

ka Taketsuru and Shinjiro Torii opened the Yamazaki distillery in Japan. His aim was to find a location that echoed that of the Scottish Highlands, and here we are today with Japanese whisky providing a suitable alternative for those consumers who know they have a palate attuned to single malt Scotch, but are looking for something a little more exotic.

This ideal of producing to the Scottish style was part of the driver for the modern day success of Karuizawa, the lost Japanese distillery. One of the men responsible for rescuing the last remaining casks of this now legendary single malt is Marcin Miller, who explains that, "in 1955 when they built the distillery they were attempting to make a whisky in the most traditional way possible, and for this you can read that the founders were looking to replicate some of the more robust, successful Speyside single malts from Scotland. They imported Golden Promise from Scotland, which was distilled through small stills and then matured in sherry butts. But the result was a very different product, because of the maturation environment."

Miller contextualises this by saying that the maturation of Karuizawa is down to a "confluence of different elements: the high altitude on an active volcano; an average temperature of 10°C; humidity at a constant 80% and mists around the distillery site and warehousing every day. All this coming together at the same time, in the same place is what makes Karuizawa, Karuizawa, giving it a remarkable intensity of richness and aroma".

Certainly Karuizawa is not a Highland or Speyside single malt replicate, but very much its own product. A DNA test on Karuizawa may well reveal the family tree of Golden Promise barley grown and malted in Scotland, but it us undeniably Japanese whisky. It is this exciting diversity within the world of single malt whisky, made from three simple ingredients, using three simple stages which, with the addition of individual maturation airroir, creates one incredible, diverse and global product.

Joel Harrison is an award winning author, communicator and industry consultant, whose work has been published in over 20 countries, across 13 different languages. His writing work can be seen in publications such as The Wall Street Journal India and The Daily Telegraph in the UK. Harrison also appears regularly on British television across a number of shows as a whisky specialist. He sits as a judge for the International Wine and Spirits Competition (IWSC) where today he holds the role of a Trophy Judge and Chairman across Scotch whisky and other spirits. In 2013 Harrison was made a Keeper of the Quaich.

The new Macallan Distillery

A new era for Scotch Whisky Tourism

by Becky Paskin

Not that long ago, a curious visitor
to a whisky distillery was considered a nucance
interferring with the daily work. Today, the whisky tourists are treated
as valuable guests and the tours are tailormade
to suit everyone´s palate.

When Alfred Barnard toured the whisky distilleries of the United Kingdom in the late 19th century, there was no such thing as a gift shop. Distilleries at the time were more concerned with making whisky than entertaining visitors who happened to drop by; in fact showing any guest around a site was considered an inconvenience, taking the distillery manager away from their work.

It wasn't until the 1960s, when the Glenfarclas, Glenfiddich and Glenlivet distilleries opened their visitor centres on Speyside that the potential for whisky tourism was realised. Gradually, more distilleries on popular tourist routes added their own centres – by 1999, 44 distilleries offered visitor facilities – but it's only really been in the last decade that Scotch producers have been placing the visitor experience right alongside production at the heart of their operation. Of the 122 malt distilleries operating

Part of the visitor´s area at the new Macallan Distillery

in Scotland, over half now have visitor centres open to the public or are available to visit by appointment. Distilleries are no longer just about making whisky; they've realised the power of providing memorable experiences that connect people to their brands.

But why now? "There's definitely more awareness of Scotch whisky and social media has definitely helped with that," says Susan Morrison, Chief Executive of the Scotch Whisky Experience on Edinburgh's Royal Mile. "With greater awareness and accessibility to experts and people talking about whisky, means there's a much greater interest in Scotch whisky. Once you manage to ignite that spark in people it becomes quite voracious an appetite to learn more, experience more and visit distilleries, and that has all snowballed."

Scotch whisky distilleries are now collectively one of the biggest tourist attractions in the UK, with over 1.9 million visits during 2017 – an increase of 11% on the previous year. "These are exciting times," says Karen Betts, CEO of the Scotch Whisky Association (SWA). "Scotch whisky distilleries have invested hugely in providing world-class visitor facilities at their sites all over Scotland, and they are collaborating in establishing new whisky trails and finding new ways of telling the story of Scotch to British and foreign visitors alike."

The highest number of visitors to Scotch distilleries hail from Germany and the US – two major export markets for the industry, followed by those from India, China and Japan. Chinese visitors are so prevalent at the Scotch Whisky Experience that tours are now offered in both Mandarin and Cantonese. It's not a coincidence that more overseas visitors than ever are flocking to Scotland and seeking out a distillery experience. Organisations like VisitScotland and Moray Speyside Tourism have increased their marketing investment to attract visitors to the country, and it seems to be paying off – 2017 saw an extra 50,000 visitors compared to the previous year, representing the biggest surge in tourism in the area.

Jo Robinson, regional director for Moray Speyside at VisitScotland, says while whisky is an attractive prospect for visitors, it's Scotland's overall appeal that's prompting visits. "Whisky has to be one of the high ticket items, and certainly something particularly the Speyside brand is known for globally, but in recent years there's been more effort to package up that whisky experience with luxury products. So it's not just about selling the whisky as a standalone experience, it's about the provenance of the area, the food and drink produced there, the beautiful hotels, experiences, accommodation and things to see and do in the area."

An artist´s impression of the future global brand home for Johnnie Walker in Edinburgh

The tourist pound is now so important to the Scotch whisky industry that an unprecedented level of investment has been poured into transforming distilleries into world-class attractions, in both form and function. In the last five years, distilleries have invested over £500 million in creating tourism experiences for visitors.

Huge investments ahead

In April 2018 Diageo announced plans to invest £150m in upgrading its 12 existing distillery visitor centres, establishing specialist experiences at the soon-to-reopen Brora and Port Ellen sites, as well as build a global brand home for Johnnie Walker in Edinburgh. At the time, Cristina Diezhandino, Diageo Global Scotch Whisky Director, said: "New generations of consumers around the world are falling in love with Scotch and they want to experience it in the place where it is made and meet the people who make it. This investment will ensure that the people we attract to Scotland from around the world go home as life-long ambassadors for Scotch and for Scotland."

Similarly, Edrington pumped £140m into building a new home for Macallan in Speyside, after realising it needed more capacity. It was thought that adding an-other still house to the already fragmented Victorian distillery would create a messy home that wasn't representative of the luxury brand. Instead, the decision was taken to design a separate, monolithic, subterranean feat of engineering that has entirely disrupted expectations of the traditional distillery design, in terms of its architecture, technology and approach to the visitor experience. "What we've done is going to be fantastic for everyone," says Adele Joyce, Macallan Brand Team Project Manager, who was responsible for leading the installation of the visitor experience. "At Macallan now we will have a great number of people who are interested not only in whisky itself, but in engineering and architecture, who will then come to see the building and hopefully then be attracted to the whisky and want to learn more."

The standard distillery tour takes guests on a journey through the production plant, which is peppered with interactive installations representing Macallan's 'six pillars'. Already innovative in that the educational elements of a visitor centre are immersed in with the stills and washbacks, each installation brings Macallan's brand philosophies to life, whether gazing upon a droplet of spirit suspended in mid-air, or wandering through a moving oak forest to feel the warmth of a cask being charred.

Part of the experience at Lindores Abbey Distillery is that you can actually see the old abbey from the still house

"Everything in the building has been considered, even down to the design of the shelves in the boutique, which are made from virgin and toasted oak, just so we can continue to tell the story of the casks in the retail areas and we can make it relatable for our guests and boutique staff," Joyce says. "There are small details in everything. We've got an iconic structure, an iconic brand, so to have an iconic home to sit them in now is something that stands up there and will be noted as an incredible piece of architecture with something incredible inside it."

Another distillery blurring the boundaries between distillery and visitor attraction is the soon-to-open Holyrood distillery in Edinburgh. Taking over an empty, 180-year-old railway building across two floors, Holyrood distillery will immerse visitors in a colourful exploration of flavour as they explore. Bill Farrar, Sales and Marketing Director for Holyrood distillery, which is set to open in summer 2019, says starting with a shell has enabled the team plan the distillery around the visitor experience. "Because we are able to plan the operational side around the tourism side, we're able to make it fairly interesting and logical," he says. "We want to build a distillery that's all about flavour, and make whisky accessible to as many people as possible."

While Holyrood plans to simplify the explanation of the production process for those will little knowledge of Scotch, experts will be on-hand to answer more difficult questions on the brand's use of multiple yeast strains and barley varieties. "It's very much designed to appeal to a wide cross-section of people rather than just someone who's fanatical about single malt. But if you are fanatical about single malt, we have the expertise to take you through every little quirk and difference that we will have. You'll see smoky whisky, sweet whisky, spicy whisky and you'll be able to decide there and then which you like the best, and if you care to buy a bottle, we'd be delighted."

The visitor experience is essentially a giant shop window for the brand (which they hope results in an exit through the gift shop), so regardless of whether a distillery has stock ready to sell or not, authenticity is key. For Gareth Roberts, Director at Organic Architects, which designed Ardnamurchan, Lindores Abbey and Ncn'ean distilleries, the brand story forms the starting point of any new distillery design. "People are really brand aware these days, and from the outset, certainly the distilleries we're working on, they are looking to make it a brand home," he says. "They're fully aware of making sure that nothing they do to the building compromises the brand, and that the building, the design and the tour, the exhibition and the visitor centre, are at one with the character of the brand that they want to put out there." At Lindores, that meant considering the distillery's physical relationship to the abbey itself to communicate the location's distilling heritage. Roberts explains: "At Lindores we linked the story of the abbey and Friar John Cor by putting the stills in a big window looking down over the abbey. It completes the traditional story from 500 years ago. We all as designers have a duty to make a brilliant visitor experience for the people who are spending their time coming to the building."

Clydeside - the latest distillery to open in Glasgow

For Neil Mathieson, Managing Director of Mossburn Distillers, which operates the new Torabhaig distillery on Skye, tourism is vital in establishing a new brand, particularly if marketing budgets are scant. He says: "Tourism is a very important part of establishing a brand. If you don't encourage your disciples then they can't spread the word, and I think for malt whiskies that don't have large marketing budgets or obvious routes into distribution, you have to play the part and encourage people to understand who you are, where you are, and possibly when you come and see us."

Distillery layout and design aside, one of the most vital aspects of any visitor experience is the quality of the tours on offer. Companies may be pumping millions into designing jaw-dropping, multi-sensory experiences, but the quality of the information presented, and how it is tailored to different knowledge levels, cannot be overlooked. "What's critical, and what we've tried to focus on at Clydeside, is the quality of the tour guide," says Tim Morrison, Chairman of Glasgow's Clydeside distillery. "He or she is the focal point to portraying the brand, creating the interest for the tours, making them feel like they're part of that tour. The tour guide has such an important part to play, both with their knowledge, their presentation, their warmth and their welcome. The brand is synonymous with the distillery; if you do a lousy job with the visitor, they're not going to be very happy with your brand."

These days it's simply not enough for a tour to point out the basics of production and offer a dram at the end. "Over the last 10 years, we've certainly seen tourists expect more from their experiences – they want to fully immerse themselves in the brands," says Katie Waugh, Visitor Centre Marketing Manager for Diageo. "Guests love to hear the personal and entertaining stories from our tour guides. Consumers are more conscious about the provenance of what they eat and drink – they are seeking out experiences which educate as well as delight." Whether that's something as simple as offering a whiff of the foreshots and feints, or taking an extended exploration of local food and drink producers, distilleries cannot afford to be complacent when it comes to providing added value.

At least 14 Scotch distilleries are set to come online in the next two years, most of which will be open to visitors, but their success as tourist destinations will be determined by how attractive their proposition is to both general visitors and whisky enthusiasts alike. However, Macallan's Adele Joyce says: "Anyone doing anything in the industry to improve the guests experience can only benefit the industry as a whole." If every new distillery continues to put the visitor at the heart of the operation, the only problem whisky fans have now is deciding which to go visit first.

Becky Paskin is editor of online magazine Scotchwhisky.com, the world's leading website for Scotch whisky lovers. She was the first journalist to gain a General Certificate in Distillation with the Institute of Brewing and Distilling – a qualification usually reserved for distillery operators. Becky has been writing about drinks for over 10 years, and is a member of the society Keepers of the Quaich. She regularly presents educational whisky seminars at global drinks shows. In 2018 she co-founded #OurWhisky, a movement to challenge outdated stereotypical perceptions of the modern whisky drinker.

The Macallan
Highland Single Malt
Scotch Whisky
Cask N° 1402
1965
THE MACALLAN DISTILLERS LTD
PRODUCE OF SCOTLAND

MATURED ONLY IN
SHERRY WOOD
The MACALLAN
Single Highland Malt
Scotch Whisky
1951
ONE OF ONLY 632 BOTTLES
PRODUCE OF SCOTLAND
49.8%vol   700ml

The MACALLAN
Highland Single Malt
Scotch Whisky
First Bottled 1975
1940
THE MACALLAN DISTILLERS LTD
PRODUCE OF SCOTLAND
700 ml

MATURED ONLY IN SHERRY WOOD
YEARS 40 OLD
The MACALLAN
Highland Single Malt
Scotch Whisky
First Bottled 1979
1939
PRODUCE OF SCOTLAND
700ml

YEARS 30 OLD
The MACALLAN
Single Highland Malt
Scotch Whisky
Cask N° 6098
1973
THE MACALLAN DISTILLERY
PRODUCE OF SCOTLAND
700 ml

YEARS 21 OLD
The MACALLAN
Highland Single Malt
Scotch Whisky
Cask N° 1247
1989
PRODUCE OF SCOTLAND

MATURED ONLY IN SHERRY WOOD
YEARS 22 OLD
The MACALLAN
Highland Single Malt
Scotch Whisky
Cask N° 24706
1990
Distilled 1990 | Bottled 2013
THE MACALLAN DISTILLERS LTD

Whisky Investment
a golden opportunity

by Jonny McCormick

The interest in collecting rare whiskies has spread
like a wildfire in recent years. The next step is to view the golden liquid as
other rare commodities that can be bought and sold. Some say it´s an
opportunity to make a good return on your investment while
others feel the soul of whisky is being lost.

To begin with, the paddles raised at the back of the auction room were competing in a three-way contest between the telephone bidder to the auctioneer's left, and the commissioned bids in the book. It was May 18th 2018, late Friday afternoon, and an auction of fine whisky was underway at Bonhams Hong Kong Gallery inside the skyscrapers of Pacific Place. As the bids rose incrementally, the lithe limb movements of the auctioneer revealed an open palm whenever the phone bidder took the lead. At HK$5 million, the phone bidder bowed out, narrowing the field to a binary choice. The auctioneer gave fair warning when the bidding hit HK$7 million, scanning the faces of his colleagues managing phone bids for signs of interest. In response, he noted their curt headshakes before his salesroom staff returned to relaying the auction proceedings to their wealthy clients behind cupped hands.

Suddenly, the auctioneer's face was transformed by a look of surprise: at the last possible moment, the gentleman bidder in possession of paddle 666 indicated that he was prepared to give a little more. Accepting his bid, the hammer fell at HK$7.05 million, a final price in excess of $1 million dollars. Amidst spontaneous applause and cheering, the sale of the Macallan Valerio Adami 1926 60 year old at Bonhams became the most expensive bottle of whisky ever auctioned.

Incredibly, it took less than thirty years from the first dedicated whisky auction to the sale of the first million-dollar bottle. This was a hugely significant moment, reclaiming the record for Scotch whisky, yet reaffirming Hong Kong as the location where such records are set. For the professional who auctioned the Adami, and the Macallan Peter Blake 1926 60 year old for a marginally lower sum, it was the culmination of many years work.

"I first come across these two bottles in a European collector's display room in 2010, almost the same time as I started the first Hong Kong whisky auction," recalls Daniel Lam, Head of Fine Wine & Whisky at Bonhams, Hong Kong. By 2016 the bottles had changed hands, and he was approached about offering them at auction. Lam advised holding off: the price for Macallan was only just starting to pick up after the 2015 auction boom in Japanese whisky. They decided the ideal sale date was May 2018 and the pair was launched last March backed by a press release and video. These bottles had not been seen for thirty years, and Lam was confident the market was ready.

"I certainly felt the interest was there. With an estimate of HK$3.6 million (US$460,000) each, the highest of any alcohol in an auction at that time, we treated them like pieces of art." Potential buyers from Asia flew in to inspect the bottles, and the sale gathered momentum as word spread amongst the world's top collectors. "I knew if the Blake could fetch a good price, so would the Adami. That's why we placed the Blake in the middle of the auction and the Adami at the very end."

Bonhams Hong Kong has been a major player in the remarkable growth of Scotch whisky values over the past few years. As the market moves into whisky, so the clients are changing. "We are certainly attracting interest from wine collectors, but new whisky collectors have also emerged," reports Lam. "Around 80% of whisky sale buyers are private collectors who bid for investment or personal consumption, whereas most wine buyers are dealers, merchants, or restaurants." Lam estimates that 40% of the whisky auction market is now based on trading for investment only. "Like any collectable item, a person needs knowledge and passion, sometimes with a bit of trial and error, to justify the investment. Our focus is really on emerging whisky markets like China, Vietnam, Laos, and Cambodia where wealthy private enthusiasts tend to buy for their own consumption and have the resources to buy the best."

Whisky lovers progress from a curiosity about drinking whisky to becoming ardent whisky investors, and the pace of that metamorphosis is quickening, as Sean McGlone, Director of Whisky Auctioneer attests, "I think people get to that a lot quicker," he says. "People notice the returns on whisky very quickly and discover that they're going for a bottle that costs £200 one year, but £250 the next. That's converted a lot of drinkers and non-profit collectors, into collectors for profit. I think the increasing visibility of the process really does encourage people to start collecting for investment."

Have fashions shifted from buying-to-drink to buying-to-invest? "There's always been a healthy mix," acknowledges McGlone. "People are also fooling themselves to a degree. They think they're buying to collect, but deep down they're buying to invest.

The record breaker - Macallan Valerio Adami

Karuizawa has been a good investment in recent years

Sean McGlone, Director of Whisky Auctioneer

There have been a lot of new investors attracted to it, and I think that some people who used to invest a little, now invest a lot because they've had good returns."

Top whiskies can fetch staggering sums. Every month, whiskies sell for £5,000 to £50,000 or more on the first page of an auction's website, but who is buying them? "I would say a lot of it is business," shares McGlone. "If a bottle hits market value, then it's often being purchased by a business. People buying for business have a set price, they religiously stick to it, and they don't tend to push up the prices. If the whisky greatly exceeds market value, either a passionate collector or a very passionate drinker is buying it. They are the ones who will pay above the market value to get what they want."

More economist, less mixologist, could be a realistic description of the next wave of whisky enthusiasts. Some collectors build up an encyclopaedic knowledge of brands, bottlings, and values, more important attributes for an investor, rather than the traditional expertise concerned with understanding flavour or distillery character developed through years of sampling a broad range of bottlings.

"I think there is a degree of knowledge and skill in understanding that," admits McGlone. "If there are two releases from the distillery, do you understand which one will be better for investment? Nowadays, a lot of people look at things purely from an investment perspective."

Christian Svantesson - founder of the Single Malt Fund

Investing in a whisky fund

Trading in individual bottles is a time-consuming business, so some whisky investors are looking beyond the auction scene for profits. With varying levels of success, alternative investment schemes concerning whisky have been launched, such as the Whisky Trading Company by Holyrood Park distillery's David Robertson in 2013, and the Platinum Whisky Investment Fund in Hong Kong by Rickesh Kishnani in 2014. The Swedish-based Single Malt Fund (SMF) is the latest of these enterprises, but founder and CEO Christian Svantesson believes his approach is different, and offers whisky investors a significant range of opportunities and benefits. He says, "There are so many whisky lovers around the world that are lustily looking in different magazines at these fantastic bottles and reading tasting notes of whiskies that they dream about. Unfortunately, to invest, buy, and sell these bottles is something for the super-rich these days, the multi-millionaires, but we are offering the possibility to be part of that. Democratising these investments is an important aspect of this fund."

Svantesson's father became a collector in the mid-1970s, following the advice of a family friend to switch from collecting cognac to malt whisky, so Svantesson grew up surrounded by fine whisky,

"It's always been around and I've always appreciated it, but whisky is an acquired taste; for most teenagers in Sweden, it's a difficult drink to appreciate. Many of my whisky maniac friends fell head over heels into whisky; I don't have that relationship with it." As a young man, Svantesson bought whisky with his first pay cheque earned by washing dishes in a restaurant. "I bought the Macallan, now one of the most sought after brands, but at that time, it was just standard whisky. I liked the name and it was easy to pronounce for a Swedish teenager."

The idea of running a rare whisky alternative investment scheme would have appeared ridiculous last century when few bottles ever topped £1,000 and auctions were only convened in Scotland every three months. Svantesson distils the global success of whisky down to two factors: effective marketing by the Scotch whisky industry and the power of social media. The promotion of Scotch whisky created a lifestyle, and a culture developed around it. "Social media has done wonders for the collectors, and it all comes down to supply and demand," says Svantesson. "In Sweden, we have around 250 whisky clubs, and probably five times more when you include other whisky societies, but without social media, we would not see the scene we have today."

"Social media also reminds us of the dangers of buying and selling whisky," he discloses. "In Sweden, buying and selling is everywhere; they are selling samples, they're selling bottles, and it's totally unregulated and without shame." On a personal basis, Svantesson identifies as a drinker-collector, rather than an investor. "I usually open my bottles at one point or other," he admits. "I have never personally sold a bottle. I've only purchased and opened bottles. That's the honest truth."

The idea for the SMF started during a celebratory trip to Islay with a group of like-minded, whisky-loving friends during February 2016. Talking one evening, Svantesson, then working in venture capital, shared his thoughts with his companions, many of whom also worked in finance,

"It's such an interesting market but it's not going to get any easier," he mused. "We see trends out there, but nothing grows upwards forever." He asked his associates, "What if we launched a fund with professionally managed investments that was onshore, regulated, transparent, and open to normal whisky lovers?" Over the next eighteen months, Svantesson assembled a team of lawyers, fund managers, and financial advisors who found Sweden's laws governing alternative investment funds provided just the right conditions. It's worth noting that due to Sweden's alcohol laws, the investment body of the SMF may be in Sweden, but the operational arm is based in Dublin.

Admittedly, some whisky collectors may balk at investing their money in a fund rather having ownership and full control over the bottles, but perhaps ownership is slightly old-fashioned these days? Participation without ownership is all the rage: Netflix, Spotify, and Kindle, for example, have allowed us to dispense with our bulky DVD box sets, CD cases, and dog-eared novels. Do we really need all those unopened cartons of whisky cluttering up our homes? The advantages of investing in the SMF include the strength in numbers and the accessibility of the fund to many income brackets.

"There are whisky lovers out there who would be so happy to own a Port Ellen, a Brora, or a Macallan, one of these super bottles,' expands Svantesson. "By giving them the opportunity to be part of a fund, then they can say, 'Hey, I own this bottle.' People love this liquid, they live this liquid, and we're offering another way to interact with their hobby and this culture. There is such a magical world around whisky. It's another way to invest in something that they understand and they love. I mean, who loves a bond?"

The SMF will invest in liquid from the primary and secondary market, private collections, auctions, new releases, and they have been increasingly interested in buying mature casks. Investors receive detailed information on the performance of the fund's acquisitions and holdings. Svantesson promises, "You can follow how the fund invests in every bottle and realises each investment and you can feel part of it." An enterprise like the SMF also needs a vault, it's own Aladdin's cave if you like, where the precious bottles can be stored securely under the watchful eye of a custodian. I like to imagine that it looks like the room filled with packing cases at the end of Raiders of the Lost Ark. "Absolutely, I love that image!" laughs Svantesson.

An additional incentive for SMF investors is the right of first refusal when they liquidize their assets, which has specifically attracted some collector-investors. The team will write about the investments and explain the rationale behind their acquisitions, just like any other fund. Involvement will help investors learn more about the market, which could enhance their own whisky purchases as they become more sophisticated collectors. Svantesson expects, "Hopefully, we will bring them along on the trip and nurture their interest even further, yet do all this in a safe, transparent, and regulated way."

With the fund capped at €25M, the SMF has the potential to influence producers releasing new whiskies as well as secondary market trading. Whenever you read in the Malt Whisky Yearbook about this year's latest high value releases, bear in mind that their target customer may no longer be a private individual, but an investment fund.

"The purchase power that we have will make us yet another capable potential buyer, so we will be part of driving the price, should we choose to be part of that," comments Svantesson. "Certainly, we will add to the demand, and supply, as more liquidity is poured into the market. We see that we have a better understanding of the true market value, but a private individual may exceed the price for reasons we would never agree with." A whisky investment fund requires a diverse buying strategy, but Svantesson offers this advice about whisky collectibles; "You can divide them into two different types of rarities; ones that are created, and ones that have evolved. It seems to be accepted that the ones that have evolved are more genuine, and have a higher 'snob' value. From a market perspective, or from a collectors' perspective, as long as it is a genuine bottling, does it really matter? I say it doesn't. As a drinker, I prefer the rarity that has evolved as it has become scarcer due to consumption."

There are downsides to any investment, and those risks include the cost, potential returns, volatility of the market, and trust in the expertise of those taking the decisions. "There is a risk in investing in whisky, but we believe that the development of whisky investments has a very positive outlook for the foreseeable future," says Svantesson reassuringly. Firstly, the fund is regulated by the Swedish equivalent of the Financial Services Authority. "As an alternative investment, we are investing in something that carries a lot of risk. We wanted to lessen that risk and increase the transparency by regulating the risk." Secondly, investing in the fund will cost an annual management fee of 2.5%. "Remember these are handpicked bottles, we're not trading in paperwork," points out Svantesson. "I think it's a fair cost. There is a team of professionals who do nothing else but invest in whisky; they analyse the market, they analyse the liquid, so there is a cost that comes with that." The SMF also believes its professional approach gives it a greater chance of avoiding counterfeit whisky than an individual private collector. "We have the knowledge and the resources to properly investigate our investments to avoid buying fakes." The SMF opened to investors in 2018 with a projected lifespan of six years, telling the market that investors could reasonably expect a 10% net return per annum (i.e. a £1,000 initial investment minus the 2.5% fee at the start of each year, would deliver a net profit of £484 after 6 years, with the SMF collecting £218 in fees over the duration of the fund). Svantesson is optimistic they will achieve their target for investors, "The market has performed better than that in the past but that says nothing about the future."

Has the morality disappeared?

The arrival of the SMF, like everything else concerned with whisky investment, is an understandable manifestation of the evolution of whisky's success. Not everyone is happy with the state of affairs, however, as whisky consumers divert their budgets to spend their money at auctions or chase limited releases sold directly from the brands, and prices have risen steeply as companies try to curb flipping, the quick-sell strategy used to make short-term profits from limited editions. Fewer of us are walking into our local whisky shops to make a purchase. If you buy a rare bottle which you have no intention of drinking because you intend to profit off the back of a fellow whisky enthusiast and expect a return of four or five times higher than what you bought it for, then could there be a backlash to your actions?

There are parallels with the music industry: Ed Sheeran is championing a fight back against secondary ticketing websites re-selling event tickets to concertgoers at excessive prices, with music fans being turned away from gigs when the tickets turn out to be invalid.

Vince Fusaro – co-owner of Luvian's

Vince Fusaro has been a whisky retailer since 1983, and is co-owner of Luvian's, an original wine and spirits merchant with shops in Cupar and St. Andrews, Fife. His hard-hitting message to Scotch whisky producers about morality, honesty, and greed is clear,

"It's punters that make the market. You make the market. You have usurped the position of the collectors and punters while making a bob or two and you force them on to a treadmill that they step off at their peril. You've created a vicious circle, and it's vicious in every sense, because they've invested so much. You've forced them into this, and probably a lot of them think, 'Can I afford to get off here?'"

Fusaro explains that the Scotch Whisky Industry posts a turnover of £4 billion for sales of 1.3 billion bottles, which makes the average price of a bottle of whisky around £3, net of VAT and duty, including dry goods and maturation. "Whisky is cheap," he says. Fusaro believes that too many limited edition whiskies are being produced, and his advice to those marketing Scotch whisky would be to cut supply.

"If you are not greedy and you actually make a whisky limited to a few thousand bottles, not a few thousand cases, then you can sell out because you've created the market," he explains. Nowadays, he sometimes only takes half of his allocation of new limited editions because of overproduction; "You can't treble and quadruple production, especially with non-age statement whiskies, that is nonsense! It's pure greed; this is not market forces anymore." As a retailer, he is increasingly finding that he is the one left holding stock. "I've got things in the shop that I can't sell, because after the first flurry, no one wants them any more. It is like selling Easter eggs after Easter, what do you do with them?"

Fusaro despairs at the spiralling prices of 18, 25, and 40 year old whiskies when the 12 year old versions are heavily discounted in supermarkets: the entry level bottle is half the price it should be, the others are ten times as much. "So are we being taken for a ride?" he asks. "Oh, it's customer demand, they say. No, it's not, because you've forced people to got to auctions to realise that we're all greedy: 99% of us are greedy. I'm one of the veterans now, I've been in the trade 35 years, but I've been loyal and faithful to the whisky industry. I have promoted this wonderful liquid, and shared the stories with my customers. I should have read more about the whisky barons, I should have read more about the Pattison scandal, I should have read more about how the Irish were treated in the early 20th century to make Scotch palatable," laments Fusaro. "I feel the morality has somehow disappeared from whisky."

So what does the future hold? "It will continue until people realise the Emperor isn't wearing any clothes, and that might not be too far down the line," warns Fusaro. "Until the merry-go-round stops, it will keep going round. I love the expression; 'You can shave a man all his life but only cut his throat once.' All you have to do is cut a couple of throats and word soon gets out."

Whisky writer and photographer Jonny McCormick is Contributing Editor of Whisky Advocate magazine and one of their leading whisky reviewers. He is known as a specialist in the field of rare and collectable whiskies, and his prolific writing on the topic has made him an authority on the secondary market. He is a Keeper of the Quaich and has presented Scotch whisky tastings in Europe, North America, and Asia.

Is this a Golden Age for Scotch Whisky?

by Charles MacLean

The notion of past 'golden ages'
when everything was better dates back to Classical times.
Currently, whisk(e)y is enjoying an unprecedented boom globally,
but is the product as good as it was in the past?
And will it be followed by a bust?

The first writer I know of to apply the term 'Golden Age' to whisky is Aeneas Macdonald in 1930. In his splendid polemic Whisky he bemoans the quality of (blended) Scotch available, the lack of appreciation shown to whisky generally and the fact that malt whisky was all but unavailable.

"…there has been a tendency to abolish whisky from the table of the connoisseur to the saloon bar and the golf club smoke-room. The notion that we can possibly develop a palate for whisky is guaranteed to produce a smile of derision in any company except that of a few Scottish lairds, farmers, gamekeepers, and bailies, relics of a vanished age of gold when the vintages of the north had their students and lovers."

The Johnnie Walker blending room in the early 1920s and Kirsteen Campbell, Master Blender for Edrington and although...

But was whisky really 'better' in 'the old days'? And how far back do we have to peer to find this Arcadian era?

Ten years before Whisky appeared, the great oenophile, Professor George Saintsbury, recalled in his Notes on a Cellar Book (1920) a handful of malts he had enjoyed thirty years before, when he was Professor of English in the University of Edinburgh. He remarks that they were more full-bodied and flavourful than the whiskies currently available, and like Macdonald eschews blends.

Another professor, RJS McDowall, looked to the future in a post-script to his book The Whiskies of Scotland (1967). He was apprehensive for four reasons: the increase in capacity – "More whisky is being produced today than ever in its history"; the age at which it is bottled – "Many malt distillers sell it at the legal minimum three years, long before it is properly matured"; the marketing of cheap blends – "grain whisky flavoured slightly with very young malt whisky" and high taxation leading to reliance on export markets. He concludes: "It is only by keeping up the quality of Scotch whisky that it can maintain its unique position."

Elsewhere he cautions against automation and competition from non-Scotch whiskies:

"… there has not yet appeared, as far as I know, a plant controlled by computer. It will come but by then all the good whisky will have been consumed and our successors will have nothing to compare it with. Even today, we cannot tell what the whisky of fifty years ago was really like. It is to be hoped that the urge to make and sell whisky quickly and more cheaply will not lead to a deterioration of standards. Perhaps this has begun. I hate to think of it but, if it does, it will be replaced by whiskies from other countries for there are rain and peat in both Spain and Japan."

Notwithstanding the doubts expressed by these authorities, today it is commonplace to extoll the virtues of whiskies made in the 1960s and 1970s, and regret the fact that in blind tastings against their contemporary equivalents, they almost invariably score higher.

Better or just different?

This leads to lengthy discussions about how and why the flavours might have changed and whether such changes might take place over time in an unopened bottle. In regard to the latter, the Scotch whisky industry says "No, or if at all, only very

...there is almost 100 years between the pictures, much of the technique and practice has remained the same

slightly (through oxidation)". But if this is the case and the whisky has the same flavour profile as the day it was filled into the bottle, then 'whiskies in the old days' were 'different', at least – I won't say 'better' – than today's…

Many changes in process took place during the 1960s and early 1970s, in the interests of economy and efficiency, and to meet the huge demand for Scotch during this era. Not all of them were beneficial to flavour, in spite of the considerable efforts made by malt distillers to replicate spirit character after such changes had been made. But their key concern was consistency, not flavour.

Flavour – the combination of aroma, texture and taste – came to pre-eminence with the rise in interest in single malt whiskies which began in the 1980s and has been gathering pace ever since. In 1980, less than one per cent of the malt whisky made was bottled as a single, and although today 90% of malt still goes for blending, sales of Scotch malt contribute around 25% to the industry's profitability.

The unprecedented growth in smaller 'craft' distilleries in recent years all over the world might certainly be described as a 'golden age' for whisky production. But it also heralds a high degree of concern for flavour: most of these new distilleries – in many countries, all of them – will, or are, offering their products for sale as single whiskies (malts, ryes, mixed grains) rather than producing for blending purposes. Accordingly, they must win consumers by releasing whiskies with flavours which appeal.

The new generation of whisky distillers is exploring how this might be achieved, often in relation to what raw materials (cereals and yeasts) are on hand locally, aspects of plant and process which might be tweaked, cask-types used for maturation. Might we be on the threshold of another 'golden age'?

The current boom is unprecedented in the history of whisky.

Thirty new distilleries opened in Scotland between 2004 and 2017, with a combined capacity to produce slightly over 73 million LPA a year. Ten of these distilleries are small (under 200,000 LPA), eleven are medium-sized (200-750,000 LPA), but nine are capable of producing in excess on one million LPA per annum. I know of a further thirty-seven distilleries which are either proposed or under construction, plus three which are being revived.

In addition to these new distilleries, many well-known distilleries have been substantially expanded.

Over the past ten years malt whisky production capacity has increased by a staggering 60.25%, from 239 million LPA in 2007 to 383 million LPA in 2017. Of course, not all distilleries operate at capacity every year: annual output is based on anticipated future requirements.

The optimism manifested by this increase in capacity is based upon the anticipated global demand for Scotch whisky over the coming decades – a remarkably difficult exercise, vulnerable to factors beyond the industry's control, including the global economy and international politics, not to mention sale of alcohol regulations, fiscal arrangements and fashion in over two hundred markets.

This huge increase in capacity is paralleled in many countries. The statistics below relate to the Big Four non-Scotch producers; very many other countries all over the world are distilling whisky for the first time.

In the USA, the number of Distilled Spirits Permits (DSPs) – the federal permit required to lawfully operate a distillery – has grown from below 100 in 2007, to 560 in 2010 to 1,825 in 2016. In 2015 alone, almost 400 DSPs were issued, a rate of more than one per day. Since 2016, more than 1,000 craft distilleries have been operating in the United States - an industry that was virtually non-existent fifteen years ago.

The number of Japanese distilleries has gone from eight to twenty since 2010, while the total export value of Japanese whisky has increased nearly tenfold from 1.07 billion yen (about $10 million) in 2006 to 10.378 billion yen (more that $100 million) in 2015.

Ireland grew from five to eighteen distilleries between 2013 and 2017, with a further sixteen proposed. Not all are small: William Grant's Tullamore Distillery has a capacity of 3.6 million LPA, and produces both malt and grain spirits. Between 2008 and 2016, sales of Irish whiskey doubled (4.4 million 9-litres cases, to 8.7 million cases in 2008) with sales projected to exceed 12 million cases by 2020, and 24 million by 2030

Canada's eight major whisky distilleries have been joined by over 100 micro-distilleries, at lease half of which are beginning to make whisky. Together, these new entrants produced less than 0.1% of the 22.5 million cases of whisky bottled in 2016. This will increase slightly as new producers' stocks begin to mature. Canada consumes just 15% of its production at home, exporting the rest to over 155 countries.

Whisky is now being made in significant quantities all over the world, and the best of the makes are high quality. They are also designed to be different to Scotch, not an immitation. But do these whiskies pose a threat to Scotch?

More to Scotch than the liquor

Scotch, especially Scotch malt, offers far broader range of ages, flavours and styles than non-Scotch, and because of the rigourous legal definition, offers a more consistent product. Simple in essence, it is also is the most complex spirit known to man, organoleptically. The provenance and romantic history of Scotch whisky is appealing: Scotland – 'le pays sauvage', 'the land of mist and mountains, clans and castles' - is intriguimg. Our climate is also perfect for the long maturation of whisky. Scotch whisky has cachet and a story to tell. Dr. Nicholas Morgan summed it up: "When you buy a bottle of Scotch, you buy a hell of a lot more than 'liquor in a bottle'. You're buying history, craft, time and tradition".

Although often now assisted by technology, the craft skills developed over very many years and generations in relation to process, maturation and blending are key to creating flavour, while the scientific bases of flavour continue to be investigated – and, happily, continue to be elusive. The industry is continually exploring ways to develop attractive flavours, while respecting the very tight legal definition of 'Scotch', such as yeast and barly varieties, longer fermentaions, stills operation and wood finishing.

Somewhat arrogantly – but with justification – the Scotch whisky industry's view is that "all roads lead to Scotch". We embrace and support non-Scotch distillers, in the knowledge that once consumers acquire a taste for whisky they are certain to explore Scotch whisky – and hopefully to settle there! After all, Scotch currently sells three times more than its nearest rival.

Scotch whisky is being exported all over the world.

Scotch is being challenged from new whiskies produced all around the world.

So, as we peer into our crystal balls…

Will demand continue to grow to meet supply? Or are we filling a lake of whisky, surplus to requirements, as happened in the early 1980s? And if we are creating a surplus in the short term, will this increase its value in years to come? Those companies which still have stocks of whisky from the previous 'whisky loch' – now at 30-40 years old – can sell them for eye-watering prices…

Although export figures have gone up and down over the past ten years, the overall trend is up, with 2017 being a record year for sales. With good reason, the Scotch whisky industry has high hopes for China, where Diageo is running a major, education-based, generic promotion of 'whisky'. Exports to Singapore were up 29.4% by value in 2017, from where most will be shipped to China. Exports to Latvia, an entrepot for Russia, were up 105% by value last year. Mexica and Brazil currently stand fourth and fifth in the league of 'best-sellers of blended Scotch by volume'.

The sheer geographical spread of the markets for Scotch offers a degree of protection if one market fails – the eggs are distributed in many baskets. Here are some examples, with by value export figures from 2017: USA +7.7%, South Africa +20.7%, France +2.1%, Germany +13.5%, Spain +5.2%…

The global whisky market is driven by the global economy, and individual markets by local economies: consumers must have sufficient disposable income to afford it. Other factors include duty and other fiscal imposts and regulations (not to mention prohibition in certain markets), availability, fashion, changing lifestyles (including health concerns), competition from other alcoholic (and now non-alcoholic) drinks.

There will be some causalties among the recently founded malt whisky distilleries, but is it better to hazard over-production now, rather then miss (global) opportunites later? The highly paid bean-counters and actuaries say 'yes' and this demonstrates great confidence in the future of Scotch.

Charles MacLean has spent the past thirty-five years researching and writing about Scotch whisky and is one of the leading authorities. He spends his time sharing his knowledge around the world, in articles and publications, lectures and tastings, and on TV and radio. His first book (Scotch Whisky) was published in 1993 and since then he has published nine books on the subject. He was elected a Keeper of the Quaich in 1992 and became Master of the Quaich in 2009. In 1997, Malt Whisky won the Glenfiddich Award and in 2003 A Liquid History won 'Best Drinks Book' in the James Beard Awards. In 2012 he also starred in Ken Loach's film The Angel's Share.

Brian Kinsman, Master Blender, William Grant & Sons

Feel The Whisky

by Ian Wisniewski

When we taste a whisky, most of us tend
to focus on the flavour. But there´s more to whisky than that
– there´s also mouthfeel. Let´s explore the reasons behind why whiskies
behave differently on our palate – let´s feel the whisky.

We love to analyse, deliberate and deliver our verdict on the flavour profile of a malt whisky. So, how is it possible that a vital element of this experience is rarely mentioned ? "When I'm tasting with people I always look at their throats, the whisky is swallowed immediately. I always ask 'how was it ?' People reply 'it went down like silk,' or 'it went down a treat.' This may allude to mouthfeel, but people usually focus totally on flavour," says Richard Paterson, Whyte & Mackay's Master Blender.

I'm fascinated by flavour but in conjunction with mouthfeel, and the amazing relationship that exists between them. "I think of it as all intertwined: the taste and the flavour, which includes the texture. I write tasting notes such as 'peaches in syrup,' to paint a picture of the taste and texture. People may not think of texture, but they appreciate it," says Sandy Hyslop, Ballantine's Master Blender.

I think of mouthfeel as the 'vehicle' which delivers flavour, but also as a primary characteristic that enhances and enlivens flavour, making it a vital part of a malt's identity.

Rachel Barrie, Master Blender, BenRiach Company

"I'm a big fan of mouthfeel, it's part of the overall sensory experience, so I don't judge a malt purely on aroma and taste. I'm looking for a nice mouth-coating texture, and I love waxyness, by which I mean a thick butteriness, verging on being oily," says Dr Bill Lumsden, Director of Distilling, Whisky Creation & Whisky Stocks, Glenmorangie.

And that highlights a fascinating aspect of mouthfeel: how much variety there is. At one end of the scale it's incredibly soft, delicate, elegant, mellow or gliding, while more tactile textures are silky, velvety, creamy or juicy, with the most indulgent being luscious. Meanwhile, some higher-strength and cask strength malts have a very delicate mouthfeel, while others way down the scale at 40% abv have a fuller-bodied, weightier mouthfeel. But then there's also plenty of variety among malts at the same alcoholic strength. So, what's going on ?

"Alcohol, water and flavour compounds all play a role in determining the mouthfeel. And more specifically it's the mix and ratio of flavour compounds, with the ratio continually changing during ageing as the level of flavour compounds extracted from the cask continues to increase. What a cask provides also depends on its origins. Bourbon barrels must be American oak, while Sherry casks can be European or American oak. American oak has a different range, but also a lower level of flavour compounds, than European oak," says Brian Kinsman, Master Blender, William Grant & Sons.

Exactly how different cask types influence mouthfeel also depends on the character and texture of the new make spirit, which is of course individual to each distillery.

"The contribution the new make spirit makes to the mouthfeel of mature malt whisky is underestimated. BenRiach new make spirit has a silky vitality which stems from the citrus, zesty freshness. Using Bourbon barrels promotes this silkiness further, with a Sherry cask also maintaining that silkiness while adding a bit more spice. Glendronach new make spirit is fuller-bodied and more robust, which harmonises with the depth and weight of flavours from a sherry cask, resulting in a rich, velvety character. But you must get the balance right. There is a sweet spot in terms of texture between the type of cask and the profile of the new make spirit," says Rachel Barrie, Master Blender, BenRiach Company.

Another vital aspect of categorising casks is the 'fill' (ie. how many times the cask has been filled to age malt whisky). A 'first fill' cask (ie. used to age malt whisky for the first time) has a higher level of flavour compounds to contribute than a second fill, as the influence of the cask diminishes with each fill.

Two of the factors that influence the mouthfeel are age and type of maturation cask

How flavours influence mouthfeel

One of the most familiar, and popular, cask-derived flavours is vanilla, which is a multi-tasking characteristic, making fruit flavours seem richer for example, while also contributing to mouthfeel.

"Vanillin is typically present at a higher level in American oak Bourbon barrels than European oak Sherry casks, and is also significantly higher in first fill Bourbon than second fill. Depending on the level of vanillin the cask contributes, this gives sweetness which also feels soft, silky and rounded on the palate," says Brian Kinsman.

Sandy Hyslop adds, "Vanillin makes a particular contribution to cask strength malt, when the intensity of the alcohol can be quite prickly, but vanillin adds sweetness and creamyness which helps to make it less astringent."

However, it's tannins that have always received the greatest praise for creating mouthfeel (while also lauded for providing structure, complexity and body).

European oak contains significantly higher tannin levels than American oak, with a related factor being the original occupant of the cask. The higher alcoholic strength of Bourbon, for instance, extracts a higher level of tannins from the oak during the ageing process compared to Sherry. And then, once the casks are being used to age malt whisky in Scotland, it's a case of factoring in the fill, as the tannin level decreases significantly in a subsequent fill.

"The higher tannin levels of a first fill Bourbon barrel give a richer, rounder mouthfeel, while also adding more dryness to the mouthfeel than a second fill. And since the year 2,000 there's been a significant increase in the number of first fill Bourbon barrels used in Scotland," says Stuart Harvey, Master Blender, Inver House Distillers.

The decreasing level of tannin in each fill of a Sherry cask has a similar influence.

"First fill Spanish oak gives the greatest level of tannins and spices from the oak, which promotes a velvety, creamy mouthfeel. This compares to second fill Spanish oak which has a sweeter, caramelised note, with less unctuous oiliness making it slightly lighter, so the mouthfeel is different," says Rachel Barry.

However, the tannin debate also raises some significant parameters.

"At their best tannins provide a good backbone of structure, and all the other flavours attach themselves to this backbone of tannin. But tannin in whisky can be very dangerous, able to spoil as well as enhance a whisky, as higher tannin levels can add astringency and bitterness," says Dr Bill Lumsden.

Another key influence on mouthfeel are fatty acid esters, which are long-chain flavour compounds (ie. comprising several molecules or more).

"A higher level of fatty acid esters gives a lovely mouthfeel that is smooth, gliding and elegant. However, the level of fatty acid esters varies quite dramatically from one malt to another," says Stuart Harvey.

This variability stems from different stages of the production regime.

"Fatty acid esters start with fermentation, particularly when using a wooden rather than stainless steel wash back, and a longer fermentation time. Fatty acid esters also come off slightly later in the distillation run because they are larger, weightier molecules, so the level of fatty acid esters also depends on the spirit cut. Malts with more fatty acid esters, such as Glendronach, tend to have a fuller-bodied mouthfeel," says Rachel Barrie.

How various characteristics determine the profile of a mature malt whisky also depends on another vital factor. Time.

"Younger whiskies are quite lively and can have peppery, prickly notes in the mouthfeel, then at 7, 8, 9 years of age they're emerging from that initial boisterous phase and becoming more savvy, with the texture becoming softer and less aggressive. This is the result of extracting flavour compounds from the cask, in conjunction with evaporation," says Richard Paterson.

Focusing on particular details is always fascinating, but these should be viewed within a broader context.

"More humid conditions, which you find at the bottom of the warehouse, result in a bit more weight in the mouthfeel, while the top of the warehouse is relatively cooler and drier, resulting in a more elegant texture," adds Richard Paterson.

How we perceive texture

Whatever a malt whisky has to offer there's also the question of how these characteristics are perceived. As our palates are individual we can all pick up similar, or different flavours from the same malt, which makes it seem logical that the mouthfeel of the same malt will also be variously perceived.

Identifying characteristics in a malt whisky is very much a team effort. This includes numerous taste buds in the tongue, which are all able to detect every flavour. When tasting a malt whisky aromas also pass from the palate through the throat and retro nasal passage (a conduit from the mouth to the nose) to reach the olfactory sense.

"The tongue and olfactory sense send independent messages to the brain, which processes all the data to provide an understanding of what's going on. However, in terms of flavour detection the nose is way ahead of the mouth, and the brain uses olfactory signals in order to validate what the tongue perceives," says Greg Tucker, a taste psychologist at The Marketing Clinic.

Despite it's amazing credentials the olfactory sense can't assess mouthfeel. This is down to the palate, but it's the nervous system rather than taste buds that do the work.

"The nervous system detects heat, temperature and texture, sending messages to the brain which unscrambles them in a fraction of a moment. Nerves in the tongue provide it with a tactile element able to detect the feel of the liquid in the mouth," says Greg Tucker.

Another amazing aspect of mouthfeel is that, just as malt whisky can reveal a sequence of flavours, the texture can also evolve. I often find that mouthfeel which is initially mellow soon changes, and a mellow overture is followed by a symphony of texture. The appearance of citrus notes, for example, can unleash juicyness, or a sudden 'wave' of citrus flavour that unfurls across the palate. Vanilla is often accentuated by a creamy texture, while rich notes can introduce lusciousness. Meanwhile, the emergence of dryness (which can be considered textural as well as a flavour) provides an effective counterpoint to an indulgent mouthfeel. So, what's behind this evolution ?

"Part of the glory of Scotch whisky is the ability to put together such a complex flavour and delivery, though flavours have associations which also influence the perception of mouthfeel. If I detect fudge as a flavour the texture will also appear to be thicker, which shows that the mouth is an imperfect detection system," says Greg Tucker.

Rachel Barrie adds, "The sense of mouthfeel changing when tasting is partly due to perception, but it's also due to physical changes in the whisky, which is warming up on the palate from room temperature, and as it heats up various volatiles (flavour compounds) are being released, which in turn influence the mouthfeel."

How we perceive flavour and mouthfeel is also influenced by a vital decision: whether or not to add water (and if so the amount). Diluting has a multi-effect. As the alcoholic strength reduces, the balance of water and alcohol changes, as does the flavour

Bill Lumsden, Director of Distilling, Whisky Creation & Whisky Stocks, Glenmorangie

profile and mouthfeel.

"I taste at cask strength and write the tasting note, then add water to see what other flavours are apparent. On the other hand, higher strength whiskies can anaesthetise the tongue, and therefore need to be diluted. But it's a tricky balance, particularly with whiskies beyond 21 years old, as at that age whisky doesn't have the muscle to withstand the added water," says Richard Paterson.

It's always a fascinating exercise to taste a malt neat, focussing on mouthfeel as much as flavour, then re-taste the whisky with a drop of water added, re-taste with a second drop added, and so on, to monitor how the mouthfeel and flavour profile evolve, and to find which option best suits your palate. (This exercise should ideally be conducted with the same measure of the same whisky in a number of identical glasses, with each glass receiving a progressively higher degree of dilution. Otherwise re-tasting and diluting whisky in the same glass means adding additional drops of water to a continually reducing volume of whisky, making the impact of each drop of water that much greater).

Knowing exactly what a malt whisky has to offer also requires a particular virtue. Patience.

"It's all about holding the whisky for long enough in the mouth, you need to take your time to allow the mouthfeel and different flavours to be fully investigated," says Richard Paterson.

Definitely. We should all investigate fully, as there's so much to say about mouthfeel. We just have to start saying it.

Ian Wisniewski is a freelance drinks writer focusing on spirits, and particularly Scotch whisky. He contributes to various publications including Whisky Magazine and is the author of ten books, including Classic Malt Whisky. He regularly visits distilleries in Scotland, in order to learn more about the production process which is of particular interest to him.

Picture of Ian Wisniewski courtesy of Finlandia vodka

Kalle Valkonen, Head Distiller at Kyrö Distillery

Moment of truth for World Whisky

by Ian Buxton

Time to leave the nest for fledglings
from distilleries all around the world. In a world so dominated
by ´The Big Five´, how will the new whiskies compare to the old?
The battle for shelf space has begun.

"Do I <u>need</u> ten Indian single malts?" asks Royal Mile Whiskies' Arthur Motley, responsible for sales and purchasing for this well-known whisky specialist. "Or ten or twelve Swedish whiskies?" "Not really", is his answer "especially", he adds, "if they hang around and take up expensive space in our shops and warehouse."

And right there we have a large part of the problem facing new world producers when trying to break into established markets. Looked at from the perspective of a UK retailer, Scotch is going to account for the majority of sales and thus fill most of their shelves. Much the same will be true in the USA, where Bourbon and rye join Scotch in squeezing the space available for any newcomer.

The established giants of whisky (Scotland, USA, Ireland, Japan and Canada) have everything going for them: reputation; heritage and deep stocks to mention just three of their entrenched advantages. So how can the new boys from Finland, Taiwan, Australia and so on hope to break in?

Well, there are some successes and perhaps lessons to be learnt.

Miika Lipiäinen, CEO of Finland's Kyrö Distillery is clear why this award-winning operation has made such a strong start. "We focus single-mindedly on Finnish wholegrain rye," he explains. "Whisky people know this is a difficult and demanding grain which therefore appeals to them – and it's a Finnish tradition, which means that our story is based on truth."

Kyrö have taken their cohesive story from just five people in 2014 to more than thirty today. As well as focusing exclusively on one grain they have concentrated their efforts on just four markets – their homeland, Germany, the UK and the USA. As a result, says Lipiäinen, it's possible for their team to be present in the market and be closely involved at all level of the trade.

Foreign market entry being both expensive and highly competitive, Kyrö have employed some 'out of the box' thinking: in the USA, for example, while they have some distribution in trendy New York establishments, most of their work is concentrated around Chicago and the Great Lakes. Why? Because, back in time, many Finnish and Nordic immigrants to the US settled in this area and up to Minnesota. Not only are these areas slightly less competitive than other US markets, but the residual folk memory and fondness for the old country gives a Finnish brand a tiny, but unique edge. Kyrö can develop from here, having built a sustainable and defensible platform of loyal consumers – that's the theory at least, and so far it seems to be working.

Something else Lipiäinen added rang true when considering the needs of retailers. "If you just create an endless stream of 'cool' bottlings, it's very hard for a person who's never heard of you to get a sense of what you're about", he told me.

Later, interviewing Arthur Motley, much the same comment was made. According to him, many smaller producers ('craft' distillers everywhere, not just in the new world category) "overproduce their range to look good at whisky shows – but that's a nightmare for the retailer", he said. "With tiny production of five or six different styles, what are we supposed to stock?" His frustration was obvious and the message clear: do one thing (or a very few) and do it well.

That's probably easier if you enjoy significant backing. David Vitale from Australia's Starward, who in December 2015 were the recipient of funding from Diageo's 'accelerator programme' Distill Ventures, sees it like this: "The one thing that new world distilleries have is a compelling flavour-led story that anchors itself in the place it is made. For us it is obviously our use of Australian wine barrels to mature our whisky. This makes the story – once you can get over the challenges – easier to tell".

The challenges don't stop once your whisky is on a shelf somewhere. Arthur Motley reflects on the prospect of an eventual shakeout across the category. "We [and other retailers] can't stock everything. The savvy buyers will become increasingly selective and curate what they really believe in." And, he might have added, what sells.

And that points to another challenge: pricing. These whiskies are, inevitably, expensive to buy. As Amrut's Ashok Chokalingam puts it "matching the pricing of the big boys of Scotland is another task". That makes these whiskies a considered choice – or a risk to ever more cash-strapped consumers. According to Miika Lipiäinen recognizing that was one reason why the current Batch 5 release of Kyrö rye will be available only in 10cl bottles. The €17 ticket is expensive per cl of alcohol, he acknowledges but "it's an opportunity to try without breaking the bank."

Such an approach, albeit expensive in packaging costs, allows many more consumers to get a sense of the brand and favours drinkers over collectors ('hurrah to that' I say!). The hope is that by 2020, when greater stocks will be available, consumers who have tried the whisky will be willing to accept a full-price bottle knowing that it represents less of a risk that they simply won't like it.

It reminds us that making whisky is a long-term business. Consider that while today we may think of Japan as a major producing nation distilling exceptionally high-quality whisky, less than twenty years ago it was hardly regarded at all and, looking further back, was dismissed as a mere novelty. It has taken many years of investment and hard work to achieve its present, enviable position.

Two 'world whiskies' – Starward and Teerenpeli

The oldest expression so far from Amrut Distillery - the 12 year old Greedy Angels

Follow the Japanese

So, could some new world whiskies follow this path? The world seems smaller these days and, with the influence of social media and greater international travel there may be a greater willingness to accept all kinds of products, not just whiskies, of hitherto unexpected origins. One person who anticipates that happening is Ashok Chokalingam of Amrut.

Indian single malt has been an unexpected success in European markets and Chokalingam sees several factors, not least the "shortage of aged whiskies in Scotland [which] gave us an opportunity to fill the gap". But, within a decade he predicts that Indian single malt will be recognized and valued as Japanese whisky has been, noting that "importers and distributors are keen to take on rest of the world whiskies as this category is growing and will grow even further".

Up to a point, cautions David Vitale. "If you are a fledgling distillery with small volumes to start with, you need to find a distributor that has the patience to give you the support you need early-on", and that may not be as easy as it sounds.

There is, however, a caveat and word of warning on the costs. "The funding of sales and marketing campaign was tough for us and we lost money for seve-ral years before we started to establish our brands to what they are today," says Chokalingam. "Amrut were able to withstand as our finances were sound [but] for a newcomer it will be tough," he adds.

David Vitale echoed that point. "With whisky, the obvious challenge is investing ahead of the curve," he said. "As a distillery, you are typically making way more whisky (for future years) than you are selling now. This obviously puts challenges on cashflow to fund your momentum. Added to this you are trying to build a brand – not just ship boxes so despite there being a huge amount of options to sell whisky, you need to be disciplined to place the whisky in the right places at the right time."

But what are the 'right places'? One strategy, of course, is to stay very small and concentrate on local markets. For some years, the Bakery Hill Distillery, which like Starward is based in Melbourne, Australia shipped supplies to the UK and France in an attempt to develop export markets. Today, however, they've pulled back as domestic interest and demand has grown to the point where virtually none of their bottles ever leave their home state of Victoria.

"We can't and don't compete with big distillers," says David Baker "but find gaps in the market they can't fill. Ours is a quality, hand-made, single barrel offer and demand is now so enormous that we have nothing left over for export!"

David Baker - founder and owner of Bakery Hill Distillery

Bakery Hill will expand but, as a family owned legacy business with no outside shareholders, they are in no hurry to do so. "The larger you grow, the larger the problems get," notes Baker adding that their success has come through fair pricing, consistent quality and "educating consumers, which is a big part of our business".

The problem for this distiller, then, is keeping up with local demand without compromising independence of ownership. For David Baker, this is "a generational project – we're here for the long term".

Other distillers, though, want to grow bigger, faster. A case in point is that other Australian newcomer, Starward. Diageo's cash allowed an expansion of production and presented the opportunity to take the brand to international markets – today Starward may be found in UK specialists at around £50 for a standard bottle, relatively mainstream pricing compared to many world whiskies with their higher unit costs (as a point of comparison, Bakery Hill's single barrel expressions retail at the equivalent of £80 for 50cl in Victoria).

Also growing is Finland's Teerenpeli. Distilling began, quietly enough, in the cellars of owner Anssi Pyysing's restaurant in Lahti but today most production takes place at the edge of town in conjunction with the family's brewery and they claim to be Finland's largest whisky distillery. Having started modestly in 2002, they can now offer a 10 year old expression and have casks laid down for even older releases in the future.

Pyysing suggests that they have had to "invent and learn totally new ways of making whisky" such as their combined beer brewing and distilling operation or the warehousing in containers. Further innovations here include environmentally-friendly production using boilers powered by wood pellets (there is no shortage of wood in Finland!) which enhances the brand's green credentials and appeals to eco-conscious consumers. Overall, he is optimistic about future prospects, especially the use of social media in brand building and marketing ("where permitted," he notes) that allow smaller brands the opportunity to compete on level terms with the larger companies.

Cask sales have also been key to their success, both generating cash and building a network of supporters to spread the word about the brand. For Pyysing, Finnish whisky is about "raising the interest towards whisky in customers who have not been familiar with it before" – which he argues strongly is actually benefitting the whole whisky industry, not just the new wave producers.

And that is an argument made by one of the largest new wave producers, Kavalan from Taiwan who, hard though it is to credit, have been around for less than fifteen years. A huge part of their success, as with Japanese whisky before them, has been the credibility brought with international awards and

Kavalan Distillery and their latest core bottling - Distillery Select

their whiskies have collected an enviable haul of top medals.

As their amiable Master Distiller Ian Chang, a familiar face at whisky shows around the globe, explains, "We were dismissed many times as attempting something impossible. But we took it step by step and with every award we won, the more convinced we were that we had a product worth sharing with the world. With every step, we brought our few supporters along with us. Gradually, we grew a bigger support base, established our distribution lines, gained trust with the experts and built our customer following."

There has been a single-minded obsession with quality at Kavalan, especially the highest standard of wood management, initially under the influence of the late Dr Jim Swan, but taken up wholeheartedly by Chang and the ownership. It's one thing to hire the best advice but, having done so, not everyone is able or willing to follow it – Kavalan are something of a shining example to others, though the deep pockets and passion of the owning Lee family make this possible on a substantial scale.

But breaking new ground is never easy. "Back then there was no such thing as 'World' whisky and we were a whisky not only made outside of the traditional whisky homelands, but also in a hot country, with no experience of making whisky, and on the unlikely island of Taiwan," says Chang. "So you can imagine how difficult it was to do anything at first."

While Kavalan's many awards have made an enduring mark though and built a customer base in global markets, a UK retailer who wished to remain anonymous made a curious observation about world whiskies. "We sell decent quantities of Swedish whisky," they told me "but largely to Swedes visiting the UK who can't get it at home!"

So international success is not all it may at first appear. But, wherever their whisky ends up, I believe we should salute these early pioneers who have truly helped forge a movement that changed the world of whisky. For good or bad – and I see little that's bad – things will never be the same again!

Ian Buxton has nearly 30 years' experience in the whisky industry. He runs his own strategic marketing consultancy; holds tastings, and writes regular columns for a number of trade and consumer magazines. As well as several corporate histories, Ian has written three titles in the bestselling 101 Whiskies series and has enjoyed great success with the companion 101 Gins To Try Before You Die. Most recently, he wrote a whisky and travel personal memoir, Whiskies Galore, and has just published 101 Rums to Try Before You Die. Ian does not plan on dying any time soon – he has a 4th edition of 101 Whiskies to prepare and then a revision of The Science & Commerce of Whisky (with Professor Paul Hughes) for the Royal Society of Chemistry.

Malt distilleries

Including the subsections:
Scottish distilleries | New distilleries | Closed distilleries
Japanese distilleries | Distilleries around the globe

Explanations

Owner: Name of the owning company, sometimes with the parent company within brackets.

Region/district: There are five protected whisky regions or localities in Scotland today; Highlands, Lowlands, Speyside, Islay and Campbeltown. Where useful we mention a location within a region e.g. Orkney, Northern Highlands etc.

Founded: The year in which the distillery was founded is usually considered as when construction began. The year is rarely the same year in which the distillery was licensed.

Status: The status of the distillery's production. Active, mothballed (temporarily closed), closed (but most of the equipment still present), dismantled (the equipment is gone but part of or all of the buildings remain even if they are used for other purposes) and demolished.

Visitor centre: The letters (vc) after status indicate that the distillery has a visitor centre. Many distilleries accept visitors despite not having a visitor centre. It can be worthwhile making an enquiry.

Address: The distillery´s address.

Tel: This is generally to the visitor centre, but can also be to the main office.

Website: The distillery's (or in some cases the owner's) website.

Capacity: The current production capacity expressed in litres of pure alcohol (LPA).

History: The chronology focuses on the official history of the distillery and independent bottlings are only listed in exceptional cases.

Tasting notes: For all the Scottish distilleries that are not permanently closed we present tasting notes of what, in most cases, can be called the core expression (mainly their best selling 10 or 12 year old).

We have tried to provide notes for official bottlings but in those cases where we have not been able to obtain them, we have turned to independent bottlers.

The whiskies have been tasted by Gavin D Smith (GS), a well-known and experienced whisky profile and author of 20 books on the subject or by Ingvar Ronde (IR).

There are also tasting notes for Japanese malts and these have all been written by Stefan Van Eycken.

All notes have been prepared especially for Malt Whisky Yearbook 2019.

Aberfeldy

[ah•bur•fell•dee]

Owner:
John Dewar & Sons
(Bacardi)

Region/district:
Southern Highlands

Founded: 1896
Status: Active (vc)
Capacity: 3 400 000 litres

Address: Aberfeldy, Perthshire PH15 2EB

Website: aberfeldy.com
Tel: 01887 822010 (vc)

Behind the development of Aberfeldy stood two of whisky history's most effective and synergistic brothers, John and Tommy Dewar. Together in 1880 they took control of the company which their father had started more than 30 years earlier.

Big brother John was methodical and controlling spending his first few years at the company consolidating the organisation. When Tommy, his younger brother, joined him he started to change the image of the company. He was an energetic entrepreneur and social dynamo and his first assignment was to establish a market in London. After this, he set off on a 2 year sales tour to the U.S and 25 other countries around the world and established partnerships and distribution channels where ever he landed.

The ever increasing demand for Dewar's whisky ultimately required having their own production. Auchnagie distillery was purchased in 1890 however it quickly became too small and the brothers decided to build a new distillery. Aberfeldy was opened in 1898 and despite the company changing hands many times throughout the years, the disitillery has continued to be a constant of John Dewer & Sons. In 2000, the award winning Dewars World of Whisky visitor centre was opened and it attracted more than 38,000 visitors last year.

The equipment consists of a 7.5 ton stainless steel mash tun, eight washbacks made of larch and three made of stainless steel with an average fermentation time of 70 hours and four stills. With an additional washback, installed in 2014, production has now escalated to 22 mashes per week and 3.4 million litres of alcohol. The owners have also invested £1.2m in a biomass boiler that will reduce greenhouse gas emissions by up to 90%.

The core range consists of **12, 16** and **21 years old**. An 18 year old, destined for duty free, was recently removed to make way for a **16 year old** and a **21 year old madeira finish**. Three recent, limited travel retail exclusives were an **18 year old port finish**, a **33 year old single cask** and a **Vintage 1999**.

History:

1896 John and Tommy Dewar embark on the construction of the distillery, a stone's throw from the old Pitilie distillery which was active from 1825 to 1867. Their objective is to produce a single malt for their blended whisky - White Label.

1898 Production starts in November.

1917 The distillery closes.

1919 The distillery re-opens.

1925 Distillers Company Limited (DCL) takes over.

1972 Reconstruction takes place, the floor maltings is closed and the two stills are increased to four.

1991 The first official bottling is a 15 year old in the Flora & Fauna series.

1998 Bacardi buys John Dewar & Sons from Diageo at a price of £1,150 million.

2000 A visitor centre opens and a 25 year old is released.

2005 A 21 year old is launched in October, replacing the 25 year old.

2009 Two 18 year old single casks are released.

2010 A 19 year old single cask, exclusive to France, is released.

2011 A 14 year old single cask is released.

2014 The whole range is revamped and an 18 year old for duty free is released.

2015 A 16 year old is released.

2018 A 16 year old and a 21 year old madeira finish are released for duty free.

Tasting notes Aberfeldy 12 years old:

GS – Sweet, with honeycombs, breakfast cereal and stewed fruits on the nose. Inviting and warming. Mouth-coating and full-bodied on the palate. Sweet, malty, balanced and elegant. The finish is long and complex, becoming progressively more spicy and drying.

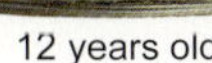
12 years old

Aberlour

[ah•bur•<u>lower</u>]

Owner:	**Region/district:**
Chivas Brothers Ltd	Speyside
(Pernod Ricard)	

Founded:	**Status:**	**Capacity:**
1879	Active (vc)	3 800 000 litres

Address: Aberlour, Banffshire AB38 9PJ

Website:	**Tel:**
aberlour.com	01340 881249

It´s no wonder that Aberlour is the best selling Scotch single malt in France. It was the first Scottish distillery acquired by the maker of pastis, Pernod Ricard, and became the founding stone of what is now the second largest operator in the Scotch business.

The single malt lost two places since last year and is now the eighth best selling single malt with 3,6 million bottles. Aberlour was one of the first distilleries to tailor its distillery tours for the discerning whisky aficionados, rather than for large groups of tourists. The basic tour lasts for two hours and includes a tasting of no less than six expressions. The start of the tour, with a history time line of Scotland and Scotch, is equally impresssive.

The distillery is equipped with a 12 ton semi-lauter mash tun, six stainless steel washbacks and two pairs of large and wide stills in a very spacious still room. To achieve the desired character of the newmake, which is fruity, the operators run a very slow distillation. With a 7.5 hour spirit cycle, the middle cut (73-63%) takes two hours to complete.

The core range of Aberlour includes **12, 16** and **18 year olds** – all being matured in a combination of ex-bourbon and ex-sherry casks. Another core expression is **Aberlour a'bunadh**, matured in ex-Oloroso casks. It is always bottled at cask strength and up to 62 different batches have been released by July 2018. A new expression was added to the core range in May 2018 - **Aberlour Casg Annamh**. Matured in ex-oloroso casks (both European and American oak) as well as ex-bourbon, this is the first in a new series. For select markets (mainly France) another four expression are available; **10 year old, 12 year old un chill-filtered, 15 year old Select Cask Reserve** and **White Oak Millennium 2004**. Two exclusives are available for duty free – a **12 year old Sherry Cask** and a **15 year old Double Cask**. There is also a cask strength bottling in the Distillery Reserve Collection, available at all Chivas´ visitor centres – a **17 year old bourbon cask matured**.

History:

1879 The local banker James Fleming founds the distillery.

1892 The distillery is sold to Robert Thorne & Sons Ltd who expands it.

1898 Another fire rages and almost totally destroys the distillery. The architect Charles Doig is called in to design the new facilities.

1921 Robert Thorne & Sons Ltd sells Aberlour to a brewery, W. H. Holt & Sons.

1945 S. Campbell & Sons Ltd buys the distillery.

1962 Aberlour terminates floor malting.

1973 Number of stills are increased from two to four.

1974 Pernod Ricard buys Campbell Distilleries.

2000 Aberlour a´bunadh is launched.

2001 Pernod Ricard buys Chivas Brothers and merges Chivas Brothers and Campbell Distilleries under the brand Chivas Brothers.

2002 A new, modernized visitor centre is inaugurated in August.

2008 The 18 year old is also introduced outside France.

2013 Aberlour 2001 White Oak is released.

2014 White Oak Millenium 2004 is released.

2018 Casg Annamh is released.

12 years old

Tasting notes Aberlour 12 year old:

GS – The nose offers brown sugar, honey and sherry, with a hint of grapefruit citrus. The palate is sweet, with buttery caramel, maple syrup and eating apples. Liquorice, peppery oak and mild smoke in the finish.

Allt-a-Bhainne

[alt a•<u>vain</u>]

Owner:
Chivas Brothers Ltd
(Pernod Ricard)

Region/district:
Speyside

Founded: **Status:** **Capacity:**
1975 Active 4 200 000 litres

Address: Glenrinnes, Dufftown, Banffshire AB55 4DB

Website: **Tel:**
- 01542 783200

The term "sister distilleries" often refers to two distilleries working on the same site – Benriach/Longmorn, Glenlossie/Mannochmore or Glen Grant/Caperdonich. Yet there is another side to the term, the one referring to the time when they were built.

Based on that, Braeval and Allt-a-Bhainne are the definite sisters. Both born from a decision made by the then-owners, Seagrams, they were founded in 1973 and 1975 respectively. A booming Scotch whisky industry called for more spirit to be made and both distilleries are situated in the area of Speyside named Glen of the Livet. But this is where the similarities stop. While Braeval has the exterior design of a 20th century Italian monastery, all dressed in white, Allt-a-Bhainne bears more of a resemblance to an East German rocket plant. None of them looks like the traditional Speyside distillery. If we go inside, there are few signs of Braeval being an efficient and "easy-to-run" distillery while at Allt-a-Bhaine on the other hand, all the equipment, from mash tun to stills, are neatly placed on the same level.

In 2015, a new, modern lauter mash gear was fitted into the existing traditional, 9 ton mash tun which had previously been equipped with rakes and ploughs. The rest of the equipment consists of eight stainless steel washbacks with a fermentation time of 48-50 hours and two pairs of stills. The distillery is currently working 7 days a week with 25 mashes resulting in 4 million litres of alcohol per year. Chivas Brothers has no distillery on Islay so, to cover their need of peated whisky for their blends, they needed to resort to other solutions. During the last few years, part of the production at Allt-a-Bhainne has therefore been peated. In 2018 it will be 30% with a phenol specification in the barley between 10 and 20ppm.

Historically, the owners have shown no interest in releasing official bottlings from the distillery. Instead we have had to rely on independent bottlers such as Aberko (Deerstalker). In autumn 2018, however, Chivas Bros launched a lightly peated **Allt-a-Bhainne NAS**, initially for the UK and Australian markets.

History:

1975 The distillery is founded by Chivas Brothers, a subsidiary of Seagrams, in order to secure malt whisky for its blended whiskies. The total cost amounts to £2.7 million.

1989 Production has doubled.

2001 Pernod Ricard takes over Chivas Brothers from Seagrams.

2002 Mothballed in October.

2005 Production restarts in May.

2018 An official, lightly peated bottling is released.

Allt-a-Bhainne NAS

Tasting notes Deerstalker 18 year old:

GS – Honey, icing sugar, lanolin; becoming buttery. Soft fruits, and finally toffee bonbons. Silky mouth-feel, slightly oily, vanilla, white pepper and tangerines. Relatively long finish and persistently spicy.

Ardbeg

[ard•beg]

Owner:	**Region/district:**
The Glenmorangie Co (Moët Hennessy)	Islay
Founded: **Status:**	**Capacity:**
1815 Active (vc)	1 400 000 litres

Address: Port Ellen, Islay, Argyll PA42 7EA

Website:	**Tel:**
ardbeg.com	01496 302244 (vc)

The increased demand for Ardbeg single malt has forced the team to do their utmost in recent years to squeeze out every drop of whisky from the current equipment. Now they´ve come to a point where a distillery expansion is the only way to go.

Starting 2018, a new still house will be built to house a total of four stills. The current still house will be re-furbished to accomodate another six washbacks. The plan is to have all the new equipment commissioned by late 2019. Meanwhile, the malt storage capacity has increased from 60 to 120 tonnes and a new boiler house has been built, housing two boilers – one lead and one back-up. Production in 2018 will be 1.4 million litres of pure alcohol and with all the new equipment in place, the capacity will rise to 2.4 million litres.

When Hiram Walker took over the distillery in 1973, they made sure the distillery was in full production until 1981 when Allied Distillers became the new owner. They already had Laphroaig in their range and with peated whisky being no way near as desirable in those days compared to today, Ardbeg was mothballed until 1989. Seven years followed where whisky was produced two months per year. Glenmorangie bought Ardbeg in 1997 and since then, the distillery has been producing 100% of its production capacity.

Sales of Ardbeg single malt is increasing rapidly. In the last two years, volumes are up by 15% and 1.2 million bottles were sold in 2017. This means Ardbeg is the fourth biggest seller on Islay after Laphroaig, Lagavulin and Bowmore.

Currently, the distillery is equipped with a 5 ton stainless steel semi lauter mash tun, six washbacks made of Oregon pine with a fermentation time of 56-57 hours and one pair of stills. A purifier is connected to the spirit still to help create the special, fruity character of the spirit. In 2018 they will be making 16-17 mashes per week, thereby accounting for 1.4 million litres of pure alcohol.

The core range, all non-chill filtered, consists of the **10 year old**, a mix of first and re-fill bourbon casks, **Uigeadail**, a marriage of bourbon and sherry casks and bottled at cask strength, **Corryvreckan**, also a cask strength and a combination of bourbon casks and new French oak and **An Oa**, a vatting of whiskies matured in several types of casks that have been married together in huge vats. The Ardbeg Day expression for 2018 was **Grooves**, with part of the whisky matured in re-toasted red wine casks. As usual, a Committee version was launched in March, bottled at 51.6% while the general release followed in June, bottled at 46%. Recent limited expressions include a **21 year old** and **Ardbeg Twenty Something** – a 23 year old made from spirit distilled in the mid-nineties when Allied Distillers used to own the distillery. It was matured in a combination of ex-bourbon and ex-oloroso sherry. It was then followed up in autumn 2018 by a second edition, **22 years old** and matured in ex-bourbon casks,

History:

1794 First record of a distillery at Ardbeg. It was founded by Alexander Stewart.

1798 The MacDougalls, later to become licensees of Ardbeg, are active on the site through Duncan MacDougall.

1815 The current distillery is founded by John MacDougall, son of Duncan MacDougall.

1853 Alexander MacDougall, John's son, dies and sisters Margaret and Flora MacDougall, assisted by Colin Hay, continue the running of the distillery. Colin Hay takes over the licence when the sisters die.

1888 Colin Elliot Hay and Alexander Wilson Gray Buchanan renew their license.

1900 Colin Hay's son takes over the license.

1959 Ardbeg Distillery Ltd is founded.

1973 Hiram Walker and Distillers Company Ltd jointly purchase the distillery for £300,000 through Ardbeg Distillery Trust.

1977 Hiram Walker assumes single control of the distillery. Ardbeg closes its maltings.

1979 Kildalton, a less peated malt, is produced over a number of years.

1981 The distillery closes in March.

1987 Allied Lyons takes over Hiram Walker and thereby Ardbeg.

History continued:

1989 Production is restored. All malt is taken from Port Ellen.

1996 The distillery closes in July and Allied Distillers decides to put it up for sale.

1997 Glenmorangie plc buys the distillery for £7 million. Ardbeg 17 years old and Provenance are launched

1998 A new visitor centre opens.

2000 Ardbeg 10 years is introduced and the Ardbeg Committee is launched.

2001 Lord of the Isles 25 years and Ardbeg 1977 are launched.

2002 Ardbeg Committee Reserve and Ardbeg 1974 are launched.

2003 Uigeadail is launched.

2004 Very Young Ardbeg (6 years) and a limited edition of Ardbeg Kildalton (1300 bottles) are launched. The latter is an un-peated cask strength from 1980.

2005 Serendipity is launched.

2006 Ardbeg 1965 and Still Young are launched. Almost There (9 years old) and Airigh Nam Beist are released.

2007 Ardbeg Mor, a 10 year old in 4.5 litre bottles is released.

2008 The new 10 year old, Corryvreckan, Rennaissance, Blasda and Mor II are released.

2009 Supernova is released, the peatiest expression from Ardbeg ever.

2010 Rollercoaster and Supernova 2010 are released.

2011 Ardbeg Alligator is released.

2012 Ardbeg Day and Galileo are released.

2013 Ardbog is released.

2014 Auriverdes and Kildalton are released.

2015 Perpetuum and Supernova 2015 are released.

2016 Dark Cove and a 21 year old are relased.

2017 An Oa, Kelpie and Twenty Something are released.

2018 Grooves is released.

Tasting notes Ardbeg 10 year old:

GS – Quite sweet on the nose, with soft peat, carbolic soap and Arbroath smokies. Burning peats and dried fruit, followed by sweeter notes of malt and a touch of liquorice in the mouth. Extremely long and smoky in the finish, with a fine balance of cereal sweetness and dry peat notes.

Ardmore

[ard•moor]

Owner:
Beam Suntory

Region/district:
Highland

Founded: 1898

Status: Active

Capacity: 5 550 000 litres

Address: Kennethmont, Aberdeenshire AB54 4NH

Website:
ardmorewhisky.com

Tel:
01464 831213

Few distilleries have had such a long and solid relationship with the same blend as Ardmore has had with Teachers. Founded by the Teacher family in 1898, Ardmore and its single malt has always been the backbone of the famous blend.

This is still the case but Teacher´s blended Scotch has experienced a decline in sales in the past couple of years. Even though it is a global brand, Teachers has heavily relied on two markets – India and Brazil. Between them, they represent more than 50% of the total sales. Brazil has, due to a severe recession, shown weak sales figures for Scotch whisky for three years in a row now. This has of course also had an impact on Teachers and last year the owners relaunched the brand including a new bottle design.

The distillery is equipped with a 12.5 ton, cast iron, semi-lauter mash tun with a copper dome, 14 Douglas fir washbacks (4 large and 10 smaller ones), as well as four pairs of stills. At the moment, Ardmore is working a 7-day week with 23 mashes per week resulting in 4.1 million litres of alcohol. Traditionally, Ardmore has been the only distillery in the region consistently producing peated whisky with a phenol specification in the barley of 12-14 ppm. Occasionally in recent years a heavily peated spirit has also been produced. The earthy Highland peat is locally sourced from St Fergus. For blending purposes, they also produce the unpeated Ardlair (around 40% of the yearly output). The fermentation time for Ardlair is longer than for regular Ardmore – 70 hours compared to 55 hours.

Ardmore serves as the signature malt in Teacher´s blended Scotch but is also released as a single malt. The core range is made up of **Legacy**, a mix of 80% peated and 20% unpeated malt, and a **12 year old Port finish** with four years in port pipes. In 2015, **Tradition** was released as a duty free exclusive together with **Triple Wood** with no age statement and matured in bourbon barrels, quarter casks and sherry puncheons. A new release in 2017 was a **20 year old**, double matured in a mix of first- and second-fill bourbon casks and the second batch was launched in 2018 together with a new **30 year old**.

History:

1898 Adam Teacher, son of William Teacher, starts the construction of Ardmore Distillery which eventually becomes William Teacher & Sons´ first distillery. Adam Teacher passes away before it is completed.

1955 Stills are increased from two to four.

1974 Another four stills are added, increasing the total to eight.

1976 Allied Breweries takes over William Teacher & Sons and thereby also Ardmore. The own maltings (Saladin box) is terminated.

1999 A 12 year old is released to commemorate the distillery's 100th anniversary. A 21 year old is launched in a limited edition.

2002 Ardmore is one of the last distilleries to abandon direct heating (by coal) of the stills in favour of indirect heating through steam.

2005 Jim Beam Brands becomes new owner when it takes over some 20 spirits and wine brands from Allied Domecq for five billion dollars.

2007 Ardmore Traditional Cask is launched.

2008 A 25 and a 30 year old are launched.

2014 Beam and Suntory merge. Legacy is released.

2015 Traditional is re-launched as Tradition and a Triple Wood and a 12 year old port finish are released.

2017 A 20 year old, double matured is released.

2018 A 30 year old is released.

Legacy

Tasting notes Ardmore Legacy:

GS – Vanilla, caramel and sweet peat smoke on the nose, while on the palate vanilla and honey contrast with quite dry peat notes, plus ginger and dark berries. The finish is medium to long, spicy, with persistently drying smoke.

Arran

[ar•ran]

Owner: Isle of Arran Distillers

Region/district: Highlands (Arran)

Founded: 1993

Status: Active (vc)

Capacity: 1 200 000 litres

Address: Lochranza, Isle of Arran KA27 8HJ

Website: arranwhisky.com

Tel: 01770 830264

At the same time as it´s business as usual at the recently expanded Arran distillery, the owners were working full time on completing their second distillery on the southern part of the island.

The construction of Lagg Distillery started in February 2017 and Arran´s Master Distiller, James MacTaggart anticipates they will be commissioning the distillery end of 2018 to start production in January/Februay 2019. Lagg will be equipped with a 4 ton mash tun, four wooden washbacks and one pair of stills. However, the production room is designed for another four washbacks and two more stills. Arran distillery in Lochranza is by far the most visited distillery in Scotland. Well over 100,000 people come here every year! When Lagg opens up to visitors in 2019, the owners expect the combined number to rise to more than 160,000.

The distillery is equipped with a 2.5 ton semi-lauter mash tun, six Oregon pine washbacks with an average fermentation time of 60 hours and four brand new stills. The owners aim to produce 600,000 litres of pure alcohol during 2018. In anticipation of moving the peated production to Lagg once it´s opened – there will, for the first time since 2004, be no peated spirit distilled at Arran this year.

The core range consists of **10, 14** and **18 year old, Robert Burns Malt** and **Lochranza Reserve**. Also included in the core range are the peated expressions **Machrie Moor** and **Machrie Moor Cask Strength**. A new expression joined the range in autumn 2018 – the distillery´s first **21 year old**. Initially, 9 000 bottles were released. A range of wood finishes include **Amarone, Port** and **Sauternes** and every year a number of **single casks**, matured either in ex-bourbon or ex-sherry are released. The second release in the limited Smuggler´s Edition range was launched in July 2017 – **The Exciseman** – and one month later, the 3rd edition of **The Bothy** appeared. In October 2017, a special bottling was released to celebrate the distillery manager´s James MacTaggart 10th anniversary with the distillery and in June 2018, **Brodick Bay**, finished in oloroso butts and the first in the new Explorer´s Series, was launched.

History:

1993 Harold Currie founds the distillery.

1995 Production starts in full on 17th August.

1998 The first release is a 3 year old.

1999 The Arran 4 years old is released.

2002 Single Cask 1995 is launched.

2003 Single Cask 1997, non-chill filtered and Calvados finish is launched.

2004 Cognac finish, Marsala finish, Port finish and Arran First Distillation 1995 are launched.

2005 Arran 1996 and two finishes, Ch. Margaux and Grand Cru Champagne, are launched.

2006 After an unofficial launch in 2005, Arran 10 years old is released as well as a couple of new wood finishes.

2007 Four new wood finishes and Gordon´s Dram are released.

2008 The first 12 year old is released as well as four new wood finishes.

2009 Peated single casks, two wood finishes and 1996 Vintage are released.

2010 A 14 year old, Rowan Tree, three cask finishes and Machrie Moor (peated) are released.

2011 The Westie, Sleeping Warrior and a 12 year old cask strength are released.

2012 The Eagle and The Devil´s Punch Bowl are released.

2013 A 16 year old and a new edition of Machrie Moor and released.

2014 A 17 year old and Machrie Moor cask strength are released.

2015 A 18 year old and The Illicit Stills are released.

2017 The Exciseman is released.

2018 A 21 year old and Brodick Bay are released.

14 years old

Tasting notes Arran 14 year old:

GS – Very fragrant and perfumed on the nose, with peaches, brandy and ginger snaps. Smooth and creamy on the palate, with spicy summer fruits, apricots and nuts. The lingering finish is nutty and slowly drying.

Auchentoshan

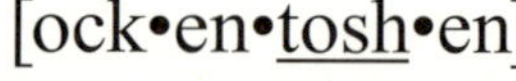

[ock•en•tosh•en]

Owner:		Region/district:
Beam Suntory		Lowlands

Founded:	Status:	Capacity:
1823	Active (vc)	2 000 000 litres

Address: Dalmuir, Clydebank, Glasgow G81 4SJ

Website:	Tel:
auchentoshan.com	01389 878561

With its proximity to Glasgow and considering the fact that it was one of only two Lowland distilleries until quite recently, it´s surprising that it took so long for Auchentoshan single malt to be recognised.

A proper visitor centre wasn´t built until 2004 and the owners were always more focused on the stable mate Bowmore. Things have changed though. Only in the last two years, sales volumes have increased by more than 60% to reach 1.4 million bottles in 2017. A decade ago, the distillery would produce around half a million litres but in the last few years, three times that volume is distilled. Auchentoshan has also been quick to liaise with an important group of influencers - the bartenders. Their collaboration with the on-trade business has attracted new, young fans.

Auchentoshan is the only distillery in Scotland doing 100% triple distillation. This means having a very narrow spirit cut. They start collecting the middle cut at 82% and stop at 80%, long before any other distillery starts collecting. The equipment consists of a semi-lauter mash tun with a 6.8 ton mash charge, four Oregon pine washbacks and three made of stainless steel, all with a fermentation time of 50 to 120 hours, and three stills. On site there are three dunnage and two racked warehouses which can hold about 20,000 casks. The plan for 2018 is to do a mixture of 10 to 15 mashes per week and 1.5 million litres of alcohol.

The core range consists of **American Oak**, a first fill bourbon maturation without age statement, **12 years, Three Woods, 18 years** and **21 years**. The former duty free range was replaced in 2015 by **Blood Oak**, without age statement and matured in a combination of bourbon and red wine casks and the 24 year old **Noble Oak**, a vatting of bourbon and oloroso casks. Two of the previous expressions, Heartwood and Springwood, may be due for a relaunch as well. A limited version named **Bartender´s Malt** was launched in summer 2017. Designed to be used in cocktails, it is a vatting of malt from five decades including whiskies matured in ex-Laphroaig casks, rum casks, red wine barriques, German oak and American oak. **Bartender´s Malt 2** was released in 2018 as well as a limited **1988 PX Cask**.

History:

1817	First mention of the distillery Duntocher, which may be identical to Auchentoshan.
1823	The distillery is founded by John Bulloch.
1823	The distillery is sold to Alexander Filshie.
1878	C.H. Curtis & Co. takes over.
1903	The distillery is purchased by John Maclachlan.
1941	The distillery is severely damaged by a German bomb raid.
1960	Maclachlans Ltd is purchased by the brewery J. & R. Tennent Brewers.
1969	Auchentoshan is bought by Eadie Cairns Ltd who starts major modernizations.
1984	Stanley P. Morrison, eventually becoming Morrison Bowmore, becomes new owner.
1994	Suntory buys Morrison Bowmore.
2002	Auchentoshan Three Wood is launched.
2004	More than a £1 million is spent on a new, refurbished visitor centre. The oldest Auchentoshan ever, 42 years, is released.
2006	Auchentoshan 18 year old is released.
2007	A 50 year old, the oldest ever Auchentoshan to be bottled, was released.
2008	New packaging as well as new expressions - Classic, 18 year old and 1988.
2010	Two vintages, 1977 and 1998, are released.
2011	Two vintages, 1975 and 1999, and Valinch are released.
2012	Six new expressions are launched for the Duty Free market.
2013	Virgin Oak is released.
2014	American Oak replaces Classic.
2015	Blood Oak and Noble Oak are released for duty free.
2017	Bartender´s Malt is launched.
2018	Bartender´s Malt 2 and 1988 PX Cask are released.

American Oak

Tasting notes Auchentoshan American Oak:

GS – An initial note of rose water, then Madeira, vanilla, developing musky peaches and icing sugar. Spicy fresh fruit on the palate, chilli notes and more Madeira and vanilla. The finish is medium in length, and spicy to the end.

Auchroisk

[ar•thrusk]

Owner:
Diageo

Region/district:
Speyside

Founded: 1974

Status: Active

Capacity: 5 900 000 litres

Address: Mulben, Banffshire AB55 6XS

Website:
malts.com

Tel:
01542 885000

While there are many examples of distilleries in Scotland that changed hands quite often, it seems likely that Auchroisk holds some kind of record. Before it even commenced distilling, there had been three owners involved.

Construction of the distillery began early in 1972 by International Distillers & Vintners (IDV). This was a constellation that had been formed ten years earlier when United Wine Traders (an agent for champagne, brandy and sherry but also with Justerini & Brooks Scotch under its umbrella), bought W & A Gilbey, famous for their gin but also with interests in the whisky business. Just a few months later, IDV was acquired by Watney Mann – at one time the second largest brewing company in the world after Guinness. But, the merry-go-round didn´t stop there. After another couple of months, Grand Metropolitan, a hotel and catering conglomerate, presented a hostile take-over bid to the board of Watney Mann and succeeded in buying the company for £400m. Two years after this initial turmoil, Auchroisk started production. In 1997, Grand Metropolitan merged with Guinness and formed Diageo who still owns the distillery.

The equipment consists of a 12 ton stainless steel semi-lauter mash tun, eight stainless steel washbacks with a fermentation time of 53 hours and four pairs of stills. Auchroisk produces 5.8 million litres of alcohol per year, currently with a nutty/malty character. This has changed over the years though and not so long ago, the style was green/grassy. This is not unusual for distilleries that produce malt mainly for blends. It all depends on what the owner predicts they will need for the coming 5 years.

The first, widely available release of Auchroisk single malt was in 1986 under the name Singleton. In 2001, it was replaced by a **10 year old** in the Flora & Fauna range. Recent, limited bottlings include a **20 year old** from 1990 and a **30 year old**, both launched as part of the Special Releases. In October 2016, it was time for the next limited Auchroisk in the Special Releases series; a **25 year old**, distilled in 1990 and bottled at 51.2%.

History:

1972 Building of the distillery commences by Justerini & Brooks (which, together with W. A. Gilbey, make up the group IDV) in order to produce blending whisky. In February the same year IDV is purchased by the brewery Watney Mann which, in July, merges into Grand Metropolitan.

1974 The distillery is completed and, despite the intention of producing malt for blending, the first year's production is sold 12 years later as single malt thanks to the high quality.

1986 The first whisky is marketed under the name Singleton.

1997 Grand Metropolitan and Guinness merge into the conglomerate Diageo. Simultaneously, the subsidiaries United Distillers (to Guinness) and International Distillers & Vintners (to Grand Metropolitan) form the new company United Distillers & Vintners (UDV).

2001 The name Singleton is abandoned and the whisky is now marketed under the name of Auchroisk in the Flora & Fauna series.

2003 Apart from the 10 year old in the Flora & Fauna series, a 28 year old from 1974, the distillery's first year, is launched in the Rare Malt series.

2010 A Manager´s Choice single cask and a limited 20 year old are released.

2012 A 30 year old from 1982 is released.

2016 A 25 year old from 1990 is released.

10 years old

Tasting notes Auchroisk 10 year old:

GS – Malt and spice on the light nose, with developing nuts and floral notes. Quite voluptuous on the palate, with fresh fruit and milk chocolate. Raisins in the finish.

Aultmore

[ault•moor]

Owner:
John Dewar & Sons
(Bacardi)

Region/district:
Speyside

Founded: 1896
Status: Active
Capacity: 3 200 000 litres

Address: Keith, Banffshire AB55 6QY

Website:
aultmore.com

Tel:
01542 881800

Between the two clusters of distilleries in the towns of Keith and Rothes, there are three quite anonymous distilleries scattered in the countryside – Glentauchers, Auchroisk and Aultmore.

All three are located next to main roads (Glentacuhers/A95, Aultmore/A96 and Auchroisk/B9103) but none of them accept visitors. Official bottlings have been scarce over the years but at least for Aultmore, things have changed for the better. Dewars relaunched their entire single malt range in 2014 when the Last Great Malts was introduced and all of a sudden, Aultmore could boast both a core range and presence in the duty free segment.

Aultmore single malt may not have been widely available until recent days but was always known to the locals. During the 20th century, fishermen from Buckie, which is situated some 10 kilometres to the north of Aultmore on Moray Firth, asked for "a nip of the Buckie Road" at inns and bars along the road. That was the secret name for Aultmore single malt and the same words are now embossed at the bottom of the Aultmore bottle. Aultmore single malt has always been revered by blenders as the perfect whisky to build up a blend. The wort is clear and the distillery uses long fermentations. This indicates a fruity and fragrant whisky but with declining lyne arms, the reflux is limited and the wide middle cut (73-61%) adds a distinct body to the newmake.

The distillery was completely rebuilt at the beginning of the 1970s and nothing is left of the old buildings from 1896. The distillery is equipped with a 10 ton Steinecker full lauter mash tun, six washbacks made of larch with a minimum fermentation time of 56 hours and two pairs of stills. Since 2008 production has been running seven days a week, which for 2018, means 16 mashes per week and just over 3 million litres of alcohol.

The core range consists of **12 year old** and an **18 year old**. The 25 year old which was released a few years back has now been discontinued. For the duty free market there is a **21 year old**.

History:

1896 Alexander Edward, owner of Benrinnes and co-founder of Craigellachie Distillery, builds Aultmore.

1897 Production starts.

1898 Production is doubled; the company Oban & Aultmore Glenlivet Distilleries Ltd manages Aultmore.

1923 Alexander Edward sells Aultmore for £20,000 to John Dewar & Sons.

1925 Dewar's becomes part of Distillers Company Limited (DCL).

1930 The administration is transferred to Scottish Malt Distillers (SMD).

1971 The stills are increased from two to four.

1991 United Distillers launches a 12-year old Aultmore in the Flora & Fauna series.

1996 A 21 year old cask strength is marketed as a Rare Malt.

1998 Diageo sells Dewar's and Bombay Gin to Bacardi for £1,150 million.

2004 A new official bottling is launched (12 years old).

2014 Three new expressions are released – 12, 25 and 21 year old for duty free.

2015 An 18 year old is released.

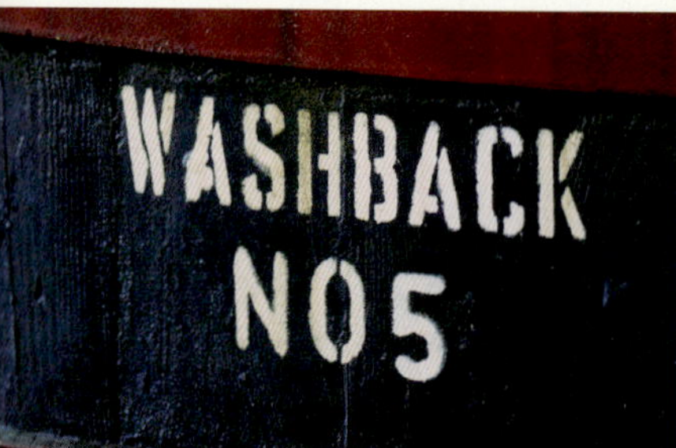

12 years old

Aultmore 12 years old:

GS – A nose of peaches and lemonade, freshly-mown grass, linseed and milky coffee. Very fruity on the palate, mildly herbal, with toffee and light spices. The finish is medium in length, with lingering spices, fudge, and finally more milky coffee.

Balblair

[bal•<u>blair</u>]

Owner:
Inver House Distillers
(Thai Beverages plc)

Region/district:
Northern Highlands

Founded: **Status:**   **Capacity:**
1790   Active (vc)   1 800 000 litres

Address: Edderton, Tain, Ross-shire IV19 1LB

Website: **Tel:**
balblair.com   01862 821273

Judging from official records, Balblair is the fourth oldest distillery in Scotland still in production, beaten only by Glenturret, Strathisla and Bowmore. Actually, there are some facts pointing to 1749 as a possible start for the distillery.

In all honesty, it should be said that the distillery buildings that we see today are of a later date (1872) when the distillery was re-built and moved half a mile to the north. Balblair has always been situated on lands belonging to the Balnagowan Estate, which was owned by clan Ross from the 1300s until 1972 when Egyptian business man Mohammed Al-Fayed, (previous owner of Harrod´s in London until 2010) bought the estate and the castle which is situated 15 kilometres south of the distillery. In 2012, the distillery opened a small but excellent visitor centre which now attracts around 4,000 visitors yearly.

The distillery is equipped with a stainless steel, 4.4 ton semi lauter mash tun, six Oregon pine washbacks with an average fermentation time of 72 hours and one pair of stills. The production target for 2018 is 14 mashes per week – six with a fermentation time of 60 hours and eight fermenting for 90 hours. The total production for 2018 will be 1.14 million litres of alcohol. On site, there are also eight dunnage warehouses with a total capacity of 22,500 casks. In 2015 the distillery converted from using heavy fuel oil to gas, thereby reducing the emission of greenhouse gases significantly.

The entire range of Balblair single malt is built on vintages rather than age statements. The current core range consists of four vintages – **1983, 1991, 2000** and **2005**. For the duty free market, three expressions were released in 2014; a **1999** and **two versions of 2004** matured in bourbon and sherry casks respectively. The oldest vintage available from the distillery at the moment is **1969**. For visitors to the distillery there is also the opportunity to bottle a **single cask** Balblair, from a selected cask which is replaced as it becomes depleted.

History:

1790   The distillery is founded by James McKeddy.

1790   John Ross takes over

1836   John Ross dies and his son Andrew Ross takes over with the help of his sons.

1872   The distillery is moved to the present location.

1873   Andrew Ross dies and his son James takes over.

1894   Alexander Cowan takes over and rebuilds the distillery

1911   Cowan is forced to cease payments and the distillery closes.

1941   The distillery is put up for sale.

1948   Robert Cumming buys Balblair for £48,000.

1949   Production restarts.

1970   Cumming sells Balblair to Hiram Walker.

1988   Allied Distillers becomes the new owner through the merger between Hiram Walker and Allied Vintners.

1996   The distillery is sold to Inver House Distillers.

2000   Balblair Elements and the first version of Balblair 33 years are launched.

2001   Thai company Pacific Spirits (part of the Great Oriole Group) takes over Inver House.

2004   Balblair 38 years is launched.

2005   12 year old Peaty Cask, 1979 (26 years) and 1970 (35 years) are launched.

2006   International Beverage Holdings acquires Pacific Spirits UK.

2007   Three new vintages replace the former range.

2008   Vintage 1975 and 1965 are released.

2009   Vintage 1991 and 1990 are released.

2010   Vintage 1978 and 2000 are released.

2011   Vintage 1995 and 1993 are released.

2012   Vintage 1975, 2001 and 2002 are released. A visitor centre is opened.

2013   Vintage 1983, 1990 and 2003 are released.

2014   Vintage 1999 and 2004 are released for duty free.

2016   Vintage 2005 is released.

Vintage 2005

Tasting notes Balblair 2005:

GS – Chocolate-flavoured ice cream, vanilla and a hint of ozone on the nose. The palate is full and oily, with big spice notes, honey, soft toffee and citrus fruit. The finish is medium in length, with malt and enduring spice.

Balmenach

[bal•<u>may</u>•nack]

Owner:
Inver House Distillers
(Thai Beverages plc)

Region/district:
Speyside

Founded: 1824
Status: Active
Capacity: 2 800 000 litres

Address: Cromdale, Moray PH26 3PF

Website: inverhouse.com
Tel: 01479 872569

In recent years, investments in Scotch whisky distilleries have been about turning the production greener. As it happens, it´s not just about controlling the impact on the environment but there is also money to be saved.

A new biogas plant was installed at Balmenach this summer to treat whisky co-products such as pot ale and spent lees. About 130 m³ of these will each day be processed by the plant and through anaerobic digestion it will be turned into 2,000 m³ of biogas. This in turn will be fed to a CHP engine to heat and power the distillery. The new facility will be integrated with an existing biomass boiler that already supplies heat to the distillery. The £3m investment will make Balmenach one of Scotland´s greenest distilleries.

Balmenach is equipped with an 8 ton stainless steel semi-lauter mash tun, with an old copper canopy. There are six washbacks made of Douglas fir with a 52 hour fermentation period, and three pairs of stills connected to worm tubs where each worm is 94 metres long. In 2018, the distillery will be doing 15 mashes per week which translates to 1.9 million litres of alcohol. Since 2012, a part of the production (up to 400,000 litres) has been heavily peated (50ppm), but in the last three years, there has been no peated production. The three dunnage warehouses currently hold 9,500 casks.

For the past nine years, gin has also been part of the production at Balmenach. Purchased neutral spirit is pumped through a vaporiser and then to a copper berry chamber where the vapours travel upwards passing five trays with different kinds of botanicals and finally end up in the condenser. Caorunn gin has become the third biggest super-premium gin in the UK and for a couple of years now, it is also possible to book a guided gin tour at the distillery.

There is no official bottling of Balmenach single malt. Aberko in Glasgow though, has been working with the distillery for a long time and, over the years, has released Balmenach under the name Deerstalker. The current expression is a 12 year old.

History:

1824 The distillery is licensed to James MacGregor who operated a small farm distillery by the name of Balminoch.

1897 Balmenach Glenlivet Distillery Company is founded.

1922 The MacGregor family sells to a consortium consisting of MacDonald Green, Peter Dawson and James Watson.

1925 The consortium becomes part of Distillers Company Limited (DCL).

1930 Production is transferred to Scottish Malt Distillers (SMD).

1962 The number of stills is increased to six.

1964 Floor maltings replaced with Saladin box.

1992 The first official bottling is a 12 year old.

1993 The distillery is mothballed in May.

1997 Inver House Distillers buys Balmenach from United Distillers.

1998 Production recommences.

2001 Thai company Pacific Spirits takes over Inver House at the price of £56 million. The new owner launches a 27 and a 28 year old.

2002 To commemorate the Queen's Golden Jubilee a 25-year old Balmenach is launched.

2006 International Beverage Holdings acquires Pacific Spirits UK.

2009 Gin production commences.

Deerstalker 12 years old

Tasting notes Deerstalker 12 years old:

GS – The nose is sweet and fruity, with sherry and chilli. Faintly savoury. Fruity and very spicy on the palate, with black pepper and hints of sherry. More chilli in the finish, plus plain chocolate-coated raisins.

Balvenie

[bal•<u>ven</u>•ee]

Owner: William Grant & Sons

Region/district: Speyside

Founded: 1892

Status: Active (vc)

Capacity: 7 000 000 litres

Address: Dufftown, Keith, Banffshire AB55 4DH

Website: thebalvenie.com

Tel: 01340 820373

Not only is Balvenie one of the most sold single malts in the world – just over 4 million bottles last year. It is also one of few distilleries in Scotland where you can follow every step of the production.

They have their own floor maltings producing 15% of their needs and there is also a coppersmith and a cooperage on site. Unlike its sister distillery on the same grounds, Glenfiddich which predominantly focus maturation in ex-bourbon barrels, Balvenie has built its fame on double maturation – ex-bourbon and ex-sherry. The first Doublewood release appeared 25 years ago and this method is still the backbone of the flavour profile. They were also one of the pioneers (together with Glenmorangie) when it came to wood finishing some of their whiskies and in 2017, the owners took yet another step in their search for new flavour profiles, when they for the first time launched two whiskies that were made from 100% peated Balvenie malt.

The distillery is equipped with an 11.8 ton full lauter mash tun, nine wooden and five stainless steel washbacks with a fermentation time of 68 hours, five wash stills and six spirit stills. For 2018, the production plan is 29 mashes per week and 7 million litres of alcohol. The main part is unpeated but each year one week of production comes from peated barley (20-40 ppm).

The core range consists of **Doublewood 12 years, Doublewood 17 years, Caribbean Cask 14 years, Single Barrel 12 years First Fill, Single Barrel 15 years Sherry Cask, Single Barrel 25 years Traditional Oak, Portwood 21 years, 30 years, 40 years** and **50 years old**. Recent limited releases include batch 5 of **Tun 1509** and batch 6 of the **Tun 1858**. Chapter four of **The Balvenie DCS Compendium** was launched in 2018 and at the same time, batch two of **The Balvenie Peat Week** (this time a 2003 vintage) was released. To celebrate the 25th anniversary of Double Wood 12 year old, a limited **25 year old** was released in autumn 2018. For Duty Free there is the **Triple Cask series (12, 16** and **25 years old)** as well as the **21 year old Madeira Cask** and the **14 year old Peated Triple Cask.**

History:

1892 William Grant rebuilds Balvenie New House to Balvenie Distillery (Glen Gordon was the name originally intended). Part of the equipment is brought in from Lagavulin and Glen Albyn.

1893 The first distillation takes place in May.

1957 The two stills are increased by another two.

1965 Two new stills are installed.

1971 Another two stills are installed and eight stills are now running.

1973 The first official bottling appears.

1982 Founder's Reserve is launched.

1996 Two vintage bottlings and a Port wood finish are launched.

2001 The Balvenie Islay Cask, with 17 years in bourbon casks and six months in Islay casks, is released.

2002 A 50 year old is released.

2004 The Balvenie Thirty is released.

2005 The Balvenie Rum Wood Finish 14 years old is released.

2006 The Balvenie New Wood 17 years old, Roasted Malt 14 years old and Portwood 1993 are released.

2007 Vintage Cask 1974 and Sherry Oak 17 years old are released.

2008 Signature, Vintage 1976, Balvenie Rose and Rum Cask 17 year old are released.

2009 Vintage 1978, 17 year old Madeira finish, 14 year old rum finish and Golden Cask 14 years old are released.

2010 A 40 year old, Peated Cask and Carribean Cask are released.

2011 Second batch of Tun 1401 is released.

2012 A 50 year old and Doublewood 17 years old are released.

2013 Triple Cask 12, 16 and 25 years are launched for duty free.

2014 Single Barrel 15 and 25 years, Tun 1509 and two new 50 year olds are launched.

2015 The Balvenie DCS Compendium is launched.

2016 A 21 year old madeira finish is released.

2017 The Balvenie Peat Week 2002 and Peated Triple Cask are released.

2018 A limited 25 year old is relased.

Tasting notes Balvenie Doublewood 12 years:

GS – Nuts and spicy malt on the nose, full-bodied, with soft fruit, vanilla, sherry and a hint of peat. Dry and spicy in a luxurious, lengthy finish.

Doublewood 12 years old

Ben Nevis

[ben nev•iss]

Owner:
Ben Nevis Distillery Ltd
(Nikka, Asahi Breweries)

Region/district:
Western Highlands

Founded: 1825
Status: Active (vc)
Capacity: 2 000 000 litres

Address: Lochy Bridge, Fort William PH33 6TJ

Website:
bennevisdistillery.com

Tel:
01397 702476

Every year, Ben Nevis ship up to 75% of their production in the form of new make to their owners in Japan. Once there, it´s used for manufacturing the popular blend Black Nikka.

An unusual routine it may seem but the whisky regulations in Japan (and in several other countries in the Far East for that matter) are far from the ones imposed by the Scotch Whisky Association in Scotland. A blend in Japan, being labelled Japanese whisky, may well contain whisky made from anywhere in the world.

Traditionally, Japanese ownership of Scotch distilleries, has proven to be a good solution (Tomatin, Bowmore etc) but in the case of Ben Nevis, one would hope for more focus from the owners on Ben Nevis as a single malt in its own right as it deserves it.

Ben Nevis is equipped with a 9.2 ton lauter mash tun, six stainless steel washbacks and two made of Oregon pine as well as two pairs of stills. Fermentation used to be 48 hours in the steel washbacks and 96 hours in the wooden ones. From 2014, however, when 24/7 production was introduced, fermentation is 48 hours in all washbacks. The plan for 2018 is to do 12-15 mashes per week and 2 million litres of alcohol. Around 50,000 litres of this will be heavily peated. Early 2018, the distillery installed an LPG boiler (gas) instead of the old one from 1990 which was fired by heavy fuel oil. In spring 2018, a bottle of Dew of Ben Nevis, allegedly produced in 1882, either at Ben Nevis or the neighbouring distillery Nevis, and discovered in a home in Toronto, was offered for sale by Prinz Beverage Group, basd in Germany and Hong Kong.

The core range consists of **MacDonald´s Ben Nevis 10 year old** and the peated **MacDonald´s Traditional Ben Nevis**. The latter, which is an attempt to replicate the style of Ben Nevis single malt from the 1880s, was introduced as a limited expression but has now become a part of the core range. There is also an 8 year old blended malt, MacDonald´s Glencoe. Recent limited releases, aimed at select markets, include a **51 year old** for France, a **50 year old** for Taiwan and a **25 year old** for Germany.

History:

1825 The distillery is founded by 'Long' John McDonald.

1856 Long John dies and his son Donald P. McDonald takes over.

1878 Demand is so great that another distillery, Nevis Distillery, is built nearby.

1908 Both distilleries merge into one.

1941 D. P. McDonald & Sons sells the distillery to Ben Nevis Distillery Ltd headed by the Canadian millionaire Joseph W. Hobbs.

1955 Hobbs installs a Coffey still which makes it possible to produce both grain and malt whisky.

1964 Joseph Hobbs dies.

1978 Production is stopped.

1981 Joseph Hobbs Jr sells the distillery back to Long John Distillers and Whitbread.

1984 After restoration and reconstruction totalling £2 million, Ben Nevis opens up again.

1986 The distillery closes again.

1989 Whitbread sells the distillery to Nikka Whisky Distilling Company Ltd.

1990 The distillery opens up again.

1991 A visitor centre is inaugurated.

1996 Ben Nevis 10 years old is launched.

2006 A 13 year old port finish is released.

2010 A 25 year old is released.

2011 MacDonald´s Traditional Ben Nevis is released.

2014 Forgotten Bottlings are introduced.

2015 A 40 year old "Blended at Birth" single blend is released.

10 years old

Tasting notes Ben Nevis 10 years old:

GS – The nose is initially quite green, with developing nutty, orange notes. Coffee, brittle toffee and peat are present on the slightly oily palate, along with chewy oak, which persists to the finish, together with more coffee and a hint of dark chocolate.

Benriach

[ben•ree•ack]

Owner:
BenRiach Distillery Company
(Brown Forman)

Region/district:
Speyside

Founded: 1897
Status: Active
Capacity: 2 800 000 litres

Address: Longmorn, Elgin, Morayshire IV30 8SJ

Website:
benriachdistillery.co.uk

Tel:
01343 862888

Even though Benriach was opened more than 120 years ago, it took until 2004 until the single malt was recognised by whisky drinkers. Admittedly, the first single malt appeared in 1994 thanks to Seagrams but it was soon forgotten.

It was Billy Walker, who took over the distillery in 2004, who realised the distillery´s real potential. One of the benefits he discovered was that the distillery had been producing small volumes of peated whisky since 1972 – an unusual practice for a Speyside distillery in the 20th century. The fact that whisky stock going back 40 years was included in the take-over, finally convinced Walker that the deal was a rare opportunity.

BenRiach distillery is equipped with a 5.8 ton traditional cast iron mash tun with a stainless steel shell, eight washbacks made of stainless steel with short (55 hours) and long fermentations (+100 hours) and two pairs of stills. The production for 2018 will be 1.8 million litres which includes 240,000 litres of peated spirit at 35ppm and 35,000 litres of triple distilled spirit. In 2013, the owners revamped the malting floor but it has only been used sporadically since the re-opening. The last time was in April 2018.

Gone from the core range since last year are the 16 and 20 year olds and a **21 year old** matured in four different types of wood has been added as well as a **12 year old**, fully matured in sherry wood. The rest of the core range consists of **Heart of Speyside** (no age), **Cask Strength, 10, 25** and **35 years old**. Peated varieties include **Birnie Moss, Curiositas 10 year old** and **Peated Quarter Cask** Two new additions to the peated range are **Temporis 21 year old** (aged in virgin oak, ex-bourbon, ex-oloroso and ex-PX casks) and **Authenticus 30 year old**. Currently, there are three different wood finishes - **22 year old Dark Rum**, the **22 year old Dunder** and the peated **22 year old Albariza**. In June 2017, the brand made its debut in the travel retail segment with **10 year old Triple Distilled** as well as duty-free versions of **Classic Quarter Cask** and **Peated Quarter Cask**. Finally, **batch 15** of the **single cask** bottlings was launched in May 2018.

History:

1897 John Duff & Co founds the distillery.

1900 The distillery is closed.

1965 The distillery is reopened by the new owner, The Glenlivet Distillers Ltd.

1972 Production of peated Benriach starts.

1978 Seagram Distillers takes over.

1985 The number of stills is increased to four.

1998 The maltings is decommissioned.

2002 The distillery is mothballed in October.

2004 Intra Trading, buys Benriach together with the former Director at Burn Stewart, Billy Walker.

2004 Standard, Curiositas and 12, 16 and 20 year olds are released.

2005 Four different vintages are released.

2006 Sixteen new releases, i.a. a 25 year old, a 30 year old and 8 different vintages.

2007 A 40 year old and three new heavily peated expressions are released.

2008 New expressions include a peated Madeira finish, a 15 year old Sauternes finish and nine single casks.

2009 Two wood finishes (Moscatel and Gaja Barolo) and nine single casks are released.

2010 Triple distilled Horizons and heavily peated Solstice are released.

2011 A 45 year old and 12 vintages are released.

2012 Septendecim 17 years is released.

2013 Vestige 46 years is released. The maltings are working again.

2015 Dunder, Albariza, Latada and a 10 year old are released.

2016 Brown Forman buys the company for £285m. BenRiach cask strength and Peated Quarter Cask are launched.

2017 10 year old Triple Distilled and Peated Cask Strength are released.

2018 A 12 and a 21 year old as well as Temporis 21 year old and Authenticus 30 year old are released.

Tasting notes BenRiach 10 year old:

GS – Earthy and nutty on the early nose, with apples, ginger and vanilla. Smooth and rounded on the palate, with oranges, apricots, mild spice and hazelnuts. The finish is medium in length, nutty and spicy.

10 years old

Benrinnes

[ben <u>rin</u>•ess]

Owner: **Region/district:**
Diageo   Speyside

Founded: **Status:**   **Capacity:**
1826   Active   3 500 000 litres

Address: Aberlour, Banffshire AB38 9NN

Website: **Tel:**
malts.com   01340 872600

In the first 40 years Benrinnes distillery had its fair share of misfortunes, including a devastating flooding and more than one owner going bankrupt. David Edward became the new owner in 1864 and his son, Alexander, took over in 1896 after his father´s death.

As a promoter of distillery projects in the Speyside area, Alexander definitely had star qualities and was an entrepreneur of great proportions; he founded Craigellachie in 1891, Aultmore in 1896 and Dallas Dhu in 1898, took over Benrinnes in 1896, Oban in 1898 and Yoker distillery in 1913. He also leased a part of his Sanquhar Estate (near Forres) to the founders of Benromach. ”Sandy” Edward died in 1946 at the age of 81.

Benrinnes was completely rebuilt in the 1950's and none of the original buildings remain. A major upgrade was made in autumn 2012 which included a full automation of the process, as well as a new control room where one operator can handle all the work. The equipment consists of an 8.5 ton semi-lauter mash tun, eight washbacks made of Oregon pine with a fermentation time ranging from 65 to 100 hours. There are also two wash stills and four spirit stills and from 1966 until a few years ago, they were run three and three with a partial triple distillation. This system has since been abandoned and one wash still will now serve two spirit stills. The spirit vapours are cooled using cast iron worm tubs which contribute to the character of Benrinnes' newmake, which is light sulphury. The wide spirit cut (73%-58%) also plays its part in creating a robust and meaty spirit. In the last couple of years, Benrinnes has been alternating between a 7-day production week and a 5-day with either 21 or 15 mashes per week.

Most of the production goes into blended whiskies – J&B, Johnnie Walker and Crawford´s 3 Star – and there is currently only one official single malt, the **Flora & Fauna 15 year old**. In 2010 a Manager´s Choice from 1996 was released and in autumn 2014 it was time for a 21 year old Special Release bottled at 57%.

History:

1826   Lyne of Ruthrie distillery is built at Whitehouse Farm by Peter McKenzie.

1829   A flood destroys the distillery and a new distillery is constructed by John Innes a few kilometres from the first one.

1834   John Innes files for bankruptcy and William Smith & Co takes over.

1864   William Smith & Co goes bankrupt and David Edward becomes the new owner.

1896   Benrinnes is ravaged by fire which prompts major refurbishment. Alexander Edward takes over.

1922   John Dewar & Sons takes over ownership.

1925   John Dewar & Sons becomes part of Distillers Company Limited (DCL).

1956   The distillery is completely rebuilt.

1964   Floor maltings is replaced by a Saladin box.

1966   The number of stills doubles to six.

1984   The Saladin box is taken out of service and the malt is purchased centrally.

1991   The first official bottling from Benrinnes is a 15 year old in the Flora & Fauna series.

1996   United Distillers releases a 21 year old cask strength in their Rare Malts series.

2009   A 23 year old is launched as a part of this year´s Special Releases.

2010   A Manager´s Choice 1996 is released.

2014   A limited 21 year old is released.

15 years old

Tasting notes Benrinnes 15 years old:

GS – A brief flash of caramel shortcake on the initial nose, soon becoming more peppery and leathery, with some sherry. Ultimately savoury and burnt rubber notes. Big-bodied, viscous, with gravy, dark chocolate and more pepper. A medium-length finish features mild smoke and lively spices.

Benromach

[ben•<u>ro</u>•mack]

Owner: Gordon & MacPhail

Region/district: Speyside

Founded: 1898

Status: Active (vc)

Capacity: 700 000 litres

Address: Invererne Road, Forres, Morayshire IV36 3EB

Website: benromach.com

Tel: 01309 675968

At a time when few distillery owners offered their single malts to the public, Gordon & MacPhail assumed the role of "official bottler" of a wide range of brands. Their part in establishing today´s huge interest in malt whisky can not be overrated.

Founded in 1895, the company realised that having a distillery of their own would benefit their business. The owner at the time, John Urquhart, decided in 1950 to place a bid on Strathisla when it was up for sale. He was willing to pay £70,000 but the distillery went to Seagrams who offered £71,000! Nevertheless, 43 years later, the company bought Benromach distillery. Celebrating the 20th anniversary of whisky production at Benromach, the owners announced that they will now expand the production into gin as well. A former malt barn will be turned into a gin distillery which will be producing Red Door Gin

The goal at Benromach is to produce a Speyside whisky, just like it used to taste back in the 1950s. This is achieved by predominantly using medium peated barley (12ppm). The distillery is equipped with a 1.5 ton semi-lauter mash tun with a copper dome and 13 washbacks made of larch (nine of which were commissioned in early 2017) with a fermentation time of 72-120 hours. There is also one pair of stills with the condensers outside. In 2018 the production will be 14 mashes per week and 400,000 litres of pure alcohol including two weeks of peated production.

The core range consists of **10** and **15 year old** and the **100 Proof**. Recent limited releases include a **35 year old**, a **1975 single cask**, a **2009 Triple Distilled** and a **20th Anniversary** bottling, released in April 2018. There are also special editions; **Organic**, the first single malt to be fully certified organic by the Soil Association and **Peatsmoke**, produced by using heavily peated barley. Recent wood finishes include **Chateau Cissac 2009** and **Sassicaia 2010** and for duty free there is the **Traveller´s Edition**. In October 2018, 575 bottles from the very first cask that was filled after the re-opening in 1998, were launched. All profits from **Benromach Cask No. 1** will be donated to charitable causes.

History:

1898 Benromach Distillery Company starts the distillery.

1911 Harvey McNair & Co buys the distillery.

1919 John Joseph Calder buys Benromach and sells it to recently founded Benromach Distillery Ltd owned by several breweries.

1931 Benromach is mothballed.

1937 The distillery reopens.

1938 Joseph Hobbs buys Benromach and sells it on to National Distillers of America (NDA).

1953 NDA sells Benromach to Distillers Company Limited (DCL).

1966 The distillery is refurbished.

1968 Floor maltings is abolished.

1983 Benromach is mothballed.

1993 Gordon & McPhail buys Benromach.

1998 The distillery is once again in operation.

1999 A visitor centre is opened.

2004 The first bottle distilled by the new owner is 'Benromach Traditional'.

2005 A Port Wood finish (22 years old) and a Vintage 1968 are released together with the Benromach Classic 55 years.

2006 Benromach Organic is released.

2007 Peat Smoke, the first heavily peated whisky from the distillery, is released.

2008 Benromach Origins Golden Promise is released.

2009 Benromach 10 years old is released.

2011 New edition of Peatsmoke, a 2001 Hermitage finish and a 30 year old are released.

2013 A Sassicaia Wood Finish is released.

2014 Three new bottlings are launched; a 5 year old, 100 Proof and Traveller´s Edition.

2015 A 15 year old and two wood finishes (Hermitage and Sassicaia) are released.

2016 A 35 year old and 1974 single cask are released.

2017 A 1976 single cask and a 2009 Triple Distilled are released.

2018 A 20th Anniversary bottling and a Sassicaia 2010 are released.

Tasting notes Benromach 10 year old:

GS – A nose that is initially quite smoky, with wet grass, butter, ginger and brittle toffee. Mouth-coating, spicy, malty and nutty on the palate, with developing citrus fruits, raisins and soft wood smoke. The finish is warming, with lingering barbecue notes.

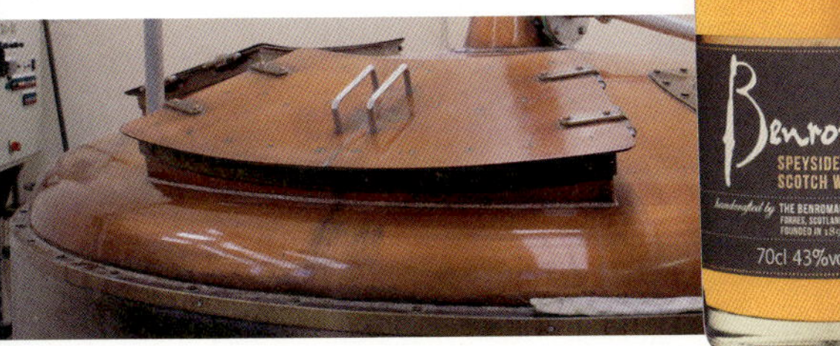

10 years old

Bladnoch

[blad•nock]

Owner: David Prior

Region/district: Lowlands

Founded: 1817

Status: Active (vc)

Capacity: 1 500 000 litres

Address: Bladnoch, Wigtown, Wigtonshire DG8 9AB

Website: bladnoch.com

Tel: 01988 402605

It has now been three years since the Australian entrepreneur David Prior assumed ownership of Bladnoch distillery and the stills were fired up again in May 2017 for the first time since 2009.

Back then it was owned by Raymond Armstrong who ressurected the closed distillery which had been deemed surplus by the owners at the time, Diageo. The new owner is now working on a visitor centre with the plan to open it in April 2019. The current distillery manager, Ian MacMillan, has been in the industry for 46 years and during the past 25 years he refurbished and re-branded the three distilleries owned by Burn Stewart Distillers. A firm believer in traditional production methods, Ian has taken on the stewardship of Bladnoch in the same way which includes exploring the ways Lowland malts were produced in the 1800s.

The distillery is equipped with a 5 ton stainless steel semi-lauter mash tun, six Douglas fir washbacks with a combination of short (76 hours) and long (100 hours) fermentations and two pairs of stills. The plan for 2018 is to do 7-9 mashes per week and 750-900,000 litres of pure alcohol. A small part of heavily peated production started already in 2017 and will continue in 2018.

When the new owners took over, the deal included several thousand casks of whisky dating back to the 1980s. Where needed, MacMillan re-filled whiskies from inferior casks into quality wood and in November 2016, the first new whiskies were released, initially in Australia but later rolled out into other markets as well. The range includes **Samsara** with no age statement and matured in ex-bourbon and casks that had contained Californian red wine, the 15 year old **Adela** matured in ex-oloroso casks and the 25 year old **Talia**. The latter had been matured in a mix of bourbon and sherry casks and finished in new American oak. Two more Talia expressions have since been released - a **25 year old port finish** and a **27 year old bourbon cask finish**. For the 200th anniversary, a **Vintage 1988** finished in moscatel casks was released as well as **10 year old** matured in ex-bourbon. The owners also have a blended Scotch under the name Pure Scot.

History:

1817 Founded by Thomas and John McClelland.

1878 John McClelland's son Charlie reconstructs and refurbishes the distillery.

1905 Production stops.

1911 Dunville & Co. buys T. & A. McClelland Ltd. Production is intermittent until 1936.

1937 Dunville & Co. is liquidated and Bladnoch is wound up. Ross & Coulter from Glasgow buys the distillery after the war. The equipment is dismantled and shipped to Sweden.

1956 A. B. Grant (Bladnoch Distillery Ltd.) takes over and restarts production with four new stills.

1964 McGown and Cameron becomes new owners.

1973 Inver House Distillers buys Bladnoch.

1983 Arthur Bell and Sons take over.

1985 Guiness Group buys Arthur Bell & Sons which, from 1989, are included in United Distillers.

1988 A visitor centre is built.

1993 United Distillers mothballs Bladnoch in June.

1994 Raymond Armstrong buys Bladnoch in October.

2000 Production commences in December.

2003 The first bottles from Armstrong are launched, a 15 year old cask strength from UD casks.

2008 First release of whisky produced after the take-over in 2000 - three 6 year olds.

2009 An 8 year old of own production and a 19 year old are released.

2014 The distillery is liquidated.

2015 The distillery is bought by David Prior.

2016 Samsara, Adela and Talia are released.

2017 Production starts again and a Vintage 1988 is released.

2018 A 10 year old is released.

Samsara

Tasting notes Bladnoch Samsara:

GS – The nose is slightly savoury, with soft spices and tinned peaches with cream. Sweet on the palate, with passion fruit and vanilla. Long in the finish with ripe pears, and increasingly dry spices, plus a suggestion of tannins.

Blair Athol

[blair ath•ull]

Owner: | **Region/district:**
Diageo | Southern Highlands

Founded: | **Status:** | **Capacity:**
1798 | Active (vc) | 2 800 000 litres

Address: Perth Road, Pitlochry, Perthshire PH16 5LY

Website: | **Tel:**
malts.com | 01796 482003

The distilleries in Scotland attract more visitors than ever before and Diageo announced in spring 2018 that they will invest £1.5bn in a huge Johnnie Walker experience in Edinburgh and at the same time expand visitor centres at four of their sites.

Blair Athol is not one of them but on the other hand it managed to attract more people in 2017 than any other distillery in the company. No less than 86,000 came to see the distillery, an increase by 23% compared to the previous year. Blair Athol has one of the best locations in Scotland, a few hundred metres from the busy A9 going from Edinburgh up to Inverness. A new feature at the distillery is a used mash tun from Clynelish which has been turned into a whisky tasting bar!

Bell´s blended whisky was introduced in 1896 and from the very start, single malt from Blair Athol was a vital component. The connection became stronger when Bell´s acquired the distillery in 1933. The independence of Arthur Bell & Sons lasted much longer than most of the old family companies and it wasn´t until 1985 that they were sold to Guinness and later became a part of Diageo. There was a time in the 1970s when every third bottle of blended whisky that was sold in the UK was Bell´s.

The equipment of Blair Athol distillery consists of an 8.2 ton semi-lauter mash tun, six washbacks made of stainless steel and two pairs of stills. The part of the spirit which goes into Bell´s is matured mainly in bourbon casks, while the rest is matured in sherry casks. The last couple of years, the distillery has been working a 5-day week with 12 mashes per week and around 2 million litres of alcohol. This also means a scheme of short (46 hours) and long (104 hours) fermentations. A very cloudy wort gives Blair Athol newmake a nutty and malty character.

The output today is still used for Bell´s whisky and the only official bottling is the **12 year old Flora & Fauna**. In autumn 2017, however, a **23 year old**, matured in ex-bodega European oak butts was released as part of the Special Releases. There is also a **distillery exclusive** bottling with no age statement.

History:

1798 John Stewart and Robert Robertson found Aldour Distillery, the predecessor to Blair Athol. The name is taken from the adjacent river Allt Dour.

1825 The distillery is expanded by John Robertson and takes the name Blair Athol Distillery.

1826 The Duke of Atholl leases the distillery to Alexander Connacher & Co.

1860 Elizabeth Connacher runs the distillery.

1882 Peter Mackenzie & Company Distillers Ltd of Edinburgh (future founder of Dufftown Distillery) buys Blair Athol and expands it.

1932 The distillery is mothballed.

1933 Arthur Bell & Sons takes over by acquiring Peter Mackenzie & Company.

1949 Production restarts.

1973 Stills are expanded from two to four.

1985 Guinness Group buys Arthur Bell & Sons.

1987 A visitor centre is built.

2003 A 27 year old cask strength from 1975 is launched in Diageo's Rare Malts series.

2010 A distillery exclusive with no age statement and a single cask from 1995 are released.

2016 A distillery exclusive without age statement is released.

2017 A 23 year old is released as part of the Special Releases.

12 years old

Tasting notes Blair Athol 12 years old:

GS – The nose is mellow and sherried, with brittle toffee. Sweet and fragrant. Relatively rich on the palate, with malt, raisins, sultanas and sherry. The finish is lengthy, elegant and slowly drying.

Bowmore

[bow•moor]

Owner: | **Region/district:**
Beam Suntory | Islay

Founded: | **Status:** | **Capacity:**
1779 | Active (vc) | 2 000 000 litres

Address: School Street, Bowmore, Islay, Argyll PA43 7GS

Website: | **Tel:**
bowmore.com | 01496 810441

The good people of Bowmore have been extremely busy in the last two years, launching a new range for duty free, re-launching their core range while at the same time releasing extremely old vintages as well as introducing a completely new series of special bottlings.

This follows a change in the structure of ownership where Beam and Suntory joined forces. At the same time Rachel Barrie, master blender for Bowmore, Glen Garioch and Auchentoshan, left the company in 2017 to join BenRiach Distillers with Ron Welsh assuming overall responsibility for the blending of all whiskies in the company. Welsh has worked with Beam since 2005 (and Allied Domecq since 1992) where he developed the use of quarter casks for both Laphroaig and Ardmore.

The distillery is one of only a few Scottish distilleries with its own floor maltings, with 30% of the malt requirement being produced in-house. The remaining part is bought from Simpson's. Both parts have a phenol specification of 25 ppm and are always mixed on a 1:3 ratio, with 2 tons in house malt and 6 tons of malt from Simpsons before mashing. The distillery has an eight ton stainless steel semi-lauter mash tun, six washbacks made of Oregon pine, with both short (48 hours) and long (100 hours) fermentations and two pairs of stills. The 27,000 casks are stored in two dunnage and one racked warehouse. In 2018, they will be doing 14 mashes per week, seven short and seven long fermentations, which amounts to 1.8 million litres of alcohol.

The core range for domestic markets includes **No. 1**, **12 years, 15 years** (with the name Darkest having been dropped), **18 years** and **25 years**. The duty free line-up was completely revamped last year and all the old varieties are gone. The new range since spring 2017 is **10 year old** (Dark and Intense), **15 year old** (Golden and Elegant) and **18 year old** (Deep and Complex). A limited release was made in autumn 2016, highlighting the influence from Vault No. 1 where some of the warehouse walls are actually found below sea level. The first expression, bottled at 51.5% was called **Bowmore Vault Edition** with the added "Atlantic Sea Salt". A third instalment named **Peat Smoke** is due for release in autumn 2018. A limited release of impressive age appeared in late 2016 – the fifth and final edition of the famous **Black Bowmore** distilled in 1964. In autumn 2017 a **50 year old**, distilled in 1966, was released which was followed by a **Vintage 1965** in 2018. A new range, highlighting how wine casks interact with Bowmore single malt, was introduced in autumn 2017. The first two bottlings in the Vintner's Trilogy were the **18 year old Double Matured Manzanilla** and a **26 year old** which had received a second maturation (for 13 years) in ex-wine barriques. The third expression, a **27 year old** with a finish in port pipes, was released in summer 2018. Finally, there were two bottlings for Feis Ile 2018; a **15 year old** (53.8%) matured in oloroso sherry casks and a rare and limited **1989 (28 years old)** from a bourbon cask.

History:

1779 Bowmore Distillery is founded by David Simpson and becomes the oldest Islay distillery.

1837 The distillery is sold to James and William Mutter of Glasgow.

1892 After additional construction, the distillery is sold to Bowmore Distillery Company Ltd, a consortium of English businessmen.

1925 J. B. Sheriff and Company takes over.

1929 Distillers Company Limited (DCL) takes over.

1950 William Grigor & Son takes over.

1963 Stanley P. Morrison buys the distillery and forms Morrison Bowmore Distillers Ltd.

1989 Japanese Suntory buys a 35% stake in Morrison Bowmore.

1993 The legendary Black Bowmore is launched.

1994 Suntory now controls all of Morrison Bowmore.

1996 A Bowmore 1957 (38 years) is bottled at 40.1% but is not released until 2000.

1999 Bowmore Darkest with three years finish on Oloroso barrels is launched.

2000 Bowmore Dusk with two years finish in Bordeaux barrels is launched.

2001 Bowmore Dawn with two years finish on Port pipes is launched.

2002 A 37 year old Bowmore from 1964 and matured in fino casks is launched in a limited edition of 300 bottles (recommended price £1,500).

2003 Another two expressions complete the wood trilogy which started with 1964 Fino - 1964 Bourbon and 1964 Oloroso.

2004 Morrison Bowmore buys one of the most out standing collections of Bowmore Single Malt from the private collector Hans Sommer. It totals more than 200 bottles and includes a number of Black Bowmore.

History continued:

2005 Bowmore 1989 Bourbon (16 years) and 1971 (34 years) are launched.

2006 Bowmore 1990 Oloroso (16 years) and 1968 (37 years) are launched. A new and upgraded visitor centre is opened.

2007 An 18 year old is introduced. 1991 (16yo) Port and Black Bowmore are released.

2008 White Bowmore and a 1992 Vintage with Bordeaux finish are launched.

2009 Gold Bowmore, Maltmen´s Selection, Laimrig and Bowmore Tempest are released.

2010 A 40 year old and Vintage 1981 are released.

2011 Vintage 1982 and new batches of Tempest and Laimrig are released.

2012 100 Degrees Proof, Springtide and Vintage 1983 are released for duty free.

2013 The Devil´s Casks, a 23 year old Port Cask Matured and Vintage 1984 are released.

2014 Black Rock, Gold Reef and White Sands are released for duty free.

2015 New editions of Devil´s Cask, Tempest and the 50 year old are released as well as Mizunara Cask Finish.

2016 A 9 year old, a 10 year old travel retail exclusive and Bowmore Vault Edit1on are released as well as the final batch of Black Bowmore.

2017 No. 1 is released together with three new expressions for travel retail.

2018 Vault Edit1on Peat Smoke and Vintner´s Trilogy are launched.

Tasting notes Bowmore 12 year old:

GS – An enticing nose of lemon and gentle brine leads into a smoky, citric palate, with notes of cocoa and boiled sweets appearing in the lengthy, complex finish.

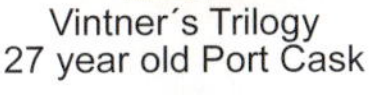

Vintner´s Trilogy
27 year old Port Cask

18 years old
Travel Retail

Vault Edition
Atlantic Sea Salt

No. 1

12 years old

25 years old

Braeval

[bre•<u>vaal</u>]

Owner:	**Region/district:**
Chivas Brothers (Pernod Ricard)	Speyside
Founded: **Status:**	**Capacity:**
1973 Active	4 200 000 litres

Address: Chapeltown of Glenlivet, Ballindalloch, Banffshire AB37 9JS

Website:	**Tel:**
-	01542 783042

There is a saying about family businesses that the first generation creates, the second spends and the third destroys. That could be a fitting description of the founders of Braeval distillery – Seagram´s.

Joseph E. Segram & Sons was founded already in the 1800s but is was in 1928, when the Canadian Sam Bronfman and his company Distillers Corporation took over, that Seagram Co eventually became the biggest alcoholic drinks company in the world. Mr Sam, as he was often called, was a clever businessman who took advantage of the alcohol prohibition in neighbouring USA to strengthen his position. In 1949 he went on to buy Chivas Brothers, thereby entering into the Scotch whisky business.

Sam Bronfman died in 1971 and was succeeded by his son Edgar. It was during his time in the company that Braeval, Allt-a-Bhainne and Glen Keith were built and Glenlivet became a part of the company. His son Edgar Jr. took over in 1994 and having spent time in Hollywood as a script writer and producer, he decided to expand the family company into the entertainment business. This decision proved to be a disastrous one. In 2000, Bronfman was forced to find a business partner and the French conglomerate Vivendi took over. Shortly after, Vivendi sold off the beverage division to Pernod Ricard and Diageo and Seagrams seized to exist.

The equipment at Braeval consists of a 9 ton stainless steel mash tun which was equipped with traditional rakes until 2016 when the tun was equipped with a modern lauter gear. Furthermore, there are 13 stainless steel washbacks with a fermentation time of 70 hours and six stills. There are two wash stills with aftercoolers and four spirit stills, and with the possibility of doing 26 mashes per week, the distillery can now produce 4.2 million litres per year.

A **16 year old single cask**, available at Chivas´ visitor centres is the only offical bottling. From time to time independent bottlers have made releases and it has also been used for the bottling of Deerstalker.

History:

1973 The distillery is founded by Chivas Brothers (Seagram´s) and production starts in October.

1975 Three stills are increased to five.

1978 Five stills are further expanded to six.

1994 The distillery changes name to Braeval.

2001 Pernod Ricard takes over Chivas Brothers.

2002 Braeval is mothballed in October.

2008 The distillery starts producing again in July.

2017 The first official bottling, a 16 year old single cask, is released.

16 years old

Tasting notes Braeval 16 year old:

GS – Marzipan, milk chocolate-coated Turkish Delight and orange peel on the nose. The palate is sweet and fruity, with stewed apples, sugared almonds, nutmeg and ginger. Medium to long in the finish, consistently sugary and spicy.

Whisky
the way I see it

Alistair McDonald
Distillery Manager
The Clydeside Distillery

You´re Islay born and bred – what made you decide to leave the island?

I started at Bowmore serving my time as an Apprentice Distillery Engineer and to attain my college education I was offered a move to Glasgow to allow me to complete this while working between Auchentoshan Distillery and our Springburn blending operation.

After several years as manager of a well-known distillery such as Auchentoshan – what made you decide to take on the job as Clydeside Distillery manager?

After 33 years it was a big decision to leave such a highly profiled distillery but the opportunity to rejoin the Morrison family who I first started my career with and be involved in a brand new distillery in the heart of Glasgow overseeing the project install through to comissioning and then creating and developing an exciting new make spirit, was too much of a lure not to be a part of. These opportunities dont come around very often and I wanted to use my previous years of experience to help bring to life this exciting new distillery and spirit.

Please describe your day-to-day job.

My day to day job consists of managing a small team of production operators and overseeing the production processes to ensure they are being kept consistent to maintain a high quality spirit. Also looking after the health and safety side of the site is very important to myself and the team. Hosting industry partners, journalists and whisky enthusiasts is also another part of the role that I enjoy very much. We have a very small team at the Clydeside and it can be "all hands to the pump" at times so very seldom are two days the same.

What would be your worst nightmare as a distillery manager?

After creating an exciting new premium Clydeside Single Malt and not having the stock behind us to fulfill our customer demands or requirements.

Glasgow has a history of being a whisky town. In what way is that important to you and the distillery?

It´s of significant importance to ourselves at The Clydeside that we have brought whisky distilling back to a city that has lost so many of its distilleries over the years and to give Glaswegians the opportunity to have a quality single malt that they can call their own! Hopefully the rebirth of distilling in a city that once had over 30 (legal) distilleries may continue in years to come.

Your location is soaked with whisky history. How is that evident when visiting the distillery and how important do you think it is to have a story to tell when you open up a new distillery?

The distillery is part of the Pumphouse building which once controlled the access gate to the Queens dock allowing ships to export whisky all over the world from the Clyde. This is very important as we are bringing back to life the link between whisky and the Clyde with the opening of our new distillery on the banks of the river. Also our chairman Tim Morrison`s Great Grand father, John Morrison, constructed the Queens dock and Pumphouse in 1877 and this concludes a remarkable family connection with the distillery and the dock which has a very interesting history that our vistiors love to learn about.

You´re in the Lowlands. Has that affected the way you distill Clydeside whisky?

Yes. We are creating a typical Lowland style as this is our location and want the brand to be recognised as a premium Lowland single malt. Some new distilleries are creating various expressions lightly/heavily peated etc. but we want The Clydeside to have its own consistent identity and be recognised as an established brand before experimenting with various expressions.

Whisky tourism has become increasingly important to producers of Scotch in recent years. What have you done at Clydeside in order to give the visitor a unique experience?

Our visitors will have a unique experience taking a step back in time to the history of the Pumphouse, Queens Dock, distilling in Glasgow and the Morrison family dating back to 1877 before embarking on a tour of our Distillery with breath taking view's of the River Clyde from the Stillhouse. Visitors have access to our cafe, as well as our specialist whisky shop which includes a premium retail area for collectors.

The classic end of a whisky tour is a dram. With no whisky from your own production to pour, how have you solved that?

We have purchased a parcel of casks from a well known whisky distilling company to give our visitors the oppurtunity to taste 3 single malts of different regions, all at 10 year old and 40% abv to appreciate the difference in style of each region until our own single malt is available and ready for tasting.

What does Scotch whisky mean to you?

Scotch whisky for me is part of our national identity which has played a major part in my life, providing me with a very interesting and enjoyable career. It is also a very satisfying reward to sip and savour at the end of a busy week.

The history of Scotch whisky has had its ups and downs over the years. How do you see the future for Scotch in the next 10-15 years?

I have been involved in the industry since 1984 and seen the ups and downs but over the last 10-15 years single malt has continued to grow from strength to strength and with all the emerging markets I can only see this trend continuing for the next 10 -15 years and beyond.

Bruichladdich

[brook•lad•dee]

Owner: Rémy Cointreau   **Region/district:** Islay

Founded: 1881   **Status:** Active (vc)   **Capacity:** 1 500 000 litres

Address: Bruichladdich, Islay, Argyll PA49 7UN

Website: bruichladdich.com   **Tel:** 01496 850221

Ever since Mark Reynier and Simon Coughlin together with other investors bought the mothballed Bruichladdich in 2000, the distillery has become known for its will to experiment, innovate and break new ground.

Their view on terroir, how the location where the barley has been grown influences the spirit, is well-known. So is their will to try out odd varieties such as the old bere barley (only Arran and Springbank have done the same) and releasing bottlings made from organically grown barley (in common with Benromach and Deanston). In 2017, they also did 5 mashes with rye grown on Islay. The unmalted rye was mixed with malted barley and the experiment will continue in 2018.

The distillery is equipped with a 7 ton cast iron, open mash tun with rakes, dating back to 1881 when the distillery was founded. There are six washbacks of Oregon pine with a fermentation time between 70 and 105 hours and two pairs of stills. All whisky produced is based on Scottish barley, 33% of which comes from Islay and with 5% being organically grown. During 2018, they will be doing 9-10 mashes per week, resulting in 1 million litres of alcohol. The breakdown of the three whisky varieties during 2018 are 60% Bruichladdich, 30% Port Charlotte and 10% Octomore. There are currently 13 warehouses on site with three more being built in 2018. The malting floors at Bruichladdich were closed in 1961 but there are now definite plans to start their own malting again within the next three years. The idea is to move the bottling facility to a new location on site and build a malting plant where the current bottling plant is located. No time table for commencement of the work has yet been presented.

Bruichladdich single malt was unpeated between 1962 and 1994 but today, there are three main lines in the distillery´s production; unpeated Bruichladdich, heavily peated Port Charlotte and the ultra-heavily peated Octomore. The core expressions for **Bruichladdich** are **The Classic Laddie, Islay Barley 2010** and **Black Art 5**. The range for **Port Charlotte** was completely revamped in 2018 (including new bottle design) and the core range now consists of the **10 year old**, bottled at 50% and replacing PC Scottish barley (although the new expression is also made from 100% Scottish barley) and **2011 Islay Barley**. The duty free range is made up of **The Laddie Eight, Bruichladdich 1990, Port Charlotte MC:01** (distilled in 2009 and matured in marsala casks) and **Octomore 08.2**. Recent limited expressions include **Bruichladdich Bere Barley 2008, Bruichladdich The Organic Barley 2009, Port Charlotte MRC:01 2010** (matured in Bordeaux casks) and **Octomore 08.1, 08.3** and **08.4**. In November 2017, the **Rare Cask** series was launched which was made up of three Bruichladdich bottlings distilled in 1984-1986. Finally, there were two special bottlings of Port Charlotte for Feis Ile 2018; **The Heretic**, five casks from different maturations, distilled in 2001 and **The Distillery Valinch**, a single oloroso butt distilled in 2005.

History:

1881   Barnett Harvey builds the distillery with money left by his brother William III to his three sons William IV, Robert and John Gourlay.

1886   Bruichladdich Distillery Company Ltd is founded and reconstruction commences.

1929   Temporary closure.

1936   The distillery reopens.

1938   Joseph Hobbs, Hatim Attari and Alexander Tolmie purchase the distillery through the company Train & McIntyre.

1938   Operations are moved to Associated Scottish Distillers.

1952   The distillery is sold to Ross & Coulter.

1960   A. B. Grant buys Ross & Coulter.

1961   Own maltings ceases.

1968   Invergordon Distillers take over.

1975   The number of stills increases to four.

1983   Temporary closure.

1993   Whyte & Mackay buys Invergordon Distillers.

1995   The distillery is mothballed in January.

1998   In production again for a few months.

2000   Murray McDavid buys the distillery from JBB Greater Europe for £6.5 million.

2001   The first distillation (Port Charlotte) is on 29th May and the first distillation of Bruichladdich starts in July. In September the owners' first bottlings from the old casks are released, 10, 15 and 20 years old.

2002   The world's most heavily peated whisky is produced on 23rd October when Octomore (80ppm) is distilled.

2004   Second edition of the 20 year old (nick-named Flirtation) and 3D, also called The Peat Proposal, are launched.

2005   Several new expressions are launched - the second edition of 3D, Infinity, Rocks, Legacy

History continued:

2006 The first official bottling of Port Charlotte; PC5.

2007 New releases include Redder Still, Legacy 6, PC6 and an 18 year old.

2008 New expressions include the first Octomore, Bruichladdich 2001, PC7 and Golder Still.

2009 New releases include Classic, Organic, Black Art, Infinity 3, PC8, Octomore 2 and X4+3 - the first quadruple distilled single malt.

2010 PC Multi Vintage, Organic MV, Octomore/3_152, Bruichladdich 40 year old are released.

2011 The first 10 year old from own production is released as well as PC9 and Octomore 4_167.

2012 Ten year old versions of Port Charlotte and Octomore are released as well as Laddie 16 and 22, Bere Barley 2006, Black Art 3 and DNA4. Rémy Cointreau buys the distillery.

2013 Scottish Barley, Islay Barley Rockside Farm, Bere Barley 2nd edition, Black Art 4, Port Charlotte Scottish Barley, Octomore 06.1 and 06.2 are released.

2014 PC11 and Octomore Scottish Barley are released.

2015 PC12, Octomore 7.1 and High Noon 134 are released.

2016 The Laddie Eight, Octomore 7.4 and Port Charlotte 2007 CC:01 are released.

2017 Black Art 5 and 25 year old sherry cask are launched. The limited Rare Cask series is launched.

2018 The Port Charlotte range is revamped and a 10 year old and Islay Barley 2011 are released.

Tasting notes Bruichladdich Scottish Barley:

GS – Mildly metallic on the early nose, then cooked apple aromas develop, with a touch of linseed. Initially very fruity on the gently oily palate. Ripe peaches and apricots, with vanilla, brittle toffee, lots of spice and sea salt. The finish is drying, with breakfast tea.

Tasting notes Port Charlotte Scottish Barley:

GS – Wood smoke and contrasting bonbons on the nose. Warm Tarmac develops, with white pepper. Finally, fragrant pipe tobacco. Peppery peat and treacle toffee on the palate, with a maritime note. Long in the finish, with black pepper and oak.

Tasting notes Octomore Scottish Barley:

GS – A big hit of sweet peat on the nose; ozone and rock pools, supple leather, damp tweed. Peat on the palate is balanced by allspice, vanilla and fruitiness. Very long in the finish, with chilli, dry roasted nuts and bonfire smoke.

Bere Barley 2008

Black Art 5

The Organic 2009

The Classic Laddie Scottish Barley

Port Charlotte
Islay Barley 2011

Port Charlotte
10 year old

Bunnahabhain

[buh•nah•hav•enn]

Owner:
Distell International Ltd.

Region/district:
Islay

Founded: **Status:** **Capacity:**
1881 Active (vc) 2 700 000 litres

Address: Port Askaig, Islay, Argyll PA46 7RP

Website: **Tel:**
bunnahabhain.com 01496 840646

The setting of Bunnahabhain, right on the sound of Islay and overlooking Jura, is no less than stunning. The distillery itself, however, has been due for an extensive upgrade for a long time,

Finally it is about to happen. Some of the warehouses and a few distillery village houses will be demolished with new warehouses being built closer to the sea. The remaining buildings will all be refurbished. Phase two is the creation of a new, purpose built visitor centre which will hopefully be ready to open for Feis Ile 2019. The entire project, which will last for three years, will cost £11m.

The distillery is equipped with a 12.5 ton traditional stainless steel mash tun, six washbacks made of Oregon pine and two pairs of stills. The fermentation time varies between 48 and 110 hours. The production for 2018 will be 2.1 million litres, split between 35% peated and 65% unpeated. The peated volume has more than doubled compared to last year and the peating level has also increased slightly to 35-45ppm.

The core range consists of **12, 18** and **25 year olds** (all in new packaging) as well as a **40 year old**. The two peated expressions, Toiteach and Ceobanach have been replaced with **Toiteach a Dha** (meaning Smoky Two in Gaelic), without age statement and matured in both bourbon and sherrycasks. Another no age statement addition to the range appeared in 2017 in the shape of **Stiùireadair**, matured in first and re-fill sherry casks. Recent limited releases include **Moine Oloroso**, a **1980 vintage**, a **14 year old PX finish**, a **12 year old Moine brandy finish** and, most recently, a **20 year old Palo Cortado** and a **9 year old Moine matured in red wine casks**. There are three travel retail exclusives – **Cruach-Mhòna** which comprises of young, heavily peated Bunnahabhain, **Eirigh Na Greine**, a vatting of whisky from bourbon, sherry and red wine casks and the sherry-matured **An Cladach**. Finally, there is one distillery exclusive – a **12 year old** finished in **palo cortado** casks - and two special bottlings for Feis Ile 2018, a peated **2007 Moine Oloroso finish** and a **15 year old**, finished in **Spanish Oak**.

History:

1881 William Robertson of Robertson & Baxter, founds the distillery together with the brothers William and James Greenless, owners of Islay Distillers Company Ltd.

1883 Production starts in earnest in January.

1887 Islay Distillers Company Ltd merges with William Grant & Co. in order to form Highland Distilleries Company Limited.

1963 The two stills are augmented by two more.

1982 The distillery closes.

1984 The distillery reopens. A 21 year old is released to commemorate the 100th anniversary.

1999 Edrington takes over Highland Distillers and mothballs Bunnahabhain but allows for a few weeks of production a year.

2001 A 35 year old from 1965 is released during Islay Whisky Festival.

2002 A 35 year old from 1965 is released during Islay Whisky Festival. Auld Acquaintance 1968 is launched at the Islay Jazz Festival.

2003 Edrington sells Bunnahabhain and Black Bottle to Burn Stewart Distilleries for £10 million. A 40 year old from 1963 is launched.

2004 The first limited edition of the peated version is a 6 year old called Moine.

2005 Three limited editions are released - 34 years old, 18 years old and 25 years old.

2006 14 year old Pedro Ximenez and 35 years old are launched.

2008 Darach Ur is released for the travel retail market and Toiteach (a peated 10 year old) is launched on a few selected markets.

2009 Moine Cask Strength is released.

2010 The peated Cruach-Mhòna and a limited 30 year old are released.

2013 A 40 year old is released.

2014 Eirigh Na Greine and Ceobanach are released.

2017 Moine Oloroso, Stiùireadair and An Cladach are released.

2018 Toiteach a Dha and a 20 year old Palo Cortado are released.

Tasting notes Bunnahabhain 12 years old:

GS – The nose is fresh, with light peat and discreet smoke. More overt peat on the nutty and fruity palate, but still restrained for an Islay. The finish is full-bodied and lingering, with a hint of vanilla and some smoke.

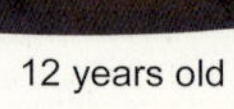

12 years old

Caol Ila

[cull eel•a]

Owner: Diageo
Region/district: Islay

Founded: 1846
Status: Active (vc)
Capacity: 6 500 000 litres

Address: Port Askaig, Islay, Argyll PA46 7RL

Website: malts.com
Tel: 01496 302760

The two Islay distilleries owned by Diageo today were both taken over by the company´s predecessor DCL in 1927. After that the development and use of the two distilleries would differ greatly.

Lagavulin would eventually become one of the single malt superstars, not least after being selected as one of the six Classic Malts in 1988. Caol Ila on the other hand was demolished and re-built in the early 1970s to be used as a producer of peated malt for the owner´s blends. Apart from the standard treatment, a bottling in the Flora & Fauna range, that all Diageo distilleries received, it would last until 2002 before an entire range was presented.

By then, the interest from whisky enthusiasts in peated malts had grown and it was impossible for the owners to ignore the potential. Within a few years the range consisted of half a dozen expressions. At the same time, the distillery remained an important supplier of malt for Diageo´s blends and so in 2011, the distillery underwent an upgrade which increased the capacity to 6.5 million litres. The distillery is due for more attention in the next couple of years. As part of a £150m investment by Diageo in whisky tourism, the visitor centre is targeted for a substantial upgrade.

Caol Ila is equipped with a 13 ton full lauter mash tun, eight wooden washbacks and two made of stainless steel and three pairs of stills. In recent years, the distillery has been doing 26 mashes per week which amounts to 6.5 million litres of alcohol. Caol Ila is known for its peated whisky but, depending on the requirement from the blending team, unpeated new-make is also produced.

The core range consists of **Moch** without age statement, **12, 18** and **25 year old, Distiller´s Edition** with a moscatel finish and **Cask Strength**. The release for Islay Festival 2018 was a **10 year old** that had been matured in refill American oak hogsheads and rejuvenated European oak butts. As usual, Caol Ila was also represented by an unpeated expression in the Special Releases 2018. This time it was a **15 year old**. But that was not all – in the range there could also be found an unsually old Caol Ila, a **35 year old** bottling of the peated version, matured in a combination of American and Europan oak.

History:

1846 Hector Henderson founds Caol Ila.

1852 Henderson, Lamont & Co. is subjected to financial difficulties and Henderson is forced to sell Caol Ila to Norman Buchanan.

1863 Norman Buchanan sells to the blending company Bulloch, Lade & Co. from Glasgow.

1879 The distillery is rebuilt and expanded.

1920 Bulloch, Lade & Co. is liquidated and the distillery is taken over by Caol Ila Distillery.

1927 DCL becomes sole owners.

1972 All the buildings, except for the warehouses, are demolished and rebuilt.

1974 The renovation, which totals £1 million, is complete and six new stills are installed.

1999 Experiments with unpeated malt.

2002 The first official bottlings since Flora & Fauna/ Rare Malt appear; 12 years, 18 years and Cask Strength (c. 10 years).

2003 A 25 year old cask strength is released.

2006 Unpeated 8 year old and 1993 Moscatel finish are released.

2007 Second edition of unpeated 8 year old.

2009 The fourth edition of the unpeated version (10 year old) is released.

2010 A 25 year old, a 1999 Feis Isle bottling and a 1997 Manager´s Choice are released.

2011 An unpeated 12 year old and the unaged Moch are released.

2012 An unpeated 14 year old is released.

2013 Unpeated Stitchell Reserve is released.

2014 A 15 year old unpeated and a 30 year old are released.

2016 A 15 year old unpeated is released.

2017 An 18 year old unpeated is released.

2018 Two bottlings in the Special Releases - a 15 year old and a 35 year old.

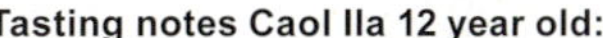

35 years old

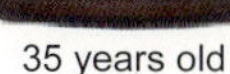

Tasting notes Caol Ila 12 year old:

GS – Iodine, fresh fish and smoked bacon feature on the nose, along with more delicate, floral notes. Smoke, malt, lemon and peat on the slightly oily palate. Peppery peat in the drying finish.

Cardhu

[car•<u>doo</u>]

Owner: Diageo

Region/district: Speyside

Founded: 1824

Status: Active (vc)

Capacity: 3 400 000 litres

Address: Knockando, Aberlour, Moray AB38 7RY

Website: malts.com

Tel: 01479 874635

Today, more than 60 distilleries in Scotland have opened their doors to visitors but in the early 1960s this was not the case. At that time the owners saw their distilleries merely as production plants with trade secrets that should be closely guarded.

The first company to acknowledge the marketing benefits of inviting consumers to see the production was William Grant & Sons and they opened a visitor centre at Glenfidddich in 1969. They were also the first to brand and market a single malt on a global scale with their Glenfiddich Straight Malt in 1963 The first competitor to follow suit, was DCL who launched Cardhu single malt in 1965. Cardhu was also first in the DCL stable of distilleries to have a visitor centre. It was rebuilt in 1998, focusing on the distillery as the spiritual home of the blend Johnnie Walker. Today, the facilities are too small to welcome the increasing number of visitors. Soon, however, it´s time for another upgrade.

Diageo announced in April 2018 that £150m will be invested in whisky tourism with the major part of the sum allocated to a brand new Johnnie Walker experience in Edinburgh. Four distilleries, representing the "four corners of Scotland", will also receive a substantial share of the investment – alongside Cardhu, it will be Glenkinchie, Caol Ila and Clynelish.

Cardhu distillery is equipped with an 8 ton stainless steel full lauter mash tun with a copper top, ten washbacks (eight made of Douglas fir and two of stainless steel), all with a fermentation time of 75 hours and three pairs of stills. Four of the wooden washbacks are new, having replaced four old ones made of larch. In 2018, Cardhu will be working a 7-day week with 21 mashes per week and a production of 3.4 million litres of alcohol.

Cardhu is Diageo´s third best selling single malt after The Singleton and Talisker with 2,7 million bottles sold in 2018. The core range from the distillery is **12, 15** and **18 year old** and two expressions without age statement – **Amber Rock** and **Gold Reserve,** both bottled at 40%. There is also a **Special Cask Reserve** matured in rejuvenated bourbon casks and in 2016 a **distillery exclusive** was released.

History:

1824 John Cumming applies for and obtains a licence for Cardhu Distillery.

1846 John Cumming dies and his wife Helen and son Lewis takes over.

1872 Lewis dies and his wife Elizabeth takes over.

1884 A new distillery is built to replace the old.

1893 John Walker & Sons purchases Cardhu for £20,500.

1908 The name reverts to Cardow.

1960 Reconstruction and expansion of stills from four to six.

1981 The name changes to Cardhu.

1998 A visitor centre is constructed.

2002 Diageo changes Cardhu single malt to a vatted malt with contributions from other distilleries in it.

2003 The whisky industry protests sharply against Diageo's plans.

2004 Diageo withdraws Cardhu Pure Malt.

2005 The 12 year old Cardhu Single Malt is relaunched and a 22 year old is released.

2009 Cardhu 1997, a single cask in the new Manager´s Choice range is released.

2011 A 15 year old and an 18 year old are released.

2013 A 21 year old is released.

2014 Amber Rock and Gold Reserve are launched.

2016 A distillery exclusive is released.

Amber Rock

Tasting notes Cardhu 12 years old:

GS – The nose is relatively light and floral, quite sweet, with pears, nuts and a whiff of distant peat. Medium-bodied, malty and sweet in the mouth. Medium-length in the finish, with sweet smoke, malt and a hint of peat.

Websites to watch

scotchwhisky.com
Without a doubt the best whiskysite there is! It covers every possible angle of the subject in an absolutely brilliant way.

whiskyfun.com
Serge Valentin, one of the Malt Maniacs, is almost always first with well written tasting notes on new releases.

whiskyreviews.blogspot.com
Ralfy does this video blog with tastings and field reports in an educational yet easy-going and entertaining way.

maltmadness.com
Our all-time favourite with something for everyone. Managed by the founder of Malt Maniacs, Johannes van den Heuvel.

edinburghwhiskyblog.com
Mainly run by Chris White these days it´s about reviews of new releases and news from the whisky world.

whiskycast.com
The best whisky-related podcast on the internet and one that sets the standard for podcasts in other genres as well.

nonjatta.com
An excellent blog with a wealth of interesting information on Japanese whisky and Japanese culture.

whiskyintelligence.com
The best site on all kinds of whisky news. The first whisky website you should log into every morning!

whisky-news.com
Apart from daily news, this site contains tasting notes, distillery portraits, lists of retailers, events etc.

thewhiskylady.net
Anne-Sophie Bigot´s mission is "to remove the dusty cliché that whisky is only an old man´s drink" and she does it so well!

malt-review.com
Mark, Jason and Adam provide very honest and comprehensive reviews on whiskies as well as well-written features.

meleklerinpayi.com
I don´t read Turkish but, since Burkay Adalig´s blog is the 7th most visited whisky blog in the world (!), a lot of people do.

whiskynotes.be
This blog is almost entirely about tasting notes (and lots of them, not least independent bottlings) plus some news.

whiskyforeveryone.com
Educational site, perfect for beginners, with a blog where both new releases and affordable standards are reviewed.

blog.thewhiskyexchange.com
A knowledgeable team from The Whisky Exchange write about new bottlings and the whisky industry in general.

whisky-distilleries.net
Ernie Scheiner describes more than 130 distilleries in both text and photos and we are talking lots of great images!

connosr.com
This whisky social networking community is a virtual smorgasbord for any whisky lover!

canadianwhisky.org
Davin de Kergommeaux presents reviews, news and views on all things Canadian whisky. High quality content.

whiskyisrael.co.il
Gal Granov is definitely one of the most active of all bloggers. Well worth checking out daily!

spiritsjournal.klwines.com
Reviews about whiskies and the whisky industry in general by David Driscoll from the US retailer K&L Wines.

thewhiskywire.com
Steve Rush mixes reviews of the latest bottlings with presentations of classics plus news, interviews etc.

bestshotwhiskyreviews.com
Jan van den Ende presents his honest opinions on everything from cheap blends to rare single cask bottlings.

scotch-whisky.org.uk
The official site of SWA (Scotch Whisky Association) with i.a. press releases and publications about the industry.

whiskysaga.com
Brilliant blog by Norwegian whisky enthusiast Thomas Öhrbom - not least on every detail relating to Nordic whiskies.

whiskysponge.com
The brilliantly sarcastic blog by Angus Macraild is where everyone in the business secretely wants to be mentioned.

speller.nl
Thomas and Ansgar Speller explore the world of whisky and they´ve been to more distilleries than most people.

thewhiskeywash.com
Since 2015, this great team of whisky writers has brought us initiated reviews and recently they started a podcast as well.

whiskeyreviewer.com
This is a web magazine covering the world of whisky through news, reviews, features and interviews.

thewhiskyphiles.com
An incredibly comprehensive blog filled no just with well written reviews but also news, comments, distillery profiles...

spiritedmatters.com
When Billy Abbott, known from The Whisky Exchange website, writes something it´s always thoughtful and interesting.

whiskywaffle.com
Enjoy the no-nonsense reviews and comments about affordable whiskies and not just the latest unobtainable single cask.

allthingswhisky.com
Even though postings sometimes occur intermittently, these reviews and musings are always an interesting read.

Clynelish

[cline•leash]

Owner: Diageo

Region/district: Northern Highlands

Founded: 1967

Status: Active (vc)

Capacity: 4 800 000 litres

Address: Brora, Sutherland KW9 6LR

Website: malts.com

Tel: 01408 623003 (vc)

Heading north on the A9, it´s a 40 minute drive from Glenmorangie to the next distillery, Clynelish. To reach the next two distilleries on the Scottish mainland (Pulteney and Wolfburn), it´s another 1,5 hours in the car.

In other words, the distilleries are not as close to each other in this part of Scotland as they are in Speyside. This is also one of the explanations why the rather frugal visitor centre at Clynelish fails to attract more than 4,000 visitors annually. However, things are about to change. This became apparent in April 2018 when Diageo announced a £150m investment in whisky tourism over three years. The main part will be focused on a Johnnie Walker Experience in Edinburgh but large sums will also be invested in four distilleries playing a significant part in the Johnnie Walker profile and representing the "four corners of Scotland" – Clynelish, Caol Ila, Cardhu and Glenkinchie.

And as if that´s not enough – the second distillery on the site, Brora which was closed in 1983, will open up again, probably in 2020, after a substantial upgrade and renovation. The only equipment left in the old buildings are the stills, feints receiver, spirit receiver and the spirit safe.

Following a year-long upgrade which was completed in June 2017, the distillery is now equipped with a 12.5 ton full lauter mash tun, 8 wooden washbacks and two made of stainless steel. The still room, with its three pairs of stills, has stunning views towards the village of Brora and the North Sea. Clynelish is usually operational 7-days a week, producing around 4.8 million litres of alcohol. Approximately 6,000 casks of Clynelish are stored in the two old Brora warehouses next door, but most of the production is matured elsewhere.

The main part of the production is used for blends, mainly Johnnie Walker Gold Label. Official bottlings include a **14 year old** and a **Distiller´s Edition**, with an Oloroso Seco finish. Recent limited bottlings include **Clynelish Select Reserve** which has been launched two years in a row as part of the annual Special Releases.

History:

1819 The 1st Duke of Sutherland founds a distillery called Clynelish Distillery.

1827 The first licensed distiller, James Harper, files for bankruptcy and John Matheson takes over.

1846 George Lawson & Sons become new licensees.

1896 James Ainslie & Heilbron takes over.

1912 James Ainslie & Co. narrowly escapes bankruptcy and Distillers Company Limited (DCL) takes over together with James Risk.

1916 John Walker & Sons buys a stake of James Risk's stocks.

1931 The distillery is mothballed.

1939 Production restarts.

1960 The distillery becomes electrified.

1967 A new distillery, also named Clynelish, is built adjacent to the first one.

1968 'Old' Clynelish is mothballed in August.

1969 'Old' Clynelish is reopened as Brora and starts using a very peaty malt.

1983 Brora is closed in March.

2002 A 14 year old is released.

2006 A Distiller´s Edition 1991 finished in Oloroso casks is released.

2009 A 12 year old is released for Friends of the Classic Malts.

2010 A 1997 Manager´s Choice single cask is released.

2014 Clynelish Select Reserve is released.

2015 Second version of Clynelish Select Reserve is released.

2017 The distillery produces again after a year long closure for refurbishing.

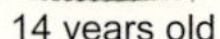
14 years old

Tasting notes Clynelish 14 year old:

GS – A nose that is fragrant, spicy and complex, with candle wax, malt and a whiff of smoke. Notably smooth in the mouth, with honey and contrasting citric notes, plus spicy peat, before a brine and tropical fruit finish.

Cragganmore

[crag•an•moor]

Owner: **Region/district:**
Diageo   Speyside

Founded: **Status:**   **Capacity:**
1869   Active (vc)   2 200 000 litres

Address: Ballindalloch, Moray AB37 9AB

Website: **Tel:**
malts.com   01479 874700

A phrase commonly used these days for any producing company is "the route-to-market". Having a great product doesn´t necesarrily equate to success. You also need to have a plan how to get it to your customers.

For Cragganmore, their route-to-market was through the blending company James Watson & Co. Founded in 1815 and based in Dundee, they bought the entire output from the distillery ever since the start in 1869. Cragganmore single malt was used in their blends, not least the popular Watson´s Number 10. James Watson never owned Cragganmore – it was in the hands of the founding family, Smith, until 1923 – but four other distilleries were bought by the blenders; Glen Ord, Pulteney, Balmenach and Parkmore.

The company took a major blow in summer of 1906 when one of their bonded warehouses in Dundee with one million gallons of spirit caught fire but the company managed to continue its business. After several changes in ownership, with closures and re-openings, James Watson and Co finally ceased to operate in 1981. Cragganmore, on the other hand, enjoyed a solid reputation as one of the top malts for blending. But it did not stop at that. In 1988 it was selected as one of the original six Classic malts, representing Speyside in the range.

The distillery is equipped with a 6.8 ton stainless steel full lauter mash tun with a copper canopy and six washbacks made of Oregon pine with a 60 hour fermentation time. There are two large wash stills with sharply descending lyne arms and two considerably smaller spirit stills with boil balls and long, slightly descending lyne arms. In 2018, the distillery will be working a 5-day week which translates to 1.65 million litres of alcohol.

For many years, Cragganmore single malt has given character to the Old Parr blend - a brand that sells around 12 million bottles every year. The official core range of Cragganmore is made up of a **12 year old** and a **Distiller's Edition** with a finish in Port pipes. In 2016, a **special vatting** appeared as part of the Special Releases.

History:

1869 John Smith, who already runs Glenfarclas distillery, founds Cragganmore.

1886 John Smith dies and his brother George takes over operations.

1893 John's son Gordon, at 21, is old enough to assume responsibility for operations.

1901 The distillery is refurbished and modernized with help of the famous architect Charles Doig.

1912 Gordon Smith dies and his widow Mary Jane supervises operations.

1917 The distillery closes.

1918 The distillery reopens and Mary Jane installs electric lighting.

1923 The distillery is sold to the newly formed Cragganmore-Glenlivet Distillery Co. where Mackie & Co. and Sir George Macpherson-Grant of Ballindalloch Estate share ownership.

1927 White Horse Distillers is bought by DCL which thus obtains 50% of Cragganmore.

1964 The number of stills is increased from two to four.

1965 DCL buys the remainder of Cragganmore.

1988 Cragganmore 12 years becomes one of six selected for United Distillers´ Classic Malts.

1998 Cragganmore Distillers Edition Double Matured (port) is launched for the first time.

2002 A visitor centre opens in May.

2006 A 17 year old from 1988 is released.

2010 Manager´s Choice single cask 1997 and a limited 21 year old are released.

2014 A 25 year old is released.

2016 A Special Releases vatting without age statement and a distillery exclusive are released.

12 years old

Tasting notes Cragganmore 12 years old:

GS – A nose of sherry, brittle toffee, nuts, mild wood smoke, angelica and mixed peel. Elegant on the malty palate, with herbal and fruit notes, notably orange. Medium in length, with a drying, slightly smoky finish.

Craigellachie

[craig•ell•ack•ee]

Owner:
John Dewar & Sons
(Bacardi)

Region/district:
Speyside

Founded: 1891
Status: Active
Capacity: 4 100 000 litres

Address: Aberlour, Banffshire AB38 9ST

Website:
craigellachie.com

Tel:
01340 872971

Dufftown may have six distilleries and Rothes four but many whisky enthusiasts coming to Speyside tend to stay in Craigellachie, situated by the junction of the A941 and the A95.

There is only one distillery in the town and while producing excellent spirit, it is not open to visitors. Instead it is two hotels and, not least their whisky bars, that attract the visitors. The oldest is Craigellachie Hotel, established in 1893 by Alexander Edward who also founded the distillery. His aim was to attract well-to-do Victorians who wanted to come to Scotland for fishing and shooting. The hotel had a downturn following a series of changes in ownership but since 2014, when it was taken over by the London business man Piers Adam, the hotel has received a facelift. The Quaich Bar can offer 1,000 different whiskies. The Highlander Inn down the road, was acquired in 2005 by Duncan Elphick, former general manager at Craigellachie Hotel. He took with him the hotel's bar manager Tatsuya Minagawa and since 2015, he is now the owner. The range in the bar may be smaller (around 400 whiskies) but is also very personalised due to Tatsuya's many years in the whisky business.

Craigellachie distillery is equipped with a Steinecker full lauter mash tun, installed in 2001, which replaced the old, open cast iron mash tun. There are also eight washbacks made of larch with a fermentation time of 56-60 hours and two pairs of stills. Both stills are attached to worm tubs. The old cast iron tubs were exchanged for stainless steel in 2014 and the existing copper worms were moved to the new tubs. Production in 2018 will be 21 mashes per week and 3.9 million litres of alcohol.

Apart from a 14 year old, which at times could be hard to get hold of, there was no official bottling of Craigellachie until 2014, when the brand was re-launched. Three new expressions (**13, 17 and 23 year old**) were released for selected domestic markets. This was followed by a range for duty free, **19, 31 and 33 year old**, where the two first have now been discontinued. Two small batch releases were added to the duty free range in 2018 – a **24 year old** and a **17 year old** with palo cortado finish.

History:

1890 The distillery is built by Craigellachie–Glenlivet Distillery Company which has Alexander Edward and Peter Mackie as part-owners.

1891 Production starts.

1916 Mackie & Company Distillers Ltd takes over.

1924 Peter Mackie dies and Mackie & Company changes name to White Horse Distillers.

1927 White Horse Distillers are bought by Distillers Company Limited (DCL).

1930 Administration is transferred to Scottish Malt Distillers (SMD), a subsidiary of DCL.

1964 Refurbishing takes place and two new stills are bought, increasing the number to four.

1998 United Distillers & Vintners (UDV) sells Craigellachie together with Aberfeldy, Brackla and Aultmore and the blending company John Dewar & Sons to Bacardi Martini.

2004 The first bottlings from the new owners are a new 14 year old which replaces UDV's Flora & Fauna and a 21 year old cask strength from 1982 produced for Craigellachie Hotel.

2014 Three new bottlings for domestic markets (13, 17 and 23 years) and one for duty free (19 years) are released.

2015 A 31 year old is released.

2016 A 33 year old and a 1994 Madeira single cask are released.

2018 A 24 year old and and a 17 year old palo cortado -finish are released for duty free.

13 years old

Tasting notes Craigellachie 13 years old:

GS – Savoury on the early nose, with spent matches, green apples and mixed nuts. Malt join the nuts and apples on the palate, with sawdust and very faint smoke. Drying, with cranberries, spice and more subtle smoke.

Dailuaine

[dall•yoo•an]

Owner: Diageo	**Region/district:** Speyside
Founded: 1852	**Status:** Active	**Capacity:** 5 200 000 litres

Address: Carron, Banffshire AB38 7RE

Website: malts.com	**Tel:** 01340 872500

When you take the small road from the A95 towards Carron, after a minute or so you will see a number of warehouse roofs on your left side. It´s almost as if you and your car will be landing on top of them.

They belong to Dailuaine but haven´t been used since 1989 which is a pity as they are some of the most beautiful dunnage warehouses in Speyside. This is not the only feature at Dailuaine that has been mothballed. The floor maltings were replaced by a Saladin box in 1960 (these days the malt comes from any of the commercial maltsters) but the wonderful malting floors are still in pristine condition. Of a later date is the dark grains plant at the back of the site which was used to process draff and pot ale into cattle feed. For the past few years though, this has been silent.

Dailuaine has cemented its place in whisky history thanks to a new innovation that was tested here for the first time in 1889. At that time the architect, Charles Cree Doig, constructed the first pagoda roof (as it was named later) to make it easier to ventilate the smoke coming from the kiln. Unfortunately, the roof collapsed in 1917 but the same design can still be seen today at many of the distilleries around Scotland although the vast majority of them these days are just ornamental.

Dailuaine distillery is equipped with a stainless steel, 11.2 ton full lauter mash tun, eight washbacks made of larch, plus two stainless steel ones placed outside and three pairs of stills. In 2015, the fermentation time was changed to help achieve a more waxy character to the spirit. The reason for the change was that Clynelish distillery has been closed for refurbishing. That is the only Diageo distillery so far that has accounted for this style which is so important for some blends. During 2018 they will be doing four short fermentations (80 hours) per week and eight long (107 hours) amounting to 2.6 million litres of pure alcohol.

Dailuaine is one of many distilleries whose main task is to produce malt whisky which is to become part of blended Scotch. The only core bottling is the **16 year old Flora & Fauna**. In autumn 2015, a **34 year old** from 1980 was launched as part of the Special Releases.

History:

1852 The distillery is founded by William Mackenzie.

1865 William Mackenzie dies and his widow leases the distillery to James Fleming, a banker from Aberlour.

1879 William Mackenzie's son forms Mackenzie and Company with Fleming.

1891 Dailuaine-Glenlivet Distillery Ltd is founded.

1898 Dailuaine-Glenlivet Distillery Ltd merges with Talisker Distillery Ltd and forms Dailuaine-Talisker Distilleries Ltd.

1915 Thomas Mackenzie dies without heirs.

1916 Dailuaine-Talisker Company Ltd is bought by the previous customers John Dewar & Sons, John Walker & Sons and James Buchanan & Co.

1917 A fire rages and the pagoda roof collapses. The distillery is forced to close.

1920 The distillery reopens.

1925 Distillers Company Limited (DCL) takes over.

1960 Refurbishing. The stills increase from four to six and a Saladin box replaces the floor maltings.

1965 Indirect still heating through steam is installed.

1983 On site maltings is closed down and malt is purchased centrally.

1991 The first official bottling, a 16 year old, is launched in the Flora & Fauna series.

1996 A 22 year old cask strength from 1973 is released as a Rare Malt.

1997 A cask strength version of the 16 year old is launched.

2000 A 17 year old Manager´s Dram matured in sherry casks is launched.

2010 A single cask from 1997 is released.

2012 The production capacity is increased by 25%.

2015 A 34 year old is launched as part of the Special Releases.

Tasting notes Dailuaine 16 years old:

GS – Barley, sherry and nuts on the substan-tial nose, developing into maple syrup. Medium-bodied, rich and malty in the mouth, with more sherry and nuts, plus ripe oranges, fruitcake, spice and a little smoke. The finish is lengthy and slightly oily, with almonds, cedar and slightly smoky oak.

16 years old

Dalmore

[dal•moor]

Owner:
Whyte & Mackay Ltd (Emperador Inc)

Region/district:
Northern Highlands

Founded: 1839

Status: Active (vc)

Capacity: 4 300 000 litres

Address: Alness, Ross-shire IV17 0UT

Website: thedalmore.com

Tel: 01349 882362

Dalmore single malt has lived through two different periods of fame. The first was in the late 1800s when it was one of the first single malts to be exported to all corners of the world.

Then followed a time, especially after the 1960 amalgamation with long standing customer Whyte & Mackay, when the produce was destined to become a part of the blended whisky. Surprisingly, considering Dalmore´s current reputation in the whisky market, it would last until the early 2000s before Dalmore once again carved out a niche for itself as a high-end single malt. Initiated by the new owners at the time, Vivian Imerman and Robert Tchenguiz, and the long-serving master blender, Richard Paterson, Dalmore was transformed into a prestige whisky.

The distillery is equipped with a 10.4 ton stainless steel, semi-lauter mash tun, eight washbacks made of Oregon pine with a fermentation time of 50 hours and four pairs of stills. All the wash stills have peculiar flat tops while the spirit stills are equipped with water jackets, which allow cold water to circulate between the reflux bowl and the neck of the stills, thus increasing the reflux. The owners expect to do 22 mashes per week during 2018, producing close to 4 million litres.

The core range consists of **12, 15, 18** and **25 year old, 1263 King Alexander III** and **Cigar Malt**. A new addition to the range in spring 2018 was the **Port Wood Reserve**. Initially matured in ex-bolurbon casks, halft of the stock was transferred into tawny port pipes for additional maturation and then married together with the ex-bourbon casks. **Valour**, exclusive to travel retail, was joined in 2016 by **Regalis** with a finish in Amoroso casks, **Luceo** with a final maturation in Apostoles casks and **Dominium** finished in Matusalem casks. Recent limited bottlings include new versions of the **35** and **40 year old**, a new range called **Vintage Port Collection** with three different expressions and, in spring 2018, a **45 year old**. The current distillery exclusive is a **Vintage 2000**, finished for 5 years in Californian Merlot barriques.

History:

1839 Alexander Matheson founds the distillery.

1867 Three Mackenzie brothers run the distillery.

1891 Sir Kenneth Matheson sells the distillery for £14,500 to the Mackenzie brothers.

1917 The Royal Navy moves in to start manufacturing American mines.

1920 The Royal Navy moves out and leaves behind a distillery damaged by an explosion.

1922 The distillery is in production again.

1956 Floor malting replaced by Saladin box.

1960 Mackenzie Brothers (Dalmore) Ltd merges with Whyte & Mackay.

1966 Number of stills is increased to eight.

1982 The Saladin box is abandoned.

1990 American Brands buys Whyte & Mackay.

1996 Whyte & Mackay changes name to JBB (Greater Europe).

2001 Through management buy-out, JBB (Greater Europe) is bought from Fortune Brands and changes name to Kyndal Spirits.

2002 Kyndal Spirits changes name to Whyte & Mackay.

2007 United Spirits buys Whyte & Mackay. A 15 year old, and a 40 year old are released.

2008 1263 King Alexander III is released.

2009 New releases include an 18 year old, a 58 year old and a Vintage 1951.

2010 The Dalmore Mackenzie 1992 is released.

2011 More expressions in the River Collection and 1995 Castle Leod are released.

2012 The visitor centre is upgraded and Constellaton Collection is launched.

2013 Valour is released for duty free.

2014 Emperador Inc buys Whyte & Mackay.

2016 Three new travel retail bottlings are released as well as a 35 year old and Quintessence.

2017 Vintage Port Collection is launched.

2018 The Port Wood Reserve is released.

12 years old

Tasting notes Dalmore 12 years old:

GS – The nose offers sweet malt, orange marmalade, sherry and a hint of leather. Full-bodied, with a dry sherry taste though sweeter sherry develops in the mouth along with spice and citrus notes. Lengthy finish with more spices, ginger, Seville oranges and vanilla.

Dalwhinnie

[dal•whin•nay]

Owner: Diageo

Region/district: Speyside

Founded: 1897

Status: Active (vc)

Capacity: 2 200 000 litres

Address: Dalwhinnie, Inverness-shire PH19 1AB

Website: malts.com

Tel: 01540 672219 (vc)

Occasionally, a producer of Scotch will launch a special bottling of their single malt bearing the name of a retiring distillery manager to acknowledge their long time service in the company.

Rarely, if ever, is this honour bestowed upon a member of the staff who´s not in a managerial position. One exemption was the distillery exclusive bottling from Dalwhinnie launched in spring 2018. Matured in re-fill bourbon and bottled at 48%, it was named Lizzie´s Dram. Lizzie Stewart started her career at Dalwhinnie in 1987 following in the footsteps of her mother and brother. Eventually, she became Scotland´s first female operator in malt distilling. Since then, things have progressed and today it is quite common to see women involved in the production of Scotch. Not least Diageo have lead the way with ten of their 28 malt whisky distillery managers currently being women.

The distillery is equipped with a 7.3 ton full lauter mash tun and six wooden washbacks with the fermentation split into four short sessions at 60 hours and six long, fermenting over the weekend, at 110 hours. There is one pair of stills, replaced in 2018, attached to worm tubs which were replaced with new ones in 2015. In February and March 2018 the distillery was closed when the two stills were exchanged for new ones. The 5-day production week for 2018 means 10 mashes per week which gives 1.4 million litres of alcohol in the year. Dalwhinnie is one of Diageo´s best selling single malts and comes in at sixth place with 1.2 million bottles sold in 2017. It is also a key malt in two major Scotch blends – Buchanans and Black & White. The latter increased sales by no less than 33% in 2017 and now sells 29 million bottles, mainly in Brazil, Mexico and Colombia.

The core range is made up of a **15 year old** and a **Distiller's Edition** with a finish in oloroso casks. A new addition, **Dalwhinnie Winter´s Gold**, was released in July 2015. Autumn 2015 saw the release of a limited **25 year old** and in 2018, **Lizzie´s Dram**, the distillery exclusive was launched.

History:

1897 John Grant, George Sellar and Alexander Mackenzie commence building the facilities. The first name is Strathspey.

1898 The owner encounters financial troubles and John Somerville & Co and A P Blyth & Sons take over and change the name to Dalwhinnie.

1905 Cook & Bernheimer in New York, buys Dalwhinnie for £1,250 at an auction.

1919 Macdonald Greenlees & Willliams Ltd headed by Sir James Calder buys Dalwhinnie.

1926 Macdonald Greenlees & Williams Ltd is bought by Distillers Company Ltd (DCL) which licences Dalwhinnie to James Buchanan & Co.

1930 Operations are transferred to Scottish Malt Distilleries (SMD).

1934 The distillery is closed after a fire in February.

1938 The distillery opens again.

1968 The maltings is decommissioned.

1987 Dalwhinnie 15 years becomes one of the selected six in United Distillers´ Classic Malts.

1991 A visitor centre is constructed.

1992 The distillery closes and goes through a major refurbishment costing £3.2 million.

1995 The distillery opens in March.

2002 A 36 year old is released.

2006 A 20 year old is released.

2010 A Manager´s Choice 1992 is released.

2012 A 25 year old is released.

2014 A triple matured bottling without age statement is released for The Friends of the Classic Malts.

2015 Dalwhinnie Winter´s Gold and a 25 year old are released.

2016 A distillery exclusive without age statement is released.

2018 Lizzie´s Dram, a distillery exclusive bottling, is released.

15 years old

Tasting notes Dalwhinnie 15 years old:

GS – The nose is fresh, with pine needles, heather and vanilla. Sweet and balanced on the fruity palate, with honey, malt and a very subtle note of peat. The medium length finish dries elegantly.

Deanston

[deen•stun]

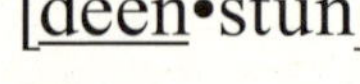

Owner:	**Region/district:**
Distell International Ltd.	Southern Highlands
Founded: **Status:**	**Capacity:**
1965 Active (vc)	3 000 000 litres

Address: Deanston, Perthshire FK16 6AG

Website:	**Tel:**
deanstonmalt.com	01786 843010

Deanston distillery is comparatively young and the hamlet bearing the same name was formed as late as the early 1800s. It all has to do with a cotton mill and a weavery founded by the Buchanan brothers in the late 18th century.

The company employed thousands of workers who all needed somewhere to live. A village was built around the plant and eventually, they even embossed their own coins which could only be used in the local stores. In 1965 the mill hade to close but James Finlay & Co, together with whisky broker Brodie Hepburn transformed it into a whisky distillery the following year.

Deanston is equipped with a red 10.5 ton traditional open top, cast iron mash tun and eight washbacks made either of stainless steel or corten steel. Since January 2018, the distillery has moved to 7-day production which means 13 mashes per week (2.4 million litres in the year) and a fermentation time of 85 hours. There are also two pairs of stills with ascending lyne arms. Together with Clynelish and Dailuaine, Deanston is the only distillery in Scotland producing a waxy new make. One way to obtain that character is a long fermentation. Having started in 2000, organic spirit is being produced every year. Due to the demand for "traditional" Deanston single malt, the volume of organic spirit has been reduced to 10,000 litres during 2018. In 2012 a visitor centre was opened which today is one of the best in the industry.

The core range is **12 18 year old, Virgin Oak** matured in first fill bourbon and with a 1-3 months finish in virgin oak casks and the **15 year old Organic**. Recent limited releases include a **40 year old**, a **Vintage 2008** that has matured in **red wine casks** and another **Vintage 2008** (released in 2018) with a **brandy finish**. For visitors, there is a reward in the form of some exclusive bottlings – curerntly a **2002 Marsala finish** and a **1999 Muscat finish**. Following a try-out with three expressions exclusive to duty-free stores in the US, a **10 year old Bordeaux** red wine cask finish was recently launched for global travel retail.

History:

1965 A weavery from 1785 is transformed into Deanston Distillery by James Finlay & Co. and Brodie Hepburn Ltd Brodie Hepburn also runs Tullibardine Distillery.

1966 Production commences in October.

1971 The first single malt is named Old Bannockburn.

1972 Invergordon Distillers takes over.

1974 The first single malt bearing the name Deanston is produced.

1982 The distillery closes.

1990 Burn Stewart Distillers from Glasgow buys the distillery for £2.1 million.

1991 The distillery resumes production.

1999 C L Financial buys an 18% stake of Burn Stewart.

2002 C L Financial acquires the remaining stake.

2006 Deanston 30 years old is released.

2009 A new version of the 12 year old is released.

2010 Virgin Oak is released.

2012 A visitor centre is opened.

2013 Burn Stewart Distillers is bought by South African Distell Group for £160m

2014 An 18 year old cognac finish is released in the USA.

2015 An 18 year old is released.

2016 Organic Deanston is released.

2017 A 40 year old and Vintage 2008 are released.

2018 A 10 year old Bordeaux finish is released for duty free.

12 years old

Tasting notes Deanston 12 years old:

GS – A fresh, fruity nose with malt and honey. The palate displays cloves, ginger, honey and malt, while the finish is long, quite dry and pleasantly herbal.

Dufftown

[duff•town]

Owner:
Diageo

Region/district:
Speyside

Founded: 1896

Status: Active

Capacity: 6 000 000 litres

Address: Dufftown, Keith, Banffshire AB55 4BR

Website:
malts.com
thesingleton.com

Tel:
01340 822100

Peter Mackenzie, one of the founders of Dufftown distillery, also became a successful whisky blender with great achievements, not least on the American market.

Prohibition, however, put a lot of pressure on the company and in 1933 it was acquired by Arthur Bell & Sons. Peter Mackenzie, however, is not forgotten, as one of his blended whiskies, The Real Mackenzie, is available for purchase even today.

Dufftown distillery is equipped with a 13 ton full lauter mash tun, 12 stainless steel washbacks and three pairs of stills. All stills furthermore have sub coolers. The style of Dufftown single malt is green and grassy which is achieved by a clear wort and long fermentation (75 hours minimum). Dufftown is one of few distilleries where the wash stills are smaller than the spirits stills. In a seven day week, no less than 165 still runs are completed (110 in the wash stills and 55 in the spirits stills) which clearly shows what a busy distillery Dufftown is. Dufftown has been working 24/7 since 2007 and during 2018 they will be producing 6 million litres of alcohol.

The core range, which received a substantial upgrade in terms of packaging in 2018, consists of **The Singleton of Dufftown 12, 15 and 18 year old**. At the same time, a new expression was added to the line-up - **Malt Master´s Selection**. Without age statement, the whisky has been matured in a combination of bourbon and sherry casks with a high proportion of refill casks. In 2013 a new range exclusive to duty free was launched. The first two releases were **Trinité** and **Liberté** and yet a third release, **Artisan**, was added in spring of 2014. Also in 2014, two new bottlings were released for domestic markets; Tailfire and Sunray and the two were later followed by Spey Cascade. Following the recent revamp of the range, all these three are now about to be discontinued. Limited releases appear from time to time. The latest two, released in 2016, were exclusive to Hong Kong – a **21 year old** matured in sherry casks and a **25 year old** from ex bourbon casks.

History:

1895 Peter Mackenzie, Richard Stackpole, John Symon and Charles MacPherson build the distillery Dufftown-Glenlivet in an old mill.

1896 Production starts in November.

1897 The distillery is owned by P. Mackenzie & Co., who also owns Blair Athol in Pitlochry.

1933 P. Mackenzie & Co. is bought by Arthur Bell & Sons for £56,000.

1968 The floor maltings is discontinued and malt is bought from outside suppliers. The number of stills is increased from two to four.

1974 The number of stills is increased from four to six.

1979 The stills are increased by a further two to eight.

1985 Guinness buys Arthur Bell & Sons.

1997 Guinness and Grand Metropolitan merge to form Diageo.

2006 The Singleton of Dufftown 12 year old is launched as a special duty free bottling.

2008 The Singleton of Dufftown is made available also in the UK.

2010 A Manager´s Choice 1997 is released.

2013 A 28 year old cask strength and two expressions for duty free - Unité and Trinité - are released.

2014 Tailfire, Sunray and Spey Cascade are released.

2016 Two limited releases are made - a 21 year old and a 25 year old.

2018 Malt Master´s Selection is released.

Singleton of Dufftown 12 year

Tasting notes Dufftown 12 years old:

GS – The nose is sweet, almost violet-like, with underlying malt. Big and bold on the palate, this is an upfront yet very drinkable whisky. The finish is medium to long, warming, spicy, with slowly fading notes of sherry and fudge.

Edradour

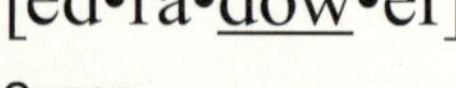

[ed•ra•<u>dow</u>•er]

Owner:
Signatory Vintage
Scotch Whisky Co. Ltd

Region/district:
Southern Highland

Founded: 1825
Status: Active (vc)
Capacity: 260 000 litres

Address: Pitlochry, Perthshire PH16 5JP

Website: edradour.com
Tel: 01796 472095

It has been a few years since Edradour could call itself Scotland's smallest distillery with almost 15 distilleries producing smaller volumes these days. Since January 2018 the distillery has also expanded to become even larger.

On the other side of the burn, a replica of the original distillery has been built. This includes an open, traditional cast iron mash tun with a mash size of 1.1 tons and also the distillery "trademark" - an unusual Morton refrigerator to cool the wort. There are four washbacks made of Oregon pine with space left to install another two in the future. The dumpy wash still and the spirit still are attached to a worm tub on the outside. New warehouses have been erected next to the new still house and on site there are now 6 racked warehouses and four dunnage with a capacity of holding 25,000 casks.

With 6 mashes per week at each distillery during 2018 they will produce 260,000 litres of alchol, but with two more washbacks and running double shifts, the theoretical capacity could be 500,000 litres. Due to rapidly increasing demand for the unpeated Edradour, there has been no peated production (for Ballechin) the past two years but during 2018 they will be doing 25,000 litres. Whenever peated production occurs, it will be in the old distillery.

The core range consists of **10 year old, 12 year old Caledonia Selection** (oloroso finish), **Cask Strength Sherry 14 year old,** and **Cask Strength Bourbon 10 year old**. There is also the peated **Ballechin 10 year old**. The Straight From The Cask range is made up of a number of expressions, all fully matured in different casks; **Edradour 2006 Madeira, 2008 Sherry, 2007 Rum, 2007 Sauternes, 2007 Burgundy** and **2003 Chardonnay** and **Ballechin 2004 Burgundy, 2004 Port** and **2005 Bordeaux**. Recent limited releases include three Edradour finishes; **16 year old Barolo, 17 year old Bordeaux** and **21 year old Oloroso** as well as the interesting **8 year old vatting** of sherry matured Edradour and bourbon matured Ballechin.

History:

1825 Probably the year when a distillery called Glenforres is founded by farmers in Perthshire.

1837 The first year Edradour is mentioned.

1841 The farmers form a proprietary company, John MacGlashan & Co.

1886 John McIntosh & Co. acquires Edradour.

1933 William Whiteley & Co. buys the distillery.

1982 Campbell Distilleries (Pernod Ricard) buys Edradour and builds a visitor centre.

1986 The first single malt is released.

2002 Edradour is bought by Andrew Symington from Signatory for £5.4 million. The product range is expanded with a 10 year old and a 13 year old cask strength.

2003 A 30 year old and a 10 year old are released.

2004 A number of wood finishes are launched as cask strength.

2006 The first bottling of peated Ballechin is released.

2007 A Madeira matured Ballechin is released.

2008 A Ballechin matured in Port pipes and a 10 year old Edradour with a Sauternes finish are released.

2009 Fourth edition of Ballechin (Oloroso) is released.

2010 Ballechin #5 Marsala is released.

2011 Ballechin #6 Bourbon and a 26 year old PX sherry finish are relased.

2012 A 1993 Oloroso and a 1993 Sauternes finish as well as the 7th edition of Ballechin (Bordeaux) are released.

2013 Ballechin Sauternes is released.

2014 The first release of a 10 year old Ballechin.

2015 Fairy Flag is released.

2017 New releases include an 8 year old vatting of Edradour and Ballechin.

2018 The new distillery is commissioned.

12 years old

Tasting notes Edradour 10 years old:

GS – Cider apples, malt, almonds, vanilla and honey ar present on the nose, along with a hint of smoke and sherry. The palate is rich, creamy and malty, with a persistent nuttiness and quite a pronounced kick of slightly leathery sherry. Spices and sherry dominate the medium to long finish.

Fettercairn

[fett•er•cairn]

Owner: Whyte & Mackay (Emperador)
Region/district: Eastern Highlands

Founded: 1824
Status: Active (vc)
Capacity: 3 200 000 litres

Address: Fettercairn, Laurencekirk, Kincardineshire AB30 1YB

Website: fettercairndistillery.co.uk
Tel: 01561 340205

Fettercairn has never had a high profile amongst whisky enthusiasts even though the owners over the years have made attempts to make it more visible.

In 2002, they dropped the brand name Old Fettercairn and introduced Fettercairn 1824, launching a 12 year old followed up by some old expressions. Seven years later 1824 was scrapped and instead a unicorn, inspired by the crest of the founder, appeared on the bottles and Fior and Fasque were released. Finally, in August 2018, an entire new range with four expressions was introduced – still with the unicorn on the label. Initially the whiskies were available in the UK before being rolled out to other markets, including Taiwan, France, Germany and the US.

Recently revealed documents show that an unusual experiment was going on at Fettercairn in 1951. In an attempt to speed up maturation, the distillery director at the time, circulated new make through "active chemical" thereby reducing the maturation from 10 years to a few hours. The trials were stopped when the Board of Trade officials feared that it could undermine the Scotch whisky industry should foreign distilleries try to imitate the process.

Fettercairn distillery is equipped with a traditional, 5 ton cast iron mash tun and eleven washbacks with a fermentation time of 60 hours. There are two pairs of stills with a feature making Fettercairn unique among Scottish distilleries (although a similar technique is used at Dalmore). When collecting the middle cut, cooling water is allowed to trickle along the outside of the spirit still necks and is collected at the base for circulation towards the top again. This is done in order to increase reflux and thereby produce a lighter and cleaner spirit. For some time, the owners also produced heavily peated spirit (55ppm), but there has been no peated production for the last couple of years. The producion goal for 2018 is 18 mashes per week and 1.5 million litres of alcohol.

The new range consists of a **12 year old** and a **28 year old**, both matured in ex-bourbon casks. There is also a **40 year old** with a finish in palo cortado sherry casks and a **50 year old**, finished in tawny port pipes for five years.

History:

1824 Sir Alexander Ramsay founds the distillery.

1830 Sir John Gladstone buys the distillery.

1887 A fire erupts and the distillery is forced to close for repairs.

1890 Thomas Gladstone dies and his son John Robert takes over. The distillery reopens.

1912 The company is close to liquidation and John Gladstone buys out the other investors.

1926 The distillery is mothballed.

1939 The distillery is bought by Associated Scottish Distillers Ltd. Production restarts.

1960 The maltings discontinues.

1966 The stills are increased from two to four.

1971 The distillery is bought by Tomintoul-Glenlivet Distillery Co. Ltd.

1973 Tomintoul-Glenlivet Distillery Co. Ltd is bought by Whyte & Mackay Distillers Ltd.

1974 The mega group of companies Lonrho buys Whyte & Mackay.

1988 Lonrho sells to Brent Walker Group plc.

1989 A visitor centre opens.

1990 American Brands Inc. buys Whyte & Mackay for £160 million.

1996 Whyte & Mackay and Jim Beam Brands merge to become JBB Worldwide.

2001 Kyndal Spirits buys Whyte & Mackay from JBB Worldwide.

2002 The whisky changes name to Fettercairn 1824.

2003 Kyndal Spirits changes name to Whyte & Mackay.

2007 United Spirits buys Whyte & Mackay. A 23 year old single cask is released.

2009 24, 30 and 40 year olds are released.

2010 Fettercairn Fior is launched.

2012 Fettercairn Fasque is released.

2018 A new range is launched; 12, 28, 40 and 50 year old.

Tasting notes Fettercairn 12 years old:

IR – A delicious combination of pineapple, banana and mango together with coffee beans, cured ham and dried flowers. Still fruity on the palate but also becomes more spicy and malty and with a bit of mint at the end.

12 years old

Glenallachie

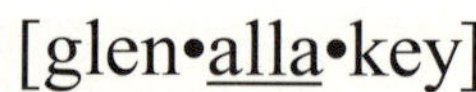

[glen•alla•key]

Owner:
The Glenallachie Distillers Co.

Region/district:
Speyside

Founded: 1967

Status: Active

Capacity: 4 000 000 litres

Address: Aberlour, Banffshire AB38 9LR

Website:
www.theglenallachie.com

Tel:
01236 422120

It´s been a year now since Billy Walker and his associates took over Glenallachie from Chivas Brothers and not totally surprising, the change in ownership has already started to show.

In March 2018, no less than six different single casks were released to commemorate the 50th anniversary of the opening of the distillery. A few months later, the new owners launched a new core range of a single malt that hade been rarely bottled by the previous owners. Included in the deal when the distillery was sold were two blended Scotch brands – MacNair´s and White Heather. The former has been relaunched as a blended malt including heavily peated Islay whisky as well as Speyside malts (including Glenallachie) while White Heather will continue as a blend, bottled as a 21 year old!

The distillery is equipped with a 9.7 ton semi-lauter mash tun, six washbacks made of mild steel, but lined with stainless steel, plus another two washbacks which were brought in from Caperdonich when that was demolished in 2011. There are also two pairs of unusually wide stills with horizontal condensers. During the first year under new ownership, the distillery produced 750,000 litres of pure alcohol. On site, there are 16 warehouses (2 dunnage, 2 palletised and 12 racked). The new owners have decided to fill newmake into casks at three different strengths to achieve different flavour profiles – 63,5%, 68% and 72%. They will also be doing at least 20% heavily peated production every year using barley with an 80ppm phenol specification.

Under Chivas´ regime, Glenallachie single malt used to be a key ingredient in one of the top selling blends in France – Clan Campbell. With the new owners, a range of **single casks** was released in March 2018 – distilled in 1978 until 1991. A few months later a core range was unveiled; a **10 year old cask strength, 12, 18** and **25 year old**. All of them are non-chill filtered and without artificial colouring and bottled either at cask strength or 46-48%.

History:

1967 The distillery is founded by Mackinlay, McPherson & Co., a subsidiary of Scottish & Newcastle Breweries Ltd. William Delmé Evans is architect.

1985 Scottish & Newcastle Breweries Ltd sells Charles Mackinlay Ltd to Invergordon Distillers which acquires both Glenallachie and Isle of Jura.

1987 The distillery is decommissioned.

1989 Campbell Distillers (Pernod Ricard) buys the distillery, increases the number of stills from two to four and takes up production again.

2005 The first official bottling for many years is a Cask Strength Edition from 1989.

2017 Glenallachie Distillery Edition is released and the distillery is sold to The Glenallachie Consortium.

2018 A series of single casks is released followed by a core range consisting of 12, 18 and 25 year old.

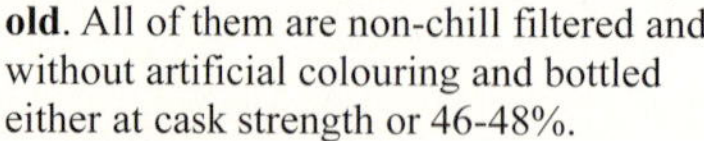

12 years old

Tasting notes Glenallachie 12 years old:

IR – Baked apples with almonds and custard, lemon zest and pine needles on the nose. Rich and lively on the palate, sweet spices, ginger, bananas, liquorice, raisins and hints of pepper.

Glenburgie

[glen•<u>bur</u>•gee]

Owner:	**Region/district:**
Chivas Brothers	Speyside
(Pernod Ricard)	

Founded:	**Status:**	**Capacity:**
1810	Active	4 250 000 litres

Address: Glenburgie, Forres, Morayshire IV36 2QY

Website:	**Tel:**
-	01343 850258

For a long time there have been semi-official bottlings of Glenburgie single malt from Gordon & MacPhail, mainly a 10 year old and other independent bottlers have also released their fair share. The owners themselves have been more reluctant.

The odd cask strength bottlings from Chivas Brothers have surfaced from time to time, available for purchase in the company´s visitor centres. In autumn 2017, however, an entire new range with official bottlings, not only from Glenburgie, but also Miltonduff and Glentauchers was launched. All three are 15 years old and were first released in the duty free segment before being rolled out to domestic markets.

What these three whiskies have in common is that they are vital parts of Ballantine´s and the name of the blend prominently features on the labels. Ballantine´s is the second most sold Scotch in the world with a 17% increase in volume during the past four years. In 2017 it sold 83 million bottles. As succesful as it may be, it is the single malt category that has been growing rapidly in recent years and Chivas Brothers obviously wants to tie in with that trend.

Glenburgie distillery was founded in 1810 as Kilnflat distillery, but the buildings that we see today are of a much later date, having been built in 2003 when the old distillery was demolished. Glenburgie is equipped with a 7.5 ton full lauter mash tun, 12 stainless steel washbacks and three pairs of stills. In older days, the fermentation time used to be around 70 hours, but has now been reduced to 52. The majority of the production is filled into bourbon casks and a part thereof is matured in four dunnage, two racked and two palletised warehouses.

The new official bottling is a **15 year old** aged in ex-bourbon casks and bottled at 40%. A **17 year old** cask strength in the range The Distillery Reserve Collection is also available at Chivas´ visitor centres.

History:

1810 William Paul founds Kilnflat Distillery. Official production starts in 1829.

1870 Kilnflat distillery closes.

1878 The distillery reopens under the name Glenburgie-Glenlivet, Charles Hay is licensee.

1884 Alexander Fraser & Co. takes over.

1925 Alexander Fraser & Co. files for bankruptcy and the receiver Donald Mustad assumes control of operations.

1927 James & George Stodart Ltd (owned by James Barclay and R A McKinlay since 1922) buys the distillery which by this time is inactive.

1930 Hiram Walker buys 60% of James & George Stodart Ltd.

1936 Hiram Walker buys Glenburgie Distillery in October. Production restarts.

1958 Lomond stills are installed producing a single malt, Glencraig. Floor malting ceases.

1981 The Lomond stills are replaced by conventional stills.

1987 Allied Lyons buys Hiram Walker.

2002 A 15 year old is released.

2004 A £4.3 million refurbishment and reconstruction takes place.

2005 Chivas Brothers (Pernod Ricard) becomes the new owner through the acquisition of Allied Domecq.

2006 The number of stills are increased from four to six in May.

2017 A Glenburgie 15 year old is released.

15 years old

Tasting notes Glenburgie 15 years old:

IR – Very fruity on the nose with notes of pears, apple pie, honey, marzipan and roasted nuts. The palate reveals tropical fruits, white chocolate, marmalade, vanilla and caramel.

Glencadam

[glen•ka•dam]

Owner:
Angus Dundee Distillers

Region/district:
Eastern Highlands

Founded: 1825
Status: Active
Capacity: 1 300 000 litres

Address: Brechin, Angus DD9 7PA

Website: glencadamwhisky.com
Tel: 01356 622217

Few whisky companies have kept such a low profile as Angus Dundee Distillers. As early as 1948, Sidney Hillman formed a company with the name Burn Stewart which bought and sold whisky from different producers.

In time his son, Terence "Terry" Hillman, joined and Burn Stewart remained family owned until it was sold in 1988. The same year Terry founded Angus Dundee Distillers with the same business concept – purchasing of whisky to be blended and sold on. Today, Terry is 85 years old and still sits on the company board which is controlled but his two children Aaron and Tania. Other than Glencadam and Tomintoul single malt, Angus Dundee produces a large number of blends – including Scottish Royal, Glen Parker, The Dundee and Parker's. These are blended in enourmous steel tanks of which 16 sit at Glencadam. From here the spirit is sent to the bottling plant in Coatbridge east of Glasgow before being sent to over 70 markets globally.

One of the more long term owners of Glencadam was the blending company Gilmour Thomson & Co from Glasgow. They took over in 1891 and sold it to Hiram Walker in 1954. For them, Glencadam single malt was an important part of their blended whisky Royal Blend which was said to be Edward VII's favourite whisky,

Glencadam distillery is equipped with a traditional, 4.9 ton cast iron mash tun, six stainless steel washbacks with a fermentation time of 52 hours and one pair of stills. The external heat exchanger on the wash still is from the fifties and perhaps the first in the business. On site are two dunnage warehouses from 1825, three from the 1950s and one modern racked. The distillery is currently working a 7 day week, which enables 16 mashes per week and 1.3 million litres of alcohol.

Two years ago, six new bottlings were added and the core range now consists of **Origin 1825, 10, 13, 18** (new), **21** and **25 year old**. Also in the core range are two wood finishes; a **17 year old port finish** and a **19 year old oloroso finish**. Recent limited editions include a **28 year old single sherry cask** from 1989.

History:

1825 George Cooper founds the distillery.

1827 David Scott takes over.

1837 The distillery is sold by David Scott.

1852 Alexander Miln Thompson becomes the owner.

1857 Glencadam Distillery Company is formed.

1891 Gilmour, Thompson & Co Ltd takes over.

1954 Hiram Walker takes over.

1959 Refurbishing of the distillery.

1987 Allied Lyons buys Hiram Walker Gooderham & Worts.

1994 Allied Lyons changes name to Allied Domecq.

2000 The distillery is mothballed.

2003 Allied Domecq sells the distillery to Angus Dundee Distillers.

2005 The new owner releases a 15 year old.

2008 A re-designed 15 year old and a new 10 year old are introduced.

2009 A 25 and a 30 year old are released in limited numbers.

2010 A 12 year old port finish, a 14 year old sherry finish, a 21 year old and a 32 year old are released.

2012 A 30 year old is released.

2015 A 25 year old is launched.

2016 Origin 1825, 17 year old port finish, 19 year old oloroso finish, an 18 year old and a 25 year old are released.

2017 A 13 year old is released.

10 years old

Tasting notes Glencadam 10 years old:

GS – A light and delicate, floral nose, with tinned pears and fondant cream. Medium-bodied, smooth, with citrus fruits and gently-spiced oak on the palate. The finish is quite long and fruity, with a hint of barley.

GlenDronach

[glen•<u>dro</u>•nack]

Owner:
Benriach Distillery Co
(Brown Forman)

Region/district:
Highlands

Founded: 1826

Status: Active (vc)

Capacity: 1 400 000 litres

Address: Forgue, Aberdeenshire AB54 6DB

Website:
glendronachdistillery.co.uk

Tel:
01466 730202

The distillery was founded by James Allardes (often referred to as Allardice), a local farmer and businessman. Among his aquaintances was the Marquis of Huntly, later to become 5th Duke of Gordon.

The Duke whose properties stretched from Deeside in the South to Elgin in the North, could attest that the majority of his tenants were involved illegally in whisky production. Instead of becoming morally indignant, he proposed to parliament in London that there should be penalties for illicit distillers whilst making it simpler for those who wished to obtain a licence and distil leagally. His proposal was approved and in 1823 The Spirits Act was passed. The result was the application of hundreds of distilleries during the following year. Glendronach, one of the first applicants, received its licence in 1826.

The equipment consists of a 3.7 ton cast iron mash tun with rakes, nine washbacks made of larch with a fermentation time of 60 to 90 hours and two pairs of stills. The plan is to produce 1.2 million litres of alcohol in 2018. The distillery has made increasingly larger volumes of peated spirit, and for 2018 it will be around 150,000 litres with a phenol specification of 38ppm.

The core range is **The Hielan 8 years, Original 12 years, Allardice 18 years, Parliament 21 years** and **Grandeur 25 years** where the 9th release was made in February 2018. The popular 15 year old Revival has been out of the range for a while, but the plan is to re-introduce it again in autumn 2018. A new addition to the core range appeared in 2015 with the first (at least in modern times) **Peated GlenDronach**. Without age statement, the whisky has been matured in bourbon casks and then finished in a combination of oloroso and PX sherry casks. This was followed up in autumn 2017 with the finish **Peated Port Wood**. There are four wood finishes; **12 year old Sauternes, 14 year old Virgin Oak, 18 year old Tawny Port** and **19 year old Madeira** plus a limited **14 year old Marsala**. Batch 16 of the **single casks** appeared in February 2018 and batch number 7 of the **cask strength** expression appeared in May, The first GlenDronach for duty free appeared in autumn 2018 when **10 year old Forgue** and **16 year old Boynsmill** were released.

History:

1826 The distillery is founded by a consortium with James Allardes as one of the owners.

1837 Parts of the distillery is destroyed in a fire.

1852 Walter Scott (from Teaninich) takes over.

1887 Walter Scott dies and Glendronach is taken over by a consortium from Leith.

1920 Charles Grant buys Glendronach for £9,000.

1960 William Teacher & Sons buys the distillery.

1966 The number of stills is increased to four.

1976 Allied Breweries takes over William Teacher & Sons.

1996 The distillery is mothballed.

2002 Production is resumed on 14th May.

2005 The distillery closes to rebuild from coal to indirect firing by steam. Reopens in September. Chivas Brothers (Pernod Ricard) becomes new owner through the acquisition of Allied Domecq.

2008 Pernod Ricard sells the distillery to the owners of BenRiach distillery.

2009 Relaunch of the whole range including 12, 15 and 18 year old.

2010 A 31 year old, a 1996 single cask and a total of 11 vintages and four wood finishes are released. A visitor centre is opened.

2011 The 21 year old Parliament and 11 vintages are released.

2012 A number of vintages are released.

2013 Recherché 44 years and a number of new vintages are released.

2014 Nine different single casks are released.

2015 The Hielan, 8 years old, is released.

2016 Brown Forman buys the distillery. Peated GlenDronach and Octaves Classic are released.

2017 A range of new single casks is released.

2018 Two bottlings for duty free are released - 10 year old Forgue and 16 year old Boynsmill.

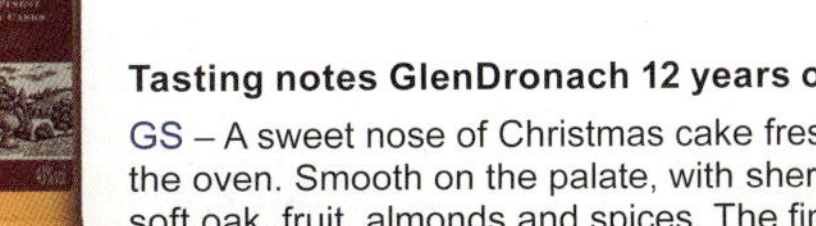

12 years old Original

Tasting notes GlenDronach 12 years old:

GS – A sweet nose of Christmas cake fresh from the oven. Smooth on the palate, with sherry, soft oak, fruit, almonds and spices. The finish is comparatively dry and nutty, ending with bitter chocolate.

Glendullan

[glen•dull•an]

Owner: Diageo   **Region/district:** Speyside

Founded: 1897   **Status:** Active   **Capacity:** 5 000 000 litres

Address: Dufftown, Keith, Banffshire AB55 4DJ

Website: www.thesingleton.com   **Tel:** 01340 822100

Glendullan is one of three Diageo distilleries working under the brand name The Singleton, Glen Ord and Dufftown being the other two.

A total of 6.2 million bottles of Singleton were sold in 2017 - a remarkable figure considering the brand has only existed for 12 years. Although no official figures are presented, it is commonly accepted that Glen Ord represents the greater proportion of sales.

Glendullan distillery is situated just one minute`s drive east of Glenfiddich and was built in 1897 by William Williams – a blender from Aberdeen. The working distillery we see today is of a much later date, built in 1972 and the two plants operated simultaneously until 1985 when the old distillery was closed. These buildings are now used by Diageo´s engineering team which delivers maintenance to 23 Diageo distilleries, bio plants and dark grain facilities across Scotland. The old distillery, with one pair of stills, had a capacity of one million litres a year.

The distillery is equipped with a 12 ton full lauter stainless steel mash tun, 8 washbacks made of larch and two made of stainless steel with a fermentation time of 75 hours to promote a green/grassy character of the whisky, as well as three pairs of stills. In 2018 the distillery will be doing 21 mashes per week, producing 5 million litres of alcohol.

The recently re-packaged core range of **Singleton of Glendullan** consists of **12, 15** and **18 year old**. There is also a range exclusive to duty free, The Singleton Reserve Collection with **Classic** (matured in American oak), **Double Matured** (matured separately in American and European oak and then married together) and **Master´s Art** (with a finish in Muscat casks). The Forgotten Drops Series was created in autumn for both Glen Ord and Glendullan with the aim to present old and limited expressions. The first for Glendullan, in spring 2018, was a **40 year old**, the oldest whisky ever released from the distillery. Two more expressions in the series are expected in autumn 2018 and 2019 respectively.

History:

1896 William Williams & Sons, a blending company with Three Stars and Strahdon among its brands, founds the distillery.

1902 Glendullan is delivered to the Royal Court and becomes the favourite whisky of Edward VII.

1919 Macdonald Greenlees buys a share of the company and Macdonald Greenlees & Williams Distillers is formed.

1926 Distillers Company Limited (DCL) buys Glendullan.

1930 Glendullan is transferred to Scottish Malt Distillers (SMD).

1962 Major refurbishing and reconstruction.

1972 A brand new distillery is constructed next to the old one and both operate simultaneously during a few years.

1985 The oldest of the two distilleries is mothballed.

1995 The first launch of Glendullan in the Rare Malts series is a 22 year old from 1972.

2005 A 26 year old from 1978 is launched in the Rare Malts series.

2007 Singleton of Glendullan is launched in the USA.

2013 Singleton of Glendullan Liberty and Trinity are released for duty free.

2014 A 38 year old is released.

2015 Classic, Double Matured and Master´s Art are released.

2018 The Forgotten Drops 40 years old is released.

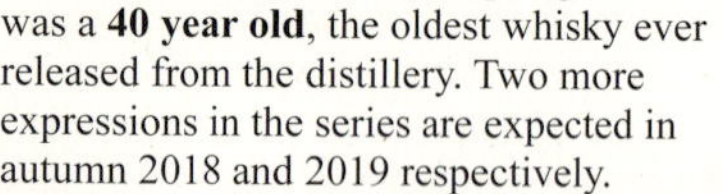

12 years old

Tasting notes Singleton of Glendullan 12 years:

GS – The nose is spicy, with brittle toffee, vanilla, new leather and hazelnuts. Spicy and sweet on the smooth palate, with citrus fruits, more vanilla and fresh oak. Drying and pleasingly peppery in the finish.

Glen Elgin

[glen el•gin]

Owner:
Diageo

Region/district:
Speyside

Founded: **Status:** **Capacity:**
1898 Active 2 700 000 litres

Address: Longmorn, Morayshire IV30 8SL

Website: **Tel:**
malts.com 01343 862100

After a quick glimpse of the equipment setup at Glen Elgin, you would be inclined to think that a rather robust and heavy single malt was being made here. In fact – the reality is quite the opposite.

Six stills with declining lyne arms don´t call for much reflux and heading out into the yard, there are six wooden wormtubs to cool the spirit vapours which generally means a heavy spirit. However, a slow distillation and, not least, long fermentations (between 80 and 120 hours) work against the perceived notions and the result is a fruity whisky but still with a lot of depth.

No wonder Glen Elgin single malt has always been a favourite amongst blenders. It can work wonders in a blended Scotch but it has also enjoyed some fame as a single malt, already in 1977. Later on it appeared as one of many in the Flora & Fauna range but in 2002, Diageo decided to give four of their brands some more attention and the Hidden Malts range was launched. Comprised of Glen Elgin, Caol Ila, Clynelish and Glen Ord, Hidden Malts existed for several years. Today three of the whiskies are included in the extended Classic Malts range while Glen Ord has become part of the hugely succesful Singleton family.

The distillery is equipped with an 8.4 ton Steinecker full lauter mash tun from 2001, nine washbacks made of larch and six small stills. The distillery alternates between 12 and 16 mashes per week. Three of the washbacks were installed as late as 2012 in the extended tun room, which meant that the production capacity increased by 50%. The stills are connected to six wooden worm tubs where the spirit vapours are condensed. A new boiler was installed in 2014, replacing the two, old existing ones.

Glen Elgin single malt is an integral part of the White Horse blended Scotch which sells around 20 million bottles every year in key markets spread across the world: Japan, Greece, Brazil and South Africa. The only official bottling is a **12 year old,** but a **limited 18 year old**, matured in ex-bodega European oak butts was one of the Special Releases in 2017.

History:

1898 The former manager of Glenfarclas, William Simpson and banker James Carle found Glen Elgin.

1900 Production starts in May but the distillery closes just five months later.

1901 The distillery is auctioned for £4,000 to the Glen Elgin-Glenlivet Distillery Co. and is mothballed.

1906 The wine producer J. J. Blanche & Co. buys the distillery for £7,000 and production resumes.

1929 J. J. Blanche dies and the distillery is put up for sale again.

1930 Scottish Malt Distillers (SMD) buys it and the license goes to White Horse Distillers.

1964 Expansion from two to six stills plus other refurbishing takes place.

1992 The distillery closes for refurbishing and installation of new stills.

1995 Production resumes in September.

2001 A 12 year old is launched in the Flora & Fauna series.

2002 The Flora & Fauna series malt is replaced by Hidden Malt 12 years.

2003 A 32 year old cask strength from 1971 is released.

2008 A 16 year old is launched as a Special Release.

2009 Glen Elgin 1998, a single cask in the new Manager´s Choice range is released.

2017 An 18 year old is launched as part of the Special Releases.

12 years old

Tasting notes Glen Elgin 12 years old:

GS – A nose of rich, fruity sherry, figs and fragrant spice. Full-bodied, soft, malty and honeyed in the mouth. The finish is lengthy, slightly perfumed, with spicy oak.

Glenfarclas

[glen•<u>fark</u>•lass]

Owner: **Region/district:**
J. & G. Grant   Speyside

Founded: **Status:**   **Capacity:**
1836   Active (vc)   3 500 000 litres

Address: Ballindalloch, Banffshire AB37 9BD

Website: **Tel:**
glenfarclas.com   01807 500257

With the sixth generation working at the distillery, Glenfarclas is one of the oldest family-owned distilleries in Scotland. There was a time though when external owners were brought in and it could have ended with a disaster.

In 1896, the infamous Pattison brothers joined the company as partners. Two years later they were accused of fraud on a scale that would bring the entire Scotch whisky industry to its knees. Needless to say, this was not the time to "be in bed" with the Pattisons who went into liquidation. Fortunately the agreement between Glenfarclas and the brothers opened up for the Grant family to buy out their shares from the liquidator and the distillery was once again wholly owned by the Grant family.

Glenfarclas is known for its devotion to sherry casks, an expensive way to mature whisky nowadays as ex-sherry casks can be hard to come by. Glenfarclas way of solving this has been to build a 25 year long relationship with José y Miguel Martin bodega which supplies all their casks.

The distillery is equipped with a 16.5 ton semi-lauter mash tun and twelve stainless steel washbacks with a minimum fermentation time of 60 hours but on average it is currently 102 hours. There are three pairs of directly fired stills (very rarely seen these days) and the wash stills are equipped with rummagers. This is a copper chain rotating at the bottom of the still to prevent solids from sticking to the copper. During 2018, the distillery will do around 8 mashes per week which means 2 million litres of pure alcohol. A number of new dunnage warehouses have recently been built and the owners can now store 96,000 casks on site. Glenfarclas single malt has always been highly ranked among whisky aficionados and close to two million bottles are sold annually.

The Glenfarclas core range consists of the **8, 10, 12, 15, 21** and **25 year old**, as well as the lightly sherried **Glenfarclas Heritage** which comes without an age statement and the **105 Cask Strength**. The latter was the first commercially available cask strength single malt and to celebrate the 50th anniversary of the launch, a **22 year old** version was launched in 2018. There is also a **17 year old** destined for the USA, Japan and Sweden. The **30** and **40 year olds** are limited but new editions occur regularly. An **18 year old** exclusive to travel retail was launched in 2014 and in 2018, a **2004 single cask** was released for the Speyside Festival. The owners quite often make spectacular limited releases and the rarity of the expressions clearly show the impressive selection that they have available in their warehouses. In the past four years they have released a series of bottlings called The Generations Range which included whiskies made in the 1950s! The owners also continue to release bottlings in their **Family Casks** series with vintages ranging from 1954 to 2003. Finally, every year the owners produce special limited bottlings for their biggest markets.

History:

1836 Robert Hay founds the distillery on the original site since 1797.

1865 Robert Hay passes away and John Grant and his son George buy the distillery. They lease it to John Smith at The Glenlivet Distillery.

1870 John Smith resigns in order to start Cragganmore and J. & G. Grant Ltd takes over.

1889 John Grant dies and George Grant takes over.

1890 George Grant dies and his widow Elsie takes over the license while sons John and George control operations.

1895 John and George Grant take over and form The Glenfarclas-Glenlivet Distillery Co. Ltd with the infamous Pattison, Elder & Co.

1898 Pattison becomes bankrupt. Glenfarclas encounters financial problems after a major overhaul of the distillery but survives by mortgaging and selling stored whisky to R. I. Cameron, a whisky broker from Elgin.

1914 John Grant leaves due to ill health and George continues alone.

1948 The Grant family celebrates the distillery's 100th anniversary, a century of active licensing. It is 9 years late, as the actual anniversary coincided with WW2.

1949 George Grant senior dies and sons George Scott and John Peter inherit the distillery.

1960 Stills are increased from two to four.

1968 Glenfarclas is first to launch a cask-strength single malt. It is later named Glenfarclas 105.

1972 Floor maltings is abandoned and malt is purchased centrally.

1973 A visitor centre is opened.

1976 Enlargement from four stills to six.

History continued:

2002 George S Grant dies and is succeeded as company chairman by his son John L S Grant

2003 Two new gift tins are released (10 years old and 105 cask strength).

2005 A 50 year old is released to commemorate the bi-centenary of John Grant´s birth.

2006 Ten new vintages are released.

2007 Family Casks, a series of single cask bottlings from 43 consecutive years, is released.

2008 New releases in the Family Cask range. Glenfarclas 105 40 years old is released.

2009 A third release in the Family Casks series.

2010 A 40 year old and new vintages from Family Casks are released.

2011 Chairman´s Reserve and 175th Anniversary are released.

2012 A 58 year old and a 43 year old are released.

2013 An 18 year old for duty free is released as well as a 25 year old quarter cask.

2014 A 60 year old and a 1966 single fino sherry cask are released.

2015 A 1956 Sherry Cask and Family Reserve are released.

2016 40 year old, 50 year old, 1981 Port and 1986 cask strength are released.

2018 A 22 year old version of the 105 Cask Strength is released.

Tasting notes Glenfarclas 10 year old:

GS – Full and richly sherried on the nose, with nuts, fruit cake and a hint of citrus fruit. The palate is big, with ripe fruit, brittle toffee, some peat and oak. Medium length and gingery in the finish.

105 Cask Strength

50 years old

12 years old

18 years old

Family Cask 1959

21 years old

40 years old

Glenfiddich

[glen•<u>fidd</u>•ick]

Owner:
William Grant & Sons

Region/district:
Speyside

Founded: **Status:**
1886   Active (vc)

Capacity:
13 700 000 litres

Address: Dufftown, Keith, Banffshire AB55 4DH

Website:
glenfiddich.com

Tel:
01340 820373 (vc)

A huge upgrade is underway at Glenfiddich and when the next Yearbook is published around September 2019, the already large distillery will be even bigger with a capacity of producing 20 million litres.

The caveat is of course that the extensive work is going according to plans. It usually does though, when William Grant is involved. Huge projects such as Girvan grain distillery, Ailsa Bay malt distillery and the Tullamore distillery in Ireland have all been completed according to schedule.

The ongoing expansion is of course due to the fact that the demand for Glenfiddich single malt is on the rise. In 2011, it was the first single malt Scotch to sell more than one million cases (12 million bottles) in one year. In 2017 sales amounted to 15.6 million bottles and Glenfiddich single malt is around 50% of the company´s total sales in terms of value. In 1963 William Grant and Glenfidddich became the first to systematically promote a single malt around the world including television commercials. This gave Glenfiddich the position of the world´s best-selling single malt, a position it still maintains today.

Currently, Glenfiddich is equipped with two, stainless steel full lauter mash tuns – both with a 10 ton mash. There are 32 washbacks made of Douglas fir with a minimum fermentation time of 68 hours but typically 72. Two still rooms hold a total of 11 wash stills and 20 spirit stills. All the stills in still house number 2 are directly fired using gas. The production for 2018 will be 68 mashes per week and 13.65 million litres of pure alcohol. The ongoing expansion includes a new tun room and a new still house. In terms of equipment there will be one more mash tun, 16 washbacks, 5 wash stills and 10 spirit stills.

The core range consists of **12, 15, 18, 21, Excellence 26, 30** and **40 year old**. The **Rich Oak 14 year old** has now been removed from the core range and is an exclusive to Canada. There is also a **14 year old** bourbon matured available only in the US. Recent limited releases include **Glenfiddich The Original**, an attempt to replicate the flavour profile of Straight Malt from the early 1960s, the **38 year old Glenfiddich Ultimate** and a **50 year old**. A special range is called Experimental Series where **IPA Experiment** with a finish in IPA beer casks and **Project XX** where the casks were selected by 20 brand ambassadors are ongoing items. A third bottling, the **21 year old Winter Storm** finished in Canadian icewine casks, was released in spring 2018 followed by **Fire & Cane** in July. The latter is a smoky whisky finished in rum casks. In 2014, the **Glenfiddich Gallery** was introduced where Malt Master, Brian Kinsman, has selected special casks. Included in the duty free range are three Age of Discovery bottlings; **Madeira cask, Bourbon cask** and **Red Wine cask finish** as well as the Cask Collection with **Select Cask, Reserve Cask, Vintage Cask** and **Finest Solera**. Another duty free exclusive is **Glenfiddich Rare Oak 25 years**. Finally, a **15 year old Distillery Edition** is available at the distillery and selected duty free markets.

History:

1886   The distillery is founded by William Grant, 47 years old, who had learned the trade at Mortlach Distillery. The equipment is bought from Mrs. Cummings of Cardow Distillery. The construction totals £800.

1887   The first distilling takes place on Christmas Day.

1892   William Grant builds Balvenie.

1898   The blending company Pattisons, largest customer of Glenfiddich, files for bankruptcy and Grant decides to blend their own whisky. Standfast becomes one of their major brands.

1903   William Grant & Sons is formed.

1957   The famous, three-cornered bottle is introduced.

1958   The floor maltings is closed.

1963   Glennfiddich becomes the first whisky to be marketed as single malt in the UK and the rest of the world.

1964   A version of Standfast's three-cornered bottle is launched for Glenfiddich in green glass.

1969   Glenfiddich becomes the first distillery in Scotland to open a visitor centre.

1974   16 new stills are installed.

2001   1965 Vintage Reserve is launched in a limited edition of 480 bottles. Glenfiddich 1937 is bottled (61 bottles).

2002   Glenfiddich Gran Reserva 21 years old, finished in Cuban rum casks is launched. Caoran Reserve 12 years is released. Glenfiddich Rare Collection 1937 (61 bottles) is launched and becomes the oldest Scotch whisky on the market.

2003   1973 Vintage Reserve (440 bottles) is launched.

2004   1991 Vintage Reserve (13 years) and 1972 Vintage Reserve (519 bottles) are launched.

History continued:

2005 Circa £1.7 million is invested in a new visitor centre.

2006 1973 Vintage Reserve, 33 years (861 bottles) and 12 year old Toasted Oak are released.

2007 1976 Vintage Reserve, 31 years is released.

2008 1977 Vintage Reserve is released.

2009 A 50 year old and 1975 Vintage Reserve are released.

2010 Rich Oak, 1978 Vintage Reserve, the 6th edition of 40 year old and Snow Phoenix are released.

2011 1974 Vintage Reserve and a 19 year old Madeira finish are released.

2012 Cask of Dreams and Millenium Vintage are released.

2013 A 19 year old red wine finish and 1987 Anniversary Vintage are released. Cask Collection with three different expressions is released for duty free.

2014 The 26 year old Glenfiddich Excellence, Rare Oak 25 years and Glenfiddich The Original are released.

2015 A 14 year old for the US market is released.

2016 Finest Solera is released for travel retail. Two expressions in the Experimental Series are launched; Project XX and IPA Experiment.

2017 Winter Storm is released.

2018 A new expression in the Experimental Series is released - Fire & Cane.

Tasting notes Glenfiddich 12 year old:

GS – Delicate, floral and slightly fruity on the nose. Well mannered in the mouth, malty, elegant and soft. Rich, fruit flavours dominate the palate, with a developing nuttiness and an elusive whiff of peat smoke in the fragrant finish.

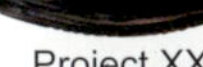

Project XX

Fire & Cane

IPA Experiment

12 years old

Reserve Cask

Vintage Cask

Distillery Edition 15 years old

Winter Storm

Glen Garioch

Glen Garioch is one of Scotland's oldest distilleries but the story seemed to be coming to an end in 1968 when the owners at the time, DCL, closed production. For a long time the water supply had been a huge problem and they contemplated closing for good.

After all, they had more than 40 other distilleries at their disposal. One man who owned only one distillery was Stanley P Morrison who purchased Bowmore in 1963. He was convinced that he could find a viable water source and placed a bid for Glen Garioch. A local "diviner" (so called as they can 'smell' out water), by the name of Alec "Digger" Grant successfully discovered a source så plentiful that production could increase 10 fold once the distillery opened again in 1973.

Glen Garioch single malt is typically unpeated, but smoky notes can easily be detected in expressions distilled before 1994 when their own floor maltings closed. Until then, the malt was peated with a phenol specification of 8-10ppm. The distillery is equipped with a 4 ton full lauter mash tun, eight stainless steel washbacks with a fermentation time of 72 hours, one wash still and one spirit still (replaced in 2016). There is also a third still, which has not been used for a long time. The spirit is tankered to Glasgow, filled into casks and returned to the distillery's four warehouses. During 2018 the production will be 7 mashes per week and around 450,000 litres in the year.

The core range is the **1797 Founder's Reserve** (without age statement) and a **12 year old**, both of them bottled at 48%. Recent limited releases include **Virgin Oak**, fully matured in virgin American white oak – and a selection of **Vintage** expressions including **1986, 1991, 1995** and **1999**. The first chapter of a new range of cask strength bottlings called **Glen Garioch Renaissance Collection** was released in 2014 with a 15 year old and the fourth and final installment came in 2018 by way of an **18 year old**.

[glen gee•ree]

Owner:
Beam Suntory

Region/district:
Eastern Highlands

Founded:
1797

Status:
Active (vc)

Capacity:
1 370 000 litres

Address: Oldmeldrum, Inverurie, Aberdeenshire AB51 0ES

Website:
glengarioch.com

Tel:
01651 873450

History:

1797 John Manson founds the distillery.

1798 Thomas Simpson becomes licensee.

1825 Ingram, Lamb & Co. bcome new owners.

1837 The distillery is bought by John Manson & Co.

1884 The distillery is sold to J. G. Thomson & Co.

1908 William Sanderson buys the distillery.

1933 Sanderson & Son merges with the gin maker Booth's Distilleries Ltd.

1937 Booth's Distilleries Ltd is acquired by Distillers Company Limited (DCL).

1968 Glen Garioch is decommissioned.

1970 It is sold to Stanley P. Morrison Ltd.

1973 Production starts again.

1978 Stills are increased from two to three.

1994 Suntory controls all of Morrison Bowmore Distillers Ltd.

1995 The distillery is mothballed in October.

1997 The distillery reopens in August and from now on, it is using unpeated malt.

2004 Glen Garioch 46 year old is released.

2005 15 year old Bordeaux Cask Finish is launched. A visitor centre opens in October.

2006 An 8 year old is released.

2009 Complete revamp of the range - 1979 Founders Reserve (unaged), 12 year old, Vintage 1978 and 1990 are released.

2010 1991 vintage is released.

2011 Vintage 1986 and 1994 are released.

2012 Vintage 1995 and 1997 are released.

2013 Virgin Oak, Vintage 1999 and 11 single casks are released.

2014 Glen Garioch Renaissance Collection 15 years is released.

2018 The fourth and final installment of the Rennaisance Collection is released.

12 years old

Tasting notes Glen Garioch 12 years old:

GS – Luscious and sweet on the nose, peaches and pineapple, vanilla, malt and a hint of sherry. Full-bodied and nicely textured, with more fresh fruit on the palate, along with spice, brittle toffee and finally dry oak notes.

Whisky
the way I see it

Karen Fullerton
Global Brand Ambassador
The Glenmorangie Company

You´ve been working in the whisky business now for sixteen years - could you please tell us how your whisky interest started?

I started my career in the drinks industry just over 20 years ago in wine sales. During this time I completed my Wine and Spirits Education Trust to advanced level which helped to build my knowledge within the wine and spirits sector but also opened up my senses to appreciate the difference between an average and excellent quality beverage. I got my first dream job when I moved back to Scotland in 2002 to work for The Glenmorangie Company, as business development manager, North of Scotland. Within a couple of years I was promoted to be the first female Scottish Brand Ambassador for USA. For the last 8 years I have been based at our headquarters in Edinburgh working on a global role.

Your current position at Glenmorangie is that of the Global Brand Ambassador for both Glenmorangie and Ardbeg. What does that mean?

It is an incredibly fun and diverse role. The fun part is to be working with so many departments within the business, from sales and marketing to the Glenmorangie and Ardbeg distilleries, as well as the whisky creation team. A big part of my role is to implement and host The Moet Hennessy Scotch whisky academy; another part of my role is to travel to various markets around the world educating the trade on everything that makes Glenmorangie and Ardbeg unique in how we create our single malt Scotch whisky. I also host VIP whisky dinners for our key partners.

I know that your time at Glenmorangie has also included working with whisky creation – a task not often performed by a brand ambassador. What did you do and what did you learn from that period?

I have always been interested in the origins of flavour whether it's with beer, whisky or wine. I have just completed my Brewing and Distilling Diploma, by distance learning, at Heriot Watt University. A world class course, I would strongly recommend it to anyone who is interested in pursuing a career in this arena. I am lucky to have the kind support of Dr Bill Lumsden, Gillian Macdonald, Brendan McCarron and the team to share new product development ideas. I also attend regular seminars/ workshops at The Scotch Whisky Research Institute which keeps me informed with science and technology.

Glenmorangie has been a forerunner when it comes to selecting the proper wood for maturation. How did this start?

Our wood management harks back to the SPUR Project (Support for Products Under Research) which was part-funded by a grant for innovative research, from the Department of Trade and Industry in the early 1980's. This project involved a comprehensive investigation of our existing wood, and involved a number of chromatography tests as well as the investigations by specially trained sensory evaluation panels at Pentlands Research Institute (now called The Scotch Whisky Research Institute). From this research is the reason why we only fill our ex-bourbon American white oak casks two

times and it was also at this time when our slow growth designer casks were born and we started pioneering wood finishing.

You were also involved in establishing and running The Glenmorangie Company Academy. Please tell us more.

I learned from working in sales that you don't have the time to go through every aspect of what makes Scotch whisky so amazing with your key customers. However, if you are able to immerse your team within the natural enviroment that inspired the whisky creation, you can bring the different expressions to life within your portfolio and hopefully that information will be shared with their own personal story.

In your profession, you´ve been to more countries than I can think of – which ones are your favourites and why?

Georgia, South Africa, Germany, Russia and Switzerland predominately because of the people, the culture, the incredible landscape and the fabulous nature.

I know, at least in some markets, people sometimes may be prejudiced against women working in the whisky business. During your years working as a brand ambassador, do you feel that things have changed for the better?

Sadly prejudice will always exist, however I am glad to say the industry is in a very healthy place and it's great to see such a diverse demographic of people enjoying Scotch whisky around the world. As with any premium beverage, if you have an appreciation of the aroma, taste and flavour that is unique to different products... it is as simple as that.

There is a lot of discussion on how to get the younger generation (millenials or what ever we would like to call them) interested in Scotch whisky. What would you say is the best way?

It all comes down to doing the basics right: education on the category; help to uncover the incredible spectrum of aroma and flavour you can discover from one Scotch whisky to another; highlighting different ways of enjoying Scotch whisky (i.e. straight, on the rocks or as a cocktail); and finally, continuing to be open minded and unprejudiced in how we position the category.

What does Scotch whisky mean to you?

A spirit with great character!

The history of Scotch whisky has had its ups and downs over the years. How do you see the future for Scotch in the next 10-15 years?

That's a tough question...who knows what is around the corner as to what's not? Having said that, I strongly believe the future of Scotch whisky is in a good place. If we continue to be open minded and share what makes this magnificent product so special in a responsible way, along with how the Scotch Whisky Association is doing an incredible job of keeping the integrity of the category – I think it´s all good!

Glenglassaugh

[glen•glass•ock]

Owner: | **Region/district:**
Glenglassaugh Distillery Co | Highlands
(BenRiach Distillery Co.) |

Founded: | **Status:** | **Capacity:**
1875 | Active (vc) | 1 100 000 litres

Address: Portsoy, Banffshire AB45 2SQ

Website: | **Tel:**
glenglassaugh.com | 01261 842367

The revival in 2008 of Glenglassaugh, a distillery that had been closed for more than 22 years, came as a pleasant surprise to any whisky lover. The name of the buyer was equally surprising.

Nobody in the industry had ever heard of The Scaent Group - a Dutch-registered investment company founded in 2003. Their main business was in energy trading, construction and telecom and they had no record of investments in the world of spirits. Now they wanted to buy a whisky distillery. They approached the whisky consultant Stuart Nickerson and asked him to come up with suitable prospects. On two occasions, a deal was very close to come through but stumbled at the finish line. Anxious to fulfill his clients needs, Nickerson got in touch with Highland Distillers (Edrington) asking if the mothballed Glenglassaugh might be up for sale and everything fell into place. The start could have gone smoother though. In September 2007, before the deal had been finalised, copper thieves broke into the mothballed distillery causing damages worth £100,000.

The equipment of the distillery consists of a 5.2 ton Porteus cast iron mash tun with rakes, four wooden washbacks and two stainless steel ones with a fermentation time between 54 and 80 hours and one pair of stills. The production is 800,000 litres of pure alcohol, of which 40,000 litres is peated (30ppm). The main part (85%) is filled to be used as single malt while the rest is sold externally.

The core range is **Revival**, finished in oloroso casks, **Evolution**, matured in American oak and **Torfa** which is peated (20ppm) and without age statement. Limited releases include **30, 40** and **51 year old**, as well as single casks in the **Rare Cask Series** where batch four was released in autumn 2018. The second release of **Octaves Classic** and **Octaves Peated**, matured around 7 years in small casks holding around 60 litres appeared at the same time. Autumn 2017 saw the first release of a wood finish series from the distillery - **Port, PX Sherry, Peated Port** and **Peated Virgin Oak**. All expressions started out in ex-bourbon and were bottled at 46%.

History:

1873 The distillery is founded by James Moir.

1887 Alexander Morrison embarks on renovation work.

1892 Morrison sells the distillery to Robertson & Baxter. They in turn sell it on to Highland Distilleries Company for £15,000.

1908 The distillery closes.

1931 The distillery reopens.

1936 The distillery closes.

1957 Reconstruction takes place.

1960 The distillery reopens.

1986 Glenglassaugh is mothballed.

2005 A 22 year old is released.

2006 Three limited editions are released - 19 years old, 38 years old and 44 years old.

2008 The distillery is bought by the Scaent Group for £5m. Three bottlings are released - 21, 30 and 40 year old.

2009 New make spirit and 6 months old are released.

2010 A 26 year old replaces the 21 year old.

2011 A 35 year old and the first bottling from the new owners production, a 3 year old, are released.

2012 A visitor centre is inaugurated and Glenglassaugh Revival is released.

2013 BenRiach Distillery Co buys the distillery and Glenglassaugh Evolution and a 30 year old are released.

2014 The peated Torfa is released as well as eight different single casks and Massandra Connection (35 and 41 years old).

2015 The second batch of single casks is released.

2016 Octaves Classic and Octaves Peated are released.

2017 Three wood finishes are released.

2018 Batch four in the Rare Cask series is launched.

Evolution

Tasting notes Glenglassaugh Evolution:

GS – Peaches and gingerbread on the nose, with brittle toffee, icing sugar, and vanilla. Luscious soft fruits dipped in caramel figure on the palate, with coconut and background stem ginger. The finish is medium in length, with spicy toffee.

Glengoyne

[glen•goyn]

Owner: Ian Macleod Distillers

Region/district: Southern Highlands

Founded: 1833

Status: Active (vc)

Capacity: 1 100 000 litres

Address: Dumgoyne by Killearn, Glasgow G63 9LB

Website: glengoyne.com

Tel: 01360 550254 (vc)

In 2003 Edrington, owners at the time of Glengoyne and several other distilleries, decided to re-evaluate their brands and strategy. A decision was made to sell off what was considered non-core brands and focus on the biggest sellers.

Bunnahabhain was sold to Burn Stewart in April and just a few weeks later, Glengoyne went to Ian Macleod. The aim was to concentrate on Macallan, Highland Park, Famous Grouse and Cutty Sark. Fifteen years later, Edrington has made a similar move when they´ve announced that Glenturret and the Cutty Sark brand are up for sale. Even though Glengoyne was considered surplus in 2003, Edrington had taken good care of the distillery over the years. It was rebuilt and expanded and the single malt was launched in the 1990s. However, it was after the Ian Macleod take-over that the brand started to make a name for itself. An extensive (and costly) investment in high quality sherry wood, an expansion of the range and huge investments in their visitor centre have paid off. The single malt is selling well and 75,000 visitors come to the distillery in the Trossachs every year.

The distillery is equipped with a 3.8 ton semi lauter mash tun. There are also six Oregon pine washbacks, as well as the rather unusual combination of one wash still and two spirit stills. Both short (56 hours) and long (110 hours) fermentations are practised. In 2018, the production will be 920,000 litres of alcohol.

The core range consists of **10, 12, 18, 21** and **25 year old**. There is also batch six of the **cask strength** which for the first time was 100% matured in sherry casks. Recent limited releases include a **30 year old** and batch 6 of the popular **The Teapot Dram**. The line-up for duty free was completely revamped in April 2018. The 15 year old Distiller´s Gold was replaced by a range called Spirit of Oak with no less than four expressions - all of them heavily influenced by sherry casks; **Cuartillo** (American oak oloroso), **Balbaine** (European oak oloroso), **28 year old** (a combination of American and European oak oloroso) and **Glengoyne PX** (American and European oak with a finish in PX casks).

History:

1833 The distillery is licensed under the name Burnfoot Distilleries by the Edmonstone family.

1876 Lang Brothers buys the distillery and changes the name to Glenguin.

1905 The name changes to Glengoyne.

1965 Robertson & Baxter takes over Lang Brothers and the distillery is refurbished. The stills are increased from two to three.

2001 Glengoyne Scottish Oak Finish (16 years old) is launched.

2003 Ian MacLeod Distillers Ltd buys the distillery plus the brand Langs from the Edrington Group for £7.2 million.

2005 A 19 year old, a 32 year old and a 37 year old cask strength are launched.

2006 Nine "choices" from Stillmen, Mashmen and Manager are released.

2007 A new version of the 21 year old, two Warehousemen´s Choice, Vintage 1972 and two single casks are released.

2008 A 16 year old Shiraz cask finish, three single casks and Heritage Gold are released.

2009 A 40 year old, two single casks and a new 12 year old are launched.

2010 Two single casks, 1987 and 1997, released.

2011 A 24 year old single cask is released.

2012 A 15 and an 18 year old are released as well as a Cask Strength with no age statement.

2013 A limited 35 year old is launched.

2014 A 25 year old is released.

2018 A new range for duty free is released – Cuartillo, Balbaine, a 28 year old and Glengoyne PX.

12 years old

Tasting notes Glengoyne 12 years old:

GS – Slightly earthy on the nose, with nutty malt, ripe apples, and a hint of honey. The palate is full and fruity, with milk chocolate, ginger and vanilla. The finish is medium in length, with milky coffee and soft spices.

Glen Grant

[glen grant]

Owner: Campari Group   **Region/district:** Speyside

Founded: 1840   **Status:** Active (vc)   **Capacity:** 6 200 000 litres

Address: Elgin Road, Rothes, Banffshire AB38 7BS

Website: glengrant.com   **Tel:** 01340 832118

Until 2002, Glen Grant held the position as the second best-selling single malt in the world after Glenfiddich and if we go back 30 years, it sold more than 500,000 cases per year. The future looked bright but a change in ownership affected its development.

Already in the 1950s, Glen Grant had joined forces with Glenlivet and a few years later, the owners had established Glen Grant as the best-selling single malt in the expanding Italian market. In 1978, the two distilleries were sold to Seagrams. They were not bad owners - on the contrary, they rationalised and expanded the distillery. But their interest lay in blends and in particular Chivas Regal. The lion´s share of Glen Grant went into the famous blend and the next owner, Pernod Ricard, continued to prioritize this too.

The result meant that Glen Grant lost its position amongst the top sellers, and the trend has continued under Campari's ownership. In 2017 the brand sold 3.5 million bottles which ranks them 9th in the world. Glen Grant has never been widely marketed throughout the important American market, but with a 15 year old exclusive, the owners have decided to give it a serious try. And not only there – since 2018 Glen Grant is available also in Canada.

The distillery is equipped with a 12.3 ton semi-lauter mash tun, ten Oregon pine washbacks with a minimum fermentation time of 48 hours and four pairs of stills. The wash stills are peculiar in that they have vertical sides at the base of the neck and all eight stills are fitted with purifiers. This gives an increased reflux and creates a light and delicate whisky. A new, extremely efficient £5m bottling hall was inaugurated in 2013. It has a capacity of 12,000 bottles an hour and Glen Grant is the only one of the larger distillers bottling the entire production on site. In 2015 a second line for the premium range was installed. During 2018, the operators will split their time between the distillery and the bottling plant, doing 20 mashes per week for 20 weeks which will amount to 2 million litres of pure alcohol.

The Glen Grant core range consists of **Major´s Reserve** with no age statement, a **5 year old** sold in Italy only and a **10 year old**. Two further additions to the core range were made in 2016 – a **12 year old** matured in both bourbon and sherry casks and an **18 year old** bourbon matured. Summer 2016 also saw the introduction of a **12 year old non chill-filtered** expression for the duty free market. In early 2018, a **15 year old**, matured in first fill bourbon and bottled at 50% was launched for the American market as well as for duty free. Recent limited editions include **Glen Grant Fiodh**, 43 years old and exclusive to Singapore. Older expressions are rarely released by the owners but can from time to time be found in the range from Gordon & MacPhail. Recently a collection of six bottlings distilled from 1950 to 1955 was launched by the independent bottler.

History:

1840 The brothers James and John Grant, managers of Dandelaith Distillery, found the distillery.

1861 The distillery becomes the first to install electric lighting.

1864 John Grant dies.

1872 James Grant passes away and the distillery is inherited by his son, James junior (Major James Grant).

1897 James Grant decides to build another distillery across the road; it is named Glen Grant No. 2.

1902 Glen Grant No. 2 is mothballed.

1931 Major Grant dies and is succeeded by his grandson Major Douglas Mackessack.

1953 J. & J. Grant merges with George & J. G. Smith who runs Glenlivet distillery, forming The Glenlivet & Glen Grant Distillers Ltd.

1961 Armando Giovinetti and Douglas Mackessak found a friendship that leads to Glen Grant becoming the most sold malt whisky in Italy.

1965 Glen Grant No. 2 is back in production, but renamed Caperdonich.

1972 The Glenlivet & Glen Grant Distillers merges with Hill Thompson & Co. and Longmorn-Glenlivet Ltd to form The Glenlivet Distillers.

1973 Stills are increased from four to six.

1977 The Chivas & Glenlivet Group (Seagrams) buys Glen Grant Distillery. Stills are increased from six to ten.

2001 Pernod Ricard and Diageo buy Seagrams Spirits & Wine, with Pernod acquiring Chivas Group.

History continued:

2006 Campari buys Glen Grant for €115m.

2007 The entire range is re-packaged and re-launched and a 15 year old single cask is released. Reconstruction of the visitor centre.

2008 Two limited cask strengths - a 16 year old and a 27 year old - are released.

2009 Cellar Reserve 1992 is released.

2010 A 170th Anniversary bottling is released.

2011 A 25 year old is released.

2012 A 19 year old Distillery Edition is released.

2013 Five Decades is released and a bottling hall is built.

2014 A 50 year old and the Rothes Edition 10 years old is released.

2015 Glen Grant Fiodh is launched.

2016 A 12 year old and an 18 year old are launched and a 12 year old non chill-filtered is released for travel retail.

2017 A 15 year old is released for the American market.

2018 A 15 year old is released for the duty free market.

Tasting notes Glen Grant 12 year old:

GS – A blast of fresh fruit – oranges, pears and lemons – on the initial nose, before vanilla and fudge notes develop. The fruit carries over on to the palate, with honey, caramel and sweet spices. Medium in length, with cinnamon and soft oak in the finish.

12 years old

12 years old
non chill-filtered

18 years old

10 years old

The Major's Reserve

Glengyle

[glen•gajl]

Owner: | **Region/district:**
Mitchell´s Glengyle Ltd | Campbeltown

Founded: | **Status:** | **Capacity:**
2004 | Active | 750 000 litres

Address: Glengyle Road, Campbeltown,
Argyll PA28 6LR

Website: | **Tel:**
kilkerran.com | 01586 551710

The distillery was founded by William Mitchell, member of a family that can truly be called a Campbeltown whisky dynasty. Since the early 1800s until today, members of the Mitchell family have been involved in at least four distilleries.

It all started around 1660 when the Mitchells first came to Campbeltown from the Lowlands as farmers. In the early 19th century, Archibald Mitchell was distilling whisky without a license. On the same site, Springbank was founded in 1828 and taken over by two of Archibald´s sons – John and William. Eventually, William joined his two other brothers, Hugh and Archibald Jr., at Riechlachan distillery and then, in 1872, he founded Glengyle. Meanwhile, their sister Mary had become involved with Drumore distillery. John and his son Alexander continued to develop Springbank while Glengyle was sold in 1919 to West Highland Malt Distilleries and closed soon thereafter. A chequered history followed when the buildings were used as a worskhop, a rifle shooting range and a feed store. In 2000, Hedley Wright, great great grandson of John Mitchell and owner of Springbank, bought the premises and turned it into a working distillery once again.

The distillery is equipped with a 4.5 ton semi-lauter mash tun, two washbacks made of boat skin larch and two made of Douglas fir. The fermentation varies between 72 and 110 hours. There is also one set of stills. Malt is obtained from the neighbouring Springbank and the same staff also runs operations. The capacity is 750,000 litres, but considerably smaller amounts have been produced over the years. The plan for 2018 is an increase from the previous year, but it shouldn´t involve more than 82,000 litres made up of "regular" Kilkerran and 20,000 litres of heavily peated spirit.

After many years of Work in Progress, the first core **12 year old** was launched in August 2016. It was a vatting of bourbon- (70%) and sherry-matured (30%) whisky. The owners had plans for only one bottling but due to demand, they made another two and more is to be expected. In spring 2017, an **8 year old** was launched with a third batch planned for late autumn 2018.

History:

1872 The original Glengyle Distillery is built by William Mitchell.

1919 The distillery is bought by West Highland Malt Distilleries Ltd.

1925 The distillery is closed.

1929 The warehouses (but no stock) are purchased by the Craig Brothers and rebuilt into a petrol station and garage.

1941 The distillery is acquired by the Bloch Brothers.

1957 Campbell Henderson applies for planning permission with the intention of reopening the distillery.

2000 Hedley Wright, owner of Springbank Distillery and related to founder William Mitchell, acquires the distillery.

2004 The first distillation after reconstruction takes place in March.

2007 The first limited release - a 3 year old.

2009 Kilkerran "Work in progress" is released.

2010 "Work in progress 2" is released.

2011 "Work in progress 3" is released.

2012 "Work in progress 4" is released.

2013 "Work in progress 5" is released and this time in two versions - bourbon and sherry.

2014 "Work in progress 6" is released in two versions - bourbon and sherry.

2015 "Work in progress 7" is released in two versions - bourbon and sherry.

2016 Kilkerran 12 years old is released.

2017 Kilkerran 8 year old cask strength is released

12 years old

Tasting notes Kilkerran 12 year old:

GS – Initially, quite reticent on the nose, then peaty fruit notes develop. Oily and full on the palate, with peaches and more overt smoke, plus an earthy quality. Castor oil and liquorice sticks. Slick in the medium-length finish, with slightly drying oak and enduring liquorice.

Whisky
the way I see it

Angus MacRaild
Whisky consultant and organiser
of the Old & Rare Show

Photo: Marcel van G

I believe you were quite young when you were first intro-duced to Scotch whisky. Please tell us more.

My Dad used to have the occasional bottle of malt whisky around the house, usually Laphroaig. I remember being allowed a tiny sip of this when I was about 4-5 years old and I was instantly fascinated by its taste. From then on I'd often ask about whisky, read the backs of bottles and get a wee taste. As a young teenager I'd read books about it and it really just grew from there.

How did you come up with the idea to arrange the Old & Rare Show in Glasgow, what is it all about and how would you describe the people attending?

Ever since visiting old bottle festivals in Europe I had thought it would be great to do something celebrating older whiskies in Scotland – the country where they were made. I mentioned this to my good friend Jonny McMillan who also co-organises Dramboree and he was very keen to do it so we started looking into the idea of a rare whisky festival. Finance was a hurdle for us so we spoke to Sukhinder at The Whisky Exchange about the possiblity of sponsor-ship. They had also been considering the idea of an old bottle show in Scotland so Sukhinder suggested a partnership, something which worked well for us so we went from there. In the end it worked out pretty much exactly as we envisaged, which is a show that really holds up and celebrates the greatest whiskies ever made. Of course these whiskies are crazy expensive now but we try to make sure the show offers something to every level of finance and interest. This was our second year and we had everyone from some of the world's most serious collectors, new enthusiasts from Asia, people that don't often travel from the USA and Russia and students and young drinks professionals from Edinburgh and Glasgow – all keen to come and learn and enjoy types of whisky they would really struggle to find elsewhere.

In an interview, you said there was a turning point in the whisky market around 2009 and that the time before that could be called "the age of innocence". What did you mean by that?

I mean that was a time before a really big proliferation of know-ledge and awareness about whisky, and in particular high quality, malt whisky. It was before prices started to go crazy and you saw real diversification of the secondary market. It was a time when there was less cynicism; fewer individuals coming into whisky solely with commercial or investment ambitions; you could still buy some pretty remarkable bottles for attractive, 'drinkable' prices. I would characterise it as the tipping point when knowledge prolife-rated via the internet and created a subsequent knock-on effect on value – and crucially 'perception' of value – and that in turn led to a broader change in mindset about whisky. Now, you could argue that as a result we live in an age of cynicism, or an age of maturity.

You´ve become known to advocate whiskies produced in the 40s, 50s and 60s. Are they superior to whiskies produced today or just different?

I belive they are superior. But I'm not really advocating just for those whiskies. My argument is for the methods and ingredients that made those levels of quality. As a whisky lover I want, for myself and everyone else, to drink and enjoy the best possible quality whiskies. It's really an argument against the forces of uniformity and homogenisation. An argument that says yes you can have mass production to feed the blends on a commerical level that sustains that sector of your industry. But there is also a demand for a different style, one driven more by distinct distillery personality; distillate over wood; fruit, wax and texture over sweetness and vanilla. My argument is we know exactly how to make whiskies of these characteristics and quality so why the hell aren't more people doing it? I don't believe the commercial argument – that it's too time consuming and costly – works anymore in a world where plenty people are willing to pay good money for good whisky. The whisky world is big enough to have people making both styles. I think Dornoch will do it, and I am interested to see if Diageo will do it with Brora and Port Ellen. I really hope so, I think it would be a spectacular missed opportunity if they don't do something really special with those projects.

What does Scotch whisky mean to you?

A great bottle of whisky can be the foundation of cherished shared memories with diverse people in the most mundane of locations. Similarly a humble or basic whisky can be uplifted to something remarkable by the people you're with or place you drink it. It's this continual overlap of friends, places, memories and flavours that whisky can thread itself between which I love. When it's at its best Scotch Whisky is hard to beat for flavour; its inherent ability to ignite conversation and ideas; and its adaptability to all scenes of life from moments of celebration to pathos. And it speaks to that part of my identity which is Scottish - to have a spirit which can be so evocative of its place of origin but which has gone out into the world and become this iconic drink is a remarkable thing.

The history of Scotch whisky has had its ups and downs over the years. How do you see the future for Scotch in the next 10-15 years?

Well, for starters I think the industry has a bad habit of forgetting its history. The problem with Scotch is that its arcs of fortune tend to outlast the common human lifespan so it's easy to see a decade of growth and start rubbing your hands with glee when you look at India or China or wherever looks profitable – especially if your pri-mary goal is your own, understandable, professional advancement and not the generational caretaking of your industry. There's no rea-son Scotch can't go from boom to bust again in the next couple of decades. I think over the next 10-15 years you'll see a huge amount of competition for attention from the new-start distilleries, many of which aren't making interesting whisky so you'll also see some closures there I expect. I think you'll also see continued growth and interest in single malt as it's a product which people tend to fall in love with and stay in love with. And I also think you'll see unprece-dented levels of disruption – social and economic – from the forces of climate change and the ways in which we begin to seriously try and tackle this as a planet. I'm not sure any industry, let alone whisky, is fully prepared for this and the changes in process, laws and socio-economic re-structuring it will bring.

Glen Keith

[glen <u>keeth</u>]

Owner:	**Region/district:**
Chivas Brothers	Speyside
(Pernod Ricard)	

Founded:	**Status:**	**Capacity:**
1957	Active	6 000 000 litres

Address: Station Road, Keith, Banffshire AB55 3BU

Website:	**Tel:**
-	01542 783042

For a long time, the owners of Glen Keith, Chivas Brothers, have focused on a select few of their distilleries when it comes to single malt bottlings. The rest have had to accept the role of being producers of malt for blends.

In the last year though, things have changed. Malts from all the distilleries have been bottled at cask strength and sold at the company's vistor centres and not only that. A handful have also been graced by core expressions that are widely available. Glen Keith is one of them, with a Distillery Edition launched in autumn 2017. Definitely a salutary move from one of the big producers but we probably shouldn't expect a wider range in the future. Glen Keith single malt still serves as an important part of several of the company's blends - Chivas Regal, 100 Pipers and Passport to name but a few. The latter was created by Jimmy Laing in the 1960s when Seagrams still owned Chivas Brothers. In the last ten years the brand has grown by more than 300% and it's the number one standard blend in Brazil and number two in Mexico.

Following 13 years of no production, Chivas Brothers started to reignite the work at the distillery in spring 2012. The old Saladin maltings were demolished and part of that area now holds a new building with a Briggs 8 ton full lauter mash tun and six stainless steel washbacks. In the old building there are nine washbacks made of Oregon pine and six, old but refurbished stills. The distillery was re-opened in April 2013 and now has the capacity to do 6 million litres with the possibility of producing 40 mashes per week. For a short period in the 1970s, Glen Keith produced two unusual single malts named Craigduff and Glenisla. They were never released by the owners but the independent bottler Signatory, has bottled them both.

Until recently, the only current, official bottling of Glen Keith single malt was a 17 year old cask strength available at Chivas' visitor centres. In autumn 2017 though, a **Distillery Edition** without age statement was launched – matured in ex-bourbon casks.

History:

1957 The Distillery is founded by Chivas Brothers (Seagrams).

1958 Production starts.

1970 The first gas-fuelled still in Scotland is installed, the number of stills increases from three to five.

1976 Own maltings (Saladin box) ceases.

1983 A sixth still is installed.

1994 The first official bottling, a 10 year old, is released as part of Seagram's Heritage Selection.

1999 The distillery is mothballed.

2001 Pernod Ricard takes over Chivas Brothers from Seagrams.

2012 The reconstruction and refurbishing of the distillery begins.

2013 Production starts again.

2017 A Distillery Edition is launched.

Distillery Edition

Tasting notes Glen Keith Distillery Edition:

IR – Sweet and fruity on the nose with notes of toffee and apples. Smooth on the palate, vanilla, tropical fruits, marzipan, sponge cake, honey, pears and a hint of dry oak in the finish.

Glenkinchie

[glen•kin•chee]

Owner: **Region/district:**
Diageo   Lowlands

Founded: **Status:**   **Capacity:**
1837   Active (vc)   2 500 000 litres

Address: Pencaitland, Tranent,
East Lothian EH34 5ET

Website: **Tel:**
malts.com   01875 342004

More than 40,000 visitors find their way to Glenkinchie every year and a little more than a year ago, the visitor centre got a substantial upgrade. But that wasn't enough. By 2020, at the latest, the distillery will have new facilities catering to the tourists.

This is all part of a plan that Diageo revealed in April 2018. No less than £150m will be invested in whisky tourism with the major part of the sum allocated to a brand new Johnnie Walker experience in Edinburgh. Four distilleries, reprsenting the "four corners of Scotland", will also receive a substantial share of the investment – apart from Glenkinchie, it´s Cardhu, Caol Ila and Clynelish. One excuisite and unique feature in the visitor centre, is an 18 metre long distillery model scale 1:6 which was built for the British Empire Exhibition in 1924 (picture below).

Glenkinchie is equipped with a full lauter mash tun (9 tons) and six wooden washbacks with a fermentation time of 66-110 hours. There are two stills and while it has often been said that their wash still is the biggest in Scotland, that is not true. However it has the biggest charge – 21,000 litres. In 2017, the distillery will be working a 5-day week with 10 mashes, producing around 2 million litres of alcohol.

While the matured Glenkinchie is a grassy and fairly delicate Lowland whisky, the equipment and distilling regime suggests something different. Both stills have steeply descending lyne arms with no reflux at all to get rid of heavier compounds and minimal copper contact. The wormtub also indicates a heavy spirit and the newmake is indeed both sulphury and robust. After 12 years of maturation, however, the spirit transforms completely.

Glenkinchie is one of the six original Classic Malts, representing The Lowlands. The core range consists of a **12 year old** and a **Distiller´s Edition** with a finish in amontillado sherry casks. There is also a new **distillery exclusive** with an 18 months finish in sherry casks. In October 2016, a **24 year old**, distilled in 1991 and bottled at 57.2% was launched as part of the Special Releases.

History:

1825 A distillery known as Milton is founded by John and George Rate.

1837 The Rate brothers are registered as licensees of a distillery named Glenkinchie.

1853 John Rate sells the distillery to a farmer by the name of Christie who converts it to a sawmill.

1881 The buildings are bought by a consortium from Edinburgh.

1890 Glenkinchie Distillery Company is founded. Reconstruction and refurbishment is on-going for the next few years.

1914 Glenkinchie forms Scottish Malt Distillers (SMD) with four other Lowland distilleries.

1939-
1945 Glenkinchie is one of few distilleries allowed to maintain production during the war.

1968 Floor maltings is decommissioned.

1969 The maltings is converted into a museum.

1988 Glenkinchie 10 years becomes one of selected six in the Classic Malt series.

1998 A Distiller's Edition with Amontillado finish is launched.

2007 A 12 year old and a 20 year old cask strength are released.

2010 A cask strength exclusive for the visitor centre, a 1992 single cask and a 20 year old are released.

2016 A 24 year old and a distillery exclusive without age statement are released.

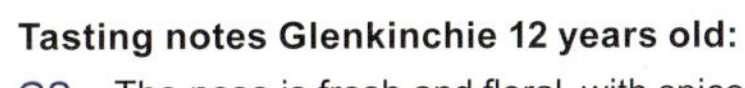

12 years old

Tasting notes Glenkinchie 12 years old:

GS – The nose is fresh and floral, with spices and citrus fruits, plus a hint of marshmallow. Notably elegant. Water releases cut grass and lemon notes. Medium-bodied, smooth, sweet and fruity, with malt, butter and cheesecake. The finish is comparatively long and drying, initially rather herbal.

Glenlivet

[glen•<u>liv</u>•it]

Owner: **Region/district:**
Chivas Brothers   Speyside
(Pernod Ricard)

Founded:	**Status:**	**Capacity:**
1824	Active (vc)	21 000 000 litres

Address: Ballindalloch, Banffshire AB37 9DB

Website: **Tel:**
theglenlivet.com   01340 821720 (vc)

In spring 2015, the owners of Glenlivet announced that their biggest seller, the 12 year old, would be discontinued to be replaced by Founder´s Reserve without an age statement.

Many Glenlivet fans all over the world were sceptical to say the least. Replacing an aged whisky with a NAS bottling was not well received, at least to start with. The reason for the move was that Chivas Bros simply didn´t have enough aged stock in the warehouses. Three years later, the scene has changed. The classic 12 year old is being re-introduced to market after market. At the same time the Founder´s Reserve managed to attract many consumers, both old and new. Last year alone, that particular expression managed to sell no less than 3 million bottles! That volume of just one bottling equals the sales of the entire Talisker range with ten different expressions.

Sales of Glenlivet have been remarkably good in recent years. Volumes have increased by 57% from 2010 to 2017 when almost 13 million bottles were sold. This positive trend has put some pressure on the owners to increase production. An expansion of the distillery has been underway for some time now and in summer 2018 the new extension of the distillery was commissioned bringing the total capacity to 21 million litres of alcohol – by far the largest malt distillery in Scotland.

With the new addition, the distillery is now equipped with two Briggs full lauter mash tuns, each with a 13.5 ton charge. The 16 wooden washbacks have been complemented by another 16 made of stainless steel. Fourteen pairs of stills are divided with four pairs in the oldest still room, three in the beautiful room that was built in 2010 and another seven in the third and latest still room.

The core range of Glenlivet is made up of **Founder´s Reserve, 12 year old, 12 year old Excellence, 15 year old French Oak Reserve, 18 year old, 21 year old Archive** and **Glenlivet XXV.** A new addition to the range appeared in May 2018 when **Captain´s Reserve,** with a finish in cognac casks, was released. A special range of non-chill filtered whiskies called Nàdurra include: **Nàdurra Oloroso Cask Strength, Nàdurra First Fill Selection Cask Strength** and **Nàdurra Peated Whisky Cask Finish.** All three are available at cask strength but also bottled at 48% for duty free. The smoky notes in the latter come from a finish in casks that had previously held peated Scotch whisky. The travel retail range also includes **Master Distiller´s Reserve, Master Distiller´s Reserve Solera Vatted,** as well as **Master Distiller´s Reserve Small Batch,** all without age statement. In 2014 a 50 year old became the first bottling in a new range, The Winchester Collection with a third edition, **Vintage 1967,** released in September 2018. Over the years, the owners have released mystery bottlings where very little was revealed about the content. The idea is to challenge the customers and get them to think about the whisky from their own perspective. The very latest bottling was **The Glenlivet Code** which was released in spring 2018.

History:

- **1817** George Smith inherits the farm distillery Upper Drummin from his father Andrew Smith who has been distilling on the site since 1774.
- **1840** George Smith buys Delnabo farm near Tomintoul and leases Cairngorm Distillery.
- **1845** George Smith leases three other farms, one of which is situated on the river Livet and is called Minmore.
- **1846** William Smith develops tuberculosis and his brother John Gordon moves back home to assist his father.
- **1858** George Smith buys Minmore farm and obtains permission to build a distillery.
- **1859** Upper Drummin and Cairngorm close and all equipment is brought to Minmore which is renamed The Glenlivet Distillery.
- **1864** George Smith cooperates with the whisky agent Andrew P. Usher and exports the whisky with great success.
- **1871** George Smith dies and his son John Gordon takes over.
- **1880** John Gordon Smith applies for and is granted sole rights to the name The Glenlivet.
- **1890** A fire breaks out and some of the buildings are replaced.
- **1896** Another two stills are installed.
- **1901** John Gordon Smith dies.
- **1904** John Gordon's nephew George Smith Grant takes over.
- **1921** Captain Bill Smith Grant, son of George Smith Grant, takes over.
- **1953** George & J. G. Smith Ltd merges with J. & J. Grant of Glen Grant Distillery and forms the company Glenlivet & Glen Grant Distillers.
- **1966** Floor maltings closes.
- **1970** Glenlivet & Glen Grant Distillers Ltd merges with Longmorn-Glenlivet Distilleries Ltd and Hill Thomson & Co. Ltd to form The Glenlivet Distillers Ltd.

History continued:

1978 Seagrams buys The Glenlivet Distillers Ltd. A visitor centre opens.

1996 The visitor centre is expanded, and a multimedia facility installed.

2000 French Oak 12 years and American Oak 12 years are launched

2001 Pernod Ricard and Diageo buy Seagram Spirits & Wine. Pernod Ricard thereby gains control of the Chivas group.

2004 This year sees a lavish relaunch of Glenlivet. French Oak 15 years replaces the previous 12 year old.

2005 Two new duty-free versions are introduced – The Glenlivet 12 year old First Fill and Nadurra. The 1972 Cellar Collection (2,015 bottles) is launched.

2006 Nadurra 16 year old cask strength and 1969 Cellar Collection are released.

2007 Glenlivet XXV is released.

2009 Four more stills are installed and Nadurra Triumph 1991 is released.

2010 Another two stills are commissioned and capacity increases to 10.5 million litres. Glenlivet Founder´s Reserve is released.

2011 Glenlivet Master Distiller´s Reserve is released for the duty free market.

2012 1980 Cellar Collection is released.

2013 The 18 year old Batch Reserve and Glenlivet Alpha are released.

2014 Nadurra Oloroso, Nadurra First Fill Selection, The Glenlivet Guardian´s Chapter and a 50 year old are released.

2015 Founder´s Reserve is released as well as two new expressions for duty free; Solera Vatted and Small Batch.

2016 The Glenlivet Cipher and the second edition of the 50 year old are launched.

2018 Captain´s Reserve and Code are released. A new distillery is commissioned.

Tasting notes Glenlivet 12 year old:

GS – A lovely, honeyed, floral, fragrant nose. Medium-bodied, smooth and malty on the palate, with vanilla sweetness. Not as sweet, however, as the nose might suggest. The finish is pleasantly lengthy and sophisticated.

Tasting notes Glenlivet Founder´s Reserve:

GS – The nose is fresh and floral, with ripe pears, pineapple, tangerines, honey and vanilla. Medium-bodied, with ginger nuts, soft toffee and tropical fruit on the smooth palate. Soft spices and lingering fruitiness in the finish.

Master Distiller´s Reserve Solera Vatted

Master Distiller´s Reserve

The Glenlivet Code

Founder´s Reserve

21 years old Archive

Nàdurra Peated

Captain´s Reserve

12 years old

Glenlossie

[glen•loss•ay]

Owner: Diageo
Region/district: Speyside

Founded: 1876
Status: Active
Capacity: 3 700 000 litres

Address: Birnie, Elgin, Morayshire IV30 8SS

Website: malts.com
Tel: 01343 862000

Glenlossie was closed in January 2018 and production will not resume until April/May 2019. The reason is an extensive upgrade, similar to the one happening at Knockando.

New compressor room, yeast room and control room are all on the list as well as automation of the still house. All electrical equipment, cables, pumps and pipework will be replaced and a general upgrade of buildings will also take place. The only new equipment relating directly to distilling, will be another two washbacks, external and made of stainless steel to complement the existing eight made from larch.

Usually, more washbacks will mean increased capacity but not in this case. The 3.7 million litres were based on working a 7-day week with short fermentations (65 hours). However, the green/oily character of the newmake is dependent on a mix of short and long fermentations (mainly longs at 104 hours) so the additional washbacks will enable the distillery to achieve that character even when they will be working 7 days a week.

After the upgrade, the distillery will be equipped with an 8 ton stainless steel full lauter mash tun, eight washbacks made of larch and two made of stainless steel. There are three pairs of stills with the spirit stills equipped with purifiers between the lyne arms and the condensers, thus increasing the reflux. Next to Glenlossie lies the much younger Mannochmore distillery and except for the two distilleries, a dark grains plant and a bio-plant, the site also holds fourteen warehouses that can store 250,000 casks of maturing whisky.

Together with Glenkinchie and Linkwood, Glenlossie is one of the major contributors to the Haig Gold Label blend. During the early 1970s this famous brand was the first Scotch to sell one million cases (12 million bottles) in a year in the UK alone. A few years ago, the Haig brand was extended with two all-grain versions – Haig Club and Haig Club Clubman. The two whiskies are aimed to the on-trade market for use in cocktails and drinks. The only official bottling of Glenlossie available today is a **10 year old**.

History:

1876 John Duff, former manager at Glendronach Distillery, founds the distillery. Alexander Grigor Allan (to become part-owner of Talisker Distillery), the whisky trader George Thomson and Charles Shirres (both will co-found Longmorn Distillery some 20 years later with John Duff) and H. Mackay are also involved in the company.

1895 The company Glenlossie-Glenlivet Distillery Co. is formed. Alexander Grigor Allan passes away.

1896 John Duff becomes more involved in Longmorn and Mackay takes over management of Glenlossie.

1919 Distillers Company Limited (DCL) takes over the company.

1929 A fire breaks out and causes considerable damage.

1930 DCL transfers operations to Scottish Malt Distillers (SMD).

1962 Stills are increased from four to six.

1971 Another distillery, Mannochmore, is constructed by SMD on the premises. A dark grains plant is installed.

1990 A 10 year old is launched in the Flora & Fauna series.

2010 A Manager´s Choice single cask from 1999 is released.

10 years old

Tasting notes Glenlossie 10 years old:

GS – Cereal, silage and vanilla notes on the relatively light nose, with a voluptuous, sweet palate, offering plums, ginger and barley sugar, plus a hint of oak. The finish is medium in length, with grist and slightly peppery oak.

Whisky
the way I see it

Marc Pendlebury
Founder and owner of
WhiskyBrother

I know your whisky career started with a blog but tell us what led up to that and why you started blogging?

I had been interested in whisky for a while and was spending all my spare time on whisky. Although South Africa is a big whisky market, there weren't regular activities, events, or outlets for a whisky enthusiast, so the blog was a way for me to connect and share my passion with other whisky enthusiasts.

What made you decide to open up a whisky shop in Johannesburg in 2012?

Johannesburg didn't have a dedicated whisky store, and as a whisky consumer I found it frustrating to buy my whisky from general bottle stores who couldn't provide any information or recommendations and lacked variety. I believe whisky is a specialty product that deserves a specialist environment. I knew many other local whisky enthusiasts, who I met through my blog, who felt the same way and so, I decided to take the plunge and try create such a store myself.

A few years later you opened up a bar. What gave you that idea?

As a whisky lover I would never go out to drink whisky because there was nowhere in the city that catered to whisky lovers in terms of selection, pricing, specialisation, service; nor would my whisky friends and customers. I've visited and been inspired by the many amazing whisky bars across the world and always thought it would be great to try to set one up in Joburg.

Since 2017 you also organise The Only Whisky Show in Johannesburg. Please tell us more.

There are a few whisky shows (including the biggest in the world) that tour South Africa, and they all have their audience, but for me, none really captured the smaller dedicated shows that are available in more developed whisky markets. Too often the shows have other alcohols available and/or become a battleground for the big brands and their marketing budgets. I wanted a show that focused exclusively on whisky, provided a level playing field for all exhibitors, had interesting whiskies available for tasting even, if they weren't available in the market, and where whisky enthusiasts could learn and share their passion.

What are your future plans? Expansion into other cities?

I hope and plan to have a presence in other cities, but only in due time. I'm in no hurry. WhiskyBrother's singular focus is whisky, and so, if there is an audience for us that makes it viable to continue expanding, then we will. Outside of that, we have lots of plans but are currently working on increasing the number of exclusive and single cask releases we stock, to provide more variety.

What kind of misconceptions about whisky do you encounter and what is your best advice for a person ready to start their whisky journey?

I suspect the misconceptions I hear in SA are the same all over the world: the peaty taste comes from the water, older is better, blends are not as good, distillery X is better because it's higher/older/newer/more expensive… and so on. One of the misconceptions I don't hear, but have come to realise, is that people think whisky is more expensive than other spirits. I simply don't think that is true. Can it be more expensive? Of course, but it doesn't have to be. With a limited budget you can still participate and engage as a whisky enthusiast – swap samples, attend shows, join/create whisky clubs, buy books/magazines, etc.! Advice wise, it's not groundbreaking but, I recommend malt newcomers try taste as many whiskies as they can and learn about what they are tasting. You can't truly appreciate what's in your glass if you don't know anything about it, and if you can't compare it to other whiskies.

How would you describe the South African whisky scene today?

Whisky is the number one consumed spirit in South Africa, but the market is dominated by big commercial brands that dominate whisky globally. We have millions of "whisky drinkers" who are very brand loyal and drink the same whisky all the time but know very little about it. Thankfully there is a small, but ever growing, dedicated community of whisky enthusiasts across the country who are passionate about whisky and are always looking to try new things. These are the people WhiskyBrother caters to.

In 2017 you became a Keeper of the Quaich. Please tell us what that is and what it means to you.

The Keepers of the Quaich is an international, invite-only society that recognises individuals who have shown outstanding commitment to the Scotch Whisky industry. It is by far the greatest honour I have received, and one I am still not wholly sure I deserve (just yet- but I'll keep trying!). To be in the same company as the legends of the Scotch whisky industry is incredibly humbling, particularly for a small South African whisky company.

What does Scotch whisky mean to you?

Very simply, scotch (and whisky in general) is my life. Apart from the fact it is my livelihood, it is my passion and drive. As ridiculous as it may sound, if I had more time in my day, I would spend it on whisky. Whisky connects me to a whole world of wonderful people, fascinating history, an incredible production process, and an unmatched array and depth of flavours.

The history of Scotch whisky has had its ups and downs over the years. How do you see the future for Scotch in the next 10-15 years?

The next decade and a half will be very interesting as we see the multitude of new distilleries get their products to market, and consumers can decide based on the quality of the product, not just speculators spending absurd amounts on first releases on auctions. I don't think all these new producers will find a market and it's inevitable others will join the stables of the big multi-national companies. I do, however, hope that the increased competition and capacity, of both new and existing distilleries, will allow prices to normalise.

Glenmorangie

[glen•<u>mor</u>•run•jee]

Owner:
The Glenmorangie Co
(Moët Hennessy)

Region/district:
Northern Highlands

Founded: 1843
Status: Active (vc)
Capacity: 6 000 000 litres

Address: Tain, Ross-shire IV19 1PZ

Website:
glenmorangie.com

Tel:
01862 892477 (vc)

In January 2018, the owners of Glenmorangie announced that they were about to expand the distillery´s capacity. Glenmorangie couldn't have started the celebration of their 175th Anniversary in a better way.

The expansion may not be as grandiose as the ones happening at certain competitors, (Glenfiddich, Glenlivet and Macallan), but on the other hand, it's only been nine years since the distillery last increased its capacity. The planned expansion will take the capacity from 6 to 7 million litres and the work is expected to be completed in 2019. In 2017 Glenmorangie took a significant step towards a more sustainable production when an anaerobic digestion plant was installed, where microorganisms break down by-products such as pot ale and spent lees. Since 2007 Glenmorangie has held the 4th spot amongst the world's most sold single malts and over that time they have increased sales volumes with 60%. For the past three years, volumes have been pretty stable – around 6 million bottles per year.

The distillery is currently equipped with a full lauter mash tun with a charge of 10 tons, 12 stainless steel washbacks with a fermentation time of 52 hours and six pairs of stills. They are the tallest in Scotland and the still room is one of the most magnificent to be seen. Production for 2018 will be 28 mashes per week which equates to 5.5 million litres in the year. A new stillhouse with space for two additional stills is being built at the moment together with a building which will house two more washbacks.

The core range consists of **Original** (10 year old), **18 year old** and three 12 year old wood finishes: **Quinta Ruban** (port), **Nectar D´Or** (Sauternes) and **Lasanta** (sherry). Included in the core range is also **Signet**. For a while, the **25 year old** was discontinued but it is now back in the range. A series of bottlings, called Private Edition, started in 2009 with the release of the sherried **Sonnalta PX**. This has been followed up once a year with Finealta, Artein, Ealanta, Companta, Tùsail, Milsean and Bacalta. The new release for 2018 was **Spìos**. The bottling is an exciting experiment where the whisky has been matured fully in first-fill American oak that previously contained rye whiskey. For the travel retail market, there is **Dornoch, Duthac, Tayne, Tarlogan** and a **19 year old**. In January 2018 **Cadboll** was added to the range. Matured in ex-bourbon casks, the whisky was then finished in barriques that had been used to hold Muscat and Sémillon wines. In 2016, the first bottling in a new series of vintage malts (Bond House No. 1) was released - **Grand Vintage Malt 1990**. This was followed in spring 2018 by **Grand Vintage Malt 1989** and in autumn by **Grand Vintage Malt 1993** with a 15 year extra maturation in ex-Madeira casks. Other recent limited releases include the re-launched **Astar**, **A Midwinter night´s Dram** and **Glenmorangie Pride 1974** - the oldest Glenmorangie so far. To celebrate the 175th anniversary, a **16 year old** single first-fill ex-bourbon cask, bottled at 53.1%, was released in June 2018.

History:

1843 William Mathesen applies for a license for a farm distillery called Morangie, which is rebuilt by them. Production took place here in 1738, and possibly since 1703.

1849 Production starts in November.

1880 Exports to foreign destinations such as Rome and San Francisco commence.

1887 The distillery is rebuilt and Glenmorangie Distillery Company Ltd is formed.

1918 40% of the distillery is sold to Macdonald & Muir Ltd and 60 % to the whisky dealer Durham. Macdonald & Muir takes over Durham's share by the late thirties.

1931 The distillery closes.

1936 Production restarts in November.

1980 Number of stills increases from two to four and own maltings ceases.

1990 The number of stills is doubled to eight.

1994 A visitor centre opens. September sees the launch of Glenmorangie Port Wood Finish which marks the start of a number of different wood finishes.

1995 Glenmorangie´s Tain l´Hermitage (Rhone wine) is launched.

1996 Two different wood finishes are launched, Madeira and Sherry. Glenmorangie plc is formed.

1997 A museum opens.

2001 A limited edition of a cask strength port wood finish is released in July, Cote de Beaune Wood Finish is launched in September and Three Cask (ex-Bourbon, charred oak and ex-Rioja) is launched in October for Sainsbury's.

2002 A Sauternes finish, a 20 year Glenmorangie with two and a half years in Sauternes casks, is launched.

History continued:

2003 Burgundy Wood Finish is launched in July and a limited edition of cask strength Madeira-matured (i. e. not just finished) in August.

2004 Glenmorangie buys the Scotch Malt Whisky Society. The Macdonald family decides to sell Glenmorangie plc (including the distilleries Glenmorangie, Glen Moray and Ardbeg) to Moët Hennessy at £300 million. A new version of Glenmorangie Tain l´Hermitage (28 years) is released and Glenmorangie Artisan Cask is launched in November.

2005 A 30 year old is launched.

2007 The entire range gets a complete makeover with 15 and 30 year olds being discontinued and the rest given new names as well as new packaging.

2008 An expansion of production capacity is started. Astar and Signet are launched.

2009 The expansion is finished and Sonnalta PX is released for duty free.

2010 Glenmorangie Finealta is released.

2011 28 year old Glenmorangie Pride is released.

2012 Glenmorangie Artein is released.

2013 Glenmorangie Ealanta is released.

2014 Companta, Taghta and Dornoch are released.

2015 Túsail and Duthac are released.

2016 Milsean, Tayne and Tarlogan are released.

2017 Bacalta, Astar and Pride 1974 are released.

2018 Spios, Cadboll and Grand Vintage Malt 1989 are released.

Tasting notes Glenmorangie Original 10 year old:

GS – The nose offers fresh fruits, butterscotch and toffee. Silky smooth in the mouth, mild spice, vanilla, and well-defined toffee. The fruity finish has a final flourish of ginger.

Spios

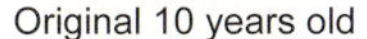

19 years old

Cadboll

Original 10 years old

Astar

Nectar D´Or

Glen Moray

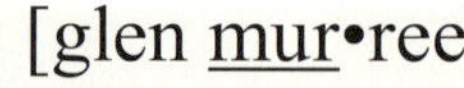

[glen mur•ree]

Owner:
La Martiniquaise (COFEPP)

Region/district:
Speyside

Founded: 1897

Status: Active (vc)

Capacity: 5 700 000 litres

Address: Bruceland Road, Elgin,
Morayshire IV30 1YE

Website:
glenmoray.com

Tel:
01343 542577

Ten years ago, Glen Moray saw a change in owner-ship from one French company to another. The effect couldn't have been greater. From a life in the sha-dows of Glenmorangie and Ardbeg to a place in the sun with a substantial range and increased capacity.

Celebrating its 120th anniversary last year, the distillery has seen an increase in sales of 22% in the last two years to reach 1.5 mil-lion bottles in 2017. The owners, La Martiniquaise, is the second largest spirits business in France after Pernod Ricard and they've also shown rapid growth in recent years. In 2016, the turnover reached a symbolic €1bn. Significant brands on the whisky side include two Scotch blends, Label 5 and Sir Edward's, both just below the Top 10 blends in the world.

Since 2016, the distillery is equipped with an 11 ton full lauter mash tun. There are 14 stainless steel washbacks placed outside with a fermentation time of 50-60 hours and nine stills. The three old wash stills were converted to spirit stills which make it a total of six and three new wash stills were constructed by Frilli in Italy. The current capacity is 5.7 million litres of alcohol, but the owners have the option of reintroducing the old mash tun, adding a few more washbacks and two more wash stills which would increase the capacity to 8.9 million litres. In 2018, the distillery will be producing 4.8 million litres, of which 200,000 litres will be heavily peated (50ppm) spirit.

The core range consists of **Classic, Classic Port Finish, Classic Chardonnay Finish, Classic Sherry Finish** and **Classic Peated**. Furthermore, we can also find a **12, 15** and **18 year old**. A new expression was released in the UK in autumn 2018 - **10 year old Fired Oak** with some of the spirit matured in virgin oak while the rest came from ex-bourbon casks. Also in the pipeline is a no age statement version with a two year **finish in cider casks**. Recent limited releases include batch 4 of the **25 year old Port finish** and, to celebrate last year's 120th anniversary, **Glen Moray Mastery**, a vatting of five different vintages. Finally, a **1998 PX finish** and a **2010 Peated PX finish** can be found exclusively at the visitor centre.

History:

1897 Elgin West Brewery, dated 1830, is reconstructed as Glen Moray Distillery.

1910 The distillery closes.

1920 Financial troubles force the distillery to be put up for sale. Buyer is Macdonald & Muir.

1923 Production restarts.

1958 A reconstruction takes place and the floor maltings are replaced by a Saladin box.

1978 Own maltings are terminated.

1979 Number of stills is increased to four.

1996 Macdonald & Muir Ltd changes name to Glenmorangie plc.

1999 Three wood finishes are introduced - Chardonnay (no age) and Chenin Blanc (12 and 16 years respectively).

2004 Louis Vuitton Moët Hennessy buys Glenmorangie plc and a 1986 cask strength, a 20 and a 30 year old are released.

2006 Two vintages, 1963 and 1964, and a new Manager's Choice are released.

2007 New edition of Mountain Oak is released.

2008 The distillery is sold to La Martiniquaise.

2009 A 14 year old Port finish and an 8 year old matured in red wines casks are released.

2011 Two cask finishes and a 10 year old Chardonnay maturation are released.

2012 A 2003 Chenin Blanc is released.

2013 A 25 year old port finish is released.

2014 Glen Moray Classic Port Finish is released.

2015 Glen Moray Classic Peated is released.

2016 Classic Chardonnay Finish and Classic Sherry Finish are released as well as a 15 and an 18 year old.

2017 Glen Moray Mastery is launched.

2018 10 year old Fired Oak is released.

12 years old

Tasting notes Glen Moray 12 years old:

GS – Mellow on the nose, with vanilla, pear drops and some oak. Smooth in the mouth, with spicy malt, vanilla and summer fruits. The finish is relatively short, with spicy fruit.

Glen Ord

[glen ord]

Owner: Diageo
Region/district: Northern Highlands
Founded: 1838
Status: Active (vc)
Capacity: 11 000 000 litres
Address: Muir of Ord, Ross-shire IV6 7UJ
Website: malts.com
Tel: 01463 872004 (vc)

The single malt from Glen Ord is sold under the brand name The Singleton together with two other whiskies – Glendullan and Dufftown. Introduced just 12 years ago, the brand has become the best-selling single malt in the Diageo range.

A total of 6.2 million bottles were sold in 2017. The owners never reveal sales figures separately for the three sub brands but it´s no secret that Glen Ord is number one, available mainly in Asia and at the distillery visitor centre. Glen Ord is probably the only distillery in Scotland which over the years has had three types of maltings on site – from the traditional floor maltings via Saladin boxes to the drum maltings which are used today. The barley is soaked for two days in 18 steeping vessels and then germinated for four days in the 18 drums. There are four kilns to dry the malt – two that are always used for unpeated production and two where they exchange between using peat and hot air. The total capacity is 45,000 tons per year and, apart for their own need, they produce malt mainly for Talisker but also for a few other Diageo distilleries. Recently, with Port Ellen maltings closed for maintenance, they also deliver malt to Caol Ila and Lagavulin.

Since 2011, Glen Ord distillery has been expanded rapidly in several stages and with the latest expansion in 2015, the distillery now has a capacity of 11 million litres. The complete set of equipment comprises of two stainless steel mashtuns, each with a 12.5 ton mash. There are 22 wooden washbacks with a fermentation time of 75 hours and no less than 14 stills.

The core range is the **Singleton of Glen Ord 12, 15 and 18 year old**. A sub-range, The Singleton Reserve Collection, is exclusive to duty free and consists of **Signature, Trinité, Liberté** and **Artisan**. The Forgotten Drops Series was created in 2017 for both Glen Ord and Glendullan with the aim to present old and limited releases. The first for Glen Ord was a **41 year old**, the oldest whisky ever released from the distillery. Two more expression in the series are expected in autumn 2018 and 2019 respectively. A 14 year old also appeared in the 2018 Special Releases.

History:

1838 Thomas Mackenzie founds the distillery.

1855 Alexander MacLennan and Thomas McGregor buy the distillery.

1870 Alexander MacLennan dies and the distillery is taken over by his widow who marries the banker Alexander Mackenzie.

1877 Alexander Mackenzie leases the distillery.

1878 Alexander Mackenzie builds a new still house and barely manages to start production before a fire destroys it.

1896 Alexander Mackenzie dies and the distillery is sold to James Watson & Co. for £15,800.

1923 John Jabez Watson, James Watson's son, dies and the distillery is sold to John Dewar & Sons. The name changes from Glen Oran to Glen Ord.

1961 A Saladin box is installed.

1966 The two stills are increased to six.

1968 Drum maltings is built.

1983 Malting in the Saladin box ceases.

1988 A visitor centre is opened.

2002 A 12 year old is launched.

2003 A 28 year old cask strength is released.

2004 A 25 year old is launched.

2005 A 30 year old is launched as a Special Release from Diageo.

2006 A 12 year old Singleton of Glen Ord is launched.

2010 A Singleton of Glen Ord 15 year old is released in Taiwan.

2011 Two more washbacks are installed, increasing the capacity by 25%.

2012 Singleton of Glen Ord cask strength is released.

2013 Singleton of Glen Ord Signature, Trinité, Liberté and Artisan are launched.

2015 The Master´s Casks 40 years old is released.

2017 A 41 year old reserved for Asia is released.

2018 A 14 year old triple-matured is launched as part of the Special Releases.

14 years old

Tasting notes Glen Ord 12 years old:

GS – Honeyed malt and milk chocolate on the nose, with a hint of orange. These characteristics carry over onto the sweet, easy-drinking palate, along with a biscuity note. Subtly drying, with a medium-length, spicy finish.

Glenrothes

[glen•roth•iss]

Owner:	Region/district:
The Edrington Group	Speyside
(the brand is owned by Berry Bros)	

Founded:	Status:	Capacity:
1878	Active	5 600 000 litres

Address: Rothes, Morayshire AB38 7AA

Website:	Tel:
theglenrothes.com	01340 872300

Bottling according to vintage, like they do in the wine business, is a rare bird in the whisky world. The first distillery who introduced it, and one of just two that practice it, was Glenrothes and now they have decided to abandon the procedure.

Actually, Glenrothes single malt hasn´t been available as an official bottling for that long. It was launched in 1987 as a 12 year old. Seven years later, the brand owners at the time, Berry Brothers, made the bold step to start releasing vintages. The only other distillery that followed suit a few years later was Balblair. Bottling by vintage definitely made Glenrothes stand out but in 2008, the owners decided to complement the range by releasing expressions without vintage. The first one was Robur Reserve and this was followed by other bottlings. In 2017, Edrington reclaimed ownership of the brand after seven years with Berry Brothers at the helm. One year later, the new owners declared that vintages are now a thing of the past and a new range with age statements was launched in September 2018.

Glenrothes distillery is equipped with a 5.5 ton stainless steel full lauter mash tun. Twelve washbacks made of Oregon pine are in one room, whilst an adjacent tun room houses eight stainless steel washbacks – all of them with a 58 hour fermentation time. The magnificent still house has five pairs of stills performing a very slow distillation. In 2018, the distillery will be doing 44 mashes per week, producing just over 4 million litres of alcohol.

All the old expressions in the core range have disappeared and the same goes for the vintages. They have been replaced by Soleo Collection which is based on whiskies that have matured 100% in sherry casks. The range consists of **10 year old, 12 year old, Whisky Maker´s Cut, 18 year old** and **25 year old**. There is also a second range in the pipeline called **Aqua Collection** which will be sold on-line. The current duty free range will continue until September 2019; **Robur Reserve, Manse Reserve, Elder´s Reserve, Minister´s Reserve** and the **25 year old Ancestor´s Reserve**.

History:

1878 James Stuart & Co. begins planning the new distillery with Robert Dick, William Grant and John Cruickshank as partners.

1879 Production starts in December.

1884 The distillery changes name to Glenrothes-Glenlivet.

1887 William Grant & Co. joins forces with Islay Distillery Co. and forms Highland Distillers Company.

1897 A fire ravages the distillery.

1903 An explosion causes substantial damage.

1963 Expansion from four to six stills.

1980 Expansion from six to eight stills.

1989 Expansion from eight to ten stills.

1999 Edrington and William Grant & Sons buy Highland Distillers.

2002 Four single casks from 1966/1967 are launched.

2005 A 30 year old is launched together with Select Reserve and Vintage 1985.

2008 1978 Vintage and Robur Reserve are launched.

2009 The Glenrothes John Ramsay, Alba Reserve and Three Decades are released.

2010 Berry Brothers takes over the brand.

2011 Editor´s Casks are released.

2013 2001 Vintage and the Manse Brae range are released.

2014 Sherry Cask Reserve and 1969 Extraordinary Cask are released.

2015 Glenrothes Vintage Single Malt is released.

2016 Peated Cask Reserve and Ancestor´s Reserve are released.

2017 The brand returns to Edrington and The Glenrothes Wine Merchant´s Collection is introduced.

2018 The entire range is revamped and four new bottlings with age statements are introduced.

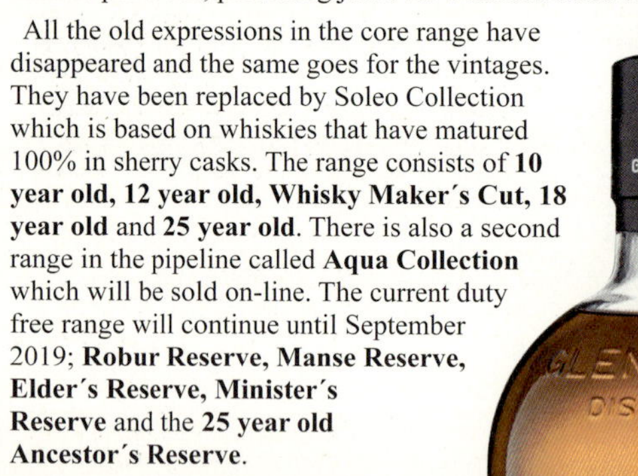

12 years old

Tasting notes Glenrothes Soleo 12 year old:

IR – Fresh and fruity on the nose with notes of strawberries/raspberries and a hint of cinnamon. The taste if fruity and spicy with notes of pear, cinnamon, nutmeg, lemon zest and, in the finish, brown sugar and a little ginger.

Whisky
the way I see it

Tristan Stephenson
Whisky entrepreneur and author

Your CV includes job titles such as bartender, writer, barista, whisky ambassador, spirits consultant etc. What is the common denominator here?

I guess the link between everything I do is flavour. I'm fascinated by taste and flavour and every time my career has shifted in direction it has been thanks to my own curiosities that surround flavour — how we experience it, how we manipulate it, and how we communicate it.

There are such strong links between the industries I have been involved in from both a flavour and science perspective. The way a steak cooks on a barbecue has links to how a coffee bean roasts, how peat reek is produced and why direct-fired stills produce a different style of new make spirit. I've found that a broader understanding of mechanisms such as these has given me a finer appreciation of their effects on a finished product.

You were the co-founder of Fluid Movement, an attempt to challenge the stuffines of the on-trade business. One of the ways was the opening of Black Rock bar in London. What distinguishes that bar from others?

The aim of Black Rock was to do away with the dogma that many people see when they think about whisky. We wanted to democratise whisky and create a space that was accepting of new initiates and aficionados alike. At virtually every turn during the design stages we challenged ourselves to think of the first principles of enjoying a glass of whisky, and then attempted to weave that in to the fabric of the bar.

We have filtered running water taps on every table; the mood and lighting of the bar are more akin to a hip-hop club than a 'traditional' whisky bar; and the whole room is dominated by a 5 ton English oak tree trunk that seats up to 20 people and houses two cocktail maturation channels that sit within the table itself.

But perhaps the most important thing about Black Rock is our commitment to demystifying whisky flavour. We believe that flamboyant language has its place in the category, but for many people, simplicity is the key to appreciation. All of our whiskies in Black Rock are organised by flavour, each sitting in one of six cabinets: smoke, fruit, fragrance, balance, sweet and spicy. Whiskies that sit higher in the cabinet are lighter in style and whiskies that sit lower in the cabinet are heavier. This allows guests to select a product based entirely on it flavour profile rather than by its country of origin or region, which in these days of increased variety and innovation, often means very little in the context of flavour.

After that you launched Whisky Me. What is that and what made you do it?

Whisky Me was less an idea than it was the next obvious step down this pathway of malt whisky demystification (I might yet claim the word 'dewhyskification/dewhiskyfication'!) by getting good quality product in to the hands of those who want to learn more but feel the category is too elitist (and too expensive) to gain a foot holding.

Convenience culture will become a growing trend in alcohol over the next few years. We are seeing it already in deliveries-to-your-door and a growing range of RTD products, and I think there's opportunities for spirits too. Whisky Me delivers a PET pouch of single malt whisky through your letterbox every month for £7. We fill the pouches with whisky that we genuinely enjoy and the expressions tend to be 15yo and over and typically retail for £60 a bottle. The service is backed up by a 1-minute video of the distillery that we shoot on location with our drone. The branding is disruptive in so far as it doesn't conform to what you might consider 'traditional' malt whisky packaging and it is designed to be that way. We prefer to let the liquid do the talking, which is as it should be.

The whisky industry is often talking about how to reach the Millenials or Generation Y or whatever you wan´t to call them. In your opinion, what´s the best way of getting the young generation interested in whisky?

I think the best way to engage with any demographic is to speak their language without patronising. Millenials and Gen Y seek value and provenance in the products they buy. Provenance isn't a problem where whisky is concerned, but value is trickier. That's because value is contingent on balancing price with appreciation. If you don't appreciate a product you will never find value in it. That's why the education piece is so important to whisky.

Your work is very much centred around finding new ways of enjoying spirits yet at the same time you devote a lot of space in your book An Odyssey of Malt, Bourbon and Rye Whiskies to history. How important is the history and tradition to Scotch whisky?

I think that history is simply another way that we can appreciate the value of whisky. Understanding where a product has come from, how geography has conspired with economic and socio-political events to have shaped its flavour, who the people were that made it, and how a distillery has evolved over the years. These things add value to a product and hopefully give us a reason to pause and reflect when we're enjoying a glass.

What does Scotch whisky mean to you?

I consider myself an amateur historian and scientist. Whisky combines both of those passions perfectly and not only that, it tastes delicious too!

The history of Scotch whisky has had its ups and downs over the years. How do you see the future for Scotch in the next 10-15 years?

Besides that which I have already mentioned, I see Scotch continuing its return back in to mixed drinks. When I first began bartending, I rarely made scotch cocktails and by request of the guest I would typically would only mix it with soda or ginger. We are now seeing a much welcomed return of the whisky highball, which has inspired bartenders to riff new and ingenious variants. Single malt whisky is no longer so sacrosanct that we can't mix it and as result there are some incredible malt whisky cocktails being turned out of the top bars. I think that scotch, with its Scottish provenance, depth and breadth of flavours, and rich histoy, has the potential rise up as the next big mixing spirit…in the UK at least.

Glen Scotia

[glen sko•sha]

Owner:
Loch Lomond Group
(majority owner Exponent)

Region/district:
Campbeltown

Founded: 1832
Status: Active (vc)
Capacity: 800 000 litres

Address: High Street, Campbeltown, Argyll PA28 6DS

Website: glenscotia.com
Tel: 01586 552288

It takes time and a bit of planning to visit the three distilleries in the remote Campbeltown. For those who find the journey too long, the owners of Glen Scotia have come up wth a solution. They bring the experience to the consumer.

The Glen Scotia Grand Tour, which kicked off in London in March 2018, is an interactive pop-up event which reproduces the distillery and the surroundings through props, virtual projections and, of course, a selection of Glen Scotia single malt. After London, the tour will be rolled out internationally to other countries including the USA.

Glen Scotia is equipped with a traditional 2.8 ton cast iron mash tun, nine washbacks made of stainless steel with an average fermentation time of 120 hours and one pair of stills. The shortest fermentation time is 70 hours but can reach over 100 hours. For some years, the distillery had a very short middle cut, starting to collect the spirit at 71% and stopping at 68%. This has now changed and they come off spirit at 63%, at least for the unpeated distillations. The production in 2018 will be 10 mashes per week resulting in 520,000 litres of pure alcohol, of which 10% is a combination of medium peated (20ppm) and heavily peated (55ppm) spirit. At the moment, the distillery is working on a transition from heavy fuel oil to LPG gas for the boiler.

The range was revamped in spring 2015 and the core bottlings are now **Double Cask** (matured in bourbon casks and with a 3-4 months finish in PX sherry), **15 year old** (finished in oloroso casks), **18 year old** (finished in oloroso casks), **25 year old** (matured in ex-bourbon casks and married for 12 months in first fill bourbon) and the gently peated **Victoriana** which has been bottled at cask strength. The owners also released the first bottlings for duty free in 2017; the **Glen Scotia Campbeltown 1832** finished in PX sherry casks and a **16 year old**. A number of **single cask** bottlings available only at the distillery, have been released, most of them in connection with the open day of the distillery in May every year.

History:

1832 The families of Stewart and Galbraith start Scotia Distillery.

1895 The distillery is sold to Duncan McCallum.

1919 Sold to West Highland Malt Distillers.

1924 West Highland Malt Distillers goes bankrupt and Duncan MacCallum buys back the distillery.

1928 The distillery closes.

1930 Duncan MacCallum commits suicide and the Bloch brothers take over.

1933 Production restarts.

1954 Hiram Walker takes over.

1955 A. Gillies & Co. becomes new owner.

1970 A. Gillies & Co. becomes part of Amalgated Distillers Products.

1979 Reconstruction takes place.

1984 The distillery closes.

1989 Amalgated Distillers Products is taken over by Gibson International and production restarts.

1994 Glen Catrine Bonded Warehouse Ltd takes over and the distillery is mothballed.

1999 The distillery re-starts under Loch Lomond Distillery supervision using labour from Springbank.

2000 Loch Lomond Distillers runs operations with its own staff from May onwards.

2005 A 12 year old is released.

2006 A peated version is released.

2012 A new range (10, 12, 16, 18 and 21 year old) is launched.

2014 A 10 year old and one without age statement are released - both heavily peated.

2015 A new range is released; Double Cask, 15 year old and Victoriana.

2017 A 25 year old and an 18 year old as well as two bottlings for duty-free are released.

Double Cask

Tasting notes Glen Scotia Double Cask:

GS – The nose is sweet, with bramble and redcurrant aromas, plus caramel and vanilla. Smooth mouth-feel, with ginger, sherry and more vanilla. The finish is quite long, with spicy sherry and a final hint of brine.

Glen Spey

[glen <u>spey</u>]

Owner:
Diageo

Region/district:
Speyside

Founded: 1878

Status: Active

Capacity: 1 400 000 litres

Address: Rothes, Morayshire AB38 7AU

Website:
malts.com

Tel:
01340 831215

Of the four distilleries located in Rothes, found between Dufftown and Elgin, Glen Grant is the largest with a magnificent visitor centre and a world famous brand of single malt.

Glenrothes has dedicated fans that couldn't imagine missing out on a new bottling from the distillery and Speyburn single malt was recently re-launched at the same time as the distillery's capacity was doubled. The fourth distillery on the other hand, Glen Spey, doesn't make much noise. With the least capacity of the four and a very frugal bottling of their single malt, it's one of the lesser known distilleries in Scotland. It was built in 1878, the same year as the neighbouring Glenrothes and the initiator of the two projects was James Stuart who, at that time, ran Macallan distillery. He withdrew from the construction of Glenrothes at an early stage and focused on Glen Spey instead. Twenty years later it became the first distillery in Scotland to be bought by an English company, W&A Gilbey, who then went on to buy Knockando and Strathmill

The distillery is equipped with a 4.4 ton semi-lauter mash tun, eight stainless steel washbacks with both short (46 hours) and long (100 hours) fermentations and two pairs of stills. Heating of the stills is usually made by using internal coils or pans but the wash stills at Glen Spey have radiators. The two spirit stills are equipped with purifiers which add reflux and also help eliminate the heavier esters. Due to a cloudy wort, the Glen Spey new make is nutty and slightly oily. Even though a new control room was installed in 2017, Glen Spey is still run largely as a manual distillery. In 2017, the distillery will be doing 18 mashes per week (ten short and eight long) and 1.5 million litres of pure alcohol in the year.

The single malt from Glen Spey has its biggest importance in the blend J&B, where it is one of the signature malts and the only official single malt is the **12 year old Flora & Fauna** bottling. In 2010, two limited releases were made – a **1996 single cask** from new American Oak and a **21 year old** with maturation in ex-sherry American oak.

History:

1878 James Stuart & Co. founds the distillery which becomes known by the name Mill of Rothes.

1886 James Stuart buys Macallan.

1887 W. & A. Gilbey buys the distillery for £11,000 thus becoming the first English company to buy a Scottish malt distillery.

1920 A fire breaks out and the main part of the distillery is re-built.

1962 W. & A. Gilbey combines forces with United Wine Traders and forms International Distillers & Vintners (IDV).

1970 The stills are increased from two to four.

1972 IDV is bought by Watney Mann which is then acquired by Grand Metropolitan.

1997 Guiness and Grand Metropolitan merge to form Diageo.

2001 A 12 year old is launched in the Flora & Fauna series.

2010 A 21 year old is released as part of the Special Releases and a 1996 Manager´s Choice single cask is launched.

12 years old

Tasting notes Glen Spey 12 years old:

GS – Tropical fruits and malt on the comparatively delicate nose. Medium-bodied with fresh fruits and vanilla toffee on the palate, becoming steadily nuttier and drier in a gently oaky, mildly smoky finish.

Glentauchers

[glen•tock•ers]

Owner:
Chivas Brothers
(Pernod Ricard)

Region/district:
Speyside

Founded: 1897
Status: Active
Capacity: 4 200 000 litres

Address: Mulben, Keith, Banffshire AB55 6YL

Website:
-

Tel:
01542 860272

The name James Buchanan in intricably linked with Glentauchers distillery. He became one of the great whisky barons in the late 1800s and unlike the majority of his competitors, who had inherited their position from their fathers, he was a selfmade man.

The fact that he was unburdend by the inheritence of a family business clearly worked in his favour. Unbiased and unrestricted he anaylised the preferences of the English customers. His conclusion was that a soft and delicate blend would be prefered over the more flavourful and inconsistent self whisky (as single malts were called at the time). His Buchanan Blend became a success and in 1895 he secured a Royal Warrant from Queen Victoria and the Prince of Wales. Two years later, together with his business partner and mentor W P Lowrie, he opened his first distillery, Glentauchers, to secure his needs for malt whisky. Later on, he would become the owner of two more distilleries – Bankier and Convalmore. In the beginning of the 20th century, he was the owner of the biggest one-man whisky business in the world!

The distillery is equipped with a 12.2 ton stainless steel full lauter mash tun. There are six washbacks made of Oregon pine and three pairs of stills. The distillery is now doing 18 mashes per week and a total of 4 million litres per year. Most of the process at Glentaucher´s is done mechanically using traditional methods. The thought behind this is that new employees and trainees from Chivas Brothers will be able to work here for a while to learn the basic techniques of whisky production.

The role of Glentauchers has always been to produce malt whisky for blends - first for Buchanans Black & White, later on for Teachers and today it is an integral part of Ballantines. Official bottlings have been more or less non-existent but in 2017 a **15 year old** was launched as a part of the Ballantine´s Single Malt Series (together with Glenburgie and Miltonduff). There is also a **15 year Distillery Reserve Collection**, exclusively sold at Chivas´ visitor centres.

History:

1897 James Buchanan and W. P. Lowrie, a whisky merchant from Glasgow, found the distillery.

1898 Production starts.

1906 James Buchanan & Co. takes over the whole distillery and acquires an 80% share in W. P. Lowrie & Co.

1915 James Buchanan & Co. merges with Dewars.

1923 Mashing house and maltings are rebuilt.

1925 Buchanan-Dewars joins Distillers Company Limited (DCL).

1930 Glentauchers is transferred to Scottish Malt Distillers (SMD).

1965 The number of stills is increased from two to six.

1969 Floor maltings is decommissioned.

1985 DCL mothballs the distillery.

1989 United Distillers (formerly DCL) sells the distillery to Caledonian Malt Whisky Distillers, a subsidiary of Allied Distillers.

1992 Production recommences in August.

2000 A 15 year old Glentauchers is released.

2005 Chivas Brothers (Pernod Ricard) become the new owner through the acquisition of Allied Domecq.

2017 A 15 year old is released in the Ballantine´s Single Malt Series.

15 years old

Tasting notes Glentauchers 15 years old:

IR – Delicious on the nose, both floral and fruity, vanilla, pastry, heather and honey. Still fruity on the palate with additional notes of roasted nuts, toffee and milk chocolate..

Glenturret

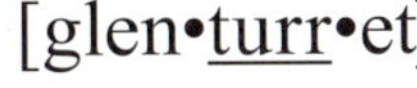

[glen•turr•et]

Owner: The Edrington Group

Region/district: Southern Highlands

Founded: 1775

Status: Active (vc)

Capacity: 340 000 litres

Address: The Hosh, Crieff, Perthshire PH7 4HA

Website: theglenturret.com

Tel: 01764 656565

When a distillery changes hands, it is often an affair between two companies already involved in the spirits business. In the case of closed distilleries being re-opened, the picture is quite often another.

Recent examples are yoghurt millionaire David Prior taking over Bladnoch and the Dutch-based investment company Scaent buying Glenglassaugh. From the 1950s we have perhaps the best example of a private person saving a distillery for posterity. By 1957, Glenturret had been closed for more than 30 years. Enter James Fairlie who bought the buildings and managed to find second hand equipment at Tullibardine. Fairlie did have some background in the whisky business, having worked at a blending company in Glasgow but it was as a whisky enthusiast he had fallen in love with the old site. His idea was to make a malt whisky using traditional methods. In that sense he was very much a pioneer of today's craft movement. Following a surprising announcement in June 2018 by the owners, Edrington, it now remains to be seen who will be the next owner. The distillery has been put up for sale and this also means that the well-known visitor centre The Famous Grouse Experience, receiving more than 70,000 visitors every year, will be closing. The Famous Grouse blend though will still remain with Edrington.

Glenturret is equipped with a stainless steel, open mash tun, the only one left in Scotland where the mash is stirred by hand. There are eight Douglas fir washbacks with a fermentation time of up to 120 hours and one pair of stills. From April 2018 to March 2019, the distillery will be producing 170,000 litres of alcohol. The main part of this, 140,000 litres, will be unpeated Glenturret, while the remaining part is made up of the heavily peated (80ppm in the barley) Ruadh Maor, which is used mainly for blends.

The core range consists of **10 year old, Glenturret Sherry, Glenturret Triple Wood** and **Glenturret Peated**. Recent limited releases include two 29 year olds - **Cameron´s Cut** and **Jamieson´s Jigger Edition** - as well as the **Peated Drummond Edition**, 100% peated Glenturret, bottled at cask strength and available only at the distillery.

History:

1775 Whisky smugglers establish a small illicit farm distillery named Hosh Distillery.

1818 John Drummond is licensee until 1837.

1826 A distillery in the vicinity is named Glenturret, but is decommissioned before 1852.

1852 John McCallum is licensee until 1874.

1875 Hosh Distillery takes over the name Glenturret Distillery and is managed by Thomas Stewart.

1903 Mitchell Bros Ltd takes over.

1921 Production ceases and the buildings are used for whisky storage only.

1929 Mitchell Bros Ltd is liquidated, the distillery dismantled and the facilities are used as storage for agricultural needs.

1957 James Fairlie buys the distillery and re-equips it.

1959 Production restarts.

1981 Remy-Cointreau buys the distillery and invests in a visitor centre.

1990 Highland Distillers takes over.

1999 Edrington and William Grant & Sons buy Highland Distillers for £601 million. The purchasing company, 1887 Company, is a joint venture between Edrington (70%) and William Grant (30%).

2002 The Famous Grouse Experience, a visitor centre costing £2.5 million, is inaugurated.

2003 A 10 year old Glenturret replaces the 12 year old as the distillery´s standard release.

2007 Three new single casks are released.

2013 An 18 year old bottled at cask strength is released as a distillery exclusive.

2014 A 1986 single cask is released.

2015 Sherry, Triple Wood and Peated are released.

2016 Fly´s 16 Masters is released.

2017 Cameron´s Cut, Jamieson´s Jigger Edition and Peated Drummond Edition are launched.

10 years old

Tasting notes Glenturret 10 years old:

GS – Nutty and slightly oily on the nose, with barley and citrus fruits. Sweet and honeyed on the full, fruity palate, with a balancing note of oak. Medium length in the sweet finish.

Highland Park

[hi•land park]

Owner:
The Edrington Group

Region/district:
Highlands (Orkney)

Founded: 1798
Status: Active (vc)
Capacity: 2 500 000 litres

Address: Holm Road, Kirkwall, Orkney KW15 1SU

Website: highlandparkwhisky.com
Tel: 01856 874619

Highland Park is doing well at the moment. If we back up five years, the brand was suffering from lower sales volumes. There was a considerable shortage of whiskies aged 10-15 years in the warehouses due to an irregular production in the late 1990s.

This problem is now history. Sales in 2017 increased by 24% and reached the highest level ever – 1.7 million bottles! The rebranding of the entire core range as well as an unprecedented release of completely new expressions during 2017, probably helped boost the figures. The character of Highland Park single malt relies heavily on the peat that they are using to dry the malt. As opposed to mainland malt where trees have played an important part and Islay malt which is influenced by trees but also marine vegetation, Orkney malt is characterised by the presence of heather and this gives the matured whisky a different and lighter phenolic aroma and taste.

The distillery is equipped with a semi-lauter mash tun, twelve Oregon pine washbacks with a fermentation time between 50 and 80 hours, and two pairs of stills. The mash tun has a capacity of 12 tons but is only filled to 50%. The plan for 2018 is to do 17 mashes per week for 6 months and then increase to 22 mashes which means a total of 2.3 million litres of alcohol. Highland Park is malting 30% of its malt themselves and there are five malting floors with a capacity of almost 36 tons of barley. The phenol content is 30-40 ppm in its own malt and the malt which has been bought from Simpson´s is unpeated. There are also 19 dunnage warehouses and four racked on site.

The core range of Highland Park consists of **10 year old Viking Scars, 12 year old Viking Honour, 18 year old Viking Pride** as well as **25, 30** and **40 year olds**. The duty free range, called the Warrior Series, has been around for several years now and in 2018 a major part of the existent bottlings were replaced by new expressions. The more expensive ones, **Ragnvald** and **Thorfinn**, are still available while **Svein, Einar, Harald** and **Sigurd** have been discontinued. Instead, four new expressions were launched in autumn 2018; **Spirit of the Bear** (40% and matured mainly in American oak ex-sherry), **Loyalty of the Wolf** (14 years old, bottled at 42.3% and matured in a combination of American oak ex-sherry and ex-bourbon), **Wings of the Eagle** (16 years old, bottled at 44.5% and predominantly from European oak ex-sherry) and a duty free version of the **18 year old Viking Pride** bottled at the higher strength of 46%. **Voyage of the Raven** is a limited edition also available in travel retail. Recent limited expressions include a new edition of the **50 year old**, the second installment in the Viking Legend series, **Valknut** (where the locally grown barley variety Tartan was used as part of the recipe), the 17 year old **The Dark, Full Volume** distilled in 1999 and **Dragon Legend**, part of the core range but only available in Europe in the same way that **Magnus** is an exclusive to the US. Add to this a huge number of single casks destined for certain markets.

History:

1798 David Robertson founds the distillery. The local smuggler and businessman Magnus Eunson previously operated an illicit whisky production on the site.

1816 John Robertson, an Excise Officer who arrested Magnus Eunson, takes over production.

1826 Highland Park obtains a license and the distillery is taken over by Robert Borwick.

1840 Robert´s son George Borwick takes over but the distillery deteriorates.

1869 The younger brother James Borwick inherits Highland Park and attempts to sell it as he does not consider the distillation of spirits as compatible with his priesthood.

1895 James Grant (of Glenlivet Distillery) buys Highland Park.

1898 James Grant expands capacity from two to four stills.

1937 Highland Distilleries buys Highland Park.

1979 Highland Distilleries invests considerably in marketing Highland Park as single malt which increases sales markedly.

1986 A visitor centre, considered one of Scotland's finest, is opened.

1997 Two new Highland Park are launched, an 18 year old and a 25 year old.

1999 Highland Distillers are acquired by Edrington Group and William Grant & Sons.

2000 Visit Scotland awards Highland Park "Five Star Visitor Attraction".

2005 Highland Park 30 years old is released. A 16 year old for the Duty Free market and Ambassador´s Cask 1984 are released.

History continued:

2006 The second edition of Ambassador´s Cask, a 10 year old from 1996, is released. New packaging is introduced.

2007 The Rebus 20, a 21 year old duty free exclusive, a 38 year old and a 39 year old are released.

2008 A 40 year old and the third and fourth editions of Ambassador´s Cask are released.

2009 Two vintages and Earl Magnus 15 year are released.

2010 A 50 year old, Saint Magnus 12 year old, Orcadian Vintage 1970 and four duty free vintages are released.

2011 Vintage 1978, Leif Eriksson and 18 year old Earl Haakon are released.

2012 Thor and a 21 year old are released.

2013 Loki and a new range for duty free, The Warriors, are released.

2014 Freya and Dark Origins are released.

2015 Odin is released.

2016 Hobbister, Ice Edition, Ingvar and King Christian I are released.

2017 Valkyrie, Dragon Legend, Voyage of the Raven, Shiel, Full Volume, The Dark and The Light are released.

2018 New bottlings in the duty free range include Spirit of the Bear, Loyalty of the Wolf and Wings of the Eagle. The limited Valknut is also released.

Tasting notes Highland Park 12 year old:

GS – The nose is fragrant and floral, with hints of heather and some spice. Smooth and honeyed on the palate, with citric fruits, malt and distinctive tones of wood smoke in the warm, lengthy, slightly peaty finish.

Dragon Legend

Valknut

Voyage of the Raven

10 years old

12 years old

Loyalty of the Wolf

Inchgower

[inch•gow•er]

Owner: Diageo

Region/district: Speyside

Founded: 1871

Status: Active

Capacity: 3 200 000 litres

Address: Buckie, Banffshire AB56 5AB

Website: malts.com

Tel: 01542 836700

In his groundbreaking book on whisky distilleries in the United Kingdom, published in 1887, Alfred Barnard dedicated six pages to Inchgower. Just for comparison – Glenfarclas and Glenmorangie got one each and Macallan was dismissed in seven lines.

Perhaps the fact that the founder and owner, Alexander Wilson, invited him for dinner influenced his appraisal. On the other hand, Barnard writes that the whisky is "...much appreciated by connoisseurs" and that it is "sold principally in England and exported to the Colonies".

Today, almost all the production of Inchgower single malt goes into blends while the three distilleries mentioned above are all mega stars in the whisky world. It just goes to show that the ambition and the focus of a distillery owner plays an important part as to whether or not a single malt will become a well known brand in its own right

The distillery is equipped with an 8.4 ton stainless steel semilauter mash tun and six washbacks made of Oregon pine. There are also 2 pairs of stills with a fairly unusual middle cut. Starting at 70% to avoid the fruity esters and cutting at 55% to catch the more robust flavours. This, together with a cloudy wort, gives a robust and nutty/spicy flavour to the newmake which makes Inchgower a perfect signature malt in Bell´s blended Scotch. In 2017, the distillery was closed from June-October to replace the five existing malt bins with three larger ones. The production plan for 2018 is a 5-day operation which means short (40-45 hours) and long (90-92 hours) fermentations.

Inchgower is situated on the south side of Moray Firth and is difficult to miss as it is situated just at the A98 near the small fishing port of Buckie. If one is driving from Elgin towards Banff, it is even easier to spot the distillery as the name appears on the roof. Besides the official **Flora & Fauna 14 year old**, there have also been a few limited bottlings of Inchgower single malt. The most recent was a **27 year old** in autumn 2018 which was part of the yearly Special Releases.

History:

1871 Alexander Wilson & Co. founds the distillery. Equipment from the disused Tochineal Distillery, also owned by Alexander Wilson, is installed.

1936 Alexander Wilson & Co. becomes bankrupt and Buckie Town Council buys the distillery and the family's home for £1,600.

1938 The distillery is sold on to Arthur Bell & Sons for £3,000.

1966 Capacity doubles to four stills.

1985 Guinness acquires Arthur Bell & Sons.

1987 United Distillers is formed by a merger between Arthur Bell & Sons and DCL.

1997 Inchgower 1974 (22 years) is released as a Rare Malt.

2004 Inchgower 1976 (27 years) is released as a Rare Malt.

2010 A single cask from 1993 is released.

2018 A 27 year old is launched as part of the Special Releases.

27 years old

Tasting notes Inchgower 14 years old:

GS – Ripe pears and a hint of brine on the light nose. Grassy and gingery in the mouth, with some acidity. The finish is spicy, dry and relatively short.

Jura

[joo•rah]

Owner: Whyte & Mackay (Emperador Inc)

Region/district: Highlands (Jura)

Founded: 1810

Status: Active (vc)

Capacity: 2 400 000 litres

Address: Craighouse, Isle of Jura PA60 7XT

Website: isleofjura.com

Tel: 01496 820240

Almost twenty years ago a desision was made to re-rack most of the stock into high quality bourbon casks to improve the quality. Some five years later, the strategy started to pay off and sales figures increased dramatically.

Now, the owners are ready to take the next step which means a complete overhaul of the entire range. No less than ten new expressions were launched during spring 2018. Jura is currently the third best selling single malt in the UK after Glenfiddich and Glenmorangie and sells almost 2 million bottles globally.

Jura distillery is equipped with a 5 ton semi-lauter mash tun, six stainless steel washbacks with a fermentation time of 54 hours and two pairs of stills – the second tallest in Scotland. Working a 7-day week since 2011, they will be doing 28 mashes per week and 2,3 million litres of alchol during 2018, which will include around 7% of peated production (at 50ppm).

The entire core range has been discontinued and is now replaced by **Journey** (matured in American oak), **10 year old** (finished in oloroso sherry casks), **12 year old** (also an oloroso finish), **Seven Wood** (a vatting of whiskies matured in seven types of French oak as well as ex-bourbon barrels) and **18 year old** (finished in red wine casks). All the expressions have an amount of peated Jura in the recipe. Turas-Mara, exclusive to duty free, has been replaced by no less than four new expressions in a range called **Sherry Cask Collection; The Sound, The Road, The Loch** and **The Paps**. All of them have been finished in PX casks that have held sherry for varying amounts of time. A fifth duty free version, exclusive to Asia, is the **12 year old The Bay**. Recent limited releases include the **20 year old One and All**, a vatting of whiskies from at least five different types of casks and the 18 year old **One for You** which was released in 2018. Due to the intense work on the new range, there was no special bottling for the Jura Tastival this year.

History:

1810 Archibald Campbell founds a distillery named Small Isles Distillery.

1853 Richard Campbell leases the distillery to Norman Buchanan from Glasgow.

1867 Buchanan files for bankruptcy and J. & K. Orr takes over the distillery.

1876 Licence transferred to James Ferguson & Sons.

1901 Ferguson dismantles the distillery.

1960 Charles Mackinlay & Co. extends the distillery. Newly formed Scottish & Newcastle Breweries acquires Charles Mackinlay & Co.

1963 The first distilling takes place.

1985 Invergordon Distilleries acquires Charles Mackinlay & Co., Isle of Jura and Glenallachie from Scottish & Newcastle Breweries.

1993 Whyte & Mackay (Fortune Brands) buys Invergordon Distillers.

1996 Whyte & Mackay changes name to JBB (Greater Europe).

2001 The management buys out the company and changes the name to Kyndal.

2002 Isle of Jura Superstition is launched.

2003 Kyndal reverts back to its old name, Whyte & Mackay. Isle of Jura 1984 is launched.

2004 Two cask strengths (15 and 30 years old) are released in limited numbers.

2006 The 40 year old Jura is released.

2007 United Spirits buys Whyte & Mackay. The 18 year old Delmé-Evans and an 8 year old heavily peated expression are released.

2008 A series of four different vintages, called Elements, is released.

2009 The peated Prophecy and three new vintages called Paps of Jura are released.

2012 The 12 year old Jura Elixir is released.

2013 Camas an Staca, 1977 Juar and Turas-Mara are released.

2014 Whyte & Mackay is sold to Emperador Inc.

2016 The 22 year old "One For The Road" is released.

2017 The limited One and All is released.

2018 A new core range is released; 10, 12 and 18 year old as well as Journey and Seven Wood.

Tasting notes Jura 10 years old:

GS – Resin, oil and pine notes on the delicate nose. Light-bodied in the mouth, with malt and drying saltiness. The finish is malty, nutty, with more salt, plus just a wisp of smoke.

12 years old

Kilchoman

[kil•ho•man]

Owner:
Kilchoman Distillery Co.

Region/district:
Islay

Founded:
2005

Status:
Active (vc)

Capacity:
460 000 litres

Address: Rockside farm, Bruichladdich,
Islay PA49 7UT

Website:
kilchomandistillery.com

Tel:
01496 850011

Building a new distillery on Islay, the Holy Grail for many whisky lovers and the ultimate goal for a whisky pilgrimage, could be seen as arrogance bordering on blasphemy. Anthony Wills, though, managed to pull it off.

With the distillery established in 2005, he has proved any possible critics wrong by producing a classic Islay single malt. By demand he now needs to expand the distillery and at the time of writing, a new stillhouse, mash house and tun room are being built. Some time in autumn 2018, there will be a second distillery unit mirroring the existing one completely and thereby doubling the capacity.

Meanwhile, a new malting floor and kiln have been opened which means that the distillery is now able to produce 30% of their malt requirement themselves, typically with a phenool content of 20ppm. The rest (50ppm) is bought from Port Ellen. Further evidence of the distillery´s success are the five new warehouses that will be built within the next couple of years.

Currently, the distillery is equipped with a 1.2 ton stainless steel semi-lauter mash tun, six stainless steel washbacks with an average fermantation time of 90 hours and one pair of stills. The distillery is currently doing 10 mashes per week which translates to 230,000 litres of alcohol. With the expansion completed, the distillery will be able to do 460,000 litres of pure alcohol per year.

The core range consists of **Machir Bay** and **Sanaig**. The latter was released in 2016 and has been matured in a combination of ex-bourbon and ex-oloroso sherry casks. Limited, but regular releases are the sherry matured **Loch Gorm** and **100% Islay**. Recent, limited releases include the **Original Cask Strength**, the **2009 Vintage** as well as the second release of a **four year old**, matured fully in **ruby port** casks and a **Sauternes cask finish**. The special Feis Ile 2018 bottling was an **11 year old cask strength** version matured in ex-bourbon barrels. For the UK duty free market there is **Coull Point** and for global duty free, **Saligo Bay** is available.

History:

2002 Plans are formed for a new distillery at Rockside Farm on western Islay.

2005 Production starts in June.

2006 A fire breaks out in the kiln causing a few weeks´ production stop but malting has to cease for the rest of the year.

2007 The distillery is expanded with two new washbacks.

2009 The first single malt, a 3 year old, is released on 9th September followed by a second release.

2010 Three new releases and an introduction to the US market. John Maclellan from Bunnahabhain joins the team as General Manager.

2011 Kilchoman 100% Islay is released as well as a 4 year old and a 5 year old.

2012 Machir Bay, the first core expression, is released together with Kilchoman Sherry Cask Release and the second edition of 100% Islay.

2013 Loch Gorm and Vintage 2007 are released.

2014 A 3 year old port cask matured and the first duty free exclusive, Coull Point, are released.

2015 A Madeira cask maturation is released and the distillery celebrates its 10th anniversary.

2016 Sanaig and a Sauternes cask maturation are released.

2017 A Portugese red wine maturation and Vintage 2009 are released.

2018 Original Cask Strength and 2009 Vintage are released.

Machir Bay

Tasting notes Kilchoman Machir Bay:

GS – A nose of sweet peat and vanilla, undercut by brine, kelp and black pepper. Filled ashtrays in time. A smooth mouth-feel, with lots of nicely-balanced citrus fruit, peat smoke and Germolene on the palate. The finish is relatively long and sweet, with building spice, chili and a final nuttiness.

Kininvie

[kin•in•vee]

Owner: William Grant & Sons

Region/district: Speyside

Founded: 1990

Status: Active

Capacity: 4 800 000 litres

Address: Dufftown, Keith, Banffshire AB55 4DH

Website: -

Tel: 01340 820373

When Kininvie started production in 1990, it was the first distillery to open in Scotland since 1975. It would take another five years until the next one was due (Arran) and then another ten until Kilchoman was fired up.

In 30 years, only three malt distilleries were founded compared to the last 18 years when 30 new distilleries have seen the light of day. The recent explosion of new distilleries have everything to do with the demand for malt whisky and in a sense, the same applied to Kininvie. The difference is that today, the new producers' ambition is to bottle their product whereas Kininvie's role was to take the pressure off Glenfiddich and Balvenie as a filler for the company's blends – Grants and Clan MacGregor.

William Grant & Sons rarely spoke of Kinivie, simply because it was never intended to be bottled on its own. Things changed though, when a whisky innovation team, spearheaded by Kevin Abrook, decided the company should showcase their hidden gems as well. Girvan single grain was promoted as was Ailsa Bay single malt and Kininvie joined them with several single malt releases.

Kininvie distillery consists of one still house with three wash stills and six spirit stills, tucked away behind Balvenie. There is a 9.6 ton stainless steel full lauter mash tun which is placed next to Balvenie's in the Balvenie distillery and ten Douglas fir washbacks with a minimum fermentation time of 75 hours can be found in two separate rooms next to the Balvenie washbacks. Production in 2018 will be 20 mashes per week which means a total of 4.2 million litres of pure alcohol.

It wasn't until autumn 2013 that Kininvie single malt was launched under its own name for the first time. A 23 year old was released Taiwan and later in the UK, USA and selected European markets. The end of 2015 saw the release of a **23 year old** core bottling. A **17 year old** is available in duty free and three, limited **25 year old** single casks named First Drops, were launched in 2015.

History:

1990 Kininvie distillery is inaugurated and the first distillation takes place on 25th June.

1994 Another three stills are installed.

2006 The first expression of a Kininvie single malt is released as a 15 year old under the name Hazelwood.

2008 In February a 17 year old Hazelwood Reserve is launched at Heathrow's Terminal 5.

2013 A 23 year old Kininvie is launched in Taiwan.

2014 A 17 year old and batch 2 of the 23 year old are released.

2015 Batch 3 of the 23 year old is released and later in the year, the batches are replaced by a 23 year old signature bottling. Three 25 year old single casks are launched.

23 years old

Tasting notes Kininvie 17 years old:

GS – The nose offers tropical fruits, coconut and vanilla custard, with a hint of milk chocolate. Pineapple and mango on the palate, accompanied by linseed oil, ginger, and developing nuttiness. The finish dries slowly, with more linseed, plenty of spice, and soft oak.

Knockando

[nock•<u>an</u>•doo]

Owner:
Diageo.

Region/district:
Speyside

Founded:
1898

Status:
Active

Capacity:
1 400 000 litres

Address: Knockando, Morayshire AB38 7RT

Website:
malts.com

Tel:
01340 882000

For more than fifty years, W & A Gilbey, to most of us known as a gin producer, were the owners of Knockando distillery. When they bought Glen Spey in 1887, they were the first English company to own a Scottish distillery.

At that time the Gilbey brothers were not known for their gin. That production did not start until 1895. They actually started as wine traders but the ravaging of the vinelouse in France in the 1860s led them to the whiskey business and Glen Spey. The following years, they purchased another two distilleries, Strathmill and Knockando. The single malts from all three distilleries would eventually become a vital part of the J&B blend. This was created in the 1930s to suit the American taste for a light, blended whisky. Today, the brand is in spot number five on the top list, selling around 40 million bottles every year. They stopped filling casks at the distillery several years ago. Instead it is tankered away to other distilleries and some of the casks are returned for maturation in two dunnage and two racked warehouses.

The distillery is equipped with a small (4.4 ton), semi-lauter mash tun, eight Douglas fir washbacks and two pairs of stills. Knockando has always worked a five-day week with 16 mashes per week, 8 short fermentations (50 hours) and 8 long (100 hours). In 2018, however, the distillery will be closed for a major refurbishing in similar with Glenlossie. Knockando´s nutty character, a result of the cloudy worts coming from the mash tun, has given it its fame. However, in order to balance the taste, the distillers also wish to create the typical Speyside floral notes by using boiling balls on the spirit stills to increase reflux.

Knockando is Diageo´s 8th most sold single malt (600,000 bottles in 2017) and has for many years been especially popular in France, Spain and Greece. The core range consists of **12 year old, 15 year old Richly Matured, 18 year old Slow Matured** and the **21 year old Master Reserve**. In 2011 a 25 year old matured in first fill European oak was released as part of the Special Releases.

History:

1898 John Thompson founds the distillery. The architect is Charles Doig.

1899 Production starts in May.

1900 The distillery closes in March and J. Thompson & Co. takes over administration.

1903 W. & A. Gilbey purchases the distillery for £3,500 and production restarts in October.

1962 W. & A. Gilbey merges with United Wine Traders (including Justerini & Brooks) and forms International Distillers & Vintners (IDV).

1968 Floor maltings is decommissioned.

1969 The number of stills is increased to four.

1972 IDV is acquired by Watney Mann who, in its turn, is taken over by Grand Metropolitan.

1978 Justerini & Brooks launches a 12 year old Knockando.

1997 Grand Metropolitan and Guinness merge and form Diageo; simultaneously IDV and United Distillers merge to United Distillers & Vintners.

2010 A Manager´s Choice 1996 is released.

2011 A 25 year old is released.

12 years old

Tasting notes Knockando 12 years old:

GS – Delicate and fragrant on the nose, with hints of malt, worn leather, and hay. Quite full in the mouth, smooth and honeyed, with gingery malt and a suggestion of white rum. Medium length in the finish, with cereal and more ginger.

Knockdhu

A visit to a distillery should be on the to-do list of any whisky enthusiast and there are plenty in Scotland that are open to tourists. Once you´ve been to a few, you tend to look for the smaller ones that are off the beaten track to broaden your perspective.

Knockdhu is the perfect example. Traditionally run and with a range of single malts that have become quite well-known to aficionados around the world, it was just a matter of time until whisky lovers would come knocking on the door to have a look. As time passed by, the friendly crew let them have a peek and answered questions. After a while, a tour guide was hired and currently there are two tours daily. The next step is to build a small visitor centre, which will hopefully open up in summer 2019, with a view to building something on a grander scale in the future.

Knockdhu distillery is equipped with a 5 ton stainless steel lauter mash tun, eight washbacks made of Oregon pine, with fermentation time now increased to 65 hours and one pair of stills with worm tubs. For 2018 they plan to do an average of 14 mashes per week which means a total of 1.5 million litres of alcohol. Around 20% of that will be heavily peated (45ppm). The spirit is filled mainly into bourbon casks with an additional 15% of sherry butts.

The core range consists of **12, 18, 24, 35 years old** and the limited **Vintage 1975** where the stock is almost depleted. The latter, released in 2015, is the oldest expression yet to be released by the owner. In addition to that there is the peated range where almost ten different expressions have replaced each other over the past few years. The latest addition from 2017, **Peatheart**, however is destined to become a part of the core range. Up until now, the phenol content on the label has referred to the ppm in the matured whisky. With Peatheart (40ppm), the owners have decided to state the ppm of the malted barley. Every year a new vintage is released and in spring 2017 it was a **2002** which replaced the 2000. In 2015, two new expressions were released for duty-free; **Black Hill Reserve** and the peated (13.5ppm) **Barrow**. Both have matured in bourbon casks and they were complemented by **Rùdhan** in autumn 2016.

[nock•doo]

Owner:
Inver House Distillers
(Thai Beverages plc)

Region/district:
Highland

Founded: **Status:**   **Capacity:**
1893   Active (vc)   2 000 000 litres

Address: Knock, By Huntly, Aberdeenshire AB54 7LJ

Website:
ancnoc.com

Tel:
01466 771223

History:

1893 Distillers Company Limited (DCL) starts construction of the distillery.

1894 Production starts in October.

1930 Scottish Malt Distillers (SMD) takes over production.

1983 The distillery closes in March.

1988 Inver House buys the distillery from United Distillers.

1989 Production restarts on 6th February.

1990 First official bottling of Knockdhu.

1993 First official bottling of anCnoc.

2001 Pacific Spirits purchases Inver House Distillers at a price of $85 million.

2003 Reintroduction of anCnoc 12 years.

2004 A 14 year old from 1990 is launched.

2005 A 30 year old from 1975 and a 14 year old from 1991 are launched.

2006 International Beverage Holdings acquires Pacific Spirits UK.

2007 anCnoc 1993 is released.

2008 anCnoc 16 year old is released.

2011 A Vintage 1996 is released.

2012 A 35 year old is launched.

2013 A 22 year old and Vintage 1999 are released.

2014 A peated range with Rutter, Flaughter, Tushkar and Cutter is introduced.

2015 A 24 year old, Vintage 1975 and Peatlands are released as well as Black Hill Reserve and Barrow for duty free.

2016 Vintage 2001, Blas and Rùdhan are released.

2017 Vintage 2002 and Peatheart are released.

12 years old

Tasting notes anCnoc 12 years old:

GS – A pretty, sweet, floral nose, with barley notes. Medium bodied, with a whiff of delicate smoke, spices and boiled sweets on the palate. Drier in the mouth than the nose suggests. The finish is quite short and drying.

Lagavulin

[lah•gah•<u>voo</u>•lin]

Owner: Diageo
Region/district: Islay

Founded: 1816
Status: Active (vc)
Capacity: 2 530 000 litres

Address: Port Ellen, Islay, Argyll PA42 7DZ

Website: malts.com
Tel: 01496 302749 (vc)

This year's Feis Ile marked a change of stewardship at the Lagavulin distillery. For seven years, Georgie Crawford has as the manager supervised the daily work at the distillery but has also become a familiar face to all the visitors coming back year after year.

She is now leaving but will still remain on the island where she was born. Her future role is to bring Port Ellen distillery back to life after having been closed since 1983. Her successor at Lagavulin is Colin Gordon, who's recently been managing Port Ellen maltings and before that Inchgower and Roseisle distilleries.

Despite a small dip in 2017, Lagavulin is still the second best-selling malt on Islay (Laphroaig being number one). Close to 2.2 million bottles were sold in 2017 which makes it the fourth best-selling malt in the Diageo stable. The positive trend put a pressure on the distillery team. The question was how to increase volume without a huge investment and, most importantly, without compromising the quality of the spirit. For the last two years, the solution has been a more efficient cleaning system in the stillhouse which gave space for one more mash per week without interfering with fermentation times or run times in the stills.

On a peninsula next to the distillery stands the ruins of Dunyvaig Castle (picture next page). In the 14th and 15th centuries it was used by the clan Macdonald (or Lord of the Isles) to protect the island from attacks from the sea. In August 2018, a team of 40 archaeologists and experts, began an excavation of the site, funded by Lagavulin distillery, in order to learn more about the castle and its history.

The distillery is equipped with a 4.4 ton stainless steel full lauter mash tun, ten washbacks made of larch with a 55 hour fermentation cycle and two pairs of stills. The spirit stills are actually larger than the wash stills and are filled almost to the brim. This diminishes the copper contact and that, together with a slow distillation, creates the rich and pungent character of Lagavulin single malt. Bourbon hogsheads are used, almost without exception, for maturation and all of the new production is stored on the mainland. The distillery is working 24/7 and the volume is between 2.5 and 2.6 million litres of alcohol.

The core range of Lagavulin is unusually limited and only consists of a **12 year old cask strength** (which actually forms part of the Special Releases but new bottlings appear every year), a **16 year old** and the **Distiller's Edition**, a Pedro Ximenez sherry finish. A fourth addition to the permanent range appeared in autumn 2017 in the way of an **8 year old** bottled at 48%. Recent limited bottlings include three bottlings in 2016 to celebrate the distillery's bicentenary – an 8 year old (later to become part of the core range), a **25 year old** bottled at cask strength and matured in sherry casks and a single cask **Lagavulin 1991**. The Islay Festival special release for 2018, bottled at 53.9%, was an **18 year old** of refill and rejuvenated hogsheads and bodega sherry butts.

History:

1816 John Johnston founds the distillery.

1825 John Johnston takes over the adjacent distillery Ardmore founded in 1817 by Archibald Campbell and closed in 1821.

1836 John Johnston dies and the two distilleries are merged and operated under the name Lagavulin. Alexander Graham, a wine and spirits dealer from Glasgow, buys the distillery.

1861 James Logan Mackie becomes a partner.

1867 The distillery is acquired by James Logan Mackie & Co. and refurbishment starts.

1878 Peter Mackie is employed.

1889 James Logan Mackie passes away and nephew Peter Mackie inherits the distillery.

1890 J. L. Mackie & Co. changes name to Mackie & Co. Peter Mackie launches White Horse onto the export market with Lagavulin included in the blend. White Horse blended is not available on the domestic market until 1901.

1908 Peter Mackie uses the old distillery buildings to build a new distillery, Malt Mill, on the site.

1924 Peter Mackie passes away and Mackie & Co. changes name to White Horse Distillers.

1927 White Horse Distillers becomes part of Distillers Company Limited (DCL).

1930 The distillery is administered under Scottish Malt Distillers (SMD).

1952 An explosive fire breaks out and causes considerable damage.

1962 Malt Mills distillery closes and today it houses Lagavulin's visitor centre.

1974 Floor maltings are decommisioned and malt is bought from Port Ellen instead.

1988 Lagavulin 16 years becomes one of six Classic Malts.

History continued:

1998 A Pedro Ximenez sherry finish is launched as a Distillers Edition.

2002 Two cask strengths (12 years and 25 years) are launched.

2006 A 30 year old is released.

2007 A 21 year old from 1985 and the sixth edition of the 12 year old are released.

2009 A new 12 year old appears as a Special Release.

2010 A new edition of the 12 year old, a single cask exclusive for the distillery and a Manager´s Choice single cask are released.

2011 The 10th edition of the 12 year old cask strength is released.

2012 The 11th edition of the 12 year old cask strength and a 21 year old are released.

2013 A 37 year old and the 12th edition of the 12 year old cask strength are released.

2014 A triple matured for Friends of the Classic Malts and the 13th edition of the 12 year old cask strength are released.

2015 The 14th edition of the 12 year old cask strength is released.

2016 An 8 year old and a 25 year old are launched as well as the yearly 12 year old cask strength.

2017 A new edition of the 12 year old cask strength is released.

2018 An 18 year old is released for Feis Ile.

Tasting notes Lagavulin 16 year old:

GS – Peat, iodine, sherry and vanilla merge on the rich nose. The peat and iodine continue on to the expansive, spicy, sherried palate, with brine, prunes and raisins. Peat embers feature in the lengthy, spicy finish.

| Distiller´s Edition | 25 years old | 8 years old |

| 16 years old | 12 years old cask strength |

Laphroaig

[lah•froyg]

Owner: Beam Suntory   **Region/district:** Islay

Founded: 1815   **Status:** Active (vc)   **Capacity:** 3 300 000 litres

Address: Port Ellen, Islay, Argyll PA42 7DU

Website: laphroaig.com   **Tel:** 01496 302418

Today, it´s difficult to understand that there was a time when peated whisky was seen merely as a way to add some weight and flavour to blended whiskies. Enjoying it as a single malt was not an option.

Nowadays, peated whisky is not just restricted to Scotland. All around the world smoky single malts have become a natural part of the range. The question is, when did this yearn for smoky whiskies start and who started it? It´s probably fair to say that Laphroaig played a crucial part. In the 1930s, the owner of the distillery, Ian Hunter, travelled in the US creating an interest in the smoky style and Laphroaig was sold as a single malt. In the 1940s and 1950s, it was available as a 10 year old and since 2001, it has been the most popular of the Islay malts with 3.7 million bottles sold in 2017.

Laphroaig is equipped with a 5.5 ton stainless steel full lauter mash tun and six stainless steel washbacks with an average fermentation time of 50-55 hours. The distillery uses an unusual combination of three wash stills and four spirit stills, all fitted with ascending lyne arms. It is one of very few distilleries with its own maltings which produces 20% of its requirements. The own malt has a phenol specification of 40-60ppm, while the remaining malt from Port Ellen or the mainland lies between 35 and 45ppm. The distillery is running at full capacity which means 3.3 million litres in the year. Due to increased sales volumes, discussions about an increase of production at the distillery have been ongoing for the past two years and while the exact plans have not been revealed, the distillery will be expanded within the next couple of years. Laphroaig has one of the best visitor centres in the industry with a wide variety of tours at different levels.

The core range consists of **Select** without age statement, **10 year old, 10 year old cask strength** (10th batch released in 2018), **Quarter Cask, Triple Wood** and a **25 year old**. A new addition to the range, **Lore**, was launched in 2016. With no age statement, the whisky has been matured in a combination of first fill bourbon barrels, quarter casks and oloroso hogsheads. The travel retail range was recently modified, with some of the old varieties being replaced by **Four Oak** and the **1815 Edition**. Four Oak, is a vatting from four different casks while The 1815 Edition is a mix of first-fill, heavily charred bourbon barrels and new European oak hogsheads. **PX Cask** is also a part of the duty free range. Recent limited releases include a **30 year old** from late 2016, followed in autumn 2017 by a **27 year old** with a maturation in first-fill ex-bourbon barrels and refill quarter casks and a **28 year old** in autumn 2018, matured in a combination of quarter casks, ex-bourbon barrels and oloroso sherry butts. The **Cairdeas** range include two recent bottlings exclusively for the Friends of Laphroaig (available from the distillery and online); **Quarter Cask** bottled at 57.2% and the **15 year old** – both matured in ex-bourbon casks. The Feis Ile bottling for 2018 was an **8 year old Cairdeas**, matured for six years in ex-bourbon and then finished for another two years in ex fino sherry casks.

History:

1815 Brothers Alexander and Donald Johnston found Laphroaig.

1836 Donald buys out Alexander and takes over operations.

1837 James and Andrew Gairdner found Ardenistiel a stone's throw from Laphroaig.

1847 Donald Johnston is killed in an accident in the distillery when he falls into a kettle of boiling hot burnt ale. The Manager of neigh-bouring Lagavulin, Walter Graham, takes over.

1857 Operation is back in the hands of the Johnston family when Donald's son Dougald takes over.

1860 Ardenistiel Distillery merges with Laphroaig.

1877 Dougald, being without heirs, passes away and his sister Isabella, married to their cousin Alexander takes over.

1907 Alexander Johnston dies and the distillery is inherited by his two sisters Catherine Johnston and Mrs. William Hunter (Isabella Johnston).

1908 Ian Hunter arrives in Islay to assist his mother and aunt with the distillery.

1924 The two stills are increased to four.

1927 Catherine Johnston dies and Ian Hunter takes over.

1928 Isabella Johnston dies and Ian Hunter becomes sole owner.

1950 Ian Hunter forms D. Johnston & Company

1954 Ian Hunter passes away and management of the distillery is taken over by Elisabeth "Bessie" Williamson, who was previously Ian Hunters PA and secretary.

1967 Seager Evans & Company buys the distillery through Long John Distillery, having already acquired part of Laphroaig in 1962. The number of stills is increased from four to five.

1972 Bessie Williamson retires. Another two stills are installed bringing the total to seven.

History continued:

1975 Whitbread & Co. buys Seager Evans (now renamed Long John International) from Schenley International.

1989 The spirits division of Whitbread is sold to Allied Distillers.

1991 Allied Distillers launches Caledonian Malts. Laphroaig is one of the four malts included.

1994 HRH Prince Charles gives his Royal Warrant to Laphroaig. Friends of Laphroaig is founded.

1995 A 10 year old cask strength is launched.

2001 A 40 year old is released.

2004 Quarter Cask is launched.

2005 Fortune Brands becomes new owner.

2007 A vintage 1980 (27 years old) and a 25 year old are released.

2008 Cairdeas, Cairdeas 30 year old and Triple Wood are released.

2009 An 18 year old is released.

2010 A 20 year old for French Duty Free and Cairdeas Master Edition are launched.

2011 Laphroaig PX and Cairdeas - The Ileach Edition are released.

2012 Brodir and Cairdeas Origin are launched.

2013 QA Cask, An Cuan Mor, 25 year old cask strength and Cairdeas Port Wood Edition are released.

2014 Laphroaig Select and a new version of Cairdeas are released.

2015 A 21 year old, a 32 year old sherry cask and a new Cairdeas are released and the 15 year old is re-launched.

2016 Lore, Cairdeas 2016 and a 30 year old are released.

2017 Four Oak, The 1815 Edition and a 27 year old are released.

2018 A 28 year old and Cairdeas Fino are released.

Tasting notes Laphroaig Select:

GS – The nose offers chocolate and malt notes set against peat, citrus fruit and iodine. Citrus fruit is most apparent on the relatively light palate, along with ginger, cinnamon and dried fruits. The peat is muted. The finish offers bright spices, new oak and medicinal notes.

Tasting notes Laphroaig 10 year old:

GS – Old-fashioned sticking plaster, peat smoke and seaweed leap off the nose, followed by something a little sweeter and fruitier. Massive on the palate, with fish oil, salt and plankton, though the finish is quite tight and increasingly drying

Select

Quarter Cask

Lore

28 years old

The 1815 Edition

10 years old

Triple Wood

Cairdeas Fino

Linkwood

[link•wood]

Owner:
Diageo

Region/district:
Speyside

Founded: 1821
Status: Active
Capacity: 5 600 000 litres

Address: Elgin, Morayshire IV30 8RD

Website: malts.com
Tel: 01343 862000

In the whisky world of today it is popular to talk about single estate distilleries and "grain-to-glass" production. It lends a certain authenticity to the brand when everything is produced and manufactured locally.

Sometimes we tend to forget that this was the way all Scotch was produced until the early 1900s. Linkwood is one example. Built on the vast Seafield Estates, on the southern outskirts of Elgin, it was run by the estate factor Peter Brown for many years. The barley came from the fields of the estate and the by-products were fed to the cattle. Peter's son William took over in 1872, demolished the distillery and built a new one. By this time, Linkwood single malt had earned a reputation of being one of the best to use for the popular blends of the time. Linkwood managed to keep its independence in 1925 when a huge number of distilleries were aqcuired by the giant of the time – DCL/SMD. It only lasted for eight years when Linkwood finally was absorbed into the company which we today know as Diageo.

The old part of the distillery, which stopped producing in 1996, was equipped with worm tubs and had a slightly different character than the Linkwood of today. On two occasions during 2011-2013, the distillery has been expanded. The old distillery buildings facing Linkwood Road were demolished and an extension of the current still house, which houses two of the stills and the tunroom, was conducted. The only original buildings from 1872 left standing are No. 6 warehouse and the redundant, old kiln with the pagoda roof. The set up of equipment now is one 12.5 ton full lauter mash tun, 11 wooden washbacks and three pairs of stills. The fermentation time during 5-day week production varies between 65 and 105 hours. Production during the last couple of years has varied between 3.6 and 5.6 million litres of alcohol, depending on having a 5 or 7 day production week.

The only official core bottling is a **12 year old Flora & Fauna**. In October 2016, a **37 year old** distilled in 1978 and bottled at 50.3%, was launched as part of the Special Releases.

History:

1821 Peter Brown founds the distillery.

1868 Peter Brown passes away and his son William inherits the distillery.

1872 William demolishes the distillery and builds a new one.

1897 Linkwood Glenlivet Distillery Company Ltd takes over operations.

1902 Innes Cameron, a whisky trader from Elgin, joins the Board and eventually becomes the major shareholder and Director.

1932 Innes Cameron dies and Scottish Malt Distillers takes over in 1933.

1962 Major refurbishment takes place.

1971 The two stills are increased by four. Technically, the four new stills belong to a new distillery referred to as Linkwood B.

1985 Linkwood A (the two original stills) closes.

1990 Linkwood A is in production again for a few months each year until 1996.

2002 A 26 year old from 1975 is launched as a Rare Malt.

2005 A 30 year old from 1974 is launched as a Rare Malt.

2008 Three different wood finishes (all 26 year old) are released.

2009 A Manager's Choice 1996 is released.

2013 Expansion of the distillery including two more stills.

2016 A 37 year old is released.

12 years old

Tasting notes Linkwood 12 years old:

GS – Floral, grassy and fragrant on the nutty nose, while the slightly oily palate becomes increasingly sweet, ending up at marzipan and almonds. The relatively lengthy finish is quite dry and citric.

Whisky
the way I see it

Mark Van Der Vijver
International Commercial Manager
The Scotch Malt Whisky Society

You have been working for The Scotch Malt Whisky Society since 2004. What is your background and what made you decide to start working for the Society?

My experience was in hospitality and venue management and I joined the SMWS to open and launch our new Members' Rooms at 28 Queen Street in Edinburgh, an opportunity I couldn't pass up.

Started in 1983 by Pip Hills, it seems that the SMWS was ahead of its time selling single cask malt whisky. What influence did the Society have on the interest in single malts that we see today?

The Society founders were maverick and adventurous when the whisky industry was struggling, and their vision allowed people to discover the complexity and flavours of single cask single malts. By setting up the SMWS as a membership organisation, the Society provided an opportunity for whisky enthusiasts to discover, learn, appreciate and share single malt whisky. The Society was instrumental in driving the interest and education in single cask, single malt whisky and today we are perceived as the world's leading authority.

Since 2015, when Glenmorangie sold the Society, there has been a definitive change in the way you operate. For example, you have recently attached a number of partner bars across Europe. Please explain the strategy you have today.

We are focussed on creating great membership experiences. That means offering members a variety of fun and informative ways to get involved and share our single cask whiskies. We have a programme of tasting events, pop-up bars, a presence at whisky festivals and our partner bar network. We're looking to increase opportunities for members to share their experiences online, and also encourage them to host their own SMWS-related activities. Our approach to whisky hasn't changed much since we started in 1983. We continue to offer around 25 new single cask malts every month, exclusive to SMWS members.

Some independent bottlers are struggling these days to find interesting casks (or any cask for that matter). When the producers are focusing more on single malts, how does that affect you?

We have great relationships with producers in Scotland and elsewhere and have enjoyed their support over the years. Our focus on single casks and a constant variety of styles and distilleries means we have a different approach to planning our stocks. Also, because we don't reveal the name of the distillery it means that some doors are more likely to be open to us than would be the case otherwise. Either way, we have a robust stock management plan and are in a good position with over 100 different makes of Scotch in our warehouses and plenty of variety for our members for years to come.

Are independent bottlings a thing for a small number of whisky enthuisasts or is there an interest from the general whisky consumer as well?

It depends on the whisky. Some need more of an introduction and explanation, so buying without trying or getting advice can be daunting for less experienced whisky drinkers. But there's no reason why a specialist bottling won't be of interest to everyone. We recognise that our unique approach needs that kind of support. That's part of the reason why we're a membership club and that we offer tasting notes, content, advice and opportunities for tastings. We're keen to involve everyone, regardless of their experience or knowledge. It's supposed be fun after all!

Is there anything the whisky producers could learn from independent bottlers or are their hands tied due to corporate decisions?

There's room for everyone and the big producers and independent bottlers occupy different territories with different approaches. The SMWS has always had a different approach as an unconventional and entertaining club with some of the world's most expectional whiskies at the heart of everything that we do.

The SMWS is not just about Scotch whisky anymore. Please tell us a bit about your expansion into rum, gin, armagnac etc.

In 2017, the Society introduced our Single Cask Spirits collection, having previously experimented and released some non-Scotch and non-whisky. These spirits are distinctive and have their own bottle presentation, offering members an even greater range of flavours and experiences. The SMWS takes the same approach with the selection and quality of its rums, cognacs, armagnacs, gins and bourbons as we do with our Scotch. We also continue to release international whiskies including Japanese, English, Indian, so members are constantly surprised.

What does Scotch whisky mean to you?

As a South African, it's a privilege to work in an industry with such a rich heritage. My great great grandfather was also a wine and spirits merchant in Edinburgh, working near the Society's home at The Vaults, so the family connection adds a special dimension for me.

The history of Scotch whisky has had its ups and downs over the years. How do you see the future for Scotch in the next 10-15 years?

The future is promising as we see investments in new distilleries and prioritisation of visitor centres for education, growing interest and appreciation from whisky consumers and the continued recognition of the value and credibility of Scotch whisky across the globe. Scotch will benefit from the growth of international whiskies that introduce consumers to the category, but Scotch will always remain special and authentic.

Loch Lomond

[lock low•mund]

Owner:
Loch Lomond Group
(majority owner Exponent Private Equity)

Region/district:
Western Highlands

Founded: 1965 **Status:** Active **Capacity:** 5 000 000 litres

Address: Lomond Estate, Alexandria G83 0TL

Website: lochlomonddistillery.com **Tel:** 01389 752781

Loch Lomond is a distillery that insists on doing things their own way. With four different types of stills, and at least 13 styles of whisky, it is a distillery unlike any other in Scotland. In its diversity, it almost resembles a Japanese distillery.

It has been the odd one out ever since the opening in 1966 but it is in recent years, with new owners coming in 2014, that we can see a strategy in how they blend, bottle and brand their whisky. The combined skills of long time serving master distiller and blender John Peterson and the new master blender Michael Henry, have made Loch Lomond interesting to whisky enthusiasts.

Loch Lomond distillery is equipped with one 9 ton full lauter mash tun complemented by ten 25,000 litres and eleven 50,000 litres washbacks – all made by stainless steel. The set-up of stills differs completely from any other distillery in Scotland. There are two, traditional, copper pot stills and six straight neck pot stills where the swan necks have been replaced by rectifying columns. Furthermore, there is one Coffey still used for continuous distillation. And if this wasn´t enough, an additional distillery with column stills producing grain whisky is housed in the same building. For the grain side of production there are twelve 100,000 litres and eight 200,000 litres washbacks. Its total capacity is 5 million litres of malt spirit and 18 million litres of grain.

The core range is divided between three brands; **Loch Lomond** with **Original**, a **12** and an **18 year old**; **Inchmurrin**, also with a **12** and an **18 year old** but a **Madeira wood finish** as well and **Inchmoan**, recently re-introduced in a new range called Loch Lomond Island Collection with a **12 year old** and a **1992 vintage**. An extensive duty-free range has been developed recently with **Loch Lomond Single Grain, Signature** blended Scotch and a **12 year old** single malt together with **Inchmurrin Madeira finish** and the new **10 year old single cask**. One limited expression during last year stands out – a **50 year old Loch Lomond**! Distilled in the straight necked pot stills in 1967, matured for 31 years in refill American oak and with the final two decades in a European oak hogshead, this is the oldest bottling from the owners, so far.

History:

1965 The distillery is built by Littlemill Distillery Company Ltd owned by Duncan Thomas and American Barton Brands.

1966 Production commences.

1971 Duncan Thomas is bought out.

1984 The distillery closes.

1985 Glen Catrine Bonded Warehouse Ltd buys Loch Lomond Distillery.

1987 The distillery resumes production.

1993 Grain spirits are also distilled.

1997 A fire destroys 300,000 litres of maturing whisky.

1999 Two more stills are installed.

2005 Inchmoan and Craiglodge as well as Inchmurrin 12 years are launched.

2006 Inchmurrin 4 years, Croftengea 1996 (9 years), Glen Douglas 2001 (4 years) and Inchfad 2002 (5 years) are launched.

2010 A peated Loch Lomond with no age statement is released as well as a Vintage 1966.

2012 New range for Inchmurrin released – 12, 15, 18 and 21 years.

2014 The distillery is sold to Exponent Private Equity. Organic versions of 12 year old single malt and single blend are released.

2015 Loch Lomond Original Single Malt is released together with a single grain and two blends, Reserve and Signature.

2016 A 12 year old and an 18 year old are launched.

2017 This year´s releases include Inchmoan 12 year old and Inchmurrin 12 and 18 year old.

2018 A 50 year old Loch Lomond is released.

Loch Lomond Original

Tasting notes Loch Lomond Original:

GS – Initially earthy on the nose, with malt and subtle oak. The palate is rounded, with allspice, orange, lime, toffee, and a little smokiness. Barley, citrus fruits and substantial spiciness in the finish.

Longmorn

[long•morn]

Owner:
Chivas Brothers
(Pernod Ricard)

Region/district:
Speyside

Founded: **Status:** **Capacity:**
1894 Active 4 500 000 litres

Address: Longmorn, Morayshire IV30 8SJ

Website: **Tel:**
- 01343 554139

For many years, Longmorn single malt has been described as one of the best hidden gems in Scotch whisky. It has always been the backbone of many of the famous blends but in terms of official bottlings, the owners have never taken a clear stand.

It was launched as a 15 year old in 1993, became very popular but was replaced by a 16 year old in 2007. Nine years later, the whisky was rebranded. A bottling with no age statement was complemented by a new 16 year old and a 23 year old. New packaging and a rather hefty price increase made the campaign look a bit like Diageo´s relaunch of Mortlach a few years earlier. The owners themselves, also state that with the new range, they are targeting customers who are looking for luxurious whisky. In the case of Longmorn, the two versions with age statements are not at all that easy to come by and the re-branding wasn´t supported by a website for the brand.

Longmorn distillery is equipped with a modern 8.5 ton Briggs full lauter mash tun which replaced the old, traditional tun in 2012. At the same time, seven of the eight, old stainless steel washbacks were moved to the new tun room and an additional three were installed. The eight, onion-shaped stills with declining lyne arms are big and fitted with sub-coolers and the wash stills have external heat exchangers. The production capacity was also increased in 2012 by 30% to 4.5 million litres. During 2018, the production runs for five days per week with 18 mashes. This means roughly 3 million litres of alcohol over the year. The style of the newmake is fruity yet robust.

In 2015, **The Distiller´s Choice** (with no age statement) replaced the 16 year old as the only core bottling. Or at least so it was said. A year later though, the **16 year old** was back with a higher proportion of first fill casks. At the same time, a **23 year old** was released. The 16 year old cask strength in the new range, The Distillery Reserve Collection, which was released two years ago has now been discontinued.

History:

1893 John Duff & Company, which founded Glenlossie already in 1876, starts construction. John Duff, George Thomson and Charles Shirres are involved in the company. The total cost amounts to £20,000.

1894 First production in December.

1897 John Duff buys out the other partners.

1898 John Duff builds another distillery next to Longmorn which is called Benriach (at times aka Longmorn no. 2). Duff declares bankruptcy and the shares are sold by the bank to James R. Grant.

1970 The distillery company is merged with The Glenlivet & Glen Grant Distilleries and Hill Thomson & Co. Ltd. Own floor maltings ceases.

1972 The number of stills is increased from four to six. Spirit stills are converted to steam firing.

1974 Another two stills are added.

1978 Seagrams takes over through The Chivas & Glenlivet Group.

1994 Wash stills are converted to steam firing.

2001 Pernod Ricard buys Seagram Spirits & Wine together with Diageo and Pernod Ricard takes over the Chivas group.

2004 A 17 year old cask strength is released.

2007 A 16 year old is released replacing the 15 year old.

2012 Production capacity is expanded.

2015 The Distiller´s Choice is released.

2016 A 16 year old and a 23 year old are released.

Tasting notes Longmorn Distiller´s Choice:

GS – Barley sugar, ginger, toffee and malt on the sweet nose. The palate reveals caramel and milk chocolate, with peppery Jaffa orange. Toffee, barley and a hint of spicy oak in the medium-length finish.

The Distiller´s Choice

Macallan

[mack•al•un]

Owner: **Region/district:**
Edrington Group   Speyside

Founded: **Status:**   **Capacity:**
1824   Active (vc)   15 000 000 litres

Address: Easter Elchies, Craigellachie, Morayshire
AB38 9RX

Website: **Tel:**
themacallan.com   01340 871471

The new Macallan distillery was commissioned in November 2017. The term means that you do a number of trials to make sure everything is working and that the spirit is up to standard.

But it wasn´t until summer 2018 that it was opened to the public. What they encountered, was a distillery unlike any other in Scotland. Shaped like five hills with meadow grass on the roof tops, it blends in very well with the surrounding landscape. One of the five "hills" houses the new visitor center with an art gallery and six different rooms representing the six pillars that define the style of Macallan single malt. The visitors will also be able to see the Macallan archive – a collection of more than 400 different bottles.

The new distillery is equipped with a full lauter mash tun with a 17 ton mash. There are 21 washbacks made of stainless steel that can hold 68,000 litres each. The fermentation time is 60 hours. There are 12 wash stills, each paired to two spirit stills - a total of 36 stills. The capacity is 15 million litres of pure alcohol per year. The old distillery has been mothballed, ready to be used if needed. With a capacity of 11 million litres, it is equipped with two mash tuns (8.3 and 6.7 tons respectively), 22 stainless steel washbacks and six made of wood, seven wash stills and 14 spirit stills.

The core range of Macallan has gradually evolved and now consists of three styles; **Sherry Oak** (100% maturation in sherry casks) was the only available version until 2004 when Fine Oak was introduced and it is also the style that once made Macallan famous. Today it is represented by **12, 18, 25** and **30 years old**. Fine Oak means, at least in the eyes of some Macallan fans, a controversial step away from the classic Macallan because bourbon matured whisky was also involved. In hindsight it proved a succesful addition to the range. Fine Oak has recently changed name to **Triple Cask** and is reprsented by **12, 15** and **18 year old**. **Double Cask**, finally, is the youngest addition to the range and is currently made up of a **12 year old** and **Gold** without age statement. In this case, Double cask means a mix of sherry casks from both American and European oak.The previous 1824 range exclusive for duty free was replaced by The Macallan Quest Collection, a new set of four bottlings in January 2018; **Quest** (bottled at 40%) has been matured in a combination of ex-bourbon and ex-sherry, **Lumina** (41.3%) has been matured in sherry casks, both American and European oak, **Terra** (43.8%) uses first fill ex-sherry casks as does **Enigma** (44.9%). All expression are without age statement. A range of prestige bottlings called The Macallan Masters Decanter Series includes; **Reflexion, No 6** and **M**. Recent limited releases include **Edition No. 4, Classic Cut** (bottled at 58.4%) and, last but not least, a **72 year old**, the oldest release from the distillery to date. The release was limited to 600 decanters. In July 2018, 725 Lalique decanters of the rare **M Black** were released and at the same time **Genesis** was launched to celebrate the new distillery. Finally, starting in autumn 2017, a range of 13 single casks (**Exceptional Single Cask**) were released, all of them sherry matured.

History:

1824 The distillery is licensed to Alexander Reid under the name Elchies Distillery.

1847 Alexander Reid passes away and James Shearer Priest and James Davidson take over.

1868 James Stuart takes over the licence. He founds Glen Spey distillery a decade later.

1886 James Stuart buys the distillery.

1892 Stuart sells the distillery to Roderick Kemp from Elgin. Kemp expands the distillery and names it Macallan-Glenlivet.

1909 Roderick Kemp passes away and the Roderick Kemp Trust is established to secure the family's future ownership.

1965 The number of stills is increased from six to twelve.

1966 The trust is reformed as a private limited company.

1968 The company is introduced on the London Stock Exchange.

1974 The number of stills is increased to 18.

1975 Another three stills are added, now making the total 21.

1984 The first official 18 year old single malt is launched.

1986 Japanese Suntory buys 25% of Macallan-Glenlivet plc stocks.

1996 Highland Distilleries buys the remaining stocks. 1874 Replica is launched.

1999 Edrington and William Grant & Sons buys Highland Distilleries for £601 million through The 1887 Company with 70% held by Edrington and 30% by William Grant & Sons. Suntory still holds 25% in Macallan.

2000 The first single cask from Macallan (1981) is named Exceptional 1.

History continued:

2001 A new visitor centre is opened.

2002 Elegancia replaces 12 year old in the duty-free range. 1841 Replica, Exceptional II and Exceptional III are also launched.

2003 1876 Replica and Exceptional IV, single cask from 1990 are released.

2004 Exceptional V, single cask from 1989 is released as well as Exceptional VI, single cask from 1990. The Fine Oak series is launched.

2005 New expressions are Macallan Woodland Estate, Winter Edition and the 50 year old.

2006 Fine Oak 17 years old and Vintage 1975 are launched.

2007 1851 Inspiration and Whisky Maker´s Selection are released as a part of the Travel Retail range. 12 year old Gran Reserva is launched in Taiwan and Japan.

2008 Estate Oak and 55 year old Lalique are released.

2009 The mothballed No. 2 stillhouse is re-opened. The Macallan 1824 Collection and a 57 year old Lalique bottling is released.

2010 Oscuro is released for Duty Free.

2011 Macallan MMXI is released for duty free.

2012 Macallan Gold, the first in the new 1824 series, is launched.

2013 Amber, Sienna and Ruby are released.

2014 1824 Masters Series (with Rare Cask, Reflexion and No. 6) is released.

2015 Rare Cask Black is released.

2016 Edition No. 1 and 12 year old Double Cask are released.

2017 Folio 2 is released. The new distillery is commissioned.

2018 Fine Oak changes name to Triple Cask, The Quest Collection is released for duty free and Macallan M Black and Genesis are launched.

Tasting notes Macallan 12 year old Sherry oak:

GS – The nose is luscious, with buttery sherry and Christmas cake characteristics. Rich and firm on the palate, with sherry, elegant oak and Jaffa oranges. The finish is long and malty, with slightly smoky spice.

Tasting notes Macallan 12 year old Triple Cask:

GS – The nose is perfumed and quite complex, with marzipan and malty toffee. Expansive on the palate, with oranges, marmalade, milk chocolate and oak. Meidum in length, balanced and comparatively sweet.

Gold   12 yo Sherry Oak   12 yo Triple Cask

Enigma   Edition No 4   Terra

Double Cask 12 yo   Rare Cask Black   Reflexion   Rare Cask

Macduff

[mack•duff]

Owner:
John Dewar & Sons Ltd
(Bacardi)

Region/district:
Highlands

Founded: **Status:** **Capacity:**
1960   Active   3 400 000 litres

Address: Banff, Aberdeenshire AB45 3JT

Website: **Tel:**
lastgreatmalts.com   01261 812612

Single malt from Macduff constitutes the backbone of William Lawson – a blend established in 1889. But it wasn´t until Martini & Rossi took over in 1963 that volumes began to increase.

In the last ten years sales volumes of William Lawson have increased by 140% and in 2017, 37 million bottles were sold. In 2012 it surpassed Bacardi´s other Scotch blend, Dewars, and is now the sixth best selling Scotch in the world. Traditional strongholds for the brand such as France and Spain have in later years been complemented by Russia, Latin America and, more recently, Africa (Kenya, Nigeria etc). A slogan that has been used frequently in ads is "No rules! Great Scotch!", and the marketing of the brand involves adding ice and cola to the whisky. The single malt from Macduff, which has been sold under the brand name The Deveron since 2015, has also been selling well lately going from 175,000 bottles in 2012 to 600,000 in 2017 – a remarkable achievement! The distillery is beautifully located on the banks of the River Deveron, east of Banff on the Moray Firth coast.

Macduff is equipped with a 6.75 ton stainless steel semi-lauter mash tun and nine washbacks made of stainless steel with a fermentation time of 55 hours. There is also a rather unusual set-up of five stills – two wash stills and three spirit stills. In order to fit the stills into the still room, the lyne arms on four of the stills are bent in a peculiar way and on one of the wash stills it is U-shaped. In 2018 the distillery will be doing 26 mashes per week for 48 weeks, producing 3.4 million litres of alcohol.

Official bottlings from Macduff have always been made under the name Glen Deveron. When a completely new range of bottlings was launched in 2015, the name had changed to The Deveron. The core range now consists of a **10 year old**, exclusive to France, as well as a **12** and **18 year old**. For duty free, a new range was launched in 2013 under the name The Royal Burgh Collection encompassing a **16**, a **20** and a **30 year old**.

History:

1960 The distillery is founded by Marty Dyke, George Crawford, James Stirrat and Brodie Hepburn (who is also involved in Tullibardine and Deanston). Macduff Distillers Ltd is the name of the company.

1964 The number of stills is increased from two to three.

1967 Stills now total four.

1972 William Lawson Distillers, part of General Beverage Corporation which is owned by Martini & Rossi, buys the distillery from Glendeveron Distilleries.

1990 A fifth still is installed.

1993 Bacardi buys Martini Rossi (including William Lawson) and eventually transfered Macduff to the subsidiary John Dewar & Sons.

2013 The Royal Burgh Collection (16, 20 and 30 years old) is launched for duty free.

2015 A new range is launched - 10, 12 and 18 years old.

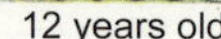
12 years old

Tasting notes The Deveron 12 years old:

GS – Soft, sweet and fruity on the nose, with vanilla, ginger, and apple blossom. Medium-bodied, gently spicy, with butterscotch and Brazil nuts. Caramel contrasts with quite dry spicy oak in the finish.

Mannochmore

[man•och•moor]

Owner:	**Region/district:**
Diageo	Speyside

Founded:	**Status:**	**Capacity:**
1971	Active	6 000 000 litres

Address: Elgin, Morayshire IV30 8SS

Website:	**Tel:**
malts.com	01343 862000

Mannochmore was built in those happy days when optimism was high and whisky production booming. Following prohibition in the US and World War II, blended Scotch whisky had created a position as the leading spirits category in the world.

By the time Mannochmore started producing, no less than eleven new distilleries had already been opened and there were four more to follow within the next couple of years. It was quite common in those days to build a new distillery on the site of an old one and run them simultaneously. Then, in most cases, the older distillery closed within a couple of years; Clynelish/Brora (new distillery opened 1968 with the old closing 1983), Teaninich (1970/1984), Linkwood (1971/1996) and Glendullan (1972/1985). One exception was the construction of Mannochmore on the grounds of Glenlossie in 1971. Except for Mannochmore being closed for a couple of years, both distilleries continued to produce during the hardships of the 1980s up until today. Today the distillery is mainly a reliable supplier of malt whisky for Diageo´s blended brands.

The Glenlossie/Mannochmore complex is a busy site (eventhough Glenlossie is currently closed for refurbishing) with 14 warehouses holding 250,000 casks from many of Diageo´s distilleries. There is a dark grains plant converting pot ale into cattle feed, as well as a newly installed biomass burner turning draff into steam which will power the entire site. And, of course, there are two distilleries with Glenlossie having been built almost a hundred years before Mannochmore.

Since 2013 the distillery is equipped with an 11.1 ton Briggs full lauter mash tun, eight wooden washbacks and another eight external made of stainless steel and four pairs of stills. Clear wort and long fermentations (up to 100 hours) creates a new-make spirit with a fruity character and the distillery is currently running a 7-day production.

The only current official bottling is a **12 year old Flora & Fauna**. In autumn 2016, a **25 year old** distilled in 1990 and bottled at 53.4%, was launched as part of the Special Releases.

History:

1971 Distillers Company Limited (DCL) founds the distillery on the site of their sister distillery Glenlossie. It is managed by John Haig & Co. Ltd.

1985 The distillery is mothballed.

1989 In production again.

1992 A Flora & Fauna series 12 years old becomes the first official bottling.

2009 An 18 year old is released.

2010 A Manager´s Choice 1998 is released.

2013 The number of stills is increased to four.

2016 A 25 year old cask strength is released.

12 years old

Tasting notes Mannochmore 12 years old:

GS – Perfumed and fresh on the light, citric nose, with a sweet, floral, fragrant palate, featuring vanilla, ginger and even a hint of mint. Medium length in the finish, with a note of lingering almonds.

Miltonduff

Scotch whisky exports hit a record high in 2017 with both volumes and value increasing. Even though blends still dominate the picture, the biggest growth comes in the single malt category.

Volumes are around 10% of total sales but the value on the other hand now represents an impressive 28% of the total. No wonder then that many producers are eager to shift some of their whisky stock to single malt bottlings. This is evidenced not least by Chivas Brothers which for the first time have widely released expressions from three of their distilleries, previously reserved only for blends.

The three distilleries are Miltonduff, Glenburgie and Glengassaugh, whose malt whisky for decades, have been important components contributing to Ballantines. Obviously the lion´s share of the three single malts still goes into the blend - after all, it´s the second most sold Scotch whisky in the world. Furthermore, to highlight the link between the famous blend and the new single malts the entire range is called Ballantine´s Single Malt Series.

Miltonduff distillery is equipped with an 8 ton full lauter mash tun with a copper dome, 16 stainless steel washbacks with a fermentation time of 56 hours and six, large stills. The lyne arms are all sharply descending which allows for very little reflux. This makes for a rather robust and oily new make in contrast to the lighter and more floral Glenburgie – another key malt in Ballantines. In 1964, two Lomond stills were installed at Miltonduff. They were equipped with columns with adjustable plates with the intention of distilling different styles of whisky from the same still. They were dismantled in 1981 but the special whisky produced in the still, Mosstowie, can still, with a bit of luck, be found.

The new official bottling is a **15 year old** matured in ex-bourbon casks. There is another bottling from the owners but only available at the Chivas´ visitor centres - a **19 year old**, matured in first fill bourbon barrels and part of the Distillery Reserve Collection.

15 years old

[mill•ton•<u>duff</u>]

Owner: **Region/district:**
Chivas Brothers   Speyside
(Pernod Ricard)

Founded: **Status:**   **Capacity:**
1824   Active   5 800 000 litres

Address: Miltonduff, Elgin, Morayshire IV30 8TQ

Website: **Tel:**
-                01343 547433

History:

1824 Andrew Peary and Robert Bain obtain a licence for Miltonduff Distillery. It has previously operated as an illicit farm distillery called Milton Distillery but changes name when the Duff family buys the site it is operating on.

1866 William Stuart buys the distillery.

1895 Thomas Yool & Co. becomes new part-owner.

1936 Thomas Yool & Co. sells the distillery to Hiram Walker Gooderham & Worts. The latter transfers administration to the newly acquired subsidiary George Ballantine & Son.

1964 A pair of Lomond stills is installed to produce the rare Mosstowie.

1974 Major reconstruction of the distillery.

1981 The Lomond stills are decommissioned and replaced by two ordinary pot stills, the number of stills now totalling six.

1986 Allied Lyons buys 51% of Hiram Walker.

1987 Allied Lyons acquires the rest of Hiram Walker.

1991 Allied Distillers follow United Distillers´ example of Classic Malts and introduce Caledonian Malts in which Tormore, Glendro-nach and Laphroaig are included in addition to Miltonduff. Tormore is later replaced by Scapa.

2005 Chivas Brothers (Pernod Ricard) becomes the new owner through the acquisition of Allied Domecq.

2017 A 15 year old is released.

Tasting notes Miltonduff 15 years old:

IR – Fresh citrus and honey on the nose together with heather, ginger and peaches. More spicy on the palate with cinnamon and clove, vanilla, honey, red berries and liquorice.

Mortlach

[mort•lack]

Owner: Diageo

Region/district: Speyside

Founded: 1823

Status: Active

Capacity: 3 800 000 litres

Address: Dufftown, Keith, Banffshire AB55 4AQ

Website: mortlach.com, malts.com

Tel: 01340 822100

Mortlach is a distillery and a single malt that has always been revered by the aficionados. It has no visitor centre and so when the distillery occasionally opens its gates during the Speyside Whisky Festival, tickets sell out instantly.

Its fame came largely from the heavily sherried and meaty 16 year old official bottling. This was discontinued and a new range of Mortlachs was introduced in 2014. However, the new expressions never seemed to take off, perhaps partly due to a substantial increase in price. The owners admitted the range had disappointed whisky fans and three new whiskies were launched in autumn 2018 - all with age statements.

The distillery is equipped with a 12 ton full lauter mash tun and six washbacks made of larch, currently with 6 short fermentations (55 hours) and 6 long (110 hours). There are three wash stills and three spirit stills where the No. 3 pair acts as a traditional double distillation. The low wines from wash stills No. 1 and 2 are directed to the remaining two spirit stills according to a certain distribution. In one of the spirit stills, called Wee Witchie, the charge is redistilled twice and, with all the various distillations taken into account, it could be said that Mortlach is distilled 2.81 times. All the stills are attached to worm tubs for cooling the spirit vapours. Five of the tubs are made from wood and one (number 3 wash still) is made from stainless steel. During 2018, the distillery will be working a 5-day week with 12 mashes/week with a target of making 2.6 million litres.

The previous range with Rare Old, Special Strength, 18 year old and 25 year old relied heavily on maturation in ex-bourbon barrels even if there was a presence of sherry butts in some of them. With the new bottles, it´s the other way around - the two older ones have been matured in ex-sherry casks while the youngest is a vatting of ex-sherry and ex-bourbon. The range now consists of **12 year old Wee Witchie, 16 year old Distiller´s Dram** and the **20 year old Cowie´s Blue Seal.**

History:

1823 The distillery is founded by James Findlater.

1824 Donald Macintosh and Alexander Gordon become part-owners.

1831 The distillery is sold to John Robertson for £270.

1832 A. & T. Gregory buys Mortlach.

1837 James and John Grant of Aberlour become part-owners. No production takes place.

1842 The distillery is now owned by John Alexander Gordon and the Grant brothers.

1851 Mortlach is producing again after having been used as a church and a brewery for some years.

1853 George Cowie joins and becomes part-owner.

1867 John Alexander Gordon dies and Cowie becomes sole owner.

1896 Alexander Cowie joins the company.

1897 The number of stills is increased from three to six.

1923 Alexander Cowie sells the distillery to John Walker & Sons.

1925 John Walker becomes part of Distillers Company Limited (DCL).

1964 Major refurbishment.

1968 Floor maltings ceases.

1996 Mortlach 1972 is released as a Rare Malt.

1998 Mortlach 1978 is released as a Rare Malt.

2004 Mortlach 1971, a 32 year old cask strength is released.

2014 Four new bottlings are released - Rare Old, Special Strength, 18 year old and 25 year old.

2018 A new range is presented; 12 year old Wee Witchie, 16 year old Distiller´s Dram and 20 year old Cowie´s Blue Seal.

Tasting notes Mortlach 12 years old:

IR – Fresh and intense on the nose with notes of sherry, apple cider, dark plums, tobacco and toffee. The palate is robust with orange marmalade, dark chocolate, espresso and chili pepper.

12 years old

Oban

[oa•bun]

Owner:	**Region/district:**
Diageo	Western Highlands
Founded: **Status:**	**Capacity:**
1794 Active (vc)	870 000 litres
Address: Stafford Street, Oban, Argyll PA34 5NH	
Website:	**Tel:**
malts.com	01631 572004 (vc)

Not only did the two Stevenson brothers, John and Hugh, build the distillery. They played a vital part in transforming Oban from the tiny fishing hamlet it was in the late 1700s into a modern and thriving town.

The two brothers had arrived in Oban around 1780 and they soon started a business that would be the foundation of their future wealth. They bought the small island of Belnahua, southwest of Oban, and opened a slate quarry. Together with another four islands (Easdale, Luing and Seil), Belnahua formed what was known as Slate Islands. For 200 years, starting in 1630, these four islands dominated the slate industry in Scotland with up to 8 million slates produced per year.

Many of these slates went into building the houses when Oban was growing but they were also exported to markets as far away as Australia. In time, the importance of the quarries in Slate Islands diminished and in 1955, the last slate quarry in Scotland ceased production. But the Stevenson brothers were industrial in many ways. They were involved in construction work, ship building and also started a tannery and a brewery before founding Oban distillery in 1793.

The equipment consists of a 7 ton traditional stainless steel mash tun with rakes, four washbacks made of European larch and one pair of stills. Attached to the stills is a rectangular, stainless steel, double worm tub to condense the spirit vapours. One washback will fill the wash still twice. However, the character of Oban single malt is dependent on long fermentations (110 hours), hence they can only manage six mashes per week, giving it five long fermentations and one short (65 hours). The production for 2018 will be slightly more than 800,000 litres.

The core range consists of **Little Bay, a 14 year old,** an **18 year old** exclusive for USA and a **Distiller's Edition** with a montilla fino sherry finish. In 2018, the fourth release of an Oban single malt in the yearly Special Releases appeared. This time it was **21 year old** matured in refill sherry butts.

History:

1793 John and Hugh Stevenson found the distillery.

1820 Hugh Stevenson dies.

1821 Hugh Stevenson's son Thomas takes over.

1829 Bad investments force Thomas Stevenson into bankruptcy. His eldest son John takes over.

1830 John buys the distillery from his father's creditors for £1,500.

1866 Peter Cumstie buys the distillery.

1883 Cumstie sells Oban to James Walter Higgins who refurbishes and modernizes it.

1898 The Oban & Aultmore-Glenlivet Co. takes over with Alexander Edwards at the helm.

1923 The Oban Distillery Co. owned by Buchanan-Dewar takes over.

1925 Buchanan-Dewar becomes part of Distillers Company Limited (DCL).

1931 Production ceases.

1937 In production again.

1968 Floor maltings ceases and the distillery closes for reconstruction.

1972 Reopening of the distillery.

1979 Oban 12 years is on sale.

1988 United Distillers launches Classic Malts and Oban 14 year old is included.

1998 A Distillers' Edition is launched.

2002 The oldest Oban (32 years) so far is launched.

2004 A 1984 cask strength is released.

2009 Oban 2000, a single cask, is released.

2010 A no age distillery exclusive is released.

2013 A limited 21 year old is released.

2015 Oban Little Bay is released.

2016 A distillery exclusive without age statement is released.

2018 A 21 year old is launched as a part of the Special Releases.

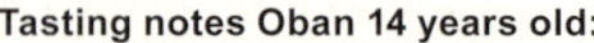

21 years old

Tasting notes Oban 14 years old:

GS – Lightly smoky on the honeyed, floral nose. Toffee, cereal and a hint of peat. The palate offers initial cooked fruits, becoming spicier. Complex, bittersweet, oak and more gentle smoke. The finish is quite lengthy, with spicy oak, toffee and new leather.

Pulteney

[poolt•ni]

Owner:
Inver House Distillers
(Thai Beverages plc)

Region/district:
Northern Highlands

Founded: 1826
Status: Active (vc)
Capacity: 1 800 000 litres

Address: Huddart St, Wick, Caithness KW1 5BA

Website: oldpulteney.com
Tel: 01955 602371

In the last couple of years, sales of single malts have increased rapidly while many blends have been struggling. In the two years from 2014 to 2016, only eight of the top 35 single malts showed declining volumes. One of them was Old Pulteney.

With two core expressions gone in the last year (the 17 and the 21 year old) it seemed the owners were facing a temporary lack of older whiskies. Inver House are also big on the blending side and this part of the business may have taken a toll on the stocks of aged Pulteney single malt. However, in August 2018, the owners presented an entirely new core range consisting of four expressions in completely new packaging.

Pulteney is located in Wick and not only was the distillery closed between 1930 and 1951, but the entire town was dry. A law gave communities in Scotland the right to implement prohibition similar to the one that was enforced in the USA, provided a majority of the population voted for it. The ban was enforced in 1922 and it lasted until 1947 before pubs in Wick were allowed to serve alcohol again.

The distillery is equipped with a stainless steel semi-lauter mash tun with a copper canopy. There are seven washbacks made of stainless steel with a fermentation time between 50 and 110 hours. The wash still, equipped with a huge boil ball and a very thick lye pipe, is quaintly chopped off at the top. Both stills use stainless steel worm tubs for condensing the spirit. Around 1.6 million litres of alcohol are produced yearly.

The new core range of Old Pulteney consists of **12 years old**, matured in ex-bourbon casks and bottled at 40%, the smoky **Huddart** without age statement. and **15** and **18 years old**, both matured in a combination of ex-bourbon and ex-sherry casks. The duty free range is made up of **Noss Head**, matured in ex-bourbon American oak, and **Duncansby Head** and **Dunnet Head,** a mix of ex-bourbon and ex-sherry. They were complemented by two vintages in 2017 – **1990** and **2006**. A **1983 Vintage** was released at the same time.

History:

1826 James Henderson founds the distillery.

1920 The distillery is bought by James Watson.

1923 Buchanan-Dewar takes over.

1930 Production ceases.

1951 In production again after being acquired by the solicitor Robert Cumming.

1955 Cumming sells to James & George Stodart, a subsidiary to Hiram Walker & Sons.

1958 The distillery is rebuilt.

1959 The floor maltings close.

1961 Allied Breweries buys James & George Stodart Ltd.

1981 Allied Breweries changes name to Allied Lyons.

1995 Allied Domecq sells Pulteney to Inver House Distillers.

1997 Old Pulteney 12 years is launched.

2001 Pacific Spirits (Great Oriole Group) buys Inver House at a price of $85 million.

2004 A 17 year old is launched.

2005 A 21 year old is launched.

2006 International Beverage Holdings acquires Pacific Spirits UK.

2010 WK499 Isabella Fortuna is released.

2012 A 40 year old and WK217 Spectrum are released.

2013 Old Pulteney Navigator, The Lighthouse range (3 expressions) and Vintage 1990 are released.

2014 A 35 year old is released.

2015 Dunnet Head and Vintage 1989 are released.

2017 Three vintages (1983, 1990 and 2006) are released together with a 25 year old.

2018 A completely new core range is launched; 12 years old, Huddart, 15 years old and 18 years old.

12 years old

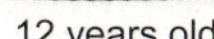

Tasting notes Old Pulteney 12 years old:

GS – The nose presents pleasingly fresh malt and floral notes, with a touch of pine. The palate is comparatively sweet, with malt, spices, fresh fruit and a suggestion of salt. The finish is medium in length, drying and decidedly nutty.

Royal Brackla

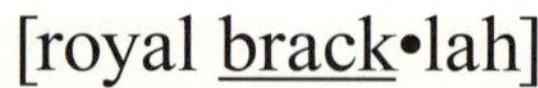

[royal brack•lah]

Owner:	Region/district:
John Dewar & Sons (Bacardi)	Highlands

Founded:	Status:	Capacity:
1812	Active	4 100 000 litres

Address: Cawdor, Nairn, Nairnshire IV12 5QY

Website:	Tel:
lastgreatmalts.com	01667 402002

Once you´ve left Elgin, "capital" of the distillery-clotted Speyside, and drive west on the A96 towards Inverness, you stop seeing pagoda roofs every five minutes.

After a while, you might be able to spot Glenburgie to your left and you will pass by Benromach at Forres but before you reach Inverness, there´s only one distillery left in this area and that is Royal Brackla. It lies off the beaten track on the B9090 sideroad a few kilometres south of Nairn. But if the distillery is hidden in a geographical sense, its single malt has always been very present in the minds of blenders.

The character of the whisky lends itself very well to a lot of blends. There are several factors contributing to this style; clear wort, long fermentations (70 hours), long foreshots (30 minutes), a slow distillation and ascending lyne arms on the stills to create as much reflux as possible during the distillation.

In similar with Royal Lochnagar, the distillery can boast of once having held a royal warrant. It was granted already in 1835 by William IV but since the warrant expires five years after the monarch has died the brand is no longer a holder.

Royal Brackla is equipped with a 12.5 ton full lauter mash tun. There are six wooden washbacks and another two made of stainless steel which have been placed outside. Finally, there are also two pairs of stills. In 2018, the distillery will be doing 17 mashes per week which translates to 4 million litres of alcohol which is more or less the full capacity of the distillery. In 2015 a biomass boiler (fired with wood-chips) replaced the old, heavy fuel oil boiler. Not only will this contribute to a 5,000 ton reduction of CO^2 emissions, but it will also be 50% more energy efficient.

The new core range introduced in 2015 and replacing the previous 10 year old, consists of a **12, 16** and **21 year old**. There are no limited releases but a 25 year old version of Dewar´s blend was released in autumn 2017 which had been finished in casks that had previously been used to mature Royal Brackla single malt.

History:

1812 The distillery is founded by Captain William Fraser.

1833 Brackla becomes the first of three distilleries allowed to use 'Royal' in the name.

1852 Robert Fraser & Co. takes over the distillery.

1897 The distillery is rebuilt and Royal Brackla Distillery Company Limited is founded.

1919 John Mitchell and James Leict from Aberdeen purchase Royal Brackla.

1926 John Bisset & Company Ltd takes over.

1943 Scottish Malt Distillers (SMD) buys John Bisset & Company Ltd and thereby acquires Royal Brackla.

1964 The distillery closes for a big refurbishment **-1966** and the number of stills is increased to four. The maltings closes.

1970 Two stills are increased to four.

1985 The distillery is mothballed.

1991 Production resumes.

1993 A 10 year old Royal Brackla is launched in United Distillers´ Flora & Fauna series.

1997 UDV spends more than £2 million on improvements and refurbishing.

1998 Bacardi–Martini buys Dewar´s from Diageo.

2004 A new 10 year old is launched.

2014 A 35 year old is released for Changi airport in Singapore.

2015 A new range is released; 12, 16 and 21 year old.

12 years old

Tasting notes Royal Brackla 12 years old:

GS – Warm spices, malt and peaches in cream on the nose. The palate is robust, with spice and mildly smoky soft fruit. Quite lengthy in the finish, with citrus fruit, mild spice and cocoa powder.

Royal Lochnagar

[royal loch•nah•gar]

Owner: Diageo
Region/district: Eastern Highlands

Founded: 1845
Status: Active (vc)
Capacity: 500 000 litres

Address: Crathie, Ballater, Aberdeenshire AB35 5TB

Website: malts.com
Tel: 01339 742700

There are three distilleries, of which only two are currently operating, that have the word Royal attached to their distillery names. The reason for this is that they at one time or another were granted a Royal Warrant by the monarch at the time.

In the case of Lochnagar, it was the unlikely story of the owner John Begg inviting his "neighbours" in 1848, Queen Victoria and Prince Albert, to come and visit the distillery. Prince Albert had recently acquired Balmoral Castle, just a kilometre away, and the royals apparently took a liking to the whisky and awarded Begg a Royal Warrant.

The thing is that a royal warrant only lasts five years after the granting regent has passed away (unless it´s revoked for other reasons) and the last king to acknowledge Lochnagar under these circumstances was George V and so since 1941, the distillery is not per definition a supplier to the Royal household and neither is Royal Brackla. In fact the only two companies involved in the whisky business that currently hold a Royal Warrant are Laphroaig and Berry Brothers.

The distillery is equipped with a 5.4 ton open, traditional stainless steel mash tun. There are two wooden washbacks (a third that hadn´t been used for years has now been removed), with short fermentations of 70 hours and long ones of 110 hours. The two stills are quite small with a charge in the wash still of 6,100 litres and 4,000 litres in the spirit still and the spirit vapours are condensed in cast iron worm tubs. The whole production is filled on site with 1,000 casks being stored in its only warehouse, while the rest is sent to Glenlossie. Four mashes per week during 2018 will result in 450,000 litres of pure alcohol.

Royal Lochnagar is the signature malt of the best selling Scotch blend in Korea – Windsor. The core range of single malts consists of the **12 year old** and **Selected Reserve**. The latter is a vatting of casks, usually around 18-20 years of age. In autumn 2015 one of the oldest bottlings from the distillery was launched, a **36 year old single cask**.

History:

1823 James Robertson founds a distillery in Glen Feardan on the north bank of River Dee.

1826 The distillery is burnt down by competitors but Robertson decides to establish a new distillery near the mountain Lochnagar.

1841 This distillery is also burnt down.

1845 A new distillery is built by John Begg, this time on the south bank of River Dee. It is named New Lochnagar.

1848 Lochnagar obtains a Royal Warrant.

1882 John Begg passes away and his son Henry Farquharson Begg inherits the distillery.

1896 Henry Farquharson Begg dies.

1906 The children of Henry Begg rebuild the distillery.

1916 The distillery is sold to John Dewar & Sons.

1925 John Dewar & Sons becomes part of Distillers Company Limited (DCL).

1963 A major reconstruction takes place.

2004 A 30 year old cask strength from 1974 is launched in the Rare Malts series (6,000 bottles).

2008 A Distiller´s Edition with a Moscatel finish is released.

2010 A Manager´s Choice 1994 is released.

2013 A triple matured expression for Friends of the Classic Malts is released.

2016 A distillery exclusive without age statement is released.

12 years old

Tasting notes Royal Lochnagar 12 years old:

GS – Light toffee on the nose, along with some green notes of freshly-sawn timber. The palate offers a pleasing and quite complex blend of caramel, dry sherry and spice, followed by a hint of liquorice before the slightly scented finish develops.

Scapa

[ska•pa]

Owner:
Chivas Brothers
(Pernod Ricard)

Region/district:
Highlands (Orkney)

Founded: 1885
Status: Active
Capacity: 1 300 000 litres

Address: Scapa, St Ola, Kirkwall, Orkney KW15 1SE

Website: scapawhisky.com
Tel: 01856 876585

One may wonder why two distillers (Townsend and Macfarlane) based in Glasgow decided to build a distillery in Orkney. Especially in the 1880s when the islands appeared much more remote than today.

One thing is clear though - the stunning location, with its marvellous view of the Scapa Bay, can be matched only by a few Scottish distilleries. Therefore, it was long overdue when the owners finally opened a visitor centre in April 2015. But the location is not just about whisky. After Germany's surrender in the First World War in 1918, the allied forces ordered the German navy to sail to Scapa Flow and lay anchor. The French wished to use the ships to rebuild their navy, while the English wanted them to be scrapped. However, before any decision could be made, a German Admiral, Ludwig von Reuter and his crew, in June 1919 were successful in sinking 52 of the 74 vessels to prevent them from being used by any of the allied forces. During the following 15 years most were recovered and sold for scrap. The wrecks that remain have become a popular site for sports divers.

The equipment consists of a 3 ton semi-lauter mash tun with a copper dome, twelve washbacks and two stills. Until recently, there were eight washbacks with four of them made from Corten steel but with four new ones added in summer 2018, all twelve are now made of stainless steel. At the same time, the boiler was also replaced. Due to the increased production, fermentation time is down to 52 hours from the previous 160. The wash still, sourced from Glenburgie distillery, is only one of two surviving Lomond stills in the industry but on the Scapa still, the adjustable plates have been removed.

The previous 16 year old has been replaced by **Scapa Skiren**, which was introduced in 2015. Matured in first fill bourbon, it doesn´t carry an age statement. This was followed up in autumn 2016 with **Scapa Glansa**, matured in American oak and then finished in casks that previously held peated whisky. There are also two cask strength distillery exclusives – a **10 year old first fill sherry** and a **15 year old first fill bourbon**. These two can also be found at the other Chivas visitor centres.

History:

1885 Macfarlane & Townsend founds the distillery with John Townsend at the helm.

1919 Scapa Distillery Company Ltd takes over.

1934 Scapa Distillery Company goes into voluntary liquidation and production ceases.

1936 Production resumes.

1936 Bloch Brothers Ltd (John and Sir Maurice) takes over.

1954 Hiram Walker & Sons takes over.

1959 A Lomond still is installed.

1978 The distillery is modernized.

1994 The distillery is mothballed.

1997 Production takes place a few months each year using staff from Highland Park.

2004 Extensive refurbishing takes place at a cost of £2.1 million. Scapa 14 years is launched.

2005 Production ceases in April and phase two of the refurbishment programme starts. Chivas Brothers becomes the new owner.

2006 Scapa 1992 (14 years) is launched.

2008 Scapa 16 years is launched.

2015 The distillery opens for visitors and Scapa Skiren is launched.

2016 The peated Glansa is released.

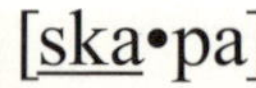

Scapa Skiren

Tasting notes Scapa Skiren:

GS – Lime is apparent on the early nose, followed by musty peaches, almonds, cinnamon, and salt. More peaches on the palate, with tinned pear and honey. Tingling spices in the drying finish, which soon becomes slightly astringent.

Speyburn

[spey•burn]

Owner:
Inver House Distillers
(Thai Beverages plc)

Region/district:
Speyside

Founded: | **Status:** | **Capacity:**
1897 | Active | 4 500 000 litres

Address: Rothes, Aberlour, Morayshire AB38 7AG

Website:
speyburn.com

Tel:
01340 831213

Back up ten years and Speyburn was very much a single malt under the radar – at least in Europe. In the US though, it has been a brand to reckon with for a long time, not least for historical reasons, having had an American owner in the past.

In the last few years though, the range has been expanded and it now includes seven different expressions. With the recent upgrade of the distillery, it seems the owners have their minds set on an increased exposure of the brand.

An impressive expansion of the distillery was completed in 2015. The expansion had cost £4m and included a new 6.25 ton stainless steel mash tun. Four of the six wooden washbacks were kept but they have also expanded with no less than 15 washbacks made of stainless steel. Finally, the existing wash still was converted to a spirit still of exactly the same shape as the other one, while a new and much larger wash still was installed. The two spirit stills are connected to a worm tub while the wash still is fitted with a shell and tube condenser. The fermentation time has also been lengthened from the original 48 hours to a minimum of 72 hours. During 2018 the distillery will be working on a 5-day production with 27 mashes per week, equating to approximately 3 million litres of pure alcohol. In 1900, Speyburn was the first distillery to abandon floor malting in favour of a new method – drum malting. In the late sixties, the malting closed but the equipment is still there to see, protected by Historic Scotland.

The core range of Speyburn single malt is a **10 year old,** a **15 year old** and **Bradan Orach** without age statement. In 2015, **Arranta Casks** was released as a limited USA exclusive and this was followed up in 2017 by **Companion Casks**, matured in first fill ex Buffalo Trace bourbon casks. Recently, expressions designated for the duty free market have also been released. The **10 year old,** a combination of ex-bourbon and ex-sherry is bottled at 46% as opposed to the standarad 40% and there is also a **Hopkins Reserve** that has been matured in casks that previously held a peated whisky.

History:

1897 Brothers John and Edward Hopkins and their cousin Edward Broughton found the distillery through John Hopkins & Co. They already own Tobermory. The architect is Charles Doig. Building the distillery costs £17,000 and the distillery is transferred to Speyburn-Glenlivet Distillery Company.

1916 Distillers Company Limited (DCL) acquires John Hopkins & Co. and the distillery.

1930 Production stops.

1934 Productions restarts.

1962 Speyburn is transferred to Scottish Malt Distillers (SMD).

1968 Drum maltings closes.

1991 Inver House Distillers buys Speyburn.

1992 A 10 year old is launched as a replacement for the 12 year old in the Flora & Fauna series.

2001 Pacific Spirits (Great Oriole Group) buys Inver House for $85 million.

2005 A 25 year old Solera is released.

2006 Inver House changes owner when International Beverage Holdings acquires Pacific Spirits UK.

2009 The un-aged Bradan Orach is introduced for the American market.

2012 Clan Speyburn is formed.

2014 The distillery is expanded.

2015 Arranta Casks is released.

2017 A 15 year old and Companion Casks are launched.

2018 Two expressions for duty free are released - a 10 year old and Hopkins Reserve.

10 years old

Tasting notes Speyburn 10 years old:

GS – Soft and elegant on the spicy, nutty nose. Smooth in the mouth, with vanilla, spice and more nuts. The finish is medium, spicy and drying.

Speyside

[spey•side]

Owner:
Speyside Distillers Co.

Region/district:
Speyside

Founded: **Status:**
1990   Active

Capacity:
600 000 litres

Address: Glen Tromie, Kingussie, Inverness-shire PH21 1NS

Website:
speysidedistillery.co.uk

Tel:
01540 661060

History:

1956 George Christie buys a piece of land at Drumguish near Kingussie.

1957 George Christie starts a grain distillery near Alloa.

1962 George Christie (founder of Speyside Distillery Group in the fifties) commissions the drystone dyker Alex Fairlie to build a distillery in Drumguish.

1986 Scowis assumes ownership.

1987 The distillery is completed.

1990 The distillery is on stream in December.

1993 The first single malt, Drumguish, is launched.

1999 Speyside 8 years is launched.

2000 Speyside Distilleries is sold to a group of private investors including Ricky Christie, Ian Jerman and Sir James Ackroyd.

2001 Speyside 10 years is launched.

2012 Speyside Distillers is sold to Harvey´s of Edinburgh.

2014 A new range, Spey from Speyside Distillery, is launched (NAS, 12 and 18 year old).

2015 The range is revamped again. New expressions include Tenné, 12 years old and 18 years old.

2016 "Byron´s Choice - The Marriage" and Spey Cask 27 are released.

2017 Trutina and Fumare are released.

A good product is the obvious starting point if you wish to succeed in the whisky business. Another important side is branding and marketing. The industry is full of examples where producers do their utmost to create an interesting story about their whisky.

In the case of Speyside distillery and Spey whisky, their creativity includes a link to Lord Byron. Supposedly, the famous poet sent a cask of Spey whisky to King George III to celebrate his marriage to Annabella Milbanke in 1815. Since Speyside distillery was founded 175 years after the marriage, the whisky obviously had been produced elsewhere in the Speyside area.

Be that as it may, when John Harvey McDonough took over Speyside six years ago, it was a boost for both the distillery and the brand. His connections in the Far East, not least in Taiwan, have helped him establish the brand as one of the top sellers in that market. The small distillery is beautiful and set in stunning surroundings but is at the same time a bit remote and difficult to find. For that reason, the owners have decided to open up a visitor experience in nearby Aviemore. Named The Snug after a local pub, the centre will stock the distillery´s range and host tastings.

The distillery is equipped with a 4.2 ton semi-lauter mash tun, four stainless steel washbacks with a 70-120 hour fermentation time and one pair of stills. For the last couple of years they have been working a 6 day week with a total production of 600,000 litres of alcohol.

The core range of Spey single malt is made up of **Tenné** (with a 6 months port finish), **18 year old** (sherry matured), **Chairman´s Choice** and **Royal Choice**. The latter two are multi-vintage marriages from both American and European oak. Two new core bottlings were added in 2017; **Trutina** which is a 100% bourbon maturation and **Fumare**, similar to Trutina but distilled from peated barley. Also part of the core range is **Beinn Dubh** which replaced the black whisky Cu Dubh. The 12 year old which used to be a part of the range has been discontinued. Recent limited releases include a **single cask** for the Spirit of Speyside Festival 2018 as well as single cask releases for select markets.

Trutina

Tasting notes Spey Trutina:

IR – A floral nose, with lemon, granola, shortbread and dried grass. A sweet start on the palate, honey, white chocolate, sweet red apples and then ends with a dry, oaky note.

Whisky
the way I see it

Jackie Thomson
Visitor Centre Manager
Ardbeg Distillery

You have been a part of Ardbeg ever since it was bought and resurrected by Glenmorangie. What were your first feelings when you came to the distillery in 1997?

First feelings were naturally ones of trepidation. For me a new location, new distillery, new people. For the guardians of Ardbeg so much history in a place. Lots to live up to! Excitement, fluttery tummy, recognising what Islay meant in the world of whisky, single track roads, a little disappointment at how Ardbeg looked. I have to admit that Ardbeg and Islay had not previously been on my holiday list. Intense and real enthusiasm. I was pregnant so life was blooming in so many ways.

The visitor centre opened the year after and today, when nearly 15,000 people come every year it is like they are making a pilgrimage. What was it like in the first years?

It was fun. And hard work. And all about building a team. Visitors were more inquisitive, rather than knowledgable. Ardbeg had been out of bounds for so long that it's re-opening brought visitors who loved Islay malts and peaty whisky. In a way there was a little more naivety about the distillery. Ardbeg needed investment – it was run down having been, from the 60's to the 80's, sporadically producing spirit. People were naturally curious and those first years were free and easy and all about warmly involving visitors to share in Ardbeg's re-opening.

I realise you have many different types of visitors. How do you try to cater to each group?

Every visitor who walks through the door of Ardbeg has different desires and needs and expectations, but every visitor should be greeted with warmth and sincerity. I often say that tourism and the act of visiting a place can be very transient in nature. On Islay coming to the island transcends this and people came twice or three times a year. Which actually makes them friends and not merely a passing exchange of information. Love to give a group of single malt lovers an experience and memory they may not forget! An oyster on the Atlantic, a chocolate fondue on the back of a quad bike up the hill, a tasting in a cave, some scallops under the cliffs of the Oa. It does get harder though.....!

The visitor centre is of course there to attend to visitors from all parts of the world but does it also have a significance to the local Islay community?

Yes – absolutely! We started in the visitor centre with a few tables and chairs and a bowl of soup. The visitor centre has evolved so much over the years. We are as happy to see local visitors from Portnahaven as we are to welcome guests from Paraguay. Ardbeg really did push the visitor experience to a different level 20 years ago on Islay. So as well as greeting single malt lovers when visiting their 50th distillery, local ladies coming out for a tasty lunch, a group who love Ardbeg passing through on a tall ship, celebrating the wedding of Committee members, hosting a Spanish themed flamenco dinner or holding a meeting for the local development group, I'd like to think Ardbeg has been a hub for much more than drinking whisky.

How important is the visitor centre as a marketing tool for the whisky compared to other channels and types of promotion?

Hugely so. The distillery is the birthplace of the spirit and the whisky. I think in the broadest sense. There is a very strong team spirit which prevails at Ardbeg and a loyalty which manifests itself in many ways.... from staff nights out at the pub, to visitors who tattoo themselves with The Ardbeg logo, to the spirit of co-operation which carries through Ardbeg lovers the world over. The distillery has a feeling and that is the feeling we want Ardbeg drinkers to feel when they imbibe in a wee dram. Wherever they may be.

All the tour guides and visitor centre staff are the ones in hand to hand combat learning the information, instilling the personality and disseminating the information. Each of them tactically astute at marketing... even though they don't always realise it!

The Feis Ile has become bigger every year and with a couple of new distilleries being built, it will grow in the years to come. How important is the Feis to Ardbeg and to Islay and is their a risk it will grow out of proportion?

We love the Islay Festival of Malt and Music and I can still cast my mind back to when we knew the names of most of the visitors who came to enjoy the Festival. It has become an incredibly busy event where distilleries can really push and pull visitors in all directions. There is no doubt that it will continue to expand and grow in the coming years. But there is also a greater force at work. Tourism and businesses have grown so rapidly on Islay over the past 20 years that there are worrying strains being placed upon the island's infrastucture – roads, transport links, ferry and plane, accommodation and places to eat. Distilleries are expanding and the world is getting smaller – with people seeking destinations which are remote and safe with good spirit. Islay ticks all the boxes. Whilst Islay benefits socially and economically from the arrival of Islay malt lovers, the island groans from the sheer numbers of people wanting to travel, eat, drink and stay on the island.

What does Scotch whisky mean to you?

If you stand back and think about what Scotch whisky is it is really simple. It is a drink which inspires strong emotions and can make people happy and sad. Whisky can bring people together and be the fuel for a passsion that burns deeply. It embodies the land, people and language of Scotland. Whisky is unselfish and is to be shared amongst kindred spirits.

The history of Scotch whisky has had its ups and downs over the years. How do you see the future for Scotch in the next 10-15 years?

We need to trust consumers – whisky drinkers are knowledgeable folk. They know good whisky when they taste it. I'd love to think that we can listen to what they want and the ideas they have. Crossing ideas within the industry – from restaurateurs, bartenders and owners, chefs and creatives. More collaboration. Whisky is a long game.... not short-term thinking but really looking to build on firm foundations. Wish people would stop being so cynical sometimes and just enjoy their dram.

Springbank

[spring•bank]

Owner:
Springbank Distillers
(J & A Mitchell)

Region/district:
Campbeltown

Founded: 1828
Status: Active (vc)
Capacity: 750 000 litres

Address: Well Close, Campbeltown, Argyll PA28 6ET

Website: springbankwhisky.com
Tel: 01586 551710

History:

1828 The Reid family, in-laws of the Mitchells (see below), founds the distillery.

1837 The Reid family encounters financial difficulties and John and William Mitchell buy the distillery.

1897 J. & A. Mitchell Co Ltd is founded.

1926 The depression forces the distillery to close.

1933 The distillery is back in production.

1960 Own maltings ceases.

1969 J. & A. Mitchell buys the independent bottler Cadenhead.

1979 The distillery closes.

1985 A 10 year old Longrow is launched.

1987 Limited production restarts.

1989 Production restarts.

1992 Springbank takes up its maltings again.

1997 First distillation of Hazelburn.

1998 Springbank 12 years is launched.

1999 Dha Mhile (7 years), the world's first organic single malt, is launched.

2000 A 10 year old is launched.

2001 Springbank 1965 'Local barley' (36 years), 741 bottles, is launched.

2002 Number one in the series Wood Expressions is a 12 year old with five years on Demerara rum casks.

2004 Springbank 10 years 100 proof is launched as well as Springbank Wood Expression bourbon, Longrow 14 years old, Springbank 32 years old and Springbank 14 years Port Wood.

2005 Springbank 21 years, the first version of Hazelburn (8 years) and Longrow Tokaji Wood Expression are launched.

2006 Longrow 10 years 100 proof, Springbank 25 years, Springbank 9 years Marsala finish, Springbank 11 years Madeira finish and a new Hazelburn 8 year old are released.

It´s not that unusual today that a distillery decides to introduce a separate sub-range of bottlings where they can showcase a different style of whisky compared to the core brand.

Tomintoul/Old Ballantruan, Tomatin/Cu Bocan and Edradour/Ballechin are a few examples. Not to mention Bruichladdich with three different versions. First out though, was Springbank. In 1973, they started to distill heavily peated malt which later would be known as Longrow. In 1997, it was time for yet another style when the triple distilled Hazelburn was first produced. Both of them represent a small percentage of the production but then again, only 140,000 litres of Springbank are made every year.

In 2009, the distillery introduced Springbank Open Day where visitors could experience the distillery, tastings and all sorts of activities. Since 2014, this has expanded to become Campbeltown Malts Festival, including also Glengyle and Glen Scotia distilleries. In time for the 2018 festival, Springbank opened a new shop and visitor centre, expanding the number and type of tours they could offer. Another, more hands-on activity that the distillery can offer is the whisky school which runs every summer with former distillery manager Frank McHardy as headmaster. For a week, the "students" will get involved and learn about all the steps in traditional whisky making.

The distillery is equipped with a 3.5 ton open cast iron mash tun, six washbacks made of Scandinavian larch with a fermentation time of up to 110 hours, one wash still and two spirit stills. The wash still is unique in Scotland, as it is fired by both an open oil-fire and internal steam coils. Ordinary condensers are used to cool the spirit vapours, except in the first of the two spirit stills, where a worm tub is used. Springbank is also the only distillery in Scotland that malts its entire need of barley using own floor maltings.

Springbank produces three distinctive single malts with different phenol contents in the malted barley. Springbank is distilled two and a half times (12-15ppm), Longrow is distilled twice (50-55 ppm) and Hazelburn is distilled three times and unpeated. When Springbank is produced, the malted barley is dried using 6 hours of peat smoke and 30 hours of hot air, while Longrow requires 48 hours of peat smoke. In 2018 a total of 175,000 litres will be produced of which 10% is Longrow and 10% Hazelburn.

The core range is **Springbank 10, 15** and **18 year old**, as well as **12 year old cask strength**. There are also limited but yearly releases of a **21 year old** and a **25 year old**. Longrow is represented by **Longrow without age statement,** the **18 year old** and the **Longrow Red**. The latest edition of the latter was an 11 year old finished in casks that had held cabernet franc red wine. Finally, there is **Hazelburn** where the core range consists of a **10 year old** and the new **Hazelburn Sherry Wood 13 year old**, replacing the 12 year old. Recent, limited editions include **Springbank Local Barley 10 year old,** a **14 year old Springbank** matured in bourbon casks and a **14 year old Longrow Sherry Wood.**

History continued:

2007 Springbank Vintage 1997 and a 16 year old rum wood are released.

2008 The distillery closes temporarily. Three new releases of Longrow - CV, 18 year old and 7 year old Gaja Barolo.

2009 Springbank Madeira 11 year old, Springbank 18 year old, Springbank Vintage 2001 and Hazelburn 12 year old are released.

2010 Springbank 12 year old cask strength and a 12 year old claret expression together with new editions of the CV and 18 year old are released. Longrow 10 year old cask strength and Hazelburn CV are also new.

2011 Longrow 18 year old and Hazelburn 8 year old Sauternes wood expression are released.

2012 Springbank Rundlets & Kilderkins, Springbank 21 year old and Longrow Red are released.

2013 Longrow Rundlets & Kilderkins, a new edition of Longrow Red and Springbank 9 year old Gaja Barolo finish are released.

2014 Hazelburn Rundlets & Kilderkins, Hazelburn 10 year old and Springbank 25 years old are launched.

2015 New releases include Springbank Green 12 years old and a new edition of the Longrow Red.

2016 Springbank Local Barley and a 9 year old Hazelburn barolo finish are released.

2017 Springbank 14 year old bourbon cask and Hazelburn 13 year old sherrywood are released.

2018 Local Barley 10 year old, 14 year old Longrow Sherry Wood and a new Longrow Red are released.

Tasting notes Springbank 10 years old:

GS – Fresh and briny on the nose, with citrus fruit, oak and barley, plus a note of damp earth. Sweet on the palate, with developing brine, nuttiness and vanilla toffee. Long and spicy in the finish, coconut oil and drying peat.

Tasting notes Longrow NAS:

GS – Initially slightly gummy on the nose, but then brine and fat peat notes develop. Vanilla and malt also emerge. The smoky palate offers lively brine and is quite dry and spicy, with some vanilla and lots of ginger. The finish is peaty with persistent, oaky ginger.

Tasting notes Hazelburn 10 years old:

GS – Pear drops, soft toffee and malt on the mildly floral nose. Oiliness develops in time, along with a green, herbal note and ultimately brine. Full-bodied and supple on the smoky palate, with barley and ripe, peppery orchard fruits. Developing cocoa and ginger in the lengthy finish.

12 years old c.s.   18 years old   21 years old

Local Barley    Longrow Red

Springbank 10 years   Hazelburn 10 years    Longrow

Strathisla

[strath•eye•la]

Owner: **Region/district:**
Chivas Bros (Pernod Ricard)   Speyside

Founded: **Status:**   **Capacity:**
1786   Active (vc)   2 450 000 litres

Address: Seafield Avenue, Keith,
Banffshire AB55 5BS

Website: **Tel:**
chivas.com   01542 783044

The single malt from Strathisla has plenty of fans but a visit to the distillery will be focused much more on Chivas Regal – the blend which relies heavily on Strathisla malt.

James and John Chivas established Chivas Brothers in 1857 and over the years they released several brands. However, it was with the launch of Chivas Regal in 1909, that Chivas became a household name for whisky connoiseurs. In the 1970s, before the interest in single malts had taken off in a big way, it was considered the pinnacle of Scotch whisky by many consumers.

Since 2012, however, the brand has been on a slippery slope, losing 17% of its volume and in 2016 it was passed by Grant´s on the top list of blends and it now occupies the fourth place. In 2017, the brand sold 50 million bottles. The owners seem well aware of the situation and in December 2017, a new ad agency, McCann, was called in to take care of global advertising for the brand. The Chivas Regal core range is made up of 12, 18 and 25 year old with several limited editions having been launched over the years. The most recent are Chivas Regal Ultis from 2016, which is the first blended malt in the portfolio, and, released in 2017, a Chivas Regal which had been finished in casks made of the rare Japanese mizunara oak.

The distillery is equipped with a 5.12 ton traditional mash tun with a raised copper canopy, seven washbacks made of Oregon pine and three of larch – all with a 54 hour fermentation cycle. There are two pairs of stills in a cramped, but very charming still room. The wash stills are of lantern type with descending lyne arms and the spirit stills have boiling balls with the lyne arms slightly ascending. Most of the spirit produced at Strathisla is piped to nearby Glen Keith distillery for filling or to be tankered away.

The core expression is the **12 year old** but there is also one cask strength bottling in the new range The Distillery Reserve Collection which can be found at Chivas´ visitor centres; a **17 year old** bottled at 57.9%.

History:

1786 Alexander Milne and George Taylor found the distillery under the name Milltown, but soon change it to Milton.

1823 MacDonald Ingram & Co. purchases the distillery.

1830 William Longmore acquires the distillery.

1870 The distillery name changes to Strathisla.

1880 William Longmore retires and hands operations to his son-in-law John Geddes-Brown. William Longmore & Co. is formed.

1890 The distillery changes name to Milton.

1942 Jay Pomeroy acquires a majority of the shares in William Longmore & Co. Pomeroy is jailed as a result of dubious business transactions and the distillery goes bankrupt in 1949.

1950 Chivas Brothers buys the run-down distillery at a compulsory auction for £71,000 and starts restoration.

1951 The name reverts to Strathisla.

1965 The number of stills is increased from two to four.

1970 A heavily peated whisky, Craigduff, is produced but production stops later.

2001 The Chivas Group is acquired by Pernod Ricard.

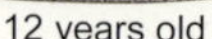

12 years old

Tasting notes Strathisla 12 years old:

GS – Rich on the nose, with sherry, stewed fruits, spices and lots of malt. Full-bodied and almost syrupy on the palate. Toffee, honey, nuts, a whiff of peat and a suggestion of oak. The finish is medium in length, slightly smoky and a with a final flash of ginger.

Strathmill

[strath•**mill**]

Owner: **Region/district:**
Diageo   Speyside

Founded: **Status:**   **Capacity:**
1891   Active   2 600 000 litres

Address: Keith, Banffshire AB55 5DQ

Website: **Tel:**
malts.com   01542 883000

If you´ve been on a guided tour of a distillery, you´ve seen the "fancy" parts – mashtun, washbacks and the shining copper stills. But hidden below is a maze of pipes, valves and wires that are equally important to the final product.

Every now and then, a distillery built in the 1800s needs a complete revamp that will enable it to work for another 50-100 years. Some years ago, Diageo´s focus was on building new distilleries or increasing the capacity at the exisiting ones. At the moment, it seems the aim is to make sure the existing distilleries perform reliably and consistently in years to come. And, not least important, that the production complies with todays environmental standards and regulations

Currently, both Knockando and Glenlossie are closed for a massive overhaul of the respective plants and it´s not unlikely that Strathmill may be next in line. Founded in the late 1800s, it has been producing malt whisky to become a part of the J&B blend ever since. Its obscurity on the single malt market is reflected in the location of the distillery - hidden away down a side road by the river Isla in Keith.

The equipment at Strathmill consists of a 9.1 ton stainless steel semi-lauter mash tun and six stainless steel washbacks. Currently, the distillery is working a 5-day week which means both short (65 hours) and long (120 hours) fermentations, producing around 2 million litres of pure alcohol in the year. There are two pairs of stills and Strathmill is one of few distilleries still using purifiers on the spirit stills. This device is mounted between the lyne arm and the condenser and acts as a mini-condenser, allowing the lighter alcohols to travel towards the condenser and forcing the heavier alcohols to go back into the still for another distillation. The result is a lighter spirit. In Strathmill´s case both purifiers and condensers are fitted on the outside of the still house to optimize energy savings.

The only official bottling is the **12 year old Flora & Fauna**, but a limited **25 year old** was launched in 2014 as part of the Special Releases.

History:

1891   The distillery is founded in an old mill from 1823 and is named Glenisla-Glenlivet Distillery.

1892   The inauguration takes place in June.

1895   The gin company W. & A. Gilbey buys the distillery for £9,500 and names it Strathmill.

1962   W. & A. Gilbey merges with United Wine Traders (including Justerini & Brooks) and forms International Distillers & Vintners (IDV).

1968   The number of stills is increased from two to four and purifiers are added.

1972   IDV is bought by Watney Mann which later the same year is acquired by Grand Metropolitan.

1993   Strathmill becomes available as a single malt for the first time since 1909 as a result of a bottling (1980) from Oddbins.

1997   Guinness and Grand Metropolitan merge and form Diageo.

2001   The first official bottling is a 12 year old in the Flora & Fauna series.

2010   A Manager´s Choice single cask from 1996 is released.

2014   A 25 year old is released.

12 years old

Tasting notes Strathmill 12 years old:

GS – Quite reticent on the nose, with nuts, grass and a hint of ginger. Spicy vanilla and nuts dominate the palate. The finish is drying, with peppery oak.

Talisker

[tal•iss•kur]

Owner: Diageo

Region/district: Highlands (Skye)

Founded: 1830
Status: Active (vc)
Capacity: 3 300 000 litres

Address: Carbost, Isle of Skye, Inverness-shire IV47 8SR

Website: malts.com
Tel: 01478 614308 (vc)

Talisker and Brora share the same background in the sense that they were both founded against the background of one of the darker chapters of Scottish history – The Highland Clearances.

In the early 1800s, land-owners across northern Scotland wanted to increase the yield of their land to create even more wealth. One easy way was to enter into large-scale sheep farming. Sheep need pasture and farmers which for centuries had held land were driven from their homes to make room for the sheep. Thousands of families were ruthlessly evicted, some of them forced to seek work in the coal mines or in the fishing industry while many saw no other opportunity but to emigrate to Australia or America. In Brora, the Marquis of Stafford was the landowner and he also founded Brora distillery in 1819. On Skye, the MacAskill brothers managed the Talisker Estate, owned by the MacLeods. They continued the eviction of farmers started by the previous leaseholder and they also founded Talisker distillery in 1830.

Through reduced shutdowns and by introducing one extra mash per week, the team at Talisker have managed to produce 3.3 million litres of alcohol – a new record for the distillery! It remains to be seen if this will be enough to cover future needs of the malt. In the last two years alone, sales have increased by 20% to just over 3 million bottles in 2017 and it´s now one of the Top 10 single malts in the world.

The distillery is equipped with a stainless steel lauter mash tun with a capacity of 8 ton, eight washbacks made of Oregon pine and five stills (two wash stills and three spirit stills), all of which are connected to wooden worm tubs. The wash stills are equipped with a special type of purifiers, which use the colder outside air, and have a u-bend in the lyne arm. The purifiers and the peculiar bend of the lyne arms allow for more copper contact and increase the reflux during distillation. The fermentation time is quite long (65-75 hours) and the middle cut from the spirit still is collected between 76% and 65% which, together with the phenol specification, gives a medium peated spirit. Production in 2018 will be 20 mashes per week which accounts for 3.3 million litres of alcohol.

Talisker's core range consists of **Skye** and **Storm**, both without age statement, **10, 18, 25** and **30 year old, Distiller's Edition** with an Amoroso sherry finish, **Talisker 57⁰ North** which is released in small batches, and **Port Ruighe**, finished in ruby port casks. There is also **Dark Storm**, the peatiest Talisker so far, which is exclusive to duty free. A second bottling for duty free, **Neist Point**, was launched in 2015. A new range of limited bottlings was introduced in summer 2018 – the Bodega Series which will explore the impact of different sherry cask finishes. The first instalment was a **40 year old** which had been finished in casks that once held 40 year old amontillado sherry. Finally, an **8 year old** matured in first fill ex-bourbon and bottled at 59.4% was launched in autumn 2018 as part of the yearly Special Releases.

History:

1830 Hugh and Kenneth MacAskill found the distillery.

1848 The brothers transfer the lease to North of Scotland Bank and Jack Westland from the bank runs the operations.

1854 Kenneth MacAskill dies.

1857 North of Scotland Bank sells the distillery to Donald MacLennan for £500.

1863 MacLennan experiences difficulties in making operations viable and puts the distillery up for sale.

1865 MacLennan, still working at the distillery, nominates John Anderson as agent in Glasgow.

1867 Anderson & Co. from Glasgow takes over.

1879 John Anderson is imprisoned after having sold non-existing casks of whisky.

1880 New owners are now Alexander Grigor Allan and Roderick Kemp.

1892 Kemp sells his share and buys Macallan Distillery instead.

1894 The Talisker Distillery Ltd is founded.

1895 Allan dies and Thomas Mackenzie, who has been his partner, takes over.

1898 Talisker Distillery merges with Dailuaine-Glenlivet Distillers and Imperial Distillers to form Dailuaine-Talisker Distillers Company.

1916 Thomas Mackenzie dies and the distillery is taken over by a consortium consisting of, among others, John Walker, John Dewar, W. P. Lowrie and Distillers Company Limited (DCL).

1928 The distillery abandons triple distillation.

1960 On 22nd November the distillery catches fire and substantial damage occurs.

1962 The distillery reopens after the fire.

History continued:

1972 Own malting ceases.

1988 Classic Malts are introduced, Talisker 10 years included. A visitor centre is opened.

1998 A new stainless steel/copper mash tun and five new worm tubs are installed. Talisker is launched as a Distillers Edition with an amoroso sherry finish.

2004 Two new bottlings appear, an 18 year old and a 25 year old.

2005 To celebrate the 175th birthday of the distillery, Talisker 175th Anniversary is released. The third edition of the 25 year old cask strength is released.

2006 A 30 year old and the fourth edition of the 25 year old are released.

2007 The second edition of the 30 year old and the fifth edition of the 25 year old are released.

2008 Talisker 57° North, sixth edition of the 25 year old and third edition of the 30 year old are launched.

2009 New editions of the 25 and 30 year old are released.

2010 A 1994 Manager´s Choice single cask and a new edition of the 30 year old are released.

2011 Three limited releases - 25, 30 and 34 year old.

2012 A limited 35 year old is released.

2013 Four new expressions are released – Storm, Dark Storm, Port Ruighe and a 27 year old.

2014 A bottling for the Friends of the Classic Malts is released.

2015 Skye and Neist Point are released.

2016 A distillery exclusive without age statement is released.

2018 A 40 year old, the first in the new Bodega Series, and an 8 year old Special Release are launched.

Tasting notes Talisker 10 years old:

GS – Quite dense and smoky on the nose, with smoked fish, bladderwrack, sweet fruit and peat. Full-bodied and peaty in the mouthy; complex, with ginger, ozone, dark chocolate, black pepper and a kick of chilli in the long, smoky tail.

Tasting notes Talisker Storm:

GS – The nose offers brine, burning wood embers, vanilla, and honey. The palate is sweet and spicy, with cranberries and blackcurrants, while peat-smoke and black pepper are ever-present. The finish is spicy, with walnuts, and fruity peat.

Port Ruighe

Storm

Skye

8 years old

Dark Storm

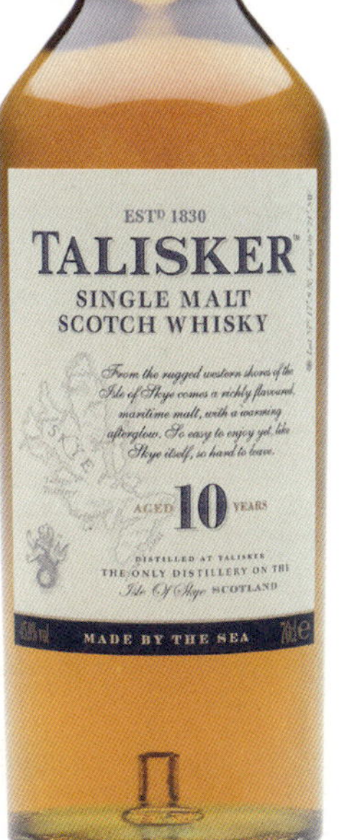

10 years old

Bodega Series 40 yo

Distiller´s Edition

Tamdhu

[tam•<u>doo</u>]

Owner:
Ian Macleod Distillers

Region/district:
Speyside

Founded: **Status:**
1897   Active

Capacity:
4 000 000 litres

Address: Knockando, Aberlour,
Morayshire AB38 7RP

Website:
tamdhu.com

Tel:
01340 872200

The very slim chance of the Saladin maltings at Tamdhu ever working again came to an end in spring 2018 when they were demolished. The area will now be used for a new malt in-take and a storage bin system.

Sad as that may be, the ressurection of Tamdhu, not only as a working distillery, but also as producer of a range of single malts, definitely makes up for the loss. In 2011 the distillery was considered surplus by the owners, Edrington. Still, it came as a surprise to most when the distillery was offered for sale. One would have thought that the distillery would contribute by producing malt whisky for Famous Grouse and Cutty Sark. When Ian Macleod took over, it proved to be a blessing. The long neglected brand was reborn and can now be found in markets globally.

The distillery is equipped with an 11.8 ton semilauter mash tun, nine Oregon pine washbacks with a fermentation time of 59 hours and three pairs of stills. There are a total of 16 warehouses (a mix of dunnage, racked and palletized) and the plans are to build another eight. Production for 2018 will be 16 mashes per week which translates to 3.1 million litres for the entire year. Planning permission has been granted to build a cooperage for cask repairs and works on that will probably start in late 2018.

The owners, Ian Macleod, are committed to maturing Tamdhu single malt in sherry casks but the flavour is further enhanced by the fact that they are using both American and European oak. The core range consists of a **10 year old** matured in first and second fill sherry casks and the non-chill filtered **Batch Strength**. A **12 year old** was released globally in August 2018 and a **15 year old** core bottling is also due for release in late 2018/early 2019. Limited releases include an extraordinary **50 year old**, matured in a first fill European oak sherry butt released in 2017 to celebrate the 120th anniversary of the distillery. Recently, we have seen the release of **Dalbeallie Dram** (part of the Collectors Journey 01) and the 120th Anniversary **Single Cask Distillery Team Limited Edition**.

History:

1896   The distillery is founded by Tamdhu Distillery Company, a consortium of whisky blenders with William Grant as the main promoter. Charles Doig is the architect.

1897   The first casks are filled in July.

1898   Highland Distillers Company, which has several of the 1896 consortium members in managerial positions, buys Tamdhu Distillery Company.

1911   The distillery closes.

1913   The distillery reopens.

1928   The distillery is mothballed.

1948   The distillery is in full production again in July.

1950   The floor maltings is replaced by Saladin boxes when the distillery is rebuilt.

1972   The number of stills is increased from two to four.

1975   Two stills augment the previous four.

1976   Tamdhu 8 years is launched as single malt.

2005   An 18 year old and a 25 year old are released.

2009   The distillery is motballed.

2011   The Edrington Group sells the distillery to Ian Macleod Distillers.

2012   Production is resumed.

2013   The first official release from the new owners – a 10 year old.

2015   Tamdhu Batch Strength is released.

2017   A 50 year old is released.

2018   A 12 year old and the Dalbeallie Dram are released

Tasting notes Tamdhu 10 years old:

GS – Soft sherry notes, new leather, almonds, marzipan and a hint of peat on the nose. Very smooth and drinkable, with citrus fruit, gentle spice and more sweet sherry on the palate. Persistent spicy leather, with a sprinkling of black pepper in the finish.

10 years old

Tamnavulin

[tam•na•<u>voo</u>•lin]

Owner:
Whyte & Mackay (Emperador)

Region/district:
Speyside

Founded: 1966
Status: Active
Capacity: 4 000 000 litres

Address: Tomnavoulin, Ballindalloch,
Banffshire AB3 9JA

Website:
www.tamnavulinwhisky.com

Tel:
01807 590285

For the second year in a row, Tamnavulin was a part of the Speyside Whisky Festival in May 2018 with tours being offered to the public. This was an excellent opportunity for whisky enthusiasts to get acquainted with a fairly anonymous distillery.

But this wasn´t the first time the distillery catered to visitors. Until the late 1990s, an old carding mill on the site was used as a visitor centre. The beautiful building, where farmers would bring their sheep fleeces to be made into wool, can still be seen down in the glen and there has actually been discussions about using it once again for tourism purposes.

Tamnavulin distillery is equipped with a full lauter mash tun with an 11 ton capacity, nine washbacks made of stainless steel with a fermentation time of 60 hours (an increase from the previous 48) and three pairs of stills. The wash stills, with horizontal lyne arms, are all equipped with subcoolers while the spirit stills with their descending lyne arms have purifiers. Like so many other distilleries, Tamnavulin is now changing from heavy oil to gas to fuel their boiler. During 2018, the owners will be doing 18 mashes per week which means a total of 3.5 million litres of alcohol. From 2010 to 2013, part of the yearly production (around 5%) was heavily peated with a phenol specification in the barley of 55ppm. There has been no peated production since.

The character of Tamnavulin new make is slightly grassy with a 25 minute foreshot and a middle cut running from 75% down to 60%. These days, the spirit always goes into first fill bourbon and part of it is then finished in sherry casks. However, it hasn´t always been that way and recently a re-racking programme, similar to the one the owners did with Jura, has beeen implemented. The result is a vast improvement of the quality of the whisky.

There used to be an official 12 year old bottling but this was discontinued years ago. In 2016, however, a new **Tamnavulin Double Cask** with a sherry finish, was released as an exclusive for the UK market to celebrate the distillery´s 50th anniversary. Since then it has been launched into other markets as well.

History:

1966 Tamnavulin-Glenlivet Distillery Company, a subsidiary of Invergordon Distillers Ltd, founds Tamnavulin.

1993 Whyte & Mackay buys Invergordon Distillers.

1995 The distillery closes in May.

1996 Whyte & Mackay changes name to JBB (Greater Europe).

2000 Distillation takes place for six weeks.

2001 Company management buy out operations for £208 million and rename the company Kyndal.

2003 Kyndal changes name to Whyte & Mackay.

2007 United Spirits buys Whyte & Mackay. Tamnavulin is opened again in July after having been mothballed for 12 years.

2014 Whyte & Mackay is sold to Emperador Inc.

2016 Tamnavulin Double Cask is released.

Double Cask

Tasting notes Tamnavulin Double Cask:

GS – The nose offers malt, soft toffee, almonds and tangerines. Finally, background earthiness. Smooth on the palate, with ginger nut biscuits, vanilla and orchard fruits, plus walnuts. The finish is medium in length, with lingering fruity spice.

Teaninich

[tee•<u>ni</u>•nick]

Owner:
Diageo

Region/district:
Northern Highlands

Founded: **Status:**
1817   Active

Capacity:
10 200 000 litres

Address: Alness, Ross-shire IV17 0XB

Website:
malts.com

Tel:
01349 885001

The small town of Alness north of Inverness can boast two distilleries. One is Dalmore down by the Cromarty Firth, a distillery known to most if not all whisky drinkers. The other is the often overlooked Teaninich.

Even the location, in an industrial area south of the town centre, tells a story of a distillery focused on producing large amounts of malt for blending purposes. In the 1970s it was one of the largest distilleries in Scotland with a six million litre capacity. Today it´s even bigger but several other distilleries have also increased their capacity in the last couple of decades. Those who do know about Teaninich also know that the distilling process comprises several unique features. First of all, the malted barley is ground into a fine flour without husks in an Asnong hammer mill. This is the basis for a higher spirit yield but also means that you can use barley varieties that wouldn´t mill as well in a traditional Porteus mill with rollers. The grist is mixed with water in a conversion vessel. Once the conversion from starch to sugar is done, the mash passes through a Meura 2001 mash filter which consists of a number of mesh bags. The filter compresses the bags and the wort is collected for the next step – fermentation. The advantages are efficiency, high yield and clear wort while the drawback is that the technique is significantly more expensive.

A huge expansion of the distillery was conducted in 2015 which lead to a doubled capacity. The equipment now consists of a new filter with a 14 ton mash to cope with the larger volumes. There are also 18 wooden washbacks and two made of stainless steel – all with a fermentation time of 75 hours. Three of the original wash stills have been altered into spirit stills so that the old still house now houses all six spirit stills, while a new house has been built for the six, new wash stills. At the moment, the distillery is alternating between 16 and 28 mashes per week which gives a total of 4 million litres of pure alcohol.

The only official core bottling is a **10 year old** in the Flora & Fauna series but a limited **17 year old** matured in refill American oak was launched in autumn 2017 as part of the Special Releases.

History:

1817 Captain Hugh Monro, owner of the estate Teaninich, founds the distillery.

1831 Captain Munro sells the estate to his younger brother John.

1850 John Munro, who spends most of his time in India, leases Teaninich to the infamous Robert Pattison from Leith.

1869 John McGilchrist Ross takes over the licence.

1895 Munro & Cameron takes over the licence.

1898 Munro & Cameron buys the distillery.

1904 Robert Innes Cameron becomes sole owner of Teaninich.

1932 Robert Innes Cameron dies.

1933 The estate of Robert Innes Cameron sells the distillery to Distillers Company Limited.

1970 A new distillation unit with six stills is commissioned and becomes known as the A side.

1975 A dark grains plant is built.

1984 The B side of the distillery is mothballed.

1985 The A side is also mothballed.

1991 The A side is in production again.

1992 United Distillers launches a 10 year old Teaninich in the Flora & Fauna series.

1999 The B side is decommissioned.

2000 A mash filter is installed.

2009 Teaninich 1996, a single cask in the new Manager´s Choice range is released.

2015 The distillery is expanded with six new stills and the capacity is doubled.

2017 A 17 year old is launched as part of the Special Releases.

Tasting notes Teaninich 10 years old:

GS – The nose is initially fresh and grassy, quite light, with vanilla and hints of tinned pineapple. Mediumbodied, smooth, slightly oily, with cereal and spice in the mouth. Nutty and slowly drying in the finish, with pepper and a suggestion of cocoa powder notes.

10 years old

Tobermory

[tow•bur•<u>mo</u>•ray]

Owner: **Region/district:**
Distell International Ltd.   Highland (Mull)

Founded: **Status:**   **Capacity:**
1798   Active (vc)   1 000 000 litres

Address: Tobermory, Isle of Mull, Argyllsh. PA75 6NR

Website: **Tel:**
tobermorydistillery.com   01688 302647

Tobermory has been closed since spring 2017 and is not due to open again until May 2019. The reason is a major upgrade of the buildings and the roofs and including new equipment but a new visitor centre is also in the plans.

The distillery has been known as Tobermory from 1798 until its closure in 1930. After that it has been alternating between being called Tobermory and Ledaig, and single malt is released under both names with Ledaig being reserved for the peated versions with a phenol content of 30-40ppm. Peat was used in the olden days and was re-introduced in 1996 when Burn Stewart´s Master Blender, Ian MacMillan, decided to recreate the old style of Tobermory single malt. From 1972 to 1993 the production at Tobermory was intermittent and of varied quality. The vast majority of old Tobermory today is from 1993 and later when Burn Stewart took over. The older stock was scrutinised by Ian MacMillan with a few gems to be found. The rest was used for blending.

The distillery is equipped with a traditional 5 ton cast iron mash tun, four wooden washbacks with a fermentation time of 50 to 90 hours and two pairs of stills. Two of the stills were replaced in August 2014 with the other two being replaced during the current upgrade. All of the washbacks will also be replaced. Before the temporary closure, the production was 8 mashes per week and 750,000 litres of alcohol with a 50/50 split between Ledaig and Tobermory.

The core range from Tobermory distillery is the **10** and **18 year old Ledaig** and the **10 year old Tobermory.** Recent limited expressions include a **Tobermory 21 year old Manzanilla finish,** a **15 year old Tobermory Marsala finish,** a **13 year old Ledaig** matured in amontillado sherry casks and, released in 2018, a **12 year old Tobermory** with a fino sherry finish and two **19 year old Ledaig** finished in PX casks and oloroso casks respectively. There are a number of distillery exclusives to be found with a **2000 Tobermory Madeira finish** and a **2002 Ledaig rioja finish** as the most recent ones.

History:

1798   John Sinclair founds the distillery.

1837   The distillery closes.

1878   The distillery reopens.

1890   John Hopkins & Company buys the distillery.

1916   Distillers Company Limited (DCL) takes over John Hopkins & Company.

1930   The distillery closes.

1972   A shipping company in Liverpool and the sherrymaker Domecq buy the buildings and embark on refurbishment. When work is completed it is named Ledaig Distillery Ltd.

1975   Ledaig Distillery Ltd files for bankruptcy and the distillery closes again.

1979   The estate agent Kirkleavington Property buys the distillery, forms a new company, Tobermory Distillers Ltd and starts production.

1982   No production. Some of the buildings are converted into flats and some are rented to a dairy company for cheese storage.

1989   Production resumes.

1993   Burn Stewart Distillers buys Tobermory for £600,000.

2002   Trinidad-based venture capitalists CL Financial buys Burn Stewart Distillers for £50m.

2005   A 32 year old from 1972 is launched.

2007   A Ledaig 10 year old is released.

2008   A limited edition Tobermory 15 year old is released.

2013   Burn Stewart Distillers is sold to Distell Group Ltd. A 40 year old Ledaig is released.

2015   Ledaig 18 years and 42 years are released together with Tobermory 42 years.

2018   A 12 year old Tobermory fino sherry finish and two 19 year old Ledaig are released.

Tasting notes Tobermory 10 years old:

GS – Fresh and nutty on the nose, with citrus fruit and brittle toffee. A whiff of peat. Medium-bodied, quite dry on the palate with delicate peat, malt and nuts. Medium finish with a hint of mint and a slight citric tang.

Tasting notes Ledaig 10 years old:

GS – The nose is profoundly peaty, sweet and full, with notes of butter and smoked fish. Bold, yet sweet on the palate, with iodine, soft peat and heather. Developing spices. The finish is medium to long, with pepper, ginger, liquorice and peat.

10 years old

Tomatin

[to•mat•in]

Owner: **Region/district:**
Tomatin Distillery Co   Highland
(Takara Shuzo Co., Kokubu & Co., Marubeni Corp.)

Founded: **Status:**   **Capacity:**
1897   Active (vc)   5 000 000 litres

Address: Tomatin, Inverness-shire IV13 7YT

Website: **Tel:**
tomatin.com   01463 248144 (vc)

Sales of single malt Scotch have increased since the early 1990s and the past few years have been extra-ordinary. A number of producers focusing on sales to third parties, have realised that there´s money to be made bottling the malt themselves.

One of the best examples of this trend is Tomatin. Ten years ago, the business was still focused on supplying malt whisky for blends, especially to their Japanese owners. A new strategy was put in place and since then the number of single malt releases from the distillery has gone from two to thirty and sales from 170,000 bottles to 680,000 bottles!

The distillery is equipped with one 8 ton stainless steel mash tun, 12 stainless steel washbacks with a fermentation time from 54 to 110 hours and six pairs of stills (only four of the spirit stills are still in use). The goal is to produce 1.8 million litres in 2018, including a couple of weeks of peated production at 30-35ppm. Recently, the owners have prepared nine water beds with 28,000 plants through which spent lees containing copper, are pumped.

The core range consists of **Legacy** (without age statement), **12, 18** and **36 year old**. Included are also **Cask Strength, 14 year old port finish** and a **First Fill Bourbon** exclusive to the UK. In August 2018, a **30 year old** was added to the range. Recent limited releases include a new range focusing on the effect of different cask maturations called **Five Virtues (Wood, Fire, Earth, Water** and **Metal)**. There are also a number of vintages; **1981, 1995, 2002 Cabernet Sauvignon** and **2007 Carribean rum** as well as **Contrast**, a pack of two bottles (bourbon and sherry matured) with whiskies from six vintages. **Warehouse 6 Collection**, a new range of 40-year-old-plus whiskies, was introduced in 2016 with the latest release being a **1975 vintage**. Since 2016, the distillery´s duty free range consists of **8, 12, 15** and **40 year olds**. The smoky side of Tomatin is represented by **Cù Bòcan without age statement, Cù Bòcan Sherry, Cù Bòcan Virgin Oak, Cù Bòcan Bourbon** and four vintages; **1988, 1989, 2005** and, released in September 2017, **2006.**

History:

1897 The distillery is founded by Tomatin Spey Distillery Company.

1906 Production ceases.

1909 Production resumes through Tomatin Distillers.

1956 Stills are increased from two to four.

1958 Another two stills are added.

1961 The six stills are increased to ten.

1974 The stills now total 23 and the maltings closes.

1985 The distillery company goes into liquidation.

1986 Takara Shuzo Co. and Okara & Co., buy Tomatin through Tomatin Distillery Co.

1998 Okara & Co is liquidated and Marubeni buys out part of their shareholding.

2004 Tomatin 12 years is launched.

2005 A 25 year old and a 1973 Vintage are released.

2006 An 18 year old and a 1962 Vintage are launched.

2008 A 30 and a 40 year old as well as several vintages from 1975 and 1995 are released.

2009 A 15 year old, a 21 year old and four single casks (1973, 1982, 1997 and 1999) are released.

2010 The first peated release - a 4 year old exclusive for Japan.

2011 A 30 year old and Tomatin Decades are released.

2013 Cù Bòcan, the first peated Tomatin, is released.

2014 14 year old port finish, 36 year old, Vintage 1988, Tomatin Cuatro, Cù Bòcan Sherry Cask and Cù Bòcan 1989 are released.

2015 Cask Strength and Cù Bòcan Virgin Oak are released.

2016 A 44 year old Tomatin and two Cù Bòcan vintages (1988 and 2005) are released.

2017 New releases include Wood, Fire and Earth as well as a 2006 Cù Bòcan.

2018 A 30 year old is released.

12 years old

Tasting notes Tomatin 12 years old:

GS – Barley, spice, buttery oak and a floral note on the nose. Sweet and medium-bodied, with toffee apples, spice and herbs in the mouth. Medium-length in the finish, with sweet fruitiness.

Tomintoul

[tom•in•<u>towel</u>]

Owner: Angus Dundee Distillers

Region/district: Speyside

Founded: 1965

Status: Active

Capacity: 3 300 000 litres

Address: Ballindalloch, Banffshire AB37 9AQ

Website: tomintouldistillery.co.uk

Tel: 01807 590274

Family owned Angus Dundee Distillers were far-sighted when they bought their first distillery, Tomintoul, in 2000. Blenders and independent bottlers for 50 years, they realised that it would soon be harder to purchase casks from the the majority of distillery owners.

Simply put, they needed their own production and they were not the first either. Gordon & MacPhail had purchased Benromach in 1993 and others would follow suit - Signatory (Edradour), Murray McDavid (Bruichladdich) and Ian Macleod (Glengoyne). But compared to the others, Tomintoul is of an impressive size with a capacity of 3.3 million litres per year.

Tomintoul is equipped with a 12 ton semi lauter mash tun, six stainless steel washbacks with a fermentation time of 54-60 hours and two pairs of stills. There are currently 15 mashes per week, which means that capacity is used to its maximum, a total of 13 warehouses (racked and palletised) have a storage capacity of 120,000 casks. The malt used for mashing is unpeated, but every year since 2001, heavily peated (55ppm) spirit is produced. On the site there is also a blending centre with 14 large blending vats.

The core range consists of **Tlàth** without age statement, **10, 14, 16, 21** and **25 year old**. There are also two finishes; a **12 year old oloroso sherry** casks and a **15 year old port finish**. The peaty side of Tomintoul is re-presented by **Peaty Tang** and, as a stand alone range, **Old Ballantruan** and **Old Ballantruan 10 year old**. Two new expressions were released in 2017 – the **15 year old Peaty Tang** (40%) and a **15 year old Old Ballantruan** (50%). Recent limited releases include a **Single Sherry Cask, Five Decades, a 40 year old** and, launched in September 2018, **Tomintoul 1965 The Ultimate Cask**. The latter is the sole remaining cask from 1965 (the first year of distillation) and only 105 bottles were released.

History:

1965 The distillery is founded by Tomintoul Distillery Ltd, which is owned by Hay & MacLeod & Co. and W. & S. Strong & Co.

1973 Scottish & Universal Investment Trust, owned by the Fraser family, buys both the distillery and Whyte & Mackay.

1974 The two stills are increased to four and Tomintoul 12 years is launched.

1978 Lonhro buys Scottish & Universal Investment Trust.

1989 Lonhro sells Whyte & Mackay to Brent Walker.

1990 American Brands buys Whyte & Mackay.

1996 Whyte & Mackay changes name to JBB (Greater Europe).

2000 Angus Dundee plc buys Tomintoul.

2002 Tomintoul 10 year is launched.

2003 Tomintoul 16 years is launched.

2004 Tomintoul 27 years is launched.

2005 The peated Old Ballantruan is launched.

2008 1976 Vintage and Peaty Tang are released.

2009 A 14 year old and a 33 year old are released.

2010 A 12 year old Port wood finish is released.

2011 A 21 year old, a 10 year old Ballantruan and Vintage 1966 are released.

2012 Old Ballantruan 10 years old is released.

2013 A 31 year old single cask is released.

2015 Five Decades and a 40 year old are released.

2016 A 40 year old and Tlàth without age statement are launched.

2017 15 year old Peaty Tang and 15 year old Old Ballantruan are launched.

2018 Tomintoul 1965 The Ultimate Cask is released.

10 years old

Tasting notes Tomintoul 10 years old:

GS – A light, fresh and fruity nose, with ripe peaches and pineapple cheesecake, delicate spice and background malt. Medium-bodied, fruity and fudgy on the palate. The finish offers wine gums, mild, gently spiced oak, malt and a suggestion of smoke.

Tormore

[tor•more]

Owner:
Chivas Bros (Pernod Ricard)

Region/district:
Speyside

Founded: 1958

Status: Active

Capacity: 4 800 000 litres

Address: Tormore, Advie, Grantown-on-Spey, Morayshire PH26 3LR

Website:
tormoredistillery.com

Tel:
01807 510244

Whisky tourism in Scotland is bigger than ever with more than 1.3 million people visiting distilleries last year. Speyside is one of the hot spots and it would seem that being situated next to one of the main roads would be a blessing.

No need to lure potential tourists along a narrow and winding road. But despite Tormore distillery being right next to the busy A95 – a Speyside artery going from Aviemore to Keith – there is no sign of the owners planning to open it up to visitors. It is a shame because the distillery itself is stunning and the architecture is quite unlike any other distillery in Scotland.

Unfortunately Tormore single malt is not one of Chivas´ top priorities (despite an attempt in 2014 to re-brand it) and so with a limited presence on shop shelves, it would make little sense to open up a visitor centre. Before the 2014 re-launch, there have been two attempts to establish Tormore single malt as a brand. In 1991 it became part of Caledonian Malts, a range introduced by the owners at the time, Allied Distillers. It was later replaced in the range by Scapa. The second time was in 2004 when a 12 year old was launched under the name "The Pearl of Speyside". The name had reference to the generous stock of freshwater pearl mussels which you can find in the river Spey that flows close to the distillery.

From the outside, Tormore is without competition the most unusual looking distillery in Scotland, at least until the new Macallan was opened. Following an upgrade in 2012, Tormore is now equipped with a stainless steel full lauter mash tun, 11 stainless steel washbacks and four pairs of stills. Tormore single malt is known for its fruity and light character which is achieved by a clear wort, a slow distillation and by using purifiers on all the stills.

Nearly everything that is produced at Tormore is used for blended Scotch but there is a **14 year old** bottled at 43% and a **16 year old**, non chill-filtered, bottled at 48%. Both have been matured in American oak.

History:

1958 Schenley International, owners of Long John, founds the distillery.

1960 The distillery is ready for production.

1972 The number of stills is increased from four to eight.

1975 Schenley sells Long John and its distilleries (including Tormore) to Whitbread.

1989 Allied Lyons (to become Allied Domecq) buys the spirits division of Whitbread.

1991 Allied Distillers introduce Caledonian Malts where Miltonduff, Glendronach and Laphroaig are represented besides Tormore. Tormore is later replaced by Scapa.

2004 Tormore 12 year old is launched as an official bottling.

2005 Chivas Brothers (Pernod Ricard) becomes new owners through the acquisition of Allied Domecq.

2012 Production capacity is increased by 20%.

2014 The 12 year old is replaced by two new expressions - 14 and 16 year old.

14 years old

Tasting notes Tormore 14 years old:

GS – Vanilla, butterscotch, summer berries and light spice on the nose. Milk chocolate and tropical fruit on the smooth palate, with soft toffee. Lengthy in the finish, with a sprinkling of black pepper.

Tullibardine

[tully•<u>bar</u>•din]

Owner: **Region/district:**
Terroir Distillers   Highlands
(Picard Vins & Spiritueux)

Founded: **Status:**   **Capacity:**
1949   Active (vc)   3 000 000 litres

Address: Blackford, Perthshire PH4 1QG

Website: **Tel:**
tullibardine.com   01764 682252

Tullibardine is the wonderful story of a distillery that was deemed surplus in the aftermath of the huge decline for Scotch in the mid 1980s. Mothballed in 1994, it was revived ten years later by new owners.

A consortium of private investors (all with experience from the whisky business) took over Tullibardine with plans to include a retail village adjacent to the distillery. The property crash in 2009 radically changed the prospects. The distillery was sold to Picard in 2014. They have invested heavily which has resulted in a new visitor centre, a bottling line, a vatting hall, more warehouses and even a small cooperage used for repairing casks.

Tullibardine is also the spiritual home to the famous brand, Highland Queen. First launched in 1893 the brand had its heyday in the 1970s when it was popularly sold all over the world. In 2008, it was taken over by the Picard family. The range, with Tullibardine single malt as a key component, now consists of three blends and six single malts, the oldest being a 40 year old. The new 1561 blend is in fact the same recipe as the old classic blend Bailie Nicol Jarvie, once launched by Macdonald & Muir, former owners of Glenmorangie.

Tightly fitted into a cramped production area, the equipment consists of a 6 ton stainless steel semi-lauter mash tun, nine stainless steel washbacks with a fermentation of 55-60 hours and two pairs of stills. The production in 2018 will be around 2,6 million litres. Initially, the whole production is filled into first fill bourbon.

The core range consists of **Sovereign**, bourbon matured and without age statement, **225 Sauternes finish** (the biggest seller of the finishes), **228 Burgundy finish** and **500 Sherry finish** and two older bottlings – a **20 year old** and a **25 year old**. A new range called Custodian´s Collection was introduced in 2015 with a 50 year old as the first release. The latest in that range was **Vintage 1962**. The first cask strength Tullibardine made this century was The Murray 2004 vintage, launched in 2016. The latest expression, **The Murray Marsala Finish**, was released in October 2018.

History:

1949   The architect William Delmé-Evans founds the distillery.

1953   The distillery is sold to Brodie Hepburn.

1971   Invergordon Distillers buys Brodie Hepburn Ltd.

1973   The number of stills increases to four.

1993   Whyte & Mackay buys Invergordon Distillers.

1994   Tullibardine is mothballed.

1996   Whyte & Mackay changes name to JBB (Greater Europe).

2001   JBB (Greater Europe) is bought out from Fortune Brands by management and changes name to Kyndal (Whyte & Mackay from 2003).

2003   A consortium buys Tullibardine for £1.1 million. The distillery is in production again.

2005   Three wood finishes from 1993, Port, Moscatel and Marsala, are launched together with a 1986 John Black selection.

2006   Vintage 1966, Sherry Wood 1993 and a new John Black selection are launched.

2007   Five different wood finishes and a couple of single cask vintages are released.

2008   A Vintage 1968 40 year old is released.

2009   Aged Oak is released.

2011   Three vintages and a wood finish are released. Picard buys the distillery.

2013   A completely new range is launched – Sovereign, 225 Sauternes, 228 Burgundy, 500 Sherry, 20 year old and 25 year old.

2015   A 60 year old Custodian Collection is released.

2016   A Vintage 1970 and The Murray from 2004 are released.

2017   Vintage 1962 and The Murray Chateauneuf-du-Pape are released.

2018   The Murray Marsala Finish is released.

Sovereign

Tasting notes Tullibardine Sovereign:

GS – Floral on the nose, with new-mown hay, vanilla and fudge. Fruity on the palate, with milk chocolate, brazil nuts, marzipan, malt, and a hint of cinnamon. Cocoa, vanilla, a squeeze of lemon and more spice in the finish.

Ardnahoe Distillery under construction, 22nd August 2018

Photo: Rob Pla

New
distilleries

New distilleries are being opened in Scotland
at a rate we haven´t experienced since the great whisky boom
of the late 19th century. In the first twelve years of the new millennium,
six new malt whisky distilleries opened up in Scotland. In the next five
years, another twenty distilleries came on stream and in 2018 alone,
four more distilleries were added! There are at least another
20 distilleries in different stages of construction or planning.
In theory, this means that in a couple of years there could be a
total of 140 malt whisky distilleries operating in Scotland.

Wolfburn

[wolf•burn]

Owner:
Aurora Brewing Ltd.

Region/district:
Northern Highlands

Founded: 2013
Status: Active (vc)
Capacity: 135 000 litres

Address: Henderson Park, Thurso,
Caithness KW14 7XW

Website:
wolfburn.com

Tel:
01847 891051

The most northerly distillery on the Scottish mainland, Wolfburn, is situated in an industrial area on the outskirts of Thurso.

There are four, large, newly constructed buildings of which one is the distillery, while the other three are warehouses and a bottling plant. The owners have chosen a site that is situated 350 metres from the ruins of the old Wolfburn Distillery. Construction work commenced in August 2012 and the first newmake came off the stills at the end of January 2013.

The distillery is equipped with a 1.1 ton semi-lauter stainless steel mash tun with a copper canopy, four stainless steel washbacks with a fermentation time of 70-92 hours, holding 5,500 litres each, one wash still (5,500 litres) and one spirit still (3,600 litres). Wolfburn uses a mix of casks: approximately one third of the spirit is laid down in ex-bourbon quarter casks, a further third is in ex-bourbon

hogsheads as well as barrels, and the final third is laid down in ex-sherry butts.

The main part of the malt is unpeated and the intention is to create a smooth whisky. However, since 2014, a lightly peated (10 ppm) spirit has also been produced. The inaugural bottling from the distillery appeared in early 2016 and had a smoky profile due to the fact that it had partly been matured in quarter casks from Islay. This limited release was followed by a more widely available bourbon matured whisky which in September 2016 was re-named Northland. At the same time a second bottling appeared, Aurora, which had been partly matured in oloroso sherry casks. The core range was expanded in 2017 with Morven, the distillery´s first peated whisky and September 2018 saw the fourth expression being released - Langskip, matured in ex-bourbon barrels and bottled at 58%. A range of limited bottlings named Kylver started in summer 2016 and the fourth installment was due for release in November 2018.

Kingsbarns

[kings•barns]

Owner:
Wemyss family

Region/district:
Lowlands

Founded: 2014
Status: Active (vc)
Capacity: 600 000 litres

Address: East Newhall Farm, Kingsbarns,
St Andrews KY16 8QE

Website:
kingsbarnsdistillery.com

Tel:
01333 451300

The plans for this distillery near St Andrews in Fife, were drafted in 2008 and came to fruition in 2014 when the distillery was opened.

The idea, initiated by Doug Clement, was to restore a dilapidated farmhouse from the late 18th century and turn it into a modern distillery. Planning permission was received in March 2011 and in September 2012, the Scottish government awarded a grant of £670,000. This, in turn, led to the Wemyss family agreeing to inject £3m into the project and becoming the new owners. The family-owned company owns and operates the independent bottling company, Wemyss Malts, and also owns other companies in the field of wine and gin.

Construction began in June 2013 and the distillery was officially opened on 30th November 2014 on St Andrew´s Day. Commissioning of the distillery began in January

2015 with the first casks being filled early in March. The distillery is equipped with a 1.5 ton stainless steel mash tun, four 7,500 litre stainless steel washbacks with a fermentation time of 65-85 hours, one 7,500 litre wash still and one 4,500 litre spirit still. A slow distillation and an early cut are important to achieve the fruity character. Mainly first fill bourbon barrels are used for maturation together with STR casks (wine barriques that have been shaved, toasted and re-charred). The current yearly production is 200,000 litres of alcohol.

The first release of Kingsbarns single malt was in summer 2018 when a limited number of bottles were made available to the members of the Founder´s Club. A general release will follow in late 2018. There are also plans to release single casks each year. In summer 2017, a designated gin distillery was opened on site to produce the already succesful Darnley´s Gin.

Ballindalloch

[bal•lin•**da**•lock]

Owner: The Macpherson-Grant family

Region/district: Speyside

Founded: 2014

Status: Active (vc)

Capacity: 100 000 litres

Address: Ballindalloch, Banffshire AB37 9AA

Website: ballindallochdistillery.com

Tel: 01807 500 331

In the heart of Speyside, the owners of Ballindalloch Castle, the Macpherson-Grant family, decided in 2012 to turn a steading from 1820 into a whisky distillery.

Previous generations of the family had been involved in distilling from the 1860s and from 1923 to 1965, they owned part of Cragganmore distillery, not far away from the castle. The old farm building was meticulously renovated with attention given to every little detail and the result is an amazingly beautiful distillery which can be seen from the A95 between Aberlour and Grantown-on-Spey.

Ballindalloch distillery takes its water from the nearby Garline Springs and all the barley (currently Concerto) is grown on the Estate. All of the distillery equipment are gathered on the second floor which makes it easy for visitors to get a good view of the production. The equipment consists of an extraordinary 1 ton semi lauter, copper clad mash tun with a copper dome. There are four washbacks made of Oregon pine where the fermentation time was increased a while ago to increase the fruity character of the spirit. There are now four long fermentations (140 hours) and on short (92 hours). Finally there is a 5,000 litre lantern-shaped wash still and a 3,600 litre spirit still with a reflux ball. Both stills are connected to two wooden worm tubs for cooling the spirit vapours. The distillery is run by three persons only and, with no automation or computers. The distillery came on stream in September 2014 and was officially opened 16th April 2015 by Prince Charles. The distillery is working 5 days a week, making 100,000 litres of alcohol. The idea is to produce a robust and bold whisky, enhanced not least by the use of worm tubs. The first single malt release is expected in 2022.

The distillery is open for visitors by appointment and there is also the opportunity to take part in The Art of Whisky Making, which means spending a day with the crew and learning about whisky from mashing to warehousing.

Ardnamurchan

[ard•ne•**mur**•ken]

Owner: Adelphi Distillery Ltd

Region/district: Western Highlands

Founded: 2014

Status: Active (vc)

Capacity: 500 000 litres

Address: Glenbeg, Ardnamurchan, Argyll PH36 4JG

Website: adelphidistillery.com

Tel: 01972 500 285

The success for the independent bottler, Adelphi Distillery, has forced the owners to build their own distillery.

The chosen site is Glenbeg on the Ardnamurchan peninsula, just north of Isle of Mull. Most of the buildings were completed by August 2013, the equipment started to arrive in the autumn and, on 11th July 2014, the distillery came on stream. The distillery is equipped with a 2 tonne semi lauter mash tun made of stainless steel with a copper canopy, four wooden washbacks and three made of stainless steel, a wash still (10,000 litres) and a spirit still (6,000 litres). Minimum fermentation time is 72 hours. The production started with 2 mashes per week, then increased to five until May 2018, when it increased to an optimal level of 12, which will result in around 420,000 litres of alcohol per annum. Two different styles of whisky are produced; peated for six months of the year and unpeated for the rest. For the peated spirit, the barley has a phenol specification of 30-35ppm. The ultimate goal is to have the ability to floor malt a high proportion of their own barley as well.

Adelphi plans to release a mature spirit under the AD brand each year until 2021 when it will bottle the first Ardnamurchan Single Malt. The company also continues to forge relationships with distillers from other countries, in conjunction with Fusion Whisky Ltd., releasing international blends. To date: The Glover with Japan, The Kincardine and E&K with India, The Winter Queen with Holland and The Brisbane with Australia.

The owners have put in a lot of effort into creating a distillery with an environmental footprint as small as possible and all the power and heat requirements for the distillery come from local renewables. Adelphi Distillery is named after a distillery which closed in 1902. The company is owned by Keith Falconer and Donald Houston, with Alex Bruce as Managing Director.

Annandale

[ann•an•dail]

Owner: Annandale Distillery Co.

Region/district: Lowlands

Founded: 2014

Status: Active (vc)

Capacity: 500 000 litres

Address: Northfield, Annan, Dumfriesshire DG12 5LL

Website: annandaledistillery.com

Tel: 01461 207817

In 2010 Professor David Thomson and his wife, Teresa Church, obtained consent from the local council for the building of the new Annandale Distillery in Dumfries and Galloway in the south-west of Scotland.

The old one had been producing since 1836 and was owned by Johnnie Walker from 1895 until it closed down in 1918. From 1924 to 2007, the site was owned by the Robinson family, who were famous for their Provost brand of porridge oats. David Thomson began the restoration of the site in June 2011 with the two, old sandstone warehouses being restored to function as two-level dunnage warehouses. The distillery was in a poor condition and the mash house and the tun room was largely reconstructed while the other buildings were refurbished substantially. The old maltings, with the kiln and original pagoda roof, have been turned into an excellent visitor centre. The total cost, including restoration, construction and new equipment amounted to £10.5m.

Entering the production area of the new distillery is like walking into a beautiful village church. First you run into the 2.5 ton semi-lauter mash tun with an elegant copper dome. Then, with three wooden washbacks (a fermentation time of 72-96 hours) on each side, you are guided up to the two spirit stills (4,000 litres). Once you have reached them, you find the wash still (12,000 litres) slightly hidden behind a wall. The capacity is 500,000 litres per annum but so far they have been working one shift, which means 6 mashes per week and 250,000 litres.

The first cask was filled on 15 November 2014 and both unpeated and peated (45ppm) whisky is distilled. Finally, in June 2018, two single malts were released, both matured in ex-Buffalo Trace barrels. In both cases the whiskies, the un-peated Man O´Words and the peated (18ppm in the bottle) Man O´Swords were bottled at cask strength.

Inchdairnie

[inch•dairnie]

Owner: John Fergus & Co. Ltd

Region/district: Lowlands

Founded: 2015

Status: Active

Capacity: 2 000 000 litres

Address: Whitecraigs Rd, Glenrothes, Fife KY6 2RX

Website: inchdairniedistillery.com

Tel: 01595 510010

The majority of new and planned distilleries in Scotland (except the ones built by the biggest companies) are quite small with a capacity of 50-500,000 litres.

A rare exception is Inchdairnie, which was officially opened in May 2016, a few miles west of Glenrothes in Fife. The distillery will be able to distil 2 million litres per year with a possibility of expanding to 4 million litres. The distillery is owned by John Fergus & Co. which was founded by Ian Palmer in 2011. Palmer has 40 years of experience in the Scotch whisky industry and his latest position was general manager for Glen Turner. He is a minority share holder, with CES Whisky holding the rest of the shares.

Unusually, he distillery is equipped with a Meura mash filter, instead of a traditional mash tun. Working with a mash filter also means a hammer mill must be used to create a finer grist compared to, for example, a Porteus mill. There are four washbacks with a fermentation time of 72 hours and one pair of traditional pot stills with double condensers and aftercoolers to increase the copper to spirit ratio. The two stills are complemented by a Lomond still with six plates to provide the opportunity for triple distillation and experimental distillation. A unique yeast recipe combining beer-, wine- and distiller´s yeast is used and high gravity fermentation will create a fruitier character of the newmake.

Two main styles of whisky will be produced. Strathenry (80% of the production both unpeated and peated) will be used for blended whisky while Inchdairnie will be matured to be sold as a single malt. In November 2017, it was revealed that the distillery is also working on a rye whisky which will be called Ryelaw once bottled. According to the current SWA rules, the whisky will be categorised as a single grain Scotch whisky.

Daftmill

[daf•mil]

Owner: Francis Cuthbert **Region/district:** Lowlands
Founded: 2005 **Status:** Active **Capacity:** c 65 000 litres
Address: By Cupar, Fife KY15 5RF
Website: daftmill.com **Tel:** 01337 830303

The distillery may be one of the smallest in Scotland but few single malt releases have been more eagerly awaited by the whisky enthusiasts than the inaugural release from Daftmill.

Ever since December 2008, when the spirit legally became whisky, questions to the owners Francis and Ian Cuthbert about when the first whisky would be launched have always been answered by "when it´s ready". In 2017, they signed a distribution agreement with Berry Brothers and in May 2018, a ballot was opened for buying one of the first 629 bottles of a 12 year old matured in ex-bourbon casks. The first release was followed by a Summer Relase in June where seven casks rendered 1665 bottles.

Daftmill´s first distillation was on 16th December 2005 and around 20,000 litres are distilled in a year. It is run as a typical farmhouse distillery. The barley is grown on the farm and they also supply other distilleries. Of the total 800 tonnes that Francis Cuthbert harvests in a year, around 100 tonnes are used for his own whisky. The malting is done without peat at Crisp´s in Alloa. The equipment consists of a one tonne semi-lauter mash tun with a copper dome, two stainless steel washbacks with a fermentation between 72 and 100 hours and one pair of stills with slightly ascending lyne arms. The equipment is designed to give a lot of copper contact, a lot of reflux. The wash still has a capacity of 3,000 litres and the spirit still 2,000 litres.

Francis Cuthbert´s aim is to do a light, Lowland style whisky. In order to achieve this they have very short foreshots (five minutes) and the spirit run starts at 78% to capture all of the fruity esters and already comes off at 73%. Taking care of the farm obviously prohibits Francis from producing whisky full time. His silent season is during spring and autumn when work in the fields take all of his time. Whisky production is therefore reserved for two months in the summertime and two in the winter.

Abhainn Dearg

[aveen jar•rek]

Owner: Mark Tayburn **Region/district:** Highlands (Isle of Lewis)
Founded: 2008 **Status:** Active **Capacity:** c 20 000 litres
Address: Carnish, Isle of Lewis, Na h-Eileanan an Iar HS2 9EX
Website: abhainndearg.co.uk **Tel:** 01851 672429

In September 2008, spirit flowed from a newly constructed distillery in Uig on the island of Lewis in the Outer Hebrides.

This was the first distillery on the island since 1840 when Stornoway distillery was closed. The conditions for new distilleries being built at that time were not improved when James Matheson, a Scottish tradesman, bought the entire island in 1844. Even though he had made his fortune in the opium trade, he was an abstainer and a prohibitionist and did not look kindly on the production or use of alcohol.

The Gaelic name of the new distillery is Abhainn Dearg which means Red River, and the founder and owner is Mark "Marko" Tayburn who was born and raised on the island. Part of the distillery was converted from an old fish farm while some of the buildings are new. There are two 500 kg mash tuns made of stainless steel and two 7,500 litre washbacks made of Douglas fir with a fermentation time of 4 days. The wash still has a capacity of 2,112 litres and the spirit still 2,057 litres. Both have very long necks and steeply descending lye pipes leading out into two wooden worm tubs. Both bourbon and sherry casks are used for maturation. The plan is to use 100% barley grown on Lewis and in 2013 the first 6 tonnes of Golden Promise (15% of the total requirement) were harvested. In 2015, the owner reported that all the barley needed for the production, now came from the island. Over the years, production has been limited to around 10,000 litres of pure alcohol yearly even though the distillery has the capacity to do more.

The first release from the distillery was The Spirit of Lewis (matured for a short time in sherry casks) in 2010 and the first single malt was a limited release (2,011 bottles) of a 3 year old in October 2011, followed up by a cask strength version (58%) in 2012. The owners currently still sell Spirit of St Lewis and the 3 year old single malt. The first 10 year old single malt will be released in 2018.

Ailsa Bay

[ail•sah bey]

Owner: William Grant & Sons
Region/district: Lowlands

Founded: 2007
Status: Active
Capacity: 12 000 000 litres

Address: Girvan, Ayrshire KA26 9PT

Website: -
Tel: 01465 713091

Commissioned in September 2007, it only took nine months to build this distillery on the same site as Girvan Distillery near Ayr on Scotland´s west coast.

Initially, it was equipped with a 12,1 tonne full lauter mash tun, 12 washbacks made of stainless steel and eight stills. In August 2013 however, it was time for a major expansion when yet another mash tun, 12 more washbacks and eight more stills were commissioned, doubling the capacity to 12 million litres of alcohol.

Each washback will hold 50,000 litres and fermentation time is 60 hours for the heavier styles and 72 hours for the lighter "Balveniestyle". The stills are made according to the same standards as Balvenie's and one of the wash stills and one of the spirit stills have stainless steel condensers instead of copper. That way, they have the possibility of making batches of a more sulphury spirit if desired. A unique feature is the octangular spirit safe which sits between the two rows of stills. Each side corresponds to one specific still. To increase efficiency and to get more alcohol, high gravity distillation is used. The wash stills are heated using external heat exchangers but they also have interior steam coils. The spirit stills are heated by steam coils. In 2018, the distillery will be doing 49-51 mashes per week, producing 10 million litres of alcohol.

Five different types of spirit are produced. The most common is a light and rather sweet spirit. Then there is a heavy, sulphury style and three peated with the peatiest having a malt specification of 50ppm. The production is destined to become a part of Grant´s blended Scotch but in 2016, a peated single malt Ailsa Bay was released. In September 2018 the packaging was changed as well as the recipe, increasing both the smokiness and the sweetness.

Roseisle

[rose•eyel]

Owner: Diageo
Region/district: Highlands

Founded: 2009
Status: Active
Capacity: 12 500 000 litres

Address: Roseisle, Morayshire IV30 5YP

Website: -
Tel: 01343 832100

Roseisle distillery is located on the same site as the already existing Roseisle maltings just west of Elgin. The distillery has won several awards for its ambition towards sustainable production.

The distillery is equipped with two stainless steel, full lauter mash tuns with a 12.5 tonne charge each. There are 14 huge (115,500 litres) stainless steel washbacks and 14 stills with the wash stills being heated by external heat exchangers while the spirit stills are heated using steam coils. The spirit vapours are cooled through copper condensers but on three spirit stills and three wash stills there are also stainless steel condensers attached, that you can switch to for a more sulphury spirit. The fermentation time for a Speyside style of whisky is 90-100 hours and for a heavier style it is 50-60 hours. The plan for 2018 is to do 23 mashes per week and a total of 12 million litres of alcohol.

The total cost for the distillery was £40m and how to use the hot water in an efficient way was very much a focal point from the beginning. For example, Roseisle is connected by means of two long pipes with Burghead maltings, 3 km north of the distillery. Hot water is pumped from Roseisle and then used in the seven kilns at Burghead and cold water is then pumped back to Roseisle. The pot ale from the distillation will be piped into anaerobic fermenters to be transformed into biogas and the dried solids will act as a biomass fuel source. The biomass burner on the site, producing steam for the distillery, covers 72% of the total requirement. Furthermore, green technology has reduced the emission of carbon dioxide to only 15% of an ordinary, same-sized distillery.

Destined to be used for blends, Roseisle single malt was in autumn 2017, for the first time used in a different role. It was part of the blended malt Collectivum XXVIII where Diageo had used whiskies from all 28 malt distilleries.

Strathearn

[strath•earn]

Owner:
Tony Reeman-Clark

Region/district:
Southern Highlands

Founded: 2013 **Status:** Active **Capacity:** c 30 000 litres

Address: Bachilton Farm Steading, Methven PH1 3QX

Website: strathearndistillery.com **Tel:** 01738 840 100

This is something as unique as Scotland´s first micro-distillery. Abhainn Dearg on the Isle of Lewis has the same capacity, but the stills at Strathearn are considerably smaller.

The brainchild of Tony Reeman-Clark, it is situated a couple of miles west of Methven near Perth. Gin production was started in August 2013 and the first whisky was filled into casks in October. The distillery uses the Maris Otter barley which was abandoned by other distillers years ago due to the low yield. Reeman-Clark prefers it though, because of the flavours that it contributes. All the equipment is fitted into one room and consists of a stainless steel mash tun, two stainless steel washbacks with a fermentation time of 4-5 days, one 1,000 litre wash still and a 500 litre spirit still. Both stills are of the Alambic type with vertical tube copper condensers. When they are producing gin, they simply detach the lyne arm and mount a copper basket to the still to hold the botanicals. On the whisky side, both peated (35ppm) and un-peated whisky is produced and for maturation a variety of 50-100 litre casks are used; virgin French oak, virgin American oak and ex-sherry casks.

Reeman-Clark has also been experimenting with other types of wood like chestnut, mullberry and cherry. According to the rules, spirit matured in anything other than oak, cannot be called Scotch whisky. This problem was solved by labelling the content Uisge Beatha – the ancient name for Scotch. In early 2017, the Uisge was discontinued due to a controversy with the authorities whether or not the name Uisge was in accordance with the EU regulations. The first single malt Scotch from the distillery was released in December 2016. One hundred 50cl bottles were put up for auction and they were sold for a median price of £333. Another batch was released in September 2017. Several gins have been released including Heather Rose, Citrus and Oaked Highland and there´s also the Dunedin Golden Rum.

Eden Mill

[eden mill]

Owner:
Paul Miller

Region/district:
Lowlands

Founded: 2014 **Status:** Active (vc) **Capacity:** 80 000 litres

Address: St Andrews, Fife, KY16 0UU

Website: edenmill.com **Tel:** 01334 834038

In 2012, Paul Miller, the former Molson Coors sales director, with a background in the whisky industry, opened up the successful Eden Brewery in Guardbridge, west of St Andrews.

The site was an old paper mill and only 50 metres away, there was a distillery called Seggie which was operative between 1810 and 1860 and owned by the Haig family. As an extension of the brewery, Paul decided to build a distillery called Eden Mill Distillery. The distillery, with a capacity of 80,000 litres per year, mainly produces malt whisky, but gin is also on the map. The distillery is equipped with two wash stills and one spirit still of the alambic type. Made by Hoga in Portugal, all three stills are of the same size – 1,000 litres. Eden Mill is the first combined brewery and distillery in Scotland – a combination which has proven so successful, especially in the USA. The brewery/distillery also has a visitor centre which already attracts 20,000 visitors a year.

Whisky production started in November 2014 and the first release of a single malt appeared 24th April 2018. The 300 bottles, matured in a combination of French virgin oak, American virgin oak, and Pedro Ximinez casks sold out instantly with bottle No. 1 going for £7,100 at an auction conducted by Whisky Auctioneer. This was followed by a series of seven different 20 cl bottlings called the Hip Flask Series. All of them had been made from different mashbills and had matured in different types of casks. More releases will follow during autumn 2018.

The owners also announced their plans to expand the distillery (and brewery) by way of a £4m investment. When finished this will increase the production capacity to 200,000 litres and the goal is also to increase the number of visitors to 50,000 people per year.

Dalmunach

[dal•moo•nack]

Owner: Chivas Brothers

Region/district: Speyside

Founded: 2015

Status: Active

Capacity: 10 000 000 litres

Address: Carron, Banffshire AB38 7QP

Website: -

Tel: -

One of the newest distilleries in Scotland, and one of the most beautiful, has been built on the site of the former Imperial distillery.

Imperial distillery was built in 1897, the year of Queen Victoria´s Diamond Jubilee so no surprise where the distillery got its name. On the top of the roof there was even a large cast iron crown to mark the occasion. The founder was Thomas Mackenzie who at the time already owned Dailuaine and Talisker. The timing was not the best though. One year after the opening, the Pattison crash brought the whisky industry to its knees and the distillery was forced to close. Eventually it came into the hands of DCL (later to become Diageo) who owned it from 1916 until 2005, when Chivas Brothers took over. It was out of production for 60% of the time until 1998 when it was mothballed. The owners probably never planned to use it for distillation again as it was put up for sale in 2005 to become available as residential flats. Soon after, it was withdrawn from the market and, in 2012, a decision was taken to tear down the old distillery and build a new. Demolition of the old distillery began in 2013 and by the end of that year, nothing was left, except for the old warehouses.

Construction on the new Dalmunach distillery started in 2013 and it was commissioned in October 2014. The exceptional and stunning distillery is equipped with a 13 ton Briggs full lauter mash tun (the charge recently changed from 12 to 13 tonnes), 16 stainless steel washbacks with a fermentation time of 54 hours and 4 pairs of stills of a considerable size - 30,000 litres. The stills are positioned in a circle with a hexagonal spirit safe in the middle. The distillery, which cost £25m to build, has a capacity of 10 million litres and was officially opened in 2015 by Nicola Sturgeon, First Minister of Scotland. One interesting and quite spectacular feature is the use of part of an old Imperial washback in the main entrance.

Glasgow

[glas•go]

Owner: Liam Hughes, Ian McDougall

Region/district: Lowlands

Founded: 2015

Status: Active

Capacity: 270 000 litres

Address: Deanside Rd, Hillington, Glasgow G52 4XB

Website: glasgowdistillery.com

Tel: 0141 4047191

When Glasgow Distillery was opened in Hillington Business Park, it became the first new whisky distillery in Glasgow in modern times.

There were stills within the Strathclyde grain distillery producing the malt whisky Kinclaith from 1958-1975 but Liam Hughes, Mike Hayward and Ian McDougall had the intention of building the first proper malt distillery in Glasgow in more than hundred years. Backed up by Asian investors, the distillery was ready to start production in February 2015.

The first product to be bottled was the Makar gin which now exists in several versions. The owners have also bottled old (26-28 years), sourced single malts under the name Prometheus. The first single malt from their own production appeared in June 2018. Aged in ex-bourbon barrels and finished in virgin oak, the whisky is called 1770 Glasgow Single Malt, named after Glasgow´s first distillery which was founded at Dundashill in 1770.

The first distillation of whisky was unpeated but since then peated spirit (50ppm) is also part of the production and since January 2017, triple distillation is also practised one month per year. The distillery is located in an industrial area and the owners have no plans for a visitor centre. The distillery is equipped with a one ton mash tun, seven wash backs (5,400 litres each) with a minimum fermentation of 72 hours, one 2,500 litre wash still, one 1,400 litre spirit still and one 450 litre gin still - all from Firma Carl in Germany. Starting with 75,000 litres, since 2017 they are more or less on full production and an already planned expansion is due to be finished by 2019. This means yet another pair of stills, seven more washbacks and a total capacity of 500,000 litres. The expansion has been prompted by the success of their Makar gin but also by the interest in their inaugural single malt release.

Harris

[har•ris]

Owner: Isle of Harris Distillers Ltd.

Region/district: Highlands (Isle of Harris)

Founded: 2015

Status: Active (vc)

Capacity: 230 000 litres

Address: Tarbert, Isle of Harris, Na h-Eileanan an Iar HS3 3DJ

Website: harrisdistillery.com

Tel: 01859 502212

Almost ten years ago, Anderson Bakewell had conjured up an idea that has now resulted in a distillery which has come to fruition on the Isle of Harris.

Bakewell, who has been connected to the island for more than 40 years, acquired the services of Simon Erlanger for the company's benefit at an early stage. Erlanger, a former marketing director for Glenmorangie, is now MD of the new distillery, while Bakewell is chairman of the company. Construction started in 2014 and the distillery came into production in September 2015. The total cost for the whole project was £11.4m, but that sum probably also covered the cost for barley and casks until the first whisky is ready to be bottled. The distillery, located in Tarbert, is the second distillery after Abhainn Dearg on Lewis to be located in the Outer Hebrides.

The equipment consists of a 1.2 tonne semi lauter mash tun made of stainless steel but clad with American oak, 5 washbacks made of Oregon pine and with a fermentation time of 3-4 days, one 7,000 litre wash still and a 5,000 litre spirit still - both with descending lyne arms and made in Italy. Currently the distillery is doing 5 mashes per week. The style of the whisky, which will be called Hearach (the Gaelic word for a person living on Harris), will be medium peated with a phenol specification in the barley of 12-14ppm. The first spirit to be distilled in September 2015 was gin and this was followed by whisky in December. The gin has already been released and apart from traditional botanicals, local ingredients are also used such as sugar kelp.

Together with three other distilleries (Talisker and Torabhaig on Skye and Isle of Raasay), Harris distillery launched a new whisky route called Hebridean Whisky Trail on 15th August 2018 – www.hebrideanwhisky.com.

Lone Wolf

[loan wolf]

Owner: Brewdog plc.

Region/district: Highlands

Founded: 2016

Status: Active

Capacity: 450 000 litres

Address: Balmacassie Commercial Park, Ellon, Aberdeenshire AB41 8BX

Website: lonewolfspirits.com

Tel: 01358 724924

Founded in 2007 by James Watt and Martin Dickie, Brew Dog has grown to become the biggest independent brewery in the UK and is also the fastest-growing drinks producer in the country.

A decision was made in 2014 to also open a distillery on the premises in Ellon, outside of Aberdeen. To manage the distillery, Steven Kearsley who has a background at several Diageo distilleries, was called in. Steven was determined that this should not be "just another" whisky distillery. To use his own words, it is multi-faceted and by that he means they will not limit themselves to just a few styles of spirits. Apart from malt whisky, there will also be grain and rye, bourbon style whiskey, vodka, gin and rum on offer.

The adjacent brew house provides the wash for the distillery which has the following equipment; one 3,000 litre pot still with an 8 plate rectification column which will be used for stripping the wash for vodka, whisky and rum, another 3,000 litre still with a 60-plate column is used for the final distillation of vodka and whisky, a 600 litre pot still is dedicated to gin and brandy production, while a 50 litre pot still is used for research and experimentation. The idea is to have an innovative distillery where, for example, cherry or apple wood may be used for drying the barley or different types of wood may be used for maturation. First production was gin and vodka and following a few prototype releases, the first bottles were launched in spring 2017. Current expressions include Gunpowder Gin, Single Malt Barrel-Aged Vodka made from 100% malted barley and Cranachan Vodka which has been steeped in raspberries for 12 hours after the distillation. Whisky production is ongoing with experiments being done with different mash bills. In 2017, Lowe Wolf became one of the first Scottish distilleries in modern times to distil a rye whisky.

Arbikie

[ar•bi•ki]

Owner: The Stirling family	**Region/district:** Eastern Highlands
Founded: 2015	**Status:** Active	**Capacity:** 200 000 litres

Address: Inverkeilor, Arbroath, Angus DD11 4UZ

Website: arbikie.com

Tel: 01241 830770

The Stirling family has been farming since the 17th century and the 2000-acre Arbikie Highland Estate in Angus has now been in their possession for four generations.

The three brothers (John, Iain and David) started their careers within other fields but have now returned to the family lands to open up a single-estate distillery. The definition of a single-estate distillery is that, not only does the whole chain of production take place on site, but all the ingredients are also grown on the farm. Ballindalloch is one example but Arbikie is the first to produce both brown and white spirits.

The first vodka from potatoes was distilled in October 2014 which was followed by gin in May 2015. Trials with malt whisky, started in March 2015, have gone over to full production since October 2015.

The barley is grown in fields of their own and then sent to Boorts malt in Montrose, 7 miles away. The distillery, which is based in an old barn at the farm, is equipped with a stainless steel, semi-lauter mash tun with a 0.75 ton charge, four washbacks (two 4,400 litre and two 9,000 litre), one 4,000 litre wash still and one 2,400 litre spirit still. For the final stage of vodka and gin production, there is also a 40 plate rectification column. The whisky is mainly matured in ex bourbon barrels and ex sherry hogsheads. At the moment the Stirlings don´t intend to launch their first single malt whisky any time soon. The plan is to release it at the age of 14 in 2030.

In common with a few other distilleries in Scotland, Arbikie started trials with rye whisky production in December 2015. Although not legally a whisky (it´s under 3 years), the first rye spirit was released in spring 2018. Two styles are produced - one that is in line with the SWA rules and another using American methods.

Dornoch

[dor•nock]

Owner: Phil and Simon Thompson	**Region/district:** Northern Highlands
Founded: 2016	**Status:** Active	**Capacity:** 30 000 litres

Address: Castle Street, Dornoch, Sutherland, IV25 3 SD

Website: dornochdistillery.com

Tel: 01862 810 216

Along with their parents, Phil and Simon Thompson have been running the Dornoch Castle Hotel in Sutherland for fifteen years.

The hotel is famous for its outstanding whisky bar and the two brothers are passionate about whisky and other spirits. So passionate in fact that they decided to convert a 135-year old fire station into a distillery. The building is only 47 square metres and the brothers have struggled to fit all the equipment into the limited space. The distillery is equipped with a 300 kg stainless steel, semi-lauter mash tun from China, seven washbacks made of oak from Eastern Europe, a 1,000 litre wash still and a 600 litre spirit still. Both stills, made by Hoga in Portugal, have shell and tube condensers. The stills are directly fired using gas but they are also equipped with steam coils as an alternative heating method. There is also a 2,000 litre still with a column from Holland for the production of gin and other spirits. The distillery

has a yearly capacity of 30,000 litres of pure alcohol of which approximately 15,000 litres are dedicated to whisky. The first distillation was gin in October 2016 and whisky production commenced in January 2017. Around 100 casks of single malt had been filled in July 2018. A range of experimental batches of the gin were released during spring 2017 and in November the same year, the brothers finally launched their key expression - Thompson Bros Organic Highland Gin.

Their interest in "old-style" whiskies produced in the 1960s and earlier also has an influence on the production. All the barley is floor malted, often using old heritage varieties and different strains of brewer´s yeast is used instead of distiller´s yeast. The first two year´s of success have taken the brothers by surprise and beginning of August 2018, the launched a second row of crowdfunding in order to move the distillery up the road to a larger site and expand the production.

Torabhaig

[tor•a•<u>vaig</u>]

Owner: **Region/district:**
Mossburn Distillers   Highlands (Skye)

Founded: **Status:**   **Capacity:**
2016   Active (vc)   500 000 litres

Address: Teangue, Sleat, Isle of Skye IV44 8RE

Website: **Tel:**
www.torabhaig.com   01471 833447

The idea to build a second distillery on Skye (with Talisker being the first) was presented several years ago by the late Sir Iain Noble.

He had chosen a 19th century listed farm building near Torabhaig on the southeast coast as a suitable location, but the plans were never realized until after Sir Iain had died in 2010. A new company, Mossburn Distillers, took over the plans and after a planning consent was granted, the first phase of restoration was completed in December 2014. Chris Anderson, a former head of distilling for Dewar´s blend was responsible for the construction of the distillery. By June 2016, most of the equipment had been installed and production started in January 2017.

The distillery is equipped with a 1.5 ton stainless steel mash tun with a copper top. There are eight washbacks made of Douglas fir with a fermentation time of around 72 hours, one 8,000 litre wash still and one 5,000 litre spirit still, made by Forsyth in Rothes. In 2017, 250,000 litres will be produced, rising to 420,000 litres in 2018. The owners aim to produce a heavily peated whisky with a phenol specification of 30ppm in the malted barley. The cost to build the distillery was around £5m and this also includes a visitor centre which opened in March 2018.

In anticipation of the first single malts from the distillery, the owners have launched a range of whiskies from other distilleries called Mossburn´s Signature Casks. Two expression, both blended malts, have appeared so far - one made up of whiskies from the Islands and one from Speyside.

Mossburn Distillers was founded in 2013 and is owned by Marussia Beverages, a Dutch company specialising in spirits and fine wine. That company in turn is actually a part of the privately owned Swedish group Haydn Holding. So, for the first time in history, we now have a Swedish owned malt distillery in Scotland!

Isle of Raasay

[ajl ov r<u>a</u>ssay]

Owner: **Region/district:**
R&B Distillers   Highlands (Raasay)

Founded: **Status:**   **Capacity:**
2017   Active (vc)   200 000 litres

Address: Borodale House, Raasay, By Kyle IV40 8PB

Website: **Tel:**
rbdistillers.com   01478 470177

This new Island distillery on Raasay, east of the Isle of Skye, could be defined as a "bi-product" coming from the plans to build a distillery in the Borders.

Since 2010 Alasdair Day has planned for a new distillery in the south of Scotland. The funding, however, became an issue but was resolved when Alasdair teamed up with Bill Dobbie, entrepreneur and co-founder of online dating site Cupid. As the new company was formed, the plans for yet another distillery took shape. The idea was to turn Borodale House, a derelict Victorian hotel on the island of Raasay, into a distillery or at the least the distillery visitor´s centre. Planning approval was granted in February 2016 and the company was named R&B Distillers (Raasay and Borders). When work on the distillery got underway, the owners also decided that the project in the Borders should be put on hold until the distillery on Raasay had been built.

The Raasay Distillery, which started production 12th September 2017, is equipped with a 1 ton mash tun, six stainless steel washbacks, temperature controlled by cooling jackets and with a fermentation time of up to 115 hours, one 5,000 litre wash still and a 3,600 litre spirit still equipped with a separate purifier. Both stills were made by Frilli in Italy. The production started with one shift, 5 days a week but since July 2018, they have moved to two shifts which will mean almost 188,000 litres of pure alcohol in a year. The actual capacity on 7 days and two shifts is 200,000 litres. The first production at the distillery was heavily peated (45ppm) which will be blended with unpeated whisky to achieve what will become the house style.

A visitor´s centre opened in summer 2017 and the view from the distillery is one of Scotland´s most spectacular. In anticipation of their own whisky, a lightly peated, sourced single malt Scotch named Raasay While We Wait, finished in French oak Tuscan wine casks, is offered to the visitors.

Lindores Abbey

[linn•doors aebi]

Owner:
The Lindores Distilling Co.

Region/district:
Lowlands

Founded:
2017

Status:
Active (vc)

Capacity:
260 000 litres

Address: Lindores Abbey House, Abbey Road, Newburgh, Fife KY14 6HH

Website:
lindoresabbeydistillery.com

Tel:
01337 842547

The famous, first written record of whisky was a letter to Friar John Cor, a monk at the Abbey of Lindores, dated 1494 where, by order of King James IV, he was instructed to make "aqua vitae, VIII bolls of malt".

More than five hundred years later, whisky is again produced at Lindores Abbey in Fife. Drew and Helen McKenzie Smith, whose family for a century has owned the land on which the ruins of the abbey stands, built a distillery which was commissioned in December 2017. The location is stunning and with all the production equipment on one level you have a spectacular view of the surroundings. Behind the washbacks you catch a glimpse of Dundee and from the stills you look down on the abbey ruins with the river Tayne in the background.

All the barley used in the production comes from the owner's own farm which makes Lindores Abbey Distillery one of few producers in Scotland of single estate whisky (others being Ballindalloch and Arbikie). The equipment consists of a 2 ton semi lauter mash tun with a copper lid, four Oregon pine washbacks (with space for another four in the future) with a fermentation time between 90 and 115 hours, one 10,000 litre wash still and two 3,500 litre spirit stills. The foreshots are 15-20 minutes and the spirit cut starts at 75% and goes down to 65%. The idea behind having two spirit stills is to allow for more copper contact during distillation. The production goal for 2018 is 130,000 litres of pure alcohol.

The style of the whisky will be light and fruity and they also produce Aqua Vitae as it was made during the 15th century, which they infuse with herbs and plants growing around the Abbey. An excellent visitor centre with a wide range of activities, including whisky and champagne afternoon teas (!), is also a part of the distillery.

The Clydeside

[klajdsajd]

Owner:
Morrison Glasgow Distillers

Region/district:
Lowlands

Founded:
2017

Status:
Active (vc)

Capacity:
500 000 litres

Address: 100 Stobcross Road, Glasgow G3 8QQ

Website:
theclydeside.com

Tel:
0141 2121401

Since 2012, Tim Morrison had been working on the idea of building a whisky distillery in Glasgow and it would be difficult to find a person better suited for the task.

Morrison represents the fourth generation of one of Scotland's best known whisky families. Originally a whisky broker, Tim Morrison's father, Stanley P Morrison eventually created Morrison Bowmore Distillers and acquired three distilleries - Bowmore, Glen Garioch and Auchentoshan. The company is today owned by Beam Suntory and Tim Morrison has long left the company. Instead he took over the independent bottler AD Rattray and expanded that business by opening up a first class shop and whisky centre in Kirkoswald in Ayrshire. The Clydeside Distillery though, is run from a different company - Morrison Glasgow Distillers.

The distillery is beautifully situated on the river Clyde with well-known attractions such as the Riverside Museum, Glasgow Science Centre and the SEC Centre as its closest neighbours. The equipment consists of a 1.5 ton semi lauter mash tun, 8 stainless steel washbacks, a 7,500 litre wash still and a 5,000 litre spirit still. The foreshots are 15 minutes with a slow distillation and the cutpoints for the spirit run are 76-71%. Production started in autumn 2017 and the aim is to produce a light, Lowland style whisky.

An excellent visitor centre has been constructed within the old Pump House building from 1877 while an adjacent, modern building houses the distillery. Apart from a variety of tours, the distillery shop also offers a wide range of whiskies including new make spirit from the distillery itself. A special twist to the distillery story is that Tim Morrison's great grandfather built the Pump House which was used to power the hydraulic gates allowing ships in and out of the Queens Dock.

Ncn´ean

[nook•knee•anne]

Owner:
Ncn´ean Distillery Ltd.

Region/district:
Western Highlands

Founded: 2017
Status: Active (vc)
Capacity: 100 000 litres

Address: Drimnin, By Lochaline PA80 5XZ

Website: ncnean.com

Tel: 01967 421698

Drimnin Estate, which overlooks the Isle of Mull in the west, is located on the Morvern peninsula in the Western Highlands. The 7,000 acre estate was bought by Derek and Louise Lewis in 2001.

Their daughter Annabel Thomas, a former strategy consultant in London, is the initiator of this new distillery which, when it was in the planning stage, was called Drimnin but later changed name to Ncn`ean after a witch-queen according to Gaelic folk tales. In early 2016, the company received a £513,000 grant from the Scottish government and construction work began later that year. The late Dr. Jim Swan acted as consultant and in March 2017, the distillery came on stream.

It is equipped with a one ton semi lauter mash tun, four stainless steel washbacks with a fermentation time between 65 and 115 hours. Furthermore there is a 5,000 litre wash still and a 3,500 litre spirit still. All the malted barley used is organic and the owners strive to make all aspects of production as environmentally friendly as possible including a wood chip boiler and recycling waste heat through the temperature controlled warehouses. Production in the first year was just over 90,000 litres.

The owners produce a light and fruity whisky with maturation predominantly in ex-bourbon and red wine casks. There will also be plenty of space for experimentation, including trials with different yeast strains. Since opening, the distillery has received an organic certification from BDA. A visitor centre opened in July 2017 and the first bottling of the whisky is planned for spring 2020. In September 2018, however, the very first product from the distillery was launched. Unlike many other start ups, it was not a new-make or a gin but a botanical spirit made using various wild herbs and flowers found around the distillery.

The Borders

[boar•ders]

Owner:
The Three Stills Co. Ltd.

Region/district:
Lowlands

Founded: 2017
Status: Active (vc)
Capacity: 2 000 000 litres

Address: Commercial Road, Hawick TD9 7AQ

Website: thebordersdistillery.com

Tel: 01450 374330

On the 6th of March 2018, the first whisky distillery in the Borders in 180 years started production and the distillery opened to the public a few weeks later.

Behind the Borders Distillery in Hawick is a company called The Three Stills Company which was founded in 2013. The owners include four men who had all previously worked for William Grant & Sons – George Tait, Tony Roberts, John Fordyce and Tim Carton. Unlike some other new distillery projects, a sum of £10m had been secured before they applied for a planning permission. The owners also include private investors as well as companies in the UK and abroad. In 2015, the company purchased a site in Hawick which had been occupied by an electric company and then by an engineering firm. Starting in August 2016, the beautiful buildings, dating from the late 1880s, were meticulously renovated and turned into a distillery. It is equipped with a 5 ton mash tun, eight stainless steel washbacks, two wash stills and two spirit stills with all equipment provided by Forsyths in Rothes. The capacity is quite large, 2 million litres, and the aim is to produce an un-peated, floral whisky. Other spirits will also be produced, including gin using local botanicals and there is also a dedicated gin still on site. During the first year, the plan is to produce 1.6 million litres of spirit.

The owners also have plans to install a bio plant on the site. Using anaerobic digestion technique, by-products from the distillation will be converted into biogas which will help power the distillery. The company has already released a blended Scotch from sourced whisky called Clan Fraser. The first bottling of spirit actually made at the distillery appeared in July 2018 when William Kerr´s Borders Gin was launched.

Aberargie

[aber•ar•jee]

Owner:
The Perth Distilling Co.

Region/district:
Lowlands

Founded: 2017

Status: Active

Capacity: 750 000 litres

Address: Aberargie, Perthshire PH2 9LX

Website: -

Tel: 01738 787044

The distillery was built on the same grounds in Fife as Morrison & Mackay, independent bottler and producer of Scottish liqueurs, and a company which can trace it´s roots back to 1982.

Founded as John Murray & Co., the company was taken over in 2005 by Kenny Mackay and Brian Morrison, once the chairman of Morrison Bowmore, and his son Jamie. The production of liqueurs, especially Columba Cream, continued while bottling of Scotch single malts (The Carn Mor) was added to the business. Later on, they also took over the Old Perth brand from Whyte & Mackay and relaunched it as a blended malt. The company name was changed to Morrison & Mackay in 2014.

At the same time, the Morrison´s of the company decided to build a distillery on the premises and founded a company called The Perth Distilling Company. Construction work started in summer 2016 and the first spirit was distilled in November 2017.

The distillery is equipped with a 2 ton semilauter mash tun, six stainless steel washbacks with a fermentation time of 72 hours, one 15,000 litre wash still and one 10,000 litre spirit still. The stills were made by Forsyths and are both heated with panels instead of coils or pans. With a maturation in a mixture of first fill sherry butts, first fill bourbon barrels and second fill sherry/bourbon casks, the owners are aiming for a fruity character which will be enhanced by occasional peated spirit runs. The barley variety that they are using is Golden Promise, grown in fields owned by the Morrison family and that surround the distillery.

With the Morrison & Mackay blending and bottling facility next to the distillery, every step of the production (except malting) will take place on site.

GlenWyvis

[glen•wivis]

Owner:
GlenWyvis Distillery Ltd.

Region/district:
Highlands

Founded: 2017

Status: Active (vc)

Capacity: 140 000 litres

Address: Upper Docharty, Dingwall IV15 9UF

Website: glenwyvis.com

Tel: 01349 862005

In 2015, the local farmer John McKenzie, came up with the idea to establish a distillery that was owned by the local people – the first ever 100% community-owned distillery.

A planning application was submitted to the local council in March 2016 and by summer more than £2.5 million had been raised via a community share offer with more than 3,000 people investing. Construction started in January 2017 and later that year, the owners managed to hire one of the most experienced distillers in Scotland as the manager – Duncan Tait – who over the years had been managing several of the Diageo distilleries. The first distillation was on the 30th of January 2018 and the goal is to produce around 50,000 litres of pure alcohol the first year, moving to 55,000 litres in 2019.

The distillery is equipped with a 0.5 ton semi lauter mash tun, six washbacks made of stainless steel with a fermentation time of 72-120 hours, one 2,500 litre wash still and one 1,700 litre spirit still. The unpeated spirit, which will mainly be filled into American oak, will be matured in dunnage warehouses on site. The style of the newmake is a combination o fruity and green/grassy. A dedicated gin still was installed in spring 2018 and gin production started in beginning of June with the first release on the shelf a few weeks later.

The distillery is located in Dingwall, north of Inverness but this is not the first distillery in the town. In 1879, Ben Wyvis was founded and it went on producing until 1926 when it was closed. The area, however, is famous for yet another distillery – namely Ferintosh. It was built across the Cromarty Firth from Dingwall in 1689 by members of the Forbes family. To compensate the Forbes for loss of land during the Jacobite uprising, the family was allowed to produce and sell whisky free of duty for almost a century.

Ardnahoe

[ard•na•<u>hoe</u>]

Owner:
Hunter Laing & Company

Region/district:
Islay

Founded: **Status:**
2017   Active (vc)

Capacity:
1,000,000 litres

Address: Isle of Islay, Port Askaig PA46 7RU

Website:
ardnahoedistillery.com

Tel:
01496 840711

For an independent bottler, to have your own distillery has become increasingly important. Being able to trade casks from your own production for mature malt is a huge advantage.

There is, of course, also the benefit of being able to create your own brand for the future. Independent bottler Hunter Laing decided in 2016, it was time to build their own distillery. With the owner´s, Stewart Laing, family hailing from Islay, the Hebridean island seemed the proper place to build it. Planning permission to build Ardnahoe distillery on the northeast coast near Bunnahabhain, was granted in 2016 and two years later it was time for the first distillation.

The distillery is equipped with a 2.5 ton semi lauter mash tun, four washbacks made from Oregon pine, one wash still (12,500 litres) and one spirit still (9,000 litres), both with extremely long lyne arms. The distillery, which will be very manual without computers, is equipped with worm tubs (the only ones on Islay). The aim is to produce a variety of single malts from unpeated to peated whiskies on several levels (from 5ppm up to 40ppm). The estimated cost for the distillery is £8m and it will have an annual capacity of 1,000,000 litres of alcohol, although 200,000 litres will be the initial target. In February 2017, the legendary Jim McEwan, who retired from Bruichladdich in 2015, joined the team as production director.

Ardnahoe is the first new distillery on the island since Kilchoman was opened in 2005 and the 9th on Islay. The location is stunning and since it´s a split level distillery, the stunning view from the still house is the Sound of Islay with Isle of Jura in the distance. A distillery visitor centre with a shop is due to open soon after the distillery has commenced producing. Meanwhile, Hunter Laing has been present with a pop-up store during the last two Islay Festivals to build an interest in the distillery.

First releases

An incredible year with inaugural bottlings from five distilleries – Eden Mill, Annandale, Daftmill, Kingsbarns and Glasgow.

Distilleries per owner

c = closed, d = demolished, mb = mothballed, dm = dismantled

Diageo
Auchroisk
Banff (d)
Benrinnes
Blair Athol
Brora (c)
Caol Ila
Cardhu
Clynelish
Coleburn (dm)
Convalmore (dm)
Cragganmore
Dailuaine
Dallas Dhu (c)
Dalwhinnie
Dufftown
Glen Albyn (d)
Glendullan
Glen Elgin
Glenesk (dm)
Glenkinchie
Glenlochy (d)
Glenlossie
Glen Mhor (d)
Glen Ord
Glen Spey
Glenury Royal (d)
Inchgower
Knockando
Lagavulin
Linkwood
Mannochmore
Millburn (dm)
Mortlach
North Port (d)
Oban
Pittyvaich (d)
Port Ellen (dm)
Roseisle
Royal Lochnagar
St Magdalene (dm)
Strathmill
Talisker
Teaninich

Pernod Ricard
Aberlour
Allt-a-Bhainne
Braeval
Caperdonich (d)
Dalmunach
Glenburgie
Glen Keith
Glenlivet
Glentauchers
Glenugie (dm)
Imperial (d)
Inverleven (d)
Kinclaith (d)
Lochside (d)
Longmorn
Miltonduff
Scapa
Strathisla
Tormore

Edrington Group
Glenrothes
Glenturret
Highland Park
Macallan

Inver House (Thai Beverage)
Balblair
Balmenach

Glen Flagler (d)
Knockdhu
Pulteney
Speyburn

John Dewar & Sons (Bacardi)
Aberfeldy
Aultmore
Craigellachie
Macduff
Royal Brackla

William Grant & Sons
Ailsa Bay
Balvenie
Glenfiddich
Kininvie
Ladyburn (dm)

Whyte & Mackay (Emperador)
Dalmore
Fettercairn
Jura
Tamnavulin

Beam Suntory
Ardmore
Auchentoshan
Bowmore
Glen Garioch
Laphroaig

Distell International
Bunnahabhain
Deanston
Tobermory

Benriach Dist. Co. (Brown Forman)
Benriach
Glendronach
Glenglassaugh

Loch Lomond Group
Glen Scotia
Littlemill (d)
Loch Lomond

J & A Mitchell
Glengyle
Springbank

Glenmorangie Co. (LVMH)
Ardbeg
Glenmorangie

Angus Dundee Distillers
Glencadam
Tomintoul

Ian Macleod Distillers
Glengoyne
Rosebank (c)
Tamdhu

Campari Group
Glen Grant

Isle of Arran Distillers
Arran

Signatory
Edradour

Tomatin Distillery Co.
Tomatin

J & G Grant
Glenfarclas

Rémy Cointreau
Bruichladdich

David Prior
Bladnoch (c)

Gordon & MacPhail
Benromach

La Martiniquaise
Glen Moray

Ben Nevis Distillery Ltd (Nikka)
Ben Nevis

Picard Vins & Spiritueux
Tullibardine

Harvey´s of Edinburgh
Speyside

Kilchoman Distillery Co.
Kilchoman

Cuthbert family
Daftmill

Mark Tayburn
Abhainn Dearg

Aurora Brewing Ltd
Wolfburn

Strathearn Distillery Ltd
Strathearn

Annandale Distillery Co.
Annandale

Adelphi Distillery Co.
Ardnamurchan

Wemyss
Kingsbarns

Mcpherson-Grant family
Ballindalloch

Paul Miller
Eden Mill

Isle of Harris Distillers
Harris

The Glasgow Distillery Company
Glasgow Distillery

John Fegus & Co. Ltd
Inchdairnie

Stirling family
Arbikie

Brewdog plc
Lone Wolf

Thompson family
Dornoch

Mossburn Distillers
Torabhaig

R & B Distillers
Isle of Raasay

The Lindores Distilling Company
Lindores Abbey

Morrison Glasgow Distillers
Clydeside

Ncn´ean Distillery Ltd.
Ncn´ean

The Three Stills Co.
The Borders

The Glenallachie Distillers Co.
Glenallachie

The Perth Distilling Company
Aberargie

GlenWyvis Distillery Ltd.
GlenWyvis

Hunter Laing
Ardnahoe

Closed
distilleries

The distilleries on the following pages
have all been closed and some of them even demolished.
New releases from a few of them appear on a regular basis
but for most of them chances are very slim of ever finding another bottling.
One is also tempted to say that none of the distilleries will ever be opened
again but recent developments clearly show that you can never
be certain. In October 2017, Diageo announced that they had
plans to re-start Brora and Port Ellen and the following day,
Ian Macleod Distillers declared that Rosebank would
be reinstated as a working distillery as well.

Brora

[bro•rah]

Owner: Diageo

Region/district: Northern Highlands

Founded: 1819

Status: Closed

Capacity: 800,000 litres

Address: Brora, Sutherland KW9 6LR

Website: malts.com

Tel: 01408 623003 (vc)

Although founded under the name Clynelish distillery in 1819, it is under the name Brora that the single malt has enjoyed its newfound fame during the past two decades.

The distillery was built in the time referred to as the Highland Clearances. Many land-owners wished to increase the yield of their lands and consequently went into large-scale sheep farming. Thousands of families were ruthlessly forced away and the most infamous of the large land-owners was the Marquis of Stafford who founded Clynelish (Brora) in 1819.

The distillery had a chequered history until 1896 when the brewer and whisky broker James Ainslie assumed ownership. He rebuilt the distillery including increasing the capacity and soon Clynelish single malt enjoyed a good reputation amongst blenders. In 1967 the owners, DCL, decided to build a new, modern distillery on the same site. This was given the name Clynelish and it was decided the old distillery, with a capacity of 1 million litres of alcohol, should be closed. Shortly after, the demand for peated whisky, especially for the blend Johnnie Walker, increased and the old site re-opened but now under the name Brora and the "recipe" for the whisky was changed to a heavily peated malt.

Brora was closed in 1983 but the single malt was not forgotten. From 1995 United Distillers regularly released different expressions of Brora in the Rare Malts series. The last appeared in 2003. In 2002 a new range was created, called Special Releases and bottlings of Brora have appeared ever since, eventually earning a cult status amongst whisky aficionados.

Since the old buildings were intact with some of the equipment left (two stills, the feints receiver, the spirit receiver and the brass safe), rumours surfaced from time to time that the distillery would be reopened. Still, it came as a major surprise in October 2017 when Diageo announced that both Brora and Port Ellen, would be resurrected. With a capacity of 800,000 litres of alcohol, the plan is to start production at Brora sometime in 2020. Very little stock remains of the old Brora single malt and from 2018, this will be released separately and not in connection with the Special Releases.

History:

1819 The Marquis of Stafford, 1st Duke of Sutherland, founds the distillery as Clynelish Distillery.

1827 The first licensed distiller, James Harper, files for bankruptcy and John Matheson takes over.

1828 James Harper is back as licensee.

1833 Andrew Ross takes over the license.

1846 George Lawson & Sons takes over.

1896 James Ainslie & Heilbron takes over and rebuilds the facilities.

1912 Distillers Company Limited (DCL) takes over together with James Risk.

1925 DCL buys out Risk.

1930 Scottish Malt Distillers takes over.

1931 The distillery is mothballed.

1938 Production restarts.

1960 The distillery becomes electrified (until now it has been using locally mined coal from Brora).

1967 A new distillery is built adjacent to the first one, it is also named Clynelish and both operate in parallel from August with the new distillery named Clynelish A and the old Clynelish B.

1969 Clynelish B is closed in April but reopened shortly after as Brora and starts using a heavily peated malt until 1973.

1975 A new mashtun is installed.

1983 Brora is closed in March.

1995 Brora 1972 (20 years) and Brora 1972 (22 years) are launched as Rare Malts.

2002 A 30 year old is the first bottling in the Special Releases.

2014 The 13th release of Brora – a 35 year old.

2015 The 14th release of Brora – a 37 year old.

2016 The 15th release of Brora – a 38 year old.

2017 The 16th release of Brora - a 34 year old. Diageo announces that the distillery will re-open in 2020.

34 years old

Port Ellen

[port ell•en]

Owner:
Diageo

Region/district:
Islay

Founded: **Status:** **Capacity:**
1825 Dismantled -

Admittedly, Port Ellen has a place in whisky history due to the last 15 years of increasingly expensive bottlings but there´s another reason why the distillery is of historical importance.

Shortly after it had opened in 1824, a new device was tested at the distillery – the spirit safe. It was invented by Aeneas Coffey, one of the men behind the continuous still, and obviously the test went well. Spirit safes now exist at all distilleries in Scotland.

The founder of the distillery, Alexander Mackay, went bankrupt a few months after the distillery had opened and instead it was a relative of his, John Ramsay, who would run the distillery until the late 1800s and with great success. There was no intention of ever bottling the spirit as a single malt – all the production went to blends. In 1930 the distillery was mothballed and didn´t reopen until 1967. The final era would last but 16 years and in 1983 the distillery was closed for good (or so it would seem). Ten years before the closure, a huge drum maltings was opened on the site and this continues to produce malted barley for several of the Islay distilleries. At its height, Port Ellen was equipped with four stills, producing 1.7 million litres of alcohol.

And so time went by and few people cared much about Port Ellen even though it was released twice in the Rare Malts range (1998 and 2000). It wasn´t until 2001, when the first Port Ellen Special Release turned up that things started to change and the malt became a cult whisky. The announcement from Diageo in early October 2017 that not only Port Ellen but also Brora would be re-opened caught everyone off guard. In the case of Port Ellen, a new distillery will have to be built in the courtyard between the maltings and the old warehouses. The old drawings of the equipment still exist and one pair of stills with shell and tube condensers will be fabricated. The plan is to have the distillery, with an 800,000 litre capacity up and running sometime in 2020. There will also be a visitor centre, or brand home as Diageo calls it. There is still some stock of old Port Ellen left but going forward, this will not be launched in the Special Releases as it used to be.

History:

1825 Alexander Kerr Mackay assisted by Walter Campbell founds the distillery. Mackay runs into financial troubles after a few months and his three relatives John Morrison, Patrick Thomson and George Maclennan take over.

1833 John Ramsay, a cousin to John Morrison, comes from Glasgow to take over.

1836 Ramsay is granted a lease on the distillery from the Laird of Islay.

1892 Ramsay dies and the distillery is inherited by his widow, Lucy.

1906 Lucy Ramsay dies and her son Captain Iain Ramsay takes over.

1920 Iain Ramsay sells to Buchanan-Dewar who transfers the administration to the company Port Ellen Distillery Co. Ltd.

1925 Buchanan-Dewar joins Distillers Company Limited (DCL).

1930 The distillery is mothballed.

1967 In production again after reconstruction and doubling of the number of stills from two to four.

1973 A large drum maltings is installed.

1980 Queen Elisabeth visits the distillery and a commemorative special bottling is made.

1983 The distillery is mothballed.

1987 The distillery closes permanently but the maltings continue to deliver malt to all Islay distilleries.

2001 Port Ellen cask strength first edition is released.

2014 The 14th release of Port Ellen - a 35 year old from 1978.

2015 The 15th release of Port Ellen - a 32 year old from 1983.

2016 The 16th release of Port Ellen - a 37 year old from 1978.

2017 The 17th release of Port Ellen - a 37 year old from 1979. Diageo announces that the distillery will re-open in 2020.

37 years old

Rosebank

[rows•bank]

Owner:
Ian Macleod Distillers

Region/district:
Lowlands

Founded: **Status:**
1840   Closed

Capacity:
6-800,000 litres

Address: Falkirk FK1 4DS

Website:
rosebank.com

Tel:
-

It´s probably no exaggeration to say that the 9th and 10th October 2017 were two days that shook the whisky world. At least that part of the world which is made up of enthusiasts and collectors.

On the first day, Diageo announced that they had decided to open up two closed distilleries – Port Ellen and Brora. The surprise within the whisky community hadn´t subsided when the next day, Ian Macleod Distillers, owners of Glengoyne and Tamdhu, sent out a press release stating that they were about to reopen the closed Rosebank distillery. If at all possible, the latter piece of news was perhaps slightly less surprising. After all, rumours about a possible resurrection of Rosebank had been afloat a couple of times in recent years but nothing came to fruition. On the other hand, Diageo had sold the site to British Waterways in 2002 and so it was not up to them whether or not a distillery could be built on the same site.

Eventually Ian Macleod bought the property from Scottish Canals, (British Waterways' successor) and the trademark and stock from Diageo. One problem remained though – there was very little equipment left. In late December 2008, the stills and the mash tun had been stolen and so the new owners would have to equip the distillery anew with mash tun, three stills, washbacks and worm tubs. The aim is to produce 6-800,000 litres from 2019.

Established in 1798, Rosebank single malt enjoyed a good reputation during most of its lifespan even though the distillery also produced its fair share of grain whisky which was common especially in the Lowlands at the time. Most of the production went into blends but in 1982, Rosebank 8 year old single malt became a part of the owners Ascot Malt Cellar range together with Lagavulin, Talisker and Linkwood. Six years later, The Classic Malts saw the light of day and when the owners were to decide which malt to represent the Lowlands, their choice was Glenkinchie. What tipped the scale was the latter distillery´s closeness to Edinburgh – a fact that would guarantee plenty of visitors.

History:

1840   James Rankine founds the distillery.

1845   The distillery is expanded.

1864   Rankine buys Camelon Distillery on the west bank of the Forth-Clyde canal.

1894   Rosebank Distillery Company is formed.

1914   Rosebank, togehter with Clydesdale, Glenkinchie, St. Magdalene and Grange form Scottish malt Distillers (SMD).

1919   SMD becomes a part of Distillers company Limited (DCL).

1982   DCL launches the series The Ascot Malt Cellar with Rosebank, Linkwood, Talisker, Lagavulin and two blendeed malts.

1993   The distillery closes in June.

2002   The buildings are bought by British Waterways.

2008   The stills and other equipment are stolen.

2017   The site is bought from Scottish Canals by Ian Macleod Distillers and at the same time they acquire the trademark and stocks from Diageo.

21 years old

Banff

Owner:	Region:	Founded:	Status:
Diageo	Speyside	1824	Demolished

The distillery has a tragic history of numerous fires, explosions and bombings. The most spectacular incident was when a lone Junkers Ju-88 bombed one of the warehouses in 1941. The distillery was closed in 1983 and the buildings were destroyed in a fire in 1991.

Ben Wyvis

Owner:	Region:	Founded:	Status:
Whyte & Mackay	N Highlands	1965	Dismantled

Built on the same site as Invergordon grain distillery, the distillery was equipped with one mash tun, six washbacks and one pair of stills. The stills are in use today at Glengyle distillery. Production stopped in 1976 and in 1977 the distillery was closed and dismantled.

Caperdonich

Owner:	Region:	Founded:	Status:
Chivas Bros.	Speyside	1897	Demolished

Founded by the owners of Glen Grant. Five years after the opening, the distillery was shut down but was re-opened again in 1965 under the name Caperdonich. In 2002 it was mothballed yet again. Sold in 2010 to Forsyth´s in Rothes and the buildings were demolished.

Coleburn

Owner:	Region:	Founded:	Status:
Diageo	Speyside	1897	Dismantled

Coleburn was used as an experimental workshop where new production techniques were tested. In 1985 the distillery was mothballed and never opened again. Since 2014, the warehouses are used by Aceo Ltd, who owns the independent bottler Murray McDavid.

Convalmore

Owner:	Region:	Founded:	Status:
Diageo	Speyside	1894	Dismantled

This distillery is still intact and can be seen in Dufftown next to Balvenie distillery. The buildings are used by William Grant´s for storage while Diageo still holds the rights to the brand. In the early 20th century, distilling of malt whisky in continuous stills took place. Closed in 1985.

Dallas Dhu

Owner:	Region:	Founded:	Status:
Diageo	Speyside	1898	Closed

The distillery is still intact, equipment and all, but hasn´t produced since 1983. Today it is run by Historic Scotland as a museum which is open all year round. In 2013 a feasibility study was commissioned to look at the possibilities of re-starting production again.

Glen Albyn

Owner:	Region:	Founded:	Status:
Diageo	N Highlands	1844	Demolished

One of three Inverness distilleries surviving into the 1980s. In 1866 the buildings were transformed into a flour mill. but then converted back to a distillery in 1884 and continued producing whisky until 1983 when it was closed. Three years later the distillery was demolished.

Glenesk

Owner:	Region:	Founded:	Status:
Diageo	E Highlands	1897	Demolished

Operated under many names; Highland Esk, North Esk, Montrose and Hillside. In 1968 a large drum maltings was built adjacent to the distillery and the Glenesk maltings still operate today under the ownership of Boortmalt. The distillery building was demolished in 1996.

Glen Flagler

Owner:	Region:	Founded:	Status:
InverHouse	Lowlands	1965	Demolished

Glen Flagler was one of two malt distilleries (Killyloch being the other) that were built on the site of Garnheath grain distillery. Killyloch was closed in the early 1970s, while Glen Flagler continued to produce until 1985. A year later, Garnheath was closed only to be demolished in 1988.

Glenlochy

Owner:	Region:	Founded:	Status:
Diageo	W Highlands	1898	Demolished

Glenlochy was one of three distilleries in Fort William at the beginning of the 1900s. For a period of time, the distillery was owned by Joseph Hobbs who, after having sold the distillery to DCL, bought the second distillery in town, Ben Nevis. Glenlochy was closd in 1983.

Glen Mhor

Owner:	Region:	Founded:	Status:
Diageo	N Highlands	1892	Demolished

Glen Mhor was one of the last three Inverness distilleries and probably the one with the best reputation when it comes to the whisky that it produced. Glen Mhor was closed in 1983 and three years later the buildings were demolished. Today there is a supermarket on the site.

Glenugie

Owner:	Region:	Founded:	Status:
Chivas Bros	E Highlands	1831	Demolished

Glenugie produced whisky for six years before it was converted into a brewery. In 1875 whisky distillation started again, but production was very intermittent until 1937 when Seager Evans took over. Following several ownership changes, the distillery closed in 1983.

Glenury Royal

Owner:	Region:	Founded:	Status:
Diageo	E Highlands	1825	Demolished

The founder of Glenury was the eccentric Captain Robert Barclay Allardyce, the first to walk 1000 miles in 1000 hours in 1809. The distillery closed in 1983 and part of the building was demolished a decade later with the rest converted into flats.

Imperial

Owner:	Region:	Founded:	Status:
Chivas Bros	Speyside	1897	Demolished

In over a century, Imperial distillery was out of production for 60% of the time, but when it produced it had a capacity of 1,6 million. In 2012, the owners announced that a new distillery would be built. The old distillery was demolished and in 2015 Dalmunach distillery was commissioned.

Inverleven

Owner:	Region:	Founded:	Status:
Chivas Bros	Lowlands	1938	Demolished

Inverleven was built on the same site as Dumbarton grain distillery, equipped with one pair of traditional pot stills. In 1956 a Lomond still was added. Inverleven was mothballed in 1991 and finally closed. The Lomond still is now working again since 2010 at Bruichladdich.

Killyloch

Owner:	Region:	Founded:	Status:
InverHouse	Lowlands	1965	Demolished

Publicker Industries converted a paper mill in Airdrie into a grain distillery (Garnheath) and two malt distilleries (Glen Flagler and Killyloch). Killyloch (originally named Lillyloch after the water source) was closed in the early 1970s, while Glen Flagler continued to produce until 1985.

Kinclaith

Owner:	Region:	Founded:	Status:
Chivas Bros	Lowlands	1957	Demolished

The last malt distillery to be built in Glasgow and constructed on the grounds of Strathclyde grain distillery by Seager Evans. In 1975 it was dismantled to make room for an extension of the grain distillery. It was later demolished in 1982.

Ladyburn

Owner:	Region:	Founded:	Status:
W Grant & Sons	Lowlands	1966	Dismantled

In 1963 William Grant & Sons built their huge grain distillery in Girvan in Ayrshire. Three years later they also decided to build a malt distillery on the site which was given the name Ladyburn. The distillery was closed in 1975 and finally dismantled during the 1980s.

Littlemill

Owner:	Region:	Founded:	Status:
Loch Lomond Co.	Lowlands	1772	Demolished

Scotland's oldest working distillery until production stopped in 1992. Triple distillation was practised until 1930. In 1996 the distillery was dismantled and part of the buildings demolished and in 2004 much of the remaining buildings were destroyed in a fire.

Lochside

Owner:	Region:	Founded:	Status:
Chivas Bros	E Highlands	1957	Demolished

Most of the output from the distillery was made for blended whisky. One of the owners combined grain and malt whisky production. In 1992 the distillery was mothballed and five years later all the equipment and stock were removed. The distillery buildings were demolished in 2005.

Millburn

Owner:	Region:	Founded:	Status:
Diageo	N Highlands	1807	Dismantled

The oldest of those Inverness distilleries that made it into modern times. With one pair of stills, the capacity was 300,000 litres. In 1985 it was closed and three years later all the equipment was removed. The buildings are now a hotel and restaurant owned by Premier Inn.

North Port

Owner:	Region:	Founded:	Status:
Diageo	E Highlands	1820	Demolished

The names North Port and Brechin are used interchangeably on the labels of this single malt. The distillery had one pair of stills and produced 500,000 litres per year. Closed in 1983, it was dismantled piece by piece and was finally demolished in 1994 to make room for a supermarket.

Pittyvaich

Owner:	Region:	Founded:	Status:
Diageo	Speyside	1974	Demolished

Built by Arthur Bell & Sons on the same ground as Dufftown distillery. For a few years in the 1990s, Pittyvaich was also a back up plant for gin distillation (Gordon's gin). The distillery was mothballed in 1993 and has now been demolished.

St Magdalene

Owner:	Region:	Founded:	Status:
Diageo	Lowlands	1795	Dismantled

The distillery came into ownership of DCL in 1912 and was at the time a large distillery with 14 washbacks, five stills and with the possibility of producing more than one million litres of alcohol. Ten years after the closure in 1983, the distillery was re-built into flats.

Japanese Whisky
Making it / Faking it

by Stefan Van Eycken

Japanese whisky has received accolades from all over the world in recent years and rightly so. But there is a darker side to Japanese whisky production. The lack of proper rules, regulating what constitutes a Japanese whisky, can sometimes confuse the consumers.

Most 'news' about Japanese whisky has become rather predictable as of late: less of it available in retail, age statements removed, prices going up, auction records smashed, new distilleries popping up left and right… To most whisky enthusiasts, it has all become a bit old hat. However, the big noise this year, and it is a much needed and long overdue noise, spotlights a rather more sinister side of the Japanese whisky scene: the lack of regulations as far as whisky making is concerned and the increasing abuse of this open playing field by cunning producers.

Over the past few months, savvy consumers, commentators and a few bona fide producers have become increasingly vocal about the 'confusion' caused by the proliferation of pragmatic Japanese whisky makers – or as some would call them: 'whisky fakers'.

To say that whisky-making regulations in Japan are loose is a major understatement. If they were any looser, you'd be able to sell tap water as Japanese whisky. For starters, there is nothing that defines whisky as Japanese in terms of geographical indication. If you have a license to make whisky and you are putting something that can be called whisky – and there's considerable latitude here, too – in a bottle in Japan, you're making Japanese whisky, to all intents and purposes, regardless of where in the world it comes from. There is nothing regulating the maturation of whisky – no vessels specified in terms of materials and/or size and no minimum period of maturation, either. Neutral spirit and flavorings can be mixed in without any problem, as long as it's mentioned on the back label. Worried about quality? Well, as long as 10% of the volume in the bottle is malt or grain whisky, you're good. Don't worry about the rest. Stills can be made out of any material. You can bottle under 40%ABV. The more you look for constraints, the more you realize Japan is like a carte blanche for the creative whisky maker – which can be exhilarating, for sure, but when demand is high and money is easy, an open playing field can easily become a festering ground for opportunism and charlatanerie.

Focusing on all areas open to 'creative enterprise' is beyond the scope of this article, so we'll limit this discussion to one of two issues that consumers have become most concerned about in recent months: the use of bulk whisky imported from abroad in 'Japanese' whisky. The recategorization of spirits that started life as shochu (and awamori) as Japanese 'whisky' in the U.S. is a thorny issue of a slightly different nature that merits an article of its own.

The use of whisky imported in bulk from abroad by whisky makers in Japan is hardly a recent development. The practice is rooted in the fact that whisky producers in Japan operate as hermetically sealed businesses: nothing leaves the company unless it's as a product ready for retail. There are no whisky brokers and there's no swapping of stock. That leaves two options: create as much variety as possible in-house and/or bring in variety (or volume) from outside the country, in the case of whisky mostly from Scotland, and to a lesser extent, from the U.S. and Canada.

Just focusing on Scotland, it's clear that most whisky producers pursue both options side by side. HM Revenue & Customs – the UK government department responsible for the collection of taxes – lists 30 Japanese bulk importers of whisky. A third of those are companies that operate proper whisky distilleries, and this includes the big boys as well as the smaller, so-called craft distillers. The past 5 years have seen a marked increase in the volume of bulk exports of Scotch whisky to Japan. Comparing figures for 2013 with the last available ones, for 2017, shows a five-fold increase in the volume of bulk blended malt (1.4m lpa in 2017), an eight-fold increase in the volume bulk of blended whisky (0.7m lpa) and a three-fold increase in the volume of grain whisky exported to Japan (1.7m lpa). Overall, the volume of bulk whisky flowing from Japan to Scotland has quadrupled over the past 5 years – and that's just looking at Scotland.

Another recent development is the proliferation of new Japanese whisky brands without a clear pedigree – which brings us to the remaining two thirds on HMRC's list, i.e. those without the equipment to actually distill proper whisky. It doesn't take a genius to put two and two together. How, in Japan, can you produce a Japanese whisky if you don't have the proper equipment to make whisky? The intuitive answer would be: you can't. The actual answer is: piece of cake. You bring in stock from abroad, and merely by bringing it into the country and moving it around a bit – recasking and revatting being optional – it is magically transformed into Japanese whisky once you put it in the bottle… if that's what you want, that is.

Bona fide whisky makers like Ichiro Akuto of Chichibu Distillery see this as 'whisky laundering'. The problem is not the fact that whisky imported in bulk is used. Ichiro himself does that: "We don't make grain whisky, so we simply have to import grain whisky from abroad. Also, blending whisky from all over the world is very informative." Ichiro's flagship blended whisky Malt & Grain (White Label) contains whisky from all 5 major whisky-producing regions and he is upfront about it. The front label clearly states that the product is "World Blended Whisky" and the back label clearly identifies the origin of the components. This is not a legal requirement, however. It's a simple matter of honesty and transparency – that is to say: of ethics.

It is a sad sign of the times that, as of late, the Japanese whisky category has attracted 'whisky makers' that have no qualms about presenting products as 'Japanese whisky' – either explicitly, by labeling them as such, or implicitly in their presentation and branding – in spite of the use, in whole or in part, of whisky imported in bulk from abroad. Seeking to make a quick yen by feeding off the prestige of Japanese whisky, these producers are either hiding behind non-disclosure arguments or simply retort that legally they are not doing anything wrong, so what's the problem? Ethics, would be the short answer to that one, but that's not something that can be enforced. Caught up in the smoke and mirrors, more and more consumers are starting to lose faith. Who are the good guys and who are the bad ones?

For the time being, caveat emptor is the order of the day when buying Japanese whisky, but not everyone has the time, the desire and/or access to clear, unequivocal information to do some due diligence. Unless the Japanese whisky industry decides to tackle this issue head on with a sense of urgency, it's likely – as a prominent drinks writer remarked to me – "it will just keep getting out of hand, to the point where we don't know what the hell we're drinking anymore". In other words, a "Wild East" situation: utter chaos, a loss of trust and the erosion of a reputation that has taken nearly a century to build up.

Stefan Van Eycken grew up in Belgium and Scotland and moved to Japan in 2000. Editor of Nonjatta, he is also the man behind the 'Ghost Series' bottlings and the charity event 'Spirits for Small Change'. He is regional editor (Japan) for Whisky Magazine UK, and a regular contributor to Whisky Magazine Japan and France. His book "Whisky Rising: The Definitive Guide to the Finest Whiskies and Distillers from Japan" is available in English, Chinese and Japanese.

Akkeshi

Owner: **Location:**   **Founded:**   **Capacity:**
Kenten Jitsugyo   Hokkaido   2015   40,000 l

Malt whisky range:
Akkeshi New Born Foundations

Asaka

Owner: **Location:**   **Founded:**   **Capacity:**
Sasanokawa Shuzo   Fukushima P.2015   42,000 l

Malt whisky range:
none yet

Akkeshi distillery is located in the town of the same name on the east coast of Hokkaido. It's quite a remote area with particularly harsh winters, where temperatures can drop to -20°C. This can make whisky production rather challenging, so the maintenance season here is in the winter, rather than in the summer.

The distillery is located near the sea and surrounded by beautiful wetlands with an abundance of peat. This is no coincidence. Company president Keiichi Toita is an aficionado of Islay malts so that's where the inspiration came from. The inspiration, equipment and methods used may be Scottish, but his goal is to create a whisky that is shaped by the Akkeshi environment: "an aroma and flavour like nothing found elsewhere". They've already got the perfect pairing sorted out as Akkeshi is the only town in Japan where oysters can be shipped out all year round.

Production began in the fall of 2016. After a year of distilling, their warehouse was full, so they built a second one across from the distillery. This year, they built a third one close to the sea (above sea level). Featuring a sophisticated racking system, this one can hold around 1,300 casks – a mix of barrels, butts and puncheons – so they should be good for a while. There's also a new blenders room next to Warehouse 3, overlooking the Pacific Ocean.

There's lots in the pipeline at Akkeshi distillery. Worth highlighting are the "All Star" Experimental Casks laid down this year. These are made from local mizunara oak (not just Hokkaido, but Akkeshi mizunara) and hold spirit distilled from local barley (barley of the Ryofu cultivar, grown in Furano, Hokkaido).

This year also saw the first official releases coming out of Akkeshi, in small 200ml bottles: New Born Foundations 1, a vatting of non-peated spirit matured in ex-bourbon wood for 5-14 months (released in February 2018) and Foundations 2 (released in August), which was also matured in ex-bourbon (for 8-17 months) but peated and more indicative of the house style we can expect in the future. Two more New Born releases are to follow in 2019, in anticipation of the release of the first Akkeshi Single Malt in 2020 – just in time for the Tokyo Olympics.

Sasanokawa Shuzo are the unsung heroes of the current craft whisky movement in Japan. If they hadn't come to the rescue when Ichiro Akuto was trying to save the old Hanyu stock from being poured down the drain by the unsympathetic new owners of his father's company in 2004, there may have been no Chichibu distillery and no Ichiro to inspire a new generation of whisky makers.

Fortunately, Sasanokawa agreed to provide space in their warehouses for the 400-odd casks of Hanyu and the rest is history, as they say.

But Sasanokawa Shuzo has a whisky history of its own. The company was founded in 1765 and they turned their hand to whisky making straight after World War II, when there was a scarcity of rice (throwing a spanner in the works of their sake business) but a huge demand for whisky (particularly from the side of the Allied occupation). Sasanokawa applied for a license to make whisky in 1945 and the year after they got to work. Their focus was on the lowest grade of blended whisky.

As the economy recovered so did people's palates, so Sasanokawa – looking to up their game – started making whisky in makeshift stills (not made out of copper!) Sales weren't always great but the structure of the company kept their whisky business afloat. Sake making took up 2/3 of the year, so the remaining 1/3 the staff was kept busy making whisky.

To mark the 250th anniversary of the company in 2015, Sasanokawa decided to set up a proper malt whisky distillery. By the end of the year, two small pot stills (2,000 litres and 1,000 litres) had been installed in a vacant warehouse, and by June 2016 the distillery was ready to start producing. It is the most compact distillery in Japan, with all processes from milling to filling taking place under one roof. It's also the most hands-on distillery, with everything from carrying and feeding the barley to the mill to cleaning the equipment and everything in between done by hand.

During the past season, their second, a new type of yeast was used for 20 batches and a wider variety of cask types was filled into (including wine, brandy, rum and ex-Islay malt casks). For their next season, production staff will be doubled from 2 to 4. This will allow them to take productivity up a notch whilst keeping standards high. Watch this space.

Chichibu

Owner: Venture Whisky **Location:** Saitama P. **Founded:** 2007 **Capacity:** 60,000 l

Malt whisky range:
Occasional limited releases

Fuji Gotemba

Owner: Kirin Holdings **Location:** Shizuoka P. **Founded:** 1973 **Capacity:** 2,000,000 l

Malt whisky range:
17 year old Small Batch and occasional limited releases

Chichibu distillery is a very modest operation, but the staff dream big and work hard. There's a 2,400 litre mashtun (manually stirred with a wooden paddle!), 8 mizunara washbacks and a pair of 2,000 litre pot stills.

Every year, about 10% of production is dedicated to local barley so there is an area for floor malting. There are 4 warehouses and there's also a fully-operational cooperage.

Since 2010, Ichiro and his team have been making regular trips to Hokkaido to buy mizunara wood and the two in-house coopers have been perfecting their mizunara-barrel-making skills since 2016. The big challenge this year was getting hold of home-grown mizunara wood. It took almost 3 years of exploring the mountains in Chichibu but the persistence paid off: in May 2018, they finally managed to get Chichibu-grown mizunara.

Other big news from the Venture Whisky stable this year was the announcement that they will soon start distilling in their brand new second distillery. Some things will be the same: the location (a stone's throw from their present distillery), the staff operating the distillery, the yeast used for fermentation and the shape of the pot stills (straight heads with descending lynarms and shell-in-tube condensers), but some things will be markedly different. The size of the operation will be bigger: 2 tonnes of malted barley per batch, bigger washbacks (15,000 litres) and bigger stills (10,000 and 7,000 litres respectively.). Interestingly, the washbacks will be made of French oak, which is rather unique, and both stills will be direct heated.

The latest 'big' release (6,700 bottles, which is a huge outturn by Chichibu standards) was the IPA Cask Finish, which was very well received by fans at home and abroad.

Tasting note IPA Cask Finish:
Very hop and citrus driven on the nose. On the palate, all that plus tons of honey, a mixture of orchard fruits and tropical fruits and silver fir essential oil. Long and lingering finish with citrus peel and a green sappiness balanced by sweeter malty / biscuity notes.

Serious whisky producers in Japan try to do as much as possible in-house. No other distillery exemplifies this as much as Fuji Gotemba.

The distillery was established in 1972 by Kirin Brewery Co., J.E. Seagram & Sons and Chivas Brothers as a comprehensive whisky manufacturing plant where everything – from malt and grain whisky distilling to blending and bottling – could be done on site. Unlike most Japanese distilleries, which followed Scottish whisky-making practice, Fuji Gotemba adopted production techniques from the U.S. and Canada, as well. After Seagram started selling off its beverage assets worldwide, Kirin became the sole owner of Fuji Gotemba Distillery.

In addition to malt whisky, three types of grain whisky are made at the distillery using a multi-column still, a kettle and a doubler in a modular way. Understandably, given this production set up, most new products coming out of Fuji Gotemba are blended whiskies. These are put together by Chief Blender Jota Tanaka and his team and are well worth seeking out. The flagship Fuji-Sanroku 50°, which was re-thought in 2016, is an example of their innovative approach: it uses heavy-style, bourbon-type whisky as the key grain, rather than the top dressing.

Those keen to try a Fuji Gotemba malt should look out for the 17yo Small Batch or one of the recent 12yo Red Wine Cask Finish single casks. With regards to the latter, Tanaka points out "We get high quality French oak casks used for the ageing of red wine at Chateau Mercian, which is part of the Kirin group."

If the timing is right you may be able to pick up one of the Distiller's Select Single Malt bottlings (there is also a Single Grain) which is put together ever year in the spring by the team at the distillery, rather than by the Chief Blender and his team.

Tasting note Fuji Gotemba Single Malt 17yo Small Batch:

A smorgasbord of fruity delights (Poire belle Hélène, pineapple tarts and over-ripe mangoes). The fruity notes gain in intensity on the palate, accompanied by candied ginger and a gentle, peppery spiciness. The finish is long and lingering with a hint of burdock in the afterglow.

Hakushu

Owner: Beam Suntory
Location: Yamanashi P.
Founded: 1973
Capacity: 4,000,000 l

Malt whisky range:
NAS, 18, 25 year old plus occasional limited releases

Built 50 years after the first Suntory – and first Japanese – malt whisky distillery, Hakushu distillery is nestled in a vast forest area at the foot of Mt Kaikomagatake in the Southern Alps.

The original distillery was equipped with 6 pairs of stills. In 1977, capacity was doubled and another 6 pairs of stills added in a building next to "Hakushu 1". With its 4 mashtuns, 44 washbacks and 24 stills, Hakushu (1+2) was the biggest distillery in the world at the time. In 1981, Suntory built a new distillery, "Hakushu 3" or "Hakushu East" on the site, and decided to phase out production at "1+2" in favor of "3". This may seem a bit silly, but if you know that "1+2" had big stills, all of the same shape and size, and "3" had a variety of stills with different shapes, sizes, lyne-arm orientations, heating methods and condenser types, you can hazard a guess as to why Suntory did what they did: quantityas opposed to diversity and quality.

The distillery as it's operative now is Hakushu 3, albeit with the addition of two pairs of pot stills in 2014, bringing the total to 8 pairs. There is a small grain whisky facility at Hakushu since 2010. The first, official release coming out of that facility was part of the limited "The Essence of Suntory Whisky" trilogy, launched in February 2018: a 4yo Hakushu Rye Type Single Grain.

The Hakushu single malt was introduced in 1994, at a time when whisky consumption in Japan had been on the decline for a decade. It has always been in the shadow of its bigger brother, The Yamazaki, but over the last few years, it started attracting more and more critical acclaim. Just as The Hakushu was ready to step out into the limelight, Suntory was forced to remove the much-loved 12yo from the market. With the 18 and 25yo all but impossible to find in the wild, that means the only Hakushu single malt likely to cross your path is the no-age-statement entry expression.

Tasting note Hakushu NAS:
Green in all senses of the word. Cucumber and mint on the nose. On the palate, mossy twigs and citrus, with faint smoke emerging later on. The finish is long and woody.

Kanosuke

Owner: Komasa Jozo
Location: Kagoshima P.
Founded: 2017
Capacity: 110,000 l

Malt whisky range:
none yet

A few years ago, Kyushu didn't have any whisky distilleries. Now, it has two and both in the same prefecture, Tsunuki and Kanosuke. Clearly, there is something in the air.

Kanosuke distillery is the youngest of the two. It is owned by Komasa Jozo, one of the leading shochu makers in the area. Their claim to fame is 'Mellowed Kozuru', a barrel-aged shochu developed by the second president of the company Kanosuke Komasa and launched in 1957.

The idea to establish a whisky distillery was born in 2015 and the project was spearheaded by Yoshitsugu Komasa, who represents the fourth generation of the family to play a leading role in the company. As location for the new distillery, they picked some vacant land next to three warehouses where the company's shochu is matured. The location itself is stunning. The distillery overlooks the East China Sea and Fukiage beach, which is the longest beach in Japan.

Kanosuke Komasa had a vision to build a brand home for Mellowed Kozuru on that piece of land, so in recognition of his contribution to the company, the decision was made to name the distillery after him. The equipment was installed in the summer of 2017 – a 6,000 litre mash tun, 5 stainless steel washbacks and 3 pot stills of 6,000, 3,000 and 1,600 litre capacity respectively, all with wormtub condensers. This peculiar set up allows for various double distillation permutations as the middle one can function as either wash or spirit still.

Production officially started on November 13, 2017, so it's still early days. For the first season, the priority in terms of wood filled into was: first, ex-sherry butts, of which they filled around 30; then, re-charred ex-shochu casks, of which about 100 were filled; and after that, ex-bourbon casks. To mark the opening of the distillery to the public, a limited edition of Kanosuke new make was released on April 28, 2018.

One of the plans for the future is to use their shochu-making know-how to produce a rice whisky. This would be done in the copper pot stills, using Kagoshima rice and their in-house shochu yeast. There are other exciting things planned, but all in good time.

Miyagikyo

Owner: Nikka Whisky
Location: Miyagi P.
Founded: 1969
Capacity: 3,000,000 l
Malt whisky range:
NAS and occasional limited releases

Nagahama

Owner: Nagahama Roman Beer Co.
Location: Shiga P.
Founded: 2016
Capacity: undiscl.
Malt whisky range:
none yet

Miyagikyo is Nikka's second distillery – the yin to Yoichi's yang, in a way. Legend has it that it took Masataka Taketsuru three years to find the perfect site for his second distillery.

He settled on the valley that brings the Hirosegawa and Nikkagawa (no relation to the company name) rivers together because of the quality of the water, the suitable humidity and the crisp air. The decision was made on May 12, 1967. Apparently, there were some other candidate sites in the area to be visited later that day, but Taketsuru scooped some water out of the Nikkagawa, tasted it with some Black Nikka he had on him and that was it.

Construction started in 1968 and was completed the following year. Originally known as 'Sendai', the distillery was renamed 'Miyagikyo' when Asahi took control of Nikka in 2001. At present, Miyagikyo is equipped with 22 steel washbacks and 8 huge pot stills of the 'boil ball' type with upward lyne arms, encouraging reflux which – given the slow distillation method (steam-heated) – results in a lighter, cleaner spirit. The site also houses two enormous Coffey stills imported by Taketsuru from Scotland. Moved from Nishinomiya in 1999, these are used to produce grain whisky (Coffey Grain) but, occasionally, are used to distill malted barley (Coffey Malt). Since the summer of 2017, they're also churning out Coffey Gin and Coffey Vodka.

In September 2015, Nikka discontinued the entire Miyagikyo range because of stock shortages. It was replaced with a new NAS expression, which is the only permanently available Miyagikyo single malt until further notice. If you want a glimpse of the different facets of Miyagikyo, you have to make a trip out to the distillery where you can pick up three so-called "Key Malt" bottlings: "Fruity & Rich", "Malty & Soft" and "Sherry & Sweet".

Tasting note Miyagikyo NAS (2015 release):

Apples and pears on the nose with grassy and light floral elements; dried fruits, vanilla and anise on the palate, with a tiny bit of bitterness and some milk chocolate on the finish.

Nagahama Distillery is the smallest distillery in Japan at the time of writing. It is located in the picturesque town of the same name in Shiga and was set up in a record time of 7 months.

The owners didn't have to start from scratch, because the distillery is, in fact, an extension of Nagahama Roman (with the emphasis on the second syllable, as in "romantic") Brewery, which was established in 1996 as a brewpub. The first half of the whisky-making process – mashing and fermentation – takes place in the equipment used for beer-making. For the second half of the process, a small "still room" was created behind the bar counter.

Inspired by some of the new wave of craft distillers in Scotland (Strathearn and Eden Mill, in particular), the team at Nagahama decided to go for small stills with alembic heads of the type seen more often in calvados, cognac or pisco distillation than in whisky making. They started with a 1,000 litre wash still and a 500 litre spirit still, but this year, they took out the small spirit still, and put in 2 new 1,000 litre stills. Two of these identical stills are used as wash stills and one as a spirit still. If they want to produce more they will have to relocate as three is indeed a crowd as far as this stillroom is concerned.

The motto of the 2018 season was "Challenge & Experiment" and that's what they've been doing. Three types of barley were used: non-peated, medium (20ppm) and heavily peated (40ppm). They've also been distilling using some of the specialty malts from their brewing side (Caramel Munich and roasted malt), and they've been filling into a plethora of cask types, including quarter sherry casks as well as Fino and Amontillado butts.

Up until now, releases coming out of Nagahama distillery have all been new make – unpeated and peated – with or without a tiny cask for DIY maturation. One of the plans for next year is to release some aged whisky. This will be young – too young to call 'whisky' in most countries, but not in Japan – but it will give us an idea of what the house style may turn out to be.

Nukada

Owner:
Kiuchi Shuzo

Location:
Ibaraki P.

Founded:
2016

Capacity:
5,000 l

Malt whisky range:
none yet

Saburomaru

Owner:
Wakatsuru Shuzo

Location:
Toyama P.

Founded:
ca. 1990

Capacity:
7,000 l

Malt whisky range:
occasional releases

The distillery was set up by Kiuchi Shuzo in a corner of their Hitachino Nest brewhouse in 2016 and has been fairly under-the-radar since.

Head distiller Isamu Yoneda's uses a 1kl hybrid still to make whisky as well as gin. Most of last year's whisky production has been pot still grain whisky, made from mixed barley-and-rice mashes. Yoneda also has plans to make a barley-and-buckwheat whisky. Production is down a bit compared with last year, but that's in part because Kiuchi Shuzo has been busy with a much bigger whisky project: a brand new distillery in the Mt. Tsukuba area, with two large pot stills that should be operative by January 2019.

Up until last year, malt whisky was produced at Saburomaru distillery using an alumite pot still of the type commonly used in shochu-making.

After a successful crowdfunding campaign, parts of the distillery were upgraded, including the pot still, which got a copper swanneck. This year, a brand new mashtun was installed, which increased production efficiency. There's more good news: towards the end of the year, they will have gone the whole hog, when two proper copper pot stills made by a local factory in Takaoka city will be installed. These will both be 3,000 litre lantern type stills with downward lynearms.

Okayama

Owner:
Miyashita Shuzo

Location:
Okayama P.

Founded:
2011

Capacity:
7,000 l

Malt whisky range:
Okayama Single Malt Whisky

Sakurao

Owner:
Chugoku Jozo

Location:
Hiroshima P.

Founded:
2018

Capacity:
t.b.d.

Malt whisky range:
none yet

Miyashita Shuzo has been making sake since 1915. In 1994, they became one of the pioneers of Japanese craft beer.

In 2003, the company had the bright idea to distill some hoppy beer in their stainless steel shochu still and put the spirit in American white oak casks. Pleased with the way this was developing, they decided to have a go at producing malt whisky. They acquired their license in 2011 and started double-distilling batches in their shochu still – but stainless steel and whisky are awkward bedfellows so in 2015, they installed a copper hybrid still. They are keen on using as much local barley as they can, which comes at a price, but is worth the effort, according to the company.

Sakurao is the latest pin on the distillery map of Japan, but the liquor company behind it is not exactly a new-kid-on-the-block.

They started 'producing' whisky in 1938, but exactly how is lost in the mists of time. In 2003, they launched the Togouchi brand, but the expressions in that range are all made up of whisky imported in bulk from abroad. To mark the 100th anniversary of the company, a proper whisky distillery was set up at the company's main site. Half of the production is non-peated and the other half lightly-peated (20ppm). Everything is double distilled in one hybrid still at the distillery. For the second distillation, the column is used. The first casks filled were sherry butts.

Shinshu

Owner:	Location:	Founded:	Capacity:
Hombo Shuzo	Nagano P.	1985	80,000 l

Malt whisky range:
Komagatake (various limited edition releases)

Shizuoka

Owner:	Location:	Founded:	Capacity:
Gaia Flow Distilling	Shizuoka P.	2015	60,000 l

Malt whisky range:
none yeat

Mars Shinshu was built at the peak of whisky consumption in Japan, but the trouble with peaks is that they are followed by a fall –in the case of Japan, a 25-year long decline.

Parent company Hombo Shuzo had been making whisky since 1949. Initially, they simply blended sourced components with neutral spirits, but from 1960, they distilled proper malt whisky in various places. It was a history of starts and stops, at the mercy of nebulous market forces. In 1985, they moved their whisky operation to Shinshu but with a gradually shrinking domestic market, they were forced to mothball their distillery in 1992. In 2011, with whisky booming again, they fired up the stills once more. Production used to be limited to the winter months, but now it's closer to a typical year-round production schedule with a silent summer season, albeit a longer one than at most distilleries (about 2 months). Since 2014, the distillery has received some much-needed upgrades. The old pot stills were replaced with brand new ones and in 2018, the 5 rusty cast-iron washbacks got new company in the form of 3 Douglas fir washbacks. With increased production in mind, the old bottling hall was remodeled into a maturation warehouse in the spring of 2018.

In terms of malted barley used, four types of distillate are made at Mars Shinshu: non-peated and peated at 3.5, 20 and 50ppm. Keen to explore the influence of climate on the maturation process, some Mars Shinshu spirit has been sent to Tsunuki in Kagoshima and Yakushima island annually since 2014. The company has released a string of limited editions showcasing how impressive the results are. There is very little pre-1992 stock left, but the past season has seen two old Komgatake releases: a 1988 single cask and a Komagatake 27yo, which was a vatting of American white oak and ex-sherry casks.

Tasting note Komagatake Kohiganzakura:

Fabulous nose with stewed orchard fruits, guava jam and apple peel. On the palate: soft oak, orchard fruits again, citrus and a touch of spice. The finish is long and lingering on cotton candy and caramel sauce.

Shizuoka distillery is without a shadow of a doubt the most ingeniously designed distillery in Japan.

Inspired by Karuizawa distillery, everything from milling to filling (the barley and casks, resp.) takes place under one roof, but in different 'rooms'. Another thing that's carefully considered is the way in which the landscape – small green tea farms and forested mountains – is visible from various points in the distillery building. Also, the 'visitor experience' is integrated into the design of the distillery, which is the exception rather than the rule in Japan.

Following a visit to Kilchoman distillery in 2012, Gaia Flow founder Taiko Nakamura started thinking about setting up a distillery of his own back home. He set up a liquor import company to get a foot in the door of the drinks business, and kept working on his distillery project. Shizuoka distillery was officially opened on February 25, 2017.

Up until last year, there were 5 washbacks at the distillery: four made from Oregon pine and one made from local, Shizuoka cedar. In February 2018, three more Shizuoka cedar washbacks were installed, bringing the total to 8. There's room for 4 more but no word on if and when new washbacks will be added in the near future. The stillhouse has 3 pot stills: one from the old Karuizawa distillery and a new pair made by Forsyths in Scotland. Both of the new stills have a bulge (or boil ball). Interestingly, Nakamura opted for direct (wood-fired) heating for the wash still. The old Karuizawa still and the new spirit still are steam heated.

Initially, the staff at the distillery used the indirectly-heated pot stills, as the process is easier to control. On March 23, 2017, the directly-fired wash still was used for the first one. In addition to the development of a car park and outdoor facilities, the big project this year was the construction of Warehouse No.2. Unlike No.1, which is of the dunnage type, the new warehouse is racked. It's expected to hold up to 3,000 casks so they're good for a while.

From November 2018, the site is open to the public and tours can be booked online from the distillery website. There's exciting news for enthusiasts abroad keen to follow the progress of Shizuoka distillery more closely, too. Up until now, the Shizuoka Private Cask program was limited to the Japanese market. In 2019, it will be made available in selected foreign markets, giving interested parties the chance to choose from new make distilled with the Karuizawa wash still or with the wood fired still.

Tsunuki

Owner: Hombo Shuzo **Location:** Kagoshima P. **Founded:** 2016 **Capacity:** 90,000 l

Malt whisky range:
none yet

White Oak

Owner: Eigashima Shuzo **Location:** Hyogo P. **Founded:** 1984 **Capacity:** 60,000 l

Malt whisky range:
Akashi NAS and occasional, limited releases

Towards the end of 2015, Hombo Shuzo surprised friend and foe when they announced they were in the process of setting up a second distillery in their homebase of Tsunuki in Kagoshima.

This was a first for a craft producer in Japan, and it seemed like a strange move to lots of people at the time. Surely, they could have made arrangements to produce more at Mars Shinshu distillery? More, yes – but they weren't interested in just more. What they were after was diversity: new types of spirit.

The very first distillation was on October 27th (stripping run) and 28th (spirit run). The distillery is the playground of Tatsuro Kusano, the 30-year old head distiller. Kusano learned the ropes at Mars Shinshu under distillery manager Koki Takehira, but he has own vision for Tsunuki and an inquisitive mind. Some things are the same: the season runs roughly parallel with Mars Shinshu, i.e. September to June) and the barley used is the same, too: non-peated, lightly-peated, medium peated and heavily peated. But there are marked differences, too – not just in terms of the equipment in place, but the approach to making whisky.

This season, Kusano moved from a one ton batch to a 1,1 ton batch size, in preparation for the addition of 100g of specialty malts (caramelized and roasted malts) in some batches. In addition to various beer yeasts, he's also trialed some in-house shochu yeast – always in combination with their regular distillers yeast. The past season, Kusano has also introduced more variety in the width of the middle cut. For next season, he is trying to source malted barley that is smoked, not with peat but instead using cherry wood, pear wood and so on – just one of the many little projects at the back of his mind.

With the exception of two special editions of young distillate released in October 2017, nothing produced at Tsunuki distillery has been bottled yet. It's still early days. One thing is for sure: Tsunuki won't be a one-trick pony. Between the different types of spirit, the creativity of the team, the wide variety of casks used and the three different maturation locations (home, at Mars Shinshu and on Yakushima island), there's bound to be a Mars Tsunuki with your name on it in a few years' time.

There's a new wind blowing through Eigashima. Whisky making used to be a marginal enterprise and they didn't participate in any whisky shows in Japan.

Not because they were "too cool for school", but because they were humble and didn't have much to bring to shows anyway. That has slowly been changing and now, if there is a whisky festival somewhere in Japan, chances are they'll have a little table with some interesting new releases. No crowds and no hype, but the quality is there nowadays –which wasn't always the case in the past. On paper, this is the oldest whisky producer in Japan – having acquired a distilling license in 1919, four years before Yamazaki. It took them four decades to get their act together, though, and another four decades to release their first single malt (an 8 year old in 2007).

Since last year, the company has expanded its whisky-making season to 7 months. Having used lightly-peated malt (5ppm) for years, they switched to three types this year: non-peat, lightly-peated (albeit 10ppm) and heavily-peated (60ppm) malt this season. During the silent season, their pot stills will get a long overdue upgrade. All production is matured on site and they mostly fill into ex-bourbon wood, but they also have sherry butts, cognac casks, wine, tequila and recharred ex-barley shochu casks, as well as virgin oak.

Early in 2018, the oldest expression in almost a decade was released, a stunning 10 year old Akashi, matured in an 'old sherry butt'. In November 2018, another very interesting limited edition Akashi came out. A first for whisky as far as we know, this was matured in casks that previously held sake.

Tasting note Akashi NAS:
The deep colours and surprisingly warm nose, tips you off that there´s a sherry influence. There´s a peach tea and autumn fruits when you sip, and a fairly short finish.

Yamazaki

Owner:	Location:	Founded:	Capacity:
Beam Suntory	Osaka P.	1923	6,000,000 l

Malt whisky range:
NAS, 12, 18, 25 years old and occasional limited releases.

A lone visionary by the name of Shinjiro Torii had the guts to build the first malt whisky distillery in Japan in 1923.

A lot of water has flown through the condensers since but Yamazaki is still at the forefront of Japanese whisky-making, in terms of quality and quantity. Torii was a pragmatic man, so he decided to build his distillery close to center of commerce at the time, Osaka. The distillery started out with two pot stills but has been reconfigured and expanded many times over the years, first in 1957, and most recently in 2013, when four pot stills were added bringing the count to 16. There's plenty of variety in terms of heating method, shape, size, lyne-arm orientation and condenser type. Since 1988, eight of the washbacks are wooden whereas the other nine are stainless steel. With different peating levels for the barley, different yeast strains and a plethora of cask types, the variety of whisky types created at Yamazaki distillery is quite staggering.

Launched in 1984, The Yamazaki was not the first Japanese single malt, as is often erroneously reported – that honour goes to some limited edition Karuizawas from the mid-70s – but it was the first generally available single malt in Japan. These days, 'generally available' has to be taken with a pinch of salt. Of the theoretical range of NAS, 12, 18 and 25yo, the age-statement expressions are becoming like unicorns… reputed to exist but when was the last time you saw one?

Limited editions and single casks have become scarce and this year there wasn´t even a release of the Yamazaki Limited Edition. The only new Yamazaki single malt bottling in 2018 is the 12yo Peated Release but that was available to the bar trade only. At least, we should be thankful that the wonderful 12yo hasn't been taken off the market yet.

Tasting note Yamazaki NAS:

Zesty nose, with some sawdust and strawberry. Lots of bourbon influences on the palate, with creamy vanilla, creme brulee, but also some spice. A relatively short, sharp finish. Superb for its price bracket.

Yoichi

Owner:	Location:	Founded:	Capacity:
Nikka Whisky	Hokkaido	1934	2,000,000 l

Malt whisky range:
NAS and occasional limited releases.

It's a well-known story by now: after leaving his previous employer in 1934, Masataka Taketsuru set up his own distillery.

He settled on the town of Yoichi, up in Hokkaido, because the locale and climate conditions reminded him of Scotland, where he had studied whisky making. The first spirit ran off the stills in 1936, with the first product launched in 1940. Initially equipped with a single still that doubled as spirit and wash still, the distillery now houses 6 stills. Coal-heated and featuring straight heads and downward lyne arms, these produce a robust spirit. Although the 'house style' is peaty and heavy, Yoichi is set up to create a wide range of distillates. Between various peating levels, yeast strains, fermentation times, distillation methods and maturation types, it is said that Yoichi is capable of producing 3,000 different types of malt whisky.

In September 2015, the entire Yoichi range (which included a no-age statement expression as well as a 10, 12, 15 and 20yo) was axed and replaced with a single option: a new NAS. In the domestic market, Nikka has been focusing on creating 'limited edition' variations of its ubiquitous cheap blended whisky, Black Nikka. Worldwide, it wants to keep the star of its premium blended malt whisky Taketsuru shining .

Much to the dismay of fans worldwide, single malt releases don't seem to be a priority for the company for the time being. The only way to get your hands on something special is to visit the distillery where a selection of so-called "key malts" (NAS) is available for purchase – if you're lucky, that is. There's a choice of three: "Woody & Vanillic", "Peaty & Salty" and "Sherry & Sweet". For the time being, those are the only Yoichi single malt expressions out there.

Tasting note Yoichi NAS, (2015 release):

Barley sweetness, pencil shavings, over-ripe orchard fruits and soft smoke on the nose; oak and peat lead the dance on the palate with some candied orange peel thrown in; the finish is earthy and vegetal, with some tea on the side.

Oskar Bruno - Distillery Manager, Agitator Distillery in Sweden

Distilleries
around the globe

Including the subsections:
Europe
North America | Australia & New Zealand
Asia | Africa | South America

When we talk about the Big Five in a whisky context, we refer to the traditional five whisky producing countries; Scotland, Ireland, USA, Canada and, added in recent years, Japan. Together they represent an overwhelmingly large share of all whisky produced. Admittedly, India is the single biggest producer but since almost all the whisky from the country is made from molasses rather than any cereal, it doesn´t meet the standard definition of whisky that we have in Europe or North America.

If we focus on malt whisky, Scotland is even more dominant but volumes aren´t everything and with hundreds of new malt whisky distilleries from Iceland and Italy to Argentina and Israel, the world of whisky has become increasingly more exciting. These distilleries are by no means a homogenous group. While some of them transcend the boundaries and challenge rules and regulations, others meticulously follow traditions that go back hundreds of years.

In what sense they will be able to change the whisky world as we see it, depends very much on the availability of their products. Volumes need to be significant and distribution is vital. Read more about these issues in Ian Buxton´s article on pages 58-63. Meanwhile, let´s just marvel at a whisky world that is growing every day.

Europe

Austria

Destillerie Haider

Roggenreith, founded in 1995

www.whiskyerlebniswelt.at

  In the small village of Roggenreith in northern Austria, the Haider family has been distilling whisky since 1995 and three years later, the first Austrian whisky was released. In 2005, they opened up a Whisky Experience World with guided tours, a video show, whisky tasting and exhibitions. The wash is allowed to ferment for 72 hours before it reaches either of the two 450 litre Christian Carl copper stills. The desired strength is reached in one single distillation, thanks to the attached column. The main part (70%) of the whisky production is made from rye while the rest is from malted barley. Seven different bottlings (including peated versions) are present in the core range while several limited releases are launched regularly. Some of the latest include a malted rye with a finish in port casks as well as 12 year old verisons of both the rye and the single malt.

Broger Privatbrennerei

Klaus, founded in 1976 (whisky since 2008)

www.broger.info

  The production of whisky at this distillery owned by the Broger family is supplementing the distillation and production of eau de vie from apples and pears. The distillery is equipped with a 150 litre Christian Carl still. The total volume of whisky produced in a year is 2,500 litres. The current range of whiskies consists of five expressions; Triple Cask, Medium Smoked (smoked using beech wood), Burn Out (heavily peated), Riebelmais (corn whisky) and the limited Distiller´s Edition which has been maturing in madeira casks.

Jasmin Haider, CEO of Destilleri Haider

Other distilleries in Austria

Reisetbauer

Kirchberg-Thening, founded in 1994 (whisky since 1995)

www.reisetbauer.at

  Specialising in brandies and fruit schnapps, a range of malt whiskies is also produced. The distillery is equipped with five 350 litre stills. The 70 hour-long fermentation takes place in stainless steel washbacks. The current range of whiskies have all been matured in casks that have previously contained Chardonnay and Trockenbeerenauslese and include a 7, a 12 and a 15 year old.

Destillerie Rogner

Rappottenstein, founded in 1997

www.destillerie-rogner.at

  Originally a producer of spirits from fruits and berries, whisky has recently been added to the range. The range consists of Rogner Waldviertel Whisky 3/3 (two versions, malted and unmalted). Rye Whisky No. 13 and a single malt, Whisky No. 2. A lightly peated, limited release from rye and barley, has also been released to celebrate the 20th anniversary.

Destillerie Weutz

St. Nikolai im Sausal, founded in 2002

www.weutz.at

  The distillery added whisky to the range in 2004 when they started a cooperation with a local brewer. Some of the whiskies are produced in the traditional Scottish style such as the peated Black Peat. Others are more unorthodox, for example Franziska - based on elderflower.

Old Raven

Neustift, founded in 2004

www.oldraven.at

  More than 250,000 litres of beer are produced yearly and the wash from the brewery is used for distillation of whisky. The triple distilled Old Raven comes in three expressions – Old Raven, Old Raven Smoky and the recently released limited edition Old Raven Black Edition.

Waldviertler Granit Destillerie

Waidhofen/Thaya, founded in 1995

www.granitdestillerie.at

  The distillery has from 1995 established a comprehensive product portfolio of liquers and schnapps from all kinds of berries and fruit. Whisky production started in 2006 and the owner has released two smoked single malts, but is also working with rye and dinkel.

Destillerie Hermann Pfanner

Lauterach, founded in 1854

www.pfanner-weine.com

  In 2005, more than 150 years after the foundation, the owners expanded into whisky production. The two core expressions are Pfanner Single Malt Classic and Single Malt Red Wood with a maturation in red wine casks. There are also two recent limited releases; the smoky Pfanner Whisky X-peated and a 4 year old matured in Austrian oak.

Keckeis Destillerie

Rankweil, founded in 2003

www.destillerie-keckeis.at

  Whisky production started in 2008 and today one expression, Keckeis Single Malt is for sale as well as the new make Keckeis

Baby Malt. Part of the barley has been smoked with beech and maturation takes place in small ex-sherry casks.

Dachstein Destillerie

Radstadt, founded in 2007

www.mandlberggut.com

Apart from production of various spirits from berries, malt whisky is also produced. Maturation takes place in a mix of casks – new Austrian oak, ex-sherry casks and red wine casks. Their only release so far is the five year old Rock-Whisky which is distilled 2,5 times.

Edelbrennerei Franz Kostenzer

Maurach/Achensee, founded in 1998, whisky since 2006

www.schnaps-achensee.at

A huge range of different spirits, mainly from fruits and berries, as well as whisky is produced. Several expressions under the name Whisky Alpin have been released including a 6 year old single malt with a sherry cask finish, a 6 year old 100% single malt rye and a 3 year old single malt with smoky notes from beech wood.

Brennerei Ebner

Absam, founded in 1930

www.brennereiebner.at

Whisky production in this combination of a guesthouse, brewery and distillery, started in 2005. Whisky is just a small component of the business but, besides a single malt from barley, Pauli has also released whiskies made from maize, dinkel and wheat.

Belgium

The Owl Distillery

Grâce Hollogne, founded in1997

www.belgianwhisky.com

The first commercial bottling of Belgium's first single malt, 'The Belgian Owl', appeared in November 2008 and the core expression today is the un-chillfiltered Belgian Owl, a 3 year old bottled at 46% or at cask strength. Recent limited releases from the owner, Etienne Bouillon, include a 42 months old, bottled at cask strength and the 5 year old Eternity. The distillery is equipped with a 2.1 ton mash tun, four washbacks and two stills that had previously been used at Caperdonich distillery in Speyside. All the barley used for production comes from farms close to the distillery.

Het Anker Distillery

Blaasveld, founded in 1471 (whisky since 2003)

www.hetanker.be

Charles Leclef started out as a brewer and currently maintains this role at Brouwerij Het Anker. In 2010, he started a distillery of his own at the Leclef family estate, Molenberg, at Blaasveld. The wash still has a capacity of 3,000 litres and the spirit still 2,000 litres. The first bottles under the name Gouden Carolus Singe Malt, appeared on the market in 2008. The core expression is the 3 year old Gouden Carolus Single Malt. Limited expressions are released yearly with one of the latest being Muscad'Or with a 10 months finish in muscat casks.

Other distilleries in Belgium

Kempisch Vuur

Zandhoven, founded in 2011

www.kempisch-vuur.be

The distillery is equipped with a German continuous still and the spirit is matured for 18 months in ex bourbon casks and then

another 18 months in quarter casks from Laphroaig. The first batch was released in March 2016 and several releases have followed. The annual production is around 1.000 litres of pure alcohol.

Czech Republic

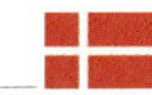

Gold Cock Distillery

Founded in 1877

www.rjelinek.cz

The whisky is produced in three versions – a 3 year old blended whisky, a 12 year old single malt and different versions of Small Batch single malt. Production was stopped for a while but after the brand and distillery were acquired by R. Jelinek a.s., the leading Czech producer of plum brandy, the whisky began life anew. The malt whisky is double distilled in 500 litre traditional pot stills.

Denmark

Stauning Whisky

Stauning, founded in 2006

www.stauningwhisky.dk

The first Danish purpose-built malt whisky distillery entered a more adolescent phase in 2009, after having experimented with two small pilot stills bought from Spain. More stills were installed in 2012. The preconditions, however, were completely changed in December 2015 when it was announced that Diageo´s incubator fund project, Distil Ventures, would spend £10m to increase the capacity of Stauning. In August 2018, it became evident what

The new stills at Stauning

the investment had meant to the distillery. A new distillery with no less than 24 copper stills, all directly fired, was opened. The floor malting were increased to 1,000 m² and the total production capacity is now 900,000 litres of pure alcohol. So far, two core expressions of single malt have been launched – Peated Reserve and Traditional Reserve. A variety of the smoked whisky, where heather has been used to dry the malted barley, have also been released and there is also a rye whisky in the range together with several limited bottlings.

Braunstein

Köge, founded in 2005 (whisky since 2007)

www.braunstein.dk

Denmark's first micro-distillery, built in an already existing brewery in Køge, just south of Copenhagen. The wash comes from the own brewery. A Holstein type of still, with four plates in the rectification column, is used for distillation. Around 40% of the required barley is ecologically grown in Denmark. The lion's share of the whisky is stored in ex-bourbon (peated version) and first fill Oloroso casks (unpeated) from 190 up to 500 litres. The first release from the distillery and the first release of a malt whisky produced in Denmark was in 2010. The most recent releases include Library Collection 18:1, matured in a combination of PX sherry and new French oak and Edition No: 9, matured in an oloroso cask.

Other distilleries in Denmark

Fary Lochan Destilleri

Give, founded in 2009

www.farylochan.dk

The main part of the malted barley is imported from the UK but they also malt some of it themselves. The five day fermentation takes place in stainless steel washbacks and distillation is done in traditional copper pot stills. The first whisky was released in 2013 and a number of bottlings have been released since then. One of the latest was the 5 year old single cask Rum Edition in late 2017.

Trolden Distillery

Kolding, founded in 2011

www.trolden.com

The distillery is a part of the Trolden Brewery and the wash from the brewery is fermented for 4-5 days before a double distillation in a 325 litre alembic pot still. The first release of a single malt was Nimbus in 2014. In December 2017, the sherried and lightly peated Nimbus No. 4 was released.

Nordisk Brænderi/Thy Whisky

Fjerritslev, founded in 2009 (whisky since 2011)

www.nordiskbraenderi.dk, www.thy-whisky.dk

The ecological barley used for the production is grown in fields surrounding the distillery. In the first 6-7 years they have managed to fill around 35 small casks of which eight have been released under the name Thy Whisky, the first in 2014 and the latest one, a first fill oloroso maturation, in summer 2018.

Nyborg Destilleri

Nyborg, founded in 1997 (whisky since 2009)

www.fioniawhisky.com

Originally opened in 2009 as an extension to an already existing brewery, the distillery moved in 2017 to new premises. The new distillery is equipped with washbacks made of oak and two copper pot stills with attached columns. The first release of Isle of Fionia single malt was in 2012. There are three ranges of single malt available; the aged Isle of Fionia, Ardor without age statement and Adventurous Spirit. The last expressions include special bottlings.

Braenderiet Limfjorden

Roslev, founded in 2013

www.braenderiet.dk

The distillery moved in spring 2018 to a new location and at the same time a brewery was added. Apart from peated and unpeated single malt and rye, the distillery also produces gin and rum. The first single malt was released in July 2016.

Ærø Whisky

Ærøskøbing, founded in 2013

www.ærøwhisky.dk

This microdistillery has been working on the small island of Ærø since 2013 using stills from Portugal. In 2016, new and larger stills made in Germany were installed and the production increased. The first bottling (made from the pilot still) was a bourbonmatured single cask released in March 2017.

Mosgaard Whisky

Oure, founded in 2015

www.mosgaardwhisky.dk

Alambic stills made in Portugal are used for the distillation and the aim is to produce 20,000 bottles per year. The first whisky release isn´t due until 2019 but the owners have already released malt spirit under the name Young Malt.

England 

St. George´s Distillery

Roudham, Norfolk, founded in 2006

www.englishwhisky.co.uk

St. George´s Distillery near Thetford in Norfolk was started by father and son, James and Andrew Nelstrop, and came on stream in December 2006. This made it the first English malt whisky distillery for over a hundred years. In December 2009, it was time for the release of the first legal whisky called Chapter 5 (the first four chapters had been young malt spirit). This has been followed by several more chapters with four of them still in the range; 14 (unpeated), 15 (heavily peated), 16 (peated sherry cask) and 17

David Fitt, distillery manager, St. George´s Distillery

(triple distilled). The core range however consists of The English Original and The English Smokey with The English Rum Cask being a limited yet yearly release. There is also a range called Founder´s Private Cellar where rar and limited bottlings appear. The very latest (in November 2017) was the distillery´s first 10 year old single malt. In 2017 a new and innovative sub range was introduced – The Norfolk. Three expressions have been bottled so far, Malt 'n' Rye made with malted barley and rye, matured in bourbon casks, Farmers where no less than eight different grains were used and Parched, a single grain.

The distillery is equipped with a stainless steel semi-lauter mash tun with a copper top and three stainless steel washbacks with a fermentation time of 85 hours. There is one pair of stills, the wash still with a capacity of 2,800 litres and the spirit still of 1,800 litre capacity. First fill bourbon barrels are mainly used for maturation and all the whiskies from the distillery are un chill-filtered and without colouring. The distillery also has an excellent, newly expanded visitor centre, including a shop with more than 300 different whiskies. More than 50,000 people travel here every year.

Cotswolds Distillery

Stourton, founded in 2014

www.cotswoldsdistillery.com

The distillery is the brainchild of Dan Szor, who acquired an estate with two stone buildings and converted them into a distillery with a visitor centre. Production of both whisky and gin started in September 2014. There are three stills; one wash still (2,400 litres), one spirit still (1,600 litres) and a Holstein still (500 litres) for production of gin and other spirits. The rest of the equipment includes a 0.5 ton mash tun and eight stainless steel wash backs. The first product for sale was their Cotswolds Dry Gin in 2014 while the first single malt, the 3 year old Odyssey, was launched in 2017. The inaugural release was a vatting of 70% reconditioned red wine casks and 30% first fill ex-bourbon. A widely available bottling was released in November. In early 2018, the distillery started experimenting with rye whisky and in August the owners made their first trials producing rum. In June 2018, Cotswolds hosted the second World Whisky Forum with speakers an delegates from all around the world.

Lakes Distillery

Bassenthwaite Lake, founded in 2014

www.lakesdistillery.com

Headed by Paul Currie, who was the co-founder of Isle of Arran distillery, a consortium of private investors founded the distillery. Production started in autumn 2014 and the £2,5m distillery is equipped with two stills for the whisky production, each with both copper and stainless steel condensers, and a third still for the distillation of gin. The capacity is 240,000 litres of pure alcohol and to help create a cash flow, the company launched a British Isles blended whisky called The One in autumn 2013. Also gin and vodka are being distilled. The very first bottle of the distillery´s single malt, The Lakes Malt Genesis, was sold on 29th June 2018 at an auction fetching a staggering £7,900. More bottles were offered to members of the Founder´s Club in September and that same month saw the first installment in a four-year collection of single malts called The Quatrefoil Collection.

Spirit of Yorkshire Distillery

Hunmanby, founded in 2016

www.spiritofyorkshire.com

Plans for the distillery started in 2014 when Tom Mellor and David Thompson, the company directors, decided to make Yorkshire's first single malt whisky. The distillery is actually situated in two separate locations with a one ton mash tun and two 10,000 litre washbacks standing at Tom´s farm which also houses a brewery while the 5,000 litre wash still and a 3,500 litre spirit still are 2,5 miles down the road in Hunmanby. All the barley comes from the farm, is malted by Muntons and the fermented wash is tankered to the distillery every week. The two pot stills are equipped with 4 plate columns and currently 50% of the production is distilled using the columns to achieve a lighter character of the new make. The distillery was commissioned in May 2016. The distillery also has a visitor centre with daily tours. In December 2017, the owners released their first malt spirit called Distillery Projects Maturing Malt. The third installment was in summer 2018 which was later followed by spirit that had matured in PX sherry casks.

Other distilleries in England

The London Distillery Company

London, founded in 2012

www.londondistillery.com

Founded in 2012 by whisky expert Darren Rook (who left the company in early 2018) and former microbrewery owner, Nick Taylor, the distillery started distilling gin at the beginning of 2013. The owners have one still designated for gin while a second still is used exclusively for whisky production. The first release in March 2013 was Dodd´s Gin. In December 2013 they got the licence to produce whisky and production started shortly thereafter. The last couple of years, the production has taken place in two sites, in Battersea and Bermondsey.

Adnams Copper House Distillery

Southwold, founded in 2010

www.adnams.co.uk

Adnams Brewery in Suffolk installed a new brewhouse in their Sole Bay Brewery in 2008. Left with a redundant, old building, they decided to convert it into a distillery. Distillation began in December 2010 and, apart from whisky – gin, vodka and absinthe are also produced. Two more stills were installed in early 2016. The first two whiskies from the distillery were released in 2013 – Single Malt No. 1, and Triple Grain No. 2 from malted barley, oats and wheat and matured in new American oak. Several whiskies have been added to the range since then, one of the latest being one made from 75% rye and 25% malted barley.

Single malts from Lakes and Cotswolds

Chase Distillery

Rosemaund Farm, Hereford, founded in 2008

www.chasedistillery.co.uk

William Chase, who founded Tyrrell´s Crisps, sold the company in 2008 and instead started a distillery on his farm in Hereford. Chase´s main product is Chase Vodka made from potatoes and gin has also become part of their range. By the end of 2011, the first whisky was distilled and since then around 40 casks are filled every year but no bottling has yet been released. The distillery is equipped with a copper still from Carl in Germany with a five plate column and an attached rectification column with another 42 plates.

Bimber Distillery

London, founded in 2015

www.bimberdistillery.co.uk

This is one of three distilleries in London currently producing whisky. The floor malted barley is bought from Warminster Maltings and the spirit is distilled in two copper stills made by Hoga in Spain – a 1,000 litre wash still and a 600 litre spirit still. The owners have already released a vodka but since the distillation of whisky did not commence until May 2016, the first bottled single malt can´t be expected until mid 2019. However, a blended 6-month-old malt spirit from bourbon, sherry and virgin oak casks has already been released.

Copper Rivet Distillery

Chatham, founded in 2016

www.copperrivetdistillery.com

Situated in an old pump house in the Chatham Docks, this distillery is owned by the Russell family. There is one copper pot still with a column attached as well as a special gin still. Dockyard Gin and Vela Vodka were released early on and in April 2017, Son of a Gun, an 8 week old grain spirit made from rye, wheat and barley, was released. The first single malt will be called Masthouse and is due for release in 2020.

Dartmoor Distillery

Bovey Tracey, founded in 2016

www.dartmoorwhiskydistillery.co.uk

Starting the distillery, the founders, Greg Millar and Simon Crow acquired a 50 year old alembic still in Cognac which hadn´t been used since 1994. The brought it to England, refurbished it and attached a copper "wash warmer" to pre warm the wash and increase the copper contact. The distillery is situated in Devon, just north of Torquay and the first distillation was in February 2017.

Isle of Wight Distillery

Newport, founded in 2015

www.isleofwightdistillery.com

The founders, Conrad Gauntlett and Xavier Baker, have years of combined experience in wine production and brewing but this is their first distillation venture. The fermented wash is bought from a local brewery and distilled in hybrid copper stills. The first whisky was distilled in December 2015 and the owners also produce vodka and Mermaid Gin.

Durham Whisky

Durham, founded in 2014 (whisky since 2018)

www.durhamwhisky.co.uk

The distillery was founded in 2014 with the aim to produce gin and vodka. In 2018, the owners decided to relocate to larger premises in Durham and whisky was added to the range. Using local malt, the distillery is equipped with a 1,200 litre wash still and a 1,000 litre spirit still.

Cooper King Distillery

Sutton-on-the-Forest, founded in 2018

www.cooperkingdistillery.co.uk

Inspired by a trip to whisky distilleries in Australia, Abbie Neilson and Chris Jaume decided to build a distillery of their own in Yorkshire. Equipped with a Tasmanian copper pot still, the distillery released its first gin in summer 2018 and the aim is to start whisky production in the autumn. The distillery practises a combination of vacuum distillation and traditional distillation

Finland 

Teerenpeli

Lahti, founded in 2002

www.teerenpeli.com

The original distillery, located in the company´s restaurant in central Lahti, is equipped with one wash still (1,500 litres) and one spirit still (900 litres). A completely new distillery, with one 3,000 litre wash still and two 900 litre spirit stills, was opened in 2015 in the same house as the brewery and today the old distillery serves as a "laboratory" producing peated spirit, gin, brandy etc. The first Teerenpeli Single Malt was launched as a 3 year old in 2005. The core range now consists of a 10 year old matured in bourbon casks, Kaski which is a 100% sherry maturation and Portti which is a 3 year old with another 1.5 years in port casks. Recent limited releases include Rasi, a moscatel finish, Karhi (madeira finish), Aura which has been matured in the brewery´s own porter casks and the smoky Suomi 100 to celebrate the 100th anniversary of Finland´s declaration of independence.

Other distilleries in Finland

Helsinki Distilling Company

Helsinki, founded in 2014

www.hdco.fi

Whisky production started in September 2014. The distillery is equipped with one mash tun, three washbacks and two stills. The first gin was released in October 2014 and more gin and akvavit but also a one year old malt spirit has followed since. On the whisky side, the focus is on rye but also single malt made from barley. The first release was a 100% malted rye in autumn 2017.

Valamo Distillery

Heinävesi, founded in 2014

www.valamodistillery.com

The distillery is situated at the Valamo Monastery in eastern Finland. Experimental distillation started in 2011 in a small, 150 litre still. In 2015, production began in earnest when the distillery was equipped with a 5,000 litre mash tun, four stainless steel washbacks and a 1,000 litre Carl still. A 5 year old, matured in first fill bourbon casks, from the early days of the distillery has already been released.

France 

Distillerie Warenghem

Lannion, Bretagne, founded in1900 (whisky since 1994)

www.distillerie-warenghem.com

Leon Warenghem founded the distillery at the beginning of the 20th century and in 1967, his grandson Paul-Henri Warenghem, together with his associate, Yves Leizour, took over the reins. They moved the distillery to its current location on the outskirts of

Lannion in Brittany. Gilles Leizour, Yves' son, took over at the end of the 1970's and it was he who added whisky to the Warenghem range. WB (stands for Whisky Breton), a blend from malted barley and wheat both distilled in a pot still, saw the light in 1987 and Armorik – the first ever French single malt – was released in 1998. At this time, Warenghem was the only whisky distillery operating in France. The distillery is equipped with a 6,000 litre semi-lauter mashtun, six stainless steel washbacks and two, traditional copper pot stills (a 6,000 litre wash still and a 3,500 litre spirit still). They only operate one run per day, five days a week. Around 180,000 litres of pure alcohol (including 20% grain whisky) are produced yearly.

The single malt core range consists of Armorik Édition Originale and Armorik Sherry Finish. Both are around 4 years old, bottled at 40%, have matured in ex-bourbon casks plus a few months in sherry butts for sherry finish and are sold in supermarkets in France. Armorik Classic, a mix of 4 to 8 year old whiskies from ex-bourbon and sherry casks and the 7 year old Armorik Double Maturation which has spent time in both new oak and sherry wood are earmarked for export as well as the Armorik Sherry Cask. Armorik Millésime (always a 2012 distillation) is a single cask bottling released every year while Maître De Chai is another annual, limited release. Warenghem has also distilled rye whisky which was first released in 2014 under the name Roof Rye and in early 2018, the first peated expression, Triagoz, was released. David Roussier, who now runs the business, is planning to change the name Warenghem to Armorik for the whisky distillery in 2019

Glann ar Mor

Pleubian, Bretagne, founded in 1999

www.glannarmor.com

The owner of Glann ar Mor Distillery in Brittany, Jean Donnay, already started his first trials back in 1999. He then made some changes to the distillery and the process and regular production commenced in 2005. The distillery is very much about celebrating the traditional way of distilling malt whisky. The two small stills are directly fired and Donnay uses worm tubs for condensing the spirit. He practises a long fermentation in wooden washbacks and the distillation is very slow. For maturation, a variety of casks are used (first fill bourbon, ex-Sauternes casks, PX sherry etc.) and when the whisky is bottled, there is neither chill filtration nor caramel colouring. The full capacity is 50,000 bottles per year but the actual production is less than 10,000 bottles. There are two versions of the whisky – the unpeated Glann ar Mor and the peated Kornog. Core expressions are usually bottled at 46% but every year a number of limited releases are made including single casks and cask strength bottlings. In 2015, Donnay also released his first rye whisky - Only Rye, made from 100% malted rye.

Distillerie des Menhirs

Plomelin, Bretagne, founded in 1986 (whisky since 1998)

www.distillerie.bzh

Originally a portable column still distillery, Guy Le Lay and his wife Anne-Marie decided in 1986 to settle down for good and the first lambig with the name Distillerie des Menhirs was released in 1989. Shortly after, Guy Le Lay came up with the idea of producing a 100% buckwheat whisky. Eddu Silver was launched in 2002, followed by Eddu Gold in 2006, Eddu Silver Brocéliande in 2013 and Eddu Diamant in 2015. Ed Gwenn (white cereal in English), aged for 4 years in ex-cognac barrels, was released for the first time in 2016 and in 2017, the third release in the Collector´s Range (Eddu Dan Ar Braz) appeared.

Distillerie Rozelieures

Rozelieures, Grand Est, founded in 1860 (whisky since 2003)

www.whiskyrozelieures.com

Hubert Grallet and his son-in-law, Christophe Dupic started with whisky production in 2003 and launched the Glen Rozelieures brand in 2007. Four versions are currently available: the first two are aged in ex-fino sherry casks, the third is lightly peated and aged in Sauternes casks and the fourth is peated. Fully automated in 2017 and with a production of 200 000 litres, Rozelieures distillery is now largest distillery in France. Since 2015, with the help of two other farmers, Rozelieures is independent in energy with its own biogas plant a few hundred meters from the distillery. In 2018, Christophe Dupic inaugurated his malting plant, with an annual capacity of 2,000 tons. Rozelieures is also bottled under the brand name Lughnasadh for the Clair de Lorraine chainstore and supply single malt whisky to the new independent bottler Maison Benjamin Kuentz.

Distillerie Lehmann

Obernai, Grand Est, founded in 1850 (whisky since 2001)

www.distillerielehmann.com

The story of Lehmann distillery starts in 1850 when the family of the actual owner set up a still in Bischoffsheim. Yves Lehmann inherited the facility in 1982 but decided to move all the equipment to a new distillery in 1993. The first regular bottling from the distillery, aged for seven years in Bordeaux casks, was launched in 2008 under the brand Elsass Whisky. The range now includes Elsass Origine (4-6 years) and Elsass Gold (6-8 years), both matured in ex-white wine casks, and Elsass Premium (8 years) matured in ex-Sauternes casks.

Miclo

Lapoutroie, Grand Est, founded in 1970 (whisky since 2012)

www.distillerie-miclo.com

Gilbert Miclo, the grandfather of Bertrand Lutt, the current manager, founded the distillery in 1970, specialising in fruit spirits. It is equipped with four Holstein waterbath pot stills and since 2012, wort from a local brewery is fermented and distilled into malt whisky. Under the brand name Welche's, three different whiskies were released in December 2016 - Welche, Welche Fine Tourbe, Welche Tourbé. In June 2018, Miclo released Welche Cherry Cask Finish, a

Warenghem Distillery

small batch of four casks (ex-burgundy and sauternes) matured for 6 years and with a finish in an ex-cherry eau-de-vie cask.

Domaine des Hautes-Glaces

Saint Jean d´Hérans, Auvergne-Rhône Alpes, founded in 2009
(whisky since 2013)

www.hautesglaces.com

At an altitude of 900 metres in the middle of the French Alps, Jérémy Bricka and Frédéric Revol decided to produce whisky from barley to bottle. Apart from growing their own barley, all the parts of whisky production take place at the distillery – malting, brewing, distillation, maturation and bottling. Not only have they set out to create the first French single estate whisky, they are doing it organically. All of their cereal (mainly barley, but also rye) is harvested, malted, distilled and aged field by field and without any chemicals. Principium, the first whisky made at the distillery has been available since June 2014. Domaine des Hautes Glaces was bought by Rémy Cointreau in 2015 and a second distillery, destined to open in 2019, is currently being built. The standard line-up includes two whiskies, Les Moissons Malt (100% malted barley) and Les Moissons Rye (100% malted rye). Single cask bottlings such as Ceros or Secale (rye), Flavis, Tekton or Ampelos (barley) are released from time to time.

Rouget de Lisle

Bletterans, Bourgogne-Franche Comté, founded in 1994
(whisky since 2006),

www.brasserie-rouget-lisle.com

Rouget de Lisle is a micro-brewery created by Bruno Mangin and his wife. In 2006, they commissioned the Brûlerie du Revermont to distil whisky for them. The first Rouget De Lisle single malt whisky was released in 2009 and in 2012, Bruno Mangin bought his own still. Current bottlings are from the numerous casks he filled during his association with the Tissot family and which lie maturing in his own warehouse. The very first 100% Rouget de Lisle whisky is still a few years away as the owner wants to release it as a 10 year old.

Domaine Mavela

Corsica, founded in 1991 (whisky since 2001)

www.domaine-mavela.com

Since 2001 whisky is produced in Corsica. The creators of P&M are the brewer Dominique Sialleli, also responsible for the creation of Pietra beer in 1996, and Jean-Claude Venturini who set up the Mavela distillery in 1991. Distilled in a Holstein still and aged in ex-Corsican muscat casks, the P&M single malt was sold for the first time in 2004 and its unique taste of the Corsican maquis

surprised many whisky lovers. End of 2017, the distillery released its first 12 year old and in 2018, Fanu Venturini and his brother Lisandru, who now run the distillery, unveiled a completely new range of three expresions: P&M Signature, P&M Red Oak (aged in ex-red-wine casks) and P&M Tourbé (peated).

Distillerie Claeyssens de Wambrechies

Wambrechies, Hauts de France, founded in 1817
(whisky since 2000)

www.wambrechies.com

Owned by the Belgian company Grandes Distilleries de Charleroi, Claeyssens is one of the oldest in France. The distillery was originally famous for its genever, the traditional spirit consumed in the north of France, in Belgium and in Holland. The first whisky, a 3 year old, was released in 2003 followed by an 8 year old in 2009. In 2013, two 12 year old bottlings were released: one aged in madeira casks and another in sherry casks, and in September 2017 a limited 8 year old from sherry casks was launched to celebrate the distillery´s 200th anniversary. Wambrechies whisky is also the heart of Bellevoye's triple malt whisky, launched by the independent bottler Sirech & Co at the end of 2015.

Distillerie Brunet

Cognac, Nouvelle Aquitaine, founded in 1920
(whisky since 2006)

www.drinkbrenne.com

In 2006, Stéphane Brunet made the bold move to start whisky production in the Poitou-Charentes region - famous for its cognac production. His whisky, Tradition Malt, was launched in 2009 and was launched in the USA by whisky enthusiast Allison Parc under the brand Brenne. Each version, bottled at 40% comes from a single cask. In September 2015 a 10 year old version was released in small quantities in the USA. Since 2015 Brenne Cuvée Spéciale is also available in France. In 2017, the brand was acquired by Samson & Surrey with Allison Parc still being involved.

Other distilleries in France

Distillerie Meyer

Hohwarth, Grand Est, founded in 1958 (whisky since 2004)
www.distilleriemeyer.fr

Founded by Fridolin Meyer in 1958, and joined by his son Jean-Claude in 1975, Meyer soon became one of the most awarded distillers in France. At the beginning of the 2000's, Jean-Claude together with his two sons, Arnaud and Lionel, decided to start whisky production as well. They launched two no-age statement

Domaine Mavela in Corsica

whiskies in 2007, just one year before the sudden death of Jean-Claude. There are currently three different versions: Meyer's Pur Malt (a single malt), Meyer's Blend Supérieur and Oncle Meyer Blend Supérieur. Meyer created a little buzz, in France, at the end of 2016 by releasing the most expensive French whisky ever: a limited 12 year old – Hommage à JC Meyer – at the staggering price of 1 000 euros.

Distillerie Gilbert Holl

Ribeauvillé, Grand Est, founded in 1979 (whisky since 2000)

www.gilbertholl.com

In 1979, Gilbert Holl began to distill occasionally in the back of his wine and spirits shop but it wasn´t until the beginning of 2000, that he finally started producing also whisky. His first bottling, Lac'Holl, was put on sale in 2004 and was followed by Lac'Holl Junior in 2007 and Lac'Holl Vieil Or in 2009. In 2015, Lac'Holl Junior was replaced by Lac'Holl Or. The oldest whiskies, 10 and 12 year olds, can only be found at the distillery.

Distillerie Hepp

Uberach, Grand Est, founded in 1972 (whisky since 2005)

www.distillerie-hepp.com

A family-owned distillery with a no-age statement core expression by the name Tharcis Hepp. Two limited editions have also been released, the first one aged in ex-plum cask, the second one under the name Johnny Hepp. As well as producing their own whisky, Hepp also distils for Meteor, the brewery that supplies the wort to some Alsatian distilleries. Meteor Single Malt Whisky has been released in summer 2017 for the first time.

Brûlerie du Revermont

Nevy sur Seille, Bourgogne-Franche Comté, founded in 1991 (whisky since 2003)

www.marielouisetissot-levin.com

For many years, the Tissot family were travelling distillers offering their services to wine producers in the area. Relying upon a very unique distillation set-up, a Blavier still with three pots, designed and built for the perfume industry, they have been producing single malt whisky since 2003. Pascal and Joseph Tissot launched their own whisky brand Prohibition in 2011. Aged in "feuillettes" (114 litres half-casks coopered specially for macvin and vin de paille french wines), the whisky is bottled without colouring.

Distillerie Bertrand

Uberach, Grand Est, founded in 1874 (whisky since 2002)

www.distillerie-bertrand.com

The distillery manager, Jean Metzger, gets the malt from a local brewer and then distils it in Holstein type stills. Two different types of whisky are produced. One is a non-chill filtered single malt with a maturation in both new barrels and ex Banyuls barrels. The other is a single cask matured only in Banyuls barrels. They have also experimented with maturation in a lot of other different ex-wine casks, and the new range became known as Cask Jaune.

Distillerie de Northmaen

La Chapelle Saint-Ouen, Normandie, founded in 1997 (whisky since 2002)

www.northmaen.com

Northmaen is a craft brewery founded in 1997 by Dominique Camus and his wife. Every year since 2005, they have bottled and sold Thor Boyo, a 3 year old single malt, distilled in a small, mobile pot still. Several more releases have followed with the peated Fafnir from 2015 as one of the latest. The still is not portable anymore but now works in a real distillery.

Brasserie Michard

Limoges, Nouvelle Aquitaine, founded in 1987 (whisky since 2008)

www.bieres-michard.com

Started as a brewery, Jean Michard began to also produce whisky in 2008. Using their own unique yeast, the first batch of their whisky, released in 2011, was highly original and very fruity. Available in an 800 bottle limited edition, it was followed by a second batch in late 2013. Jean Michard has now retired and the still does not work very often but a brand new bottle and packaging design has been recently launched, announcing a new start.

Bercloux

Bercloux, Nouvelle Aquitaine, founded in 2000 (whisky since 2014)

www.distillerie-bercloux.fr

After many trials, Philippe Laclie opened his own brewery in 2000. In 2007 he decided to diversify by buying some Scotch whisky and finishing it for a few months in Pineau des Charentes barrels. At the beginning of 2014, Philippe took the next step and invested around 100,000 euros, buying an 800 litre column still. After the first trial runs in June 2014, regular whisky production started in September. The first bottlings of Bercloux (3 and 9 months old) were released at the end of 2015 and in 2017, a 9 months old peated version was launched.

Dreumont

Neuville-en-Avesnois, Hauts de France, founded in 2005 (whisky since 2011)

www.ladreum.com

Passionate about beer, Jérôme Dreumont decided to open a distillery as well in 2005. In 2011 he built his own 300 litre still and has since then been filling only one cask per year. His first whisky, distilled from a mix of peated and non-peated barley, was launched in March 2015 and was followed by more releases in 2016 and 2017.

Distillerie du Castor

Troisfontaines, Grand Est, founded in 1985 (whisky since 2011)

www.distillerie-du-castor.com

Founded by Patrick Bertin, the distillery produces both fruit and pomace brandies. It is equipped with two small stills which have been used since 2011 by Patrick's son to distill single malt whisky. The malt is brewed by a local brewery and the distillate is aged in ex-white wine casks and finished in ex-sherry casks. The first release appeared in June 2015 under the name St Patrick.

La Roche Aux Fées

Sainte-Colombe, Bretagne, founded in 1996 (whisky since 2010)

www.distillerie-larocheauxfees.com

Gonny Keizer installed a micro-brewery in 1996 and became the first female master-brewer in France. In 2010, Gonny and her husband Henry bought a 400 litre portable automatic batch still. The still is wood-heated and equipped with a worm-tub condenser and the first spirit was put into cask in 2010. The first Roc'Elf bottling, distilled from three malted cereals (barley, wheat, oat), was released in January 2016 followed by a second in early 2017.

Distillerie Castan

Villeneuve Sur Vère, Occitanie, founded in 1946 (whisky since 2010)

www.distillerie-castan.com

In 2010, Sébastien Castan decided to permanently house the portable still that had been in the family for three generations in a proper distillery. The same year, he distilled his first whisky and aged the spirit in ex-Gaillac wine casks. In 2016, a brewery was built to supply the beer. The range consists of five bottlings: Villanova Berbie (ex-white wine casks), Gost (new cask), Terrocita (peated), Roja (ex-red wine casks) and Segala (rye).

Domaine de Bourjac

Broquiès, Occitanie, founded in 1994 (whisky since 2012)

www.domainedebourjac.com

With help from a local fruit eau-de-vie distiller, wine producer Olivier Toulouse produced a malt whisky in 2010. The first bottles of DDB were released in 2015 and that same year, Olivier bought an old Charentais type still which he refurbished in order to put it to its original use: direct distillation with smoke recuperation through a tube wrapped around the kettle to help the heat repartition. Around 400 bottles of organic whisky is produced yearly.

La Quintessence

Herrberg, Grand Est, founded in 2008 (whisky since 2013)

www.distillerie-quintessence.com

In 2008 Nicolas Schott took over the family distillery in Herrberg in order to continue the production of fruit spirits (raspberry, pear, plum, quetsche or quince) and also liqueurs (spices or asperule). End of 2016, the 34 year old distiller surprised everyone with the release of his first single malt whisky, Schott's, bottled at 42%.

La Piautre

Ménitré Sur Loire, Pays de Loire, founded in 2004 (whisky since 2014)

www.lapiautre.fr

Ten years after Yann Leroux and Vincent Lelièvre had founded a brwery, they decided to start malting their own barley and to start experiments with distillation. La Piautre is now equipped with a Charentais direct-fire heated still. The company released its three first Loire Valley whiskies in January 2018: Malt, Tourbé and Seigle.

Leisen

Malling, Grand Est, founded in 1898 (whisky since 2012)

www.distillerie-leisen-petite-hettange.fr

Since 1898, the Leisen family has distilled fruit spirits but also spirits made from rye and barley. The distillery is equipped with two Carl stills (250 and 350 litres respectively). In 2018, Jean-Marie Leisen released his first bottles under the JML brand.

Germany

Whisky-Destillerie Blaue Maus

Eggolsheim-Neuses, 1980

www.fleischmann-whisky.de

The oldest malt whisky distillery in Germany distilling their first whisky in 1983. It took, however, 15 years before the first whisky, Glen Mouse 1986, appeared. A completely new distillery became operational in April 2013. All whisky from Blaue Maus are single cask and there are around ten single malts in the range. Some of them are released at cask strength while others are reduced to 40%. An unusual experiment started in 2016 when the owners transported some casks to the island of Sylt in the North Sea. They were lowered into the sea to continue the maturation process. Because of the tide, every six hours the casks were exposed to the air. When the whisky was released it was named Sylter Tide.

Slyrs Destillerie

Schliersee, founded in 1928 (whisky since 1999)

www.slyrs.de

The malt, smoked with beech, comes from locally grown grain and the spirit is distilled in 1,500 litre stills. The non chill-filtered whisky is called Slyrs after the original name of the surrounding area, Schliers. The core expressions are a 3 year old bottled at 43% and matured in new American oak and the 51 which has matured in casks that previously held sherry, port or sauternes and is bottled at 51%. In 2015, the distillery´s first 12 year old whisky was released and other limited editions occur from time to time, including a variety of wood finishes. The latest limited release is the single cask Altitude 453.

Hammerschmiede

Zorge, founded in 1984 (whisky since 2002)

www.hammerschmiede.de

In keeping with many other small whisky producers on mainland Europe, Hammerschmiede´s main products are spirits from fruit, berries and herbs and whisky distilling was only embarked on in 2002. In 2014, Alexander Buchholz, started the construction of a new still house with additional stills making it a total of five. The first bottles were released in 2006. The core range consists of three expressions; Glen Els Journey with a blend of different maturations, Ember, which is woodsmoked and the X Series. The latter range, introduced in 2016, represents the best whiskies from the distillery, ten years or older. A subrange from the distillery is called Alrik represented by experimental maturations and finishes.

Other distilleries in Germany

Spreewood Distillers

Schlepzig, founded in 2004 (whisky production)

www.stork-club-whisky.com

Founded by Torsten Römer, the distillery changed hands in autumn 2016 when Spreewood Distillers took over. The distillery had a history of producing a wide range of spirits but the new owners decided to focus entirely on whisky and rum. The new range is called Stork Club with a Single Malt bottled at 47% and a Straight Rye bottled at 55%. Limited releases include a single Bordeaux red wine cask.

Brennerei Heinrich

Kriftel, founded in 1983 (whisky since 2009)

www.brennerei-henrich.de, www.gilors.de

The first whisky release from the distillery was the 3 year old single malt Gilors in 2012. The two core expressions, Gilors fino sherry matured and Gilors port matured, are both 3 years old. Recent limited editions include Gilors Peated (made from peated malt and matured for three years in bourbon casks) and a 7 year old, finished in PX casks.

Bayerwald-Bärwurzerei und Spezialitäten-Brennerei Liebl

Kötzting, founded in 1970 (whisky since 2006)

www.coillmor.com

Around 30,000 litres of whisky are produced annually and in 2009 the first bottles bearing the name Coillmór were released. There is a wide range aged between 4 and 8 years currently available. Recent limited editions include a 10 year old single malt matured in port casks and a 5.5 year old matured in sauternes casks.

Brennerei Höhler

Aarbergen, founded in 1895 (whisky since 2001)

www.brennerei-hoehler.de

The first whisky from the distillery was released in 2004 as a 3 year old. A couple of the more recent releases of their Whesskey (so called since it is from the province Hessen) include versions made from rye, oat, triticale and pilsner.

Stickum Brennerei (Uerige)

Düsseldorf, founded in 2007

www.stickum.de

The wash comes from their own brewery and the distillation takes place in a 250 litre column still. The single malt is called BAAS and the first bottling (a 3 year old) was released in 2010. In 2014 the owners released their first 5 year old whiskies.

Preussische Whiskydestillerie

Mark Landin, founded in 2009

www.preussischerwhisky.de

The spirit is distilled very slowly five to six times in a 550 litre copper still with a rectification column and is then matured in casks made of new, heavily toasted American white oak, German fine oak or German Spessart oak. Since 2013 only organic barley is used. The first whisky was launched as a 3 year old in December 2012. From 2015, all the whiskies have been at least 5 years old.

Kleinbrennerei Fitzke

Herbolzheim-Broggingen, founded in 1874 (whisky since 2004)

www.kleinbrennerei-fitzke.de

The first release of the Derrina single malt was in 2007 and new batches have been launched ever since including a lightly peated. The different varieties of Derrina are either made from malted grains (barley, rye, wheat, oats etc.) or unmalted (barley, oats, buckwheat, rice, triticale, sorghum or maize).

Glina Whiskydestillerie

Werder a.d. Havel, founded in 2004

www.glina-whisky.de

After 12 years of production, the distillery moved to larger premises in 2016, thereby ten-folding the capacity. Around 1,000 casks are now filled yearly. The first Glina Single Malt was released in 2008. Most of the whiskies are between 3 and 5 years old and have matured in a variety of casks. Around 80% of the production is malt whisky while the rest is made using rye.

Rieger & Hofmeister

Fellbach, founded in 1994 (whisky since 2006)

www.rieger-hofmeister.de

The first release was in 2009 and currently there are four expressions in the range – a single malt matured in pinot noir casks, a malt & grain (50% wheat, 40% barley and 10% smoked barley) from chardonnay casks, a malted rye and a single grain. A peated single malt is due for release in 2023

Kinzigbrennerei

Biberach, founded in 1937 (whisky since 2004)

www.biberacher-whisky.de

The first release from the distillery in 2008 was Badische Whisky, a blend made from wheat and barley. Two years later came the 4 year old Biberacher Whisky, the first single malt and in 2012, the range was expanded with Schwarzwälder Rye Whisky and the smoky single malt Kinzigtäler Whisky.

Destillerie Kammer-Kirsch

Karlsruhe, founded in1961 (whisky since 2006)

www.kammer-kirsch.de

The distillery is working together with the brewery Landesbrauerei Rothaus, where the brewery delivers a fermented wash to the distillery and they continue distilling a whisky called Black Forest Rothaus Single Malt Whisky. The whisky was launched for the first time in 2009 and every year in March, a new batch is released. Recent limited releases include a 2017 pinot noir finish

Brennerei Ziegler

Freudenberg, founded in 1865

www.brennerei-ziegler.de

One characteristic that distinguishes Ziegler from most other distilleries is that the maturation takes place not only in oak casks, but also in casks made of chestnut! Their current core bottling is a 5 year old called Aureum 1865 Single Malt and there is also a cask strength version. Limited releases occur regularly with the lightly peated The Bruce as one of the more recent.

Michael Schultz - owner of Glina Whiskydestillerie

Alt Enderle Brennerei

Rosenberg/Sindolsheim, founded in 1991 (whisky since 1999)

www.alt-enderle-brennerei.de

The first whisky distillation was in 2000 and the owners now have a wide range of Neccarus Single Malt for sale from a 4 year old to an 18 year old! The latest limited release was the 7 year old, smoky Terrador with a finish in rum casks.

AV Brennerei

Wincheringen, founded in 1824 (whisky since 2006)

www.avadisdistillery.de

Around 2,000 bottles are released yearly and the oak casks from France have previously been used for maturing white Mosel wine. Threeland Whisky is between 3 and 6 years old and the range also consists of finishes in oloroso and port casks.

Birkenhof-Brennerei

Nistertal, founded in 1848 (whisky since 2002)

www.birkenhof-brennerei.de

The first release from the distillery in 2008 was the 5 year old rye Fading Hill. This was followed a year later by a single malt. The most recent bottling was the 4 year old Master Edition, launched in December 2017. Since 2015, peated whisky is also produced.

Brennerei Faber

Ferschweiler, founded in 1949

www.faber-eifelbrand.de

Established as a producer of eau-de vie from fruits and berries, whisky has been included in the poduction during the last few years. The only whisky so far is a single malt that has matured for 6 years in barrels made of American white oak.

Steinhauser Destillerie

Kressbronn, founded in 1828 (whisky since 2008)

www.weinkellerei-steinhauser.de

The main products are spirits which are derived from fruits, but whisky also has its own niche. The first release was the single malt Brigantia which appeared in 2011. It was triple distilled and more releases have followed since.

Weingut Simons

Alzenau-Michelbach, founded in 1879 (whisky since 1998)

www.feinbrenner.eu

All the whisky was produced in a 150 litre still until 2013 when a new Holstein still was installed, raising the whisky production from 300 litres per year to 3-5,000 litres. A single pot still whisky has since been released and the first whisky from the new still, a 100% rye, was launched in 2016.

Nordpfälzer Edelobst & Whiskydestille

Winnweiler, founded in 2008

www.nordpfalz-brennerei.de

The first release was in 2011, a 3 year old single malt by the name Taranis with a full maturation in a Sauternes cask and in 2013 a 4 year old from ex-bourbon casks with an Amarone finish was launched. Regular releases have occured since, the latest in September 2017.

Dürr Edelbranntweine

Neubulach, founded in 2002

www.blackforest-whiskey.com

The first release from the distillery, the 4 year old Doinich Daal, reached the market in 2012. The latest release, batch 4 in December 2017, with two expressions, Eichenacker and Alte Hau, had matured in a combination of casks (wine, bourbon, cognac).

Tecker Whisky-Destillerie

Owen, founded in 1979 (whisky since 1989)

www.tecker.eu

Apart from a variety of eau de vie and other spirits, around 1,500 litres of whisky is produced annually. The core expression is the 10 year old Tecker Single Malt matured for five years in ex-bourbon barrels, followed by five yers in oloroso casks. There is also a single grain aged for 18 years in bourbon, cognac and sherry barrels.

Märkische Spezialitäten Brennerei

Hagen, whisky since 2010

www.msb-hagen.de

The spirit is distilled four times, matured in ex-bourbon barrels for 12 months and then brought to a cave, with low temperature and high humidity, for further maturation. The first whisky, the 3 year old Tronje van Hagen, was released in 2013. The whisky has now been renamed DeCavo.

Sperbers Destillerie

Rentweinsdorf, founded in 1923 (whisky since 2002)

www.salmsdorf.de

At the moment, four different expressions have been released, all of them 7 years old – single malt matured in bourbon casks, single malt matured in a mix of sherry and bourbon casks, a sherrymatured single malt bottled at cask strength, as well as,a single grain whisky from a mix of bourbon, sherry and Spessart oak casks.

Brennerei Feller

Dietenheim-Regglisweiler, founded in 1820
(whisky since 2008)

www.brennerei-feller.de

In 2012, the first single malt, the 3 year old Valerie matured in bourbon casks, was released. It was recently followed by two 5 year olds, finished in sherry- and amarone-casks respectively and a 4 year old finished in a madeira cask.

Marder Edelbrände

Albbruck-Unteralpfen, founded in 1953 (whisky since 2009)

www.marder-edelbraende.de

The first release in 2013 was the 3 year old Marder Single Malt matured in a combination of new American oak and sherry casks. One thousand bottles were released and the latest edition, a 5 year old matured in a combination of bourbon and port, was launched in 2015.

Destillerie Drexler

Arrach, whisky since 2007

www.drexlers-whisky.de

Apart from spirits made from herbs, fruits and berries, malt whisky has been produced since 2013. The first release was Bayerwoid in 2011 which was followed up by No. 1 Single Cask Malt Whisky and a 100% malted rye whisky. The latest edition of the No. 1 single cask was 4 years old.

Edelbrände Senft

Salem-Rickenbach, founded in 1988 (whisky since 2009)

www.edelbraende-senft.de

The first 2,000 bottles of 3.5 year old Senft Bodensee Whisky were released in 2012 and they were later followed by a cask strength version (55%).

Schwarzwaldbrennerei Walter Seger

Calw-Holzbronn, founded in 1952 (whisky since 1990)

www.krabba-nescht.de

The first single malt was launched in 2009 and at the moment, the owner has two expressions in the range; the 6 year old Black-Wood single malt matured in amontillado sherry casks and an 8 year old wheat whisky.

Landgasthof Gemmer

Rettert, founded in 1908 (whisky since 2008)

www.landgasthof-gemmer.de

The only single malt released from the distillery is the 3 year old Georg IV which has matured for two years in toasted Spessart oak casks and finished for one year in casks that have contained Banyuls wine. Around 800 litres are produced per year.

St Kilian Distillers

Rüdenau, founded in 2015

stkiliandistillers.com

St Kilian is one of few German distilleries designated to make whisky and nothing else. The distillery was built with the aid of David Hyne of Cooley and Great Northern Distillery fame, including stills from Forsyths. The first whisky will not be ready to launch until 2018 but five spirits at different ages have been released. The distillery has a capacity of 200,000 litres of alcohol.

Hausbrauerei Altstadthof

Nürnberg, founded in 1984

www.hausbrauerei-altstadthof.de

The first German distillery to produce organic single malt. The current range consists of the 4 year old Ayrer´s Red matured in new American oak, Ayrer´s PX, finished in PX sherry casks and Ayrer´s Bourbon, matured in bourbon barrels. A limited expression called Louis XVI, released in 2018, had been matured in a combination of casks that had previously held Bordeaux wine and cognac.

Destillerie Mösslein

Zeilitzheim, founded in 1984 (whisky since 1999)

www.frankenwhisky.de

Originally a winery, whisky production was brought on board in 1999. The first whisky was released in 2003 and the core range consists of a single malt and a grain whisky, both 5 years old. In 2017, the first 12 year old, Ernest 25, was released.

Brennerei Josef Druffel

Oelde-Stromberg, founded in 1792 (whisky since 2010)

www.brennerei-druffel.de

The first single malt, Prum, was released in 2013 and had matured in a mix of different casks (bourbon, sherry, red wine and new Spessart oak) and was finished in small casks made of plum tree! In 2015, a 5 year old version was released.

Brauhaus am Lohberg

Wismar, whisky since 2010

brauhaus-wismar.de, hinricusnoyte.de

The first release of Baltach single malt was in December 2013. It was a 3 year old with a finish in sherry casks. The latest edition of Baltach, finished in PX sherry casks was released in May 2018 and a peated version is due in 2019.

Wild Brennerei

Gengenbach, founded in 1855 (whisky since 2002)

www.wild-brennerei.de

Two 5 year old whiskies have been released so far – Wild Whisky Single Malt which has matured for three years in American white oak and another two in either sherry or port casks and Blackforest Wild Whisky, made from unmalted barley.

Brennerei Volker Theurer

Tübingen, founded in 1991

www.schwaebischer-whisky.de

Located in a guesthouse, the released its first whisky as a 7 year old in 2003 and since then they have released Sankt Johann, an 8 year old single malt and the 9 year old Tammer. Theurer is also selling a blended whisky called Original Ammertal Whisky.

Lübbehusen Malt Distillery

Emstek, founded in 2014

theluebbehusen.com

The distillery has one of the largest pot stills in the country, where whisky made from peated Scottish malt is distilled. The first release, a 3 year old, appeared in autumn 2017. Rye whisky is also produced and attached to the distillery is a visitor centre.

St. Kilian Distillery in beautiful surroundings

Burger Hofbrennerei

Burg, founded in 2007 (whisky since 2012)

sagengeister.de

Apart from distillates from fruits and berries, the distillery also produces whisky made from malted barley. Maturation is in small (100 litres) casks made of American white oak. The first release of Der Kolonist single malt was in spring 2015.

Number Nine Spirituosen-Manufaktur

Leinefelde-Worbis, founded in 1999 (whisky since 2013)

ninesprings.de

The production of liqueurs was expanded in 2013 to include rum, gin and whisky. The first single malt was launched in 2016 while one of the latest, Peated Breeze Edition, appeared in spring 2018.

Edelbrennerei Schloss Neuenburg

Freyburg, founded in 2012

schlossbrennerei.eu

Small volumes of single malt whisky are produced with the spirit maturing for two years in new, German oak and then for another year in pinot noir casks. The first release was in August 2016.

Gutsbrennerei Joh. B. Geuting

Bocholt Spork, founded in 1837 (whisky since 2010)

muensterland-whisky.de

The first releases from this distillery, two single malts and two single grain, appeared in September 2013. More releases of the J.B.G. Münsterländer Single Malt have followed, the latest a 3.5 year old matured in sherry casks.

Sauerländer Edelbrennerei

Kallenhardt, founded in 2000 (whisky since 2004)

sauerlaender-edelbrennerei.de

The first release of the Thousand Mountains McRaven appeared in 2007 as a 3 year old. The recipe was changed in 2011 from peated to unpeated and the first bottlings from the new era were launched in 2014. In 2016, the distillery was expanded when they moved the production to an old sawmill.

Destillerie Ralf Hauer

Bad Dürkheim, founded in 1989 (whisky since 2012)

sailltmor.de

The first release from the distillery appeared in 2015 with the 3 year old Saillt Mor single malt. Recent bottlings include a 4 year old matured in ex-bourbon casks, a PX sherry cask finish bottled at 59.3% and their first peated single malt (45ppm).

Destillerie Thomas Sippel

Weisenheim am Berg, founded in 1992 (whisky since 2011)

destillerie-sippel.de

Wines as well as distillates of all kinds are on the menu with whisky being introduced in 2011. The first release of the Palatinatus Single Malt came in 2014 and there are currently three expressions with different maturation.

Steinwälder Hausbrennerei

Erbendorf, founded in 1818 (whisky since 1920)

brennerei-schraml.de

A kind of whisky was made here already in the early 1900s but was then sold as "Kornbrand". When the current owner took over, the spirit was relaunched as a 10 year old single grain whisky under the name Stonewood 1880. Other releases include a wheat whisky as well as two 3 year old single malts, Dra and Smokey Monk.

Finch Whiskydestillerie

Heroldstatt, founded in 2001

finch-whisky.de

The distillery is one of Germany´s biggest with a yearly production of 250,000 litres and it is also equipped with one of the biggest pot stills in Germany - 3,000 litres. The range of whiskies is large and they are made from a variety of different grains. The age is between 5 and 8 years and included is a 5 year old single malt.

Mönchguter Hofbrennerei

Middelhagen, founded in 2006

ruegen-whisky.de

Located on the island of Rügen the distillery produces spirits from fruits and berries as well as whisky. The main product is the blended whisky Pommerscher Greif but occasional single malts have been released.

Schaubrennerei Am Hartmannsberg

Freital, founded in 2011

hartmannsberger.de

Working on a range of various spirits, the owner also produces small volumes of whisky. The first whisky was released in 2015 and the latest was a 5 year old single malt, matured in ex-sherry casks.

Old Sandhill Whisky

Bad Belzig, founded in 2012

sandhill-whisky.com

The first whisky was released as a 3 year old single malt in 2015. Since then a wide range of bottlings have been launched. The most recent are two single malts matured in port pipes and Bordeaux barriques respectively.

Bellerhof Brennerei

Owen, founded in 1925 (whisky since 1990)

bellerhof-brennerei.com

The production of whisky made from barley, wheat and rye started in 1990 and today there is one single malt in the range - the 5 year old Danne´s Gärschda Malt, available at cask strength or 43%.

Eifel Destillate

Koblenz, founded in 2009

eifel-destillate.de

Even though other spirits are produced, the focus is on whisky of all sorts. The core range consists of Single Rye, Malty Blend and Smoky Blend but several single malts can be found amongst the limitd releases. No whiskies are chill-filtered or coloured.

Iceland 

Eimverk Distillery

Reykjavik, founded in 2012

www.flokiwhisky.is

The country´s first whisky distillery emanated from an idea in 2008 when the three Thorkelsson brothers discussed the possibility of producing whisky in Iceland. In 2011 a company was formed, the first distillation was made in the ensuing year and full scale production started in August 2013. Only organic barley grown in Iceland is used for the production and everything is malted on site. Both peat and sheep dung is used to dry the malted barley. The distillery has a capacity of 100,000 litres where 50% is reserved for gin and aquavite and the rest for whisky. The first, limited release of a 3 year old whisky was in November 2017 and more bottlings are expected during 2018, including a sherry cask matured.

Republic of Ireland

Midleton Distillery

Midleton, Co. Cork, founded in 1975

www.irishdistillers.ie

Midleton is by far the biggest distillery in Ireland and the home of Jameson´s Irish Whiskey. The production at Midleton comprises of two sections – grain whiskey and single pot still whiskey. The grain whiskey is needed for the blends, where Jameson´s is the biggest seller. Single pot still whiskey, on the other hand, is unique to Ireland. This part of the production is also used for the blends but is being bottled more and more on its own.

Until recently, Midleton distillery was equipped with mash tuns both for the barley side and the grain side. After considerable research and trials however, these have now been replaced by mash filters with an astonishing increase in spirit yield from 385 litres per ton of barley to 415 litres. Two major upgrades of the distillery (in 2013 and 2017) means that Midleton is now equipped with 48 washbacks, 6 column stills and 10 pot stills. A new maturation facility with 40 warehouses has also been built in Dungourney, not far from Midleton. In autumn 2015, a new micro distillery adjacent to the existing distillery, was opened. With a production capacity of 400 casks per year, it will be used for experiments and innovation.

Of all the brands produced at Midleton, Jameson´s blended Irish whiskey is by far the biggest. In 2017 the brand sold 83 million bottles – an 11% increase compared to the previous year. Apart from the core expression with no age statement, there are 12 and 18 year olds, Black Barrel, Gold Reserve and a Vintage. Since 2015, a number of special series have been launched; Deconstructed with three bottlings – Bold, Lively and Round, The Whiskey maker´s Se-

ries with The Cooper´s Croze and The Blender´s Dog and Jameson Caskmates with two whiskies aged in stout barrels and IPA barrels. In spring 2018, Jameson Bow Street 18 years old, the first cask strength release of a Jameson, appeared. Other blended whiskey brands include Powers and the exclusive Midleton Very Rare. In recent years, Midleton has invested increasingly in their second category of whiskies, single pot still, and that range now includes Redbreast 12, 12 cask strength, 15, 21 year old, the sherrymatured Lustau Edition and the limited Redbreast Dream Cask 32 years old. Furthermore, there is Green Spot without age statement, the 12 year old Leoville Barton bordeaux finish and the Chateau Montelena finish as well as Yellow Spot 12 years old, Powers (John´s Lane, Signature and Three Swallow) and Barry Crocket Legacy. The first release of an Irish whiskey finished in virgin Irish oak in 2015, the Dair Ghaelach, was followed up by a seond edition in autumn 2017. More innovation followed in 2017 when a range of experimental whiskeys were released under the name Method and Madness. Included in the range were four expressions; a single grain finished in virgin Spanish oak, a single pot still finished in French chestnut, a single malt finished in French Limousin oak and a 31 year old single grain single cask. Two more expressions were added in summer 2018; a single pot still finished in virgin Hungarian oak and a 28 year old single pot still with six years in ex-bourbon barrels and a further 22 years in ruby port pipes.

Tullamore Dew Distillery

Clonminch, Co. Offaly, founded in 2014

www.tullamoredew.com

Until 1954, Tullamore D.E.W. was distilled at Daly´s Distillery in Tullamore. When it closed, production was temporarily moved to Power´s Distillery in Dublin, and was later moved to Midleton Distillery and Bushmill´s Distillery. William Grant & Sons acquired Tullamore D.E.W. in 2010 and in May 2013, they started to build a new distillery at Clonminch, situated on the outskirts of Tullamore. The four stills produce both malt whiskey and single pot still whiskey. The capacity is 1,8 million litres with plans to upgrade to 3,6 million in the near future. In autumn 2017, a bottling hall and a grain distillery with a capacity of doing 8 million litres of grain spirit was opened on the same site. All whiskies at Tullamore are triple distilled. Tullamore D.E.W. is the second biggest selling Irish whiskey in the world after Jameson with 13 million bottles sold in 2017. The core range consists of Original (without age statement), 12 year old Special Reserve and 14 and 18 year old Single Malts. Recent limited releases include Trilogy (a triple blend whiskey matured in three types of wood), Phoenix and Old Bonded Warehouse. As an exclusive to duty free, the Tullamore D.E.W Cider Cask Finish was launched in summer 2015 and this was followed in autumn 2017 by a Carribean Rum Cask Finish.

Cooley Distillery

Cooley, Co. Louth, founded in 1987

www.kilbeggandistillingcompany.com

In 1987, the entrepreneur John Teeling bought the disused Ceimici Teo distillery and renamed it Cooley distillery. Two years later he installed two pot stills and in 1992 he released the first single malt from the distillery, called Locke´s Single Malt. A number of brands were launched over the years. In December 2011 it was announced that Beam Inc. had acquired the distillery for $95m. In 2014, Suntory took over Beam and the new company was renamed Beam Suntory. Cooley distillery is equipped with one mash tun, four malt and six grain washbacks all made of stainless steel, two copper pot stills and two column stills. There is a production capacity of 650,000 litres of malt spirit and 2,6 million litres of grain spirit. The range of whiskies is made up of several brands. Connemara single malts, which are all more or less peated, consist of a no age, a 12 year old and a cask strength. Another brand is Tyrconnel with a core expression bottled without age statement. Other Tyrconnel varieties include three 10 year old wood finishes and the recently launched 15 year old madeira finish.

The latest Method and Madness bottlings from Midleton

Teeling Distillery

Dublin, founded in 2015

www.teelingwhiskey.com

After the Teeling family had sold Cooley and Kilbeggan distilleries to Beam in 2011, the family started a new company, Teeling Whiskey. John´s two sons, Jack and Stephen, then opened a new distillery in Newmarket, Dublin in June 2015. This was the first new distillery in Dublin in 125 years. One year after the opening, an amazing 60,000 people had been welcomed to the distillery. In summer 2017, Bacardi acquired a minority stake in Teeling Whiskey for an undisclosed sum. This is the first time Bacardi gets involved with Irish whiskey.

The distillery is equipped with two wooden washbacks, four made of stainless steel and three stills made in Italy; wash still (15,000 litres), intermediate still (10,000 litres) and spirit still (9,000 litres) and the capacity is 500,000 litres of alcohol. Both pot still and malt whisky is produced. The core range from the distillery consists of the blend Small Batch which has been finished in rum casks, Single Grain which has been fully matured in Californian red wine barrels and Single Malt - a vatting of five different whiskies that have been finished in five different types of wine casks. All these had been distilled at Cooley. The first release from their own production appeared in August 2018, limited to 250 bottles. The first general release came two months later. Recent limited bottlings include The Revival Volume V (a 12 year old finished in cognac and brandy barrels) and the Brabazon Bottling where the second release was finished in port pipes.

Walsh Whiskey Distillery

Carlow, Co. Carlow, founded in 2016

www.walshwhiskey.com

With succesful brands such as The Irishman and Writer´s Tears (both produced at Midleton), Bernard Walsh decided to open his own distillery at Royal Oak, Carlow. With a back-up from the major Italian drinks company, Illva Saronno, construction began in late 2014 and the distillery was commissioned in March 2016. the capacity is 2.5 million litres of alcohol and all types of whiskey is produced including grain- malt- and pot still whiskey. The equipment consists of a 3 ton semi-lauter mash tun, six washbacks, a 15,000 litre wash still, a 7,500 litre intermediate still and a 10,000 litre spirit still. There is also a column still for grain whiskey production. Apart from producing whiskey for its own brands, the distillery has allocated 15% of the output for a number of international partners.

Teeling Distillery in Dublin

Great Northern Distillery

Dundalk, Co. Louth, founded in 2015

www.gndireland.com

In 2013, the Irish Whiskey Company (IWC), with the Teeling family as the majority owners, took over the Great Northern Brewery in Dundalk and turned it into a distillery. When it became operational in August 2015, it was the second biggest distillery in Ireland, with the capacity to produce 3.6 million litres of pot still whiskey and 8 million litres of grain spirit. The distillery is equipped with three columns for the grain spirit production and three pot stills for producing malt and single pot still whiskey. The main part of the business will be to supply whiskey to private label brands but in 2017, the owners released their first own brand - a 14 year old single malt by the name Burke´s Irish Whiskey, which had been distilled during the family´s Cooley days.

Waterford Distillery

Waterford, Co. Waterford, founded in 2015

www.waterforddistillery.ie

Founded by the former co-owner of Bruichladdich distillery on Islay, Mark Reynier. In 2014 he bought the Diageo-owned Waterford Brewery and 16 months later, in December 2015, the first spirit was distilled. The distillery is equipped with two pot stills and one column still and, even though grain spirit will be produced, malt whiskey is the number one priority. The distillery also has a mash filter instead of a mash tun. There is a focus on local barley and Reynier is sourcing the barley from over 50 farms on 19 different soil types. The distillery has a capacity of 1 million litres but the owners have plans to go up to 3 million litres in the future. After having distilled Ireland´s first organic whiskey in 2016, Reynier recently decided to also produce the first biodynamic whiskey where the barley comes from three self-sufficient farms. They are also experimenting with different types of wood for the maturation; acacia, chestnut, mulberry, wild cherry etc.

Other distilleries in Ireland

Kilbeggan Distillery

Kilbeggan, Co. Westmeath, founded in 1757

www.kilbegganwhiskey.com

Brough back to life in 2007 by John Teeling, Kilbeggan is the oldest producing whiskey distillery in the world. The distillery, currently owned by Beam Suntory, is equipped with a wooden mash tun, four Oregon pine washbacks and two stills with one of them being 180 years old. The first single malt whiskey release from the new production came in 2010 and limited batches have been released thereafter. The core blended expression of Kilbeggan is a no age statement bottling but limited releases of aged Kilbeggan blend have occurred. There is also a Kilbeggan grain which was produced at Cooley distillery.

Pearse Lyons Distillery

Dublin, founded in 2017

www.pearselyonsdistillery.com

The founder, Dr Pearse Lyons, who passed away in March 2018, was a native of Ireland and used to work for Irish Distillers in the 1970s. In 1980 he changed direction and founded a company specializing in animal nutrition and feed supplements. In 2008, he opened a whiskey distillery in Lexington, Kentucky. Four years later, in a joint venture, he started a distillery in Carlow, Ireland. After a few years, the stills were moved to Dublin where Dr Lyons restored the old St James´ church and converted it to a distillery. The first distillation was in September 2017 but the owners are already selling three different blends and a 12 year old single malt. The whiskey is sourced but the blends all contain whiskey that was produced in Carlow before the stills were moved to Dublin.

West Cork Distillers

Skibbereen, Co. Cork, founded in 2004

www.westcorkdistillers.com

The distillery, equipped with four stills, produces both malt whiskey and grain whiskey (from barley and wheat) and some of the malting is done on site. Apart from a range of vodka, gin and liqueurs, several single malts, including a 12 year old, and blends are sold under the name West Cork. In autumn 2017, a new range called Glengarriff Collection was launched with two expressions finished in casks that had been charred using peat and bog oak.

Connacht Whiskey Company

Ballina, Co. Mayo, founded in 2016

www.connachtwhiskey.com

The distillery is equipped with three pot stills made in Canada and has the capacity to produce 300,000 litres of pure alcohol per year. The first distillation of whiskey was made in April 2016. Apart from malt whiskey and single pot still whiskey, the owners also produce vodka, gin and poitín. Sourced whiskies have been released with the most recent being the blend Brothership – a vatting of 10 year old Irish pot still and 10 year old American whiskey.

The Dingle Whiskey Distillery

Milltown, Dingle, Co. Kerry, founded in 2012

www.dingledistillery.ie

The old Fitzgerald sawmills has been transformed into a distillery with three pot stills and a combined gin/vodka still and the first production of gin and vodka was in October 2012 with whiskey production commencing in December. The first whiskey, the limited Dingle Cask No. 2, was released in December 2015 and a general release was made in autumn 2016. Batch No. 3, a marriage of bourbon and port casks, was launched in July 2018.

The Shed Distillery

Drumshanbo, Co. Leitrim, founded in 2014

www.thesheddistillery.com

Founded by entrepreneur and drinks veteran P J Rigney, the distillery cost €2m to build and is equipped with three Holstein stills with columns attached. The focus for the owners will be triple distilled single pot still whiskey but a gin has been on the market for sevral years. The first whiskey distillation was in late 2014 and an un-official release from the first cask took place in December 2017. A general release isn´t expected until 2019.

Boann Distillery

Drogheda, Co. Meath, founded in 2016

boanndistillery.ie

Assisted by the well-known whisky consultant, John McDougall, Pat Cooney built the distillery which is equipped with three Italian-made copper pot stills and a gin still. The owners have used a new technology where the copper contact is enhanced using nano-crystal coating in the lyne arms. The first distillation was in July 2018 but in common with most Irish distillery start-ups, they have already launched a sourced whiskey called The Whistler.

Glendalough Distillery

Newtown Mount Kennedy, Co. Wicklow, founded in 2012

www.glendaloughdistillery.com

For the first three years, the company acted as an independent bottler. In 2015 Holstein stills were installed and gin production began. Apart from gin, the company regularly releases sourced whiskies. The most recent expressions include a 13 year old where Japanese Mizunara oak casks have been used for the maturation. In 2016, the Canadian drinks distribution group Mark Anthony Brands invested €5.5m in the distillery.

Slane Distillery

Slane, Co. Meath, founded in 2017

www.slaneirishwhiskey.com

The Conyngham family, owners of the Slane Castle and Estate since 1703, established a whiskey brand a few years ago which became popular not least in the USA. The whiskey was produced at Cooleys but the family decided to start a distillery of their own. After an unsuccesful partnership with Camus Wine & Spirits, Brown-Forman stepped in and took over the entire project in 2015. Equipped with three copper pot stills, six column stills and washbacks made of wood, the distillery started production in spring 2018. Three types of whiskey will be produced; single malt, single pot still and grain whiskey.

Ballykeefe Distillery

Ballykeefe, Co. Kilkenny, founded in 2017

www.ballykeefedistillery.ie

A classic farm distillery and the first to operate in Kilkenny for over 200 years. The distillery is equipped with two copper pot stills and apart from whiskey (first distillation in spring 2018), gin and vodka from potatoes is also produced.

Powerscourt Distillery

Enniskerry, Co. Wicklow, founded in 2017

www.powerscourtdistillery.com

The distillery is situated at the Powerscourt Estate, owned by the Slazenger family, south of Dublin. Three pot stills were ordered from Forsyths in Scotland and distillation started in autumn 2018. Noel Sweeney from Cooley Distillery is in charge of the distillery which has a capacity of producing 1 million bottles per year.

Lough Mask Distillery

Tourmakeady, Co. Mayo, founded in 2017

www.loughmaskdistillery.com

Equipped with two alambic stills, the distillery started production in early 2018. The whiskey is double distilled and both peated and unpeated spirit will be produced. The first whiskey will be released in 2021 but both gin and vodka are already for sale.

Blackwater Distillery

Ballyduff, Co. Kerry, founded in 2014

www.blackaterdistillery.ie

Originally located in Cappoquin, Co. Waterford, the distillery moved in 2018 to Ballyduff. At that time the company was already famous for their gin. In their new distillery, equipped with three stills from Frilli in Italy, whisky will now also be produced.

Italy

Puni Destillerie

Glurns, South Tyrol, founded in 2012

www.puni.com

There are at least two things that distinguish this distillery from most others. One is the design of the distillery – a 13-metre tall cube made of red brick. The other is the raw material that they are using. Malt whisky is produced but malted barley is only one of three cereals in the recipe. The other two are malted rye and malted wheat. In 2016, however, they also started distilling 100% malted barley and anticipate to release their first whisky from that production in 2019. The distillery is equipped with five washbacks made of local larch and the fermentation time is 84 hours. There is one wash still (3,000 litres) and one spirit still (2,000 litres) and the capacity is 80,000 litres of alcohol per year. The first single malt was released in October 2015 and the current core range consists of Nova (American oak), Alba (marsala casks with a finish in Islay casks) and Sole (two years in ex-bourbon and two years in PX casks). Recent limitd editions include two 5 year olds – Gold (ex-bourbon) and Vina (marsala casks).

Liechtenstein

Brennerei Telser
Triesen, founded in 1880 (whisky since 2006)
www.telserdistillery.com

Telser is probably the only distillery in Europe still using a wood fire to heat the small stills. Production mainly comprises spirits from fruits and berries. For whisky, the distillery uses a mixture of three different malts. After a 10 day fermentation, the spirit is triple distilled and the three different spirits are blended and filled into pinot noir barriques and left to mature for a minimum of three years. The first bottling was released in 2009. The most recent expression is L´Ultimo, matured in an ex-grappa casks.

The Netherlands

Zuidam Distillers
Baarle Nassau, founded in 1974 (whisky since 1998)
www.zuidam.eu

Zuidam Distillers was started in 1974 as a traditional, family distillery producing liqueurs, genever, gin and vodka and is today managed by Patrick van Zuidam. The first release of a single malt whisky, which goes by the name Millstone, was from the 2002 production and it was bottled in 2007 as a 5 year old. The current range is a 5 year old which comes in both peated and unpeated versions, American oak 10 years, French oak 10 years, Sherry oak 12 years and PX Cask 1999. Apart from single malts there is also a Millstone 100% Rye which is bottled at 50%. Limited expressions include Vintage 1996 Oloroso (released in 2016) and a 20 year old Vintage 1996 American oak (from 2017). In 2018 a peated single PX cask distilled in 2013 was released together with a peated, double matured single malt (American oak and moscatel casks), also distilled in 2013. The distillery has been expanded over the years and the equipment now consists of one mash tun for malt whisky, one for rye and genever and 10 washbacks. Furthermore, there are a total of five stills with volumes ranging from 850 litres up to 5,000 litres. The total capacity is 280,000 litres of pure alcohol per year. But the expansion continues and more stills for a new distillery were constructed at Forsyths in Scotland during spring 2018. The distillery has also started to grow their own barley and rye at a nearby farm.

Other distilleries in The Netherlands

Us Heit Distillery
Bolsward, founded in 2002
www.usheit.com

Frysk Hynder was the first Dutch whisky and made its debut in 2005 at 3 years of age. The barley is grown in surrounding Friesland and malted at the distillery. Some 10,000 bottles are produced annually and the whisky (3 to 5 years old) is matured in a variety of casks. A cask strength version has also been released.

Kalkwijck Distillers
Vroomshoop, founded in 2009
www.kalkwijckdistillers.nl

The distillery is equipped with a 300 litre pot still still with a column attached. The main part of the production is jenever,

korenwijn and liqueurs but whisky has been distilled since 2010. In spring 2015, the first single malt was released. Eastmoor was 3 years old, made from barley grown on the estate and bottled at 40%.

Stokerij Sculte
Ootmarsum, founded in 2004 (whisky since 2011)
www.stokerijsculte.nl

The distillery is equipped with a 500 litre stainless steel mashtun, 4 stainless steel washbacks with a fermentation time of 4-5 days and two stills. The first Sculte Twentse Whisky was released in 2014 and this was followed by a 4 year old in 2016. Velthuis is now working on new recipes, including a heavily peated whisky.

Lepelaar Distillery
Texel, founded in 2009 (whisky since 2014)
www.landgoeddebontebelevenis.nl

Joscha and Inge Schoots started a brewery and shop in 2009 and continued five years later by adding distilling equipment. The business is a part of a larger crafts centre. Single malt (both peated and unpeated) as well as grain whisky and genever is produced. A first, limited release of the whisky was made for the crowd funders in 2018 and will be followed later by a general release.

Northern Ireland

Bushmill´s Distillery
Bushmills, Co. Antrim, founded in 1784
www.bushmills.com

Diageo took the market by surprise when they announced in 2014 that they were selling the distillery. This was Diageo´s only part of the increasing Irish whiskey segment and commentators struggled to see the reason for the sale. The buyer was the tequila maker Casa Cuervo, producer of José Cuervo. Diageo already owned 50% of the company´s other, upscale tequila brand, Don Julio and with the deal, they got the remaining 50% as well as $408m.

Bushmills is the second biggest of the Irish distilleries after Midleton, with a capacity to produce 4,5 million litres of alcohol a year. In 1972 the distillery became a part of Irish Distillers Group which thereby gained control over the entire whiskey production in Ireland. Irish Distillers were later (1988) purchased by Pernod Ricard who, in turn, resold Bushmill´s to Diageo in 2005 at a price tag of €295.5 million. Since the take-over, Diageo invested heavily into the distillery and it now has ten stills with a production running seven days a week, which means 4,5 million litres a year. Two kinds of malt are used at Bushmills, one unpeated and one slightly peated. The new owners, Casa Cuervo, applied for a planning permission to expand the capacity and also to build another 29 warehouses on adjacent farmland. The approval process proved to be quite difficult due to environmental objections but in August 2018, it looked as though the local council were about to give the green light.

Bushmill`s core range of single malts consists of a 10 year old, a 16 year old Triple Wood with a finish in Port pipes for 6-9 months and a 21 year old finished in Madeira casks for two years. There is also a 12 year old Distillery Reserve which is sold exclusively at the distillery and the 1608 Anniversary Edition. Black Bush and Bushmill´s Original are the two main blended whiskeys in the range but in December 2017 a third expression was added to the range – Bushmills Red Bush. The first new expression from the distillery for the domestic market in five years, Red Bush is a blend of triple distilled single malt and grain whiskey. In spring 2016, Bushmill´s launched their first whiskey exclusive for duty free, The Steamship Collection, with three special cask matured whiskies plus a number of limited releases. The first part of the series was Sherry Cask Reserve which was followed up in autumn 2016 by Port Cask Reserve and in autumn 2017 by Bourbon #3 Char Cask Reserve. Bushmill´s is the third most sold Irish whiskey after Jameson and Tullamore D.E.W.

Other distilleries in Northern Ireland

Echlinville Distillery

Kircubbin, Co. Down, founded in 2013

www.echlinville.com

After having relied on Cooley Distillery for his mature whiskey, Shane Braniff decided in 2012 to build his own distillery. Located near Kircubbin on the Ards Peninsula he started production in August 2013. The distillery was further expanded with more equipment in 2015 and in April 2016, a visitor centre opened. The distillery also has its own floor maltings. Apart from single pot still and single malt whiskey, vodka and gin is also produced. Braniff recently revived the old Dunville´s brand of blended whiskey and released a 10 year old single malt with a finish in PX sherry casks. The latest expression was Dunville´s Three Crowns Peated. All these have been made from sourced whiskey. The first bottlings from the distillery´s own production will not be released any time soon.

Rademon Estate Distillery

Downpatrick, Co. Down, founded in 2012

shortcrossgin.com

Fiona and David Boyd-Armstrong opened their distillery on the Rademon estate in 2012, which was owned by Frank Boyd, the father of Fiona. Since its inception, their main product has been Short Cross gin which quickly became a success story. In summer 2015 the production was expanded into whiskey and during the first year, around 100 barrels were filled. Through a £2.5m investment, the capacity of the distillery was further increased in 2018 with a new gin still as well as a new still for the whiskey production. More washbacks were also installed. The couple plan to release their first single malt whiskey in late 2018 or early 2019.

Norway

Det Norske Brenneri

Grimstad, founded in 1952 (whisky since 2009)

www.detnorskebrenneri.no

Founded in 1952 the company mainly produced wine from apples and other fruits. IWhisky production started in 2009 and two Holstein stills are used for the distillation. In 2012, Audny, the first single malt produced in Norway was launched. Recent bottlings

Red Bush - a new core expression from Bushmills

include Arvesölvet Kjernekar Single Cask, matured in casks that held apple aquavit and Eiktyrne Rin og Rennande, matured in ex Pineau des Charentes casks.

Other distilleries in Norway

Myken Distillery

Myken, founded in 2014

www.mykendestilleri.no

This distillery was built in Myken, a group of islands in the Atlantic ocean, 32 kilometres from mainland Norway. They distilled their first spirit in 2014 and the equipment consists of one wash still (1,000 litres), one spirit still (700 litres) and one gin still (300 litres). Both peated and unpeated whisky is produced. The first release of Myken Single Malt was in September 2018 (just 10 bottles) which was followed by another 700 bottles in November.

Arcus

Gjelleråsen, founded in 1996 (whisky since 2009)

www.arcus.no

Arcus is the biggest supplier and producer of wine and spirits in Norway with subsidaries in Denmark, Finland and Sweden. The first whisky produced by the distillery was launched in 2013. Under the name Gjoleid, two whiskies made from malted barley and malted wheat were released. More recent bottlings, some up to 5 years old, include Blindpassasjeren and Praksis 1.1 and 1.2.

Aurora Spirit

Tromsö, founded in 2016

www.auroraspirit.com

At 69.39°N, Aurora is the northernmost distillery in the world. The mash is bought from a brewery, fermented at the distillery and distilled in the 1,200 litre Kothe pot still with an attached column. Both non-peated and peated whisky will be produced. The plan is to produce at least 25,000 litres in 2020. Apart from single malt whisky, the owners also produce gin, vodka and aquavit. All their products are sold under the name Bivrost.

Oss Craft Distillery

Flesland, founded in 2016

www.osscraft.no

Specialising in gin and other spirits made from herbs and botanicals, the distillery has already launched a range of spirits under the name Bareksten (from the founder and owner Stig Bareksten). In 2017, production of malt whisky began as well.

Spain

Distilerio Molino del Arco

Segovia, foundd in 1959

www.dyc.es

The distillery has a capacity for producing eight million litres of grain whisky and two million litres of malt whisky per year. In addition to that, vodka and rum are produced and there are also in-house maltings. The distillery is equipped with six copper pot stills and there are 250,000 casks maturing on site. The big seller when it comes to whiskies is a blend simply called DYC which is around 4 years old. It is supplemented by an 8 year old blend and, since 2007, also by DYC Pure Malt, a blend of malt from the distillery and from Scottish distilleries. To commemorate the distillery's 50th anniversary in 2009, they released a 10 year old single malt.

Other distilleries in Spain

Destilerias Liber

Padul, Granada, founded in 2001

www.destileriasliber.com

Apart from whisky, the distillery produces rum, marc and vodka.
For the whisky production, the spirit is double distilled after a
fermentation of 48-72 hours. Maturation takes place in sherry casks.
The only available whisky on the market is a 5 year old single malt
called Embrujo de Granada.

Sweden

High Coast Distillery (former BOX Distillery)

Bjärtrå, founded in 2010

www.boxwhisky.se

Set in buildings from the 19th century, the distillery started
production in November 2010. Sales of their whisky, first released
in 2014, has exceeded the owners´ expectations and in 2018
the distillery was expanded. The equipment now consists of a
semilauter mash tun with a capacity of 1,5 tonnes, ten stainless steel
washbacks, two wash stills (3,800 litres) and two spirit stills (2,500
litres). The expansion has increased capacity from 100,000 litres
to 300,000. In June 2014 an excellent visitor centre was opened
which today attracts more than 10,000 visitors yearly. In 2017,
the distillery was contacted by representatives of the independent
bottler Compass Box Whisky who stated that there was a risk of
confusion between the two names. Established several years after
Compass Box, the Swedish distillery decided to change their brand
name to High Coast in order to avoid a legal claim.

The distillery makes two types of whisky – fruity/unpeated and
peated. The distillery manager, Roger Melander, wants to create a
new make which is as clean as possible by using a very slow distillation process with lots of copper contact in the still. The flavour of
the spirit is also impacted by the effective condensation using what
might be the coldest cooling water in the whisky world, namely
2-6ºC, which is obtained from a nearby river. A fermentation time
of 72-96 hours also affects the character. An interesting experiment
was started in 2016 when 100 small casks made of Japanese oak
(Quercus mongolica) were filled with new make.

The first whisky, The Pioneer, was released in June 2014. Between
3 and 4 years old, it was a vatting of unpeated and lightly peated
whisky, predominantly from bourbon casks but also a small amount
of ex-sherry. The whisky was the first in a range of four called
Early Days Collection. In 2017, the first core expression, Dàlvve,
was launched and in autumn that year, a new range, Quercus, was
introduced where four expressions highlighting the influence of the
oak will be released successively.

Mackmyra Svensk Whisky

Valbo, founded in 1999

www.mackmyra.se

Mackmyra´s first distillery was built in 1999 and, ten years later,
the company revealed plans to build a brand new facility in Gävle,
a few miles from the present distillery. In 2012, the distillery was
ready and the first distillation took place in spring of that year. The
construction of the new distillery is quite extraordinary and with
its 37 metre structure, it is perhaps one of the tallest distilleries in
the world. Since April 2013, all the distillation takes place at this
new gravitation distillery. In 2017 however, the old distillery was
re-opened as the Lab Distillery where the company aim to develop
innovative spirits in collaboration with craft distillers.

Mackmyra whisky is based on two basic recipes, one which
produces a fruity and elegant whisky, while the other is smokier.
The first release was in 2006 and the distillery now has four core
expressions; Svensk Ek, Brukswhisky, the peated Svensk Rök and,
new since 2015, MACK by Mackmyra which competes in the lower
price segment. A range of limited editions called Moment was
introduced in 2010 and consists of exceptional casks selected by
the Master Blender, Angela D`Orazio. Two of the latest editions are
Svensk Ek 2008 (maturation in small casks made of Swedish oak)
and Fjällmark where part of the whisky had matured in casks that
had previously held cloudberry wine. Seasonal expressions are also
released regularly with Gruvguld being one of the latest. The major
part of the whisky (whish was between 5 and 16 years old) was
from small casks that had matured in a abandoned mine. In 2017,
Mackmyra was also the first Swedish distillery to release a bottling
exclusively for the travel retail market – Expedition.

Spirit of Hven

Hven, founded in 2007

www.hven.com

The second Swedish distillery to come on stream, situated on
the island of Hven right between Sweden and Denmark. The
first distillation took place in May 2008. Henric Molin, founder
and owner, is a trained chemist and very concerned about what
type of yeast and grain he uses not to mention the right oak for
his casks. The distillery is equipped with a 0,5 ton mash tun, six
washbacks made of stainless steel, one wash still, one spirit still
and a designated gin still. Apart from that, a unique wooden Coffey
still was recently installed. Part of the barley is malted on site using
Swedish peat, sometimes mixed with seaweed and sea-grass, for
drying. The distillery has also expanded the whisky production to
include rye and corn. Apart from whisky, other products include
rum made from sugar beet, vodka, gin and aquavit.

Their first whisky was the lightly peated Urania, released in 2012.
The second launch was the start of a new series of limited releases
called The Seven Stars. The first expression was the 5 year old,
lightly peated Dubhe, which was followed by Merak, Phecda,
Megrez, Alioth and, in 2018, Mizar and Alcor. The first and so far

The unique wooden Coffey still at Spirit of Hven

only core expression, Tycho´s Star, was released in 2015. Upcoming releases include their first rye whisky in December 2018 while their first whisky made from corn will appear in summer 2019.

Smögen Whisky
Hunnebostrand, founded in 2010

www.smogenwhisky.se

Pär Caldenby – a lawyer, whisky enthusiast and the author of Enjoying Malt Whisky - is the founder and owner of Smögen Whisky on the west coast of Sweden. The distillery is equipped with three washbacks (1,600 litres each), a wash still (900 litres) and a spirit still (600 litres) and the capacity is 35,000 litres of alcohol a year. An interesting addition to the equipment setup was made in summer 2018 when Pär installed worm tubs to cool the spirits. Heavily peated malt is imported from Scotland and the aim is to produce an Islay-type of whisky. The first release from the distillery was the 3 year old Primör in 2014. This has over the years been followed by many limited releases. The most recent, in June 2018, was the 5 year old Sherry Quarters matured in 120 litre sherry casks made of American white oak..

Other distilleries in Sweden

Norrtelje Brenneri
Norrtälje, founded in 2002 (whisky since 2009)

www.norrteljebrenneri.se

The production consists mainly of spirits from ecologically grown fruits and berries. Since 2009, a single malt whisky from ecologically grown barley is also produced. The first bottling was released in summer 2015 and several limited editions have followed.

Gammelstilla Whisky
Torsåker, founded in 2005

www.gammelstilla.se

Unlike most of the other Swedish whisky distilleries, the owners chose to design and build their pot stills themselves. The wash still has a capacity of 600 litres and the spirit still 300 litres and the annual capacity is 20,000 litres per year. The first, limited release for shareholders was in May 2017 with a general release in January 2018 of Jern, a 4 year old matured in a combination of ex-bourbon and ex-oloroso casks.

Gotland Whisky
Romakloster, founded in 2011

www.gotlandwhisky.se

The distillery is equipped with one wash still (1,600 litres) and one spirit still (900 litres). The local barley is ecologically grown and malted on site. The floor malting is made easier through the use of a malting robot of their own construction which turns the barley. Both unpeated and peated whisky is produced and the capacity is 60,000 litres per year. The first limited release of Isle of Lime single malt was in early 2017 with a general launch in August. A new expression, Midak, was released in May 2018.

Uppsala Destilleri
Uppsala, founded in 2015

www.uppsaladestilleri.se

With a yearly production of 1,500 litres (but with a goal to increase production in the future) this is currently one of the smallest distilleries in the country. Production started in early 2016 with a 100 litre alambic still from Portugal but yet another still has already been installed. Apart from whisky, gin and rum are also produced.

Tevsjö Destilleri
Järvsö, founded in 2012

www.tevsjodestilleri.se

The owners of this combination of distillery and restaurang are primarily focused on distillation of aquavit and other white spirits and malt whisky production did not start until spring 2017. However, whisky has been produced earlier in the way of a "bourbon" with a mash bill of 70% corn, 10% malted barley, 10% unmalted barley, 5% wheat and 5% rye.

Agitator Whiskymakare
Arboga, founded in 2017

www.agitatorwhisky.se

The owners of this new distillery have chosen some rather unusual techniques in the production. Water is added during the milling in order to make the mashing more efficient. The same fermented wash is split in half and distributed to the two pairs of stills in order to achieve different characters. The stills, by the way, operate under vacuum which is extremely rare in pot still whisky making. Finally, the maturation takes place in casks where extra staves have been inserted, some of them made from chestnut. The distillery has a capacity of 500,000 litres of pure alcohol and the first distillation was made in February 2018.

Switzerland 

Whisky Castle
Elfingen, Aargau, founded in 2002

www.whisky-castle.com

The first whisky from this distillery, founded by Ruedi Käser, reached the market in 2004. It was a single malt under the name Castle Hill. Since then the range of malt whiskies has been expanded and today include Castle Hill Doublewood (3 years old matured both in casks made of chestnut and oak), Whisky Smoke Barley (at least 3 years old matured in new oak), Fullmoon (matured in casks from Hungary), Terroir (4 years old made from Swiss barley and matured in Swiss oak), Cask Strength (5 years old and bottled at 58%) and Edition Käser (71% matured in new oak casks from Bordeaux). Recent additions include Castle One and Family Reserve.

Brauerei Locher
Appenzell, founded in 1886 (whisky since 1999)

www.saentismalt.com

Brauerei Locher is unique in using old beer casks for the maturation. The core range consists of three expressions; Himmelberg, bottled at 43%, Dreifaltigkeit which is slightly peated having matured in toasted casks and bottled at 52% and, finally, Sigel which has matured in very small casks and is bottled at 40%. A range of limited bottlings under the name Alpstein is also available. The most recent, Edition XIV, was released in 2018 and had matured in beer casks for five years and then another two years in casks that had held a sweet, red wine from Spain. Snow White is another limited range where the latest release was a 5 year old with another year in casks that had previously held Marillenbrand.

Other distilleries in Switzerland

Langatun Distillery
Langenthal, Bern, founded in 2007

www.langatun.ch

The distillery was built in 2005 and under the same roof as the brewery Brau AG Langenthal. The casks used for maturation are all 225 litres and Swiss oak (Chardonnay), French oak (Chardonnay and red wine) and ex sherry casks are used. The two 5 year old core expressions are Old Deer and the peated Old Bear. Other bottlings include the single cask rye Old Eagle, a single cask "bourbon" Old Mustang, the triple matured Swiss Pipe and the organic Old Woodpecker. Recent limited bottlings include Winter Wedding, Jacob´s Dram and a Rioja cask finish.

Bauernhofbrennerei Lüthy

Muhen, Aargau, founded in 1997 (whisky since 2005)

www.brennerei-luethy.ch

The first single malt from the distillery was Insel-Whisky, matured in Chardonnay casks and released in 2008. Several releases have since followed. Starting in 2010, the yearly bottling was given the name Herr Lüthy and the 12th release from these had been matured in a combination of chardonnay casks, ex-oloroso casks and ex.bourbon barrels. Since 2016, whisky from malted rice is also produced!

Brennerei Stadelmann

Altbüron, Luzern, founded in 1932 (whisky since 2003)

www.schnapsbrennen.ch

The distillery is equipped with three Holstein-type stills and the first generally available bottling (a 3 year old) appeared in 2010. In autumn 2014, the sixth release was made, matured in a Bordeaux cask. The first whisky from smoked barley was distilled in 2012.

Etter Distillerie

Zug, founded in 1870 (whisky since 2007)

www.etter-distillerie.ch

The main produce from this distillery is eau de vie from various fruits and berries. A sidetrack to the business was entered in 2007 when they decided to distil their first malt whisky. The first release was made in 2010 under the name Johnett Single Malt Whisky and this is currently sold as a 7 year old. In 2016, a limited Johnett with a 12 months finish in Caroni rum casks was released.

Spezialitätenbrennerei Zürcher

Port, Bern, founded in 1954 (whisky from 2000)

www.lakeland-whisky.ch

The main focus of the distillery is specialising in various distillates of fruit, absinth and liqueur but a Lakeland single malt is also in the range. A limited version was released in June 2018 - an 8 year old which had matured the whole time in a Chateau d`Yquem cask.

Whisky Brennerei Hollen

Lauwil, Baselland, founded in 1999

www.single-malt.ch

The first Swiss whisky was distilled at Hollen in July 1999. In the beginning most bottlings were 4-5 years old but in 2009 the first 10 year old was released and there has also been a 12 year old, the oldest expression from the distillery so far.

Z´Graggen Distillerie

Lauerz, Schwyz, founded in 1948

www.zgraggen.ch

Focusing mainly on spirits distilled from fruits and berries, the owners also produce gin, vodka and whisky. The distillery is quite large, with a combined production of 400,000 litres per year. There are three single malts in the range – 3, 8 and 10 years old.

Wales

Penderyn Distillery

Penderyn, founded in 2000

www.penderyn.wales

In 1998 four private individuals started The Welsh Whisky Company and two years later, the first Welsh distillery in more than a hundred years started distilling. A new type of still, developed by David Faraday for Penderyn Distillery, differs from the Scottish and Irish procedures in that the whole process from wash to new make takes place in one single still. In September 2013, a second still (almost a replica of the first still) was commissioned and in June 2014, two traditional pot stills, as well as their own mashing equipment was installed. The expansion increased the production from 90,000 litres to 300,000 litres of alcohol per annum.

The first single malt was launched in 2004. The core range today is divided into two groups. Dragon consists of the Madeira finished Legend, Myth which is fully bourbon matured and Celt with a peated finish. They are all bottled at 41%. The other range is Gold with Madeira, Peated, Portwood and Sherrywood bottled at 46%. Over the years, the company has released several single casks and limited releases and a new range of whiskies called Icons of Wales was introduced in 2012 with the fifth edition, Bryn Terfel, being released in 2016. Recent limited editions also include Rich Oak and Rich Oak Single Cask. A visitor centre opened in 2008.

Other distilleries in Wales

Dà Mhìle Distillery

Llandyssul, founded in 2013

www.damhile.co.uk

Focusing on gin and grain whisky but there is also a single malt in the pipeline. Meanwhile, they have been offering aged, organic single malts that were distilled by Springbank back in the 1990s, when John Savage-Onstwedder, one of the founders, commissioned Springbank to produce the world´s first organic whisky

Aber Falls Distillery

Abergwyngregyn, founded in 2017

www.aberfallsdistillery.com

In comon with so many other distilleries, Aber Falls started producing gin and the first product was released in late 2017. Whisky, however, is also in the plan and by June 2018, onehundred casks had been filled. A visitor centre was opened in May 2018.

Lantern stills at Penderyn Distillery

North America

USA

Westland Distillery

Seattle, Washington, founded in 2011

westlanddistillery.com

Unlike most of the new craft distilleries in the USA producing whiskey, Westland Distillery did not distill other spirits to finance the early stages of production. Until November 2012, Westland was a medium sized craft distillery where they brought in the wash from a nearby brewery and had the capacity of doing 60,000 litres of whiskey per year. During the summer of 2013 the owners, the Lamb family, moved to another location which is equipped with a 6,000 litre brewhouse, five 10,000 litre fermenters and two Vendome stills (7,560 and 5,670 litres respectively). The capacity is now 260,000 litres per year. In 2017, global spirits giant Remy Cointreau bought Westland Distillery. According to Westland master distiller and co-founder Matt Hoffman, the buyer's views, not least on the influence of terroir, were very much in line with Westland's way of working. The distillery has been focusing on local barley varieties and also local peat which differs hugely from peat used in for example Scotland.

The first 5,500 bottles of their core expression, Westland American Single Malt Whiskey, were released in 2013. The current core range consists of American Oak and Peated Malt, both matured in a combination of new American oak and first fill bourbon casks and Sherry Wood which has matured in new American oak as well as in casks that previously held Oloroso and PX sherry. All three varieties have been mashed with a 5-malt grain bill and the wash has been fermented for 6 days. Over the years there have also been more than 70 different releases of single casks. Apart from experimenting with a multitude of different barley varieties, Westland is also exploring different types of oak for maturation. One of them, Garry oak, is native to the Pacific Northwest and has previously never been used for whisky maturation. Westland has so far launched two batches where 20% of the whisky was matured in casks made from Garry oak. The project even has its own designated website - westlandgarryana.com.

Balcones Distillery

Waco, Texas, founded in 2008

balconesdistilling.com

Originally founded by Chip Tate who left the company in 2014, Balcones is celebrating it's 10th anniversary this year. All of Balcones' whisky is mashed, fermented and distilled on site and they were the first to use Hopi blue corn for distillation. The core range currently consists of six expressions; Texas Single Malt, two corn whiskies made from blue corn, Baby Blue and True Blue 100, Brimstone Smoked Whiskey, Rumble (with honey, turbinado sugar and figs added to the recipe) and Texas 100 Rye - the first rye from the distillery and the latest to be added to the range. Limited expressions, some of them launched to celebrate the 10th anniversary, include two single malts, Peated and Mirador, Texas Rum, Texas Blue Corn Bourbon and True Blue Cask Strength. All whiskies are un chill-filtered and without colouring. The demand for Balcones whiskies grew rapidly and in January 2014, another four, small stills were installed. The big step though, was a completely new distillery which was built 5 blocks from the old site. Distillation started in February 2016 and the official opening was in April. The new distillery is equipped with two pairs of stills and five fermenters and they now distill approximately 350,000 litres per year.

Stranahans Whiskey Distillery

Denver, Colorado, founded in 2003

stranahans.com

Founded by Jess Graber and George Stranahan, the distillery was bought by New York based Proximo Spirits (makers of Hangar 1 Vodka and Kraken Rum among others) in 2010. Stranahans Colorado Whiskey is always made in batches aged from two to five years and since 2004, more than 200 batches have been released. Except for the core expression, the range is made up of Diamond Peak, a vatting of casks that are around 4 years old, a Single Barrel and, launched in autumn 2017, Sherry cask. The latter is a version where the classic single malt has received a finish in oloroso sherry butts. Every year in December there is the a release of the limited Snowflake edition. In December 2017 it was Quandary Peak which was a vatting of whiskies that had matured in casks that had previously contained rum, madeira, cognac, port and sangiovese red wine.

Hood River Distillers

Hood River, Oregon, 1934

hrdspirits.com

Since the foundation, the company acts as importer, distiller, producer and bottler of all kinds of spirits. Some of the products are distilled in-house while others are sourced. The role in the single malt segment came through buying Clear Creek Distillery in 2014. Founded by Steve McCarthy the distillery was one of the first to produce malt whiskey in the USA but was most famous for their eau-de-vie made from pears. The only whisky produced by the company was the peated McCarthy's Oregon Single Malt. In December 2017, Clear Creek closed their distillery in Portland in

Balcones distillery sign

order to move it to Hood River. In the meantime, the whisky can be bought at the Hood River distillery tasting room. The new Clear Creek distillery will not be open to the public.

Tuthilltown Spirits

Gardiner, New York, founded in 2003

tuthilltown.com

The distillery, 80 miles north of New York City, was founded in 2003 by Ralph Erenzo and Brian Lee. In 2010, William Grant & Sons avquired the Hudson Whiskey brand while the founders still owned the distillery. In spring 2017, William Grant followed up the deal by buying the entire company. The first products came onto the shelves in 2006 in New York and the whiskey range now consists of Hudson Baby Bourbon, a 2-4 year old bourbon made from 100% New York corn and the company´s biggest seller by far, Four Grain Bourbon (corn, rye, wheat and malted barley), Single Malt Whiskey (aged in small, new, charred American oak casks), Manhattan Rye, Maple Cask Rye and New York Corn Whiskey. The most recent limited release (November 2017) was the single barrel Empire Rye made exclusively with New York rye. There is also gin, vodka and liqueur in the range.

RoughStock Distillery

Bozeman, Montana, founded in 2005

montanawhiskey.com

The owners, Kari and Bryan Schultz, buy the 100% Montana grown and malted barley and then mill and mash it themselves. It is then fermented on the grain in two 1,000 gallon open top wooden fermenters for a 72 hour fermentation before distillation in two Vendome copper pot stills. In 2009, the first bottles of RoughStock Montana Pure Malt Whiskey were released. Since then a single barrel bottled at cask strength has been added (Black Label Montana Whiskey) and apart from whiskey made from 100% malted barley, the product range also includes whiskey made from wheat and rye and bourbon.

Copper Fox Distillery

Sperryville, Virginia, founded in 2000

www.copperfoxdistillery.com

Founded in 2000 by Rick Wasmund, the distillery moved to another site in 2006 and in November 2016, he opened up a second distillery in Williamsburg. Wasmund does his own floor malting of barley and it is dried using smoke from selected fruitwood. After mashing, fermentation and distillation, the spirit is filled into oak barrels, together with plenty of hand chipped and toasted chips of apple and cherry trees, as well as oak wood. The first single malts (known as Red Top) were just four months old but the current batches are more around 12-16 months. An older version, Blue Top, has matured for up to 42 months. Other expressions include Peachwood Single Malt and Copper Fox Rye Whiskey with a mash bill of 2/3 Virginia rye and 1/3 malted barley.

St. George Distillery

Alameda, California, founded in 1982

stgeorgespirits.com

The distillery is situated in a hangar at Alameda Point, the old naval air station at San Fransisco Bay. It was founded by Jörg Rupf, who came to California in 1979 and who was to become one of the forerunners when it came to craft distilling in America. In 1996, Lance Winters joined him and today he is Distiller, as well as co-owner. In 2005, the two were joined by Dave Smith who now has the sole responsibility for the whisky production. The main produce is based on eau-de-vie which is produced from locally grown fruit, and vodka under the brand name Hangar One. Whiskey production was picked up in 1996 and the first single malt appeared on the market in 1999. St. George Single Malt used to be sold as a three year old but, nowadays, comes to the market as a blend of whiskeys aged from 4 to 16 years. The latest release was Lot 18 in October 2018 and every lot is around 3-4,000 bottles. A new addition to the range was released in 2016. Baller is aged 3-4 years and the malt whiskey has been filtered through maple charcoal and then finished in casks that held house-made umeshu (a Japanese style of plum liqueur).

Corsair Distillery

Bowling Green, Kentucky and Nashville, Tennessee, founded in 2008

corsairdistillery.com

The two founders of Corsair, Darek Bell and Andrew Webber, first opened up a distillery in Bowling Green, Kentucky and two years later, another one in Nashville, Tennessee (followed by a second one in Nashville a few years later). In March 2018 a third site in Nashville was acquired for $6,8m. This will be used for warehousing, distilling, offices etc. Apart from producing around 20 different types of beer, the brewery is also where the wash for all the whisky production takes place. Corsair Distillery has a wide range of spirits – gin, vodka, absinthe, rum and whiskey. The number of different whiskies released is growing constantly and the owners are experimenting with different types of grain. The big sellers are Triple Smoke Single Malt Whiskey (made from three different types of smoked malt) and Ryemaggedon (made from malted rye and chocolate rye). Recent additions to the range include

Copper Fox Distillery

Hydra (made with malt that has been dried with five different types of local wood), Green Malt (100% very lightly kilned barley malt) and Grainiac - a bourbon made with 9 different grains.

House Spirits

Portland, Oregon, founded in 2004

housespirits.com

In 2015, Christian Krogstad and Matt Mount moved their distillery a few blocks to bigger premises. The main products for House Spirits used to be Aviation Gin and Krogstad Aquavit but with their new equipment they drastically increased whiskey capacity from 150 barrels per year to 4,000 barrels! The first three whiskies were released in 2009 and in 2012 it was time for the first, widely available single malt under the name of Westward Whiskey. It was a 2 year old, double pot distilled and matured in new American oak. Recent releases have been up to 5 years old and now each release is a single barrel. A limited edition made from 100% barley grown in Oregon was released in summer 2018.

Kings County Distillery

Brooklyn, New York, founded in 2010

kingscountydistillery.com

This distillery is the oldest and largest in Brooklyn. The founders, Colin Spoelman and David Haskell, have made a name for themselves as being both experimental and yet at the same time true to traditional Scottish methods of distilling whiskey. The wash is fermented for four days in open-top, wooden fermenters and they practise a double distillation with a narrow middle cut in two copper pot stills made by Forsyths in Scotland. They use organic corn from upstate New York and malted barley from the UK. The first single malt (60% unpeated and 40% peated), matured in ex-bourbon barrels was distilled in 2012 but didn't hit the market until 2016. It has then been released in batches aged between 1.5 and 4 years. In the product range is also bourbon with the unusual mash bill of 60% corn and 40% malted barley. Even more unusual is their peated bourbon! Apart from producing whiskey, Colin and David have shared their vision and knowledge in two books; The Guide to Urban Moonshining and Dead Distillers.

Virginia Distillery

Lovingston, Virginia, 2008 (production started 2015)

vadistillery.com

The whole idea for this distillery was conceived by Chris Allwood in 2007, but he left the company in 2010 and several changes in ownership have occurred since then, the last one being in spring 2016. Even though the copper pot stills arrived from Turkey in 2008 (having been bought second hand from the Turkish government), the company was struggling with the financing and the first distillation didn't take place until November 2015. The distillery has the capacity of making 1.1 million litres of alcohol and is equipped with a 3.75 ton mash tun, 8 washbacks, a 10,000 litre wash still and a 7,000 litre spirit still. Only sourced whisky (from Scotland) is currently available under their label. The first single malt from own production is expected 2020.

Long Island Spirits

Baiting Hollow, New York, founded in 2007

www.lispirits.com

Long Island Spirits, founded by Rich Stabile, is the first distillery on the island since the 1800s. The starting point for The Pine Barrens Whisky, the first single malt from the distillery, is a finished ale with hops and all. The beer is distilled twice in a potstill and matures for one year in a 10 gallon, new, American, white oak barrel. The whisky was first released in 2012 The range also includes bourbon and rye. In 2018, the distillery released the first American single malt bottled in bond. The bottled-in-bond act stipulates that the spirit must come from a single distillery, from a single season and that it must have been matured for at least four years.

Great Wagon Road Distilling Co.

Charlotte, North Carolina, founded in 2014

gwrdistilling.com

The distillery, founded by Ollie Mulligan, started with a 15 litre still but is now equipped with a 3,000 litres Kothe still in the 15,000 sq foot facility. The mash comes from a neighbouring brewery and the fermentation is made in-house in four tanks. The first batch of his Rua Single Malt was launched at Christmas 2015 and several batches have since followed, including vodka and Drumlish poteen. New releases in 2018 will include a straight Rua single malt, two finishes - port and sherry and a rye whiskey.

Hamilton Distillers

Tucson, Arizona, founded in 2011

www.hamiltondistillers.com

Having worked as a manufacturer of furniture made from local mesquite wood, Stephen Paul came up with the idea of drying barley over mesquite, instead of peat. He started his distillery using a 40 gallon still but since 2014, a 500 gallon still is in place. In spring 2015, new malting equipment was installed which made it possible to malt the barley in 5,000 lbs batches, instead of the previous 70 lbs! The first bottlings appeared in 2013 and they now have three expressions – aged Mesquite smoked (Dorado), aged unsmoked (Classic) and unaged Mesquite smoked (Clear). Recent limited releases include Winter Release and a cask strength version called Distiller's Cut.

Deerhammer Distilling Company

Buena Vista, Colorado, founded in 2010

www.deerhammer.com

The location of the distillery at an altitude of 2,500 metres with drastic temperature fluctuations and virtually no humidity, have a huge impact on the maturation of the spirit. Owners Lenny and Amy Eckstein found that their first whiskey, based on five varieties of malted barley, was ready to be released after only 9 months' maturation in December 2012. More and older batches (2 to 3 years) of their Deerhammer Single Malt have followed including a port cask finish. A new series called Progeny was launched in 2018 where the owners collaborate with other craftsmen in Colorado. So far their single malt has been finished in casks that have held cacao as well as lager.

Hillrock Estate Distillery

Ancram, New York, founded in 2011

www.hillrockdistillery.com

What makes this distillery unusual, at least in the USA, is that they are not just malting their own barley – they are floor malting it. This a technique that has been abandoned even in Scotland, except for a handful of distilleries. Jeff Baker founded the distillery in 2011 and equipped it with a 250 gallon Vendome pot still and five fermentation tanks. The first spirit was distilled in November 2011. The first release from the distillery was in 2012, the Solera Aged Bourbon. Today, the range has been expanded with a Single Malt and a Double Cask Rye. Over the years, limited bottlings have appeared such as the peated Single Malt and a Napa cabernet cask finished bourbon.

Santa Fe Spirits

Santa Fe, New Mexico, founded in 2010

www.santafespirits.com

Colin Keegan, the owner of Santa Fe Spirits, is collaborating with Santa Fe Brewing Company which supplies the un-hopped beer that is fermented and distilled in a 1,000 litre copper still from Christian Carl in Germany. The whiskey gets a hint of smokiness from mesquite. The first product, Silver Coyote released in 2011, was an unaged malt whiskey. The first release of an aged (2 years) single malt whiskey, Colkegan, was in October 2013. Since then, the range has been expanded to include also a version finished in apple brandy casks and one bottled at cask strength.

Copperworks Distilling Company

Seattle, Washington, founded in 2013

www.copperworksdistilling.com

Jason Parker and Micah Nutt, both come from a brewing background and that is also where their whiskey comes from. They obtain their wash from a local brewery and then ferment it on site. The distillery is equipped with two, large copper pot stills for the whiskey production, one smaller pot still for the gin and one column still. The whiskey is matured in 53-gallon charred, American oak barrels. The first distillation was in 2014 and the first batch of the single malt was released in September 2016. The latest batch (#12) was released in 2018 and is a combination of their two recipes - five malt and pale malt.

Rogue Ales & Spirits

Newport, Oregon, founded in 2009

www.rogue.com

The company has gradually expanded over the years and now consists of one brewery, two combined brewery/pubs, two distillery pubs and five pubs scattered over Oregon, Washington and California. The main business is still producing Rogue Ales, but apart from whiskey, rum and gin are also distilled. The first malt whiskey, Dead Guy Whiskey, was launched in 2009. In April 2016, it was time for the first straight malt whiskey - Oregon Single Malt Whiskey, aged for at least two years. It was made from barley grown and floor malted on Rogue´s own farm in Tygh Valley. Spring 2018, saw the launch of the company´s first 5 year old single malt as well as a 3 year old rye malt whiskey.

FEW Spirits

Evanston, Illinois, founded in 2010

fewspirits.com

Former attorney (and founder of a rock and roll band) Paul Hletko started this distillery in Evanston, a suburb in Chicago in 2010. It is equipped with three stills; a Vendome column still and two Kothe hybrid stills. Bourbon and rye had been on the market for a couple of years when the first single malt, with some of the malt being smoked with cherry wood, was released in 2015. In spring 2017, a limited vatting of bourbon, rye and single malt whiskies was released for the 23rd anniversary of legendary Chicago bar Delilah´s. Other limited releases include bourbons finished in Italian red wine casks and casks that had previously held American brandy.

Sons of Liberty Spirits Co.

South Kingstown, Rhode Island, founded in 2010

www.solspirits.com

Michael Reppucci started the distillery with the help of David Pickerell who was Master Distiller for Maker´s Mark for 13 years. This distillery is equipped with a stainless steel mash tun, stainless steel, open top fermenters and one 950 litre combined pot and column still from Vendome. Sons of Liberty is first and foremost a whiskey distillery, but the first product launched was Loyal 9 Vodka. In 2011 the double distilled Uprising American Whiskey was launched, made from a stout beer and it was followed in early 2014 by Battle Cry made from a Belgian style ale. Both Uprising and Battle Cry have also been released as sherry finishes.

Do Good Distillery

Modesto, California, founded in 2013

dogooddistillery.com

Founded in 2013 by six friends and family members, the goal was to make whiskey and, in particular, single malt. First production was in autumn 2014 and since autumn 2015 a number of different releases have been made; Beechwood Smoked, Peat Smoked, Cherrywood Smoked - all of them single malts - and The Nighthawk bourbon. A couple of the latest additions include The Benevolent Czar – a dark single malt from a combination of pale malt, crystal malt and chocolate malt - and a hop flavoured single malt. Due to a recent expansion of the distillery (including two more stills) the owners can now produce the equivalent of 200,000 bottles per year. In summer 2017, co-founder Jim Harrelson died from a heart attack at the age of 38.

Other distilleries in USA

Dry Fly Distilling

Spokane, Washington, founded in 2007

www.dryflydistilling.com

The first batch of malted barley was distilled in 2008 but a single malt has yet to be launched. However, several other types of whisky have been released – Bourbon 101, Straight Cask Strength Wheat Whiskey, Port Finish Wheat Whiskey, Peated Wheat Whiskey and Straight Triticale Whiskey. A new limited bottling, first released in 2015, is the triple distilled O´Danaghers which is a mix of barley, wheat and oats. A later edition (Blue Label) was a single potstill made from malted and unmalted barley.

Triple Eight Distillery

Nantucket, Massachusetts, founded in 2000

www.ciscobrewers.com

Apart from whiskey, Triple Eight also produces vodka, rum and gin. Whiskey production was moved to a new distillery in 2007. The first 888 bottles of single malt whiskey were released on 8th August 2008 as an 8 year old. To keep in line with its theme, the price of these first bottles was also $888. More releases of Notch (as in "not Scotch") have followed, aged up to 12 years.

Cedar Ridge Distillery

Swisher, Iowa, founded in 2003

www.crwine.com

Malt whiskey production started in 2005 and in 2013 the first single malt was launched. More releases of the single malt have been made since then. A range of limited releases called Silver Label Single Malts has also been introduced. Other spirits in the range include both bourbon and rye.

Nashoba Valley Winery

Bolton, Massachusetts, founded in 1978
(whiskey since 2003)

www.nashobawinery.com

Mainly about wines, the business has been expanded with a brewery and a distillery as well. In autumn 2009, Stimulus, the first single malt was released. The second release of a 5 year old came in 2010 and a 10 year old in 2015 together with a 5 year old rye.

Woodstone Creek Distillery

Cincinnati, Ohio, founded in 1999

www.woodstonecreek.com

Opened a farm winery 1999, a distillery was added to the business in 2003. The first whiskey, a five grain bourbon, was released in 2008 followed by a 10 year old single malt. Whiskey production is very small and just a handfull of releases have appeared since.

Cutwater Spirits (former spirit division of Ballast Point)

San Diego, California, founded in 2016

www.cutwaterspirits.com

In December 2015, Ballast Point Brewing was bought by Constellation Brands for the staggering sum of $1bn! The distilling side of Ballast Point, which started in 2008, was actually never a part of the deal and during 2016, a handful of executives and co-founders started a new company and distillery called Cutwater Spirits but still working with the same brands as before; Devil´s Share Whiskey, Old Grove, Fugu Vodka and Three Sheets Rum. The Devil´s Share comes in two versions - single malt and bourbon.

Edgefield Distillery

Troutdale, Oregon, 1998

mcmenamins.com

The distillery is a part of the McMenamin chain of more than 60 pubs and hotels in Oregon and Washington. More than 20 of the pubs have adjoining microbreweries and the chain's first distillery opened in 1998 at their huge Edgefield property in Troutdale with the first whiskey, Hogshead Whiskey, being bottled in 2002. Hogshead is still their number one seller. Limited releases occur every year on St Patrick´s Day under the name The Devil´s Bit. A second distillery was opened in 2011 at the company´s Cornelius Pass Roadhouse location in Hillsboro.

Town Branch Distillery

Lexington, Kentucky, 1999

lyonsspirits.com

The founder Dr Pearse Lyons, who passed away in March 2018, had an interesting background. A native of Ireland, he used to work for Irish Distillers in the 1970s. In 1980 he changed direction and founded Alltech Inc, a biotechnology company specializing in animal nutrition and feed supplements. Alltech purchased Lexington Brewing Company in 1999 and in 2008, two traditional copper pot stills were installed with the aim to produce Kentucky´s first malt whiskey. The first single malt whiskey was released in 2010 under the name Pearse Lyons Reserve and it was followed in 2011 by Town Branch bourbon and in 2014 by Town Branch Rye. In June 2018, Alltech opened yet another distillery in Pikeville - Dueling Barrels Brewery and Distillery.

Prichard´s Distillery

Kelso, Tennessee, 1999

prichardsdistillery.com

Phil Prichard started the distillery in 1999 and in 2012 the capacity was tripled with the installation of a new mash cooker and three additional fermenters. In 2014, a second distillery equipped with a new 400-gallon alembic copper still was opened at Fontanel in Nashville. The main track of the production is rum. The first single malt was launched in 2010 and later releases usually have been vattings from barrels of different age (some up to 10 years old). The whiskey range also includes rye, bourbon and a Tennessee whiskey.

Charbay Winery & Distillery

St. Helena, California, founded in 1983

www.charbay.com

With a wide range of products such as wine, vodka, grappa, pastis, rum and port, the owners decided in 1999 to also enter in to whiskey making. They wer pioneers distilling whiskey from hopped beer and over the years several releases have been made including Double-Barrel Release I, II, III and IV, Charbay R5 and S Whiskey Lot 211A. In spring 2017, the company was split in two with Marko and his wife Jenni focusing on the spirit side while Miles continues with the wine production.

High West Distillery

Park City, Utah, founded in 2007

highwest.com

The founder, David Perkins, has made a name for himself mainly as a blender of sourced rye whiskies. None of these have been distilled at High West distillery. In 2015, they opened another distillery at Blue Sky Ranch in Wanship, Utah. It started off with two 6,000 litre pot stills but the plan is to eventually have 18 washbacks and four pot stills with the possibility of producing 1,4 million litres. Even though they consider themselves blenders first and foremost, there is a single malt whiskey in the pipeline which may be released in 2020. In 2016 Constellation Brands (makers of Corona beer and Svedka vodka) bought High West Distillery for a sum of $160 million.

Cutwater Spirits Distillery

New Holland Brewing Co.

Holland, Michigan, founded in 1996 (whiskey since 2005)

www.newhollandbrew.com

After ten years, this beer brewery opened up a micro-distillery as well. The first cases of New Holland Artisan Spirits were released in 2008 and among them were Zeppelin Bend, a 3 year old (minimum) straight malt whiskey which is now their flagship brand. Included in the range are also Zeppelin Bend Reserve, matured for four years and then finished for an additional 9 months in sherry casks, Beer Barrel Bourbon and Beer Barrel Rye.

DownSlope Distilling

Centennial, Colorado, founded in 2008

www.downslopedistilling.com

The first whiskey, Double-Diamond Whiskey, was released in 2010. It was made from 65% malted barley and 35% rye and is still the core whiskey. It was followed by a number of varieties of bourbon, rye and single malt. All malt whiskies are made from floor malted Maris Otter barley.

Bull Run Distillery

Portland, Oregon, founded in 2011

www.bullrundistillery.com

The distillery is equipped with two pot stills (800 gallons each) and the main focus is on 100% Oregon single malt whiskey. First release was the sourced bourbon Temperance Trader. The first release of a single malt under the name Bull Run was a 4 year old in 2016. Shortly after that the Oregon Single Malt Whiskey was also released at cask strength (56%).

Cut Spike Distillery (formerly Solas Distillery)

La Vista, Nebraska, founded in 2009

www.cutspikedistillery.com

Originally opened as Solas distillery in 2009, it was later renamed Cut Spike distillery. In 2010 single malt whiskey was distilled and the first bottles were launched in August 2013. New batches of the 2 year old whiskey have then appeared regularly and in autumn 2017, the first single barrel version was launched.

Journeyman Distillery

Three Oaks, Michigan, founded in 2010

www.journeymandistillery.com

The first release from the distillery (Ravenswood Rye) was sourced from Koval Distillery in Ravenswood. The range of whiskies distilled at their own premises now include Last Feather Rye, Featherbone Bourbon, Silver Cross Whiskey, W.R. Whiskey, Kissing Cousins and Federalist 12 Rye. The first release of Three Oaks Single Malt Whiskey was in 2013.

Wood´s High Mountain Distillery

Salida, Colorado, founded in 2011

www.woodsdistillery.com

Whiskey is the main product at this distillery. The first expression (and current big seller), Tenderfoot Whiskey is a triple malt. The mash bill is 77% malted barley (a mix of chocolate malt and cherrywood smoked malt), 13% malted rye and 10% malted wheat. This was followed by Alpine Rye Whiskey.

Door County Distillery

Sturgeon Bay, Wisconsin, founded in 2011

www.doorcountydistillery.com

A winery founded in 1974 was complemnted by a distillery in 2011. Gin, vodka and brandy are the main products but they also make single malt whiskey. The first Door County Single Malt was released as a one year old in 2013.

Immortal Spirits

Medford, Oregon, founded in 2008

www.immortalspirits.com

A wide range of spirits are produced including gin, rum, vodka and limoncello. The only whiskey made from barley (unmalted) is the 3 year old Single Grain. The Single Barrel range of selected casks has sometimes ben represented by a single malt but currently it´s a bourbon.

Painted Stave Distilling

Smyrna, Delaware, founded in 2013

paintedstave.com

Whiskey production started in 2014, first with bourbon and rye, then followed by whiskey from malted barley. Most of the whiskey production is centered on bourbon and rye but the owners have also released Ye Old Barley Whiskey made from 100% malted barley.

Van Brunt Stillhouse

Brooklyn, New York, founded in 2012

www.vanbruntstillhouse.com

Part of the Brooklyn Spirits Trail in New York, the distillery made their first release of Van Brunts American Whiskey in 2012, a mix of malted barley, wheat and a hint of corn and rye. This has been followed by a malt whiskey from 100% malted barley, a wheated bourbon, a rye and a smoked corn whiskey.

Civilized Spirits

Traverse City, Michigan, founded in 2009

www.civilizedspirits.com

The spirits are produced at a distillery on Old Mission Peninsula, just outside Traverse City in a 1,000 litre pot still with a 24-plate column attached. The whiskey side of the business includes Civilized Single Malt (at least 3 years old), Civilized Whiskey (made from locally grown rye), Civilized White Dog Whiskey (an unoaked wheat whiskey) and Civilized Bourbon.

Square One Brewery & Distillery

St. Louis, Missouri, founded in 2006

www.squareonebrewery.com

A combined brewery and restaurant in St. Louis. Apart from rum, gin, vodka and absinthe, the owners also produce J.J. Neukomm Whiskey, a malt whiskey made from toasted malt and cherry wood smoked malt.

Maine Craft Distilling

Portland, Maine, founded in 2013

www.mainecraftdistilling.com

Currently the distillery offers vodka, gin, rum and Chesuncook, which is a botanical spirit using barley and carrot distillates as well as the Fifty Stone single malt in limited batches! The barley is floor malted on site.

3 Howls Distillery

Seattle, Washington, founded in 2013

www.3howls.com

The malted barley is imported from Scotland including a small amount of peated malt. For the distillation they use a 300 gallon hybrid still with a stainless steel belly and a copper column. Their first whiskies were released at the end of 2013, a single malt and a hopped rye and these were followed in 2014 by a rye whiskey and a bourbon.

Montgomery Distillery

Missoula, Montana, founded in 2012

www.montgomerydistillery.com

The owners mill the barley and rye to a fine flour using a hammer mill and the wash is then fermented on the grain. Distillation takes place in a Christian Carl pot still with a 21 plate column attached. The first whiskey was a rye in 2015, followed up by the 3 year old Montgomery Single Malt in November 2016. A 4 year old was released a year later and a 5 year old is due in November 2018.

Ranger Creek Brewing & Distilling

San Antonio, Texas, founded in 2010

www.drinkrangercreek.com

The owners focus on beer brewing and whiskey production. They have their own brewhouse where they mash and ferment all their beers, as well as the beer going for distillation. The first release was Ranger Creek .36 Texas Bourbon in 2011. Their first single malt, Rimfire, was launched early in 2013.

Two James Spirits

Detroit, Michigan, founded in 2013

www.twojames.com

Equipped with a 500 gallon pot still with a rectification column attached, the distillery started production in 2013. Vodka, gin, bourbon (even a peated version) and rye have already been released while a single malt is still maturing in the warehouse. Aged in ex-sherry casks the whiskey has been made from peated Scottish barley.

Brickway Brewery & Distillery (former Borgata)

Omaha, Nebraska, founded in 2013

www.drinkbrickway.com

Omaha´s first combined brewery and distillery since prohibition. All the wash for the distillation comes from their own brewery and distillation takes place in a 550 gallon Canadian wash still, and a 400 gallon spirit still from Forsyth´s in Scotland. The owners are focused on single malt whiskey but they also produce smaller amounts of bourbon and rye as well as gin and rum. Their first whisky, Borgata American Single Malt White Whisky, was released in 2014 and there is now also an aged version under the name Brickway Single Malt Whisky.

Seven Stills Distillery

San Francisco, California, founded in 2013

www.sevenstillsofsf.com

The first releases were made at Stillwater distillery in Petaluma. Since 2016, the owners have been producing their own spirit from a distillery in Bayview, an area in the San Francisco environs. The idea is to make whiskey from craft beers and the range is made up of the Core Series (in-house beer), Collaboration working with other breweries and Experimental where experimentation without boundaries is the key word.

Vikre Distillery

Duluth, Minnesota, founded in 2012

www.vikredistillery.com

Together with whisky - gin, vodka and aquavit are produced at the distillery. Whiskies include Iron Range American Single Malt, Gunflint Bourbon and Temperance River Rye. The single malt was released in March 2017. The distillery was expanded in 2016 with six new fermentation tanks.

Rennaisance Artisan Distillers

Akron, Ohio, founded in 2013

renartisan.com

Apart from whiskey, the distillery produces gin, brandy, grappa and limoncello. The first whiskey release, The King´s Cut single malt, was made from a grain bill including toasted and caramel malts and new batches appear every 6 months. An Islay style single malt is due for release in 2018

Coppercraft Distillery

Holland, Michigan, founded in 2012

coppercraftdistillery.com

The distillery is equipped with a stainless steel mash tun, six washbacks and two stills - one stripping still with stainless steel pot and copper column and a fractioning still with both pot and column made from copper. The first three whiskies - corn, wheat and malted rye - were released in summer 2014.

John Emerald Distilling Company

Opelika, Alabama, founded in 2014

www.johnemeralddistilling.com

With the wash being fermented on the grain, the main product is the Alabama Single Malt which gets its character from barley smoked with a blend of southern pecan and peach wood. The first release was made in 2015. In spring 2017, the owners also started trial distillations using triticale.

Eleven Wells Distillery

St. Paul, Minnesota, founded in 2013

11wells.com

The distillery is equipped with a 650 gallon mash tun, stainless steel open-top fermentation tanks and two stills. Whiskey is the main product and the first two releases, aged bourbon and rye, were released in 2014 followed by a wheat whiskey in 2015, but the owners have still to release a whiskey made from malted barley.

Blaum Bros. Distilling

Galena, Illinois, founded in 2012

blaumbros.com

The distillery equipment consists of a 2,000 litre mash tun, five 2,000 litre wash backs and a 2,000 litre Kothe hybrid still. Apart from gin and vodka, the first two releases were the sourced Knotter Bourbon and Knotter Rye. The first whiskey from their own production was a rye in 2015 followed by a straight bourbon in 2018. It will be a few years before the first single malt is released.

Sugar House Distillery

Salt Lake City, Utah, founded in 2014

sugarhousedistillery.net

The first release from the distillery in 2014 was a vodka, followed later that year by a single malt whisky. More releases of the single malt have followed and bourbon and rum have also been added to the range.

Venus Spirits

Santa Cruz, California, founded in 2014

venusspirits.com

Production is focused on whiskey, but gin and spirits from blue agave have also been released. The first single malt was Wayward Whiskey, made from crystal malt and released in 2015. This was followed up by a rye and later a bourbon.

Oak N´ Harbor Distillery

Oak Harbor, Ohio, founded in 2014

oaknharbordistillery.com

Only a week after the distillery started producing, their first single malt was on the shelves. Aptly named Six Days Seven Nights, it had been maturing for a week in small barrels. Since then, more and older releases have followed. Other products include bourbon, gin, apple brandy, rum and vodka.

Blue Ridge Distilling Co.

Bostic, North Carolina, founded in 2010

www.blueridgedistilling.com

The first distillation at the distillery was in June 2012 and in December the first bottles of Defiant Single Malt Whisky were released. The maturation part is very unorthodox. The spirit is matured for 60 days in stainless steel tanks with oak spirals inserted. According to the owners, this ensures a greater contact between the whisky and the wood which speeds up the maturation process. In autumn 2017, a 100% rye was added to the range.

Bent Brewstillery

Roseville, Minnesota, founded in 2014

bentbrewstillery.com

This combined brewery and distillery produces, apart from a range of beers, also gin and whiskey. No whiskies have been released so far, but one called Kursed Single Malt is currently aging in a combination of charred oak and charred apple wood.

Orange County Distillery

Goshen, New York, founded in 2013

orangecountydistillery.com

Every ingredient needed for the production is grown on the farm, including sugar beet, corn, rye, barley and even the botanicals needed for their gin. They malt their own barley and even use their own peat when needed. Since 2014, they have launched a wide range of whiskies, including corn, bourbon, rye and peated single malt. The first aged single malt was launched in summer 2015.

Key West Distilling

Key West, Florida, founded in 2013

kwdistilling.com

The main track is to produce rum but they are also distilling whiskey. The mash is brought in from Bone Island Brewing, fermented, distilled and filled into new barrels or used rum barrels. The first release of Whiskey Tango Foxtrot was in July 2015 with more batches following.

Thumb Butte Distillery

Prescott, Arizona, founded in 2013

thumbbuttedistillery.com

A variety of gin, dark rum and vodka, as well as whiskey are produced by the owners, Dana Murdock, James Bacigalupi and Scott Holderness. Rodeo Rye, Bloody Basin Bourbon, Crown King Single Malt and a limited grain whiskey have all now been released. Maris Otter barley is being used for the malt whiskies.

Seattle Distilling

Vashon, Washington, founded in 2013

seattledistilling.com

The distillery produces gin, vodka, coffee liqueur, as well as a malt whiskey. The latter, named Idle Hour was first launched in 2013 followed by more batches. The style is Irish with both malted and unmalted barley being used in the mashbill. The distillery is currently moving from Vashon Island to Olympia, 80 km southwest of Seattle.

Hewn Spirits

Pipersville, Pennsylvania, founded in 2013

hewnspirits.com

Apart from rum, gin and vodka the distillerty produces bourbon, rye and the Reclamation American Single Malt Whiskey. After maturing the malt whiskey in barrels for 1-4 months, it receives a second maturation in stainless steel vats where charred staves of chestnut and hickory wood add to the profile.

Blue Ridge Distilling

Damnation Alley Distillery

Belmont, Massachusetts, founded in 2013

damnationalleydistillery.com

A small distillery with a wide range of whiskies. Among the varieties that can be mentioned are single malt, hopped single malt, smoked single malt (smoked with fruit wood), bourbon, rye and a house whiskey from barley, corn, rye and wheat. In 2016, the first 2 year old whiskey from the distillery was launched and more releases of both single malt and rye have followed.

Wright & Brown Distilling Co.

Oakland, California, founded in 2015

wbdistilling.com

The distillery is focused on barrel aged spirits, i. e. whiskey, rum and brandy. The first whiskey was distilled in 2015 and the first product, a rye whiskey, was launched in autumn of 2016 followed by a bourbon in autumn 2017. So far, no single malt made from barley has been released.

Stark Spirits

Pasadena, California, founded in 2013

starkspirits.com

The first single malt whiskey was distilled in July 2015 and the first release was a barrel of peated single malt in February 2016. The first official distillery release of single malt (both peated and un-peated) came in February 2017. They have two stills with one reserved for all the peated production.

Cotherman Distilling

Dunedin, Florida, founded in 2015

cothermandistilling.com

All the whiskies are made from 100% malted barley. The mash is brought in from local breweries, fermented at the distillery and then distilled in a pot still and a 3-plate bubble-cap still. First launched in July 2016, several batches have followed since. Apart from whiskey – gin and vodka are also produced.

Quincy Street Distillery

Riverside, Illinois, founded in 2011

quincystreetdistillery.com

The distillery produces an impressive range of spirits including gin, vodka, absinth, bourbon, corn whiskey and rye. So far, single malt whiskey made from barley only forms a small part. The only single malt released so far is a 2 year old Golden Prairie which was launched in December 2015.

Boston Harbor Distillery

Boston, Massachusetts, founded in 2015

bostonharbordistillery.com

The distillery started production in summer 2015 and while it concentrates mainly on whiskey, it is also making a variety of spirits based on different Samuel Adams´ beers. The whiskies, currently a rye and a single malt (launched in December 2017) are released under the Putnam New England label. Apart from the distillery with its 150-gallon Vendome copper pot still, the facility consists of a shop, tasting room and an event space.

Liquid Riot Bottling Co.

Portland, Maine, founded in 2013

liquidriot.com

When Liquid Riot opened its doors, it was Maine´s first brewery/ distillery/resto-bar. At the waterfront in the Old Port, Liquid Riot produces an extensive range of beers and spirits which include bourbon, rye, oat, single malt, rum, vodka and agave spirit. Distillation is made in a German hybrid still with a 5 plate rectification column.

Old Line Spirits

Baltimore, Maryland, founded in 2014

oldlinespirits.com

The owners bought the equipment from Golden Distillery when that was about to close down and brought it to Baltimore. Distilling started in 2016 and a couple of months prior, the first Old Line single malt, two to three years old and obviously from the Golden Distillery production, was released. A peated version was also released in autumn 2017.

Cannon Beach Distillery

Cannon Beach, Oregon, founded in 2012

cannonbeachdistillery.com

The owner´s philosophy about whisky making is never to make the same spirit twice. All the whiskies are made in small batches with a new release every 2-4 months. Distillation takes place in a 380 litre Vendome still with a 6-plate column.

Witherspoon Distillery

Lewisville, Texas, founded in 2011

witherspoondistillery.com

The main products from this distillery are bourbon, rum and Bonfire (a cinnamon-infused rum), but they also make small runs of Witherspoon Single Malt which is generally aged between 1 and 2 years. The whiskey is distilled in two 1,110 litre stills and the single malt is matured in new American oak and finished in rum casks.

2ⁿᵈ Street Distilling Co

Walla Walla, Washington, founded in 2011

2ndstreetdistillingco.com

Formerly known as River Sands Distillery, the company has been around since 1968 but the distillery only started in 2011. Different types of gin and vodka are produced, as well as a single malt – R J Callaghan. It is aged for 1,5 years in charred American oak and then finished for 6 months in Hungarian oak. In 2016 a 100% malted rye, Reser´s Rye, was also released.

Sound Spirits

Seattle, Washington, founded in 2010 (whiskey since 2012)

drinksoundspirits.com

A number of different spirits are produced - gin, vodka, aquavit, liqueurs and single malt whiskey. The first release of the 3 year old Madame Damnable single malt was in 2015 and more releases have since followed. The distillery closed temporarily in September 2016 only to re-open in a new location in spring 2017.

ASW Distillery

Atlanta, Georgia, founded in 2016

aswdistillery.com

The distillery is equipped with two traditional Scottish copper pot stills but with the American twist of fermenting and distilling on the grain. Among the latest releases are Duality, made from 50% malted barley and 50% malted rye with both grains fermented and distilled in the same batch and Ameireaganach Single Malt.

Dallas Distilleries Inc.

Garland, Texas, founded in 2008

dallasdistilleries.com

The distillery is primarily focused on whiskey. The first products in their Herman Marshall range were launched in 2013. It was a bourbon and a rye and was later followed by a single malt. An unusual feature at the distillery is the open top fermenters which are made from cypress wood.

San Diego Distillery

Spring Valley, California, founded in 2015

sddistillery.com

A distillery focused almost entirely on whiskey. In March 2016 the first six whiskies were released; a bourbon, a rye and an Islay peated single malt. The next whiskey to appear was a single malt made from seven different types of brewing malt. Due to a fire in the distillery in autumn 2017, it was moved, and expanded, to a new location in spring 2018.

Alley 6 Craft Distillery

Healdsburg, California, founded in 2014

alley6.com

A small craft distillery in Sonoma county with rye whiskey as the main product. The first bottles were released in summer 2015 followed by a single malt in May 2016. The owners are experimenting with a range of different barley varieties, mainly from Germany and Belgium.

Gray Skies Distillery

Grand Rapids, Michigan, founded in 2014

grayskiesdistillery.com

In 2014, the owners bought an industrial building for their grain-to-glass distillery and a year later, the first spirit was distilled. The equipment is made up of a 1,800 litre mash kettle, four fermenters and a 2,500 litre pot still with an attached column. The first bottle of Michigan Single Malt appeared in November 2016.

Hard Times Distillery

Monroe, Oregon, founded in 2009

hardtimesdistillery.com

The first product, Sweet Baby Vodka, was followed by a wasabi-flavoured vodka, moonshine from oats and barley, Appleshine made from apple juice and, eventually, Eleventh Hour Whiskey, a single malt which is distilled twice in pot stills.

Spirit Hound Distillers

Lyons, Colorado, founded in 2012

spirithounds.com

Rum, vodka and sambucca are on the production list, but the distillery's signature spirits are gin and malt whiskey. The barley for the whiskey is grown, malted and peat-smoked in Alamosa by Colorado Malting and the whiskey released so far is straight, i.e. at least two years old. The first bottles (five single barrels) hit the shelves in summer 2015 and the first 4 year old will be released some time soon.

Arizona Distilling Company

Tempe Arizona, founded in 2012

azdistilling.com

The first release from the distillery was a bourbon sourced from Indiana. The ensuing releases, which started with Desert Durum made from wheat, have all been produced in their distillery.

Humphrey's – a single malt – was first released in late 2014 and more bottles became available in summer 2015.

Dorwood Distillery

Buellton, California, founded in 2014

dorwood-distillery.com

The distillery (which recently changed its name from Brothers Spirits) started producing malt whisky in 2016. The barley is dried using mesquite smoke and the triple distillation takes place in two reflux stills. The releases so far have been unaged but several barrels have been laid down for maturation.

Idlewild Spirits

Winter Park, Colorado, founded in 2015

idlewildspirits.com

Production of the first batch of malt whiskey was in June 2016. For maturation they has moved from 5 gallon barrels, via 10 and 30 gallons to the full-size 50 gallon barrels that he uses today. Fermentation and distillation being on the grain add to the over-all character. Their Colorado Single Malt was released in 2018.

Timber Creek Distillery

Crestview, Florida, founded in 2014

timbercreekdistillery.com

Fermentation and distillation is off the grain and, surprisingly, they use a traditional worm tub to cool the spirits – a technique that has become rare even in Scotland. Currently they have whiskies maturing made from corn, wheat, rye, barley and oat. The latest batch of Florida Single Malt was released in October 2017.

Lyon Distilling Co.

Saint Michaels, Maryland, founded in 2013

lyondistilling.com

Focusing on whiskey and rum the distillery is equipped with a 2,000 litre mash tun, stainless steel fermenters and five small pot stills. The first, unaged, malt whiskey was released in late 2015 and the first aged release came one year later.

Dirty Water Distillery

Plymouth, Massachusetts, founded in 2013

dirtywaterdistillery.com

Starting with vodka, gin and rum, the distillery expanded into malt whiskey in 2015. The first release, Bachelor Single Malt, came in 2016 and was followed by Boat For Sale Malt Whiskey which had been made using a beer from Independent Fermentations.

Long Road Distillers

Grand Rapids, Michigan, founded in 2015

longroaddistillers.com

Apart from vodka, gin and aquavit, four styles of whiskey have been released - bourbon, wheat, corn and a 6 month old whiskey made from 51% malted barley and 49% un-malted.

Motor City Gas

Royal Oak, Michigan, founded in 2014

motorcitygas.com

The owners have an experimental approach to whiskey making and use unusual and old grains (Maris Otter and Golden Promise), different yeast strains and unusual woods. The expressions so far have been both unpeated and heavily peated.

Coppersea Distilling

New Paltz, New York, founded in 2011

coppersea.com

A "farm-to-glass" distillery with the barley malted on site. Open-top wooden washbacks and direct-fired alembic stills. One of the things that make Coppersea stand out is that they don´t dry the malted barley but instead produce a mash from green, unkilned barley, The 1 year old Big Angus is made from 100% green barley.

KyMar Farm Winery & Distillery

Charlotteville, New York, founded in 2011

kymarfarm.com

Mainly producing wine, liqeurs and apple brandy. Recently though, a whiskey made from 100% malted barley and distilled in a 300 gallon hybrid and an 80 gallon alembic still, was released. After a 6 to 9 months maturation, the spirit is moved to a solera system for blending with older batches to ensure consistency.

Old Home Distillers

Lebanon, New York, founded in 2014

oldhomedistillers.com

The distillery produces bourbon, corn whiskey and malt whiskey. The mash is fermented on the grain for 4-5 days, distillation takes place in a 100 gallon hybrid column still and the spirit is matured in charred, new American oak for a minimum of seven months.

StilltheOne Distillery Two

Port Chester, New York, founded in 2010

stilltheonedistillery.com

Different kinds of whiskey are produced in a 250 gallon pot column still from Arnold Holstein. The only single malts released so far are "287" from a pale ale and "9A" made from a stout.

III Spirits

Talent, Oregon, founded in 2014

iiispirits.com

Focusing mainly on single malts. Currently there are two single malts in the range; Oregon Highlander made from a grain bill of brewer´s malt, Munich malt and crystal malt and Islay Style Peated Whisky produced from 100% heavily peated malt from Scotland.

Telluride Distilling

Telluride, Colorado, founded in 2014

telluridedistilling.com

Vodka and malt whiskey is produced in a distillery equipped with open top fermenters and a column still. Maturation is in new charred oak for two years followed by 6 months in port barrels. The first single malt was released in July 2016.

Amalga Distillery

Juneau, Alaska, founded in 2017

amalgadistillery.com

The distillery uses a 250 gallon pot still from Vendome and they are also floor malting their own barley, some of it grown in Alaska. The first single malt will be released in 2020 but both vodka and gin have already been launched.

Fainting Goat Spirits

Greensboro, North Carolina, founded in 2015

faintinggoatspirits.com

First spirits on the shelves for this distillery, as for many others, were gin and vodka. In December 2017, Fisher´s single malt whiskey was launched as a 2 year old with batch 4 being released in May 2018. Bourbon is still maturing in the warehouse.

Andalusia Whiskey

Blanco, Texas, founded in 2016

andalusiawhiskey.com

Focusing entirely on whiskey production, the owners use a 56,000 gallon tank to collect rain water for the production. The spirit is double-distilled in a 250 gallon pot still and the first single malts were released in late 2016 - Stryker, where mesquite and oak have been used to dry the barley and the lightly peated Revenant Oak. This was followed up end of 2017 by Andalusia Triple-Distilled.

Big Bottom Distilling

Hillsboro, Oregon, founded in 2015

bigbottomdistilling.com

The company started out as a blender and bottler of sourced whiskey, not least bourbon finished in different wine casks. A distillery was built in 2015 and in June 2018, their first own single malt was released.

Floor malting at Coppersea Distillery   Andrew Norman - master blender at Fainting Goat

Black Heron Spirits

West Richland, Washington, founded in 2011

blackheronspirits.com

The owner started out as a winemaker, then decided to sell the company and open a distillery instead. A wide variety of spirits are produced, including bourbon, a corn whiskey and a limited peated single malt which was first released in January 2017.

Bogue Sound Distillery

Bogue, North Carolina, founded in 2018

lyondistilling.com

The distillery is equipped with a 500-gallon still and the first spirits released included gin, vodka and rye. Recently the John A.P. Conoley single malt was added to the range.

Dark Island Spirits

Alexandria Bay, New York, founded in 2015

darkislandspirits.com

The owners produce a wide variety of spirits including gin, vodka and brandy. On the whiskey side there´s wheat, corn and bourbon and in June 2018, the first single malt was released - the 3 year old Eleanor Glen.

Golden Moon Distillery

Golden, Colorado, founded in 2008

goldenmoondistillery.com

The distillery is using four antique stills, dating from the early to mid 1900s for the production. At least 15 different kinds of spirits are distilled, one of them being a single malt, aged for a minimum of one year in new oak and then finished in used oak casks.

Jersey Spirits Distilling Co

Fairfield, New Jersey, founded in 2015

jerseyspirits.com

Apart from gin and vodka, the owners have two bourbon varieties for sale - Crossroads with a mash bill consisting of corn, rye, wheat and barley and Patriot´s Trail which is a high rye bourbon. The first distillation of a single malt was in summer 2018 which will be ready to bottle in two years..

Liberty Call Spirits

Spring Valley, California, founded in 2014

libertycalldistilling.com

The distillery, located outside San Diego, uses a variety of barley varieties for their whiskies, including caramel malts and the rare Maris Otter. Their single malt is called Old Ironsides and there is also a four grain whiskey named Blue Ridge.

Mad River Distillers

Warren, Vermont, founded in 2011

madriverdistillers.com

The distillery was built on a 150 year old farm in the Green Mountains. Focus is on rum, brandy and whiskey. The only single malt so far is Hopscotch which was first released in late 2016 with batch two launched in November 2017.

Wanderback Whiskey

Hood River, Oregon, founded in 2014

wanderback.com

The distillery was built on a 150 year old farm in the Green Mountains. Focus is on rum, brandy and whiskey. The first release of a single malt (made from four different malts) was in September as a 3 year old.

Canada 

Shelter Point Distillery

Vancouver Island, British Columbia, founded in 2009

www.shelterpointdistillery.com

In 2005, Patrick Evans and his family decided to switch from the dairy side of farming to growing crops and they bought the Shelter Point Farm just north of Comox on Vancouver Island. Eventually the idea to transform the farm into a distillery was raised and with the help of Scottish investors, the construction work began. In May 2010 all the equipment was in place including a one tonne mash tun, five washbacks made of stainless steel (5,000 litres each) and one pair of stills (a 5,000 litre wash still and a 4,000 litre spirit still). Distillation started in spring 2011 and the barley used for the distillation is grown on the farm. In May 2016, 7,000 bottles of the first single malt, 5 years old, were released. The distillery is open to experiments which was evidenced by the limited Montfort DL 14 released in autumn 2017 which was made completely from unmalted barley.

Victoria Caledonian Distillery

Victoria, British Columbia, founded in 2016

www.victoriacaledonian.com

The distillery was founded by the Scotsman Graeme Macaloney and as a helping hand he had Mike Nicolson, who previously worked at 18 distilleries in Scotland. In addition, they also acquired the services of the late Dr. Jim Swan, one of the foremost whisky consultants in the world. The distillery is equipped with a 1 ton semilauter mash tun, 7 stainless steel washbacks, a 5,500 litre wash still and a 3,600 litre spirit still from Forsyth. There is also a craft beer brewery on site. Distilling started in July 2016 and Macaloney is also planning for triple distilled pot still whiskey, as well as peated single malt once he has commissioned the planned traditional floor malting. In late 2017, the owners released the Mac Na Braiche, a 12 months malt spirit and in the range there is also sourced Scotch blended malts under the name Twa Cask Collection. A visitor centre offers tours on several levels of the distillery and the brewery, as well as tutored tastings.

Still Waters Distillery

Concord, Ontario, foundd in 2009

www.stillwatersdistillery.com

Located in Concord, on the northern outskirts of Toronto, the distillery is equipped with a 3,000 litre mash tun, two 3,000 litre washbacks and a Christian Carl 450 litre pot still. The still also has rectification columns for brandy and vodka production. The focus is on whisky but they also produce vodka, brandy and gin. Their first single malt, named Stalk & Barrel Single Malt, was released in April 2013 and it was followed in late 2014 by the first rye whisky. The current range consists of Blue Blend, Red Blend, Rye and Single Malt. A recent collaboration with BarChef has resulted in whisky cocktails in a bottle with Toasted Chamomile Old Fashioned as one of the first releases.

Glenora Distillery

Glenville, Nova Scotia, founded in 1990

www.glenoradistillery.com

Situated in Nova Scotia, Glenora was the first malt whisky distillery in Canada. The first launch of in-house produce came in 2000, a 10 year old named Glen Breton and this is still the core expression under the name Glen Breton Rare but other expressions have occured - 14, 19 and 21 year olds.. Glen Breton Ice (10 years old), the world's first single malt aged in an ice wine barrel, was launched in 2006 and since then several expressions have been launched, among them single casks and sometimes under the name Glenora. A recent limited release is the Ghleann Dubh – a 13 year old peated single malt.

Other distilleries in Canada

Victoria Spirits

Sidney, British Columbia, founded in 2008

www.victoriaspirits.com

Even though the distillery´s best-selling product is Victoria Gin, whisky production started in 2009 but has been very intermittent. The first and only single malt, Craigdarroch, was launched in early 2015. Only 250 bottles were released and more whisky can´t be expected for at least a couple of years.

Pemberton Distillery

Pemberton, British Columbia, founded in 2009

www.pembertondistillery.ca

The distillery was founded in 2009 with vodka produced from potatoes as the first product. Schramm Vodka, was launched later that year. During the ensuing year, the owner started their first trials, distilling a single malt whisky using organic malted barley. The first release was in 2013 when a limited 3 year old unpeated version was launched. Since autumn 2015, the owners have a regular expression called Pemberton Valley Organic Single Malt Whisky.

Yukon Spirits

Whitehorse, Yukon, founded in 2009

www.twobrewerswhisky.com

All of the whisky produced is made from malted grains but not only barley but also wheat and rye. The first 850 bottles of the 7 year old Two Brewer´s Yukon Single Malt Whisky were released in February 2016 and the portfolio is now based on four styles; Classic, Peated, Special Finishes and Innovative.

Okanagan Spirits

Vernon and Kelowna, British Columbia, founded in 2004

www.okanaganspirits.com

The first distillery named Okanagan was started in 1970 by Hiram Walker but it closed in 1995. In 2004, Frank Deiter, established Okanagan Spirits. A distillery was opened in Vernon and, later on, a second one was built in Kelowna. A variety of spirits made from fruits and berries as well as gin, vodka, absinthe and whisky are being produced. Since 2013, there is a single malt in the range – The Laird of Fintry.

L B Distillers

Saskatoon, Saskatchewan, founded in 2012

www.lbdistillers.ca

Founded by Michael Goldney, Cary Bowman and Lacey Crocker, in 2012. The first single malt whisky was released in summer 2016 but before that, the owners had released a fair amount of other spirits – vodka, gin and a variety of liqueurs.

Central City Brewers & Distillers

Surrey, British Columbia, founded in 2013

www.centralcitybrewing.com

What started as a brewpub has now grown to one of Canada´s largest craft brewerys. A much needed expansion followed in 2013 when they moved to a larger facility as well as adding a distillery. Apart from whisky they also produce gin and vodka. The only single malt released so far is Lohin McKinnon Single Malt including special bottlings such as peated and chocolate malt.

The Dubh Glas Distillery

Oliver, British Columbia, founded in 2015

www.thedubhglasdistillery.com

The distillery is situated at Gallagher Lake and the whisky is double distilled in an Arnold Holstein still. Even though malt whisky is the main focus, gin is also produced. Apart from Noteworthy Gin, Virgin Spirits Barley (a newmake) has also been released. First release of the single malt is expected in June 2019.

Eau Claire Distillery

Turner Valley, Alberta, founded in 2014

www.eauclairedistillery.ca

One of the first whisky distilleries in Alberta in modern times, Eau Claire opened in 2014. Their first limited single malt whisky (1,000 bottles) was released in December 2017 and a rye whisky is expected in 2018.

Glenora Distillery

Australia & New Zealand

Australia

Lark Distillery

Hobart, Tasmania, founded 1992

www.larkdistillery.com

In 1992, Bill Lark was the first person for 153 years to take out a distillation licence in Tasmania and he often referred to as the godfather of modern whisky production in Australia. Since then he has not just established himself as a producer of malt whiskies of high quality, but has also helped to off-set several new distilleries. The success of the distillery forced Bill Lark to bring in investors in the company to generate future growth and since April 2018, Australian Whisky Holdings holds a majority of the shares (56%). The whisky is double-distilled in a 1,800 litre wash still and a 600 litre spirit still and then matured in 100 litre "quarter casks". The old distillery site down in Hobart at the waterfront is now a cellar door and a showcase for Lark whisky. The core products in the whisky range are the Classic Cask at 43% and Cask Strength at 58%. Limited releases have included Heavily Peated Bourbon Cask and, to celebrate the distillery´s 25th anniversary in 2017, Revolution Release which was an experimental series of 25 different 20 litre casks.

Bakery Hill Distillery

North Balwyn, Victoria, founded 1998

www.bakeryhill.com

The first spirit at Bakery Hill Distillery, founded by David Baker, was produced in 2000 and the first single malt was launched in autumn 2003. Three different versions are available – Classic and Peated (both matured in ex-bourbon casks) and Double Wood (ex-bourbon and a finish in French Oak). As Classic and Peated are also available as cask strength bottlings, they can be considered two more varieties. Limited releases also occur with one of the latest being A Wisp of Smoke - a 9 year old peated whisky bottled at 51.7%.

Sullivans Cove Distillery

Cambridge, Tasmania, founded 1994

www.sullivanscove.com

The distillery, with Patrick Maguire at the helm since 1999, obtains wash from Cascade Brewery in Hobart and the spirit is then double distilled. In 2014 the distillery moved to a new building about four times the size of the current facility. In December 2016, the distillery was taken over by a company led by Adam Sable who was general manager of Bladnoch distillery for two years. Patrick Maguire and the rest of the team will remain with the company. The range comprises of American Oak, French Oak (where the barrels had contained port) and Double Cask. There is also Special Cask where the barrels that are used may vary from time to time.

Old Hobart Distillery

Blackmans Bay, Tasmania, founded 2005

www.overeemwhisky.com

After several years of experimenting Casey Overeem opened up his distillery in 2007. The mashing was done at Lark distillery where Overeem also had his own washbacks and the wash was made to his specific requirement. The distillation takes place in two stills (1,800 litres and 600 litres). In 2014, Old Hobart distillery was acquired by Lark Distillery Pty Ltd. The range consists of Overeem Port Cask Matured, Overeem Sherry Cask Matured and Overeem Bourbon Cask Matured - all three bottled at 43% and 60%. A limited release of single malt matured in red wine casks appeared in autumn 2017.

Hellyers Road Distillery

Burnie, Tasmania, founded 1999

www.hellyersroaddistillery.com.au

Hellyer´s Road Distillery is the largest single malt whisky distillery in Australia with a capacity of doing 100,000 litres of pure alcohol per year. The distillery is equipped with a 6.5 ton mash tun, a 40,000 litre wash still and a 20,000 litre spirit still. The pots on both stills are made of stainless steel while heads, necks and lyne arms are made of copper. Maturation takes place in ex-bourbon casks but they also use Tasmanian red wine barrels for part of it. The first whisky was released in 2006 and there are now more than ten different expression in the range, including 10 and 12 year olds, peated as well as unpeated and various finishes.

Great Southern Distilling Company

Albany, Western Australia, founded 2004

www.distillery.com.au

The distillery is located at Princess Royal Harbour in Albany. In 2015, the owners opened a second distillery in Margaret River which will is focused on gin production and in autumn 2018 a third distillery, Tiger Snake in Porongurup, started production. In a near future the combined production will be 400,000 litres of pure alcohol per year. The first expression of the whisky, called Limeburners, was released in 2008 and this is still the core bottling. Included in the range are also American Oak, Port Cask and Sherry Cask, all bottled at 43% as well as Peated which is bottled at 48%. A rye and a sour mash whisky are also sold under the brand name Tiger Snake.

Starward Distillery

Melbourne, Victoria, founded 2008

www.starward.com.au

The distillery, founded by David Vitale, was moved in October 2016 to a new and bigger site in Port Melbourne. The stills (an 1,800 litre wash still and a 600 litre spirit still) were bought from Joadja Creek Distillery in Mittagong and currently the yearly production is around 20,000 cases. The first whisky was released

Bill Lark - the Godfather of modern whisky production in Australia

under the name Starward in 2013 and the current range consists of Wine Cask (matured in Australian red wine barrels) and Solera (matured in casks that had held apera, the Australian version of sherry). In 2015, the distillery was given a major financial injection when Diageo´s incubator fund project, Distill Ventures, made a substantial investment in the distillery, increasing production to 250,000 litrs of pure alcohol per year..

Other distilleries in Australia

Nant Distillery

Bothwell, Tasmania, founded in 2007

www.nant.com.au

The distillery was founded by Keith Batt but was later taken over by Australian Whisky Holdings. The distillery is equipped with a 1,800 litre wash still, a 600 litre spirit still and wooden washbacks for the fermentation. The owners have plans to increase production by 75%. The first bottlings were released in 2010 and the current core range consists of Sherry, Port and Bourbon - all bottled at 43%.

William McHenry and Sons Distillery

Port Arthur, Tasmania, founded in 2011

www.mchenrydistillery.com.au

Equipped with a 500 litre copper pot still with a surrounding water jacket to get a lighter spirit, production started in 2012. To facilitate the cash flow, a range of different gins is also produced. The first whisky was released in May 2016 while the latest edition is a 5 year old, matured in American oak and finished in French oak.

Launceston Distillery

Western Junction (near Launceston), Tasmania, founded in 2013

www.launcestondistillery.com.au

The equipment consists of a 1,100 litre stainless steel mash tun, stainless steel washbacks, a 1,600 litre wash still and a 700 litre spirit still – both with reflux balls. The newmake is filled into

barrels which have previously held bourbon, Apera (Australian sherry) and Tawny (Australian port). The goal is to have the first whisky ready for release in summer 2018.

Black Gate Distillery

Mendooran, New South Wales, founded in 2012

www.blackgatedistillery.com

Apart from single malt whisky, the distillery produces vodka and rum. The first launch of a single malt was in early 2015 when a sherrymatured expression was released. More bottlings have followed, the latest, a 3 year old matured in port casks appeared in late 2017.

Old Kempton Distillery

Kempton, Tasmania, founded in 2013

www.oldkemptondistillery.com.au

Established as Redlands Estate Distillery in Derwent Valley, the distillery re-located in 2016 to Dysart House in Kempton and later changed the name to Old Kempton Distillery. The first spirit was distilled in March 2013 in a 900 litre copper pot still and another three stills have later been installed. The first whisky was launched in September 2015 and this has been followed by several more releases.

Archie Rose Distilling Company

Rosebery, New South Wales, founded in 2014

www.archierose.com.au

The first distillation at Archie Rose was conducted in December 2014. Apart from producing rye whisky and peated and unpeated single malt, the distillery also makes gin and vodka. The whisky is still maturing but a new make made from six different malts was released in July 2018. By June 2018, 1,000 barrels had been filled.

Timboon Railway Shed Distillery

Timboon, Victoria, founded in 2007

www.timboondistillery.com.au

Wash from a local brewery is distilled twice in a 600 litre pot still. For maturation, resized (20 litres) and retoasted ex-port, tokay and bourbon barrels are used. The first release of a whisky, matured in port barrels, was made in 2010 and some of the latest expressions have been Tom´s Cut, bottled at 58% and Christie´s Cut at 60%.

Castle Glen Distillery

The Summit, Queensland, founded in 2009

www.castleglenaustralia.com.au

Established as a vineyard in 1990, Castle Glen moved on to open up also a brewery and a distillery in 2009. Apart from wine and beer, a wide range of spirits are produced. Malted barley is imported and the first whiskey, Castle Glen Limited Edition, was released as a 2 year old in early 2012.

Joadja Distillery

Joadja, New South Wales, founded in 2014

www.joadjadistillery.com.au

The first distillation was in December 2014 when the distillery was equipped with just the one still (800 litres), used for both the wash and the spirit run. In 2015, a 2,400 litre wash still was installed together with another four washbacks. The owners plan to grow 30 acres of their own barley on the estate and also to malt it on site, using peat to dry it. The first whisky was released in autumn 2017.

Launceston Distillery

Shene Distillery

Pontville, Tasmania, founded in 2015

www.shene.com.au

Damian Mackey started distilling whisky in a small shed already in 2007. In spring 2016 the opportunity came for him to move his production to the Shene Estate at Pontville, 30 minutes north of Hobart. With four stills and a capacity of 300,000 litres this is one of the largest distilleries in Australia. The whisky is triple distilled and the first release was in August 2017.

Tin Shed Distilling Co.

Welland (Adelaide), South Australia, founded in 2013

www.iniquity.com.au

The owners opened their first distillery, Southern Coast Distillers, in 2004 with a release in 2010. Eventually it was closed and the current distillery started production in 2013. The first single malt, under the name Iniquity, was launched as a 2 year old in 2015 and several more batches have followed.

Mt Uncle Distillery

Walkamin, North Queensland, founded in 2001

www.mtuncle.com

The owners started out by producing gin, rum and vodka - all of which soon became established brands on the market. Their first single malt, The Big Black Cock, was released in April 2014, and was produced using local Queensland barley and matured for five years in a combination of French and American oak.

Loch Distillery

Loch, Victoria, founded in 2014

www.lochbrewery.com.au

This combined brewery and distillery began producing whisky in March 2015. The wash used for the whisky production comes from their own brewery. Their own gin was soon released and the first single malt was launched in July 2018.

Fanny´s Bay Distillery

Weymouth, Tasmania, founded in 2015

www.fannysbaydistillery.com.au

The distillery is equipped with a 400 litre copper pot still, a 600 litre mash tun and a 300 litre washback with a 7-8 day fermentation. The whisky starts in 20 litre port barrels and is then finished in small bourbon casks. The first whisky was released in May 2017 and it is now available in two versions - sherry and port.

Applewood Distillery

Gumeracha, South Australia, founded in 2015

www.applewooddistillery.com.au

With a background in wines and perfumes, Laura and Brendan Carter opened a distillery in the Adelaide Hills in 2015. To start with, gin, eau de vie and liqueurs were on the menu, but in summer 2015, whisky production was added. Several young malt spirits have been released but so far no whisky.

Killara Distillery

Hobart, Tasmania, founded in 2016

www.killaradistillery.com

Kristy Booth is the daughter of Bill Lark, often referred to as the godfather of Australian whisky and after 17 years working in her father´s distillery, she opened her own in summer 2016. The first whisky distillation was in August 2016 and the first bottling is due in autumnn 2018 but a succesful gin is already on the market.

Corra Linn Distillery

Relbia, Tasmania, founded in 2015

www.corralinndistillery.com.au

John Wielstra made the first distillation in his hybrid column still in autumn 2016, using a new, local barley strain that had recently been developed. He is also using his own yeast and smokes his barley using dried kelp instead of peat. The first release of single malt is expected in autumn 2018

Adams Distillery

Perth, Tasmania, founded in 2016

www.adamsdistillery.com.au

This distillery, which started producing in 2016, looks like one of the most interesting whisky projects in Australia today. After less than two years, all the equipment was up for sale to make way for a huge new distillery, five times as big as the first. The new distillery will open in December 2018 and further expansion with mutliple stills is planned already for 2019. The plan behind the major expansion is not only to produce more whisky bul also rum, gin, brandy, beer and cider.

Devil´s Distillery

Moonah, Tasmania, founded in 2015

www.devilsdistillery.com.au

Using an 1800 litre copper pot still, the distillery started production of malt whisky in 2015. They also have moonshine in their range. The first release of their Hobart single malt was in August 2018.

Spring Bay Distillery

Spring Beach, Tasmania, founded in 2015

www.springbaydistillery.com.au

A small, family-owned distillery, located on the east coast of Tasmania and equipped with a 1200 litre pot still. The first spirit released was a gin followed in autumn 2017 by the first single malt. Second bottling, bourbon matured, appeared in August 2018.

Bellarine Distillery

Drysdale, Victoria, founded in 2017

www.bellarinedistillery.com.au

Located at the unlikely address Scotchman´s Road, the distillery is equipped with four stills, producing both gin and malt whisky. Gin is in the shops but the first whisky has yet to be released.

Backwoods Distilling

Yackandandah, Victoria, founded in 2017

www.backwoodsdistilling.com.au

The distillery is equipped with a 1200 litre copper ot still with an attached column. The first distillation was in January 2018 and obviously no whisky has yet been released.

Wild River Mountain Distillery

Wondecla, Queensland, founded in 2017

www.wildrivermountaindistillery.com.au

This is one of Australia´s highest elevated distilleries, located in the Atherton Tablelands in North Queensland at a height of 870 metres. Distillation started in 2017 and the first bottlings (a corn/barley combination and a single malt) are due in December 2019.

Riverbourne Distillery

Jingera, New South Wales, founded in 2016

www.riverbournedistillery.com

Located at the head of the Molonglo River, close to Canberra, the distillery started producing whisky, rum and vodka in February 2016. The first two single malts, released in June 2018, were named The Riverbourne Identity and The Riverbourne Supremacy - an obvious nod to the movies about Jason Bourne.

The Aisling Distillery

Griffith, New South Wales, founded in 2015

www.theaislingdistillery.com.au

Since the start, around 200 barrels have been filled at this distillery which is 100% dedicated to producing malt whisky. The first release is expected in December 2018.

Darby-Norris Distillery

Kelso, Tasmania, founded in 2018

www.darbynorrisdistillery.com.au

A small distillery which started production in spring 2018. Gin and vodka have been released but the first single malt isn´t expected at least until 2020.

Coburns Distillery

Burrawang, New South Wales, founded in 2017

www.coburnsdistillery.com.au

Mark Coburn started production in spring 2017 and has so far released several versions of his gin. The single malt is still maturing. Coburns is one of very few Australian distilleries with its own peat bog for smoking the barley. Plans for the future include having no less than a set of five 5,000 litre pot stills.

New Zealand

Thomson Whisky Distillery

Auckland, North Island, founded in 2014

www.thomsonwhisky.com

The company started out as an independent bottler, sourcing their whiskies from the closed Willowbank Distillery in Dunedin, New Zealand. In April 2014, the owners opened up a small distillery based at Hallertau Brewery in North West Auckland. The wash for the distillation comes from the brewery. In February 2018, a single malt named Zeitgeist matured in virgin French oak was released and there is also Two Tone made from malted rye and barley.

Cardrona Distillery

Cardrona (near Wanaka), South Island, founded in 2015

www.cardronadistillery.com

Building on the distillery started in January 2015 and in October the first distillation was made. The distillery is equipped with 1.4 ton mash tun, six metal washbacks, one 2,000 litre wash still and a 1,300 litre spirit still. The two pot stills were made by the famous copper smiths in Scotland, Forsyth's. The production capacity is one barrel per day and the whisky will be matured in sherry casks and bourbon barrels. The owners have released a barrel-aged gin and a single malt vodka but the first single malt whisky will probably not be released until 2025..

Asia

India

Amrut Distilleries Ltd.

Bangalore, founded in 1948

www.amrutdistilleries.com

The family-owned distillery, based in Bangalore, south India, started to distil malt whisky in the mid-eighties. The equivalent of 50 million bottles of spirits (including rum, gin and vodka) is manufactured a year, of which 1,4 million bottles is whisky. Most of the whisky goes to blended brands, but Amrut single malt was introduced in 2004. It was first launched in Scotland, but can now be found in more than 40 countries. It wasn´t until 2010, however, that the brand was launched in India. The distillery, with a capacity of doing 200,000 litres of pure alcohol per year, is equipped with six washbacks with a fermentation time of 140 hours and two stills, each with a capacity of 5,000 litres. The barley is sourced from the north of India, malted in Jaipur and Delhi and finally distilled in Bangalore before the whisky is bottled without chill-filtering or colouring. The owners have had plans for a while now to build yet another distillery adjacent to the present. A new warehouse has already been built and construction of the new distillery was well underway in summer 2018.

The Amrut core range consists of unpeated and peated versions bottled at 46%, a cask strength and a peated cask strength and Fusion which is based on 25% peated malt from Scotland and 75% unpeated Indian malt. The latter, which is the biggest seller, was recently re-branded with a new design as were all the other expressions in the core range. Special releases over the years include Two Continents, where maturing casks have been brought from India to Scotland for their final period of maturation, Intermediate Sherry Matured where the new spirit has matured in

The new design of Amrut Fusion

ex-bourbon or virgin oak, then re-racked to sherry butts and with a third maturation in ex-bourbon casks, Kadhambam which is a peated Amrut matured in ex Oloroso butts, ex Bangalore Blue Brandy casks and ex rum casks and Portonova with a maturation in bourbon casks and port pipes. New editions of them all are released from time to time. A big surprise for 2013 was the release of Amrut Greedy Angels, an 8 year old and the oldest Amrut so far. That was an astonishing achievement in a country where the hot and humid climate causes major evaporation during maturation. In 2015 it was time for an even older expression, 10 years old, and in 2016, a 12 year old, the oldest whisky from India so far, was released. The highly innovative Spectrum has now reached its fourth release, this time matured in casks made of four varieties of oak. Other limited releases include the second version of Double Cask, a 5 year old combination of ex-bourbon and port pipes, the 100% malted Amrut Rye Single Malt - the first rye whisky from the company, Amalgam comprising of Amrut as well as single malts from Scotland and Asia and Con-fusion - a special bottling for members of Amrut Fever. The very latest release, in autumn 2018, was a Madeira Cask Finish.

John Distilleries Jdl

Goa, founded in 1992

www.pauljohnwhisky.com

Paul P John, who today is the chairman of the company, started in 1992 by making a variety of spirits including Indian whisky made from molasses. Their biggest seller today is Original Choice, a blend of extra neutral alcohol distilled from molasses and malt whisky from their own facilities. The brand, which was introduced in 1995/96 has since made an incredible journey. It is now one of the biggest whiskies in the world with sales of 132 million bottles in 2017. Another brand is Bangalore Malt which was the fastest growing spirit in the world in both 2016 and 2017. This is a simpler version of Original Choice and 43 million bottles were sold in 2017 - all in the state of Karnataka where the company has its head office! John Distilleries owns three distilleries and produces its brands from 18 locations in India with its head office in Bangalore. The basis for their blended whiskies is distilled in column stills with a capacity of 500 million litres of extra neutral alcohol per year. In 2007 they set up their single malt distillery which was equipped with one pair of traditional copper pot stills but in 2017, another pair of stills were added, doubling the capacity to 1.5 million litres per year. The company released their first single malt in autumn 2012 and this was followed by several single casks. In 2013 it was time for two core expressions, both made from Indian malted barley. Brilliance is unpeated and bourbon-matured while Edited, also matured in bourbon casks, has a small portion of peated barley in the recipe. At the beginning of 2014, two cask strength bottlings were released; Select Cask Classic (55,2%) and Select Cask Peated (55,5%). In 2015, finally, the third core expression was released. It was a 100% peated bottling called Bold, bottled at 46%. Recent limited releases include three 7 year old single malts; Mars Orbiter, a peated whisky matured in American oak, Oloroso, unpeated and matured in oloroso butts and Kanya, unpeated from American oak.

Other distilleries in India

Rampur Distillery

Rampur, Uttar Pradesh, founded in 1943

www.rampursinglemalt.com

This huge distillery is situated west of Delhi. It was purchased in 1972 by G. N. Khaitan and is today owned by Radico Khaitan, the fourth biggest Indian liquor company. The distillery has a capacity of producing 75 million litres of whisky based on molasses, 30 million litres of grain whisky and 460,000 litres of malt whisky per year. The first whisky brand from Radico was 8PM, which in 2017 sold 84 million bottles. The first single malt release, un-chill filtered and without age statement, appeared in May 2016.

McDowell´s Distillery

Ponda, Goa, founded in 1988 (malt whisky)

www.diageoindia.com

Established in the late 1800s, the distillery produces the second best selling Indian whisky with 285 million bottles sold in 2017. Owned by Diageo since 2014, the distillery also produces a very small amount of single malt whisky.

Israel 

The Milk & Honey Distillery

Tel-Aviv, founded in 2013

www.mh-distillery.com

Israel´s first whisky distillery was founded by Gal and Lital Kalkshtein. The distillery is equipped with a 1 ton stainless steel mash tun, four stainless steel washbacks and two copper stills (with a capacity of 9,000 and 3,500 litres each). The current production is 200,000 litres of pure alcohol while the capacity is 800,000. The first distillation was in March 2015 and in February 2016, the first in-house whisky production took place. The first 3 year old single malt, made before the final equipment was installed, was made available through Whisky Auctioneer in August 2017. The first commercial release of a single malt whisky will be at the end of 2019. Meanwhile, the owners have also released Levantine Gin and Roots, a herbal liqueur. The distillery has an active Visitor Center offering a large variety of tours and workshops.

The Golan Heights Distillery

Katzrin, founded in 2014

Founded by Canadian expat David Zibell, the distillery is equipped with two artisanal copper stills and the whisky is matured in wine casks from the nearby Golan Heights Winery. A young two-grain whisky was released in 2016 while the distillery´s first single malt aged more than three years, appeared in late 2017 as a single cask. A core expression named Ashtaroth is also underway

Pakistan 

Murree Brewery Ltd.

Rawalpindi, founded in 1860

www.murreebrewery.com

Started as a beer brewery, the assortment was later expanded to include whisky, gin, rum, vodka and brandy. The core range of single malt holds two expressions – Murree´s Classic 8 years old and Murree´s Millenium Reserve 12 years old. There is also a Murree´s Islay Reserve, Vintage Gold, which is a blend of Scotch whisky and Murree single malt.

Milk & Honey Distillery in Israel

Taiwan

Kavalan Distillery

Yanshan, Yilan County, founded in 2005
www.kavalanwhisky.com

On the 11th of March 2006 at 3.30pm, the first spirit was produced at Kavalan distillery. This was celebrated in a major way a decade later when guests and journalists from all over the world were invited for the 10th anniversary. But it was not just to celebrate 10 years of whisky production but also to witness the recent expansion of the distillery which has made Kavalan one of the ten largest malt whisky distilleries in the world! This rapid development may even have surprised the founder, entrepreneur and business man Tien-Tsai Lee, and his son, the current CEO of the company Yu-Ting Lee. Early on, it was decided that expertise from Scotland was needed to get on the right track from the beginning. Dr. Jim Swan was consulted early on and he, together with the master blender, Ian Chang, developed a strategy including production as well as the future maturation. Jim Swan sadly passed away in early 2017.

The distillery lies in the north-eastern part of the country, in Yilan County, one hour´s drive from Taipei. Following the expansion in 2016, the distillery is equipped with 5 mash tuns, 40 stainless steel washbacks with a 60-72 hour fermentation time and 10 pairs of lantern-shaped copper stills with descending lye pipes. The capacity of the wash stills is 12,000 litres and of the spirit stills 7,000 litres. Kavalan only uses a very narrow cut from the spirit run, leaving more foreshots and feints to accommodate a complex and rich flavour profile. The spirit vapours are cooled using shell and tube condensers, but because of the hot climate, subcoolers are also used.

On site, there are two five-story high warehouses, with a third expected to be completed in 2019, and the casks are tied together due to the earthquake risk. The climate in this part of Taiwan is hot and humid and on the top floors of the warehouses the temperature can reach 42°C. Hence the angel´s share is dramatic – no less than 10-12% is lost every year. At the moment, Kavalan are doing experiments aiming to reduce the angel's share to below 10%, hoping for positive results in 2020. The distillery has its own cooperage where the preparation of the wood plays an important part for the final character of the whisky. Implemented by Dr. Swan, they use a shave-toast-rechar (STR) process for some of the casks which, together with the subtropical climate, lends a very special character to the whisky.

The brand name, Kavalan, derives from the earliest tribe that inhabited Yilan, the county where the distillery is situated. Since the first bottling was released in 2008, the range has been expanded and now holds more than 19 different expressions. The best seller globally is Classic Kavalan, bottled at either 40% or 43%. In 2011, an "upgraded" version of the Classic was launched in the shape of King Car Conductor – a mix of eight different types of casks, un chill-filtered and bottled at 46%. A port finished version called Concertmaster (currently the best selling Kavalan in the USA) was released in 2009 and, later that year, two different single cask bottlings were launched under the name Solist – one ex-bourbon and one ex-Oloroso sherry. It was the launch of these two expressions that made the rest of the world aware of Taiwanese whisky.

More expressions in the Solist series have been added and the range now consists of (apart from Bourbon and Sherry) Fino, Vinho Barrique (using Portuguese wine barriques), Manzanilla, Amontillado, PX, Moscatel and Port. All of these are bottled at cask strength but in 2012 two versions bottled at 46% were also introduced – Bourbon Oak and Sherry Oak. Other releases include Podium which is a vatting of whiskies from new American oak and a selection of re-fill casks and Distillery Reserve Peaty Cask. The latter, exclusively available at the distillery visitor centre, obtains its smoky flavour from maturation in ex-Islay casks. The distillery has produced whisky from peated barley (10ppm) as well, and to launch the first bottlings from that production within 3-5 years. In May 2018 a new core expression was released – Distillery Select – which is intended to work as the entry level to the brand. Whisky is, of course, the main product for Kavalan but recently production of gin has also started with the first bottlings expected in 2018 or early 2019.

Kavalan is being exported to more than 60 countries including the USA, the UK, France, Belgium, Italy, The Netherlands, Russia, Israel and Hong Kong. Apart from Taiwan, Europe and the US are the most important markets. There is an impressive visitor centre on site with no less than one million people coming to the distillery every year. The owning company, King Car Group, with 3,000 employees, was already founded in 1956 and runs businesses in several fields; biotechnology and aquaculture, among others. It is also famous for its ready-to-drink coffee, Mr. Brown.

Kavalan Distillery and the latest core expression - Distillery Select

Other distilleries in Taiwan

Nantou Distillery

Nantou City, Nantou County, founded in 1978
(whisky since 2008)

en.ttl.com.tw

Nantou distillery is a part of the state-owned manufacturer and
distributor of cigarettes and alcohol in Taiwan – Taiwan Tobacco
and Liquor Corporation (TTL). Established as a government agency
in the early 1900s, it was renamed Taiwan Tobacco and Wine
Monopoly Bureau in 1947. Between 1947 and 1968 the Bureau
exercised a monopoly over all alcohol, tobacco, and camphor
products sold in Taiwan. It retained tobacco and alcohol monopolies
until Taiwan's entry into the WTO in 2002.

There are seven distilleries and two breweries within the TTL
group, but Nantou is the only with malt whisky production. The
distillery is equipped with a full lauter Huppmann mash tun with
a charge of 2.5 tonnes and eight washbacks made of stainless
steel with a fermentation time of 60-72 hours. There are two wash
stills (9,000 and 5,000 litres) and two spirit stills (5,000 and 2,000
litres). Malted barley is imported from Scotland and ex-sherry and
ex-bourbon casks are used for maturation. Nantou Distillery also
produces a variety of fruit wines and the casks that have stored
lychee wine and plum wine are then used to give some whiskies
an extra finish. Due to extreme temperatures during summer,
distillation only takes place from October to April. The hot and
humid climate also increases the angle´s share which is around
6-7%. Until recently, the spirit from Nantou has been unpeated,
but in 2014, trials with peated malt brought in from Scotland were
made. The main product from the distillery is a blended whisky
which comprises of malt whisky from Nantou, grain whisky from
Taichung distillery and imported blended Scotch. In 2013, two cask
strength single malt whiskies were launched – one from bourbon
casks and the other from sherry casks. The next expressions were
Omar single malt, where several versions have been released,
matured in either sherry or bourbon casks. There is also a blended
malt whisky called Yushan.

Omar - the single malt that made Nantou known to the world

Africa

South Africa 

James Sedgwick Distillery

Wellington, Western Cape, founded in 1886 (whisky since
1990)

www.threeshipswhisky.co.za

Distell Group Ltd. was formed in 2000 by a merger between
Stellenbosch Farmers' Winery and Distillers Corporation, although
the James Sedgwick Distillery was already established in 1886.
The company produces a huge range of wines and spirits including
the popular cream liqueur, Amarula Cream. James Sedgwick
Distillery has been the home to South African whisky since 1990.
The distillery has undergone a major expansion in the last years and
is now equipped with one still with two columns for production of
grain whisky, two pot stills for malt whisky and one still with six
columns designated for neutral spirit. There are also two mash tuns
and 23 washbacks. Grain whisky is distilled for nine months of the
year, malt whisky for two months (always during the winter months
July/August) and one month is devoted to maintenance. Three new
warehouses have been built and a total of seven warehouses now
hold 180,000 casks.

In Distell´s whisky portfolio, it is the Three Ships brand, introduced in 1977, that makes up for most of the sales. The range consists
of Select and 5 year old Premium Select, both of which are a
blend of South African and Scotch whiskies. Furthermore, there is
Bourbon Cask Finish, the first 100% South African blended whisky
and the 10 year old single malt. The latter was launched for the first
time in 2003 and the release in 2016 was the fifth and the first to
carry a vintage. A new range called Master´s Collection was introduced in 2015 with a 10 year old PX finish as the first release. This
was followed in 2017 by a 15 year old pinotage cask finish. Apart
from the Three Ships range, Distell also produces South Africa´s
first single grain whisky, Bain´s Cape Mountain.

In 2013 the Distell Group acquired the Scottish whisky group,
Burn Stewart Distillers, including Bunnahabhain, Tobermory and
Deanston distilleries as well as the blended whisky, Scottish Leader.
The man who tirelessly worked to bring the Three Ships single
malt to the market, was Andy Watts. After 25 years as the distillery
manager, he has now taken on a new role in the company where he
will be responsible for overseeing Distell´s entire whisky portfolio.

South America

Argentina 

La Alazana Distillery

Golondrinas, Patagonia, founded in 2011

www.laalazanawhisky.com

Located in the Patagonian Andes, the first whisky distillery in Argentina concentrating solely on malt whisky production was founded in 2011 and the distillation started in December of that year. The founders were Pablo Tognetti, an old time home brewer, and his son-in-law, Nestor Serenelli but end of 2014, Pablo Tognetti withdrew from the company. Today it´s Nestor and his wife Lila who own and run the distillery. They are both big fans of Scotch whisky and before they built the distillery, they toured Scotland to visit distilleries and to get inspiration. The owners are firm believers in the "terroir" concept where local barley and water and, not least, climate will affect the flavour of the whisky. The distillery is equipped with a lauter mash tun, four stainless steel 1,100 litre washbacks with a fermentation time of 4 to 6 days and two stills. The owners are growing their own barley and also do the malting using local peat. The house style is light and fruity but they have also filled several barrels with peated whisky. The first, limited release was made in December 2013 and in 2017, the first peated bottling, the 4 year old Haidd Merlys was launched..

Other distilleries in Argentina

Distillery Emilio Mignone & Cia

Luján, Buenos Aires province, founded in 2015

www.emiliomignoneycia.com.ar, www.emyc.com.ar

With the first distillation in November 2015, this became the second whisky distillery in Argentina. The distillery is equipped with a 300 litre open mash tun, a 250 litre washback with a 72-96 hour fermentation cycle and two stills, directly fired by natural gas. The plan for 2018 is to produce 2,000 bottles with one third being peated and the first bottling will be released in 2019. The owners are working on a second and larger distillery (10,000 litres) in Lago Puelo which should be up and running in autumn 2020.

Madoc Distillery

Dina Huapi, Rio Negro, founded in 2015

www.madocwhisky.com

The owner is one of the founders of the first Patagonian distillery, La Alazana. In 2015, he left the company and brought with him some of the equipment, as well as part of the maturing stock to build a new distillery in Dina Huapi. The existing equipment with a lauter mash tun, a washback and a copper pot still was complemented by a wash still and the first distillation took place in September 2016.

Brazil 

Union Distillery

Veranópolis, founded in 1972

www.maltwhisky.com.br

The company was founded in 1948 as Union of Industries Ltd to produce wine. In 1972 they started to produce malt whisky and two years later the name of the company was changed to Union Distillery Maltwhisky do Brasil. In 1986 a co-operation with Morrison Bowmore Distillers was established in order to develop the technology at the Brazilian distillery. Most of the production is sold as bulk whisky to be part of different blends, but the company also has its own single malt called Union Club Whisky.

Muraro Bebidas

Flores da Cunha, founded in 1953

www.muraro.com.br

This is a company with a wide range of products including wine, vodka, rum and cachaca and the total capacity is 10 million litres. Until recently, the blend Green Valley was the only whisky in the range. In 2014, however, a new brand was introduced. It has the rather misleading name Blend Seven but it appears to be a malt whisky even though it seems that essence of oak is part of the recipe. The main market for the whisky is The Carribean.

James Sedgwick Distillery

The Year
that was

Including the subsections:
The big players | The big brands | Changes in ownership
New distilleries | Bottling grapevine

From 2012 to 2016, the global alcohol consumption declined every year and in 2016 alone the volumes dropped by as much as 1.3%. It was therefore a relief for the industry to see the volumes go up by 0.1% in 2017. A small increase but the trend was broken. Wine and cider showed the most positive figures while beer continued its downward spiral. Sales of spirits grew by 1.8% to a total of 2.4bn nine-litre cases and the growth was to be found in all categories; whisky, vodka, gin, rum, tequila etc.

At the same time, all producers were well aware of a younger generation being more concerned about health and wellness. Moderate drinking may very well bring down the volumes in certain markets but on the other hand, values could continue to increase – "drink less but better". And on the horizon, there´s also the legalisation of cannabis in Canada and a number of states in the USA which may move consumers away from alcohol.

The largest spirits category is still baijiu, a Chinese spirit usually distilled from fermented sorghum. In fact, the volumes of baijiu outweigh the combined volumes of whisky, rum, gin, tequila and vodka! Most of the baijiu produced is consumed in China but if we look at spirits that are consumed globally, whisky is dominating. The category (all types of whisky) increased by 3% in 2017 reaching 372 million 9-litre cases. Only tequila/mezcal could top that growth rate (+3.6% to 33 million cases). Rum on the other hand, sometimes seen as a challenger to whisky, had flat growth selling 150 million cases. Gin, another contester, is in the midst of a change in consumer behaviour where mainstream brands are losing out to high-end, premium brands.

Starting 2013, Scotch whisky has been struggling with declining figures and in 2014 both volumes and values were down - for the first time in a decade. Part of the explanation was the poor economic climate in certain emerging markets, the ban on exports to Russia due to the conflict in the Ukraine and the ban on corporate gifting in China. In 2016, however, the trend was broken and in 2017, the value of Scotch exports reached a record high (+8.9% and beating the numbers from 2012). Volumes on the other hand were up by just 1.6% and it´s obvious that the weaker pound following the Brexit referendum in 2016 has played an important role.

Blended Scotch is by far the biggest subcategory and it managed to buck the trend of declining figures in recent years with a growth of 8% in values during 2017. The star though, in terms of growth, are single malts with an increase of more than 14% in values. While single malt volumes are still around 10% of total Scotch exports, the value is now an impressive 28.6% if you include blended malt.

SINGLE MALT SCOTCH - EXPORT

Value: +14.3% to £1.171bn

Volume: +8.1% to 122m bottles

OTHER BOTTLED SCOTCH* - EXPORT

Value: +7.8% to £2.956bn

Volume: +0.9% to 842m bottles

TOTAL SCOTCH - EXPORT

Value: +8.9% to £4.368bn

Volume: +1.7% to 1.234bn bottles

* Other bottled Scotch includes bottled blended malt, bottled blended Scotch and bottled grain Scotch whisky. Bulk expor is not included, except in the Total.

Even though Scotch whisky is exported to more than 200 countries, 78.4% of the values and 77.8% of the volumes go to the top 20 markets. In the case of single malts, 77% of the values are exported to ten countries. There are no surprises when it comes to the two biggest markets - France is number one in terms of volumes even though the numbers were down by 5.9% while USA, the number one market in terms of values, performed much better with an increase of 7.7%.

Looking at the detailed figures for each of the nine regions, all but one (Central and South America) showed positive growth figures both in terms of volumes and values.

A record year for producers of Scotch

The European Union

The European Union still maintains its position as the biggest export market for Scotch whisky which of course makes it even more important for the whisky producers that the UK government will be able to cut a favourable trade deal after Brexit. Almost 40% of the volumes are sold to markets within the union while values are a little less (31.6%). Single malts have increased steadily in the last couple of years (up 13% in 2017) but the positive thing was that blends, after negative growth in the last few years, increased in value by 11%. The interesting thing in 2017 was that volumes went up by a mere 1% while values increased by 11% - either a case of premiumisation or Scotch simply becoming more expensive!

EU — Top 3

France	volumes	-6%	values	+2%
Germany	volumes	+6%	values	+14%
Spain	volumes	-5%	values	+5%

France has been for many years, and still is, the dominant market for Scotch. In fact, in terms of volume, it is the biggest importer in the world and second to the US in terms of values. The importance of the market is evidenced by the fact that almost one third of the Scotch export in 2017 went to France. In place two and three, Spain and Germany have been rivals for many years. Spain has been a turbulent market during the last decade but both countries showed a double digit increase in 2016. In terms of volumes, 2017 was a mixed bag with Spain decreasing while shipments to Germany were up. The interesting thing though, is that in terms of values, Germany is now for the first time in second place thanks to an increase of 13.5% to £184m compared to Spain´s £175m. The fourth biggest market for Scotch in the EU (and number eight in the world) is Latvia. With 2 million people it becomes pretty obvious that the majority of the whisky isn't consumed by the people, instead, Latvia serves as a hub for exports to Russia.

North America

The second largest region, and one that accounts for one quarter of the Scotch export values, is North America. While dominated by the USA, let´s not forget two other countries - Mexico, with a presence in the top ten importers of Scotch in the world and Canada. In 2017, the region was up 2.5% in volumes and 7% in values.

North America — Top 3

USA	volumes	+7%	values	+8%
Mexico	volumes	-8%	values	-1%
Canada	volumes	+3%	values	+13%

USA had a tough act to follow with a 14% increase in values during 2016 but still managed to add another 7% to that figure in 2017. No less than 26% of the world exports of single malts go to USA which makes it an extremely important market, not least in terms of values. Whisky sales in Mexico have gone up by 75% in the last seven years and with a market share of almost 21% it is beginning to threaten the national spirit tequila, which has a 26% share. Traditionally, Mexico has been a market dominated by standard, blended Scotch and this is definitely still the biggest category. For example, sales of Black & White increased by 50% in just one year to reach more than 7 million bottles in 2017. However, in the last few years, the interest in premium spirits (blends and to a lesser degree single malts) has increased. The problem is that it´s a volatile market (like so many countries in Central and South America) and both volumes and values were in the red in 2017. Canada, finally, only import one quarter of the volumes that go to Mexico but in terms of values it´s three quarters. Purely because the interest in single malts is much larger.

Asia

The improvement in Scotch exports to Asia that could be seen last year, after several years of decline, continues. In 2016, volumes were up by 6% and while the corresponding figure for 2017 was only 1.7%, values climbed substantially more - just over 10%. Asia is the third biggest region for Scotch whisky and the second biggest in terms of volumes. As opposed to EU and North America that could be defined as mature markets, Asia is very much an emerging one with the world´s two largest countries within its borders.

Asia — Top 3

Singapore	volumes	+14%	values	+29%
Taiwan	volumes	-5%	values	-8%
India	volumes	-5%	values	+7%

In the region, India is definitely the market with the greatest potential. It has become the third biggest market in terms of volumes and the tenth in values. Just 15 years ago India was in 19th place and volumes have increased by more than 1000% since then. With Scotch having just a 1% share of the Indian spirits market, there´s room for huge increases. Especially if the current 150% import tariff on Scotch could be lowered. Singapore continues to be a huge market, third biggest in value after USA and France, but the vast majority of the whisky is re-exported to other markets in the region, not least to ASEAN countries and China. Once a reliable market for Scotch showing growth every year, Taiwan showed decreasing numbers in both value and volume for the third time in a row. Nevertheless, it is still a very important country not least when it comes to single malts. In 2017, that category continued to increase but it could not compensate for the loss in sales of blended malt and blended Scotch. It was even surpassed in 2017 by Germany and Spain in terms of values and is now in sixth place in the world. Single malt sales however are impressive. Only USA (£300m) and France (£158m) buy more than Taiwan (£94m).

There was a time, in 2003, when South Korea was the fourth biggest importer of Scotch whisky. Fourteen years later it´s not even in the top 20 with a decline during that

period of more than 70%. Thailand is another market in the region that has gone down the same track, the reasons being difficulties in the economy and political instability. Both economies have started to recover lately but it often takes a while before consumer behaviour reacts to the new circumstances.

The outlook for China is definitely better. The downturn which started in 2012 due to the governments' clampdown on corporate gifting, proved to be only temporary. The current growth (almost 50% increase in value during 2017) is driven by an increasing interest from the growing middle class. The lowering of the import duty on Scotch from 10% to 5% is of course helping to grow the market.

Central and South America

The positive figures for this region in 2016 (after three years of decline) turned out to be temporary and in 2017 the figures were again in the red. Values were down by 1% while volumes decreased by 10%. The significant difference between the two figures are due to the fact that the more expensive single malts were up by 20% while the cheaper blends dropped by more than 20%. With blends still being the dominant category by far, there is no doubt that a premiumisation of the whisky market in the region has started in earnest.

Central & South America — Top 3

Brazil	volumes	-15%	values	+1%
Dom. Republic	volumes	-11%	values	+7%
Uruguay	volumes	+4%	values	+19%

With more than 200 million people and a youthful demographic, Brazil would be an interesting market to any company regardless of their product. Even though it´s the biggest market for Scotch in the region it is also a difficult market. Beer accounts for 92% of total alcohol sales and the domestic Cachaça makes up for most of the remaining 8%. It is also a country that has been struggling with a bad economy in recent years.

Volatility is the main risk for the whisky producers doing business in the region. Political instability and uncertain economic climate make way for unpleasant surprises. One good (or bad) example of that is Venezuela which ten years ago was the fifth biggest importer of Scotch in the world. Today the market has completely collapsed and only 8% of the volumes remain. With an inflation coming close to 2000%, chances are slim that the market will recover any time soon. In Colombia, spirits were recently hit by a new 25% tax which immediately puts a stick in the wheel for the whisky producers. There are still countries in the region though that provide stability and Uruguay is one of them with a double digit increase in both values and volumes in 2017.

Africa

Apart from Eastern Europe, which is just a fifth of the African market for Scotch, this region performed the best in 2017 with a double digit increase in both values (+13%) and volumes (+13%). One should keep in mind though that these increases come from low numbers and Africa hasn´t performed that well in recent years.

Africa — Top 3

South Africa	volumes	+17%	values	+21%
Morocco	volumes	+16%	values	+8%
Nigeria	volumes	-9%	values	-21%

Traditionally, the African market for Scotch more or less equals South Africa but more countries are now gearing up, showing an interest in whisky, for example Morocco, Nigeria and Angola. Still, South Africa makes up for 70% of the volumes and 60% of the values of Scotch imported to the continent. Even more important are the impressive figures for South Africa in 2017 following three years of decline. The country is currently the ninth largest importer in the world of Scotch in terms of values.

Middle East

Values were up by 12% and volumes by 4% in this region which has become more important in recent years. Usually a strong performer when it comes to single malts, the main part of the increase last year actually came in the blended category (both bottled and in bulk).

Middle East — Top 3

UAE*	volumes	-8%	values	-1%
Lebanon	volumes	+5%	values	+24%
Israel	volumes	+22%	values	+26%

* United Arab Emirates

The biggest market in the region is still the United Arab Emirates but they are not as dominating as they used to be, even though they have 49% of the volumes and 37% of the values. The entire region performed well but it was Lebanon and Israel, two relative newcomers to Scotch, which accounted for the biggest increase. A major share of the sales to UAE are actually destined for duty free sales or for re-exporting to other countries.

Australasia

Until 2016, Australasia was the second smallest Scotch export region but some good figures have made it possible to surpass non EU-members. In 2017, values were up 4.3% and volumes by 3.8%.

Australasia — Top 3

Australia	volumes	+5%	values	+3%
New Zealand	volumes	+5%	values	+27%
New Caledonia	volumes	-2%	values	+22%

Unsurprisingly, Australia is the dominating market with 91% of the value but New Zealand in second place has shown some good figures in the last couple of years.

European non EU-members

This is the second smallest of the nine regions, responsible for only 2% of the exports. Volumes were up 10% in 2017 and values were plus 4%. Around 93% of the whisky goes to three countries - Turkey, Switzerland and Norway.

Europe (non-EU) — Top 3

Turkey	volumes	+14%	values	-1%
Switzerland	volumes	+7%	values	+14%
Norway	volumes	+5%	values	+7%

Turkey is by far the biggest market with approximately 60% of the totals. The country has for a long time favoured a preferential, three-tiered tax system where the domestic Raki is taxed substantially lower than many imported spirits including Scotch. This system, however, was abolished in 2018 and it will be interesting to see in what way this will have an impact on the figures for next year.

Eastern Europe

The smallest of all regions (1.3% of the volumes and 0.5 % of the values) is labelled Eastern Europe but with many countries in this geographical region being a part of the EU, these are in whisky export statistics a part of that larger group. Here, we are talking mainly about Russia and some of the surrounding countries. In the last few years, the figures have fluctuated significantly between years due to export restrictions against Russia because of the conflict in the Ukraine. In 2017, volumes were up 68% while values increased by 36%.

Eastern Europe — Top 3

Russia	volumes	+116%	values	+148%
Georgia	volumes	+2%	values	-1%
Montenegro	volumes	-12%	values	-6%

The biggest market in the region is Russia but the exact volumes of whisky landing in Russia are sometimes difficult to determine. Volumes of Scotch whisky going to Poland and, especially Latvia, will eventually be re-exported to Russia..

The big players

Diageo

Diageo is the world´s biggest drinks company with no less than 24 of the Top 100 best selling spirits brands under their umbrella. But the ride hasn´t been that smooth in recent years. In 2014, the company showed figures that did not please the share holders and a few years later there were also rumours about other companies looking to buy Diageo. Most probably there was little substance in those rumours and with the new CEO Ivan Menezes taking charge in 2013, the company slowly turned the ship. With the acquisition of United Spirits in India, the company is now back in the saddle as the undisputed leader of the spirits world.

The limited Jane Walker version of Black Label

The figures for the year ending 30th June 2018, showed solid growth albeit not at the same level as the year before. Organic sales were up by 5% to £12.2bn while organic operating profits increased by 7.6% to £3.7bn. The growth came from all regions with Latin America and Carribean being the star performer with an increase in operating profit of 19%. In terms of net sales, this is the smallest of Diageo´s five regions while the largest, by far, is North America (34% of net sales) followed by Europe (24%) and Asia Pacific (21%). In North America (net sales up by 4%), Scotch grew by 4% mainly driven by Johnnie Walker Black Label. Bulleit bourbon continued its growth from the last couple of years and was up by 10%. Vodka on the other hand continued to decline. Over to Europe with a 4% net sales growth led by a strong growth in gin (not least Tanqueray). Johnnie Walker grew a more modest 2% in the region while J&B continued to lose grounds in the difficult Iberian market. Finally, Asia Pacific, the third biggest market, was up by 9% and it was a solid performance in China, India and travel retail that paved the way. Johnnie Walker did well but this was offset by the decline of Windsor in Korea which continues to be a very difficult market. Recently Taiwan, which used to be a stronghold not least for single malts, has also been contracting and according to CEO Ivan Menezes, this is one reason why Diageo single malts as a whole underperformed during the year. The company´s goals for Greater China on the other hand were clearly stated by Cristina Diezhandino, global category director for Scotch and Reserve Brands, when she in an interview said that ”Our ambition is to make Scotch the number one international spirit category in China”.

Scotch is the biggest part of Diageo´s business with 25% of the net sales followed by beer (16%) and vodka 11%.

Pernod Ricard

Pernod Ricard is the second largest drinks company in the world and in the words of the company CEO, Alexandre Ricard. the "fiscal 2018 was a very strong year". Organic sales increased by 6% to €8.99bn while the profit from recurring operations increased by 6,3% to €2.36bn. Net profits were up by 13% to €1.6bn. The company has divided their market into three parts where Asia/Rest of the world is the biggest in terms of sales (+9% last year), followed by Europe (+2%) and Americas (+6%). In Asia, China and India performed well (+17% and +14% respectively) and these results must have come as a relief for the owners. Last year, the corresponding figures were just 1-2% and it´s clear that especially the figures for Martell cognac have recovered since the crackdown on corruption and extravagant gifting that the Chinese government imposed in 2012. In Europe, Germany, the UK and Eastern Europe performed well while France and Spain were a disappointment. Looking at their strategic brands, eleven out of thirteen showed growth (Royal Salute and Ricard being the exceptions) and especially Martell and Jameson (both up by14%) excelled. The Irish category leader by far, sold 83 million bottles! On the vodka side, Absolut is still number two in the world after Smirnoff and it seems as though the stagnation in recent years may have come to an end with an increase in volumes by 2% even though the brand is still in decline on the US market. Havana Club, Malibu and Beefeater are three of the biggest brands in the portfolio and they all increased by 4-6%.

On the Scotch whisky side, the company has two major blends amongst the Top 5 in the world. Ballantine´s is number two (after Johnnie Walker) and sales volumes improved by 4% to 80 million bottles while Chivas Regal (in fourth place) increased by 1% to 53 million bottles. The Glenlivet single malt is still number two in the malt category after Glenfiddich and increased their volumes by 2.5% to 12.9 million bottles in 2017.

Edrington

The company finds itself right in the midst of an exciting change of strategy. For the year 2017/2018 (ending 31 March), organic sales were up by 7% to £707m while profits dropped by 5% to £87m. The latter figure should be viewed in the light of last year's increase of 32% in profits, a figure which was influenced by the weaker pound due to the upcoming Brexit. In 2018 the Edrington Group will complete the third year of Edrington 2020, a five year strategy to increase consumer focus and accelerate growth. The plan can be summerised as follows; Perfect The Macallan, Accelerate Highland Park, Develop Super Premium, Optimise Regional Power Brands and Focus for Success.

If we start with Macallan, a new, state of the art distillery was opened to the public in 2018. The spectacular design of both the distillery and the visitor centre as well as the sheer size has been a talking piece in the Scotch whisky community for a couple of years now. Huge as it is, the distillery is but one part of a £500m investment where securing sherry-seasoned casks for maturing the whisky makes up the lion´s share. The range received a make-over in terms of new packaging and several new expressions were launched. In terms of sales, the brand reached almost 11 million bottles (up 9%) and it is more than likely that

Chivas Regal is the fourth most sold blended Scotch in the world

If we look at the brands, Johnnie Walker, the best selling Scotch in the world, increased net sales by 5% selling 220 million bottles last year which ranks the brand as the 5th best selling whisky in the world with four Indian whiskies in the lead. An attempt to make whisky more inclusive to women by launching the limited expression Jane Walker didn´t turn out exactly as the owners had hoped for. A Diageo representative explained the reason for the campaign by saying "Scotch as a category is seen as particularly intimidating by women." Some critics claimed that not only was it patronising insinuating that women didn´t "understand" whisky but if that was the case, putting a woman on the label wouldn´t change things. Diageo on the other hand said that the campaign had been misinterpreted by some consumers and that it was all about celebrating women.

The real surprise in terms of growth last year was Black & White with a 33% increase in net sales. The brand has doubled in size in five years and managed to sell almost 30 million bottles last year with Mexico, Colombia, India and South Africa as the biggest markets. On the other side of the scale, J&B, Windsor, Old Parr and Buchanan´s all showed negative growth. On the malt whisky side, all but one (Lagavulin) of the top 5 brands in the portfolio increased their volumes with The Singleton being the biggest seller but with Talisker showing the largest increase in sales – up 13% to 3 million bottles.

In April 2018, Diageo announced a £150m investment in whisky tourism in Scotland. The centre-piece will be a Johnnie Walker experience in Edinburgh but all their distillery visitor centres will be upgraded, in particular the ones at Glenkinchie, Clynelish, Caol Ila and Cardhu.

during 2018, it will be the third single malt brand to break the 1-million case barrier. Highland Park also launched a battery of new bottlings while sales volumes increased by 25% to reach 1.7 million bottles. The third single malt in the line-up is Glenrothes which was acquired by Edrington in 2017. The first year was spent on re-evaluating the range and the result appeared in autumn 2018 when new expressions with age statements replaced the vintages.

On the blended side, Cutty Sark continued to loose volume while Famous Grouse at least managed to maintain the figures from last year. A surprising announcement was made by Edrington in June 2018 when they declared that Cutty Sark and Glenturret distillery (including The Famous Grouse Experience) were up for sale. Or perhaps the move isn´t that surprising after all, seen in the light of the company´s ambition to focus on premium spirits. What appeared a bit unusual though, was that no deal with a buyer was announced. Instead the company seemed to be fishing around to see who would take the bait.

Gruppo Campari

The figures for 2017, showed an increase in net sales of 5.2% to €1816m while gross profits were up by 9.2% landing on €1075m. In the last year, the company has completed a couple of transactions in order to streamline their portfolio. Grand Marnier was acquired while Carolans and Irish Mist were disposed of, being sold to Heaven Hill Brands.

The brands in the company are divided into two groups – Global Prorities (including Aperol, Campari, Skyy and Wild Turkey) and Regional Priorities (Glen Grant, Bulldog and Espolòn). In 2017, it was the latter brands that drove the result with a 13% increase compared to the bigger brands with an 8% increase. In terms of regions, all reported an increase between 5 and 7% except for Asia which gave reason for some concern with a 0.8% decrease. Volumes of Glen Grant remained more or less at the same level as the previoys year – around 3.5 million bottles and the entire portfolio was launched in Canada for the first time. With slight declines in the third and fourth quarter of last year, the CEO Bob Kunze-Concewitz said "Looking ahead into 2018, our outlook remains fairly balanced in a still uncertain macroeconomic scenario for some emerging markets."

Beam Suntory

When Suntory bought Beam Inc in May 2014 for $16bn, a new company called Beam Suntory was formed. It is now the third largest drinks group in the world after Diageo and Pernod Ricard. The new company is owned by Suntory Holdings. Before the merger, Suntory´s portfolio included Japanese brands such as Yamazaki, Hakushu, Hibiki and Kakubin. With the deal, a range of other spirit brands have been added to the list; Jim Beam bourbon, Teacher´s blended Scotch, the two single malts Laphroaig and Ardmore, as well as Canadian Club and Courvoisier cognac.

Beam Suntory Inc is a part of Suntory Holdings´ alcoholic beverage operations which also includes beer and wine. For 2017, revenues for the entire division increased by 4.8% while operating income was down by 0.5%. Jim Beam and Maker´s Mark had an excellent year, both of them growing the volumes by 11% to reach 107 million and 23 million bottles respectively. The super premium Bourbons, Knob Creek and Basil Hayden´s, also grew at a double-digit rate. Looking at the Scotch whisky brands, Teacher´s is still showing a negative trend, dropping in volumes by 5%. The three major single malt brands on the other hand, increased their volumes; Laphroaig (+1%), Bowmore (+1.3%) and Auchentoshan (+19%).

Brown Forman

The figures for the fiscal year ending April 2018, showed net sales increasing by 8% to $3,248m while net profits increased by 7% to $717m. The company could report a sales growth from all the top ten markets including the US which accounts for 47% of the company´s sales. The backbone of Brown Forman´s business is Jack Daniel´s – the most sold American whiskey in the world and in sixth place of all whiskies that are produced. The brand grew by 6% and sold 155 million bottles. Other brands in the portfolio include Finlandia vodka (+2%), Woodford Reserve bourbon (+23%), El Jimador tequila (+8%) and, since spring 2016, BenRiach Distillery Company with BenRiach, GlenDronach and Glenglassaugh. The company also has an interest in Irish whiskey through the ownership of Slane Irish Whiskey.

The retiring CEO, Paul Varga, said "We are in the early days of capitalising on our American whiskey strategy, and believe we are extremely well-positioned to maintain the renewed momentum in our business," At the same time, the company has to deal with the consequences of President Trump´s decision to impose import duties on various products from all around the world. In June as a counter measure, Mexico placed a 25% tariff on bourbon imports and the EU followed suit in early July. Brown-Forman earns half of its revenue from the United States, with Europe accounting for a quarter and Mexico contributing around 5%.

Inver House Distillers

Inver House Distillers is a part of International Beverage Holdings which is the international arm of ThaiBev and they own and operate five distilleries in Scotland. The report for the year ending September 2017 showed decreasing sales (down by 7% to £62.7m) and also the operating profits decreased 2.8% to £7.6m. On the other hand, this was an improvement compared to last year when both turnover and profits were down by double digits. The company is still in a transition phase where they are moving away from the sales of bulk whisky in order to focus on their core brands. At the same time, the company has invested substantially in the last few years in their distilleries and warehouses. Graham Stevenson, the company´s long-standing MD, left the company last year and was succeeded by Martin Leonard.

Rémy Cointreau

The company reported a sales growth of 3.4% to €1,127 billion for the year ending March 2018. Net profits were up even more (+12%) to €151m. The biggest reason for the good figures was the continued rebound of the cognac Rémy Martin, particularly in Asia. The brand accounted for 67% of the company's sales which increased by 13%. Other spirit brands in the division Liqueurs & Spirits, which also includes Bruichladdich whisky and Botanist gin, stand for 24% of sales and the last year´s sales growth for the division was a more modest 4% . Bruichladdich is not the only whisky in the company. A few years ago the French distillery Domaine des Hautes Glaces and Westland Distillery based in Seattle also joined the stable. The single malts are still a very small part of the company´s business and in the report, CEO Valérie Chapoulad-Floquet stated that "...regarding our single malts, the main goal was to manage scarceness and build stock for the next few years."

The big brands

A version of the famous 80/20 principle is very much applicable also on the Scotch whisky business. When it comes to blends, in 2017, the twenty largest brands were responsible for 80% of the sales and in the case of malts it was 75%. The question is, with the turbulence of the whisky business in recent years and with more brands on the market, has this distribution changed at all? If we focus on just the ten biggest single malt brands, they made up 57.2% of the total malt volumes sold ten years ago and in 2017 it was 57.4%. In the case of blends, the corresponding figures are 58% versus 61%. In the same period of time, volumes of malts have gone up by 60% and blends merely by 10%. The gains in malts have been evenly split between the top tier and the rest, including many new malts that have come on the market in that time. Compared to ten years ago, there are only three new malts in the top 10 list; The Singleton, Talisker and Balvenie. The same applies to blends with William Lawsons, William Peel and Black & White being the new ones. In 2017, two of the Top 10 blends decreased in volume and two of the Top 10 malts also showed negative growth.

Blended Scotch

It´s hardly any surprise to find Johnnie Walker in the top spot as the world´s most sold Scotch. The brand sells almost three times as much as number two, Ballantine´s. But while the category leader had some great years from 2010 to 2013 when volumes rose by 22%, the trend was broken in 2014 and three years of declining volumes followed. The owners started to invest heavily in new campaigns and, depending on who delivers the figures (Drinks International and the IWSR differ here) the brand gained between 2 and 5% in volumes from 2016 to 2017 to sell between 215 and 220 million bottles. But Diageo doesn´t rely purely on new marketing campaigns. Two new, limited sub-ranges have recently been launched - Blender´s Batch and Blue Label Ghost & Rare. Just like last year, Johnnie Walker is in fifth place on the global whisky list after four Indian whiskies. Number two in blended Scotch, no surprise here either, is Ballantine´s which in the last three years has increased by 17% and sold 80 million bottles. One of their moves to increase awareness about the brand has been to release bottlings of the signature single malts that make up the blend - Miltonduff, Glenburgie and Glentauchers. In place

The extensive range from Chivas Brothers in a whisky shop in Singapore

number three, we find Grant's which is struggling to make its way back to the sales volumes of 8-10 years ago. In the last couple of years though, the trend has been positive and in 2017 it sold 53 million bottles. Hard on the heels of Grant's, just 240,000 bottles behind, is Chivas Regal. The premium blend has recently managed to re-capture some of the losses that were made in the Chinese market since 2012. Number five is J&B with 40 million bottles sold in 2017. The brand was the second biggest blend in the world up until 2006, but since then a downturn in its main market, Spain, has affected sales. A brand with an impressive growth in the last ten years (+112%) is William Lawson's. During 2017 it managed to climb two places on the top list, selling 37 million bottles. The two brands that were surpassed were Famous Grouse and William Peel which both sold around 36 million bottles (the difference between the two were only 96,000 bottles). Surprising news from Edrington (owners of Famous Grouse) in spring 2018 were that they are putting up Glenturret distillery for sale which effectively means closing down the visitor centre, The Famous Grouse Experience. For many years the best-selling Scotch blend in the important market of the USA, Dewar's is now being challenged by Johnnie Walker. Dewar's, still in place nine is struggling with decreasing sales figures and managed to sell 30 million bottles in 2017. Recent progress in emerging markets (India and China) compensated for losses made in the States. Finally, in place ten, we have a classic brand which has been out of the limelight for quite some time. Black & White was established in 1884 and had its heyday from 1920 up until the early 1960s when the decline began. In the last decade though, sales have increased by 220% (33% in the last year) and have now reached almost 28 million bottles. The impressive comeback is due to an increased demand for the whisky in Latin America.

Single Malt Scotch

To say that single malts are hot would be putting it mildly. In 2017 they made up 27% of the total values of Scotch export. If you add blended malt it adds up to just over 30%. No less than 22 of the top 25 single malts have increased their sales volumes in the last two years and since 2000, we have seen 30 new distilleries starting production in Scotland.

Every year since 1963, with one exception, Glenfiddich has been the best-selling single malt. That was the year the owners launched Glenfiddich Straight Malt, the first single malt that was promoted on a global scale. In 2017, Glenfiddich managed to sell 14.7 million bottles while their biggest competitor, Glenlivet, followed in second place with 12.9 million. The one year when Glenfiddich was second was in 2014 when Glenlivet managed to top the list. Both distilleries seem focused on future growth judging from grand expansion plans that will take them to a capacity of around 20 million litres each this year or next. Together, the two account for almost one quarter of all Scotch single malt sold globally. They are also the only two single malts that have managed to sell more than 1 million cases (12 million bottles) in one year. However, it looks like they are about to have company very soon. Edrington, the owners of the third best-selling malt The Macallan, announced in January 2018 that they were very close to the 1 million mark. Later in the year, official figures from the IWSR showed that the

brand had sold 907,000 cases in 2017 (10.9 million bottles) and with the current tailwind that the brand has, it could very well be in 2018 that they join the 1-million club. Like the top 2 distilleries, Macallan has also been working on an expansion and in late 2017, a brand new, state of the art distillery was commissioned. Compared to last year's list we have a new brand in place number four - or perhaps we should say three new brands. The Singleton was launched in 2006 and is made up of three sub-brands - Glen Ord, Dufftown and Glendullan. The brand has had tremendous success in just 12 years and managed to sell 6.2 million bottles last year. In fifth place we have yet another distillery that is optimistic about the future. Glenmorangie sold just over 6 million bottles and they too will be increasing capacity soon. With an impressive sales increase of 26% in just two years, Balvenie managed to climb two places and is now number six. It is followed by Laphroaig, the biggest seller of the Islay malts but the brand seems to have lost some of the momentum it previously had. In the last two years volumes have gone up by "only" 2% while the category as a whole grew by 11%. Laphroaig landed on 3.7 million bottles in 2017 and was followed by Aberlour which sold 3.6 million bottles. Compared to the year before that meant a decrease by 13%, the biggest loss amongst the Top 10 single malts which also meant losing two places in the Top 10 list. On the other hand, volumes of Aberlour have increased by 54% in the last decade. Finally, in tenth place for the fourth consecutive year, we have Talisker with 3 million bottles. The 13% increase compared to last year was the highest in the Top 10.

As usual, let's end up with a look at the top whiskies in North America, India and Ireland.

In North America, Jack Daniel's is the undisputed leader and the sixth most sold whisk(e)y in the world with 155 million bottles. Recent brand extensions, not least JD Tennessee Rye, have bolstered sales of the whiskey. In second place is the most sold bourbon in the world Jim Beam which enjoyed an 11% increase during 2017 selling 107 million bottles. It was followed by the Canadian whisky Crown Royal (84 million), the bourbon Evan Williams (29 million) and in fifth place, Canadian Club (24 million).

In India, we find eight of the ten most sold whiskies in the world even though they cannot be sold in the EU as whisky due to the fact that they are made from molasses rather than grain. The top 5 are the same as last year; Officer's Choice (384 million bottles), McDowell's No. 1 (284 million), Imperial Blue (228 million), Royal Stag (244 million each) and Original Choice (132 million).

The Irish whiskey industry is completely dominated by three big brands with Jameson in top spot with 83 million bottles and a growth since last year of 11%. This is followed by Tullamore Dew, 14.5 million bottles which means an increase of 12% and Bushmill's (9.4 million bottles).

Changes in ownership

One is almost tempted to write "Business as usual" and then move on to the next chapter. The latest change in ownership was in summer 2017 when Billy Walker with partners took over Glenallachie distillery from Chivas

The Singleton of Glen Ord Sensorium in Hong Kong

Brothers. Even though Pernod Ricard said the sell-off was in line with their "strategy to focus on its priority spirits and wine brands and to adjust its industrial footprint to its needs" it did come as a bit of surprise. The question was – were there more distilleries that the owners wanted to get rid of in order to streamline their production? The new owners, on the other hand were not idle after the take-over. A number of single cask releases were made in spring 2018 and this was followed by an entire core range in the summer.

Another of the big companies decided to move in the same direction as Chivas in summer 2018. Edrington announced that Glenturret distillery (including The Famous Grouse Experience) as well as the Cutty Sark blend were up for sale. Despite a long and costly campaign to raise the interest in Cutty Sark, the brand has continued to lose ground in the last 5-6 years and it´s obvious that the owners' don´t want to put more money into the blend. But what was surprising in the announcement was that, first of all, they chose to announce that they were open to offers instead of presenting a signed deal and secondly that they were willing to dispose of a visitor centre attracting more than 70,000 people every year and supporting a brand that they obviously intended to keep – The Famous Grouse. The reason for Edrington's move is their ambition to focus on premium spirits, i.e. Macallan and Highland Park and with their recent investment in the new, spectacular Macallan distillery it seems to make sense that they try to off-load some surplus brands and plants.

New distilleries

Scotland

Since the new millennium started, we have seen a virtual explosion of new distilleries opening up in Scotland. No less than 30 new malt distilleries (not counting re-openings like for instance Glenglassaugh and Bladnoch) have started production. We need to go back to the late 1800s for something similar, when 40 new distilleries were founded between 1890 and 1900. Still, it will not stop here. A number of projects are in different stages of being completed while more distilleries are currently in the planning phase. On the other hand, it seems that the hype is showing signs of slowing down. Fewer new developments have been presented this year. Some previously announced projects will clearly not come to fruition and a few distilleries, labelling themselves as a combined "gin and whisky" distillery have become aware of the short-term financial benefits of just producing gin, a spirit which doesn´t require a costly maturation. That, in combination with a visitor centre and a restaurant, clearly creates a less risky business plan compared to distilling and maturing whisky.

This chapter deals with completely new distilleries. There are ongoing projects, and one newly opened distillery, that is of such magnitude that puts all the others in the shade. Read more about the expansions of Glenfiddich and Glenlivet on pages 112 and 124 and, not least, the completely new Macallan distillery on pages 35-36 and 154.

One of the hotspots for new distilleries right now is Edinburgh with no less than three distilleries about to open within the next couple of years. The first to achieve plan-

An artist´s impression of the new Rosebank Distillery

ning permission (in August 2016) was Holyrood Distillery, founded by Kelly and Rob Carpenter and David Robertson with a long background in the Scotch whisky industry. The company has employed Jack Mayo as Head Distiller who until recently worked for The Glasgow Distillery. The distillery will be built in the 180 year old, renovated Engine Shed building next to Holyrood Park. Construction work commenced in July 2018 and with a capacity of 100,000 litres the aim is to have it up and running during 2019. The other two distilleries will be built in Leith. Patrick Fletcher and Ian Stirling submitted a planning application in September 2017 (which by August 2018 still hadn´t been approved), to build a distillery beside Ocean Terminal Shopping Centre and the Royal Yacht Britannia. Once operational, the Port of Leith distillery will be producing 400,000 litres of pure alcohol per year and there will also be a visitor centre with a shop, restaurant and bar. The second distillery in Leith, in Graham Street, is planned by Halewood Wines & Spirits who currently export wines and spirits to 90 countries around the world and they also have a shareholding in West Cork Distillers in Ireland. The new distillery will be named after John Crabbie, co-founder of North British grain distillery in 1885 and a notable whisky blender. The company submitted a planning application in May 2018 for the £7m project but so far there has been no approval granted.

With Ardnahoe becoming the 9th distillery to open on Islay in the autumn of 2018, we are now waiting for at least another two. The first to reveal their plans was the French distiller and owner of Glann ar Mor distillery in Britanny, Jean Donnay, who in 2014 received planning permission to transform an old farm just south of Bowmore into a distillery. The project, which for some time was supported by independent bottler Hunter Laing as a partner, has been crippled by adversities. The latest is a land dispute between Donnay and Hunter Laing, involving a strip of land currently owned by Hunter Laing. In November 2017 the disagreement was resolved with Hunter Laing selling the land to Donnay. At the moment it seems probable that

building of the distillery could resume. Rumours about yet another Islay distillery started to flourish two years ago and were definitely confirmed in spring 2018. This time it is Sukhinder Singh, owner of Elixir Distillers and The Whisky Exchange in London, who has the intention to build a distillery just outside Port Ellen on the road to Laphroaig. A proposal of application notice appeared in March 2018 but at the time of writing no planning application had been submitted to the council. And in a couple of years, Port Ellen will actually have two distilleries. Diageo made a very surprising announcement early October 2017 that it was their intention to bring two closed distilleries back to life – Port Ellen and Brora. In the case of Port Ellen it means new buildings and completely new equipment made from the old drawings still in the Diageo archives. With a planned production start in 2020, the distillery will have the capacity to produce 750,000 litres and there will also be a visitor centre on site.

While still in the vicinity of Islay, let´s head over to Arran where Arran Distillers are about to open up their second distillery on the island. The construction of Lagg Distillery started in February 2017 and Arran´s Master Distiller, James MacTaggart anticipates they will be commissioning the distillery end of 2018 to start production in January/February 2019. Lagg will be equipped with a 4 ton mash tun, four wooden washbacks and one pair of stills. However, the production room is designed for another four washbacks and two more stills. Arran distillery in Lochranza is by far the most visited distillery in Scotland. Well over 100,000 people come here every year. When Lagg opens up to visitors in 2019, the owners expect the combined number to rise to more than 160,000!

On the west coast of the Cowal Peninsula in the west of Scotland (just north of the isle of Bute), the village Polphail was built in the 1970s as accomodation for workers on a planned oil rig construction plant nearby. The plans for the oil rig yard never came to fruition though and the houses that had already been built turned into a ghost town which

Closed in 1983, Port Ellen Distillery will re-open again in 2020

was finally demolished in 2016. This is now the unlikely spot for a possible whisky distillery. The person behind it is none other than the previous owner of Loch Lomond distillery, Sandy Bulloch (who in fact provided the funds to demolish the 'village') and the distillery will be named Portavadie after the nearby hamlet. The planning application was approved by Argyll & Bute Council in August 2018 and the plan is to produce both whisky and gin.

Thirteen years ago, there were two working distilleries in the Lowlands – three if you count the intermittent production at Bladnoch. Today there are fourteen with The Borders distillery in Hawick, Aberargie in Fife and Clydeside Distillery in Glasgow being the latest to open. Following the current trend, there is more to come.

R&B Distillers, which recently opened their first distillery on Raasay, will now be focusing on their second in The Borders but most likely this will not be built in the next few years at least. They recently joined forces with Alasdair Day who had been nurturing plans for a distillery for a couple of years.

Plans for another distillery in The Borders have been presented by Mossburn Distillers, owners of the second distillery on Skye, Torabhaig, which opened in 2017. Planning permission was granted in December 2016 for the building of, not one, but two distilleries on the site of Jedforest Hotel near Jedburgh. The first of the two, named Jedhart Distillery, to be built will be equipped with three stills and the intention according to the owners is to "focus on small production and educating visitors on the craft of making spirit." The next stage involves building Mossburn Distillery and visitor centre with the capacity of producing 2.5 million litres per year including also grain whisky. The goal is to have Jedhart distillery up and running by 2018 while Mossburn could be producing in 2021.

Moving on to the west, The Ardgowan Distillery Company received planning permission in March 2017 to build a distillery on the Ardgowan Estate, 30 miles west of Glasgow. The initial goal was to have the 800,000 litre dis-

tillery in production by 2019 but there is still the matter of funding to be resolved. The total cost has been estimated at £17m and £982,000 was received from the Scottish government in November 2017. Recently, questions have been raised about one of the founders who apparently had been granted a much larger official funding for a wave energy firm a few years ago, a company which finally went bust.

Two malt distilleries have opened in Glasgow in the last two years and a third one is underway. Independent bottler Douglas Laing announced in July 2017 that they had plans to build a distillery on the banks of the river Clyde at Pacific Quay, just opposite the new Clydeside Distillery which opened in 2017. The total cost for the distillery is £10.7m but this also includes a bottling complex, a new corporate head office, a visitor centre, whisky laboratory and archive. Initial capacity will be 100,000 litres of pure alcohol. Planning applications, still pending decision, were submitted to Glasgow City Council in spring/summer 2018 and at that time it was also decided the name of the distillery will be Clutha.

After several years of planning (the final approval was granted in 2010), the Falkirk Distillery Company has managed to build a distillery at Salmon Inn Road, Polmont but it is still uncertain if there is actually any whisky production going on at this stage. Not far away, in Falkirk, a legendary distillery is about to be resurrected. Rosebank was established in 1798 and closed in 1993, seemingly for good. The single malt from the distillery has always been held in high esteem by whisky aficionados and rumours of a possible re-opening have been floating around over the years. Still, it came as a surprise in October 2017 when independent bottler and owner of Glengoyne and Tamdhu distilleries, Ian Macleod Distillers, declared that they had bought the old distillery buildings from Scottish Canals and the trademark and remaining whisky stock from Diageo. The goal is to re-equip the distillery and start production again in 2019/2020. The whisky will be triple distilled, just like it was before and the capacity will be 6-800,000 litres.

Campbell Meyer & Co, blenders, bottlers and exporters of whisky, own a 150,000 square ft. bonded warehouse in East Kilbride, just south of Glasgow. In spring 2016, it was announced that the company had plans to add a distillery as well. Whether or not whisky production has actually commenced is still uncertain.

Up in Speyside, The Cabrach Trust have plans to build a distillery in the village of Cabrach south of Dufftown. The idea is to convert the old Inverharroch Farm to a distillery and heritage centre and it will be operated as a social enterprise. Planning permission was received in September 2017 and the owners have hopes to start the construction towards the end of 2018. Still in Speyside, a new distillery is planned at Craggan, near Grantown-on-Spey in the Cairngorms National Park. Behind the project are none other than Gordon & MacPhail, legendary independent bottler and owner of Benromach Distillery in Forres. A planning application was submitted to the Highland Council in the summer of 2018 and if that is granted, construction would start in 2019 with the distillery ready to start producing in 2020. The architects involved is NORR who also worked on Dalmunach and the recent expansions of Glenlivet and Glenfiddich.

With Glen Wyvis having started production, there still remains a few projects north of Inverness to keep an eye on. Ardross Investments Ltd have plans to build a £15m whisky and gin distillery in Ardross, just northwest of Alness. Planning approval was granted in February 2017 and construction work started in late 2017. By summer 2018, most of the equipment was in place and the owners are hoping to start production later in the year. The distillery will have the unusually large capacity of 1 million litres of pure alcohol.

Quite possibly, Heather Nelson will be the first woman to found a Scotch whisky distillery. Co-owner of a film and TV production company, Nelson has studied at the Institute of Brewing and Distilling to gain the necessary qualification. Her planning application to build a distillery on the old World War II airbase at Fearn near Tain was submitted in March 2017 and was approved in just four weeks. The distillery will be equipped with two stills (1,000 and 600 litres respectively) and three washbacks with a capacity of producing 30,000 litres. The start of production has been delayed but the first drops may be distilled in 2018.

A bit further north, just south of Brora, lies Dunrobin Castle which attracts 85,000 visitors each year. Here, Elizabeth Sunderland, a granddaughter of the former head of Clan Sutherland, and her husband Boban Costin will build a single estate distillery housed in an old powerhouse. Planning permission was granted in late 2016 and the owners hope to have the distillery, which will produce both gin and whisky, up and running in 2019. Elizabeth Sunderland´s forefathers were the founders of Clynelish distillery in 1819 and if we head up to Brora, we have the next distillery-to-be. The old Brora distillery (next to Clynelish) was closed in March 1983. Nothing much was heard about the single malt until the mid-nineties when it was released as a Rare Malt by Diageo. In 2002 it became a yearly part of the company´s Special Releases (just like Port Ellen) and whisky aficionados around the world fell in love. Since then, another 15, increasingly expensive, releases have appeared. And so in October 2017, Diageo announced that both Brora and Port Ellen distilleries would be rebuilt with the aim to start production in 2020. In the case of Brora, most of the buildings are intact and even some of the equipment is still there. The resurrection of the two distilleries, worth £35m, is evidence of how significant single malts have become and the importance of their role in today's world of whisky.

Finally, a new distillery is planned on South Uist, the second largest island of the Outer Hebrides (Lewis & Harris being the largest). The £10m distillery, with a capacity of 300,000 litres, will be a community-run project and the plan is to have their own malting floor using local peat to dry the barley. One important feature is to use the true story of the SS Politician which sank in 1941 by the nearby island Eriskay. The ship carried 264,000 bottles of whisky and the effort by the locals 'salvaging' the whisky was immortalised by Compton Mackenzie in his novel Whisky Galore which was later made into a film.

Ireland & Northern Ireland

Since last year´s book, another five distilleries in Ireland have started producing whiskey; Ballykeefe in Kilkenny, Pearse Lyons in Dublin, Powerscourt in Wicklow, Lough Mask in Mayo and, although they have been around for a while producing gin, Blackwater in Kerry. All of them are covered in the section Distilleries around the globe.

But obviously there is more to report. A number of projects are just about to start production while others are still in the construction phase or seeking funds.

A mill dating back to 1691, less than 500 metres from St Patrick´s Cathedral in Dublin is about to be converted into The Dublin Liberties Distillery. The project has been going on for a number of years and came to a temporary halt in 2014. In March 2016, the company was bought by the UK-based drinks group, Quintessential Brands, and construction of the new distillery began. In summer 2017, Stock Spirits Group acquired 25% of Quintessential Brands and also agreed to invest another €18.3m in the new distillery. Finally, in July 2018, three stills ordered from Firma Carl in Germany arrived at the distillery and production is planned to start in the autumn of 2018.

Another distillery on the horizon in Dublin will be built by one of the heavyweights in the industry, namely Diageo. The company withdrew from the Irish whiskey scene in 2014 when they sold Bushmills. Three years later, they were ready for a comeback when they announced that not only were they about to release an Irish blend called Roe & Co but that they also had plans to build a distillery in the old Guinness power station in St James' gate. The distillery, with a capacity of 500,000 litres, is expected to start production in the first half of 2019 and a visitor centre is also in the plans.

In County Mayo, Jude and Paul Davis together with Mark Quick are working on the construction of their Nephin Distillery with a cooperage having already been opened. They expect to have the stills delivered in October or November 2018. The proposed capacity of the distillery is 500,000 litres and the use of local peat will add to the character of the whiskey. Unlike many other new distillers, Nephin will not source whiskey from other producers to sell under its own name, but prefers to wait until its own whiskey is ready to be bottled.

While still on the west coast, we can report on a few more projects. Software developer, David Raethorne, has

Darryl McNally, general manager of the Dublin Whiskey Company who are about to open a new distillery in The Liberties in Dublin

recently bought Hazelwood House in Co. Sligo and plans to restore the mansion which was built in the early 1700s. Adjacent to the house lays a factory where Raethorne will establish a craft distillery called Lough Gill, as well as a visitor´s centre. Until the distillery has been built, the company will, together with Billy Walker of BenRiach and Glenallachie fame, release mature Irish whiskey that has been bought from Cooley, under the name Athrú. Sliabh Liag Distillery in south west Donegal, received planning permission in early 2017 and are hoping to start the construction during 2018 to be able to start production in 2019. Meanwhile, a sourced blended whiskey named Silkie was released by the owners in summer 2016.

The island co-op at Cape Clear, six kilometers off the Cork coast, received planning permission in August 2016 to build a €7m distillery on the island. Unfortunately along the way, one of their major investors pulled out and the owners are now looking for other ways of funding the project. Local farmer, Liam Ahearn, and his wife, Jennifer Nickerson, have chosen the Ahearn Family farm between Clonmel and Tipperary as the designated spot for Tipperary Boutique Distillery. They have also included Jennifer´s father in the business. Stuart Nickerson is well-known to lovers of Scotch after having been the distillery manager at Glenmorangie and the mastermind behind the resurrection of Glenglassaugh. Homegrown barley will be used for the future whiskey production. In December 2017, the owners managed to secure €5m in a partnership deal with Steelworks Investments.

For eight successive generations, the Scully family have farmed the coastal lands near the resort town Clonakilty in West Cork. Michael and Helen Scully, together with members of the family, are now working on the construction of a whiskey distillery which, when ready, could be producing 100,000 cases per year. To assist them, Paul Corbett from Teeling Distillery in Dublin recently joined the team. Most of the equipment has been installed and the owners hope to start production in autumn 2018. In anticipation of their first own whiskey, sourced whiskey as well as gin will be available.

In County Longford, west of Dublin, Peter Clancy in partnership with his brother and sister is planning for a distillery on the grounds of the old post office in Lanesborough. A gin still has already been installed while the whiskey stills were being manufactured Italy at the time of writing. Apart from single malt and single pot still, Lough Ree Distillery will also be producing gin and vodka.

Neil Stewart is planning to convert a 200 year old mill in Boyle, Co. Roscommon into a whiskey distillery. The local council approved the planning application in autumn 2017 and around €5m will now be invested in the project. Apparently the celebrity actor Chris O´Dowd, a Boyle native and known from the series The IT Crowd and the movie Bridesmaids, is one of the investors.

Finally, in Northern Ireland, there are currently four ongoing projects. In Derry, the producer of cream liqueurs, Niche Drinks, were granted a permission to build a distillery in Ebrington Square. The total investment would amount to £12m with a capacity of 500,000 litres of alcohol per year. In April 2018, the American company Luxco acquired Niche Drinks but the distillery project is still ongoing. In anticipation of its own whiskey, the company has released a blend called The Quiet Man based on sourced whiskey.

Joe McGirr is the mastermind behind Boatyard Distillery in Enniskillen. The company received its planning permission in 2015 and in spring of the ensuing year, the first still was installed. The beginning of May 2016 marked the first distillation and since then the company has enjoyed quite some success with their gin and vodka. Since the start, whiskey has also been part of the plan.

Michael McKeown, founder of Matt D´Arcy & Company, has been granted a planning permission in summer 2018 for a whiskey distillery in Newry in counties Armagh and Down. Around £7m will be invested in the 100,000 litre distillery and a visitor centre and the plan is to be up and running by the end of 2019. Well before that, sourced whiskey from other distilleries will be released to build the brand.

The owner of Chateau de La Ligne vineyard in Bordeaux, Terry Cross, has plans to build a distillery within the grounds of Killaney Lodge near Carryduff. Planning approval has been secured for the £6m distillery and visitor centre.

Bottling grapevine

The "opening act" for this year simply has to be the inaugural bottlings from no less than five, more or less new distilleries. The most anticipated was in no doubt the one from Daftmill. The owner of this wee distillery in Fife has been asked questions about when his first whisky would be released for many years now and Francis Cuthbert´s answer has always been "when it´s ready". And ready it was in May 2018 when the first 629 bottles of a 12 year old came out for sale. This first release was followed by more bottles in the summer. The other four distilleries which presented their first single malts were Annandale, Eden Mill, Glasgow and Kingsbarns – all of them between 3 and 4 years of age.

But 2018 was also the year when new ranges from established producers were introduced. Glenrothes steered away from their focus on vintages and no age statement bottlings and instead introduced the Soleo collection with a 10, 12, 18 and 25 year old – all of them matured in ex-sherry casks. Pulteney announced last year that two popular expressions (17 and 21 year old) would disappear due to shortage of stock. No clues were given about any possible substitutes. In summer 2018, however, an entirely new range (in new packaging as well) was revealed with 12, 15 and 18 year olds as well as the slightly smoky Huddart. But there were more distilleries that were aiming for a total makeover, Fettercairn for instance. Having relied solely on the Fior expression for several years, the owners presented a range of four aged expressions starting with a 12 year old and then taking a leap to 28, 40 and 50 year olds. The two oldest had been finished in palo cortado and tawny port respectively.

In 2014, Diageo re-launched Mortlach or perhaps it´s more fair to say launched because the only available bottling until then was the 16 year old Flora & Fauna. It didn´t go exactly as planned with just a modest interest from the punters in the rather expensive bottlings. In 2018, the old range was scrapped to make way for the 12 year old Wee Witchie, 16 year old Distiller´s Dram and the 20 year old Cowie´s Blue Seal. Over on Jura, it was almost like Santa´s workshop with no less than 10 new expressions during the year. The old core range had to make way for a new one made up of five expressions; Journey (without age statement), 10, 12 and 18 year old as well as Seven Wood (a vatting of whiskies matured in seven types of French oak as well as ex-bourbon barrels). But it didn´t stop there. The range for travel retail also received an overhaul with a new range being launched – Sherry Cask Collection including The Sound, The Road, The Loch, The Paps and The Bay. All of them have been finished in PX casks that have held sherry for varying amounts of time.

To wrap up the section talking about new ranges, let´s finish off with Glenallachie. The distillery was taken over by Billy Walker and his partners in 2017 and it didn´t take long for them to launch a set of single casks and then in summer 2018, it was time for an entire core collection starting off with a 10 year old bottled at cask strength and followed by 12, 18 and 25 year olds, all bottled at 46%.

Bowmore continued their Vault Edition range with Peat Smoke and also released a new expression in the Vintner´s Trilogy with a 27 year old with a finish in port pipes. Remaining on Islay, Bruichladdich revamped their Port Charlotte range with a new look and two new releases – a 10 year old and 2011 Islay Barley while Bunnahabhain launched the peated Toiteach a Dha, a 20 year old palo cortado and a 9 year old Moine matured in red wine casks. Kilchoman released Original Cask Strength, a 2009 Vintage and a Sauternes cask finish and Laphroaig satisfied their Friends with two new Cairdeas expressions, Quarter Cask and a 15 year old and adding a 28 year old for the rest of their fans. Loyalty to Ardbeg was rewarded by a committee bottling (and later a general release) of the Grooves which had been matured in re-toasted red wine casks.

Macallan´s big thing of the year was obviously the opening of the new distillery but they also had time to attend to their range of whiskies. The core range is now divided into three series; the classic Sherry Oak, Triple Cask (the new name for Fine Oak) and Double Cask. Since January 2018, the range for travel retail is made up of the Quest Collection with Quest, Lumina, Terra and Enigma. A 72 year old (the oldest release from the distillery to date) and the rare M Black represented the higher end of the distillery´s offerings while Genesis, released to celebrate the new distillery, caused a traffic chaos around the distillery. Just 2,500 bottles were released for sale on the 14th August at the distillery only and they sold out in less than an hour. Police had to be called in to deal with the crowds.

Highland Park has been extremely busy in the last couple of years with plenty of new bottlings and 2018 was not an exception. The entire series destined for duty free was revamped with just a few of the old Warriors being kept in the range. The new ones, launched in autumn 2018, were Spirit of the Bear, Loyalty of the Wolf, Wings of the Eagle and a duty free version of the 18 year old Viking Pride. The owners also managed to release a new edition of the classic 50 year old as well as the second instalment in the Viking Legend series, Valknut.

Aberfeldy focused on duty free with no less than five new releases; 16 year old, 21 year old madeira finish, 18 year old port finish, a 33 year old single cask and a Vintage 1999. Glenmorangie also catered to travellers with the introduction of Cadboll but, as always, there was a new release in the Private Edition range as well. This year it was Spios which had been fully matured in casks that had previously held rye whisky. On top of that, the Grand Vintage Malt 1989 was released in spring 2018.

Glenmorangie´s old stable mate, Glen Moray, released the 10 year old Fired Oak with some of the spirit matured in virgin oak and in the pipe line is also a malt that had been finished in cider casks. Talking about finishes, Glenfiddich released Winter Storm finished in Canadian icewine casks and Fire & Cane, with an extra maturation in rum casks. Glenfiddich´s fierce competitor, Glenlivet, released a new expression in The Winchester Collection, a Vintage 1967, but also a new "mystery bottling" The Glenlivet Code, inviting customers to take a guess about the content and the maturation. And, perhaps more important, the distillery also introduced a new member of the core range by way of Captain´s Reserve with a finish in cognac casks.

Auchentoshan continued their cooperation with mixologists with Bartender´s Malt 2 and also released a 1988 PX cask while Arran released their first 21 year old while at the same time introducing Explorer´s Series with Brodick Bay, finished in oloroso butts, as the first expression.

BenRiach added two new expressions to their peated range with Temporis 21 year old and Authenticus 30 year old while GlenDronach made their debut in the travel retail range with 10 year old Forgue and 16 year old Boynsmill. Another distillery recognising the importance of duty free sales was Glengoyne when they lined up a range of no less than four bottlings for travellers; Cuartillo, Balbaine, a 28 year old and Glengoyne PX. Speyburn also wanted to be present in that segment with a 10 year old as well as Hopkins Reserve which had been matured in casks that previously held a peated whisky.

Talisker decided to highlight the impact of different sherry cask finishes with the Bodega Series with a first release of a 40 year old amontillado finish. Tobermory were into finishing as well with a 12 year old fino finish and two 19 year old Ledaigs finished in PX casks and oloroso casks. While on the same theme, Tullibardine launched the Murray Marsala Finish, Craigellachie released two bottlings for duty free; a 24 year old and a 17 year old palo cortado finish and Deanston came up with a Vintage 2008 brandy finish as well as a 10 year old Bordeaux red wine finish. Dalmore always excels in different wine maturations and released Port Wood Reserve as a new addition to the core range. At the same time, they introduced Vintage Port Collection with the third instalment being a 45 year old in spring 2018.

Old expressions are always popular, at least when you have the wallet for it, and the Loch Lomond 50 year old was definitely one to look out for. So was Tomintoul 1965 The Ultimate Cask, the sole remaining cask from 1965 (the first year of distillation). and The Singleton of Glendullan 40 year old, the oldest whisky ever released from the distillery.

Chivas Brothers have always been a bit reluctant to release single malts from their more obscure distilleries but this has changed in recent years. There were 15 year olds from Glenburgie, Miltonduff and Glentauchers in 2017 and in 2018, we saw the first official bottling, lightly peated, from Allt-a-Bhainne and even Glen Keith was granted with a release – the Distillery Edition.

Balvenie released batch two of their peated expression Peat Week and celebrated the 25th anniversary of Double Wood 12 year old with a limited 25 year old. Glen Grant pleased the American market with a 15 year old while Aberlour introduced a new member to the core range – Casg Annamh. The final chapter of Glen Garioch Rennaisance Collection was an 18 year old and Tomatin released the final two expressions in their Five Virtues series – Water and Metal. The owners of Tamdhu, Ian Macleod, continued to expand the range for Tamdhu with a 12 year old and with a 15 year old in the pipeline for next year. Springbank pleased their fans, as always, with new expressions; the Local Barley 10 year old, a 14 year old Longrow sherry wood and an 11 year old Longrow Red with a finish in cabernet franc casks

Finally, the Special Releases from Diageo were revealed already in spring 2018 (just like last year) with the aim to precede bloggers that scan the TTB (Alcohol and Tobacco Tax and Trade Bureau) website where labels need to be presented well in advance of the release. The first obvious notice was that Port Ellen and Brora are not part of the release anymore. With the imminent resurrection of both distilleries, the owners have decided to keep the stock of both whiskies for future projects, probably to coincide with the openings. Instead, this year´s release includes Carsebridge single grain 48 years old, Inchgower 27 years old, Oban 21 years old, Pittyvaich 28 years old, The Singleton of Glen Ord 14 years old, Talisker 8 years old, Lagavulin 12 years old (the usual cask strength), two Caol Ila - an unpeated 15 year old and a 35 year old - and finally Cladach, a "mystery" blended malt from coastal distilleries.

Cladach, Aberlour Casg Annamh, Jura 18 years, Fettercairn 28 years, Mortlach 20 years, Carsebridge 48 years

Independent
bottlers

The independent bottlers play an important role
in the whisky business. With their innovative bottlings, they increase
diversity. Single malts from distilleries where the owners' themselves
decide not to bottle also get a chance through the independents.
The following are a selection of the major companies.
Tasting notes have been prepared by Ingvar Ronde.

Gordon & MacPhail

www.gordonandmacphail.com

Established in 1895 the company, which is owned by the Urquhart
family, still occupies the same premises in Elgin. Apart from being
an independent bottler, there is also a legendary store in Elgin and,
since 1993, an own distillery, Benromach. In 2018, the company
announced that not only would they establish a designated gin distillery on the Benromach site but they were also to build a new malt
whisky distillery at Craggan, close to Grantown-on-Spey. Gordon &
MacPhail has an incredible variety of casks in their warehouses in
Elgin and in 2018, they revamped their portfolio of bottlings. Going
forward, there will be five distinctive ranges; Connoisseurs Choice,
a series well-known to most whisky aficionados, has received a
new look and consists of single malts bottled either at 43% or 46%.
Discovery, a new range unveiled in May 2018, is grouped under
three flavour profiles - smoky, sherry and bourbon. Distillery Labels
is a relic from a time when Gordon & MacPhail released more or
less official bottlings for several producers. Currently 10 distilleries
are represented in the range and the whisky is bottled at either 40 or
43%. Private Collection, a new range, will feature old single malts
including bottlings from closed distilleries. Generations, finally,
was first introduced in 2010. This range comprises the oldest and
rarest whiskies in stock, including previous releases such as Mortlach and Glenlivet 70 year old and, in 2015, the oldest single malt
ever bottled - a 75 year old Mortlach.

Gordon & MacPhail rarely buy matured whisky from other producers. Instead, around 95% is bought as new make spirit and filled
by the company. Some 7,000 casks are maturing in one racked and
one dunnage warehouse in Elgin, another 7,000 casks are found at
various distillers around Scotland and 20,000 casks are located in
the warehouses at Benromach.

Caol Ila 1990, 50.7%
Nose: Seductive with notes of fruit
candy, cherry trifle, French
nougat and tobacco.
Palate: Plenty of orchard fruit, sweet
cider, dry oaky notes with a hint
of smoke at the end.

Aberfeldy 1993, 58.7%
Nose: Tropical fruits, tobacco leaves
and cedar wood followed by
cinnamon, oranges and dark
chocolate.
Palate: Delicious rum notes, ripe
pineapple, banana, crème
brûlé, dark chocolate and
roasted nuts.

Berry Bros. & Rudd

www.bbr.com

Britain's oldest wine and spirit merchant, founded in 1698 has
recently opened a new shop in London. The famous address 3 St
James's Street, where the company has been since the start, has
now been returned to its appearance of 30 years ago and this will
now be a space for consultations, meetings and events. The new,
and much larger store, is just around the corner in 63 Pall Mall.
Berry Brothers had been offering their customers private bottlings
of malt whisky for years, but it was not until 2002 that they
launched Berry's Own Selection of single malt whiskies. Under the
supervision of Spirits Manager, Doug McIvor, some 30 expressions
are on offer every year. Bottling is usually at 46% but expressions

bottled at cask strength are also available. The super premium blended malt, Blue Hanger, is also included in the range. In autumn 2014 the Exceptional Casks Collection was launched, comprising of old and rare whiskies and rum. A new series called The Clasic Range was released in spring 2018. It´s made up of four bottlings of blended malt; Speyside, Islay, Sherry Cask Matured and Peated Cask Matured. At the same time, the company reintroduced their own-label gin which was first launched in 1909. In 2010, BBR sold Cutty Sark blended Scotch to Edrington and obtained The Glenrothes single malt in exchange but in 2017, BBR sold back The Glenrothes to Edrington.

Speyside Blended Malt, 44.2%
Nose: Sweet notes of honey, yellow plums and apples. Malty, dried grass and sweet, subtle smoke.
Palate: Intense and mouthcoating with waves of cereals, clove, hazelnuts and sweet smoke.

Sherry Cask Matured Blended Malt, 44.2%
Nose: Dark plums, raisins, maple syrup, walnuts, dark chocolate and a hint of smoke.
Palate: Creamy and balanced, autumnal, dark fruits, chili pepper, chocolate and cigarr smoke.

Signatory

Founded in 1988 by Andrew and Brian Symington, Signatory Vintage Scotch Whisky lists at least 50 single malts at any one occasion. The most widely distributed range is Cask Strength Collection which sometimes contains spectacular bottlings from distilleries which have long since disappeared. One good example is a very rare Glencraig 1976, 38 years old. Another range is The Unchill Filtered Collection bottled at 46%. Some of the latest bottlings released include a Linkwood 22 year old, a Glenlossie 21 year old and a very rare Dallas Dhu, distilled in 1975. Finally there is also the Single Grain Collection. Andrew Symington bought Edradour Distillery from Pernod Ricard in 2002 and the entire operations, including Signatory, are now concentrated to the distillery in Perthshire.

Ian Macleod Distillers

www.ianmacleod.com

The company was founded in 1933 and is one of the largest independent family-owned companies within the spirits industry. Gin, rum, vodka and liqueurs, apart from whisky, are found within the range and they also own Glengoyne and Tamdhu distilleries. In autumn 2017 they also revealed their plans to resurrect Rosebank Distillery in Falkirk which has been closed since 1993. Their single malt range includes The Chieftain´s, which cover a range of whiskies from 10 to 50 years old while Dun Bheagan is divided into two series – Regional Malts, 8 year old single malts expressing the character from 4 whisky regions in Scotland and Rare Vintage Single Malts, a selection of single cask bottlings from various distilleries. There are two As We Get It single malt expressions – Highland and Islay. The Six Isles blended malt contains whisky from all the whisky-producing islands while one of the top sellers is the blended malt Isle of Skye with five domestic expressions . Finally, Smokehead, a heavily, peated single malt from Islay introduced in 2006, has

become a huge success. Apart from the core expression, there is also a Smokehead Extra Black 18 years old, Smokehead Extra Rare and the limited Smokehead Rock Edition. The range was revamped in April 2018 and a new expression was added to the range – Smokehead High Voltage which is bottled at 58%. In 2016, the company acquired Spencerfield Spirit which included Edinburgh Gin as well as the blended malt Sheep Dip and Pig´s Nose blended Scotch.

Smokehead High Voltage, 58%
Nose: Herbal and green with minty notes, ripe banana, pine tree and heather smoke.
Palate: Dry and well balanced smokiness followed by chili pepper, clove, cardamom and honey.

Pig´s Nose, 40%
Nose: Slightly vegetal fruit notes hit first followed by dusty fruit spice and dried cigar leaves with a flicker of iodine.
Palate: Dried apricots with a warming spice roll onto the palate with chunky fruit cake notes.

Blackadder International

www.blackadder.se

Blackadder is owned by Robin Tucek, one of the authors of the classic whisky book, The Malt Whisky File. Apart from the Blackadder and Blackadder Raw Cask (bottled straight from the cask without any filtration at all), there are also a number of other ranges – Smoking Islay, Peat Reek, Aberdeen Distillers, Clydesdale Original and Caledonian Connections. The company has also been known for bottling unusual expressions of Amrut single malt. All bottlings are single cask, uncoloured and un chill-filtered. Most of the bottlings are diluted to 43-46% but Raw Cask is always bottled at cask strength.

Creative Whisky Company

www.creativewhisky.co.uk

David Stirk started the Creative Whisky Co in 2005 and the company exclusively bottles single casks, divided into three series: The Exclusive Malts are bottled at cask strength and vary in age between 8 and 40 years. Around 20 bottlings are made annually. This is followed by the Exclusive Regions which are single cask bottlings, bottled at 50%, from various distilleries that represent different whisky regions in Scotland. Finally there is the Exclusive Blends range. The most recent releases include a 10 year old Isle of Islay, an Ailsa Bay NAS, a 23 year old Speyside, a 23 year old Glen Keith and a 9 year old Ruadh Maor (the peated version of Glenturret). In August 2018, new owners took over with David Stirk still being involved in the business.

Duncan Taylor

www.duncantaylor.com

Duncan Taylor was founded in Glasgow in 1938 as a cask broker and trading company. In 2001, the company was acquired by Euan Shand in 2001 and operations were moved to Huntly. Duncan Taylor´s flagship brand is the blended Scotch Black Bull, a brand with a history going back to 1864. Black Bull was rebranded in 2009 by Duncan Taylor and the range consists of three core releases – Kyloe, a 12 year old and a 21 year old. There are also three limited versions, 30 year old, 40 year old and Special Reserve. In early 2018 Black Bull 10 year old rum finish was added to the range. The Black Bull brand is complimented by Smokin' which is a blend of peated Speyside, Islay and grain whisky from the Lowlands.

The portfolio also includes Rarest (single cask, cask strength whiskies of great age from demolished distilleries), Dimensions (a collection of single malts and single grains aged up to 39 years), The Octave (single malt whiskies matured for a further period in small, 50 litre ex-sherry octave casks), The Tantalus (a selection of whiskies all aged in their 40s), The Duncan Taylor Single Range (whiskies aged 30 years or more from closed distilleries) and Battlehill (a range of single malts and single grains). The blended malt category is represented by Big Smoke, a young peated whisky available in three strengths, 40%, 50% and 60%. Finally, there is also the Duncan Taylor Blended Scotch in three versions – Five Stars, 12 year old and 18 year old.

Cambus 1991 25 years old, 55.1%

Nose: Pleasant combination of dried fruit, pineapple, banana, brown sugar and vanilla.

Palate: Rich and warming with notes of liquorice, raisins, chocolate brownie, espresso and rum/raisin ice cream.

Black Bull 10 year old rum finish, 50%

Nose: Nice, fresh rum notes, boiled jasmine rice, Earl Grey and vanilla.

Palate: Smoke with tropical fruits, honey, salmiak, cardamom, cinnamon and banana.

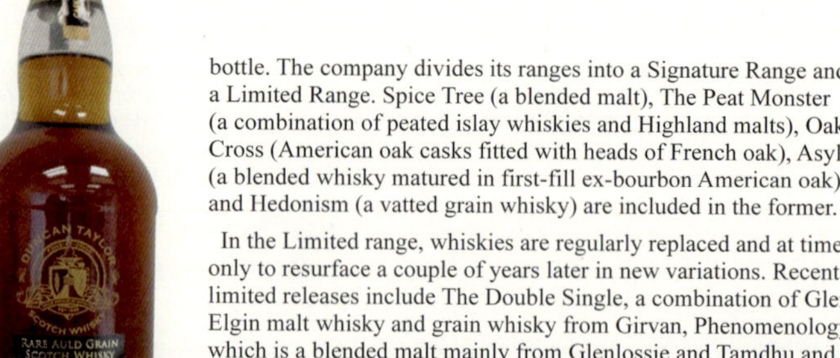

Scotch Malt Whisky Society

www.smws.com

The Scotch Malt Whisky Society, founded in 1983 and owned by Glenmorangie Co since 2003, has more than 30,000 members worldwide and apart from UK, there is a network of international branches and partner bars in 19 countries around the world. In 2015, Glenmorangie sold the SMWS to the HotHouse Club and a group of the managers. The idea from the very beginning was to buy casks of single malts from the producers and bottle them at cask strength without colouring or chill filtration. The Society has played a significant role for the interest in single cask Scotch that has exploded in recent decades. The labels do not reveal the name of the distillery. Instead there is a number but also a short description which will give you a clue to which distillery it is. Around 500 casks are bottled every year. The SMWS also arranges tastings at their different venues but also at other locations. In recent years, the range has been expanded to also include single grain, whiskies from other countries as well as rum. In July 2017, a sub-brand named Single Cask Spirits was launched for the non-malt whisky releases (rum, gin, cognac, bourbon etc) and in autumn 2017, the Society launched their first blended malt - the 10 year old Exotic Cargo.

Murray McDavid

www.murray-mcdavid.com

The company was founded in 1996 by Mark Reynier, Simon Coughlin and Gordon Wright and in 2000, they also acquired Bruichladdich distillery. In 2013 Murray McDavid was taken over by Aceo Ltd. and a year later they signed a lease for the warehouses at the closed Coleburn distillery for storing their own whiskies as well as stock belonging to clients. The bottlings are divided into six different ranges; Mission Gold (exceptionally rare whiskies bottled at cask strength), Benchmark (mature single malts bottled at 46%), Mystery Malt (single malts where the distillery is not revealed), Select Grain (single grains), The Vatting (vatted malts) and Crafted Blend (blended Scotch from their own blending). The vast majority of the releases are single casks.

Compass Box Whisky Co

www.compassboxwhisky.com

John Glaser, founder and co-owner of the company, has a philosophy which is strongly influenced by meticulous selection of oak for the casks, clearly inspired by his time in the wine business. But he also has a lust for experimenting to test the limits, which was clearly shown when Spice Tree, matured in casks containing extra staves, was launched in 2005. Glaser and Compass Box are also advocating more transparency in the industry where the customer is given as much information as possible about the contents of the

bottle. The company divides its ranges into a Signature Range and a Limited Range. Spice Tree (a blended malt), The Peat Monster (a combination of peated islay whiskies and Highland malts), Oak Cross (American oak casks fitted with heads of French oak), Asyla (a blended whisky matured in first-fill ex-bourbon American oak) and Hedonism (a vatted grain whisky) are included in the former.

In the Limited range, whiskies are regularly replaced and at times only to resurface a couple of years later in new variations. Recent limited releases include The Double Single, a combination of Glen Elgin malt whisky and grain whisky from Girvan, Phenomenology which is a blended malt mainly from Glenlossie and Tamdhu and No Name, a blended malt and the peatiest release from Compass Box yet. These were all released in autumn 2017. In spring 2018 came Hedonism The Muse, a new version of the classic blended grain and the blended Scotch Delilah´s XXV which was a celebration of the 25th anniversary of the legendary whisky bar in Chicago. A third range, Great King Street, offers blended Scotch with a 50% proportion of malt whisky and using new French oak for complexity. The first expression was called Artist´s Blend and in autumn 2014 Glasgow Blend was released. In autumn 2014, Compass Box made a long-term agreement with John Dewar & Sons where the Bacardi-owned company would supply Compass Box with stocks of whisky for future bottlings. In spring 2015 it was further announced that Bacardi had acquired a minority share of the independent bottler.

Delilah´s XXV, 48%

Nose: Mellow and rounded with notes of dried fruit, honeycomb, vanilla, sponge cake and custard.

Palate: Nice balance between sweet and dry, spicy notes, honey, marzipan and lemon curd.

Hedonism The Muse, 55%

Nose: Elegant and floral with distinct rum notes, tropical fruit and vanilla.

Palate: Still floral on the palate but also herbal with notes of violet, eucalyptus, marzipan and nutmeg.

Master of Malt

www.masterofmalt.com

Master of Malt is one of the biggest and most innovative whisky retailers in the UK. The company also has its own ranges of award-winning bottled whiskies. One range is the Single Cask Series which features natural cask strength bottlings from various distilleries. Some of the latest include a 24 year old Auchentoshan, a 29 year old Macallan, a 24 year old Glen Keith and a 14 year old Laphroaig. You can also Blend Your Own whisky on the site. Another feature is that the site has more than 6,000 of Drinks by the Dram's 30ml bottles in stock, allowing customers to personalise the contents of Drinks by the Dram Tasting Sets and spirits-filled Advent Calendars as they order. There's also a Dram Club whisky subscription service, so customers can discover new whiskies all year round.

Inchmurrin 23 years old, 54.1%

Nose: Floral and fruity with notes of pears, vanilla, heather honey and rye bread.

Palate: Creamy mouthfeel, orchard fruits, liquorice, vanilla, mushrooms, roasted nuts, honey and a hint of smoke.

Atom Brands

Part of the same Atom Drinks group as retailer Master of Malt, Atom Brands includes a number of independent bottlers. They're distributed by Maverick Drinks who also import many American craft whiskeys, including malts, from the likes of St. George Spirits, Balcones and FEW Spirits.

That Boutique-y Whisky Company
www.thatboutiqueywhiskycompany.com

Established in 2012, That Boutique-y Whisky Company's releases have all carried age statements since 2016. (Previously, the age difference between the whiskies in a single NAS batch had been as much as 30 years, but this is much less the case now.) TBWC has made it clear that they believe flavour is still the most important aspect, but are aware that customers are nonetheless interested in ages of the constituent parts. They have also offered their support to Compass Box's Campaign for Scotch Whisky. Over 250 different bottlings have now been released from more than 90 different distilleries including Springbank, Ardbeg, Mortlach, Port Ellen and Paul John. The range also includes a handful of blended malts, blends, single grains, bourbons and even ryes.

Islay #2, 25 years old, 48,7%
Nose: Sweet and fragrant smokiness, red apples, peaches, maple syrup, vanilla, menthol and thyme.
Palate: Savoury with notes of barbecue sauce and chorizo but also a lovely fruit bowl of apricots, grilled peaches and basil.

The Blended Whisky Company
www.theblendedwhiskycompany.com

The Blended Whisky Company, also established in 2012, produces The Lost Distilleries Blend and The Half-Century Blend. The Lost Distilleries Blend is made exclusively from extremely rare whiskies produced at now closed distilleries. The tenth batch is a trip down memory lane, containing grain from Port Dundas and malt from Caperdonich, Rosebank, Imperial, Mosstowie, Glen Mhor, Glenisla, Glenlochy, Craigduff, Port Ellen and Brora. The Half-Century Blend is made exclusively with whiskies over 50 years old and harks back to a time when distilleries were home to less efficient barley-strains, on-site floor maltings and inefficient brewer's yeast.

The Lost Distilleries Blend batch 10, 51%
Nose: Lively and complex with notes of tropical fruits, grape juice, aniseed, nettles, gooseberries, citrus, vanilla and chocolate.
Palate: Vanilla, butter scotch, bit of pepper, grapefruit, creme brule with a perfectly burnt crust and some woody/smokey notes at the end.

Darkness!
www.darknesswhisky.com

The first whiskies from Darkness! were released in spring 2014 and the key words for these expressions are dark and heavily sherried. To create the character, single malts are filled into specially commissioned 50 litre first fill Sherry casks where they are finished for more than 3 months. Pedro Ximénez, Oloroso, Palo Cortado, Fino and Moscatel Sherry casks have all been used (specified on each bottling) as well as hybrid PX and Oloroso casks made up with staves from each. Recent releases include a 27 year old Bladnoch finished in an PX cask and a 22 year old Tobermory finished in a Moscatel cask.

Peatside 6 year old Moscatel Cask Finish, 60,1%
Nose: Meaty and savoury, wet wool by the fireplace, burnt hay, barbecue and raisins soaked in wine.
Palate: Powerful yet youthful and vibrant, sweet smokiness with winey notes, salami, hickory, star aniseed, orange zest and baked root vegetables.

The Whisky Agency
www.whiskyagency.de

The man behind this company is Carsten Ehrlich, to many whisky aficionados known as one of the founders of the annual Whisky Fair in Limburg, Germany. His experience from sourcing casks for limited Whisky Fair bottlings led him to start as an independent bottler under the name The Whisky Agency, a business celebrating its 10th anniversary in 2018. There are several ranges including The Whisky Agency, The Perfect Dram and Specials with some unusual bottlings. A recent collaboration with The Whisky Exchange in London resulted in two releases – a 19 year old Bowmore and a 24 year old, un-named Irish distillery (quite possibly Bushmills).

North Star Spirits
www.northstarspirits.com

Founded in 2016, by Iain Croucher who was sales manager and brand ambassador for AD Rattray before deciding to go it alone. Apart from a number of single malt releases, Croucher also introduced the blended malt brand Vega in 2017. The two latest releases (in 2018) were a 40 and a 41 year old. In addition there is the 20 your old blended Scotch called Spica. North Star is not focused on just whisky from Scotland. They have bottled a 13 year old Tennessee Whiskey and there will be a small batch of Glasgow gin in the not too distant future.

A Dewar Rattray Ltd
www.adrattray.com

The company was founded by Andrew Dewar Rattray in 1868. In 2004 the company was revived by Tim Morrison, previously of Morrison Bowmore Distillers and fourth generation descendent of Andrew Dewar, with a view to bottling single cask malts from different regions in Scotland. One of its best-sellers is a single malt named Stronachie which is actually sourced from Benrinnes. There are currently two expressions, a 10 year old and the recently released 10 year old sherry finish. A peated, blended malt, Cask Islay, became available in 2011 and then again in 2013 but this time as a single malt. It was complemented in 2018 by Cask Orkney 18 year old. The AD Rattray´s Cask Collection is a range of single cask whiskies bottled at cask strength and without colouring or chill-filtration. An exciting new experiment, The Octave Project, has recently been launched by the company. It involved taking a cask from a single distillery and divide the content into four smaller casks, so called octaves. The octaves had been made from staves taken from casks that had previously contained PX sherry, Oloroso sherry, Rioja or Rum. The original whisky was then left for a period of time in the new, smaller casks. The first whiskies that were chosen for the project were Arran 6 year old, Pulteney 9 year old and Bunnahabhain 14 year old. In 2011, the company opened A Dewar Rattray´s Whisky Experience & Shop in Kirkoswald, South Ayrshire. Apart from having a large choice of whiskies for sale, there is a sample room, as well as a cask room. All the products in the shop, including personalised own label single cask bottlings, are also available on-line from www. adrattray.com.

Stronachie 10 year old Sherry Edition, 46.0%
Nose: Fruity and vibrant with notes of green tea leaves, citrus, vanilla and canned pears.
Palate: Sweet barley, honey and a hint of pepper is followed by sherry notes, eucalyptus, lemon meringue pie and dry, malty notes.

Cask Orkney 18 years old, 46%
Nose: Fresh with notes of citrus, heather, toffee, hay and green apples.
Palate: Fruity, inviting and soft on the palate, vanilla, honey, yellow plums, digestive and caramel.

Douglas Laing & Co

www.douglaslaing.com

Established in 1948 by Douglas Laing, this firm was run for many years by his two sons, Fred and Stewart. In 2013, the brothers decided to go their separate ways. Douglas Laing & Co is now run by Fred Laing and his daughter, Cara. Douglas Laing has the following brands in their portfolio; Provenance (single casks bottled at 46%), Director´s Cut (old and rare single malts), Premier Barrel (single malts in ceramic decanters), Clan Denny (mainly old single grains), Double Barrel (two malts vatted together), and Old Particular, a range of single malts and grains. A limited subrange under the Provenance label called Coastal Collection, was launched in spring 2018 and to celebrate the company´s 70th anniversary, the new XOP Platinum series was launched at the same time. The first release was a 25 year old Ardbeg.

Five years ago the company started a range that has become highly succesful. The first installment in th series that eventually was given the name Remarkable Region Malts, was Scallywag - a blended malt influenced by sherried whiskies from Speyside. More versions have followed with Scallywag 10 yer old and Scallywag Chocolate Edition 2009 (both released in 2018) being the latest. The range has been expanded over the years and now includes Timorous Beastie from the Highlands where a 10 year old in 2018 followed previous expressions. Rock Oyster (with a sherry edition released in 2017) is a blended malt combining whiskies from Islay, Arran, Orkney and Jura and can be found without age statement or as an 18 year old. The Epicurean represents the Lowlands and was introduced in 2017 while The Gauldrons, released in autumn 2017, is made from Campbeltown malts. The final regional whisky is Big Peat, a vatting of Islay malts. This was launched several years ago but was later included in

the range. A limited 25 year old Big Peat was released end of 2017. In July 2017, it was announced that Douglas Laing would also become distillers. Their chosen site in Glasgow is on the banks of the river Clyde just opposite the new Clydeside Distillery and the hope is that the distillery will be operational by the end of 2018.

The Gauldrons, 46.2%
Nose: Intense and herbal, green plants, grapefruit peel and subtle smoke.
Palate: Sweet caramel and dark sugar followed by slightly peppery notes and a hint of thyme and rosemary.

Scallywag 10 years old, 46%
Nose: Inviting with buttery toffee notes followed by pear and roasted mustard seeds.
Palate: Savoury and fruity, baked apples, vanilla, chocolate and some bitter oaky notes.

Malts of Scotland

www.malts-of-scotland.com

Thomas Ewers from Germany, bought casks from Scottish distilleries and decided in the spring of 2009 to start releasing them as single casks bottled at cask strength and with no colouring or chill filtration. Apart from ranges of Scotch single malts, Ewers has also added three ranges called Malts of Ireland, Malts of India and Whiskeys of America. At the moment he has released more than 100 bottlings and apart from a large number of single casks, there are two special series, Amazing Casks and Angel´s Choice, both dedicated to very special and superior casks. Ewers was inducted as a Keeper of the Quaich in 2016.

Hunter Laing & Co

www.hunterlaing.com

This company was formed after the demerger between Fred and Stewart Laing in 2013 (see Douglas Laing). It is run by Stewart Laing and his two sons, Scott and Andrew. The relatively new company Edition Spirits, founded by Andrew has also been absorbed into Hunter Laing with the range of single malts called First Editions. From the demerger, the following ranges and brands ended up in the Hunter Laing portfolio; The Old Malt Cask (rare and old malts, bottled at 50%), The Old and Rare Selection (an exclusive range of old malts offered at cask strength) and The Sovereign (a range of old and rare grain whiskies). A new range with the name Hepburn´s Choice was launched in spring 2014. These single malts are younger than The Old Malt Cask expressions and bottled at 46%. A little later in the year, the blended malt Highland Journey was released.

In January 2016, the company announced their intentions of building a distillery on Islay on the northeast coast near Bunnahabhain. At the time of writing minor construction details remained and the distillery was due to be commissioned during autumn 2018. Ardnahoe will have a capacity of 500,000 litres and Jim McEwan, who retired from Bruichladdich in 2015, has joined the team as production director. McEwan was also responsible for selecting six single casks of rare Islay whiskies that were released in May under the label Feis Ile 2017 Kinship. The bottles were very limited and only available during the festival. In May 2018, a second range of six Kinship bottlings were released - Highland Park, Springbank, Jura, Bowmore, Bunnahabhain and Laphroaig, all of them aged between 20 and 30 years

The Kinship Springbank 25 years old, 53,7%
Nose: Savoury and sligthly smoky, dark plums, tropical fruits, dried flowers, roasted nuts and chocolate.

Palate: Very rich with notes of orchard fruits, blueberries, chocolate, espresso and mint. Old school!

The Kinship Highland Park 21 yers old, 51.4%
Nose: Fresh with notes of dried flowers, orange peel, peaches, candy cane and a hint of smoke.
Palate: Seductive and sweet, Danish pastry, pepper, liquorice, papaya and gentle smoke.

Wemyss Malts

www.wemyssmalts.com

Founded in 2005, the family-owned independent bottler opened up their own whisky distillery at Kingsbarns in Fife in 2014. The company is mainly known for its range of blended malts of which there are three core expressions – The Hive, Spice King and Peat Chimney. These are available at 46% un chill-filtered and also in limited edition batch strength around 55%. In 2017, the family bottled a new part of their blended malt range called The Family Collection consisting of spirit sourced and fully matured by the family. There were two releases, Vanilla Burst and Treacle Chest and they were followed up in 2018 by Nectar Grove which has been finished in ex-Madeira casks. Another two releases appeared in October; Blooming Gorse, comprised of two Northern Highland malts matured in bourbon barrels and hogsheads and Flaming Feast which is a blend of one Eastern Highland and one Island single malt (both peated).

Another side of the business involves single malts. There are two ranges; one of which consists of single casks bottled at 46% or the occasional cask strength. The names of the whiskies reflect what they taste like although for some time now, the distillery name is also printed on the label. All whiskies are un chill-filtered and without colouring and in 2018, a total of 60 bottlings will be released. In 2012, the company released its first premium blended whisky, Lord Elcho, named after the eldest son of the 5th Earl of Wemyss. The Lord Elcho range has since then been expanded with a no age statement version. Finally, the family has also had great success with their Darnley´s Gin and a dedicated gin distillery was opened in June 2017 at Kingsbarns in an adjacent cottage.

Nectar Grove blended malt, 46%
Nose: Intense, sweet and prickly with floral notes, apple cider, candy sticks and honey.
Palate: Seductive and sweet with lots of fruit; oranges, apricots and peaches, also ginger, almonds and hint of menthol.

The Hive, 46%
Nose: Nice and fruity with notes of milk chocolate, bananas, sweet barley and fresh grass.
Palate: Rich honey coming through, heather, vanilla, citrus and orange marmalade.

Jewish Whisky Company

www.singlecasknation.com

A few years ago, Jason Johnstone-Yellin and Joshua Hatton, two well-known whisky bloggers, started, in alliance with Seth Klaskin, a new career as independent bottlers. The idea with Single Cask Nation somewhat reminds you of Scotch Malt Whisky Society in the sense that you have to become a member of the nation in order to buy the bottlings. Some of the more recent bottlings include a 10 year old Tamdhu with a rye finish, a 9 year old from The English Whisky Company and a 12 year old Glen Moray. They also have

American and Indian whiskies in the range including Westland, Koval, FEW Spirits and Amrut. Since 2013 the company also arranges popular whisky events under the name Whisky Jewbilee in New York, Chicago and Seattle. In 2017, the owners decided to launch a special range of whiskies that could also be found at retailers in California, Illinois, Massachusetts, New Jersey and New York, later expanded to include also DC, Delaware, Maryland and Florida. The 3rd release in summer 2018 included Invergordon 43 year old, Croftengea 10 year old and Glenrothes 20 year old.

Meadowside Blending

www.meadowsideblending.com

The company may be a newcomer to the family of independent bottlers but the founder certainly isn´t. Donald Hart, a Keeper of the Quaich and co-founder of the well-known bottler Hart Brothers, runs the Glasgow company together with his son, Andrew. There are three sides to the business – blends sold under the name The Royal Thistle, single malts labelled The Maltman and single cask single grains under the label The Grainman. A fourth range was recently introduced - Excalibur Blended Scotch where the inaugural release was 45 years old!

Elixir Distillers

www.elixirdistillers.com

The company is owned by Sukhinder Singh, known by most for his two very well-stocked shops in London, The Whisky Exchange. In the beginning of October every year, he is hosting The Whisky Show in London, one of the best whisky festivals in the world and for the last two years he has also been involved in the Old & Rare Show in Glasow. In 2005 he started as an independent bottler of malt whiskies operating under the brand name The Single Malts of Scotland. There are around 50 bottlings on offer at any time, either as single casks or as batches bottled at cask strength or at 46%. In 2009 a new range of Islay single malts under the name Port Askaig was introduced. The current core range consists of 100° Proof, 16, 19, 30 and 45 year old. Recent limited releases include 14 year old, a 33 year old single cask for USA and a 34 year old single cask for the rest of the world. Elements of Islay, a series of cask strength single malts in which all Islay distilleries are, or will be, represented was introduced a few years before Port Askaig. The list of the product range is cleverly constructed with periodical tables in mind in which each distillery has a two-letter acronym followed by a batch number, for example Ar_8 (Ardbeg) or Lp_7 (Laphroaig). The most recent bottlings, released in autumn 2018, are Bn_7, Cl_{11}, Lp_9 and Pc_5. Finally, the company also has a range called Director´s Special which showcases exceptionally old and rare single malts.

Port Askaig 14 years old, 45.8%
Nose: Dried seeweed and smoked fish, hay, coffee beans and green apples.
Palate: Fruity smokiness with sweet honey notes, peaches, apricots, salted caramel, black pepper and a bit of eucalyptus.

Mortlach 22 year old, 54.2%
Nose: Dark and powerful with chocolate, cigars, ceder wood, coffee beans and dried fruit.
Palate: Loads, and I mean loads of chocolate, Sacher torte, coffee, vanilla, liquorice, spices and pepper. A real heavy weight!

The Ultimate Whisky Company

www.ultimatewhisky.com

Founded in 1994 by Han van Wees and his son Maurice, this Dutch independent bottler has until now bottled over 850 single malts. All whiskies are un chill-filtered, without colouring and bottled at either 46% or cask strength. The van Wees family also operate one of the finest spirits shops in Europe - Van Wees Whisky World in Amersfoort - with i.a. more than 1,000 different whiskies including more than 500 single malts. In spring 2018, Han van Wees was distinguished with the role of Master of the Quaich for his many years of promoting Scotch whisky.

The Vintage Malt Whisky Company

www.vintagemaltwhisky.com

Founded in 1992 by Brian Crook, who previously had twenty years experience in the malt whisky industry, the company today is run by his three children, Andrew, Caroline and Kim. The company also owns and operates a sister company called The Highlands & Islands Scotch Whisky Co. In 2018, they acquired a former factory in Port Ellen on Islay where they hope to eventually distill a range of Islay based spirits although probably not malt whisky. The most famous brands in the range are two single Islay malts called Finlaggan and The Ileach. The latter comes in two versions, bottled at 40% and 58%. The Finlaggan range consists of Old Reserve (40%), Eilean Mor (46%), Port Finish (46%), Sherry Finish (46%) and Cask Strength (56%). Recent additions to the range include the single malt Islay Storm and the blended malt Smokestack which contains only peated malts from Islay and the Highlands. Other expressions include two blended malts, Glenalmond and Black Cuillin and, not least, a wide range of single cask single malts under the name The Cooper´s Choice. They are bottled at 46% or at cask strength and are all non coloured and non chill-filtered..

Cooper´s Choice Smokebomb Feis Ile 2018, 56%
Nose: Subtle yet charming with notes of red apples, furniture polish, smoked mackerel and barbecue sauce.
Palate: Warming, ancho chili and white pepper, honey, chocolate sponge cake, dried dates and liquorice.

Islay Storm, 40%
Nose: Fresh and vibrant with notes of burnt grass, vanilla, citrus, pears and rubber.
Palate: Sweet, medicinal smoke, honey, apples and digestives.

Svenska Eldvatten

www.eldvatten.se

Founded in 2011 by Tommy Andersen and Peter Sjögren. Since the start, more than 60 single casks, bottled at cask strength, have been released. The owners have also released their own blended malt, Glenn bottled at 50%. In their range of spirits they have aged tequila and rum and they have also launched their own rum, WeiRon Super Premium Aged Carribean Rum (both vatted and as a single cask), as well as gin and aquavit. A new, limited range called Sherry Cask Collection was launched in spring 2018. These are all blended malts of considerable age.

Wm Cadenhead & Co

www.wmcadenhead.com

This company was established in 1842 and is owned by J & A Mitchell (who also owns Springbank) since 1972. The single malts from Cadenheads are neither chill filtered nor coloured. The current range consists of Authentic Collection (single cask cask strength whiskies, exclusively sold in their own shops), World Whiskies (single malts from non Scottish distillers as well as from Scottish grain distillers) and Small Batch, a range which can be divided into three separate ranges; Gold Label (single casks bottled at cask strength), Small Batch Cask Strength (2-4 casks of whisky from the same vintage, bottled at cask strength) and Small Batch 46% (same as the previous but diluted to 46%). A fourth range is William Cadenhead Range, which consists of blended whisky as well as single malts from undisclosed distilleries. There are ten dedicated Cadenhead´s Whisky Shops in Europe with two that opened up in 2018 – in Berlin and in Vienna.

Paul John 6 years old, 56.3%
Nose: Rich and malty, dark chocolate, coconut, plums and toffee.
Palate: Robust and impressive with notes of oranges, chocolate, clove, nutmeg, salty crackers and roasted hazelnuts.

Macduff 29 years old, 55.1%
Nose: Fresh and floral, overripe apples, apple cider, lilac and rose petals.
Palate: Raisins soaked in wine, eucalyptus, citrus, ginger, lavender and goose berries.

Adelphi Distillery

www.adelphidistillery.com

Adelphi Distillery is named after a distillery which closed in 1902. The company is owned by Keith Falconer and Donald Houston, who recruited Alex Bruce from the wine trade to act as Managing Director. The company offers a range of single malts every year where the whiskies are always bottled at cask strength, uncoloured and non chill-filtered. Theer are also two recurrent brands, Fascadale and Liddesdale, where the single malt differs from batch to batch. In October 2015, the first two bottlings of a new brand saw the light of day. Together with Fusion Whisky, Adelphi launched The Glover – a unique vatting of single malt from the closed Japanese distillery Hanyu and two Scottish single malts, Longmorn and Glen Garioch. A 14 and a 22 year old (and later an 18 year old) were released. This was followed by The E&K where Amrut single malt from India was blended with Scotch malt whisky and, in spring 2018, yet another two combinations appeared – The Brisbane (Starward single malt from Australia and Glen Garioch and Glen Grant from Scotland) and The Winter Queen (malt whisky from Zuidam distillery in the Netherlands, blended with Longmorn and Glenrothes).

Since 2014, Adelphi is also operating its own distillery in Glenbeg on the Ardnamurchan peninsula. Since the opening, the owners have regularly released malt spirit (less than 3 years old) with the latest being Spirit 2018 AD. There are no plans to release the first Ardnamurchan single malt whisky until 2021.

The Winter Queen 7 years old, 52.7%
Nose: Intense with notes of sweet tobacco, dried fruit, apricots and Irish coffee. After a while, floral notes (violets and lilac) are coming through.
Palate: A bombastic dram, more of the tobacco, dates, prunes and dark cherries, roasted hazelnuts and quite a bit of spice (clove and cinnamon).

The Brisbane 5 years old, 57.5%
Nose: Autumnal and powerful, dark fruit, ripe banana, fresh wood and a bit of menthol.
Palate: Rich and mouthcoating, slightly smoky, sweet liquorice, dark chocolate, baked apples with caramel and a peppery sting.

Deerstalker Whisky Co

www.deerstalkerwhisky.com

The Deerstalker brand, which dates from 1880 was originally owned by J.G. Thomson & Co of Leith and subsequently Tennent Caledonian Breweries. It was purchased by Glasgow based Aberko Ltd in 1994 and is managed by former Tennent's Export Director Paul Aston. The Deerstalker range covers single malts as well as blended malt whiskies. Currently there are two single malts, 10 and 12 year old but a limited 13 year old was released in autumn 2017. A Deerstalker Blended Malt (Highland Edition) was launched in 2014 and in autumn 2016 the Peated Edition of Deerstalker was released.

Deerstalker Blended Malt Peated Edition, 43%
Nose: Lemons and limes blend with peated saline aromas. Warm darkness of treacle and blood oranges are in the background.
Palate: Almost liquid peat, with dark molten chocolate cake and some fresh, wild blackberries giving a lovely soft fruity edge.

Deerstalker Blended Malt Highland Edition, 43%
Nose: Sweet perfume hits with dried apricots, clover, dark roasted nuts, cloves and cinnamon.
Palate: The palate is darker than the nose with the spice mingling with spent coffee beans, a hint of ferns and dark leather.

Morrison & MacKay Whisky

www.mandmwhisky.co.uk

A relative newcomer as an independent bottler, there is nonetheless plenty of experience in the company. The Morrison part of the business name is represented by Brian Morrison (as well as his son Jamie) who´s father was the legendary Stanley P Morrison, founder of Morrison Bowmore Distilleries and at one time owner of Bowmore, Auchentoshan and Glen Garioch. After leaving Morrison Bowmore, Brian started the Scottish Liqueur Centre and the family has recently also opened a distillery in Aberargie, just south of Perth. Meanwhile the liqueur business has been expanded to also include malt whisky under the name Carn Mor. Currently there are three ranges; Carn Mor Strictly Limited, usually bottled at 46%, Celebration of the Cask which are single casks bottled at cask strength and Celebration of the Cask Black Gold with heavily sherried whiskies in focus. A fourth range of blended malts is called Old Perth.

Sansibar Whisky

www.sansibar-whisky.com

Started in 2012, this was the brainchild of the current majority owner and CEO Jens Drewitz and Carsten Ehrlich, the organizer of the famous Whisky Fair Limburg. Their idea was to create a range of high quality single malts from Scotland and to market them in connection with the well known Sansibar restaurant on the island of Sylt in northern Germany. Around 60 bottlings are produced per year and the range also includes rum.

Dramfool

www.dramfool.com

Bruce Farquhar, a whisky fan and collector for 20 years, decided in 2015 to start as an independent bottler. He sources his whisky from private individuals as well as from brokers and included in his latest releases are a 21 year old Bowmore, a 6 year old Octomore and a 22 year old ex-sherry butt from an un-named Speyside distillery.

Edinburgh Whisky Ltd.

www.edinburghwhisky.com

Two friends, Gordon Watt, a former sales director at Moët Hennessy and Gregor Mathieson with a background in the wine business and partner in the Michelin awarded Andrew Fairlie restaurant at Gleneagles, founded the company in 2013. They were later joined by Iain Hamilton. Single malt single casks are bottled under the name The Library Collection while small batch blended malts are sold under the name New Town. More ranges to be introduced during 2018/2019 are Royal Circus single malts and Old Town blended malts. The owners also have plans to open a craft distillery in central Edinburgh in the future.

Angel´s Nectar

www.angelsnectar.co.uk

For ten years Robert Ransom worked as the sales and marketing director at Glenfarclas. He left in 2014 and founded Highfern Ltd. The main product is the blended malt Angels´s Nectar which is available in two versions - First Edition (Speyside and Highland, bottled at 40%) and Rich Peat Edition (Highland, bottled at 46%). Highfern is also the UK importer for Smögen single malt and gin and Langatun Swiss single malt.

Maltbarn

www.maltbarn.com

A family company based in Germany, founded by Martin Diekmann. So far they have released just over 100 different malts (and a few cognac). The whiskies are neither coloured nor chill-filtered. The latest releases from 2018 include 21 year old Ben Nevis, 23 year old Tobermory, 26 year old Springbank and a 45 year old Speyside.

Wilson & Morgan

www.wilsonandmorgan.com

Inspired and trained by his father Mario, Fabio Rossi established the company in 1992. The first level of their whisky offerings is House Malt from undisclosed distilleries. Next comes Classic Selection, including single malts bottled at 46%. Another range is Twenties & Older which obviously is made up of older whiskies, often single casks and bottled at 50%. Finally, Cask Strength and Collecor´s Edition are all single casks that are bottled un-chill filtered and with no colouring. Since 2002, a special part of the range includes Scoth single malt finished in casks that previously held the Sicilian sweet wine Marsala.

Whisky
shops

AUSTRALIA

The Odd Whisky Coy
PO Box 471
Glenside, SA, 5065
Phone: +61 (0)417 85 22 96
www.theoddwhiskycoy.com.au
This on-line whisky specialist has an
impressive range. They are agents for
famous brands such as Springbank,
Benromach and Berry Brothers and
arrange recurrent seminars on the subject.

World of Whisky
Shop G12, Cosmopolitan Centre
2-22 Knox Street
Double Bay NSW 2028
Phone: +61 (0)2 9363 4212
www.worldofwhisky.com.au
A whisky specialist which offers a range
of 300 different expressions, most of them
single malts. The shop is also organising
and hosting regular tastings.

AUSTRIA

Potstill
Laudongasse 18
1080 Wien
Phone: +43 (0)664 118 85 41
www.potstill.org
Austria's premier whisky shop with over
1100 kinds of which c 900 are malts,
including some real rarities. Arranges
tastings and seminars and ships to several
European countries. On-line ordering.

Cadenhead Austria
Döblinger Hauptstraße 32
1190 Wien
Phone: +43 (0)677 622 476 40
www.cadenhead-vienna.at
The former shop in Salzburg is closed and
a new shop opened up in Vienna in August
2018. Focusing on the Cadenhead range
but with a wide range of other whiskies
and spirits as well.

Pinkernells Whisky Market
Alter Markt 1
5020 Salzburg
Phone: +43 (0)662 84 53 05
www.pinkernells.at
More than 400 whiskies are on offer
and they are also importers of Maltbarn,
The Whisky Chamber and Jack Wiebers.
Regular tastings.

BELGIUM

Whiskycorner
Kraaistraat 16
3530 Houthalen
Phone: +32 (0)89 386233
www.whiskycorner.be
A very large selection of single malts,
no less than 2000 different! Also other
whiskies, calvados and grappas. The site is
in both French and English.

Jurgen´s Whiskyhuis
Gaverland 70
9620 Zottegem
Phone: +32 (0)9 336 51 06
www.whiskyhuis.be
A huge assortment of more than 2,000
different single malts. Also 40 different
grain whiskies and 120 bourbons.

Huis Crombé
Doenaertstraat 20
8510 Marke
Phone: +32 (0)56 21 19 87
www.crombewines.com
A wine retailer which also covers all kinds
of spirits. A large assortment of Scotch is
supplemented with whiskies from Japan,
the USA and Ireland to mention a few.

Anverness Whisky & Spirits
Grote Steenweg 74
2600 Berchem – Antwerpen
Phone: +32 (0)3 218 55 90
www.anverness.be
Peter de Decker has established himself
as one of the best Belgian whisky retailers
where, apart from an impressive range of
whiskies, recurrent tastings and whisky
dinners play an important role.

We Are Whisky
Avenue Rodolphe Gossia 33
1350 Orp-Jauche
Phone: +32 (0)471 134556
www.wearewhisky.com
On-line retailer with a range of more than
400 different whiskies. They also arrange
3-4 tastings every month.

Dram 242
Opwijksestraat 242
9280 Lebbeke
Phone: +32 (0)477 260993
www.dram242.be
A wide range of whiskies. Apart from
the core official bottlings, they have
focused on rare, old expressions as well as
whiskies from small, independent bottlers.

CANADA

Kensington Wine Market
1257 Kensington Road NW
Calgary, Alberta T2N 3P8
Phone: +1 403 283 8000
www.kensingtonwinemarket.com
A very large range of single malt bottlings
as well as other spirits and wines. Regular
tastings in the shop. Also the home of the
Scotch Malt Whisky Society in Canada.

World of Whisky
Unit 240, 333 5 Avenue SW
Calgary
Alberta T2P 3B6
Phone: +1 587 956 8511
www.coopwinespiritsbeer.com/stores/
world-of-whisky/
Specialising in whisky from all corners of
the world. Currently there are close to 900
different whiskies in the range including
some extremely rare ones from Scotland.

DENMARK

Juul´s Vin & Spiritus
Værnedamsvej 15
1819 Frederiksberg
Phone: +45 33 31 13 29
www.juuls.dk
A very large range of wines, fortified
wines and spirits with almost 800 single
malts.

Cadenhead´s WhiskyShop Denmark
Kongensgade 69 F
5000 Odense C
Phone: +45 66 13 95 05
www.cadenheads.dk
Whisky specialist with a very good range,
not least from Cadenhead's. Nice range
of champagne, cognac and rum. Arranges
whisky and beer tastings. On-line ordering.

Whisky.dk
Sjølund Gade 12
6093 Sjølund
Phone: +45 5210 6093
www.whisky.dk
Henrik Olsen and Ulrik Bertelsen are
well-known in Denmark for their whisky
shows but they also run an on-line spirits
shop with an emphasis on whisky but also
including an impressive stock of rums.

ENGLAND

The Whisky Exchange
2 Bedford Street, Covent Garden
London WC2E 9HH
Phone: +44 (0)20 7100 0088
90-92 Great Portland Street, Fitzrovia
London W1W 7NT
Phone: +44 (0)20 7100 9888
www.thewhiskyexchange.com
An excellent whisky shop owned by
Sukhinder Singh. Started off as a mail
order business, run from a showroom in
Hanwell, but later opened up at Vinopolis

in downtown London. Moved to a new and bigger location in Covent Garden a couple of years ago and recently opened up a secodn shop in Fitzrovia. The assortment is huge with well over 1000 single malts to choose from. Some rarities which can hardly be found anywhere else are offered thanks to Singh's great interest for antique whisky. There are also other types of whisky and cognac, calvados, rum etc. On-line ordering and ships all over the world.

The Whisky Shop
(See also Scotland, The Whisky Shop)
11 Coppergate Walk
York YO1 9NT
Phone: +44 (0)1904 640300

510 Brompton Walk
Lakeside Shopping Centre
Thurrock Grays, Essex RM20 2ZL
Phone: +44 (0)1708 866255

7 Turl Street
Oxford OX1 3DQ
Phone: +44 (0)1865 202279

3 Swan Lane
Norwich NR2 1HZ
Phone: +44 (0)1603 618284

70 Piccadilly
London W1J 8HP
Phone: +44 (0)207 499 6649

Unit 7 Queens Head Passage
Paternoster
London EC4M 7DZ
Phone: +44 (0)207 329 5117

3 Exchange St
Manchester M2 7EE
Phone: +44 (0)161 832 6110

25 Chapel Street
Guildford GU1 3UL
Phone: +44 (0)1483 450900

Unit 9 Great Western Arcade
Birmingham B2 5HU
Phone: +44 (0)121 233 4416

64 East Street
Brighton BN1 1HQ
Phone: +44 (0)1273 327 962

3 Cheapside
Nottingham NG1 2HU
Phone: +44 (0)115 958 7080

9-10 High Street
Bath BA1 5AQ
Phone: +44 (0)1225 423 535

Unit 1/9 Red Mall,
Intu Metro Centre
Gateshead NE11 9YP
Phone: +44 (0)191 460 3777

Unit 201 Trentham Gardens
Stoke on Trent ST4 8AX
Phone: +44 (0)1782 644 483
www.whiskyshop.com
The largest specialist retailer of whiskies in the UK with 20 outlets. A large product range with over 700 kinds, including 400 malt whiskies and 140 miniature bottles, as well as accessories and books. They also run The W Club, the leading whisky club in the UK where the excellent Whiskeria magazine is one of the member's benefits. Shipping all over the world.

Royal Mile Whiskies
3 Bloomsbury Street
London WC1B 3QE
Phone: +44 (0)20 7436 4763
www.royalmilewhiskies.com
The London branch of Royal Mile Whiskies. See also Scotland, Royal Mile Whiskies.

Berry Bros. & Rudd
63 Pall Mall
London SW1Y 5HZ
Phone: +44 (0)800 280 2440
www.bbr.com/whisky
A legendary company that recently opned a new shop in Pall Mall. One of the world's most reputable wine shops but with an exclusive selection of malt whiskies. Also shops in Hong Kong, Singapore and Japan.

The Wright Wine & Whisky Company
The Old Smithy, Raikes Road, Skipton, North Yorkshire BD23 1NP
Phone: +44 (0)1756 700886
www.wineandwhisky.co.uk
An eclectic selection of near to 1000 different whiskies. 'Tasting Cupboard' of nearly 100 opened bottles for sampling with regular hosted tasting evenings. Great 'Collector to Collector' selection of old whiskies plus a fantastic choice of 1200+ wines, premium spirits and liqueurs.

Master of Malt
Unit 1, Ton Business Park, 2-8 Morley Rd.
Tonbridge, Kent, TN9 1RA
Phone: +44 (0)1892 888 376
www.masterofmalt.com
Online retailer and independent bottler with a very impressive range of more than 2,500 whiskies, including over 2,000 Scotch whiskies and over 1,500 single malts. In addition to whisky there is an enormous selection of gins, rums, cognacs, armagnacs, tequilas and more. The website contains a wealth of information and news about the distilleries and innovative personalised gift ideas. Drinks by the Dram 30ml samples of more than 3,300 different whiskies are also available to try before you buy a full bottle as well as a Build Your Own Tasting Set option and Dram Club monthly subscription services.

Whiskys.co.uk
The Square, Stamford Bridge
York YO4 11AG
Phone: +44 (0)1759 371356
www.whiskys.co.uk
Good assortment with more than 600 different whiskies. Also a nice range of armagnac, rum, calvados etc. The owners also have another website, www.whiskymerchants.co.uk with a huge amount of information on just about every whisky distillery in the world.

The Wee Dram
5 Portland Square, Bakewell
Derbyshire DE45 1HA
Phone: +44 (0)1629 812235
www.weedram.co.uk
Large range of Scotch single malts with whiskies from other parts of the world and a good range of whisky books. Run 'The Wee Drammers Whisky Club' with

tastings and seminars. End of October they arrange the yearly Wee Dram Fest whisky festival.

Hard To Find Whisky
1 Spencer Street
Birmingham B18 6DD
Phone: +44 (0)121 448 84 84
www.htfw.com
As the name says, this family owned shop specialises in rare, collectable and new releases of single malt whisky. The range is astounding - more than 3,000 different bottlings including no less than 402 different Macallan. World wide shipping.

Nickolls & Perks
37 High Street, Stourbridge
West Midlands DY8 1TA
Phone: +44 (0)1384 394518
www.nickollsandperks.co.uk
Mostly known as wine merchants but also has a good range of whiskies with c 300 different kinds including 200 single malts. Since 2011, they also organize the acclaimed Midlands Whisky Festival, see www.whiskyfest.co.uk

Gauntleys of Nottingham
4 High Street
Nottingham NG1 2ET
Phone: +44 (0)115 9110555
www.gauntleys.com
A fine wine merchant established in 1880. The range of wines are among the best in the UK. All kinds of spirits, not least whisky, are taking up more and more space and several rare malts can be found.

Hedonism Wines
3-7 Davies St.
London W1K 3LD
Phone: +44 (020) 729 078 70
www.hedonism.co.uk
Located in the heart of London´s Mayfair, this is a temple for wine lovers but also with an impressive range of whiskies and other spirits. They have over 1,200 different bottlings from Scotland and the rest of the world.

The Lincoln Whisky Shop
87 Bailgate
Lincoln LN1 3AR
Phone: +44 (0)1522 537834
www.lincolnwhiskyshop.co.uk
Mainly specialising in whisky with more than 400 different whiskies but also 500 spirits and liqueurs. Mailorder worldwide.

Milroys of Soho
3 Greek Street
London W1D 4NX
Phone: +44 (0)207 734 2277
shop.milroys.co.uk
A classic whisky shop in Soho with a very good range with over 700 malts and a wide selection of whiskies from around the world. On-line ordering.

Arkwrights
114 The Dormers
Highworth
Wiltshire SN6 7PE
Phone: +44 (0)1793 765071
www.whiskyandwines.com
A good range of whiskies (over 700 in stock) as well as wine and other spirits.

Regular tastings in the shop. On-line ordering with shipping all over the world.

Edencroft Fine Wines
8-10 Hospital Street, Nantwich
Cheshire, CW5 5RJ
Phone: +44 (0)1270 629975
www.edencroft.co.uk
Family owned wine and spirits shop since 1994. Around 250 whiskies and also a nice range of gin, cognac and other spirits including cigars. Worldwide shipping.

Cadenhead´s Whisky Shop
26 Chiltern Street
London W1U 7QF
Phone: +44 (0)20 7935 6999
www.whiskytastingroom.com
One in a chain of shops owned by independent bottlers Cadenhead. Sells Cadenhead's product range and c. 200 other whiskies. Regular tastings.

Constantine Stores
30 Fore Street
Constantine, Falmouth
Cornwall TR11 5AB
Phone: +44 (0)1326 340226
www.drinkfinder.co.uk
A full-range wine and spirits dealer with a good selection of whiskies from the whole world (around 800 different, of which 600 are single malts).Worldwide shipping.

House of Malt
12 Crosby Street
Carlisle CA1 1DQ
Phone: +44 (0)1228 739 713
www.houseofmalt.co.uk
A wide selection of whiskies from Scotland and the world as well as other spirits and craft ales. There are also three exclusive malts bottled by themselves.

The Vintage House
42 Old Compton Street
London W1D 4LR
Phone: +44 (0)20 7437 5112
www.sohowhisky.com
A huge range of 1400 kinds of malt whisky, many of them rare. Supplementing this is also a selection of fine wines.

Whisky On-line
Units 1-3 Concorde House, Charnley Road, Blackpool, Lancashire FY1 4PE
Phone: +44 (0)1253 620376
www.whisky-online.com
A good selection of whisky and also cognac, rum, port etc. On-line ordering with shipping all over the world.

FRANCE

La Maison du Whisky
20 rue d´Anjou
75008 Paris
Phone: +33 (0)1 42 65 03 16

6 carrefour d l´Odéon
75006 Paris
Phone: +33 (0)1 46 34 70 20

(2 shops outside France)
47 rue Jean Chatel
97400 Saint-Denis, La Réunion
Phone: +33 (0)2 62 21 31 19

The Pier at Robertson Quay

80 Mohamed Sultan Road, #01-10
Singapore 239013
Phone: +65 6733 0059
www.whisky.fr
France's largest whisky specialist with over 1200 whiskies in stock. Also a number of own-bottled single malts. La Maison du Whisky acts as a EU distributor for many whisky producers around the world. Also run a specialist rum shop and a whisky bar in Paris.

The Whisky Shop
7 Place de la Madeleine
75008 Paris
Phone: +33 (0)1 45 22 29 77
www.whiskyshop.fr
The large chain of whisky shops in the UK has now opened up a store in Paris as well.

GERMANY

Celtic Whisk(e)y & Versand
Otto Steudel
Bulmannstrasse 26
90459 Nürnberg
Phone: +49 (0)911 45097430
www.celtic-whisky.de
A very impressive single malt range with well over 1000 different single malts and a good selection from other parts of the world.

SCOMA
Am Bullhamm 17
26441 Jever
Phone: +49 (0)4461 912237
www.scoma.de
Very large range of c 750 Scottish malts and many from other countries. Holds regular seminars and tastings. The excellent, monthly whisky newsletter SCOMA News is produced and can be downloaded as a pdf-file from the website.

The Whisky Store
Am Grundwassersee 4
82402 Seeshaupt
Phone: +49 (0)8801 30 20 000
www.whisky.de
A very large range comprising c 700 kinds of whisky of which 550 are malts. Also sells whisky liqueurs, books and accessories. The website is a goldmine of information. On-line ordering.

Cadenhead´s Whisky Market
Luxemburger Strasse 257
50939 Köln
Phone: +49 (0)221-2831834
www.cadenheads.de
Good range of malt whiskies (c 350 different kinds) with emphasis on Cadenhead's own bottlings. Other products include wine, cognac and rum etc. Arranges recurring tastings and also has an on-line shop.

Pinkernells Whisky Market
Boxhagener Straße 36
10245 Berlin
Phone: +49 (0)30-22 600 610
www.pinkernells.de
An extensive range of whiskies (more than 700) and they arrange 4-5 tastings monthly. Also work as whisky consultants doing corporate events all over Germany.

Home of Malts
Hosegstieg 11
22880 Wedel
Phone: +49 (0)4103 965 9695
www.homeofmalts.com
Large assortment with over 800 different single malts as well as whiskies from many other countries. Also a nice selection of cognac, rum etc. On-line ordering.

Reifferscheid
Mainzer Strasse 186
53179 Bonn / Mehlem
Phone: +49 (0)228 9 53 80 70
www.whisky-bonn.de
A well-stocked shop with a large range of whiskies, wine, spirit, cigars and a delicatessen. Regular tastings.

Whisky-Doris
Germanenstrasse 38
14612 Falkensee
Phone: +49 (0)3322-219784
www.whisky-doris.de
Large range of over 300 whiskies and also sells own special bottlings. Orders via email. Shipping also outside Germany.

Finlays Whisky Shop
Hofheimer Str. 30
65719 Hofheim-Lorsbach
Phone: +49 (0)6192 30 90 335
www.finlayswhiskyshop.de
Whisky specialists with a large range of over 1,600 whiskies. Finlays also work as the importer to Germany of Douglas Laing, James MacArthur and Wilson & Morgan.

Weinquelle Lühmann
Lübeckerstrasse 145
22087 Hamburg
Phone: +49 (0)40-300 672 950
www.weinquelle.com
An impressive selection of both wines and spirits with over 1000 different whiskies of which 850 are malt whiskies. Also an impressive range of rums.

The Whisky-Corner
Reichertsfeld 2
92278 Illschwang
Phone: +49 (0)9666-951213
www.whisky-corner.de
A small shop but large on mail order. A very large assortment of over 2000 whiskies. Also sells blended and American whiskies. The website is very informative with features on, among others, whisky-making, tasting and independent bottlers.

World Wide Spirits
Hauptstrasse 12
84576 Teising
Phone: +49 (0)8633 50 87 93
www.worldwidespirits.de
A nice range of more than 1,000 whiskies with some rarities from the twenties. Also large selection of other spirits.

WhiskyKoch
Weinbergstrasse 2
64285 Darmstadt
Phone: +49 (0)6151 99 27 105
www.whiskykoch.de
A combination of a whisky shop and restaurant. The shop has a nice selection of single malts as well as other Scottish

products and the restaurant has specialised in whisky dinners and tastings.

Kierzek
Weitlingstrasse 17
10317 Berlin
Phone: +49 (0)30 525 11 08
www.kierzek-berlin.de
Over 400 different whiskies in stock. In the product range 50 kinds of rum and 450 wines from all over the world are found among other products. Mail order is available.

House of Whisky
Ackerbeeke 6
31683 Obernkirchen
Phone: +49 (0)5724-399420
www.houseofwhisky.de
Aside from over 1,200 different malts also sells a large range of other spirits (including over 100 kinds of rum). On-line ordering.

Wein & Whisky
Hedwigstrasse 2
12159 Berlin-Friedenau
Phone: +49 (0)30-7845010
www.world-wide-whisky.de
Large range of 1,500 different whiskies. Arranges tastings and seminars. Has a large number of rarities. Orders via email.

HUNGARY
Whisky Shop Budapest
Veres Pálné utca 7.
1053 Budapest
Phone: +36 1 267-1588
www.whiskynet.hu
www.whiskyshop.hu
Largest selection of whisky in Hungary. More than 900 different whiskies from all over the world. Even Hungarian whisky and a large selection of other fine spirits are available. Most of them can be tasted in the GoodSpirit Whisky & Cocktail Bar which operates in the same venue.

IRELAND
Celtic Whiskey Shop
27-28 Dawson Street
Dublin 2
Phone: +353 (0)1 675 9744
www.celticwhiskeyshop.com
More than 400 kinds of Irish whiskeys but also a good selection of Scotch, wines and other spirits. World wide shipping.

ITALY
Whisky Shop
by Milano Whisky Festival
Via Cavaleri 6, Milano
Phone: +39 (0)2 48753039
www.whiskyshop.it
The team behind the excellent Milano Whisky Festival also have an on-line whiskyshop with almost 500 different single malts including several special festival bottlings.

Whisky Antique S.R.L.
Via Giardini Sud
41043 Formigine (MO)

Phone: +39 (0)59 574278
www.whiskyantique.com
Long-time whisky enthusiast and collector Massimo Righi owns this shop specialising in rare and collectable spirits – not only whisky but also cognac, rum, armagnac etc. They are also the Italian importer for brands like Jack Wiebers, The Whisky Agency and Perfect Dram.

Whisky & Co.
Via Margutta, 28/29
00187 Rome
Phone: +39 (0)6 3265 0514
www.whiskyandco.it
A new and very elegant whiskyshop has recently been opened in the heart of Rome by Massimo Righi, known from Whisky Antique in Modena.

JAPAN
Liquor Mountain Co.,Ltd.
4F Kyoto Kowa Bldg.
82 Tachiurinishi-Machi,
Takakura-Nishiiru,
Shijyo-Dori, Shimogyo-Ku,
Kyoto, 600-8007
Phone: +81 (0)75 213 8880
www.likaman.co.jp
The company has more than 150 shops specialising in spirits, beer and food. Around 20 of them are designated whisky shops under the name Whisky Kingdom (although they have a full range of other spirits) with a range of 500 different whiskies. The three foremost shops are;

Rakzan Sanjyo Onmae
1-8, HigashiGekko-cho, Nishinokyo,
Nakagyo-ku, Kyoto-shi
Kyoto
Phone: +81 (0)75-842-5123

Nagakute
2-105, Ichigahora, Nagakute-shi
Aichi
Phone: +81 (0)561-64-3081

Kabukicho 1chome
1-2-16, Kabuki-cho, Shinjuku-ku
Tokyo
Phone: +81 (0)3-5287-2080

THE NETHERLANDS
Whiskyslijterij De Koning
Hinthamereinde 41
5211 PM 's Hertogenbosch
Phone: +31 (0)73-6143547
www.whiskykoning.nl
An enormous assortment with more than 1400 kinds of whisky including c 800 single malts. Arranges recurring tastings. On-line ordering. Shipping all over the world.

Van Wees - Whiskyworld.nl
Leusderweg 260
3817 KH Amersfoort
Phone: +31 (0)33-461 53 19
www.whiskyworld.nl
A very large range of 1000 whiskies including over 500 single malts. Also have their own range of bottlings (The Ultimate Whisky Company). On-line ordering.

Wijnhandel van Zuylen
Loosduinse Hoofdplein 201
2553 CP Loosduinen (Den Haag)
Phone: +31 (0)70-397 1400
www.whiskyvanzuylen.nl
Excellent range of whiskies (circa 1100) and wines. Email orders with shipping to some ten European countries.

Wijnwinkel-Slijterij
Ton Overmars
Hoofddorpplein 11
1059 CV Amsterdam
Phone: +31 (0)20-615 71 42
www.tonovermars.nl
A very large assortment of wines, spirits and beer which includes more than 400 single malts. Arranges recurring tastings. Orders via email.

Wijn & Whisky Schuur
Blankendalwei 4
8629 EH Scharnegoutem
Phone: +31 (0)515-520706
www.wijnwhiskyschuur.nl
Large assortment with 1000 different whiskies and a good range of other spirits as well. Arranges recurring tastings.

Versailles Dranken
Lange Hezelstraat 83
6511 Cl Nijmegen
Phone: +31 (0)24-3232008
www.versaillesdranken.nl
A very impressive range with more than 1500 different whiskies, most of them from Scotland but also a surprisingly good selection (more than 60) of Bourbon. Arranges recurring tastings.

Wine and Whisky Specialist van der Boog
Prinses Irenelaan 359-361
2285 GA Rijswijk
Phone: +31 70 - 394 00 85
www.passionforwhisky.com
A very good range of almost 700 malt whiskies (as well as a wide range of other spirits). World wide shipping.

NEW ZEALAND
Whisky Galore
834 Colombo Street
Christchurch 8013
Phone: +64 (0) 800 944 759
www.whiskygalore.co.nz
The best whisky shop in New Zealand with 550 different whiskies, approximately 350 which are single malts. There is also online mail-order with shipping all over the world except USA and Canada.

POLAND
George Ballantine´s
Krucza str 47 A, Warsaw
Phone: +48 22 625 48 32

Pulawska str 22, Warsaw
Phone: +48 22 542 86 22

Marynarska str 15, Warsaw
Phone: +48 22 395 51 60

Zygmunta Vogla str 62, Warsaw
Phone: +48 22 395 51 64
www.sklep-ballantines.pl

A huge range of single malts and apart from whisky there is a full range of spirits and wines from all over the world. Recurrent tastings and organiser of Whisky Live Warsaw.

Dom Whisky
Wejherowska 67, Reda
Phone: +48 691 760 000, shop
Phone: +48 691 930 000, mailorder
www.sklep-domwhisky.pl
On-line retailer who recently opened a shop in Reda. A very large range of whiskies and other spirits. Organiser of a whisky festival in Jastrzębia Góra.

RUSSIA
Whisky World Shop
9, Tverskoy Boulevard
123104 Moscow
Phone: +7 495 787 9150
www.whiskyworld.ru
Huge assortment with more than 1,000 different single malts. The range is supplemented with a nice range of cognac, armagnac, calvados, grappa and wines.

SCOTLAND
Gordon & MacPhail
58 - 60 South Street, Elgin
Moray IV30 1JY
Phone: +44 (0)1343 545110
www.gordonandmacphail.com
This legendary shop opened already in 1895 in Elgin. The owners are perhaps the most well-known among independent bottlers. The shop stocks more than 800 bottlings of whisky and more than 600 wines and there is also a delicatessen counter with high-quality products. Tastings are arranged in the shop and there are shipping services within the UK and overseas. The shop attracts visitors from all over the world.

Royal Mile Whiskies (2 shops)
379 High Street, The Royal Mile
Edinburgh EH1 1PW
Phone: +44 (0)131 2253383

3 Bloomsbury Street
London WC1B 3QE
Phone: +44 (0)20 7436 4763
www.royalmilewhiskies.com
Royal Mile Whiskies is one of the most well-known whisky retailers in the UK. It was established in Edinburgh in 1991. There is also a shop in London since 2002 and a cigar shop close to the Edinburgh shop. The whisky range is outstanding with many difficult to find elsewhere. They have a comprehensive site regarding information on regions, distilleries, production, tasting etc. Royal Mile Whiskies also arranges 'Whisky Fringe' in Edinburgh, a two-day whisky festival which takes place annually in mid August. On-line ordering with worldwide shipping.

The Whisky Shop
(See also England, The Whisky Shop)
Unit L2-02 Buchanan Galleries
220 Buchanan Street
Glasgow G1 2GF
Phone: +44 (0)141 331 0022

17 Bridge Street
Inverness IV1 1HD
Phone: +44 (0)1463 710525

93 High Street
Fort William PH33 6DG
Phone: +44 (0)1397 706164

52 George Street
Oban PA34 5SD
Phone: +44 (0)1631 570896

Unit 23 Waverley Mall
Waverley Bridge
Edinburgh EH1 1BQ
Phone: +44 (0)131 558 7563

28 Victoria Street
Edinburgh EH1 2JW
Phone: +44 (0)131 225 4666
www.whiskyshop.com
The first shop opened in 1992 in Edinburgh and this is now the United Kingdom's largest specialist retailer of whiskies with 20 outlets (plus one in Paris). A large product range with over 700 kinds, including 400 malt whiskies and 140 miniature bottles, as well as accessories and books. The own range 'Glenkeir Treasures' is a special assortment of selected malt whiskies. The also run The W Club, the leading whisky club in the UK where the excellent Whiskeria magazine is one of the member's benefits. On-line ordering.

Loch Fyne Whiskies
Main Street, Inveraray
Argyll PA32 8UD
Phone: +44 (0)800 107 1936
www.lochfynewhiskies.com
A legendary shop! The range of malt whiskies is large and they have their own house blend, the prize-awarded Loch Fyne, as well as their 'The Loch Fyne Whisky Liqueur'. There is also a range of house malts called 'The Inverarity'. On-line ordering with worldwide shipping.

Single Malts Direct
36 Gordon Street
Huntly
Aberdeenshire AB54 8EQ
Phone: +44 (0) 845 606 6145
www.singlemaltsdirect.com
Owned by independent bottler Duncan Taylor. In the assortment is of course the whole Duncan Taylor range but also a selection of their own single malt bottlings called Whiskies of Scotland. A total of almost 700 different expressions. On-line shop with shipping worldwide.

The Whisky Shop Dufftown
1 Fife Street, Dufftown
Moray AB55 4AL
Phone: +44 (0)1340 821097
www.whiskyshopdufftown.co.uk
Whisky specialist in Dufftown in the heart of Speyside, wellknown to many of the Speyside festival visitors. More than 500 single malts as well as other whiskies. Arranges tastings as well as special events during the Festivals. On-line ordering.

Cadenhead's Whisky Shop
30-32 Union Street
Campbeltown PA28 6JA
Phone: +44 (0)1586 551710
www.cadenhead.scot
Part of the chain of shops owned by independent bottlers Cadenhead. Sells Cadenhead's products and other whiskies with a good range of Springbank. On-line ordering.

Cadenhead´s Whisky Shop
172 Canongate, Royal Mile
Edinburgh EH8 8BN
Phone: +44 (0)131 556 5864
www.cadenhead.scot
The oldest shop in the chain owned by Cadenhead. Sells Cadenhead's product range and a good selection of other whiskies and spirits. Recurrent tastings. On-line ordering.

The Good Spirits Co.
23 Bath Street,
Glasgow G2 1HW
Phone: +44 (0)141 258 8427
www.thegoodspiritsco.com
A specialist spirits store selling whisky, bourbon, rum, vodka, tequila, gin, cognac and armagnac, liqueurs and other spirits. They also stock quality champagne, fortified wines and cigars. There are more than 400 single malts in the range as well as over 100 whiskies from the rest of the world.

The Carnegie Whisky Cellars
The Carnegie Courthouse, Castle Street
IV25 3SD Dornoch
Phone: +44 (0)1862 811791
www.thecarnegiecourthouse.co.uk/whisky-cellars/
Opened by Michael Hanratty in 2016, this shop has already become a destination for whisky enthusiasts from the UK and abroad. The interior of the shop is ravishing and the extensive range includes all the latest releases as well as rare and collectable bottles. UK and international shipping.

Abbey Whisky
Dunfermline KY11 3BZ
Phone: +44 (0)800 051 7737
www.abbeywhisky.com
Family run online whisky shop specialising in exclusive, rare and old whiskies from Scotland and the world. Apart from a wide range of official and independent bottlings, Abbey Whisky also selects their own casks and bottle them under the name 'The Rare Casks' and 'The Secret Casks'.

The Scotch Whisky Experience
354 Castlehill, Royal Mile
Edinburgh EH1 2NE
Phone: +44 (0)131 220 0441
www.scotchwhiskyexperience.co.uk
The Scotch Whisky Experience is a must for whisky devotees visiting Edinburgh. An interactive visitor centre dedicated to the history of Scotch whisky. This five-star visitor attraction has an excellent whisky shop with almost 300 different whiskies in stock. Reccently, after extensive refurbishment, a brand new and interactive shop was opened.

Whiski Shop
4 North Bank Street
Edinburgh EH1 2LP
Phone: +44 (0)131 225 7224
www.whiskishop.com
www.whiskirooms.co.uk
A new concept located near Edinburgh
Castle, combining a shop, a tasting
room and a bistro. Also regular whisky
tastings. Online mail order with worldwide
delivery.

Robbie's Drams
3 Sandgate, Ayr
South Ayrshire KA7 1BG
Phone: +44 (0)1292 262 135
www.robbieswhiskymerchants.com
An extensice range of whiskies available
both in store and from their on-line shop.
Specialists in single cask bottlings, closed
distillery bottlings, rare malts, limited
edition whisky and a nice range of their
own bottlings. Worldwide shipping.

The Whisky Barrel
PO Box 23803, Edinburgh, EH6 7WW
Phone: +44 (0)845 2248 156
www.thewhiskybarrel.com
Online specialist whisky shop based in
Edinburgh. They stock over 1,000 single
malt and blended whiskies including
Scotch, Japanese, Irish, Indian, Swedish
and their own casks. Worldwide shipping.

The Scotch Malt Whisky Society
www.smws.com
A legendary society with more than 20 000
members worldwide, specialised in own
bottlings of single cask Scotch whisky,
releasing between 150 and 200 bottlings
every year. Recently, the Society has also
started bottling whisky from other parts of
the world as well as gin, rum, armagnac
and other spirits.

Drinkmonger
100 Atholl Road
Pitlochry PH16 5BL
Phone: +44 (0)1796 470133

11 Bruntsfield Place
Edinburgh EH10 4HN
Phone: +44 (0)131 229 2205
www.drinkmonger.com
Owned by Royal Mile Whiskies, the idea
is to have a 50:50 split between wine and
specialist spirits with the addition of a
cigar assortment. The whisky range is a
good cross-section with some rarities and a
focus on local distilleries.

Luvian's
93 Bonnygate, Cupar
Fife KY15 4LG
Phone: +44 (0)1334 654 820

66 Market Street, St Andrews
Fife KY16 9NU
Phone: +44 (0)1334 477752
www.luvians.com
Wine and whisky merchant with a very
nice selection of more than 600 malt
whiskies.

Robertsons of Pitlochry
44-46 Atholl Road
Pitlochry PH16 5BX
Phone: +44 (0) 1796 472011
www.robertsonsofpitlochry.co.uk

With new owner since 2013, the shop has
grown to become one of Scotland´s best.
An extensive range of both whisky and gin
is complemented by single malts bottled
under their own label. There´s also an
excellent tasting room (The Bothy).

**A.D. Rattray´s Whisky Experience
& Whisky Shop**
32 Main Road
Kirkoswald
Ayrshire KA19 8HY
Phone: +44 (0) 1655 760308
www.adrattray.com
A combination of whisky shop, sample
room and educational center owned by the
independent bottler A D Rattray. Tasting
menus with different themes are available.

Robert Graham Ltd (3 shops)
194 Rose Street
Edinburgh EH2 4AZ
Phone: +44 (0)131 226 1874

111 West George Street
Glasgow G2 1QX
Phone: +44 (0)141 248 7283

254 Canongate
Royal Mile
Edinburgh EH8 8AA
Phone: +44 (0)131 556 2791
www.robertgraham1874.com
Established in 1874 this company
specialises in Scotch whisky and cigars.
A nice assortment of malt whiskies is
complemented by an impressive range of
cigars. They also bottle whiskies under
their own label.

The Jar
33 Ayr St
Troon KA10 6EB
Phone: +44 (0) 1292 319877
www.thejartroon.com
An extensive range of single malts (over
300) and Scottish gins. Specialises in rare
and collectable releases

SOUTH AFRICA
Aficionados Premium Spirits Online
M5 Freeway Park
Cape Town
Phone: +27 21 511 7337
www.aficionados.co.za
An online liquor retailer specialising in
single malt whisky. They claim to offer
the widest of range of whiskies available
in South Africa and hold regular tastings
around the country. Shipping only within
South Africa.

WhiskyBrother
Hyde Park Corner
(middle level inside shopping mall)
Johannesburg
Phone: +27 (0)11 325 6261
www.whiskybrother.com
A shop specialising in all things whisky -
apart from 400 different bottlings they also
sell glasses, books etc. Also sell whiskies
bottled exclusively for the shop. Regular
tastings and online shop. Recently opened
their own whisky bar with more than 1,000
different whiskies to try.

SWITZERLAND
P. Ullrich AG
Schneidergasse 27
4051 Basel
Phone: +41 (0)61 338 90 91
Another two shops in Basel:
Laufenstrasse 16 & Unt. Rebgasse 18
and one in Talacker 30 in Zürich
www.ullrich.ch
A very large range of wines, spirits, beers,
accessories and books. Over 800 kinds of
whisky with almost 600 single malt. On-
line ordering. Recently, they also founded
a whisky club with regular tastings (www.
whiskysinn.ch).

Eddie's Whiskies
Bahnhofstrasse/Dorfgasse 27
8810 Horgen
Phone: +41 (0)43 244 63 00
www.eddies.ch
A whisky specialist with more than 700
different whiskies in stock with emphasis
on single malts (more than 500 different).
Also arranges tastings.

Angels Share Shop
Unterdorfstrasse 15
5036 Oberentfelden
Phone: +41 (0)62 724 83 74
www.angelsshare.ch
A combined restaurant and whisky shop.
More than 600 different kinds of whisky
as well as a good range of cigars. Scores
extra points for short information and
photos of all distilleries. On-line ordering.

UKRAINE
WINETIME
Mykoly Bazhana 1E
Kyiv 02068
Phone: +38 (0)44 338 08 88
www.winetime.ua
WINETIME is the largest specialized
chain of wine and spirits shops in Ukraine.
The company runs 18 stores in 14 regions
of Ukraine.An impressive selection of
spirits with over 1000 whiskies of which
600 are malt whiskies. On-line ordering.
Also regular whisky tastings.

USA
Binny´s Beverage Depot
5100 W. Dempster (Head Office)
Skokie, IL 60077
Phone:
Internet orders, 888-942-9463 (toll free)
www.binnys.com
A chain of no less than 38 stores in the
Chicago area, covering everything within
wine and spirits. Some of the stores also
have a gourmet grocery, cheese shop and,
for cigar lovers, a walk-in humidor. Also
lots of regular events in the stores. The
range is impressive with more than 2200
whisk(e)y (740 single malts, 400 bourbons) and more. Among other products
more than 500 kinds of tequila and mezcal,
450 vodkas, 400 rums and more than 200
kinds of gin should be mentioned. And,
on top of that more than 10,000 different
wines! Online mail order service.

Statistics

The following pages have been made possible,
first and foremost thanks to kind cooperation from The IWSR.
Data has also been provided by Drinks International, The Scotch Whisky
Industry Review and the Scotch Whisky Association.

Whisk(e)y forecast (volume) by region and category 2017-2022

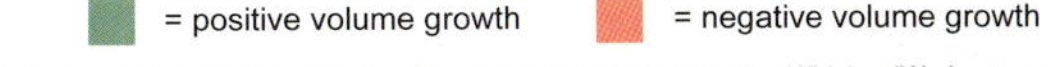

SW=Scotch Whisky, IW=Irish Whiskey, UW=US Whiskey, CW=Canadian Whisky, JW=Japanese whisky, TOT=Total.
The figures show CAGR% (Compound Annual Growth Rate) i. e. year-over-year growth rate.

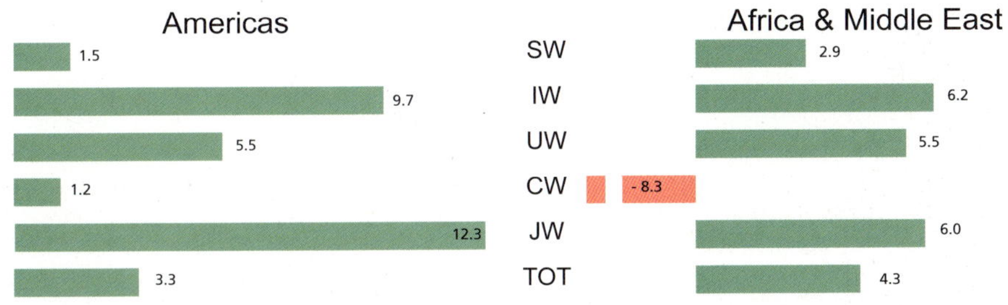

* Russia and other former Soviet Socialist Republic states

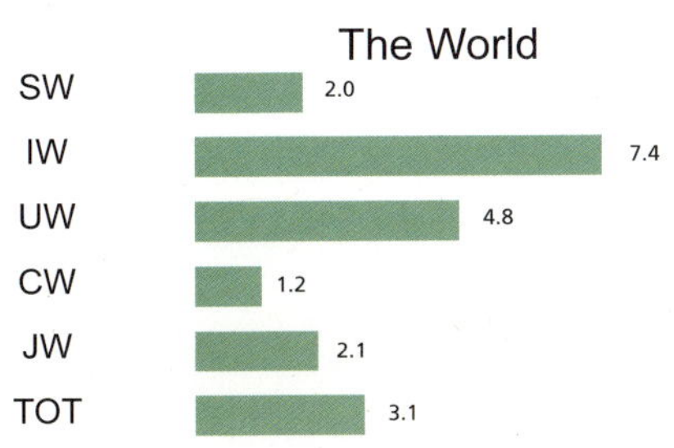

The Top 30 Whiskies of the World

Sales figures for 2017 (units in million 9-litre cases)

- Officer's Choice (Allied Blenders & Distillers), Indian whisky — 32,0
- McDowell's No. 1 (United Spirits), Indian whisky — 23,7
- Imperial Blue (Pernod Ricard), Indian whisky — 19,0
- Royal Stag (Pernod Ricard), Indian whisky — 18,7
- Johnnie Walker (Diageo), Scotch whisky — 18,3
- Jack Daniel's (Brown-Forman), Tennessee whiskey — 12,9
- Original Choice (John Distilleries), Indian whisky — 11,0
- Hayward's Fine (United Spirits), Indian whisky — 9,3
- Old Tavern (United Spirits), Indian whisky — 9,2
- Jim Beam (Beam Suntory), Bourbon — 8,9
- 8PM (Radico Khaitan), Indian whisky — 7,0
- Crown Royal (Diageo), Canadian whisky — 7,0
- Ballantine's (Pernod Ricard), Scotch whisky — 6,9
- Jameson (Pernod Ricard), Irish whiskey — 6,9
- Bagpiper (United Spirits), Indian whisky — 6,7
- Blenders Pride (Pernod Ricard), Indian whisky — 6,4
- Director's Special (United Spirits), Indian whisky — 6,1
- Kakubin (Suntory), Japanese whisky — 4,7
- Royal Challenge (United Spirits), Indian whisky — 4,6
- Grant's (Wm Grand & Sons) Scotch whisky — 4,5
- Chivas Regal (Pernod Ricard), Scotch whisky — 4,2
- Bangalore Malt (John Distilleries), Indian whisky — 3,6
- J&B (Diageo) Scotch whisky — 3,4
- William Lawson's (Bacardi), Scotch whisky — 3,1
- William Peel (Belvédère), Scotch whisky — 3,1
- Black Nikka Clear (Asahi Breweries), Japanese whisky — 3,0
- Famous Grouse (Edrington), Scotch whisky — 3,0
- Dewar's (Bacardi) Scotch whisky — 2,6
- Label 5 (La Martiniquaise), Scotch whisky — 2,6
- Evan Williams (Heaven Hill), Bourbon — 2,4

Source: Drinks International, The Millionaires Club 2018

Global Exports of Scotch by Region

Volume (litres of pure alcohol)				Value (£ Sterling)			
Region	2017	2016	chg %	Region	2017	2016	chg %
Africa	20,645,837	18,308,038	+13	Africa	189,172,758	166,699,435	+13
Asia	68,520,034	67,396,763	+2	Asia	866,853,336	785,752,330	+10
Australasia	9,282,299	8,945,599	+4	Australasia	113,526,648	108,781,275	+4
C&S America	33,651,026	37,538,506	-10	C&S America	336,371,876	339,208,739	-1
Eastern Europe	4,654,954	2,762,120	+68	Eastern Europe	23,704,619	17,406,537	+36
Europe (other)	6,397,269	5,822,396	-12	Europe (other)	94,934,930	91,136,702	+4
European Union	133,663,520	132,377,878	+1	European Union	1,382,134,101	1,241,689,593	+11
Middle East	14,655,461	14,037,184	+4	Middle East	245,071,851	217,917,206	+12
North America	54,114,317	52,769,877	+3	North America	1,116,054,150	1,040,648,531	+7
Total	**345,584,717**	**339,958,361**	**+2**	**Total**	**4,009,240,348**	**4,009,240,348**	**+9**

Source: Scotch Whisky Association

World Consumption of Blended Scotch

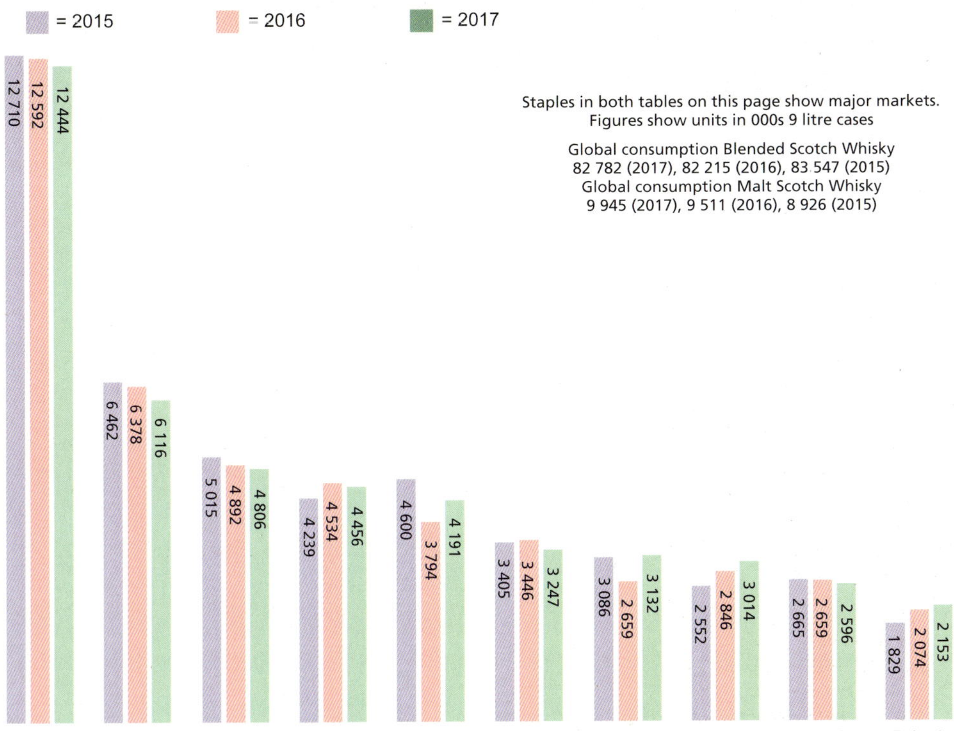

Staples in both tables on this page show major markets.
Figures show units in 000s 9 litre cases

Global consumption Blended Scotch Whisky
82 782 (2017), 82 215 (2016), 83 547 (2015)
Global consumption Malt Scotch Whisky
9 945 (2017), 9 511 (2016), 8 926 (2015)

Source: © The IWSR 2018

World Consumption of Malt Scotch

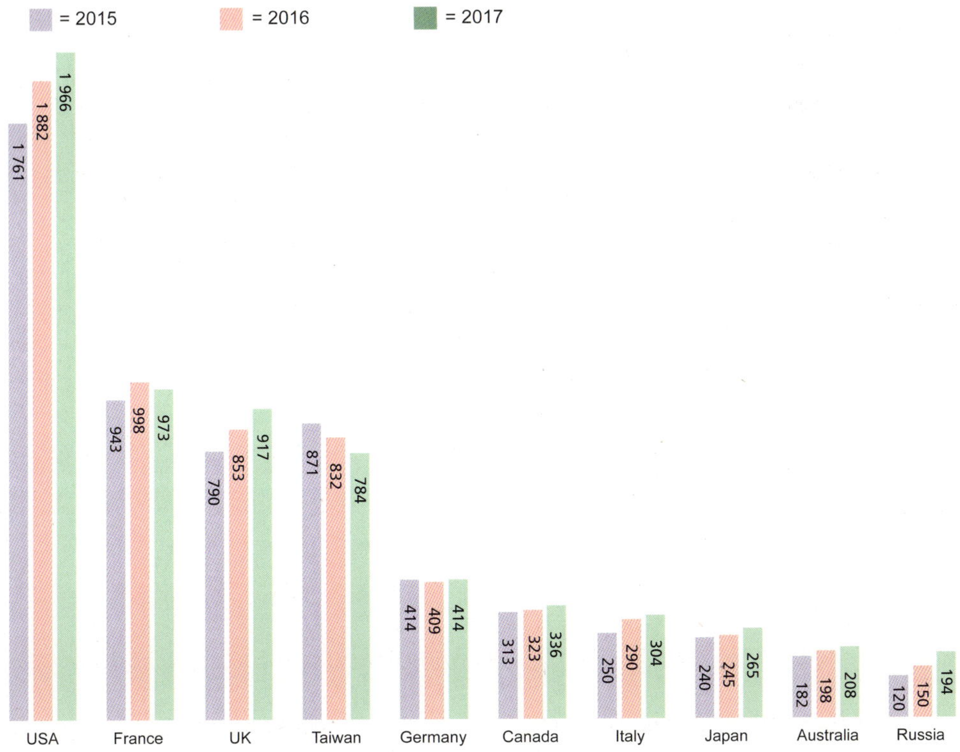

Source: © The IWSR 2018

Top 10 Scotch Malt Whisky brands - world market share %

Brand	Year	Share
Glenfiddich	2017	12,3
	2016	12,5
	2015	12,0
The Glenlivet	2017	10,8
	2016	11,0
	2015	12,0
The Macallan	2017	9,1
	2016	8,8
	2015	8,9
The Singleton Dufftown, Glendullan, Glen Ord	2017	5,2
	2016	5,2
	2015	5,4
Glenmorangie	2017	5,1
	2016	5,4
	2015	5,7
Balvenie	2017	3,4
	2016	3,2
	2015	3,0
Laphroaig	2017	3,1
	2016	3,2
	2015	3,4
Aberlour	2017	3,0
	2016	3,6
	2015	3,5
Glen Grant	2017	3,0
	2016	3,1
	2015	3,2
Talisker	2017	2,5
	2016	2,3
	2015	2,3

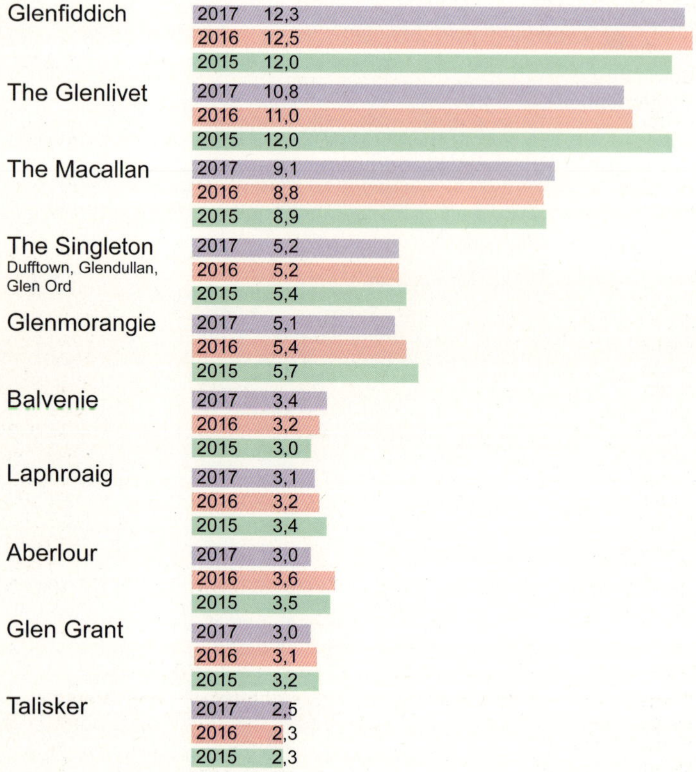

Top 10 Scotch Blended Whisky brands - world market share %

Brand	Year	Share
Johnnie Walker	2017	21,7
	2016	21,4
	2015	21,4
Ballantine´s	2017	8,1
	2016	7,8
	2015	7,1
Grant´s	2017	5,4
	2016	5,4
	2015	5,2
Chivas Regal	2017	5,4
	2016	5,3
	2015	5,3
J&B	2017	4,0
	2016	4,2
	2015	4,2
William Lawson´s	2017	3,7
	2016	3,5
	2015	3,6
Famous Grouse	2017	3,7
	2016	3,7
	2015	3,5
William Peel	2017	3,7
	2016	3,6
	2015	3,4
Dewar´s	2017	3,0
	2016	3,2
	2015	3,1
Black & White	2017	2,7
	2016	2,2
	2015	1,8

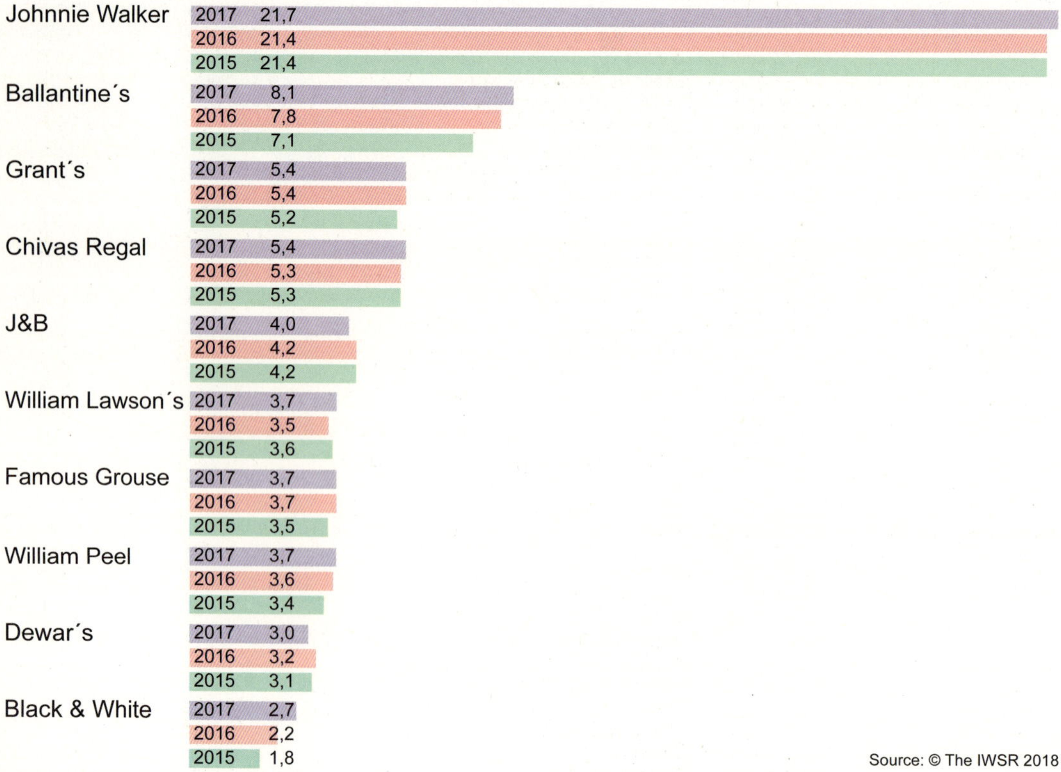

Source: © The IWSR 2018

Distillery Capacity

Litres of pure alcohol - Scottish, active distilleries only

Distillery	Capacity	Distillery	Capacity	Distillery	Capacity
Glenlivet	21 000 000	The Borders	2 000 000	Kingsbarns	600 000
Macallan	15 000 000	Bowmore	2 000 000	Speyside	600 000
Glenfiddich	13 700 000	Inchdairnie	2 000 000	Annandale	500 000
Roseisle	12 500 000	Knockdhu	2 000 000	Ardnamurchan	500 000
Ailsa Bay	12 000 000	Balblair	1 800 000	The Clydeside	500 000
Glen Ord	11 000 000	Pulteney	1 800 000	Royal Lochnagar	500 000
Teaninich	10 200 000	Bruichladdich	1 500 000	Torabhaig	500 000
Dalmunach	10 000 000	Bladnoch	1 500 000	Kilchoman	460 000
Balvenie	7 000 000	Glendronach	1 400 000	Lone Wolf	450 000
Caol Ila	6 500 000	Glen Spey	1 400 000	Glenturret	340 000
Glen Grant	6 200 000	Knockando	1 400 000	Glasgow	270 000
Dufftown	6 000 000	Ardbeg	1 400 000	Edradour	260 000
Glen Keith	6 000 000	Glen Garioch	1 370 000	Lindores Abbey	260 000
Glenmorangie	6 000 000	Glencadam	1 300 000	Harris	230 000
Mannochmore	6 000 000	Scapa	1 300 000	Arbikie	200 000
Auchroisk	5 900 000	Arran	1 200 000	Isle of Raasay	200 000
Miltonduff	5 800 000	Glenglassaugh	1 100 000	Glen Wyvis	140 000
Glen Moray	5 700 000	Glengoyne	1 100 000	Wolfburn	135 000
Glenrothes	5 600 000	Ardnahoe	1 000 000	Ballindalloch	100 000
Linkwood	5 600 000	Tobermory	1 000 000	Ncn´ean	100 000
Ardmore	5 550 000	Oban	870 000	Eden Mill	80 000
Dailuaine	5 200 000	Glen Scotia	800 000	Daftmill	65 000
Glendullan	5 000 000	Aberargie	750 000	Dornoch	30 000
Loch Lomond	5 000 000	Glengyle	750 000	Strathearn	30 000
Tomatin	5 000 000	Springbank	750 000	Abhainn Dearg	20 000
Clynelish	4 800 000	Benromach	700 000		
Kininvie	4 800 000				
Tormore	4 800 000				
Longmorn	4 500 000				
Speyburn	4 500 000				
Dalmore	4 300 000				
Glenburgie	4 250 000				
Allt-a-Bhainne	4 200 000				
Braeval	4 200 000				
Glentauchers	4 200 000				
Craigellachie	4 100 000				
Royal Brackla	4 100 000				
Glenallachie	4 000 000				
Tamdhu	4 000 000				
Tamnavulin	4 000 000				
Aberlour	3 800 000				
Mortlach	3 800 000				
Glenlossie	3 700 000				
Benrinnes	3 500 000				
Glenfarclas	3 500 000				
Aberfeldy	3 400 000				
Cardhu	3 400 000				
Macduff	3 400 000				
Laphroaig	3 300 000				
Talisker	3 300 000				
Tomintoul	3 300 000				
Aultmore	3 200 000				
Fettercairn	3 200 000				
Inchgower	3 200 000				
Deanston	3 000 000				
Tullibardine	3 000 000				
Balmenach	2 800 000				
Benriach	2 800 000				
Blair Athol	2 800 000				
Bunnahabhain	2 700 000				
Glen Elgin	2 700 000				
Strathmill	2 600 000				
Lagavulin	2 530 000				
Glenkinchie	2 500 000				
Highland Park	2 500 000				
Strathisla	2 450 000				
Jura	2 400 000				
Cragganmore	2 200 000				
Dalwhinnie	2 200 000				
Auchentoshan	2 000 000				
Ben Nevis	2 000 000				

Summary of Malt Distillery Capacity by Owner

Owner (number of distilleries)	Litres of alcohol	% of Industry
Diageo (28)	121 300 000	30,3
Pernod Ricard (13)	76 500 000	19,1
William Grant (4)	37 500 000	9,4
Edrington Group (4)	23 440 000	5,8
Bacardi (John Dewar & Sons) (5)	18 200 000	4,5
Beam Suntory (5)	14 220 000	3,6
Emperador Inc (Whyte & Mackay) (4)	13 900 000	3,5
Pacific Spirits (Inver House) (5)	12 900 000	3,2
Moët Hennessy (Glenmorangie) (2)	7 400 000	1,8
Distell (Burn Stewart) (3)	6 700 000	1,7
Campari (Glen Grant) (1)	6 200 000	1,6
Loch Lomond Group (2)	5 800 000	1,4
La Martiniquaise (Glen Moray) (1)	5 700 000	1,4
Benriach Distillery Co (3)	5 300 000	1,3
Ian Macleod Distillers (2)	5 100 000	1,3
Tomatin Distillery Co (1)	5 000 000	1,2
Angus Dundee (2)	4 600 000	1,2
The Glenallachie Consortium (1)	4 000 000	1,0
J & G Grant (Glenfarclas) (1)	3 500 000	0,9
Picard (Tullibardine) (1)	3 000 000	0,8
John Fergus & Co. (Inchdairnie) (1)	2 000 000	0,5
Nikka (Ben Nevis Distillery) (1)	2 000 000	0,5
The Three Stills Co. (The Borders) (1)	2 000 000	0,5
Rémy Cointreau (Bruichladdich) (1)	1 500 000	< 0,5
J & A Mitchell (2)	1 500 000	< 0,5
David Prior (Bladnoch) (1)	1 500 000	< 0,5
Isle of Arran Distillers (1)	1 200 000	< 0,5
Hunter Laing (Ardnahoe) (1)	1 000 000	< 0,5
The Perth Distilling Co. (Aberargie) (1)	750 000	< 0,5
Gordon & MacPhail (Benromach) (1)	700 000	< 0,5
Wemyss Malts (Kingsbarns) (1)	600 000	< 0,5
Harvey´s of Edinburgh (Speyside) (1)	600 000	< 0,5
Adelphi Distillery (Ardnamurchan) (1)	500 000	< 0,5
Annandale Distillery Co. (1)	500 000	< 0,5
Morrison Glasgow Distillers (Clydeside) (1)	500 000	< 0,5
Mossburn Distillers (Torabhaig) (1)	500 000	< 0,5
Kilchoman Distillery Co. (1)	460 000	< 0,5
BrewDog plc (Lone Wolf) (1)	450 000	< 0,5
Glasgow Distillery Company (1)	270 000	< 0,5
Others (14)	1 750 000	< 0,5
Total (122)	**400 540 000**	

Do you want to find out more in detail where the different distilleries are situated? We suggest that you pay a visit to bit.ly/daNJMP where Steffen Bräuner has plotted not only all the Scottish and Irish distilleries but there are also maps for the Americas and for distilleries from the rest of the world.
ORKNEY ISLANDS
Wick
NORTH HIGHLANDS
Isle of Lewis
Isle of Harris
SKYE
Kyle of Lockalsh
Inverness
SPEYSIDE
Loch Ness
Aberdeen
CENTRAL HIGHLANDS
Fort William
WEST HIGHLANDS
Oban
MULL
Pitlochry
EAST HIGHLANDS
Loch Tay
Dundee
Loch Lomond
Perth
St. Andrews
JURA
Stirling
Glasgow
Edinburgh
ISLAY
ARRAN
Campbeltown
Ayr
THE LOWLANDS
Dumfries
Stranraer

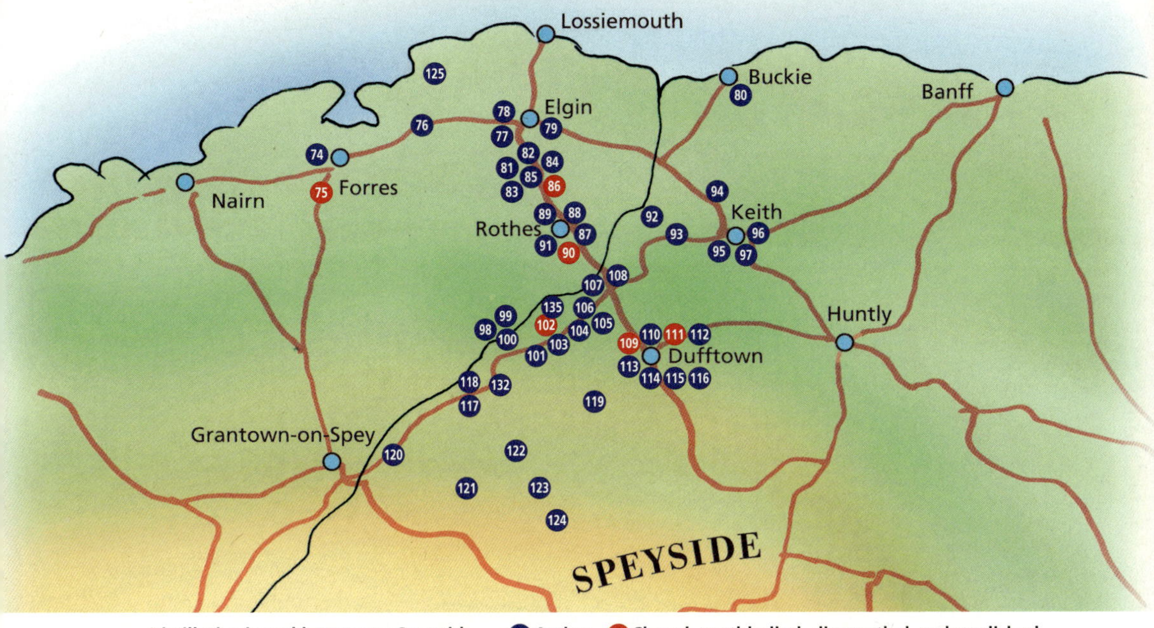

Distilleries in red letters are Speyside ● Active ● Closed, mothballed, dismantled or demolished

c = Closed, m = Mothballed, dm = Dismantled, d = Demolished

148 Aberargie	45 Deanston	51 Kinclaith (d)
39 Aberfeldy	144 Dornoch	43 Kingsbarns
106 Aberlour	110 Dufftown	114 Kininvie
129 Abhainn Dearg	136 Eden Mill	100 Knockando
127 Ailsa Bay	38 Edradour	21 Knockdhu
119 Allt-a-Bhainne	32 Fettercairn	56 Ladyburn (dm)
128 Annandale	141 Glasgow	63 Lagavulin
134 Arbikie	13 Glen Albyn (d)	64 Laphroaig
62 Ardbeg	105 Glenallachie	137 Lindores Abbey
25 Ardmore	76 Glenburgie	79 Linkwood
147 Ardnahoe	34 Glencadam	48 Littlemill (d)
131 Ardnamurchan	23 Glendronach	46 Loch Lomond
58 Arran	116 Glendullan	36 Lochside (d)
49 Auchentoshan	85 Glen Elgin	143 Lone Wolf
92 Auchroisk	35 Glenesk (dm)	84 Longmorn
94 Aultmore	101 Glenfarclas	107 Macallan
7 Balblair	112 Glenfiddich	20 Macduff
132 Ballindalloch	52 Glen Flagler (d)	81 Mannochmore
120 Balmenach	24 Glen Garioch	15 Millburn (dm)
113 Balvenie	18 Glenglassaugh	77 Miltonduff
19 Banff (d)	50 Glengoyne	115 Mortlach
30 Ben Nevis	87 Glen Grant	145 Ncn´ean
82 Benriach	60 Glengyle	33 North Port (d)
104 Benrinnes	96 Glen Keith	40 Oban
74 Benromach	55 Glenkinchie	111 Pittyvaich (d)
9 Ben Wyvis (c)	122 Glenlivet	65 Port Ellen (dm)
57 Bladnoch	31 Glenlochy (d)	4 Pulteney
37 Blair Athol	83 Glenlossie	53 Rosebank (c)
138 Borders	14 Glen Mhor (d)	125 Roseisle
66 Bowmore	8 Glenmorangie	16 Royal Brackla
124 Braeval	78 Glen Moray	27 Royal Lochnagar
5 Brora (c)	12 Glen Ord	54 St Magdalene (dm)
67 Bruichladdich	89 Glenrothes	3 Scapa
70 Bunnahabhain	61 Glen Scotia	88 Speyburn
69 Caol Ila	91 Glenspey	26 Speyside
90 Caperdonich (c)	93 Glentauchers	59 Springbank
99 Cardhu	41 Glenturret	130 Strathearn
142 Clydeside	22 Glenugie (dm)	97 Strathisla
6 Clynelish	28 Glenury Royal (d)	95 Strathmill
86 Coleburn (dm)	149 Glen Wyvis	73 Talisker
109 Convalmore (dm)	140 Harris	98 Tamdhu
118 Cragganmore	2 Highland Park	123 Tamnavulin
108 Craigellachie	133 Inchdairnie	10 Teaninich
42 Daftmill	102 Imperial (d)	72 Tobermory
103 Dailuaine	80 Inchgower	17 Tomatin
75 Dallas Dhu (c)	47 Inverleven (d)	121 Tomintoul
11 Dalmore	146 Isle of Raasay	139 Torabhaig
135 Dalmunach	71 Jura	117 Tormore
29 Dalwhinnie	68 Kilchoman	44 Tullibardine
		129 Wolfburn

2 Highland Park	51 Kinclaith (d)	100 Knockando
3 Scapa	52 Glen Flagler (d)	101 Glenfarclas
4 Pulteney	53 Rosebank (c)	102 Imperial (d)
5 Brora (c)	54 St Magdalene (dm)	103 Dailuaine
6 Clynelish	55 Glenkinchie	104 Benrinnes
7 Balblair	56 Ladyburn (dm)	105 Glenallachie
8 Glenmorangie	57 Bladnoch	106 Aberlour
9 Ben Wyvis (c)	58 Arran	107 Macallan
10 Teaninich	59 Springbank	108 Craigellachie
11 Dalmore	60 Glengyle	109 Convalmore (dm)
12 Glen Ord	61 Glen Scotia	110 Dufftown
13 Glen Albyn (d)	62 Ardbeg	111 Pittyvaich (d)
14 Glen Mhor (d)	63 Lagavulin	112 Glenfiddich
15 Millburn (dm)	64 Laphroaig	113 Balvenie
16 Royal Brackla	65 Port Ellen (dm)	114 Kininvie
17 Tomatin	66 Bowmore	115 Mortlach
18 Glenglassaugh	67 Bruichladdich	116 Glendullan
19 Banff (d)	68 Kilchoman	117 Tormore
20 Macduff	69 Caol Ila	118 Cragganmore
21 Knockdhu	70 Bunnahabhain	119 Allt-a-Bhainne
22 Glenugie (dm)	71 Jura	120 Balmenach
23 Glendronach	72 Tobermory	121 Tomintoul
24 Glen Garioch	73 Talisker	122 Glenlivet
25 Ardmore	74 Benromach	123 Tamnavulin
26 Speyside	75 Dallas Dhu (c)	124 Braeval
27 Royal Lochnagar	76 Glenburgie	125 Roseisle
28 Glenury Royal (d)	77 Miltonduff	126 Ailsa Bay
29 Dalwhinnie	78 Glen Moray	127 Abhainn Dearg
30 Ben Nevis	79 Linkwood	128 Annandale
31 Glenlochy (d)	80 Inchgower	129 Wolfburn
32 Fettercairn	81 Mannochmore	130 Strathearn
33 North Port (d)	82 Benriach	131 Ardnamurchan
34 Glencadam	83 Glenlossie	132 Ballindalloch
35 Glenesk (dm)	84 Longmorn	133 Inchdairnie
36 Lochside (d)	85 Glen Elgin	134 Arbikie
37 Blair Athol	86 Coleburn (dm)	135 Dalmunach
38 Edradour	87 Glen Grant	136 Eden Mill
39 Aberfeldy	88 Speyburn	137 Lindores Abbey
40 Oban	89 Glenrothes	138 Borders
41 Glenturret	90 Caperdonich (c)	139 Torabhaig
42 Daftmill	91 Glenspey	140 Harris
43 Kingsbarns	92 Auchroisk	141 Glasgow
44 Tullibardine	93 Glentauchers	142 Clydeside
45 Deanston	94 Aultmore	143 Lone Wolf
46 Loch Lomond	95 Strathmill	144 Dornoch
47 Inverleven (d)	96 Glen Keith	145 Ncn´ean
48 Littlemill (d)	97 Strathisla	146 Isle of Raasay
49 Auchentoshan	98 Tamdhu	147 Ardnahoe
50 Glengoyne	99 Cardhu	148 Aberargie
		149 Glen Wyvis

Distillery Index

Distillery Index

Distillery Index